THE MEANING OF THE WORD: LEXICOLOGY AND QUR'ANIC EXEGESIS

The basic intention of Qur'anic exegesis (*tafsīr*) is to understand what the text of the Qur'an means. Before attempting to understand anything of the Qur'anic worldview, its theology and ethical values, there is a need for exegetes to engage with the individual words found in the Qur'an itself. Yet, exegetes and translators, whether medieval or modern, have different theological perspectives, which influence how they do this. Many modern scholars have recognised that lexicology plays an important part in exegesis, but there are few studies of how exegetes use it to develop their interpretations of the Qur'an or that address lexicology in Qur'anic exegesis in any depth. This volume of articles begins to address this gap in the scholarship.

The Meaning of the Word provides an overview of the development of lexicological analysis in the *tafsīr* tradition, and examines how exegetes interpreted words in the Qur'an. The contributions reflect on lexicology in Qur'anic exegesis through studies of a wide range of subjects, from linguistics to literary criticism, and law and gender to mysticism; from examinations of the issue of lexicology in the Arab, Persian and Turkish worlds to its examination in the European world; and from studies of the earliest discussions of Qur'anic lexica to those made in twentieth-century Turkey and recent English translations of the Qur'an. This volume will become a subject-specific reference volume for anyone working on the interpretation of the Qur'an, as well as in Islamic Studies and the wider field of Religious Studies.

STEPHEN R. BURGE is a Research Associate at The Institute of Ismaili Studies, London. He completed his PhD at the University of Edinburgh in 2009, and has since published this as *Angels in Islam: Jalāl al-Dīn al-Suyūṭī's* al-Ḥabā'ik fī akhbār al-malā'ik (London, 2012). More recently, he has focused his attention on Qur'anic exegesis, particularly Suyūṭī's main exegetical work, *al-Durr al-manthūr fī'l tafsīr bi'l-ma'thūr*. He is also working on an edition of the *Anthology of Qur'anic Commentaries* on the 'Pillars of Islam'.

The Institute of Ismaili Studies

Qur'anic Studies Series, 13

Series editor, Omar Alí-de-Unzaga

Previously published titles:

Suha Taji-Farouki, editor,
Modern Muslim Intellectuals and the Qur'an
(2004; Paperback 2006)

Abdullah Saeed, editor,
Approaches to the Qur'an in Contemporary Indonesia
(2005)

Annabel Keeler
Sufi Hermeneutics: The Qur'an Commentary of Rashīd al-Dīn Maybudī
(2006)

Fahmida Suleman, editor,
Word of God, Art of Man: The Qur'an and its Creative Expressions
(2007; Paperback 2010)

Feras Hamza and Sajjad Rizvi, editors, with Farhana Mayer,
An Anthology of Qur'anic Commentaries,
Volume I: On the Nature of the Divine
(2008; Paperback 2010)

Toby Mayer, translator,
Keys to the Arcana: Shahrastānī's Esoteric Commentary on the Qur'an
(2009)

Travis Zadeh
The Vernacular Qur'an: Translation and the Rise of Persian Exegesis
(2012)

Martin Nguyen
Sufi Master and Qur'an Scholar: Abū'l-Qāsim al-Qushayrī and the Laṭā'if al-ishārāt
(2012)

Karen Bauer, editor,
Aims, Methods and Contexts of Qur'anic Exegesis (2nd/8th–9th/10th C.)
(2013)

Angelika Neuwirth
Scripture, Poetry and the Making of a Community: Reading the Qur'an as a Literary Text
(2014)

M. Brett Wilson
Translating the Qur'an in an Age of Nationalism: Print Culture and Modern Islam in Turkey
(2014)

Andreas Görke and Johanna Pink, editors,
Tafsīr and Islamic Intellectual History: Exploring the Boundaries of a Genre
(2014)

The Meaning of the Word

Lexicology and Qur'anic Exegesis

EDITED BY

S.R. Burge

OXFORD
UNIVERSITY PRESS

in association with

THE INSTITUTE OF ISMAILI STUDIES
LONDON

OXFORD
UNIVERSITY PRESS

Great Clarendon Street, Oxford OX2 6DP
Oxford University Press is a department of the University of Oxford.
It furthers the University's objective of excellence in research, scholarship,
and education by publishing worldwide in
Oxford New York
Auckland Cape Town Dar es Salaam Hong Kong Karachi
Kuala Lumpur Madrid Melbourne Mexico City Nairobi
New Delhi Shanghai Taipei Toronto

With offices in

Argentina Austria Brazil Chile Czech Republic France Greece
Guatemala Hungary Italy Japan Poland Portugal Singapore
South Korea Switzerland Thailand Turkey Ukraine Vietnam

Published in the United States
by Oxford University Press Inc., New York

First published 2015

British Library Cataloguing in Publication Data
Data available

Library of Congress Cataloging in Publication Data
Data available

Cover illustration:
Untitled by Khaled al-Saai. Reproduced courtesy of Khaled al-Saai.

Cover design: Russell Harris
Index by Philip Hillyer, Advanced Professional Member, Society of Indexers
Typeset by RefineCatch Ltd, Bungay, Suffolk
Printed in Great Britain on acid-free paper by
TJ International Ltd., Padstow, Cornwall

ISBN 978-0-19-872413-1

The Institute of Ismaili Studies

THE INSTITUTE OF ISMAILI STUDIES was established in 1977 with the objectives of promoting scholarship and learning on Islam, in historical as well as contemporary contexts, and fostering better understanding of Islam's relationship with other societies and faiths.

The Institute's programmes encourage a perspective which is not confined to the theological and religious heritage of Islam, but seeks to explore the relationship of religious ideas to broader dimensions of society and culture. The programmes thus *encourage* an interdisciplinary approach to Islamic history and thought. Particular attention is given to the issues of modernity that arise as Muslims seek to relate their heritage to the contemporary situation.

Within the Islamic tradition, the Institute promotes research on those areas which have, to date, received relatively little attention from scholars. These include the intellectual and literary expressions of Shiʿism in general and Ismailism in particular.

The Institute's objectives are realised through concrete programmes and activities organised by various departments of the Institute, at times in collaboration with other institutions of learning. These programmes and activities are informed by the full range of cultures in which Islam is practised today. From the Middle East, South and Central Asia, and Africa to the industrialised societies in the West, they consider the variety of contexts which shape the ideals, beliefs and practices of the faith.

In facilitating the *Qur'anic Studies Series* and other publications, the Institute's sole purpose is to encourage original research and analysis of relevant issues, which often leads to diverse views and interpretations. While every effort is made to ensure that the publications are of a high academic standard, the opinions expressed in these publications must be understood as belonging to their authors alone.

QUR'ANIC STUDIES SERIES

THE QUR'AN has been an inexhaustible source of intellectual and spiritual reflection in Islamic history, giving rise to ever-proliferating commentaries and interpretations. Many of these have remained a realm for specialists due to their scholarly demands. Others, more widely read, remain untranslated from the primary language of their composition. This series aims to make some of these materials from a broad chronological range – the formative centuries of Islam to the present day – available to a wider readership through translation and publication in English, accompanied where necessary by introductory or explanatory materials. The series will also include contextual-analytical and survey studies of these primary materials.

Throughout this series and others like it which may appear in the future, the aim is to allow the materials to speak for themselves. Not surprisingly, in the Muslim world where its scriptural sources continue to command passionate interest and commitment, the Qur'an has been subject to contending, often antithetical ideas and interpretations. This series takes no sides in these debates. The aim rather is to place on record the rich diversity and plurality of approaches and opinions which have appealed to the Qur'an throughout history (and even more so today). The breadth of this range, however partisan or controversial individual presentations within it may be, is instructive in itself. While there is always room in such matters for personal preferences, commitment to particular traditions of belief, and scholarly evaluations, much is to be gained by a simple appreciation, not always evident today, of the enormous wealth of intellectual effort that has been devoted to the Qur'an from the earliest times. It is hoped that through this objective, this series will prove of use to scholars and students in Qur'anic Studies as well as other allied and relevant fields.

Contents

Notes on Contributors

Herbert Berg is Professor in the Department of Philosophy and Religion at the University of North Carolina Wilmington. He has published widely in the field of early Qur'anic exegesis. His publications include the monograph *The Development of Exegesis in Early Islam: The Authenticity of Muslim Literature from the Formative Period* (Richmond, 2000), the edited book *Method and Theory in the Study of Islamic Origins* (Leiden, 2003) and, most recently, *Elijah Muhammad and Islam* (New York, 2009) and *Elijah Muhammad* (London, 2013).

Stephen R. Burge is a Research Associate at The Institute of Ismaili Studies, London. He completed his PhD at the University of Edinburgh in 2009, and has since published this as *Angels in Islam: Jalāl al-Dīn al-Suyūṭī's* al-Ḥabā'ik fī akhbār al-malā'ik (London, 2012). More recently, he has focused his attention on Qur'anic exegesis, particularly Suyūṭī's main exegetical work, *al-Durr al-manthūr fī'l tafsīr bi'l-ma'thūr.* He is also working on an edition of the *Anthology of Qur'anic Commentaries* on the 'Pillars of Islam'.

Ayesha S. Chaudhry is a Fellow at the Radcliffe Institute for Advanced Study at Harvard University. She is also Associate Professor of Islamic Studies and Gender Studies at the University of British Columbia. She has published widely on gender and Islam and is the author of *Domestic Violence and the Islamic Tradition: Ethics, Law and the Muslim Discourse on Gender* (Oxford, 2013).

Agostino Cilardo is Professor of the History and Institutions of the Islamic World, and Professor of Islamic Law at the Università degli Studi di Napoli 'L'Orientale'. He has published widely in the field of Islamic law, including *The Qur'ānic Term* Kalāla (Edinburgh, 2005) and an edition and translation of al-Qāḍī al-Nuʿmān's *Minhāj al-farā'iḍ* entitled *The Early History of Ismaili Jurisprudence: Law under the Fatimids* (London, 2012).

Claude Gilliot is Professor Emeritus of the Université d'Aix-Marseille and IREMAM, and a member of the Institut Dominicain d'Études Orientales (IDEO) in Cairo. He is on the editorial board of the journal *Arabica* and has published widely in the field of Qur'anic exegesis, including his monograph *Exégèse, langue et théologie en islam: L'exégèse coranique de Tabari* (Paris, 1990).

Toby Mayer is a Research Associate in the Qur'anic Studies Unit at The Institute of Ismaili Studies, London. He has published with Professor Wilferd Madelung a critical edition and translation of Shahrastānī's *Kitāb Muṣāraʿat al-falāsifa*, entitled *Struggling with the Philosopher: A Refutation of Avicenna's Metaphysics* (London, 2001), as well as an analysis and translation of Shahrastānī's exegesis of *Sūrat al-Fātiḥa* from the *Mafātīḥ al-asrār* published as *Keys to the Arcana: Shahrastānī's Esoteric Commentary on the Qur'an* (Oxford, 2009).

Christopher Melchert is Professor of Arabic and Islam at the University of Oxford. He has published widely on the hadith scholar Ibn Ḥanbal, and is now focusing his attention on the development of renunciant (*zuhd*) literature. His published works include *The Formation of the Sunni Schools of Law, 9th to 10th Centuries* (Leiden, 1997) and *Ahmad Ibn Hanbal* (Oxford, 2006).

Devin Stewart is Associate Professor of Arabic and Islamic Studies at Emory University, GA. His research has focused on Islamic law and legal education, the text of the Qur'an, Shiʿi Islam, Islamic sectarian relations, and Arabic dialectology. His work on the Qur'an includes '*Sajʿ* in the Qur'ān: Prosody and Structure', *Journal of Arabic Literature* 21 (1990) pp. 101–39; and 'Poetic License in the Qur'ān: Ibn al-Ṣā'igh al-Ḥanafī's *Iḥkām al-rāy fī aḥkām al-āy*', *Journal of Qur'anic Studies* 11 (2009), pp. 1–54.

Kees Versteegh is Professor Emeritus of the University of Nijmegen. He has published widely in the field of Arabic linguistics in both the medieval and modern periods. He was editor-in-chief of the *Encyclopaedia of Arabic Language and Linguistics* (Leiden,

2006–2009) and his published works include *The Arabic Language* (Edinburgh, 1997; 2nd edn 2014) and *Arabic Grammar and Qur'ānic Exegesis in Early Islam* (Leiden, 1993).

Stefan Wild is Professor Emeritus of the University of Bonn (Rheinische Friedrich-Wilhelms Universität Bonn). He has specialised in medieval Arabic linguistics and lexicography, as well as studies of modern Islam. His works include *Das Kitab al-ʿAin und die arabische Lexikographie* (Wiesbaden, 1965), and the two edited volumes, *The Qur'an as Text* (Leiden, 1996) and *Self-Referentiality in the Qur'ān* (Wiesbaden, 2006).

M. Brett Wilson is Assistant Professor of Religious Studies at Macalester College, MN. His research explores modernisation and religious transformation – particularly in Turkey and the late Ottoman Empire – with recent projects examining the cultural history of the Qur'an, Middle Eastern print history and Sufism. He is author of *Translating the Qur'an in an Age of Nationalism: Print Culture and Modern Islam in Turkey* (Oxford, 2014).

Travis Zadeh is Associate Professor of Religion at Haverford College, PA, where he teaches courses in Islamic intellectual and cultural history. In addition to various scholarly articles, he is the author of *Mapping Frontiers Across Medieval Islam: Geography, Translation, and the ʿAbbasid Empire* (London, 2011) and *The Vernacular Qur'an: Translation and the Rise of Persian Exegesis* (Oxford, 2012).

Note on Transliteration, Conventions and Abbreviations

Arabic transliterations follow a modified system based on the standard of the *International Journal of Middle East Studies*. Names, terms and toponyms from non-Latin alphabets are transliterated unless common in English. The genealogical sequence Muḥammad ibn Qāsim, etc., is abbreviated with 'b.' for ibn (son) and 'bt.' for bint (daughter); the definite article on the *nisba* and the *laqab* is generally dropped after its first appearance, that is, from 'al-Khargūshī' to 'Khargūshī' or 'al-Jāḥiẓ' to 'Jāḥiẓ', and so forth. Definite articles, however, are by and large maintained for formal titles, that is, al-Ḥakīm. The word imam is capitalised when referring to proper titles. Dates pertaining to Islamic history are generally indicated both in *hijrī* and Common Era forms before the sixteenth century CE, and in Common Era forms from the seventeenth century onwards. Dates marked with the abbreviation 'Sh.' in the bibliographical material correspond to the modern solar (shamsī) *hijrī* calendar used in Iran. All translations are the relevant author's unless otherwise indicated.

Abbreviations

EALL	*Encyclopedia of Arabic Language and Linguistics*, ed. Kees Versteegh *et al.* Leiden: Brill, 2005–9
EI	*Encyclopaedia of Islam*, ed., M.T. Houtsma *et al.*, 1st edition. Leiden: Brill, 1913–38
EI^2	*Encyclopaedia of Islam*, ed. H.A.R. Gibb *et al.*, 2nd edition. Leiden: Brill, 1960–2004
EI THREE	*Encyclopaedia of Islam*, ed. Kate Fleet *et al.*, 3rd edition. Leiden: Brill, 2007–

EIr	*Encyclopaedia Iranica*, ed. Ehsan Yarshater *et al.* London: Routledge and K. Paul; New York: Encyclopedia Iranica Foundation, 1982–
EQ	*Encyclopaedia of the Qur'ān*, ed. Jane Dammen McAuliffe. Leiden: Brill, 2001–6

وَعَلَّمَ ءَادَمَ ٱلْأَسْمَآءَ كُلَّهَا

And He taught Adam the names, all of them

Q. 2:31

Ἆρά γε γινώσκεις ἃ ἀναγινώσκεις;

Do you understand what you are reading?

Acts 8:30

Preface

This collection of articles is the result of a project that I first began to explore in November 2009. Whilst the project has, undoubtedly, gone through a number of twists and turns, the principal aim of this project has always been to explore how scholars engaged with words in the interpretation of the Qur'an, and how scholars incorporated discussions of the meanings of Qur'anic words into wider theological and legal debates. I greatly hope that this collection of articles will provide opportunities to reflect not only on the nature of lexicology (the study of words themselves, rather than the study of 'lexicon-making') and meaning, but also on the nature of the act of writing an exegesis of the Qur'an more broadly.

This project was built on, and developed out of, the successful 'Tafsīr Workshop: Theories and Methods in Qur'an Commentaries' run by my friend and colleague Karen Bauer at the American Academy of Religion Annual Meeting in Chicago 2008, with a follow-up workshop at the Institute of Ismaili Studies in October 2009. Karen graciously allowed me to participate in this second workshop, and it was during this that the question of lexicology and/or lexicography was mentioned frequently. I realised that it was an area of *tafsīr* studies that someone was unlikely to begin to explore on their own, but that the field would benefit from an exploration of this subject in much more detail. There are, of course, a number of people who have helped this project develop, and whom I need to thank. Firstly all of my colleagues at the Institute of Ismaili Studies have given feedback and responses to the project as it moved along, and have provided helpful advice. Particular mention must be made of Omar Alí-de-Unzaga, co-ordinator of the Qur'anic Studies Unit at the IIS, who was very much a co-developer of the project, and Farhad Daftary, Director of the IIS, who supported this project from its inception. I must also thank Karen Bauer, as this project largely arose out of her own work and workshop, and she has provided invaluable support and advice. There were a number of people who took part in the project, but who were not able to contribute to this volume, namely Jamal Ali, Michael Pregill, and Alena Kulinich; they have greatly added to this project and helped me to form my own ideas about lexicology in Qur'anic exegesis, and I am sure that others involved in this project have benefited greatly from their conference papers and lectures. Lastly, I would like to thank Eleanor Payton, who copy-edited this complex volume, and Lisa Morgan and Russell Harris, who also assisted in its publication.

To comprehend the meaning of the Qur'an is the fundamental intention of Qur'anic exegesis (*tafsīr*), and one of the most basic exegetical tools in this process is the explanation of single words (i.e. lexicology, *lugha*, *ʿilm al-lugha*). This collection of articles presents a series of analyses and discussions of how medieval and modern exegetes have engaged with questions of the meanings of words in the Qur'an. The articles approach the subject from a wide range of perspectives: from law to mysticism; from examinations of the issue of lexicology in the Arab, Persian and Turkish worlds to its examination in the European world; and from studies of the earliest discussions of Qur'anic lexica to those made in twentieth-century Turkey and recent English translations of the Qur'an. The volume does not intend to discuss specific aspects or problems of lexicology in the Qur'an, such as the use of foreign vocabulary, *hapax legemonena*, the meanings of names and so on, but is almost entirely focused on the methodologies that medieval and modern exegetes have employed in attempting to come to grips with some of the elusive, and at times the apparently not-so-elusive, vocabulary of the Qur'an.

Qur'anic Studies as a field has benefited from a vast number of studies discussing what the words in the Qur'anic text mean, particularly in the field of comparative Semitic philology, where such studies have been a staple of Western scholarship on the Qur'an for many decades. Comparative philologists have tended to focus entirely on the meaning of words in the Qur'an in its own historical context – such technical examinations of Qur'anic lexica are of great benefit to studies of the Qur'an, but I hope that this volume will illustrate that it is just as rewarding to explore how Muslim exegetes engaged with these same words, and how these words were interpreted by different people, schools and faith communities, often leading to interpretive conflict.

Theological positions taken in *kalām* controversies, Sunni–Shiʿi polemic, jurisprudence, gender debates, questions of modernism, and mysticism frequently seek authority through the mediation of the Qur'an and through the interpretation of individual words. Whilst lexicology is often regarded as playing a crucial part in this process, there are few studies of how exegetes actually approach and engage with the words of the Qur'an and their meaning. Is there, for example, an established methodology in the way in which exegetes deal with lexicology? To what extent did Arabic linguistics and lexicography influence exegesis, and vice-versa? How are discussions of individual words employed and deployed in theological and legal debates? Whilst this collection cannot answer all questions about the lexicology of the Qur'an in the vast tradition of Muslim exegesis of the Qur'an, it is hoped that these articles will generate further reflection on the ways in which Muslims, both modern and medieval, dealt with, understood, interpreted and made use of the words in the Qur'an to articulate and promote specific ideas and beliefs.

The volume is divided into four main sections. The first section ('Lexicology and the Formative Period of Qur'anic Exegesis') explores the development of ways of approaching the, sometimes difficult, lexica of the Qur'an in the earliest period of Islam. Kees Versteegh examines the earliest commentaries, and their ways of dealing with the meanings of words, and Christopher Melchert provides an analysis of early interpretations of Qur'anic lexica in non-*tafsīr* works, namely early hadith collections on *zuhd* ('asceticism' or 'renunciation'). Herbert Berg approaches the issue of the development of lexicological analysis of the Qur'an in early Islam from a different perspective, and utilises methodologies of lexical interpretation to raise questions about the role of Ibn ʿAbbās in early lexical discussions.

These early attempts to explore the meaning of lexical items in the Qur'an developed into sophisticated lexicological analyses of the Qur'an in later exegeses, as the genre of *tafsīr* became more sophisticated and nuanced. The second section ('Lexical Methodologies in Action: Four Case Studies') provides case studies of different approaches to lexical interpretation. The first two chapters in this section, by Claude Gilliot and myself, examine the *tafsīr* tradition, with Gilliot providing a detailed analysis of al-Wāḥidī's *al-Tafsīr al-baṣīṭ*. Devin Stewart and Toby Mayer present different approaches to the question of lexicology. Stewart provides a literary analysis of words in the Qur'an and the impact that rhyme had on the Qur'an and its interpretation. In mystical interpretations of the Qur'an, the words of the Qur'an were themselves often the source of spiritual reflection, and Mayer considers Shahrastānī's use of both 'formal' and metaphysical approaches to lexicology in his *Mafātīḥ al-asrār*.

Words in the Qur'an, and their interpretation, often form the basis of legal arguments, and this is explored in the third section ('Words, Interpretation and Legal Disputes'). The three chapters in this section examine three different areas of law: Agostino Cilardo studies the law of inheritance in different schools and the relationship between their interpretations of the words in the Qur'an and their legal position; Ayesha Chaudhry explores the interpretation of the word *nushūz* and the implications it has on the conception of male and female status in the medieval understanding of the Qur'anic worldview. The final article in this section, by M. Brett Wilson, provides an account and analysis of the debates about fasting in Turkey in the early twentieth century, and whether fasting was obligatory.

The debate about fasting in Turkey originated in problems and concerns about translating the Qur'an into Turkish, which, subsequently, generated much debate throughout the rest of the Islamic world at the time, particularly in Cairo. The question of translation revolves around the need for understanding the meaning of the words in the Qur'an, and the inability of a translation to convey such meanings. These ideas are explored by Travis Zadeh and Stefan Wild in the final section ('The Word in Translation: Medieval and Modern Disputes'). All of the articles in this volume describe a situation in which there are multiple interpretations of the same words. The introduction to this volume seeks to explore the different ways in which exegetes and interpreters can construct meaning, and argues that there is a need to understand the implications of the different forms of 'meaning construction'.

It is hoped that the chapters in this volume will help to illustrate the importance of lexicology in the development of interpretations of the Qur'an, and in the articulation of particular worldviews, beliefs and legal positions. The Qur'an is a complex text and not at all easy to understand, and at the very centre of interpretation is the need to understand individual words. Such studies need not be restricted to the understanding of the meanings of the words in the Qur'an in its revelatory and historical context, but can be the basis of gaining insight into how Muslims, both medieval and modern, engaged with the Qur'an and interpreted it.

Stephen Burge
London 2015

1

Introduction: Words, Hermeneutics, and the Construction of Meaning

S.R. BURGE

WHAT THE words of the Qur'an mean is, naturally, central to any understanding of the Qur'an. Before attempting to come to understand anything of the Qur'anic worldview, its theology and its ethical values, there is a need to engage with the words found in it. The essays in this volume explore the ways in which exegetes and other interpreters, such as legal theorists and translators, engage with the words of the Qur'an to generate meaning.

The question of how people read texts and respond to them has been of great concern in Biblical Studies and in philosophy more broadly, but has not been adequately addressed in Islamic Studies. This introduction will begin by looking at approaches to reading and hermeneutics in Biblical Studies and philosophy, to provide some foundation for discussion of the Qur'an and *tafsīr*. Early discussions of hermeneutics by Friedrich Schleiermacher in the nineteenth century laid the foundation for the development of a field devoted exclusively to understanding this problem.[1] Outside of Biblical Studies, Martin Heidegger's *Being and Time* and Hans-Georg Gadamer's *Truth and Method* represent attempts to understand the relationship between a reader's own context and the world of the text.[2] For Gadamer, readers have an 'historically effected consciousness' (*wirkungsgeschichtliches Bewußtsein*) that comes to influence their understanding of a text: reading is always a reflection of an individual's historical context.[3] These philosophical discussions of hermeneutics have strongly influenced the way in which the interpretation of the Bible is understood, and these ideas are worth considering in the context of the study of the Qur'an and *tafsīr*.[4]

In the early stages of the development of hermeneutic theory, Schleiermacher noted the complex relationship between reading a text on a general level and at a more specific level: considering the Bible, or a book of the Bible, as a whole against the interpretation of individual words.[5] Schleiermacher argued that the process of interpreting texts was circular (his so-called 'hermeneutic circle'), since a reader needs to understand the general Biblical worldview to interpret individual words; but at the same time, the interpretation of individual words informs the understanding of the Biblical worldview itself.[6] In the context of Islamic Studies, the implication is that the meanings exegetes give to words of the Qur'an are influenced by, and themselves influence, their interpretation of the Qur'an as whole.

Using the essays included in this volume as case studies, this introductory chapter will explore how exegetes went about this process of giving meanings to words, and the different ways in which lexical meaning can be constructed. Building on, and reacting to, the philosophical hermeneutics of figures such as Heidegger and Gadamer, as well as the emerging field of semiotics,[7] postmodern literary theorists such as Louise M. Rosenblatt, among others, have highlighted the fact that any reading is interpretative: every reader has a reaction to a text that is distinct from anyone else's reading, and the meaning and significance of individual words within the text play a part in the way in which readers receive the text and construct its meaning more generally.[8] Readers naturally bring other external texts to their reading and, to use Roland Barthes's analogy, they 'weave' these external texts into the fabric of the text being read.[9] The postmodern notion of intertextuality maintains that someone (either an author or a reader) cannot divest themselves of their life experiences; furthermore, because every reader has had different life experiences, each individual receives a text differently, resulting in a text's meaning becoming fluid and without any definitive or actual meaning.[10] For some literary theorists, a consequence of this instability of meaning was a weakening in an author's control of the text's meaning, which transferred to its reader(s).[11] However, Wolfgang Iser, in an attempt to reclaim some power for the author, presents a model in which the author and the reader are situated at opposite 'poles' and the 'text' is created in the space between these two opposing poles.[12] In this way, an author is able to encourage his or her reader to receive the text in a certain way – that is, the author is able to control the text to some extent, but the reader will still receive the text in whichever way he or she wishes, and read the author's text in light of other sources that the author may not have intended: the meaning of the text is controlled by neither the author nor the reader, but is generated through the interaction between both.

These literary and philosophical reflections on the way in which texts are received have had a great influence on the understanding and interpretation of scripture, particularly Biblical interpretation, and to a much lesser extent the interpretation of the Qur'an.[13] The Biblical scholar Rudolph Bultmann argues that exegesis is an '*existentiell* encounter' with the text, and that as a result, an exegete's interpretation is still 'determined by his own individuality, in the sense of his special biases and beliefs, his gifts and weaknesses . . .'[14] Here, the '*existentiell* encounter' with exegesis is influenced, as Bultmann argues, by an exegete's own experiences of external texts that play a part in the way he or she interprets the Bible.[15] In an Islamic Studies context, this means that *tafsīr* is generated by the interaction between how an exegete understands the world and how such a worldview can be reconciled with the text of the Qur'an.

In Biblical Studies, the term 'exegesis' is used to describe the act of developing an interpretation *out of* the text itself. The term exegesis is often coupled with its polemical counterpart 'eisegesis' – the act of developing an interpretation by bringing external ideas *into* the text that are not necessarily there. However, the usual understanding of the term exegesis – the method that is perceived as being unsullied by any reading of external texts into a text – fails to accommodate the natural influence and presence of external texts involved in the act of reading, advocated by theories of reading in both philosophical hermeneutics and postmodern literary theory. In response, George Aichele and Gary Phillips argue that all interpretation is a mixture of exegesis and eisegesis; they write: 'intertextuality disputes the reductive binary opposition of exegesis/eisegesis with "intergesis"'.[16] Aichele and Phillips locate meaning

– like Wolfgang Iser – neither inside the text nor outside of it, but argue, rather, that meaning is generated by the interaction between both the text (i.e. the scripture) and the reader (i.e. the exegete).

The way in which an exegete goes about this process is what is meant by the term hermeneutics; this consists of both the practical form that an exegete wishes to give his exegesis, and the theological and philosophical worldviews that he or she might hold.[17] For the genre of *tafsīr* this means that the commentary (i.e. the work or text itself) can determine the form that it takes – an area of *tafsīr* studies that has been given much attention recently by both Walid A. Saleh and Karen Bauer.[18] Every *tafsīr* has a specific objective and audience in mind and the content of the work is determined by these factors; so, for example, the *al-Durr al-manthūr* of Jalāl al-Dīn al-Suyūṭī (d. 911/1505) and his portions of the *Tafsīr al-Jalālayn* include different information, and even the 'occasions of revelation' material (*asbāb al-nuzūl*) differs in content in his *al-Durr al-manthūr*, the *Tafsīr al-Jalālayn*, and his work devoted to the subject, his *Lubāb al-nuqūl fī asbāb al-nuzūl*.[19]

A *tafsīr* is also influenced by an exegete's own 'pre-texts', his or her previously held theological and philosophical ideas.[20] For example, in his discussion of Q. 6:12,[21] the Muʿtazilī exegete Maḥmūd b. ʿUmar al-Zamakhsharī (d. 538/1144) writes:

> He [i.e. God] then threatens them [with punishment in the hereafter] for their neglecting to contemplate [such proofs] and for their ascription of partners to Him that have no power to create anything, by saying: *He will surely gather you to the day of Resurrection*, whereupon He will requite you for your ascription of partners [to Him].[22]

Zamakhsharī's interpretation clearly reflects two of the five Muʿtazilī principles: firstly the necessity of God's justice, and secondly that God provides both a promise of reward and a threat of punishment (*al-waʿd wa'l-waʿīd*).[23] Likewise, in order to find a Qur'anic proof for the doctrine of the imamate (*imāma*), early Shiʿis interpreted verses of the Qur'an, such as *God commands you to deliver trusts back to their owners; and when you judge between the people, that you judge with justice . . .* (Q. 4:58), in reference to the *imāma*. For example, ʿAlī

b. Ibrāhīm al-Qummī (fl. mid-fourth/tenth century) explains this verse by saying: 'It is obligatory for the imam (*farada 'alā'l-imām*) to judge between people justly (*bi'l-'adl*).'[24] Qummī's Shi'i view of the imam as a spiritual leader, alluded to here, is obviously a response that would not be entertained by Sunni exegetes. In addition, it is also extremely likely that exegeses responded to their religio-political context. In the case of hadith compilation, Andrew Newman has argued that the early Shi'i collections of Aḥmad b. Muḥammad al-Barqī (d. 274/887–8 or 280/893–4), Muḥammad b. al-Ḥasan al-Ṣaffār (d. 290/902–3) and Abū Ja'far Muḥammad al-Kulaynī (d. 328/939–40 or 329/940–41) 'may be seen as linked to, if they were not directly "the product of", broader trends and events of which the compilor himself was inherently a part'.[25] A similar influence of historical and political contexts on an exegesis is likely, and an area of *tafsīr* studies that needs and warrants further research.

The combination of the effects of both the form of a work and the author's theological or philosophical worldview on a text can be seen when comparing a particular exegesis to another work written by the same author in a different genre. The philosopher and theologian Fakhr al-Dīn al-Rāzī (d. 606/1209) provides an interesting case in point. In his *tafsīr*, the genre itself constrains him in what he can say and how he says it, since the discourse is tied to the text of the Qur'an and he can only engage with theological issues as and when the Qur'anic text provides the opportunity.[26] Rāzī does introduce philosophical and theological ideas where other exegetes do not, but such discussions must arise out of the text itself.[27] In contrast, in his theological works Rāzī is able to employ a discourse that is unfettered and unconstrained by the genre of commentary, and he can develop systematic theological arguments in a logical and sequential manner.[28] As a result, whilst he does engage with the Qur'an in his theological works, he engages with it in a completely different way. Instead of the Qur'an leading the development of ideas, the theological ideas form the basis of the *kalām*ic discourse and the Qur'an merely becomes a means of establishing credence and authority to those ideas. This can be seen throughout a work such as his *Kitāb al-Arba'īn fī uṣūl al-dīn*. In his discussion as to whether prophets are more worthy than angels, he writes:

> The members of our [Ashʿarī] school and the Shiʿa [argue] that the prophets are more worthy (*afḍal*) than angels, but the philosophers and the Muʿtazila [argue] that the heavenly angels (*al-malāʾika al-samāwiyya*) are more worthy than humans (*al-bashar*) [. . .] The first proof [is] that Adam was prostrated to by the angels, and the person being prostrated to is more worthy than the person doing the prostration. This is first made clear in His Words, Most High, *And when We said to the angels, 'Bow yourselves to Adam'.* [Q. 2:34][29]

Here, the theological idea that prophets are more worthy than angels precedes the interpretation of the verse, and the verse itself is interpreted in light of that view.[30] Whilst Rāzī does include the same point in his *tafsīr* of Q. 2:34, it is certainly not his main one, nor is it the focus of the discussion: the verse generates and demands a greater number of questions beyond that of whether angels or prophets are superior; most notably, why God commanded the angels to prostrate to something other than Him – an idea that could be interpreted as *shirk* ('associationism').[31] These two texts show quite different responses to Q. 2:34 and the question of the angelic prostration to Adam; these establish a distinction between exegesis and theological proof texting, which is not an exegetical process.[32] The roots of these different approaches to the verse are based in the different forms of genre, and the distinct aims and objectives that each entails.

Texts that engage in disputation or are advocating one particular worldview over others for doctrinal or dogmatic reasons engage with the Qur'an in a different way to exegesis. Works in the fields of law, philosophy and theology (*kalām*) use the words and verses of the Qur'an to provide proof for a specific theological or legal idea, rather than being a reflection and interpretation generated by the text of the Qur'an, which demands a different and more comprehensive response. In theological (and legal) discourses, words and verses of the Qur'an acquire a closed, forced and prescriptive meaning, since they are forming part of a larger argument, rather than being part of a response to a Qur'anic verse. The tension between open and closed interpretations distinguishes exegesis from legal and theological apologetic works, since, in contrast, the genre of *tafsīr* is typified by a desire to present a range of exegetical possibilities for interpretation and for the meanings of words themselves, cataloguing the interpretative options and leaving the meaning of the text open.[33]

This polyvalent approach is one that has been discussed in detail by Norman Calder, who argues that polyvalency is typical of *tafsīr*, and may even be the characteristic that defines it as a genre.[34] Calder also makes a distinction between two different ways in which exegetes are able to exert control over any polyvalency, namely 'the exercise of choice (hiding variety) or the expression of a preference (admitting while controlling variety)'.[35] In addition, Calder highlights the influence of hermeneutics on this process of giving a preference; regarding Zamakhsharī, he comments that he 'combines a meticulous concern for grammatical nicety with a defence of Muʿtazilī theology. These factors condition both his expressed preferences (admitting variety) and choices (implying eschewing of some possibilities).'[36] Whilst Calder's analysis of the genre of *tafsīr* is extremely helpful, it is also necessary to understand the motivations that lay behind any attempt to control or reduce the polyvalent readings available. The analysis below argues that there are two distinct reasons for reducing or challenging any potential polyvalency: one in which an exegete makes a decision based on his own analysis of the philological evidence (often from both linguistic analysis and hadith-based glosses); and another which is more highly influenced by pre-textual ideas and beliefs.

Ways of Establishing Lexical Meaning in *Tafsīr*

The discussion thus far has focused on the question of reading, hermeneutics and the formation of meaning in general terms; this volume, however, is focused on a very specific element by which exegetes, and other interpreters of the Qur'an (including translators), construct the meaning of the Qur'an. By giving a word in the Qur'an a meaning, we, as readers of an exegesis, need to ask *cui bono*? What does the exegete gain by giving that word that particular definition? In some cases there may be an underlying theological, socio-cultural or legal reason for it. The same can be equally said for translators of the Qur'an – what idea or belief is benefited by the translator translating a word in such a way? This section will outline the different ways in which individual words are given meaning by exegetes and other interpreters, and how the giving of meaning to Qur'anic lexica relates to external theological ideas.

The most obvious way in which words are given meaning is through lexicography (*ʿilm al-lugha*). Although some lexicographers see, or have seen, their works as providing authoritative accounts of how a word should be understood or spelled (the prescriptive method), many lexicons simply provide data about how a word is and has been used (the descriptive method).[37] Medieval Arabic lexicons usually provide detailed information concerning the speech of the Arabs, using poetry, the Qur'an, hadiths and proverbs as records of proper usage and meaning.[38] However, a genre of 'dictionaries of the Qur'an' (*gharīb al-Qurʾān* works; lit. 'the unusual words of the Qur'an') was also popular in the medieval period and these tend to be much more prescriptive in their handling of Qur'anic lexica, often giving single glosses for specific words, which can be seen in the *Majāz al-Qurʾān* by Abū ʿUbayda Maʿmar b. al-Muthannā (d. between 207/822 and 213/828), and Suyūṭī's *al-Mutawakkilī*.[39] Andrew Rippin comments that, in terms of providing definitions, these works 'are generally very specific as compared to being fully comprehensive for the language or for the text as a whole.'[40] This preference for prescription in *gharīb* works is still found in contemporary Arabic lexicography, both Muslim and non-Muslim. For example, the word *ṣafrāʾ* (Q. 2:69) is subject to debate in the *tafsīr* tradition, since it can indicate either yellow or black;[41] however, most *gharīb* works simply define *ṣafrāʾ* as 'yellow', with very few mentioning the debate at all.[42] The implication is that dictionaries of the Qur'an are highly influenced by the exegetical tradition, and they represent the general conclusions of the exegetes, rather than describing the ways in which the term was used by Arabs.[43] In his study of lexical interpretations of the formative period of *tafsīr*, Kees Versteegh (Chapter 2) shows that early exegetes such as Muqātil b. Sulaymān (d. 150/767) handled lexical meaning in much the same way as these 'dictionaries of the Qur'an'. Throughout his exegesis, Muqātil routinely gives words the same glosses, even when the word has been glossed very recently: for example, he glosses the word *khālidūna* ('dwell forever') with '*lā yamūtūna*' ('they will not die') in both Q. 2:81 and 2:82.[44] However, when turning to the genre of *tafsīr*, especially those working after Muḥammad b. Jarīr al-Ṭabarī (d. 310/923), it is soon discovered that many exegetes rarely, if at all, provide simple, single-word glosses of a word's meaning, nor are they purely prescriptive. Exegetes tend to provide a (possibly full) summary of the ways in which a word is used, and the meanings that it has, but at the same time an exegete often assesses these options and gives his (or her) preferred reading.[45]

Words which seem to have very little theological significance are often subjected to extensive treatment by the exegetes. For example, *Sūrat al-Falaq* begins, *Say: 'I take refuge with the Lord of the Daybreak'* (Q. 113:1). The word for daybreak (*falaq*) is disputed and can either mean 'dawn' (*ṣubḥ*), a location or place in Hell, or 'creation'. Despite the fact that it does not appear to be particularly important whether the oath is made 'with the Lord of the Daybreak' or 'with the Lord of Hell', many exegetes go to great lengths to give the meanings of *falaq*, even though they state their preference for the gloss 'dawn', as can be seen in my own essay (Chapter 6). Ṭabarī provides and describes the full range of possible interpretations of the word, yet gives an overt statement about what he thinks the word means. He is not unique in this method, since many of the other exegetes included in my sample follow the same procedure. In his comparison of the lexical methodologies of Abū'l Ḥasan 'Alī al-Wāḥidī (d. 468/1076) and Ṭabarī (Chapter 5), Claude Gilliot shows both authors giving an array of definitions for words such as *mawbiq* in Q. 18:52.[46] Whilst Ṭabarī does not give his opinion openly (as he does for *falaq*), Gilliot shows the ways in which he does manage to convey his own views: although he cites Abū 'Ubayda's interpretation of *mawbiq* as a 'promise' (*maw'id*), the fact that he includes other glosses of *mawbiq*, such as *mahlik* ('place of destruction') or *mahlak* ('perdition', 'destruction'), more prominently suggests to Gilliot that 'he [Ṭabarī] obviously does not favour it; rather, he seems to prefer the interpretation of the Kufan linguists [*mahlik*]'.[47] Wāḥidī follows a similar procedure in his discussion of the word *mawbiq*, but is more direct in his rejection of Abū 'Ubayda's view. Gilliot comments that 'Wāḥidī considers this interpretation an error (*hādhā'l-qawlu fāsidun*) from the point of view of the word and of its meaning.'[48] This methodological procedure of giving a list of possible options, but discarding some, is hermeneutically complex since it is one that provides a descriptive range of possible meanings, leaving the word open to interpretation, and yet this openness is restricted or closed by the preferred reading. The question is whether giving a preference for a particular reading is the same as giving a forced reading – that is, a reading that is directly influenced by a pre-textual idea or belief. A forced reading is not necessarily an 'incorrect' one, but it is one in which a word is forced into a specific, monovalent interpretation. Calder has noted the process of reducing polyvalency through not providing comprehensive lists of a word's meaning ('hiding variety'), and by giving a preference ('admitting while controlling variety'); but he does not differentiate between the motivations that lie behind the choice itself.[49]. A choice can be governed by external, pre-textual ideas, which creates a forced reading; or the choice can be a reflection on the linguistic evidence available. These two ways of establishing a word's meaning are very different and the two approaches need to be considered in more detail. Some lexical readings, found in some of the chapters in this volume, do appear to be influenced by pre-textual ideas and beliefs.

Ayesha S. Chaudhry presents an analysis of discussions of the word *nushūz* in medieval exegetical works (Chapter 10). The word, associated with the notion of 'disobedience', is used of women in Q. 4:34 and of men in Q. 4:128.[50] However, the exegetes' treatments of the word reveal the complexity of finding meaning for Qur'anic lexica. Chaudhry demonstrates that medieval exegetes defined *nushūz* in completely different ways depending on the gender of the person committing *nushūz*: that is, male *nushūz* is different to female *nushūz*. The exegetes are dealing with the same word, albeit appearing in different contexts; but Chaudhry shows that medieval exegetes are wilfully forgetful of their own interpretations of *nushūz*. She concludes:

> The interpretation of the same term, *nushūz*, to produce two different meanings, at times reading against the plain-sense meaning of the Qur'anic text, is significant in terms of methodology. It demonstrates that pre-modern exegetes read and interpreted the Qur'an within the context of an idealised cosmology in which a patriarchal marital structure was divinely prescribed.[51]

Chaudhry shows that the exegetes in her sample do not attempt to reconcile the two meanings of *nushūz*, and the exegetes treat them as two different words because of their different contexts – a trend that is also seen in Ṭabarī's treatment of the word *fitna*, for which he does not provide a consistent definition throughout his *tafsīr*.[52] In this case, the definitions of *nushūz* are made to reflect and conform to already existing understandings of the gender hierarchy. This is not simply an exegete giving a preference for a particular reading, but Chaudhry argues that the interpretation of *nushūz* is used to authenticate and support a specific patriarchal worldview. Discussions of contentious words like *nushūz* are both open, providing a description of the possible meanings of a word, and also forced or prescriptive. The debates about their meanings, as represented in the *tafsīr* literature, allows for a plurality of meanings, yet the divergences between husbandly and wifely *nushūz* illustrate a proof-texting interpretation that articulates the worldview of the exegetes.

Devin J. Stewart's analysis of *al-Mufradāt alfāẓ al-Qur'ān* by al-Rāghib al-Iṣfahānī (d. 422/1031) highlights a slightly different issue (Chapter 7). Stewart argues that there are a number of instances in the Qur'an where a word takes a non-standard form in order to fit in with the rhyme scheme employed in a sura, a process which Stewart calls 'cognate substitution'.[53] However, the vast majority of Muslim exegetes interpreted these non-standard forms as completely different words and ignored any possibility that they might simply have a new form for reasons of rhyme. Peter Heath, drawing on the work of Tzvetan Todorov, illustrates the way in which exegetes devote extensive material to words that appear to be easily understood, and shows that '[e]ach word becomes a trigger for interpretative processes' and that 'every word or phrase in the Qur'ān acquires enormous power for eliciting hermeneutic responses'.[54]

The exegetical view that new lexical forms are just that – i.e. words with new meanings, rather than forms that have been subject to morphological change as a result of accommodating the rhyme scheme – is also part of this exegetical response to the Qur'an in which all words and every new form is significant. Stewart argues that exegetes interpreted these cognate substitutes as different words in order to preserve the inimitability (*iʿjāz*) of the Qur'an; he writes:

> Recognition of the phenomenon of cognate substitution risked implying that God coined new forms on an ad hoc basis for particular texts in the Qur'an or that God could say one word while intending another, both of which bordered on blasphemy. Exegetes therefore argued that every difference in form implied a difference in meaning.[55]

This is a slightly separate issue to the question of polysemic and monosemic meanings of Qur'anic lexica, but it does, as in Chaudhry's study, highlight a degree of wilful ignorance and academic forgetfulness, as well as the theological limitations of meaning. Figures like al-Rāghib were well versed in rhetoric and poetics, and, Stewart argues, they must have been aware of what was happening to these words, but chose to ignore it.[56]

This process of wilfully forgetting what words can mean can also be seen in another chapter in this volume: Christopher Melchert, in his comparison of the interpretation of Qur'anic words in *tafsīr* and *zuhd* ('asceticism' or 'renunciation') traditions,[57] highlights an attempt on the part of the *mufassirūn* to ignore interpretations of which they disapproved for theological reasons (Chapter 4). In the case of *siyāḥa* ('roaming' or 'travelling') many exegetes gloss the active participle *al-sa'iḥūna* in Q. 9:112 as *al-ṣā'imūna* ('those who fast').[58] Melchert argues that the move against 'roaming', as seen in the gloss 'those who fast', is a result of a movement that found the 'roaming around' of ascetics distasteful in the context of a society where most scholars regarded sedentariness as being civilised. The *tafsīr* literature which emerged in the third/ninth century changed the meaning of *siyāḥa* to 'fasting', but the hadith literature preserved the older definition of *siyāḥa* as 'travelling'. Melchert argues that

> hadith and renunciant literature appear to preserve older interpretations of the terms *siyāḥa*, *ḥikma* and *ṣiddīq* than *tafsīr*. Either *tafsīr* is in fact less primitive than it has seemed or we must consider it strictly selective in what it recalls and what it ignores, of late first-/early eighth-century Islam.[59]

What can be seen here, as in the cases of *nushūz* and cognate substitution, is that a methodology that appears to provide a range of possible meanings for a word does not, in actual fact, always present the whole picture: the descriptiveness is selective. This selectiveness is driven by both socio-cultural and theological worldviews, making such interpretations both descriptive in the sense that they provide an account of the possible meanings of words, and forced or prescriptive in the sense that the words in the Qur'an are being used to articulate and accommodate specific external views. In these cases the preference or interpretation is not reasoned through linguistic analysis, but is defined by cultural or theological beliefs.

Understanding Complex Forms of Constructing Meaning

In the interpretations of *mawbiq*, *falaq*, *nushūz* and *siyāḥa* seen above, different ways of constructing meaning have been encountered. In all four of these examples the exegetes provide a list of possible meanings, but also give a preferred reading. However, the way in which preferences are given for *mawbiq* and *falaq* are quite different to those given for *nushūz* and *siyāḥa*. The first two preferences (*mawbiq* and *falaq*) are reached through philological and linguistic analysis of the term; the second two appear to be generated by specific worldviews. When confronted with an exegete's list of possible meanings for a word, alongside a preference, it is important to distinguish between these two types of readings, since they signify a different hermeneutic response to the Qur'anic text.

The distinction between these two types of giving a preference is hinted at in some medieval works of exegetical theory. For example, in his *Sharḥ ta'wilāt ahl al-sunnah*, 'Alā' al-Dīn al-Samarqandī (d. 539/1144),[60] commenting on the hermeneutic method of *tafsīr* and *ta'wīl* of Abū Manṣūr al-Māturīdī (d. 333/944), states:

> [As for] *ta'wīl*, it is an explanation of something that allows [for various] possibilities and of the ultimate possibility as a predominant opinion, but without a decisive affirmation (*qaṭʿ*). Thus, it [can be] said that an expression may allow such and such interpretations, and that [one of these] interpretations is more appropriate, because it is supported by fundamental sources of religion (*uṣūl*).[61]

Māturīdī uses *ta'wīl* ('interpretation')[62] to describe a method that does not force a meaning, because the reading is simply one that the exegete believes to be more appropriate. In contrast, for Māturīdī *tafsīr* comprised interpretation based on hadiths attributed to Companions of the Prophet, which, consequently, had a fixed meaning, since the Companions had direct interaction with the Prophet and knew the interpretation. Māturīdī opens his *Ta'wīlāt ahl al-sunna* with the statement: '[Concerning] the distinction between *ta'wīl* and *tafsīr*, it is said: *tafsīr* belongs to the Companions, and *ta'wīl* to the lawyers (*fuqahā'*)'.[63] However, even in the case of Māturīdī's conception of *ta'wīl*, the construction of meaning is still limited because of the preference that has been given. This way of reading and interpreting Qur'anic words is half-open and half-closed, or, perhaps neither fully descriptive nor fully prescriptive. This is quite different to the examples seen in the chapters by Chaudhry, Melchert and Stewart, in which the readings are driven by specific socio-cultural and theological motivations, and the openness of the interpretative options for lexical meaning are closed to confirm and conform to a specific worldview.

This distinction between two ways of establishing lexical meaning – by individual preference (Māturīdī's *ta'wīl*) and a more prescriptive method (Māturīdī's *tafsīr*) – is also alluded to by the Muʿtazilī theologian al-Ḥākim al-Jishumī (d. 494/1101). In the introduction to his exegetical work, *Tahdhīb fī tafsīr al-Qur'ān*, he discusses the various sciences (*ʿulūm*) of the Qur'an, and concerning *maʿnā* (meaning), he writes:

> Each word can either have one meaning, so that the only way to interpret it would be by following that meaning, or have [multiple] meanings, all of which are plausible, in which case they can be

> followed in totality or selectively. But if there is compelling evidence that only certain meanings are intended but not others, then those meanings deduced by evidence are to be followed.[64]

Here Jishumī distinguishes between a methodology that provides interpretative options, in which all possible meanings are 'plausible' and can be followed 'in totality', and another methodology in which a word with a range of possible meanings is given a preference, which, as argued above, is neither fully descriptive nor prescriptive. Lastly, Jishumī describes a methodology in which external preconceived ideas (the 'law') can close the interpretation of a word. This is made even stronger in the sentence that follows: '. . . if [a word] has a lexical meaning and a legal meaning, then the legal meaning is heeded because it is overriding'.[65] This is no longer a preferred reading, but a required one.

For some medieval theologians it is impossible to conceive of an individual holding or intending two opposing meanings for the same word at the same time; an idea that was held particularly strongly by Muʿtazilīs. For example, Abū ʿAlī Muḥammad al-Jubbāʾī (d. 303/915–16) argued that 'the meaning of an utterance is not simply a function of its verbal form, but also of the speaker's will'.[66] This means that one has to understand a word in the context of the intention (*niyya*, *irāda* or *qaṣd*) meant by the speaker when it was said. This principle can be extended to the lexical opinions of early interpreters of the Qur'an preserved in the hadith: if someone holds a belief that a word means one thing, can they intentionally give the same word a completely different meaning? In the case of *falaq*, is it logical to think ʿAbd Allāh Ibn ʿAbbās (d. ca. 68/687) believed that *falaq* meant 'dawn', a 'prison in Hell', and 'creation' simultaneously? The link between meaning (*maʿnā*) and intention (*irāda*) would suggest that one could only hold one of these interpretations at a time. The problem of having multiple definitions of the same word by one person is at the heart of Herbert Berg's analysis of the lexical hadith attributed to Ibn ʿAbbās (Chapter 3). For Berg, suspicion is cast not just on Ibn ʿAbbās, but also on his reputed 'school', since his disciples do not provide a consistent and unified front in terms of lexicology.[67] This unease with the multiple interpretations attributed to Ibn ʿAbbās does not seem to be simply a modern concern, since 'the proliferation of these deutero-Ibn ʿAbbās hadiths had, by Ṭabarī's time, forced the compiler into the awkward need to reconcile conflicting opinions'.[68]

Excursus: Mystical lexicology

The exegetes that have been encountered thus far were interested in philological and linguistic meaning, and were concerned with what words mean on a practical level. In his analysis of the *Mafātīḥ al-asrār* by Muḥammad b. ʿAbd al-Karīm al-Shahrastānī (d. 548/1153) (Chapter 8), Toby Mayer argues that Shahrastānī envisions a semantic world that works on two levels: the first is linguistic or physical meaning,[69] which is concerned with 'regular lexicology'; the second is a metaphysical layer of meaning, in which words can reveal the mysteries of the divine world. Shahrastānī himself distinguishes between these two methods, writing: 'The exegetes talk about the meanings of words and terms on the basis of lexicography and transmitted tradition; they do not discuss their arcana in regard to the harmonious order and sequence'.[70] Words, then, have both a physical and a metaphysical meaning. On this basis, Mayer concludes:

> [. . .] on one side, Shahrastānī viewed his etymology, regular lexicology and other historical treatments of the text as addressing the Qur'an *qua* inchoate, as manifest within the conditions of human history. On the other side, he viewed the arcana sections with their items of 'esoteric lexicology' and their unlocking of the text's latent semantic system through the dyadic keys as addressing the scripture *qua* eternally accomplished.[71]

Furthermore, normal linguistic rules do not necessarily apply when the lexical analysis moves into the realm of the metaphysical; indeed, Mayer shows Shahrastānī using playful and unconventional etymologies to great effect.

Shahrastānī provides a further complication to how we can understand the ways in which exegetes construct meaning for words in the Qur'an: in his handling of lexica on the physical level, Shahrastānī pursues a descriptive methodology in a similar fashion to other exegetes,[72] but on the metaphysical level, the engagement with lexicology is more 'prescriptive', and one in which there can be more than one metaphysical meaning for a word, which are all equally valid and authoritative divine truths.[73] The epistemic complexities of holding two (possibly contradictory) meanings for a word cannot really be discussed here, but metaphysical meanings of Qur'anic words are rooted in the divine and transcend the boundaries of established forms of semantic meaning.

Other, more typically Sufi, mystical exegetes engage with the words of the Qur'an in a similar way. The Persian author Rashīd al-Dīn Maybūdī (fl. sixth/twelfth century), for example, delineates his exegesis into three sections (*nawbats*): the first is a Persian translation of the Qur'anic verse; the second is an exoteric (*ẓāhir*) commentary, and the third is an esoteric (*bāṭin*) commentary.[74] In section II, Maybūdī explores lexical meanings and the different uses of the word, although Annabel Keeler comments that

> [Maybūdī] appears to be more concerned with the significance of words, and their different facets of meaning (*wujūh*) as manifested in other verses of the Qur'an. For example, when commenting on '*yawmi'l-dīn*' (Q. 1:4) he does not discuss the semantic structure of the phrase, but gives twelve different aspects of the word *dīn* as it appears in different verses of the Qur'an.[75]

Even though Maybūdī does not construct meaning through linguistic analysis, as many other exegetes do, he still presents a series of interpretative options. However, in section III, the mystical section, lexical meaning is extended through the use of *ishārāt* ('allusions' or 'allegories'), which enables, and promotes, a freer response to Qur'anic lexicology. These extensions or developments of lexical meaning represent a direct revelation of its meaning, or as Sahl al-Tustarī (d. 283/896) comments, 'the point of transcendency [*maṭla'*] is the heart's place of elevation (*ishrāf*) [from which it beholds] the intended meaning, as an understanding from God'.[76] The construction of meaning for words in the Qur'an on two separate planes of reality, the physical and the metaphysical, does not create contradictions or problems in the eyes of mystical exegetes, such as Maybūdī or Abū'l-Qāsim al-Qushayrī

(d. 465/1072). The linguistic and philological meanings of words seek to form a basis from which the mystical is developed; as Martin Nguyen notes: 'In Qushayrī's view, traditional learning and foundational knowledge serve as critical stepping stones to understanding the higher realities embedded in God's word.'[77] Mystical lexicology can complicate the ways in which words are understood to be given meaning by exegetes; however, these complications primarily arise out of the fact that mystical lexicology operates in two different spheres of meaning, the physical and the metaphysical, whereas standard exoteric exegeses focus on linguistic and philological meaning.

Is a Forced Reading Unexegetical?

The field of law is one area where preconceived religious opinions will come to the fore. As already seen, Jishumī argues that 'if [a word] has a lexical meaning and a legal meaning, then the legal meaning is heeded because it is overriding'.[78] This is similar to the view held by Muḥammad b. Idrīs al-Shāfiʿī (d. 204/820). Shāfiʿī developed a hermeneutical method that managed to accommodate existing legal principles within a revelatory framework; David R. Vishanoff comments that Shāfiʿī 'sometimes discounted or reinterpreted a revealed text in order to remain within the parameters of mainstream positive law'.[79] In many cases, the Qur'anic text is made to conform to the interpreter's already held legal views, and the way in which this can be done forms the basis of legal hermeneutic theory, except for those who take a literalist approach to Qur'anic interpretation, in which case the plain-sense reading of the Qur'an is the basis of legal decisions.[80] The need to interpret the Qur'an in light of already existing legal principles is particularly evident in Islamic inheritance law, where the interpretations of specific words, such as *walad* and *ikhwā* in Q. 4:10–11, are directly linked to preconceived and already established ideas on inheritance.[81] This process of interpreting words and verses of the Qur'an in light of already pre-textual legal ideas is analysed in detail by Agostino Cilardo (Chapter 9), who places the different legal schools' interpretations of words concerning inheritance law in the context of their own scholastic views on the division of an estate. Cilardo demonstrates that the Shiʿi author, exegete and legist Muḥammad b. al-Ḥasan al-Ṭūsī (d. 460/1067) must interpret *walad* as 'sons and daughters' to accommodate the Shiʿi convention that women can inherit; this contrasts with Sunni interpreters, who apply the term *walad* to male children only (i.e. sons), in order to maintain male inheritance rights.[82] The different legal schools can only interpret them in a single way: to do otherwise would threaten the legal position itself. In the case of legal exegesis, therefore, meaning becomes firmly prescriptive.

The question as to whether a lexical methodology that drives a forced meaning can be considered as being interpretative is complex; but, if exegesis/*tafsīr* is considered as the way in which data is collected and assessed, this forced, monovalent approach to meaning is quite different to standard *tafsīr*. This method of proof texting denies the existence of any other possibilities: there is only one meaning, no other. As a result, monovalency cannot really be considered strictly exegetical, since it is not a reflection on the text, but rather an eisegetical attempt to make the text conform to external ideas.

Are Translations Prescriptive Readings of the Qur'an?

The physical act of translation necessitates a specific response to lexical questions. Whereas exegetes have the ability to discuss a range of possibilities, a translator cannot do so. A translator, therefore, must explicitly and actively choose one reading for a word's meaning over another. This can enable translators of the Qur'an to promote particular ideas over others: for example, Laleh Bakhtiar's translation of the Qur'an is a response to her finding 'that little attention had been given to the woman's point of view'.[83]

In this volume, Stefan Wild (Chapter 13) illustrates this process in his analysis of two different 'redactions' (for want of a better word) of the Hilali–Khan translation of Q. 1:6–7, which was modified after 9/11. The two versions read:

> Guide us to the Straight Way, the way of those on whom You have bestowed Your Grace, not (the way) of those who earned Your

> Anger (such as the Jews), nor of those who went astray (such as the Christians). [1999 edition][84]

> Guide us to the Straight Way. The Way of those on whom You have bestowed Your Grace, not (the way) of those who earned Your Anger (i.e. those whose intentions are perverted; they know the Truth, yet do not follow it), nor those who went astray (i.e. those who have lost the [true] knowledge, so they wander in error, and are not guided to the Truth). [2006 revised edition][85]

The interpolations and intrusions into the text force the reader to come to specific interpretative judgements about the meaning of the verses. The move away from a polemic attack against Jews and Christians onto extremists – implied by 'those whose intentions are perverted' – shows the extent to which translation can advocate particular discourses. In his study of different translations of Mark 7:19b,[86] George Aichele distinguishes between literal and 'spiritual' translations, which advocate views associated with specific world-views or beliefs; he concludes:

> All of these translation choices constrain the reading of the text of the Gospel of Mark by eliminating alternative possibilities [. . .] In general, a literal translation will leave more reading options open than will a spiritual one, which by its nature seeks to clarify the source text.[87]

The Hilali–Khan translation and revision shows a highly 'spiritual' translation that seeks to interpret Q. 1:7 in a very specific, politicised way. Wild also highlights the politicisation of translation more generally, both in individual translations,[88] and at an institutional level, pointing to the rivalry between the King Fahd Complex in Medina and al-Azhar in Cairo in producing and authorising translations.[89] Likewise, political action on the ground, away from religious affairs, comes to affect the ways in which translations of the Qur'an are received, which is particularly the case in those translations made by Jews and Israelis. In this case, the interpretations and translations that are made are read in light of the contemporary political environment.[90]

Translation, then, enables and necessitates the articulation of certain ideas and beliefs. As Aichele notes, '[e]very translation is directed by the beliefs and values of the translator [. . .] just as every writing is directed by the ideology of the writer'.[91] The extent to which this process is pre-empted by a specific theological or political agenda is hard to establish, although some translators, especially Laleh Bakhtiar, are quite open about the way in which their translations were conditioned by a preconceived agenda. In other cases, the translation is the final product of the translator's internal discussion of a word's meaning; a process which may be similar to the exegeses of early commentators such as Muqātil b. Sulaymān. In the introduction to his translation, Yusuf Ali comments that

> In translating the Text I have aired no views of my own, but followed the received Commentators. Where they differ among themselves, I have had to choose what appeared to me to be the most reasonable opinion from all points of view. Where it is a question merely of words, I have not considered the question important enough to discuss in the Notes, but where it is a question of substance, I hope adequate explanations will be found in the Notes.[92]

Two important points can be drawn from this: (i) that translation can be an exegetical exercise, and the translation itself is the final product of the translator's internal exegetical debate made before committing to a particular translation; and (ii) the notes provide a wider frame of reference and make the translation more descriptive than prescriptive. So, whilst a translation provides single glosses for Qur'anic lexica, this may be part of an unwitnessed methodology that explores potential meanings: an outwardly forced or prescriptive approach to lexical meaning may have been the product of a methodology that has more in common with the descriptive method seen in most exegeses. However, at the same time, translations may be highly prescriptive, in cases where the Qur'an is being used as a proof text for particular worldviews. For example, Andrea Brigaglia illustrates the way in which the Nigerian translator Shaykh Naṣīru Kabarā avoids literal translations of Qur'anic phrases that are anthropomorphic, reflecting his Ashʿarī outlook.[93]

The twin issues of law and translation are discussed in detail in M. Brett Wilson's study of a debate in Turkey that took place during the early twentieth century, discussing whether the fast of Ramadan was obligatory, or whether the fast could be replaced by the payment of compensation called the *fidya* (Chapter 11). The translators and interpreters who advocated replacing the fast with the *fidya* made use of the syntactic difficulties of Q. 2:184.[94] Wilson highlights the fact that this debate is not simply an orthopractic, legal discussion about Islamic ritual, but is embedded within the wider Turkish discussions about modernity: as in Hilali–Khan, translation and politics collide. Wilson concludes:

> By revealing the ambiguity over the meaning of the word *yuṭiqūnahu*, the debate over Q. 2:184 in Turkey highlights the importance of political context in the pursuit of meaning in the Qur'an and, methodologically, provides a fascinating case of modern lexicographic analysis, and its limits, in the print-based public sphere.[95]

These discussions, as well as many other elements of the Turkish modernisation of Islam, generated much debate in other parts of the Islamic world, and are explored in detail by Travis Zadeh (Chapter 12). Zadeh highlights the link between the opposition to the translation of the Qur'an by many Muslim scholars and the doctrine of the inimitability of the Qur'an (*iʿjāz al-Qurʾān*). Part of the argument, given by both medieval and modern authors, is that non-Arabic speakers are not able to understand the full nuances of the Qur'an, and that the 'miraculousness' (*muʿjiza*) of the Qur'an cannot be conveyed in another language.[96] An element of the inimitability of the Qur'an stems from lexical meaning, its ambiguity and the philological connections that can be made between different patterns of the same root. Indeed, some theologians and legal scholars, such as ʿAlī b. Aḥmad Ibn Ḥazm (d. 456/1064), argued that one could not deduce meaning from words of the same root, but of a different pattern (i.e. one could not use the form *munfaṭir* ['be split'] in Q. 73:18 to interpret the meaning of *fāṭir* ['originator'] in Q. 35:1).[97] Others, such as some Muʿtazilīs, including Abū ʿAlī al-Jubbāʾī, argued that intention (*niyya*) was essential to meaning, and that words which had multiple meanings could not have had multiple meanings in a single speech-act.[98] However, these two positions were not predominant, and many exegetes maintained a degree of ambiguity in lexical meaning, which cannot be reproduced in translation. As a consequence, translation is inevitably prescriptive, since it cannot maintain any ambiguity that may exist.

What is Meaning For? Lexical Methodologies and Interpretation

The discussion above has highlighted a number of different ways in which lexical meaning can be constructed. These different methodologies are not simply used by different authors, but can also be found in the same work. Consequently, it is necessary to reflect on how exegetes and interpreters develop meaning, in order to facilitate accurate comparisons, and this introduction will now reflect on the construction of lexical meaning in *tafsīr* more generally. For example, exegetes such as Ṭabarī and Wāḥidī construct lexical meaning in different ways in different situations. This can, and should, be regarded as significant, since the way in which lexical meaning is constructed has a bearing on how we, as readers of an exegesis, understand the information being presented by an exegete or interpreter.

The evidence found in the articles included in this volume reveals a need to refine Calder's theories about choice in *tafsīr*. Calder's main interest is in the polyvalent nature of *tafsīr*, coupled with different means of subverting it. Calder does acknowledge the influence of hermeneutic principles on the ways in which exegetes reduce any interpretive polyvalency, but this introduction argues that, regarding the interpretation of words of the Qur'an, there is a difference between an exegete giving a preference, and when preferences are clearly underpinned by specific pre-textual ideas. The former is an evaluation of the linguistic and interpretative context, the other is influenced by beliefs held by an exegete or interpreter before coming to the text.

At its most basic level, there are two diametrically opposed methodologies to the construction of lexical meaning: the first is a methodology which provides an interpretative open description of a word's usage in Arabic. The second is a methodology that gives a single, forced or prescribed solution to a semantic question. The exploration of the ways in which exegetes and translators develop meaning for words of the Qur'an seen above has shown that this dichotomy between the descriptive and the prescriptive is not absolute, and that exegeses engage with lexical meaning in a much more complex way.

The semiotician A.J. Greimas created a way to explore and develop fields of semantic meaning through contrasting two opposed terms, and his approach will help to illustrate the different ways that exegetes construct lexical meaning (see Figure 1).[99] Greimas develops semantic meaning from a single seme (a unit of meaning or signification), which is given the symbol (S_1), and its opposite (S_2; i.e. $\neg S_1$ /'not S_1'). The seme can be a word (e.g. 'black'), an idea (e.g. 'democracy'), or even a theme or trope within a narrative (e.g. 'death' in the story of Sleeping Beauty). Greimas argues that the original seme, and its opposite (marked by the symbol ¬), also holds more complex senses of semantic meaning, which are indicated by the symbol $\tilde{S}$. In the case of the story of Sleeping Beauty, for example, the binary themes of death and life also generate the complex idea of 'being both dead *and* alive', when the princess is sleeping. Importantly, the narrative of the fairy story

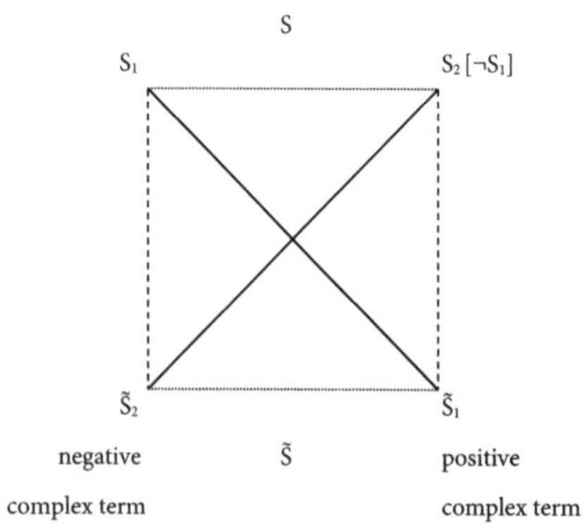

Figure 1.

does not move from 'death' to 'life' directly, but through this complex idea of 'being both dead and alive'.[100] Greimas's main objective in using the semiotic square is to show that words, concepts and signs in a binary relationship have more complex ideas lying beneath them: (i) one of which is both S_1 and S_2 ($\tilde{S}_1$), and (ii) one which is neither ($\tilde{S}_2$).

In an illustration of the way in which the semiotic square can be used, Ronald Schleifer explores the terms 'black' and 'white'.[101] In this example, 'black' (S_1) is the opposite of 'white' ($\neg S_1/S_2$), but from these two terms it is possible to develop more complex ideas: the first is a term that describes something that is both 'black and white', or a term that has 'both no colours' and 'all colours', which Schleifer calls 'colouredness' ($\tilde{S}_1$). The second is a term that is 'neither black nor white', or has 'neither all colours nor no colours', which he calls 'colourlessness' ($\tilde{S}_2$). Schleifer uses the square to place the simple terms 'black' and 'white' within wider, more complex semantic fields. The semiotic square has not just been used to describe semantic meaning, but also the relationship of ideas, technical terms and ideologies, as well as literary studies.[102] In the context of this study of how exegetes construct meaning, it is possible to explore the relationship between the opposed methods of description and prescription (see Figure 2).

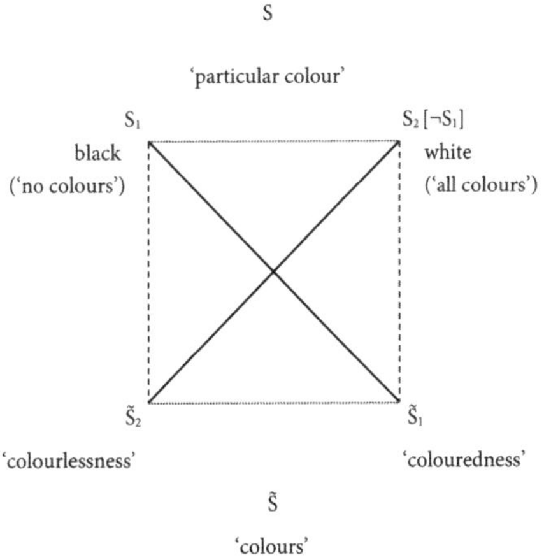

Figure 2.

The reason Greimas's square is helpful in the context of Qur'anic lexicology is that it enables a more nuanced appreciation of the ways in which the polyvalency of lexical meaning is subverted by exegetes. My analysis of the ways in which exegetes construct the meanings of words in the Qur'an has outlined four main ways of doing this: (i) the purely descriptive method (polyvalency), which produces an open interpretation; (ii) the purely prescriptive method (monovalency), which closes the potential readings of the word; (iii) a method where a list of potential meanings is given, but the exegete restricts the openness of the reading by stating a preferred option arrived at through linguistic analysis, although where other options are interpretatively valid; and (iv) a method where a list of meanings is given, but the meaning is given a closed and prescriptive definition, because of theological or socio-cultural beliefs (see Figure 3).

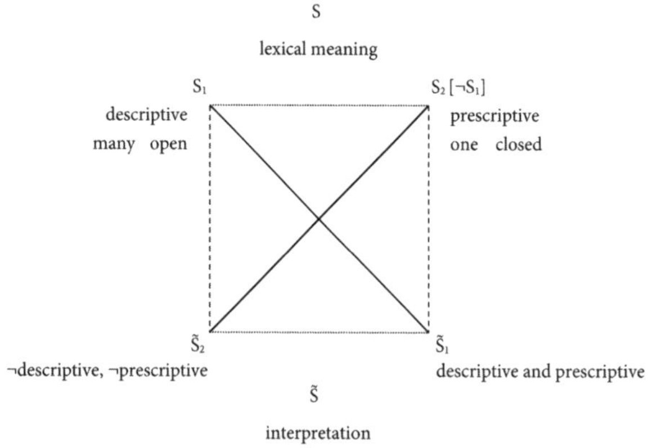

Figure 3.

When the two terms or methodologies of description and prescription (or semantic polyvalency and monovalency) are placed in the semiotic square, two complex terms emerge, which can help to delineate the different ways in which exegetes can develop lexical meaning.

The descriptive method takes a word and provides a different range of possible meanings, without giving one reading preference over any other, so the meaning of the word is left open. This method is predominantly found in lexicography (*lugha*), which attempts to provide descriptions of words' meanings in a neutral fashion.[103] The method is also found in many exegeses of the Qur'an, in those places where authors give possible options without giving a preference; it is used, for example, by Suyūṭī throughout his *al-Durr al-manthūr*,[104] but is also relatively common elsewhere. A caveat must be given that an exegete may hinder the openness of the reading by not listing every possible meaning of a given word (which Calder refers to as 'hiding variety');[105] but there are instances in which exegetes do produce open lists of possible meanings, without making any overt preference.

The prescriptive methodology is a completely different process. In this case, the starting point is not the Qur'anic word in question, but the idea, which informs the interpretation of the word and necessitates a single meaning rather than a range of meanings that could threaten the coherence of any argument being made. This is most relevant to specific discourses such as theology (*kalām*), philosophy and law, in which external ideas are rooted in the revealed scripture through the use of lexicology and other forms of argumentation. In this method, meaning is used to establish a proof (*ḥujja*) to a particular external idea or belief. However, the prescriptive method can also be found in other cases: often in *gharīb al-Qur'ān* works, in early exegeses, such as that by Muqātil b. Sulaymān (d. 150/767), and in translations of the Qur'an.

The 'descriptive and prescriptive method' is seen when the exegete provides a range of interpretations for a word's meaning, but gives a preference for a particular reading that is dictated by an external belief or idea. For example, the meaning of *nushūz* is predetermined by socio-cultural norms, and 'cognate substitutes' are interpreted differently to maintain the inimitability of the Qur'an. The way in which exegetes handle words in the Qur'an that have implications to legal theories can also introduce more prescriptive interpretations, such as in the interpretations of *walad* as either 'sons' or 'sons and daughters' in Q. 4:10–11.

The 'neither descriptive nor prescriptive method' is found most commonly in exegeses of the Qur'an, where an exegete provides a series of possibilities for a word's meaning, but gives a preference for one over any others. This methodology may also be used in translations of the Qur'an and in early exegesis, but in this case the process is hidden: the final solution to a lexical question is given, but without any of the other possibilities that were known to the exegete or translator. The 'neither descriptive nor prescriptive method' is not descriptive in the sense that a single reading is given in the preferred reading (so it is not fully polyvalent); but it is also not prescriptive, because the preference is not generated by an external idea, and other possible meanings remain equally valid (so it is not monovalent).

Typically, exegetes employ a mixture of the 'descriptive', 'descriptive and prescriptive' and 'neither descriptive nor prescriptive' methodologies in their exegeses; that is, exegesis (*tafsīr*) only operates in one part of the semiotic square (see Figure 4).

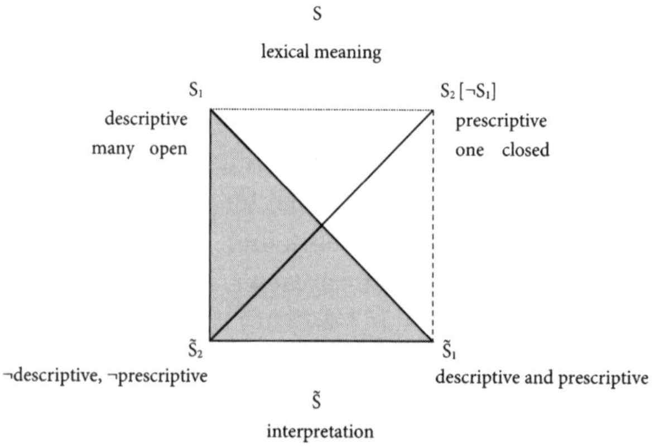

Figure 4.

As has been seen above, it is possible, for example, to find all three of these methodologies (but not the prescriptive) in Ṭabarī's *tafsīr*: his interpretation of *nushūz*, particularly in the case of wifely *nushūz*, is conditioned by socio-cultural norms; his interpretation of *falaq* provides a preferred reading based on linguistic evidence, but other meanings are valid; and in his interpretation of *mawbiq*, Ṭabarī does not give a preferred reading openly. The method that cannot easily be found in Ṭabarī's exegetical works is the purely prescriptive, providing monovalent definitions.

This exploration of the ways in which exegetes construct meaning for words in the Qur'an has shown that there are complex ways of forming lexical meaning. Furthermore, not all exegetical lexical choices or preferences are the product of the same process; some are simply preferences, and others are highly influenced by pre-textual ideas and beliefs. The two complex ways of establishing meaning – 'descriptive and prescriptive' and 'neither descriptive nor prescriptive' – help to distinguish these two types of exegetical choice: one introduces prescription, the other reduces the description. As previously discussed, these two different ways of coming to exegetical decisions are alluded to in some discussions of medieval exegetical theory. This first method ('descriptive and prescriptive') is associated by Māturīdī with *tafsīr*, since for him, interpretations found in the Hadith provide definite interpretations, but there may be a plurality of views which need to be assessed, making the approach both prescriptive and descriptive ($\tilde{S}_1$). In contrast, he views *ta'wīl* as a more open process, albeit sometimes one in which preferences are given; *ta'wīl* is concerned with 'possibility' and 'preference', which can never be properly descriptive or prescriptive ($\tilde{S}_2$). Whether or not it is appropriate to use the terms *tafsīr* and *ta'wīl* to distinguish these two methods is a different question;[106] but the distinction between giving a preference based on a personal, reflective judgement, and an opinion that is imposed on a word because of pre-textual beliefs can be made. Using Māturīdī's terms as a guide, it is possible to represent the four approaches to lexical meaning in a semiotic square (see Figure 5).

The act of translation (*tarjama*) creates a slightly different model. Since a translation must produce a single, prescriptive translation of a word, it can never be descriptive and it can never be 'neither descriptive nor prescriptive' (cf. Māturīdī's *ta'wīl*). Some translations, however, can be the product of a descriptive method that remains unseen (cf. Māturīdī's *tafsīr*); others will be highly

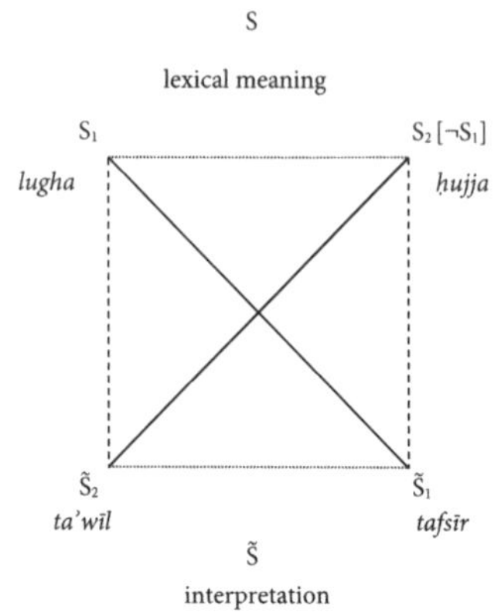

Figure 5.

prescriptive. There are also commentaries in Arabic that establish meaning in a similar fashion, such as the early exegesis of Muqātil b. Sulaymān, as well as the *Tafsīr al-Jalālayn*. With regard to lexicology, the extent to which these can be regarded as *tafsīr* or *ta'wīl* (following Māturīdī's understanding) warrants further discussion, which cannot be provided here. The construction of the meanings of words in translations of the Qur'an works in a different way to exegesis, since the genre of translation (*tarjama*) cannot accommodate descriptiveness, so translation as a whole must be confined to one side of the square (see Figure 6).

The basic function of both exegesis and translation is to generate and provide interpretations or meanings for words in the Qur'an; but the way in which the meanings of words are constructed varies greatly. Meaning can be open/polyvalent, closed/monovalent, as well as take more complex and refined forms: an exegete can reduce the potential polyvalency through giving opinions or preferences; and an exegete can introduce a degree of prescription to a lexical discussion as a result of pre-textual, external ideas and beliefs. The prescriptive methodology uses the meaning of the words in the Qur'an to support ideas, and to offer proofs (sg. *ḥujja*). Here, meaning is established not by a word's potential for a variety of meanings, but because the lexical meaning becomes a requirement

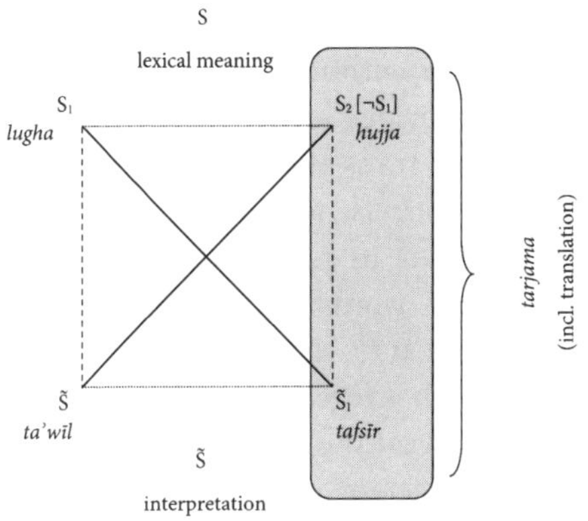

Figure 6.

(or consequence) of a previously held belief. In contrast, the descriptive methodology (*lugha*) begins by looking at a word found in the Qur'an and exploring its potential meanings. The descriptive method (even when modified with an element of prescription) is part of a wider search for the meaning of scripture, whereas the prescriptive method uses meaning to defend a specific, predefined theological belief. In this way, the construction of words' meanings are dependent on the way in which they are being approached: the prescriptive method provides a contextual framework into which meaning is placed (or forced), creating a closed and monovalent interpretative environment; the descriptive method provides a range of exegetical possibilities, creating an open and polyvalent interpretative world.[107] *Tafsīr*, however, tends to construct meaning in more complex ways, at times reducing the polyvalency through various means, or by introducing external ideas, whether theological, legal or socio-cultural, into the text.

Lexicology is not simply about semantic or philological meaning, but it is concerned with what words mean to their readers and the authors, and the significance and resonances they may have for both. As Karen Bauer comments, '*tafsīr* is each scholar's attempt to relate his world to the world of the Qur'an; it is his attempt to relate his intellectual, political and social contexts to the Quran's text'.[108] The relationship within hermeneutics between the words of the Qur'an and the wider interpretative discourse is complex. Reading, writing and translation are all subject to influence from previously held beliefs, which come into play in both the interpretation of scripture in general terms, as well as the specific handling of individual words: as Schleiermacher argued, each level of meaning feeds into the understanding of another. The different ways in which exegetes establish the meanings of the words in the Qur'an reveal the extent of the influence of external texts, as well as the different uses for giving meaning to words. The use of words as proof texts for particular ideas or beliefs shows a specific type of engagement with the Qur'an and its words. The different ways in which exegetes establish the meanings of words, the 'descriptive', the 'descriptive and prescriptive' and the 'neither descriptive nor prescriptive', highlight the different responses to words in the Qur'an within the genre of *tafsīr* itself, and the ways in which exegetes approach their personal choices and preferences.

The articles in this volume discuss the ways in which exegetes engage with words to construct the meaning of the Qur'an. It is necessary to reflect on the ways in which exegetes engage with meaning and what they hope to achieve by interpreting words in particular ways. Whilst acknowledging that external pre-textual ideas always inform the process of reading, the extent of their influence can vary depending on the word, context and approach of an exegete or translator. Exegetes and translators do not simply provide neutral descriptions of words' meanings, but seek to articulate specific ideas through them. At times this may simply be a personal preference, at others it is more thoroughly affected by external, pre-textual ideas and beliefs. Being aware of the different ways of constructing lexical meaning helps us to understand the influence of external texts on lexical meaning, as well as the way in which the meanings of words can come to direct and inform a particular reading of a Qur'anic word. The meaning of the Qur'an, taken in its most general sense, is built up from its smaller parts and the meanings of words are at its very foundation.

NOTES

1 See Friedrich D.E. Schleiermacher, *Hermeneutics and Criticism and Other Writings*, tr. and ed. Andrew Bowie (Cambridge: Cambridge University Press, 1998). Originally published as *Hermeneutik und Kritik mit besonderer Beziehung aus das Neue Testament* (Berlin: Reimer, 1838). Also see B.H. McLean, *Biblical Interpretation and Philosophical Meaning* (Cambridge: Cambridge University Press, 2012), pp. 39–43.

2 Martin Heidegger, *Being and Time*, tr. John Macquarrie and Edward Robinson (repr. Oxford: Blackwell, 1978). Originally published as *Sein und Zeit* (Tübingen: Max Niemeyer, 1927). Hans-Georg Gadamer, *Truth and Method*, tr. Joel Weinsheimer and Donald G. Marshall, 2nd rev. edn (London: Continuum, 2004). Originally published as *Wahrheit und Methode: Grundzüge einer philosophischen Hermeneutik* (Tübingen: Mohr, 1960).

3 Gadamer, *Truth and Method*, pp. 299–310.

4 For a discussion of hermeneutics in an Islamic context, see Victoria S. Harrison, 'Hermeneutics, Religious Language and the Qur'an', *Islam and Christian–Muslim Relations* 21, no. 3 (2010), pp. 207–20.

5 Schleiermacher, 'Hermeneutics and Criticism' in idem, *Hermeneutics and Criticism and Other Writings*, pp. 9–11. Schleiermacher differentiates between two types of reading, the grammatical (textual and philological reading) and the psychological (wider theological and spiritual reflection on the whole text). See also Gadamer, *Truth and Method*, pp. 184–95.

6 For a discussion of this, see McLean, *Biblical Interpretation and Philosophical Meaning*, pp. 43–4.

7 Postmodernist literary theory also developed out of the linguistic models of meaning and signification developed by Ferdinand de Sausurre, and the theories of signs (semiotics) first put forward by Charles S. Peirce.

8 Louise M. Rosenblatt, *The Reader, the Text, the Poem: The Transactional Theory of the Literary Work* (Carbondale, IL: Southern Illinois University Press, 1978), p. 13. For a longer discussion of theories of reading and *tafsīr*, see S.R. Burge, 'The Search for Meaning: *Tafsīr*, Hermeneutics, and Theories of Reading,' *Arabica* 62, no. 1 (2015), pp. 53–73.

9 See Roland Barthes, 'From Word to Text' in idem, *Image, Music, Text*, tr. Stephen Heath (repr. London: Flamingo, 1984), pp. 155–64, at pp. 159–60. Originally published as 'De l'œuvre au texte', *Revue d'esthétique* 3 (1971), pp. 225–32.

10 For an analysis of the term 'intertextuality' in postmodern literary theory, see Graham Allen, *Intertextuality: The New Critical Idiom*, 2nd edn (London: Routledge, 2011). The term is often used in the sense of 'source-criticism', but this is not what is meant by it.

11 See Roland Barthes, 'The Death of the Author' in idem, *Image, Music, Text*, pp. 142–8. Originally published as 'La mort de l'auteur', *Manteia* 5 (1968), pp. 12–17.

12 Wolfgang Iser, *The Act of Reading: A Theory of Aesthetic Response* (London: Routledge & Kegan Paul, 1978), pp. 124–51, esp. pp. 141–3.

13 Postmodernism and hermeneutic theory has attracted some Muslim thinkers, such as Mohammed Arkoun, Abdulkarim Soroush and Farid Esack; see Harrison, 'Hermeneutics, Religious Language and the Qur'an', pp. 214–19.

14 Rudolf Bultmann, 'Is Exegesis without Presuppositions Possible?' in idem, *Existence and Faith: Shorter Writings of Rudolf Bultmann*, tr. M. Ogden (London: Hodder and Stoughton Ltd., 1961), pp. 342–51, at p. 344. Originally published as 'Ist voraussetzungslose Exegese möglich', *Theologische Zeitschrift* 13 (1957), pp. 409–17. Bultmann's hermeneutic method has been critiqued by Barrie A. Wilson, 'Bultmann's Hermeneutics: A Critical Examination', *International Journal for Philosophy of Religion* 8 (1977), pp. 169–89. See also, Burge, 'The Search for Meaning', pp. 72–3.

15 See also Jay G. Williams, 'Exegesis-Eisegesis: Is there a Difference?' *Theology Today* 30 (1973), pp. 218–27.

16 George Aichele and Gary A. Phillips, 'Exegesis, Eisegesis, Intergesis', *Semeia* 69/70 (1995), pp. 7–18, at p. 14. See also Burge, 'The Search for Meaning', pp. 57–8.

17 Islamic Studies as a field has tended to use the term hermeneutics in the sense of methodology, e.g. Jane Dammen McAuliffe, 'Quranic Hermeneutics: The Views of al-Ṭabarī and Ibn Kathīr' in Andrew Rippin, ed., *Approaches to the History of the Interpretation of the Qur'ān* (Oxford: Clarendon Press, 1988), pp. 46–62; and Walid A. Saleh, 'Hermeneutics: al-Thaʿlabī' in Andrew Rippin, ed., *The Blackwell Companion to the Qur'ān* (Oxford: Blackwell, 2006), pp. 323–37.

18 Walid A. Saleh, *The Formation of the Classical Tafsīr Tradition: The Qur'ān Commentary of al-Thaʿlabī (d. 427/1035)* (Leiden: Brill, 2004), pp. 16–17; Karen Bauer, '"I Have Seen the People's Antipathy to this Knowledge": The Muslim Exegete and his Audience, 5th/11th–7th/13th Centuries' in Asad Q. Ahmed, Behnam Sadeghi and Michael Bonner, eds, *The Islamic Scholarly Tradition: Studies in History, Law, and Thought in Honor of Professor Michael Allan Cook* (Leiden: Brill, 2011), pp. 293–314. Bauer also highlights the use of *tafsīr* in sermons.

19 Cf. S.R. Burge, 'Jalāl al-Dīn al-Suyūṭī, the *Muʿawwidhatān* and the Modes of Exegesis' in Karen Bauer, ed., *Aims, Methods and Contexts of Qur'anic Exegesis (2nd/8th–9th/15th c.)* (Oxford: Oxford University Press in association with the Institute of Ismaili Studies, 2013), pp. 277–307.

20 The term 'pre-text' is used by Robert E. Innis to refer to previously read texts (in the sense of both actual written texts, and life experiences); see Robert E. Innis, 'Pragmatics of Reading', *Transactions of the Charles S. Peirce Society* 34, no. 4 (1998), pp. 869–84.

21 *Say: 'To whom belongs what is in the heavens and in the earth?' Say: 'It is God's. He has prescribed for Himself mercy. He will surely gather you to the Resurrection Day, of which there is no doubt. Those who have lost their souls, they do not believe.* Unless specified otherwise, translations of the Qur'an are from A.J. Arberry, *The Koran Interpreted* (repr., Oxford: Oxford University Press, 1998).

22 Feras Hamza and Sajjad Rizvi, with Farhana Mayer, eds, *An Anthology of Qur'anic Commentaries. Volume 1: On the Nature of the Divine* (Oxford: Oxford University Press in association with the Institute of Ismaili Studies, 2008), pp. 312–13.

23 See W. Montgomery Watt, *Islamic Philosophy and Theology*, 2nd edn (Edinburgh: Edinburgh University Press, 1985), pp. 47–52.

24 ʿAlī b. Ibrāhīm al-Qummī, *Tafsīr*, ed. Ṭayyib al-Mūsawī al-Jazā'irī (Najaf: Maṭbaʿat al-Najaf, 1387/1967), vol. 1, p. 141; for more on Shiʿi proofs for the

imamate, see Meir M. Bar-Asher, *Scripture and Exegesis in Early Imāmī Shiism* (Leiden: Brill, 1991), pp. 126–8.

25 Andrew Newman, *The Formative Period of Twelver Shīʿism: Ḥadīth as Discourse Between Qum and Baghdad* (Richmond, Surrey: Curzon, 2000), p. 51.

26 Fakhr al-Dīn al-Rāzī, *al-Tafsīr al-kabīr* (*Mafātīḥ al-ghayb*) (Tehran: Dār al-Kutub al-ʿIlmiyya, n.d.).

27 For example, Rāzī provides a long theological discussion about the sending down of the Qur'an in his exegesis of Q. 2:185 at the reference to *the month of Ramadan, wherein the Koran was sent down*; ibid., vol. 5, pp. 84–7.

28 Yasin Ceylan, *Theology and Tafsīr in the Major Works of Fakhr al-Dīn al-Rāzī* (Kuala Lumpur: International Institute of Islamic Thought and Civilization, 1996).

29 Fakhr al-Dīn al-Rāzī, *Kitāb al-Arbaʿīn fī uṣūl al-dīn* (Hyderabad: Maṭbaʿat Majlis Dāʾirat al-Maʿārif al-ʿUthmāniyya, 1353/1934–5), p. 368; cf. Rāzī's use of the Qur'an as a proof text in Binyamin Abrahamov, 'Faḫr al-Dīn al-Rāzī on the Knowability of God's Essence and Attributes', *Arabica* 49, no. 2 (2002), pp. 204–30.

30 Cf. Umberto Eco, *The Role of the Reader: Explorations in the Semiotics of Text* (Bloomington, IN: University of Indiana Press, 1979), pp. 24–7; see also Omar Alí-de-Unzaga, 'Citational Exegesis of the Qur'an: Towards a Theoretical Framework for the Construction of Meaning in Classical Islamic Thought. The Case of the *Epistles of the Pure Brethren* (*Rasāʾil Ikhwān al-Ṣafāʾ*)' in Abdou Filali-Ansary and Aziz Esmail, eds, *The Construction of Belief: Reflections on the Thought of Mohammed Arkoun* (London: Saqi Books in association with the Institute for the Study of Muslim Civilisations, 2012), pp. 168–93.

31 See Peter J. Awn, *Satan's Tragedy and Redemption: Iblīs in Sufi Psychology* (Leiden: Brill, 1983), pp. 24–33.

32 Geza Vermes makes this distinction in 'Biblical Proof-Texts in Qumran Literature', *Journal of Semitic Studies* 34 (1989), pp. 493–508, at p. 493.

33 Karen Bauer, 'Introduction' in Bauer, ed., *Aims, Methods and Contexts of Qur'anic Exegesis*, pp. 1–16, at p. 7.

34 Norman Calder, 'Tafsīr from Ṭabarī to Ibn Kathīr: Problems in the Descriptions of a Genre, Illustrated with Reference to the Story of Abraham' in G.R. Hawting and Abdul Kader A. Shareef, eds, *Approaches to the Study of the Qur'ān* (London: Routledge, 1993), pp. 101–40, at pp. 101–3.

35 Ibid., p. 103.

36 Ibid.

37 For a history of the uses of the terms 'descriptive' and 'prescriptive' in lexicography and grammar, see Henning Bergenholz and Rufus S. Gouws, 'A Functional Approach to the Choice between Descriptive, Prescriptive and Proscriptive Lexicography', *Lexikos* 20 (2010), pp. 26–51.

38 E.g. al-Khalīl b. Aḥmad, *Kitāb al-ʿAyn* (Beirut: Dār Iḥyāʾ al-Turāth al-ʿArabī, 2001); Muḥammad b. Yaʿqūb al-Fīrūzabādī, *al-Qāmūs al-muḥīṭ* (India: n.p., n.d.); Muḥammad b. Mukarram Ibn Manẓūr, *Lisān al-ʿArab*, ed. Amīn Muḥammad ʿAbd al-Wahhāb and Muḥammad al-Ṣādiq al-ʿUbaydī (Beirut: Dār Iḥyāʾ al-Turāth al-ʿArabī, 1999); Murtaḍā al-Zabīdī, *Tāj al-ʿarūs min*

jawāhir al-qāmūs, ed. ʿAbd al-Sattār Aḥmad Farāj *et al.* (Kuwait: Maṭabaʿat Ḥukūmāt al-Kuwayt, 1965–2001); and Ibn Durayd, *Kitāb Jamaharat al-lugha*, repr. (Baghdad: al-Muthanna Library, n.d.).

39 Abū ʿUbayda, *Majāz al-Qurʾān*, ed. Aḥmad Farīd al-Mazīdī (Beirut: Dār al-Kutub al-ʿIlmiyya, 2006); and Suyūṭī, *al-Mutawakkilī*, ed. and tr. William Y. Bell as *The Mutawakkili of as-Suyūṭī* (Cairo: Nile Mission Press, 1924).

40 Andrew Rippin, 'Lexicographical Texts and the Qurʾān' in idem, ed., *Approaches to the History of the Interpretation of the Qurʾān*, pp. 158–74, at p. 162.

41 For more on *ṣafrāʾ* in Q. 2:69, see Kees Versteegh, Chapter 2 in this volume, pp. 54–5; Wolfdietrich Fischer, *Farb- und Formbezeichnungen in der Sprache der altarabischen Dichtung: Untersuchungen zur Wortbedeutung und zur Wortbildung* (Wiesbaden: Otto Harrassowitz, 1965), pp. 364–5.

42 Cf. John Penrice, *A Dictionary and Glossary of the Qur'an*, repr. (Lahore: al-Biruni, 1976), p. 84; Elsaid M. Badawi and Muhammad Abdel Haleem, *Arabic-English Lexicon of Qur'anic Usage* (Leiden: Brill, 2008), p. 528; ʿAlī Akbār Qurashī, *Qāmūs-i Qurʾān* (Tehran: Dār al-Kutub al-Islāmiyya, 1973–6), vol. 4, p. 133. Arne Ambros refers to the debate about *ṣafrāʾ* in Arne A. Ambros, with Stephan Procházka, *A Concise Dictionary of Koranic Arabic* (Wiesbaden: Reichert Verlag, 2004), p. 162.

43 Cf. Calder, 'Tafsīr from Ṭabarī to Ibn Kathīr', p. 104.

44 See Versteegh, Chapter 2, p. 64, n. 53.

45 See S.R. Burge, Chapter 6 in this volume, pp. 162–3.

46 *And on the day He shall say, 'Call on My associates whom you asserted', and then they shall call on them, but they will not answer them, and We shall set a gulf (mawbiq) between them.*

47 Claude Gilliot, Chapter 5 in this volume, p. 128.

48 Ibid., p. 129.

49 Cf. Calder, 'Tafsīr from Ṭabarī to Ibn Kathīr', p. 103.

50 Q. 4:34, ... *and those that you fear may be rebellious (nushūzahunna) admonish* ...; and Q. 4:128, *If a woman fear rebelliousness (nushūzan) or aversion in her husband* ...

51 Ayesha S. Chaudhry, Chapter 10 in this volume, p. 343.

52 See Abdulkader Tayob, 'An Analytical Survey of al-Ṭabarī's Exegesis of the Cultural Symbolic Construct of *Fitna*' in Hawting and Shareef, *Approaches to the Study of the Qurʾān*, pp. 157–72; cf. Herbert Berg, 'Ṭabarī's Exegesis of the Qurʾānic Term *al-Kitāb*', *Journal of the American Academy of Religion* 63, no. 4 (1995), pp. 761–74.

53 Stewart also discusses this in 'Poetic License in the Qur'an: Ibn al-Ṣaʾigh al-Ḥanafī's *Iḥkām al-rāy fī aḥkām al-āy*', *Journal of Qur'anic Studies* 11, no. 1 (2009), pp. 1–54, at pp. 20–25.

54 Peter Heath, 'Creative Hermeneutics: A Comparative Analysis of Three Islamic Approaches,' *Arabica* 36, no. 2 (1989), pp. 173–210, at pp. 178–9. Heath is referring to Todorov's 'principle of pertinence'; Tzvetan Todorov, *Symbolism and Interpretation*, tr. Catherine Porter (Cornell: Cornell University Press, 1986), p. 28. Originally published as *Symbolisme et interpretation* (Paris: Editions du Seuil, 1978).

55 Devin J. Stewart, Chapter 7 in this volume, p. 246.

56 Cf. Alexander Key, 'Al-Raghīb al-Iṣfahānī' in Terri de Young, ed., *Essays in Arabic Literary Biography. Volume 1* (Wiesbaden: Harrassowitz, 2011), pp. 298–306. See also Stewart, 'Poetic License in the Qur'an', pp. 1–54.

57 *Zuhd* was a pietistic movement that became prominent in the early period of Islam; a body of hadith emerged which promoted *zuhd*; see Christopher Melchert's essay (Chapter 4 in this volume).

58 Q. 9:112, *Those who repent, those who serve, those who pray, those who journey . . .*

59 Melchert, Chapter 4 in this volume, p. 110.

60 See Angelika Broderson, "Alā' al-Dīn al-Samarqandī', *EI THREE* (Brill Online) [last accessed 27 June 2013].

61 Cited from Alena Kulinich, 'Representing "a Blameworthy *Tafsīr*": Muʿtazilite Exegetical Tradition in *al-Jāmiʿ fī tafsīr al-Qurʾān* of ʿAlī ibn ʿĪsā al-Rummānī (d. 384/994)' (Unpublished PhD Dissertation, School of Oriental and African Studies, University of London, 2011), p. 83 (amended slightly). The text is Kulinich's translation of ʿAlā' al-Dīn al-Samarqandī, *Sharḥ ta'wilāt ahl al-sunnah* (fragment), MS 3249, fol. 2v, Abū Rayḥān al-Bīrūnī Institute of Oriental Studies, Tashkent.

62 It should be noted that this is not always what is meant by *ta'wīl*, as it can be used, especially by Ismaili exegetes, to describe a construction of lexical meaning that is prescriptive, rather than the result of linguistic and philological analysis. For Ismaili exegetes the *ta'wīl* is forced or prescriptive, because the meaning is given through divine revelation. See Ismail K. Poonawala, 'Ismāʿīlī *ta'wīl* of the Qur'ān' in Rippin, ed., *Approaches to the History of the Interpretation of the Qur'ān*, pp. 199–222, at pp. 206–12.

63 Abū Manṣūr al-Māturīdī, *Ta'wīlāt ahl al-sunna*, ed. Fāṭima Yūsuf al-Khaymī (Beirut: Mu'assasat al-Risāla Nāshirūn, 1425/2004), p. 1. See also Ahmad Mohmed Ahmad Galli, 'Some Aspects of al-Māturīdī's Commentary on the Qur'ān', *Islamic Studies* 21, no. 1 (1982), pp. 3–22, at pp. 3–5. Māturīdī presents his theoretical understanding of *tafsīr* and *ta'wīl*, not necessarily what he does in practice. The application of the theories expounded by exegetes in their introductions do not always match an exegete's actual practice and can serve other purposes; for a discussion of introductions to *tafsīr*, see Karen Bauer, 'Justifying the Genre: A Study of Introductions to Classical Works of *Tafsīr*' in Bauer, ed., *Aims, Methods and Contexts of Qur'anic Exegesis*, pp. 39–65.

64 al-Ḥākim al-Jishumī, *Tahdhīb fī tafsīr al-Qur'ān*; translation from Suleiman A. Mourad, 'Towards a Reconstruction of the Muʿtazilī Tradition of Qur'anic Exegesis: Reading the Introduction to the *Tahdhīb* of al-Ḥākim al-Jishumī (d. 494/1101) and Its Application' in Bauer, ed., *Aims, Methods and Contexts of Qur'anic Exegesis*, pp. 101–37, at p. 104 (Ar. p. 135).

65 Ibid., p. 104 (Ar. p. 135).

66 David R. Vishanoff, *The Formation of Islamic Hermeneutics: How Sunni Legal Theorists Imagined a Revealed Law* (New Haven, CT: American Oriental Society, 2011), p. 116.

67 Herbert Berg, Chapter 3 in this volume, p. 83; cf. Claude Gilliot, 'Portrait "mythique" d'Ibn ʿAbbās', *Arabica* 32, no. 2 (1985), pp. 127–84.

68 Berg, Chapter 3 in this volume, p. 83.

69 There are three main ways of deriving meaning (*ishtiqāq*) for words: *ishtiqāq al-ṣaghīr* (etymology or the meaning of derived forms and patterns), *ishtiqāq al-kabīr* or *qalb* (meaning developed through metathesis), and *ishtiqāq al-akbar* or *ibdāl* (meaning generated through the replacement of one radical with another of a similar phonetic value). Although Shahrastānī does not use these terms, his use of 'physical' meaning is related to *ishtiqāq al-ṣaghīr* and *ishtiqāq al-kabīr*, and his 'metaphysical' lexicology is similar to *ishtiqāq al-kabīr*. For more on approaches to *ishtiqāq*, see Mustafa Shah, 'The Philological Endeavours of the Early Arabic Linguists: Theological Implications of the *tawqīf-iṣṭilāḥ* Antithesis and the *majāz* Controversy – Part I', *Journal of Qur'anic Studies* 1, no. 1 (1999), pp. 27–46, at pp. 33–5.

70 Muḥammad b. ʿAbd al-Karīm al-Shahrastānī, *Mafātīḥ al-asrār wa maṣābīḥ al-abrār*, tr. Toby Mayer as *Keys to the Arcana: Shahrastānī's Esoteric Commentary on the Qur'an* (Oxford: Oxford University Press in association with the Institute of Ismaili Studies, 2009), p. 153.

71 Toby Mayer, Chapter 8 in this volume, p. 275.

72 Ibid., p. 261.

73 Cf. Shahrastānī's exegesis of Q. 1:7, Mayer, *Keys to the Arcana*, pp. 184–5.

74 See Annabel Keeler, *Sufi Hermeneutics: The Qur'an Commentary of Rashīd al-Dīn al-Maybūdī* (Oxford: Oxford University Press in association with the Institute of Ismaili Studies, 2006), pp. 39–104.

75 Ibid., p. 52.

76 Sahl al-Tustarī, *Tafsīr*, tr. Annabel Keeler and Ali Keeler as *Tafsīr al-Tustarī* (Louisville, KY: Fons Vitae / Royal Aal al-Bayt Institute for Islamic Thought, 2011), p. 2.

77 Martin Nguyen, *Sufi Master and Scholar: Abū'l-Qāsim al-Qushayrī and the* Laṭā'if al-ishārāt (Oxford: Oxford University Press in association with the Institute of Ismaili Studies, 2012), p. 138.

78 Mourad, 'Towards a Reconstruction of the Muʿtazilī Tradition of Qur'anic Exegesis', p. 104 (Ar. p. 135).

79 Vishanoff, *The Formation of Islamic Hermeneutics*, p. 36.

80 This is particularly important for the Ẓahirīs, see ibid., pp. 66–108; and Robert Gleave, *Islam and Literalism: Literal Meaning and Interpretation in Islamic Legal Theory* (Edinburgh: Edinburgh University Press, 2012); and idem, *Scripturalist Islam: The History and Doctrines of the Akhbārī Shīʿī School* (Leiden: Brill, 2007).

81 That interpretations of specific words relevant to inheritance do not largely appear in exegeses of the Qur'an until after Shāfiʿī, indicates his influence, and also Vishanoff's main argument.

82 Agostino Cilardo, Chapter 9 in this volume, p. 297.

83 Laleh Bakhtiar, tr., *The Sublime Quran: Based on the Hanafi, Maliki and Shafii Schools of Law* (Chicago, IL: islamicworld.com, 2007), p. xliii.

84 Taqi-ud-Din al-Hilali and Muhammad Muhsin Khan, tr., *The Noble Qur'an in the English Language: A Summarized Version of At-Tabari, Al-Qurtubi, and Ibn Kathir with Comments from Sahih al-Bukhari* (Riyadh: Darussalam, 1996), p. 10.

85 Taqī al-Dīn al-Hilālī and Muḥammad Muḥsin Khān, *The Noble Qur'an. English Translation of the Meanings and Commentary*; http://www.qurancomplex.org [last accessed 20 June 2013].

86 'He [Jesus] said to them: "Then do you also fail to understand? Do you not see that whatever goes into a person from outside cannot defile, since it enters, not the heart but the stomach, and goes out into the sewer?" (Thus he declared all foods clean).' [Mark 7:18–19].

87 George Aichele, *Sign, Text, Scripture: Semiotics and the Bible* (Sheffield: Sheffield Academic Press, 1997), pp. 54–5.

88 There has been much written on this area, e.g. Abdur Rahim Kidwai, 'A Survey of English Translations of the Quran', *The Muslim World Book Review* 7, no. 4 (1987), pp. 66–71; Helmut Bobzin, 'Translations of the Qur'ān', *EQ*, vol. 4, pp. 340–58; Neal Robinson, 'Sectarian and Ideological Bias in Muslim Translations of the Qur'an', *Islam and Christian–Muslim Relations* 8, no. 3 (1997), pp. 261–78; and more region-specific studies, such as Andrea Brigaglia, 'Two Published Hausa Translations of the Qur'ān and Their Doctrinal Background', *Journal of Religion in Africa* 35, no. 4 (2005), pp. 424–49; Ziad Elmarsafy, 'Translations of the Qur'ān into Western Languages', *Religion Compass* 3, no. 3 (2009), pp. 430–39.

89 Stefan Wild, Chapter 13 in this volume, p. 432.

90 Ibid., pp. 437–40.

91 Aichele, *Sign, Text, Scripture*, p. 55.

92 Abdullah Yusuf Ali, tr., *The Meaning of the Holy Qur'ān: Qur'ānic Text (Arabic) with Revised English Translation, Commentary and Index*, 11th edn (Beltsville: Amana Publications, 1427/2006), p. xiv; cf. Brigaglia, 'Two Published Hausa Translations of the Qur'ān', pp. 436–9.

93 Brigaglia, 'Two Published Hausa Translations of the Qur'ān', pp. 440–41.

94 See also M. Brett Wilson, 'The First Translations of the Qur'an in Modern Turkey (1924–1938)', *The International Journal of Middle East Studies* 41 (2009), pp. 419–35.

95 M. Brett Wilson, Chapter 11 in this volume, p. 368.

96 See also Travis Zadeh, *The Vernacular Qur'an: Translation and the Rise of Persian Exegesis* (Oxford: Oxford University Press in association with the Institute of Ismaili Studies, 2012), pp. 214–50.

97 For more on this see Vishanoff, *The Formation of Islamic Hermeneutics*, pp. 88–91.

98 See ibid., pp. 116–17; and Richard Frank, 'Meanings Are Spoken of in Many Ways: The Earlier Arab Grammarians', *Le Muséon* 94, nos 3–4 (1981), pp. 259–319.

99 A.J. Greimas, *Sémantique structurale. Recherche de méthod* (Paris: Larousse, 1966); tr. D. McDowell, R. Schleifer and A. Velie as *Structural Semantics: An Attempt at a Method* (London: Nebraska University Press, 1983).

100 This example is taken from Bronwen Martin, 'Semiotics', *Encyclopaedia of Literary Critics and Criticism*, vol. 2, pp. 1004–12, at pp. 1008–10.

101 Ronald Schleifer, *A.J. Greimas and the Nature of Meaning: Linguistics, Semiotics and Discourse Theory* (London: Croom Helm, 1987), pp. 25–33.

102 Cf. A.J. Greimas, *Maupassant: La sémiotique du texte* (Paris: Editions du Seuil, 1976).

103 See John A. Haywood, 'The Entry in Medieval Arabic Monolingual Dictionaries: Some Aspects of Arrangement and Context' in Reinhard R.K. Hartmann, ed., *The History of Lexicography: Papers from the Dictionary*

Research Centre Seminar at Exeter, March 1986 (Amsterdam: J. Benjamins, 1986), pp. 107–13; and Rippin, 'Lexicographical Texts and the Qur'ān'.

104 Burge, Chapter 6 in this volume, pp. 172 and 180–81.

105 Calder, '*Tafsīr* from Ṭabarī to Ibn Kathīr', p. 103.

106 Andrew Rippin, 'Tafsīr', *EI*², vol. 10, pp. 83–8; cf. Galli, 'Some Aspects of al-Māturīdī's Commentary on the Qur'ān', pp. 4–5.

107 See Eco, *The Role of the Reader*, pp. 3–43.

108 Bauer, 'Introduction', in eadem, ed., *Aims, Methods and Contexts of Qur'anic Exegesis*, p. 8.

SECTION I

Lexicology and the Formative Period of Qur'anic Exegesis

2

In Search of Meaning: Lexical Explanation in Early Qur'anic Commentaries*

KEES VERSTEEGH

IN THE early period of Islam, the text of the Qur'an, accepted by all Muslims as God's revelation to the Prophet Muhammad, was transmitted in a small community of believers in the Arabian Peninsula, where Arabic was the language of the vast majority in the region. In some cases, the text of the Book itself highlights the fact that some words may have been difficult to understand, as in Q. 104:5, *what has taught you what the ḥaṭama is?* (*wa-mā adrāka mā'l-ḥaṭama?*); or Q. 101:3, *what has taught you what the qāriʿa is?* (*wa-mā adrāka mā'l-qāriʿa?*)'.[1] But there were many more lexical items in the text whose meaning must have been unclear for the believers. It would seem to be common sense to assume that, during the lifetime of the Prophet, people turned to him for help in understanding the text. Yet, most of the hadiths about the relevance of Qur'anic verses in early collections such as the *Muṣannaf* by ʿAbd al-Razzāq al-Ṣanʿānī (d. 211/827) go back to Companions rather than to the Prophet;[2] moreover, relatively few of these are concerned with the lexical meaning of Qur'anic words or expressions. Either the believers understood the meaning of most words in the revealed Book or, if they did ask about it, these explanations did not make it into the hadith literature.

* I wish to thank Stephen Burge (Institute of Ismaili Studies) for his support in writing this chapter, which went far beyond the normal duties of an editor. His comments and those of two anonymous referees made me rethink a considerable number of points.

During the first century of Islam, masses of new converts were introduced to the Qur'anic message, who could not be expected to understand it without proper knowledge of its lexicon. These converts needed help from professional interpreters. One of the earliest attempts to explain the Qur'an is traditionally ascribed to the Companion ʿAbd Allāh Ibn ʿAbbās (d. ca. 68/687), who is often cited as an authority by later scholars.[3] Three treatises are ascribed to him, and even entire *tafsīrs* were transmitted under his name. It is doubtful that these really go back to him,[4] but other commentaries have come to light that may well go back to the end of the first century and the beginning of the second century of the Hijra/eighth century CE. Some of these have been transmitted as full-fledged *tafsīrs* under the name of one exegete, for instance those by Muqātil b. Sulaymān (d. 150/767),[5] Zayd b. ʿAlī (d. 122/740) and Muḥammad al-Kalbī (d. 146/763). Others have been assembled from the quotations in later *tafsīrs*, for instance those by Mujāhid b. Jabr (d. 104/722), al-Ḍaḥḥāk b. Muzāḥim (d. ca. 106/724), al-Suddī al-Kabīr (d. 127/745), Ibn Jurayj (d. 150/767), Sufyān al-Thawrī (d. 161/778) and Maʿmar b. Rāshid (d. 153/770) in ʿAbd al-Razzāq's recension.

In these early commentaries, lexical explanation plays an important role. Difficult words are explained *ad hoc*; some words are explained with the help of the context or on the basis of the circumstances in which they were revealed (*asbāb al-nuzūl*). In some cases it is obvious that the explanation of a word is inspired by the religious or legal interpretation of the text, but in other cases it is not immediately clear why a certain meaning is preferred by the commentator. Most commentators do not content themselves only with the explanation of words, but also with their provenance: they regularly point out that some words derive from other languages, and link certain words with specific Arab tribes.

The importance of these early lexicographical attempts can hardly be overestimated. They tell us something about the preoccupations of the early believers and their perspective on the text of the Qur'an. In addition, they provide us with information about the language itself, and in particular about which words the common believers found it hard to understand. I shall first deal with the question of the authenticity of the sources, and then discuss the methods with which the commentators explained the meaning of words in the Qur'an.

Authenticity of the Early Commentaries

In his study of the development of Qur'anic exegesis, John Wansbrough suggests that the commentary literature went through a gradual evolution.[6] He couches this view in terms borrowed from the development of Talmudic commentaries on the Torah and states that the first stage of all exegetical activity in Islam was haggadic in nature, in other words, it concentrates on the narrative of the revealed text. The next stage was halakhic, focusing on the legal relevance of the text of the Qur'an. The final stage was masoretic, when commentaries started to deal with the textual and linguistic structure of the Qur'an. Wansbrough's theory presupposes a chronological development of these three types of *tafsīr* (two additional types, the rhetorical and the allegorical *tafsīr*s, will not concern us here), but this is contradicted by the fact that from the earliest stages onward, all topics were present in the commentaries, albeit to a varying degree. Thus, from the earliest period onward, one finds side by side lexical paraphrases, narrative exposition, historical explanations, textual variants (*qirā'āt*), and even a few legal and ritual issues.[7] For Wansbrough, such a combination of elements in one commentary is a strong argument against the authenticity of the text in the sense that, in his view, a commentary such as the one attributed to Kalbī is an amalgam of original remarks and later interpolation.[8] There is a certain circularity in this reasoning: since Wansbrough believes that there was a chronological development, he is unwilling to accept commentaries with a heterogeneous character as authentic.

In his study of the exegetical literature, Herbert Berg sets up a typology of commentaries according to the topics studied.[9] Basing himself on Wansbrough, Berg lists fifteen exegetical devices applied by exegetes. He aims to investigate the authenticity of the exegetical hadiths transmitted from Ibn ʿAbbās on the basis of their contents.

He concludes that in this corpus the pattern of use of the fifteen devices by the various links in the *isnād*s is inconsistent, and that it is, therefore, impossible to reconstruct any authentic texts from the early period.[10] Harald Motzki's analysis of the available exegetical sources leads to a more positive result.[11] He does not claim that all views ascribed to Ibn ʿAbbās are authentic, but argues that his method of critically examining both the contents and the *isnād*s of the sources enables him to date some of them to the last quarter of the first/seventh century.[12]

It should be pointed out here that Berg focuses on the exegetical tools used by the commentators rather than the topics addressed by them. Widening the scope of his approach to include choice of topics is more likely to bring out the individual character of each commentary. It seems reasonable to assume that, while the early commentators all share certain ideas and methods, their individual tastes and predilections in selecting topics lend each commentary its own character or, as Berg calls it, its own stylistic profile or fingerprint.[13]

This individual character shines through, even in the case of collected quotations. Of course, it is true that in the collected quotations (as against the commentaries that have been transmitted as a whole) there may be a bias, because later compilers picked out certain things that struck them as being particularly important. In the case of Ḍaḥḥāk, for instance, later compilers focused on his ideas about abrogation. Ḍaḥḥāk became known for his firm belief that all conciliatory passages about adherents of other religions in the Qur'an were abrogated by the opening verses of *Sūrat al-Tawba* (Q. 9:1–2), in which a respite (*barā'a*) is announced, after which all treaties with non-believers will be annulled.[14] This is what later generations focused on in their transmission from him, and this explains the prevalence of this point in the collected quotations. Yet, the transmitters did not concentrate on this aspect of his commentary exclusively, because from the collected quotations it is obvious that Ḍaḥḥāk had other interests as well, for instance his ideas about all topics connected with Hell.[15]

Other commentators too had a predilection for certain topics, which is manifest in the comments transmitted from them. Ibn

Jurayj, for instance, seems to have had a special interest in the role of angels; he is also keen on specifying the age of persons mentioned in the Qur'an. Such features are clearly diagnostic in determining the integrity of the text, in the sense that each commentary exhibits its own specific mix of topics and views.

The Purpose of Exegesis

Although the early commentaries sometimes deal with legal and ritual issues, their primary aim does not seem to have been to explore all legal implications of the text. Very often, verses that were used by later commentators as arguments in legal discussions are paraphrased without any obvious awareness of the implications. Thus, for instance, the famous verse Q. 5:6, *fa-ghsilū wujūhakum wa aydiyakum ilā'l-marāfiqi wa-msaḥū bi-ru'ūsikum wa arjulakum* (or: *arjulikum* or *arjulukum*) *ilā'l-kaʿbayni* (*and wash your face and your hands up till the elbows, and wipe your head clean, and* [*wash*] *your feet up till the ankles*; or: *wipe your head and your feet clean*, or *and your feet* [*the same goes for them*]), whose interpretation hinges on the choice of the case ending in the last word,[16] is simply mentioned by Muqātil in one version, without any reference to alternative readings or their implications.[17]

As a general rule, these commentators were not interested, either, in the structure of the language, but only in the underlying meaning of the text. Yet, for purposes of identification or disambiguation, they needed at least some grammatical terms, which must have gained currency at an early period. The commentators were aware of the morphological patterning of Arabic, for instance, and sometimes they offer morphological information about the pattern of a lexical item. Ḍaḥḥāk compares the word *qaṣr* ('trunks of large trees') with the word *thamr* ('fruit') because both words have a similar singular (*qaṣra*, *thamra*).[18] His purpose is to dispel any possible confusion about the identity of this lexical item, which should not be confused with the singular word *qaṣr* ('stone house'), which has the plural *quṣūr*.

The most frequently used grammatical terms in the early commentaries have to do with vocalisation and with sentence types.

These terms, too, are linked with the general purpose of the commentaries. Terms for vowels are needed to disambiguate the text and do not serve the purpose of syntactic analysis. Their primary function is to provide the commentator with a tool to distinguish between words differing only in one vowel. Thus, for instance, regarding the active participle *mukhliṣūna* ('sincere') in Q. 2:139, *we are sincerely devoted to Him* (*wa-naḥnu lahu mukhliṣūna*), one needs a term to indicate the internal *i*-vowel in order to differentiate it from the passive participle (*mukhlaṣūna*). Kalbī does so by stating that the word should be read *bi-khafḍ al-lām* ('with an *i* after the *l*').[19] The term he uses here for the internal vowel (*khafḍ*) was later used exclusively for the case ending of the genitive (in Kufan terminology, synonymous with Basran *jarr*), and not for internal vocalisation. This lack of terminological distinction between internal vowels and case endings applied to all vowels in the commentaries. It was not until the appearance of the *Kitāb Sībawayhi* at the end of the second/eighth century that it became common practice in grammatical literature to distinguish two sets of terms, one for case endings and one for internal vowels. In fact, the interchangeable use of the two sets in quotations from early commentaries constitutes a strong argument for the authenticity of these texts, contrary to Wansbrough's scepticism. In the transmission of these commentaries, the original terms are frequently maintained, rather than the 'correct' ones that had in the meantime become current.[20]

The terminology for sentence types is closely connected with the need to distinguish between different genres in the text. In order to understand the impact of a verse, one has to determine to which text type it belongs. Apparently, a classification of genres or text types in the Qur'an must have originated at a quite early time. In Muqātil's commentary, a list of text types is given which aims to cover the contents of the entire Qur'an.[21] According to this list, the Qur'an contains, among other things, general and particular statements, ambiguous and univocal verses, abrogation, parables, regulations and narrations.[22] The term 'genres' should be understood here in a very broad sense, because the distinction between genres or text types plays an important role on the level of the sentence as well. In Q. 23:82, where the unbelievers say: *when we have died and are dust and bones, will we then be resurrected?* (*a-idhā mitnā wa kunnā turāban wa ʿiẓāman a-innā la-mabʿūthūna*), exegetes, such as Muqātil, stress that it is important to clarify that this is meant as a negative exclamation (*taʿajjub wa jaḥd*), rather than a question (*istifhām*).[23]

Some of the terms used by the commentators, such as *ista'nafa* ('to begin'), are needed to indicate where one sentence ends and a new sentence begins. In commenting on Q. 57:27, *and We put compassion and mercy in the hearts of those who followed him* (*wa jaʿalnā fī qulūbi'lladhīna'ttabaʿūhā ra'fatan wa raḥmatan*), Muqātil observes that a new sentence starts (*ista'nafa al-kalām*) with the next words, *and monasticism, which they innovated, We did not prescribe for them* (*wa rahbāniyyatan ibtadaʿūhā mā katabnā ʿalayhim*).[24] By parsing the verse in this way, he implicitly rejects the interpretation that God could have put monasticism in the followers' hearts.

The commentators hardly ever bother to deal with the intricate details of grammatical structure in the Qur'an, however, and when they do so it is only because these details are indispensable for the comprehension of the text. Very rarely, they focus on deviating patterns of sentence construction. The Qur'an contains some cases of hyperbaton, which leave the contents of the verse perfectly comprehensible but may have sounded odd to those accustomed to current linguistic usage. In such cases, comments are needed not for the understanding of the verse, but in order to show how the underlying meaning would be expressed in common usage. An obvious example is that of Q. 25:59, *then, God sat upon His throne* (*thumma'stawā ʿalā'l-ʿarshi'l-Raḥmān*), which is explained by most commentators as a case of transposed word order (*muqaddam wa mu'akhkhar*) instead of *thumma'stawā'l-Raḥmān ʿalā'l-ʿarshi*, for instance by Kalbī.[25] Barring these exceptional cases of syntactic 'correction', the early commentators are interested solely in the semantic aspects of the text.

Semantic Explanation in the Early Commentaries

When a word, phrase, sentence or verse in the Qur'an needs to be explained, its meaning can be given by simple juxtaposition: for example, Suddī notes, commenting on Q. 18:40, *so that it becomes a slippery piece of barren land* (*fa-tuṣbiḥu ṣaʿīdan zalaqan*), '*al-ṣaʿīd al-amlas*' ('*al-ṣaʿīd*: the barren');[26] and Ḍaḥḥāk on Q. 4:65, *and* [*when*] *they do not find in their heart a constraint* [*to accept*] *your judgement* (*thumma lā yajidū fī anfusihim ḥarajan mimmā qaḍayta*), comments, '*ḥarajan ithman*' ('*ḥarajan*: sin').[27] This is the device most often used when the explanation consists in giving a direct equivalent or synonym of a Qur'anic word.

In some cases, especially when the explanation consists of a lengthier paraphrase or when the meaning of an entire phrase is given, exegetical connectors are used between the Qur'anic expression and the explanation, such as *qāla* or *yaqūlu* ('He [or: it] says'), *yaʿnī* ('He [or: it] means'), *ay* ('i.e.'), or *maʿnāhu* ('its meaning [is]'). The grammatical subject of the connectors is not always clearly distinguished: they may refer to God as the author of the revelation, or to the text itself.

It seems to be the case, although this is difficult to determine, that the choice of connector varies with each commentator. In Muqātil's commentary, the most frequent connectors are *yaʿnī* and, less frequently, *yaqūlu*; *ay* is used only a few times.[28] Take the following examples:

Q. 77:31 . . . *lā ẓalīlin* ***yaqūlu*** '*bāridin ẓalīlin*'
. . . *no shade* – He means 'a shade of coolness'[29]

Q. 82:1 *idhā'l-samā'u'infaṭarat* ***yaʿnī*** '*inshaqqat*'
when the heavens infaṭarat, it means 'split'[30]

Q. 2:26 *wa yahdī bihi* ***ay*** *bi-hādhā'l-mathal*
and He guides with this, i.e. 'with this parable'[31]

The distinction being made by these connectors is certainly not a strict one, and even within one commentary, connectors tend to be used interchangeably. The precise choice of exegetical connector may well have been characteristic of the individual commentary, but this is difficult to verify, since the majority of the texts derive from quotations by later authors. In principle, they transmitted these commentaries *verbatim*, but they may not have felt the need to go as far as preserving the connectors used by the source.

Some of the words explained appear to be archaic ones which had disappeared from the colloquial language of the contemporary believers; often they are *hapax legomena* (words occurring only once in the text of the Qur'an), for instance *anāmil yaʿnī 'aṭrāf al-aṣābiʿ'* (*anāmil* means 'the fingertips').[32] The explanation of a word may also involve a reference to the same word in another verse in the Qur'an, which is referred to as its *naẓīr* ('similar'; pl. *naẓā'ir*), for instance when Muqātil reinforces his interpretation of the word *furqān* in Q. 3:4 by referring to its occurrence in Q. 21:48.[33] Muqātil is credited with an entire treatise dedicated to this topic, entitled *al-Ashbāh wa'l-naẓā'ir* or *al-Wujūh wa'l-naẓā'ir*, in which the part dedicated to the *naẓā'ir* dealt systematically with the meaning of typical Qur'anic words.[34]

Some references are given systematically, so that words are paraphrased in an identical way at the vast majority of occurrences, even if they occur only a few verses apart. Thus, for instance, in Q. 21:79 the verb *ātā* is glossed with *aʿṭā* ('to give'), and the same gloss is repeated five verses below, in Q. 21:84.[35] Examples from Muqātil's commentary include *alīm* glossed with *wajīʿ* ('painful'),[36] and *jannāt* glossed with *basātīn* ('gardens').[37] This systematic replacement does not only involve substantives and verbs, but also some adverbs, such as *ayyān* glossed with *matā* ('when'),[38] and *annā* glossed with *min ayna* ('from where?').[39] Some expressions are introduced with the formula *kull shay' fī'l-Qur'ān* ('every occasion in the Qur'an'), for instance from Ḍaḥḥāk's comments, *kull shay' fī'l-Qur'ān jaʿala fa-huwa khalaqa* ('whenever "to make" [*jaʿala*] is used in the Qur'an, it means "to create" [*khalaqa*]');[40] and '*kull sulṭān fī'l-Qur'ān ḥujja*' ('every [occurrence of the word] *sulṭān* in the Qur'an [means] "proof" [*ḥujja*]').[41] This may even lead to general statements about the grammar of the Qur'anic language, as when Ḍaḥḥāk states that the disjunctive pair *aw* . . . *aw* . . . ('either . . . or . . .') always implies a choice on the part of the person to whom the statement is applied. In Q. 2:196, for instance, the provision for someone who is prevented by sickness from making the pilgrimage, which reads *then the compensation is fasting or alms or a sacrifice* (*fa-fidyatun min ṣiyāmin aw ṣadaqatin aw nusukin*), is interpreted as a set of alternatives, from which one can choose.[42]

The examples given here support the idea that the commentators had a stock list of lexical items that are systematically replaced by others. Moreover, the words in various commentaries are partly identical: the equivalence of *qisṭ* = *ʿadl* ('justice') in Q. 7:29 and 21:47, and *ghalīẓ* = *shadīd* ('violent') in Q. 31:24, is given by both Muqātil and Kalbī.[43] Sometimes, the words are paraphrased in a slightly different way, for instance Muqātil explains *alīm* in Q. 41:43 with *wajīʿ*, and Ḍaḥḥāk with *mūjiʿ*, both glosses meaning 'painful'.[44] Such parallels may suggest a common source, but much more detailed research is required to determine the exact transmission, in particular with respect to the suggestion that it was Ibn ʿAbbās who was responsible for compiling a list of Qurʾanic expressions.[45] He is mentioned by the commentators as the authority for some of the words in this category, for instance in the case of the paraphrase *sulṭān* = *ḥujja*, given by Ḍaḥḥāk and ʿAbd al-Razzāq.[46] The consistent repetition of paraphrases belonging to this category constitutes an additional argument for the integrity of the text, because their use implies an integrated approach to the text as a whole.

Some of the examples of lexical paraphrase given above, such as *qisṭ* or *sulṭān*, concern words that presumably were difficult to understand for common people without specialist knowledge of the technical lexicon of the Qurʾan. In other cases, it is clear that there were also doctrinal considerations that led to the paraphrase. Muqātil replaces the expression *a-laysa Allāh*, such as in Q. 95:8, *is God not the wisest judge?* (*a-laysaʾllāhu bi-aḥkamiʾl-ḥākimīna*), with *anā Allāhu* ('I, God . . .'), in order to emphasise the fact that these words do not express doubt on God's part, but are meant as a rhetorical statement.[47] When Abraham is called a *ḥanīf muslim* in Q. 3:67, Muqātil paraphrases this with *mukhliṣ* ('sincere').[48] This paraphrase may have originated in a desire to emphasise the difference between Islam as the religion brought by the Prophet, and *islām* as sincere submission to God.[49] Muqātil's paraphrase of *ẓulm* ('wrongdoing') with *shirk* ('polytheism') should probably be seen in light of the Muʿtazilī views on the status of the sinning believer, according to which only polytheists could be called *ẓālim*.[50]

Even when the connection with theological debates is not immediately clear, one can never completely exclude the possibility that an explanation was inspired by doctrinal considerations. Sometimes, the ideological bias is difficult to perceive and can only be reconstructed from debates elsewhere. In Muqātil's commentary, for instance, the word *mubīn* is consistently paraphrased with *bayyin*.[51] At first sight, this looks like a simple lexical paraphrase, but it turns out that the choice between these two lexical items may be connected with a doctrinal issue after all. According to Claude Gilliot, *mubīn* in the well-known collocation *kitābun mubīnun*, usually translated as 'a clear Book' (e.g. in Q. 5:15), would not mean 'clear', but 'clarifying', in accordance with its morphological status as the active participle of the causative form.[52] Gilliot interprets this phrase as a reference to earlier scriptures revealed by God, which are clarified/interpreted by the text of the Qur'an. It is very likely that Muqātil's paraphrase *bayyin* (with the meaning, 'clear') is meant to reject any interpretation of this phrase that would turn the Qur'an into a commentary/interpretation of earlier scriptures. With his choice of paraphrase, he emphasises the independent character of the Qur'anic revelation.

Another example is that of the word *khālidūna* (usually translated as 'remaining forever'), which Muqātil explains as *lā yamūtūna* ('they do not die').[53] This comment may be related to a general debate about the eternity or finiteness of punishment in Hell. According to some theologians, arguing from Q. 11:106–7 and other verses, there will be an end limit to the stay in Hell. Muʿtazilī theologians, on the other hand, believed that Hell will be created after the Last Judgement and will then exist forever.[54] The eternal punishment of the sinners was one of the consequences of their views about God's justice and His promise of reward and punishment (*al-waʿd waʾl-waʿīd*).[55] Perhaps, with his paraphrase, Muqātil just wished to emphasise that he did not believe there would be any exemption from the fire, but it is also possible that he took a position in an ongoing discussion. At any rate, the comment is more than just a lexical paraphrase.[56]

The opposite procedure to the listing of words with the same meaning throughout the Qur'an is the listing of words with different meanings in the Qur'an (this category of words is called *mutashābihāt* [lit. 'looking alike'] after Q. 3:7, which divides the verses of the Qur'an into *muḥkamāt* and *mutashābihāt*). In his treatise *al-Ashbāh wa'l-naẓā'ir*, mentioned above, Muqātil dedicates a section to this category of words under the heading of *ashbāh* ('likenesses') or *wujūh* ('aspects').[57] Some of the *mutashābihāt* not only have different meanings, but these meanings are antonymous. Examples from this category are mentioned by all commentators. The verb *ẓanna* ('to assert, assume, believe') is a good illustration of this phenomenon.[58] In the *tafsīr* attributed to him, Zayd b. ʿAlī says: '*ẓann* means certainty, but it can also mean doubt and it can mean suspicion' (*fa'l-ẓann al-yaqīn wa yakūnu al-ẓann shakkan wa yakūnu tuhman*);[59] according to Ḍaḥḥāk, it refers to secure knowledge when applied to believers, but indicates doubt when applied to unbelievers.[60] For the connotation of certainty, both Zayd b. ʿAlī and Ḍaḥḥāk refer to Q. 69:20, *I counted on meeting my account* (*innī ẓanantu annī mulāqin ḥisābiyah*). An example of *ẓann* with the connotation of uncertainty is found in Q. 38:27, *this is the assumption of the disbelievers* (*dhālika ẓannu'lladhīna kafarū*). The commentators' underlying motive is probably their wish to avoid attributing doubt to a prophet, as in the case of David in Q. 38:24, *and David realised that We had put him to the test* (*wa-ẓanna Dāwūd annamā fatannāhu*). The example of *ẓann* illustrates the fact that in the field of antonyms, doctrinal considerations are very likely to have played a role for early commentators because positing two opposed meanings for a lexical item often serves the purpose of explaining away an exegetical problem. In later literature, such lexical items with opposite meanings are called *aḍdād* (sg. *ḍidd*). Only one early commentary actually uses this term: Zayd b. ʿAlī paraphrases many words with opposite meanings, but in three cases he explicitly calls such a word a *ḍidd*.[61]

The exact problem for which the assumption of a *ḍidd* is the solution is not always immediately clear. According to Zayd b. ʿAlī, the word *ṣafrā'* ('yellow [fem.]') sometimes means 'black', as in Q. 2:69 and Q. 77:33.[62] To understand what is at stake here, one has to take into account all occurrences of the term. In Q. 77:33, *as if they are yellow camels* (*ka'annahu jimālātun ṣufrun*), yellow camels are mentioned as a simile of the splashing sparks of a fire; someone must have noted here that in Bedouin terminology dark camels are called 'yellow'.[63] This prompted a similar explanation of Q. 2:69, *He says that it is a yellow cow* (*innahu yaqūlu innahā baqaratun ṣafrā'u*). Once the word *ṣafrā'* had received the semantic extension to 'black', it became known as a *ḍidd*.[64]

The identification of *aḍdād* in the commentaries later developed into a special genre, when lexicography came into its own.[65] Lexicographers such as Muḥammad b. al-Mustanīr Quṭrub (d. 206/821) and Abū Bakr Ibn al-Anbārī (d. 328/940) compiled lists of *aḍdād* as separate treatises. They studied this phenomenon with an ulterior motive, namely to prove that the superiority of the Arabic language extended to its richness in synonyms and antonyms. This was no doubt intended as a refutation of those who criticised the Arabic language for its semantic anomalies. In the Shuʿūbiyya movement, the occurrence of homonyms and antonyms in Arabic was often presented as an example of the inferiority of that language.[66]

For the early commentators, the meaning of words was never a purely lexicographical preoccupation; their aim was the exegesis of the Qur'an, and their explanations cannot be separated from this purpose. This is particularly clear in the case of metaphorical interpretations. The text of the Qur'anic revelation contains expressions that have an obvious figurative sense. Some of the commentators do not seem to have regarded this as a problem. Ḍaḥḥāk simply states that in Q. 21:47 the word *mawāzīn* ('scales') means 'justice', since there is no mention of a real scale in this passage.[67] It becomes more complicated when God's attributes are mentioned in physical terms, such as 'hand' or 'leg', or when God is said to have sat down on His throne.[68] Some exegetes simply took such words for granted and assigned God physical attributes, for instance in Q. 68:42, where Muqātil opts for the active reading *yawma yakshifu ʿan sāqin* ('Upon the day when He bares a leg') and interprets it as referring to God's leg,[69] while most other commentators either paraphrased the word in question with an abstract word, for instance by stating that *sāq* meant 'power' in this connection, or chose the variant reading with a passive (*yukshafu*; 'shall be bared') and interpreted it as not referring to God.

In the later debate about metaphorical interpretations, Muʿtazilī exegetes were particularly active. In their wish to avoid any anthropomorphic interpretation, they applied their philological acumen to all such words as 'throne', 'arm' and 'leg', and rejected any literal interpretation of them when referring to God.[70] In their defence of the use of metaphorical interpretation as a legitimate exegetic tool, the Muʿtazilīs argued that the metaphors in the Qur'an were proof of its inimitable style (*iʿjāz al-Qurʾān*), which had always been implicitly recognised by the commentators, but not necessarily as something that should be proven.

Methodological discussions of antonyms and metaphors may have been absent in the early commentaries, yet their comments cannot be read as purely philological exercises, either. What underlies all exegetical efforts in the first two centuries of Islam is the ardent wish to understand the meaning of the revealed Book.

Explaining the Qur'an with Other Sources

Only very rarely do the early commentators refer to texts outside the Qur'an, in particular pre-Islamic poetry. There was no general injunction against referring to other texts, however, and in fact, at least two commentators make an occasional reference to a poetic line to confirm or reinforce their explanation of an expression. ʿAbd al-Razzāq, commenting on Q. 18:86, *in a muddy well* (*fī ʿaynin ḥamiʾatin*), quotes a poetic line on the authority of al-Khalīl b. Aḥmad (d. 170/786 or 175/791) in addition to the explanation from his usual source, Maʿmar b. Rāshid, to confirm Ibn ʿAbbās's reading of *ḥamiʾatin* instead of *ḥāmiʾatin*.[71] Ibn Jurayj quotes a line from Labīd to explain the meaning of the word *sabt* in Q. 2:65;[72] and he quotes a line from al-Akhṭal for the meaning of the word *ḍalla* in Q. 3:69.[73] Maybe this, too, depended on the personal predilection of the commentator.

What all commentators refer to, in different degrees, is the existence of dialectal variants (*lughāt*) within the Qur'an, but always with the aim of elucidating the text and removing ambiguities. As an example may be quoted the word *khamr* (usually translated as 'wine'), which according to Ḍaḥḥāk means 'grapes' in the ʿUmānī dialect.[74] Here, the dialectal meaning of the word is used to remove a potential confusion that might arise in Q. 12:36, where *khamr* is said to be pressed, so that the normal sense of the word becomes rather awkward.[75]

Rather frequently, the commentaries refer to the occurrence of foreign loanwords in the Qur'an, presumably for the same purpose of clarifying the text, although in this case it is unclear what the exact exegetical purpose is.[76] It is true that in some cases the foreign origin explains the fact that the word in question is not immediately comprehensible, but in other cases, one wonders whether the main motive might not have been simply intellectual curiosity on the part of the commentators.

The interest in foreign words probably goes back to the first/seventh century, because references to loanwords occur in the oldest available commentaries. The commentators sometimes assign the same word to different source languages. Thus, for instance, the word *maqālīd* ('keys') in Q. 42:12 is assigned by Mujāhid to Persian, while Muqātil believes it to be from Nabataean.[77] Yet, it is hard to escape the impression that most comments derive from a common source, which may well be connected with the Ibn ʿAbbās tradition. Mujāhid assigns the word *nāshiʾa* ('young; that which begins anew') in Q. 73:6 to Ethiopian on the authority of Ibn ʿAbbās;[78] and Sufyān al-Thawrī quotes Ibn ʿAbbās on the interpretation of *alf sana* ('a thousand years') as a translation of the Persian formula *hazar sāl*.[79] It is doubtful that the list of foreign words transmitted under Ibn ʿAbbās's name is genuine,[80] but the frequent references to Ibn ʿAbbās on the occurrence of loanwords in the Qur'an by different commentators suggest at the very least that the interest in such words goes back to the early period of Islam.

There is no trace of any reluctance in these early commentaries to accept the occurrence of foreign words in the Qur'an. Yet, some early lexicographers refused to believe in the foreign origin of any Arabic word. In spite of his Shuʿūbī leanings,[81] Abū ʿUbayda (d. between 207/822 and 213/828) states that the Qur'an contains only pure Arabic words, and that anyone claiming foreign origin for a word like *ṭāhā*, the name of Q. 20 – usually thought to derive from Nabataean – makes a big mistake.[82] In the later period of Arabic lexicography and grammar, the matter of foreign words in the Qur'an became a dogmatic issue, partly again because of questions raised by the Shuʿūbiyya movement, which thought to undermine the exclusively Arabic character of the Islamic revelation. The link between the exclusively Arabic character of the Qur'an and Arab linguistic hegemony is manifest in a discussion by Ibn Fāris (d. 395/1004). He states emphatically that everything in the Qur'an is Arabic, and that it does not make sense to recite it in Persian, since this constitutes only a translation (*tarjama*), not the miracle (*muʿjiza*) represented by the text as it was revealed in Arabic.[83] This statement combines the rejection of loanwords in the Qur'an, anti-Shuʿūbiyya sentiments, and inimitability of the Qur'an.

In those cases in which the etymology of a foreign proper name is given, it is obvious that the commentators believe this etymology may help to explain the role or history of the person with this name, for instance when Muqātil explains the name of Mūsā (Moses) from two Coptic words, *mū* ('water') and *sā* ('tree').[84] As an additional motive, etymologies may also serve to connect foreign names with Arabic roots. Thus, for instance, Muqātil derives the name Yaḥyā (John) from the root *ḥ-y-y* ('to live'), as an illustration of his miraculous birth from two aged parents 'because He brought him to life from an old man and a barren woman' (*li-annahu aḥyāhu min shaykh kabīr wa ʿajūz ʿāqir*).[85] He also connects the name Yaʿqūb (Jacob) with the word *ʿaqib* ('ankle'), because during birth, Jacob is said to have grabbed the ankle of his twin brother.[86] The source for some of these etymologies is no doubt the Jewish tradition, which became available to the commentators in the form of the so-called *isrāʾīliyyāt*, possibly through the mediation of Jewish converts.[87] There are also examples of etymologies for which a foreign source is unlikely: Suddī, for example, explains the name of Iblīs, whose original name he gives as al-Ḥārith, from the fact that after his fall he was 'driven to despair' (*ablasa mutaḥayyiran*), so that his name becomes an illustration of what happened to him.[88]

The idea that etymology may be used as a means to find out the 'real' meaning of a word becomes even more manifest when a word like *insān* ('human being') is derived from the root *n-s-y* ('to forget'): 'The reason why he is called *insān* is that [God] made a covenant with him and then he forgot (*ʿahada ilayhi fa-nasiya*).'[89]

Conclusions: From Text Interpretation to Linguistic Analysis

During the first two centuries of Islam, the main interest of scholars was the elucidation and analysis of the revealed message. Commentators were concerned to make sure that each and every word of the text was understood by the believers. In doing so, they used any information available, whether it belonged to the historical background, the narrative of the Prophet's life, or the variant readings of the text of the revelation. Yet, they concentrated on the semantics of the Qur'an. At the level of the lexicon, they replaced archaic or ambiguous words with current expressions, apparently working with a list of stock examples, which included paraphrases with a doctrinal significance. This procedure also led to the development of exegetical tools, such as the theory of antonyms (*aḍdād*), and eventually, the introduction of metaphorical meaning. Occasionally, scholarly curiosity may have been their motive, for instance, when they referred to the etymological derivation of Qur'anic words, some of which were even said to be of foreign origin.

At the end of the second/eighth century, the focus shifted from the semantic interpretation of the text of the Qur'an to the study of Arabic grammar and lexicon. Lexicographers and grammarians alike strove to explain this structure within a framework of morpho-phonological and syntactic rules. This shift in scope was accompanied by a change in the use of sources. The earliest lexicographical treatises, whether thematic word lists like the *Kitāb Khalq al-insān* and the *Kitāb al-Khayl*, both by al-Aṣmaʿī (d. 213/828), or the first real dictionary, the *Kitāb al-ʿAyn*, ascribed to al-Khalīl b. Aḥmad, treat the Qur'anic text as only one of their sources. Mohammad-Nauman Khan has shown that the *Kitāb al-ʿAyn* contains at least five hundred lemmata with Qur'anic material and betrays familiarity with the exegetical tradition, to which it refers several times.[90] Yet, the purpose of the *Kitāb al-ʿAyn* differs fundamentally from that of the commentaries: the author is concerned with the meaning of lexical items rather than with the interpretation of the revealed Book. Aṣmaʿī is even said to have occupied himself solely with poetic quotations and out of piety to have refrained from interpreting the

Qur'an and the Hadith.[91] The explanation of the Qur'an itself became increasingly the exclusive domain of *tafsīr* as a separate discipline. Polished commentaries with a balanced view of selected aspects of the text replaced the raw efforts of the early commentators. Exegesis had become a profession carried out by professional scholars.

NOTES

1 All translations of Qur'anic passages are mine.

2 Kees Versteegh, *Arabic Grammar and Qur'ānic Exegesis in Early Islam* (Leiden: Brill, 1993), pp. 65–8.

3 On the 'mythical' status of Ibn 'Abbās, see Claude Gilliot, 'Portrait "mythique" d'Ibn 'Abbās', *Arabica* 32 (1985), pp. 127–84.

4 Herbert Berg, *The Development of Exegesis in Early Islam: The Authenticity of Muslim Literature from the Formative Period* (London and New York: Curzon, 2000), pp. 129–37, and idem, Chapter 3 in this volume; for a less sceptical approach, see Isaiah Goldfeld, 'The *Tafsīr* of Abdallah b. 'Abbās', *Der Islam* 58 (1981), pp. 125–35.

5 Nicolai Sinai, 'The Qur'anic Commentary of Muqātil b. Sulaymān and the Evaluation of Early *Tafsīr* Literature' in Andreas Görke and Johanna Pink, eds, *Tafsīr and Islamic Intellectual History: Exploring the Boundaries of a Genre* (Oxford: Oxford University Press in association with the Institute of Ismaili Studies, 2014), pp. 113–43, accepts with confidence the authenticity of the text, among other reasons because of Muqātil's bad reputation, which makes it unlikely that anyone should wish to transmit the work falsely under his name. According to Gregor Schoeler, *Charakter und Authentie der muslimischen Überlieferung über das Leben Mohammeds* (Berlin and New York: de Gruyter, 1996), p. 6, n. 5, Muqātil b. Sulaymān's commentary is one of the early examples of a written text of the kind that was used exclusively in a teaching context.

6 John Wansbrough, *Quranic Studies: Sources and Methods of Scriptural Interpretation* (Oxford: Oxford University Press, 1977), pp. 119–21.

7 See Versteegh, *Arabic Grammar and Qur'ānic Exegesis*, p. 84; on legal issues, see Miklos Muranyi, 'Neue Materialien zur *Tafsīr*-Forschung in der Moscheebibliotek von Qairawan' in Stefan Wild, ed., *The Qur'ān as Text* (Leiden: Brill, 1996), pp. 225–55; legal and ritual issues are often implicit in discussions of abrogation in the commentaries, see John Burton, *The Sources of Islamic Law: Islamic Theories of Abrogation* (Edinburgh: Edinburgh University Press, 1990); for the development of *qirā'āt* in the commentaries, see Mustafa Shah, 'The Quest for the Origins of the *Qurrā'* in the Classical Islamic Tradition', *Journal of Qur'anic Studies* 7, no. 2 (2005), pp. 1–35; and Shady Hekmat Nasser, *The Transmission of the Variant Readings of the Qur'ān: The Problem of* Tawātur *and the Emergence of* Shawādhdh (Leiden: Brill, 2013).

8 Wansbrough calls such non-fitting elements 'intrusions' and attributes them to 'editorial reformulation' (*Quranic Studies*, pp. 132, 138–45); cf. Andrew Rippin, 'Al-Zuhrī, *Naskh al-Qur'ān* and the Problem of Early *Tafsīr* Texts', *Bulletin of the School of Oriental and African Studies* 47 (1984), pp. 22–43. On

the *Tafsīr al-Kalbī*, see also Marco Schöller, '*Sīra* and *Tafsīr*: Muḥammad al-Kalbī on the Jews of Medina' in Harald Motzki, ed., *The Biography of Muḥammad: The Issue of the Sources* (Leiden: Brill, 2000), pp. 18–48.

9 Berg, *The Development of Exegesis in Early Islam*, pp. 148–56.

10 Ibid., pp. 226–30; for critical remarks about this method of analysis, see also Harald Motzki, 'The Question of the Authenticity of Muslim Traditions Reconsidered: A Review Article' in Herbert Berg, ed., *Method and Theory in the Study of Islamic Origins* (Leiden: Brill, 2003), pp. 211–58.

11 Harald Motzki, 'The Origins of Muslim Exegesis. A Debate' in Harald Motzki with Nicolet Boekhoff-van der Voort and Sean W. Anthony, *Analysing Muslim Traditions: Studies in Legal, Exegetical and Maghāzī Ḥadīth* (Leiden: Brill, 2010), pp. 231–303.

12 Ibid., pp. 297–8.

13 Berg, *The Development of Exegesis in Early Islam*, pp. 119–20, 137.

14 al-Ḍaḥḥāk b. Muzāḥim, *Tafsīr al-Ḍaḥḥāk: Jamʿ wa dirāsa wa taḥqīq*, ed. Muḥammad Shukrī al-Zāwiyyatī (Cairo: Dār al-Salāma, 1419/1999), no. 947, also ibid. nos 953, 1417, 2223.

15 Kees Versteegh, 'The Name of the Ant and the Call to Holy War: al-Ḍaḥḥāk ibn Muzāḥim's Commentary on the Qur'ān' in Nicolet Boekhoff-van der Voort, Kees Versteegh and Joas Wagemakers, eds, *The Transmission and Dynamics of the Textual Sources of Islam: Essays in Honour of Harald Motzki* (Leiden: Brill, 2011), pp. 279–99.

16 John Burton, 'The Qur'an and the Practice of *wuḍū*'', *Bulletin of the School of Oriental and African Studies* 51 (1988), pp. 21–58.

17 Muqātil b. Sulaymān, *Tafsīr Muqātil b. Sulaymān*, ed. ʿAbd Allāh Maḥmūd Shiḥāta (Cairo: al-Hayʾa al-Miṣriyya al-ʿĀmma li'l-Kitāb, 1979–89), vol. 1, p. 455, ll. 14ff.; the editor vocalises *arjulakum*, which is the Sunni version; in Muqātil b. Sulaymān, *Tafsīr al-khams miʾat āya min al-Qurʾān al-karīm*, ed. Isaiah Goldfeld (Shfaram: Al-Mashriq Press, 1980), p. 21, no mention is made of alternative readings, either, but the paraphrase *fīhā taqdīm yaʿnī fa-ghsilū arjulakum ilā'l-kaʿbayni* shows that *arjulakum* is indeed the most likely reading.

18 Ḍaḥḥāk, *Tafsīr*, no. 2802.

19 Muḥammad al-Kalbī, *Tafsīr*, MS 4224 Chester Beatty Library, Dublin, fol. 183r, l. 6.

20 Versteegh, *Arabic Grammar and Qurʾānic Exegesis*, pp. 125–30.

21 Muqātil, *Tafsīr*, vol. 1, p. 27, ll. 11–17.

22 Kees Versteegh, 'Grammar and Exegesis: The Origins of Kufan Grammar and the *Tafsīr Muqātil*', *Zeitschrift der Deutschen Morgenländischen Gesellschaft* 67 (1990), pp. 206–42, at pp. 226ff.

23 Muqātil, *Tafsīr*, vol. 3, p. 163, l. 10; see also Versteegh, *Arabic Grammar and Qurʾānic Exegesis*, pp. 153–4.

24 Muqātil, *Tafsīr*, vol. 4, p. 246, l. 9.

25 Kalbī, *Tafsīr*, fol. 152r, l. 6.

26 Abū Muḥammad Ismāʿīl b. ʿAbd al-Raḥmān al-Suddī al-Kabīr, *Tafsīr al-Suddī al-Kabīr*, ed. Muḥammad ʿAṭā Yūsuf (al-Manṣūra: Dār al-Wafāʾ, 1993), p. 335, l. 11.

27 Ḍaḥḥāk, *Tafsīr*, no. 590.

28 A cursory count of the first twenty verses of Q. 2, Q. 4, Q. 5 and Q. 6 reveals that within a total of 372 exegetical remarks, Muqātil uses *yaʿnī* 184 times (50 per cent), *yaqūlu* thirty-two times (8 per cent), and juxtaposition without a connector 154 times (42 per cent); *ay* is used by him only twice in these verses.

29 Muqātīl, *Tafsīr*, vol. 4, p. 545, l. 16.

30 Ibid., vol. 4, p. 613, l. 2.

31 Ibid., vol. 1, p. 95, l. 7.

32 Ibid., vol. 1, p. 298, l. 9; according to Shawkat M. Toorawa, 'Hapaxes in the Qurʾān: Identifying and Cataloguing Lone Words (and Loanwords)' in Gabriel Said Reynolds, ed., *New Perspectives on the Qurʾān: The Qurʾān in its Historical Context 2* (London: Routledge, 2011), pp. 193–246, the function of these *hapax legomena* is to evoke wonder and amazement.

33 Muqātil, *Tafsīr*, vol. 1, p. 262.

34 See Wansbrough, *Quranic Studies*, pp. 211–12.

35 Muqātil, *Tafsīr*, vol. 3, pp. 88–9.

36 Of the seventy-two occurrences of *alīm/alīman* in the Qur'an, sixty (83.3 per cent) are glossed with *wajīʿ*: Muqātil, *Tafsīr, s.v.* Q. 2:10; 104, 174, 178; Q. 3:21, 77, 177, 188; Q. 4:138, 161, 173; Q. 5:73, 94; Q. 6:70; Q. 7:73; Q. 8:32; Q. 9:3, 34, 39, 61, 79, 90; Q. 10:4; Q. 11:26, 48; Q. 11:102; Q. 12:25; Q. 14:22; Q. 15:50; Q. 16:63, 104, 117; Q. 17:10; Q. 22:25; Q. 24:19, 63; Q. 25:37; Q. 26:201; Q. 29:23; Q. 33:8; Q. 36:18; Q. 37:38; Q. 41:43; Q. 42:21, 42; Q. 44:11; Q. 45:8, 11; Q. 46:24, 31; Q. 48:16, 17, 25; Q. 51:37; Q. 61:10; Q. 67:28; Q. 71:1; Q. 73:13; Q. 76:31; Q. 84:24. There are twelve instances where a different gloss or no gloss is given: Muqātil, *Tafsīr, s.v.* Q. 3:91; Q. 4:18; Q. 5:36; Q. 9:74; Q. 10:88, 97; Q. 31:7; Q. 34:5; Q. 43:65; Q. 58:4; Q. 59:15; Q. 64:5. [Statistics kindly provided by Stephen Burge.]

37 Of the sixty-nine occurrences of *jannāt*, thirty-four (49.2 per cent) are glossed with *basātīn*: Muqātil, *Tafsīr, s.v.* Q. 2:25; Q. 3:15, 195; Q. 4:57; Q. 5:12; Q. 6:99; Q. 9:100; Q. 14:23; Q. 15:45; Q. 16:31; Q. 18:31, 107; Q. 20:76; Q. 22:14, 23; Q. 23:19; Q. 26:57, 134; Q. 36:34; Q. 42:22; Q. 44:25, 52; Q. 47:12; Q. 48:5; Q. 50:9; Q. 51:15; Q. 52:17; Q. 54:54; Q. 58:22; Q. 65:11; Q. 66:8; Q. 71:12; Q. 78:16; Q. 85:11. However, in those cases in which *basātīn* is not given, none were given a different gloss; see Muqātil, *Tafsīr, s.v.* Q. 3:136, 198; Q. 4:13, 122; Q. 5:65, 85, 119; Q. 6:141; Q. 9:21, 72 (twice), 89; Q. 10:9; Q. 13:4, 23; Q. 19:61; Q. 22:56; Q. 25:10; Q. 26:147; Q. 31:8; Q. 32:19; Q. 35:33; Q. 37:43; Q. 38:50; Q. 40:8; Q. 48:17; Q. 56:12; Q. 57:12; Q. 61:12 (twice); Q. 64:9; Q. 68:34; Q. 70:35; Q. 74:40; Q. 98:8. [Statistics kindly provided by Stephen Burge.]

38 Every occurrence of *ayyān* is glossed with *matā*; see Muqātil, *Tafsīr, s.v.* Q. 7:187; Q. 16:21; Q. 27:65; Q. 51:12; Q. 75:6; and Q. 79:42. [Statistics kindly provided by Stephen Burge.]

39 Of the twenty-eight occurrences, twenty-one (75 per cent) gloss *annā* with *min ayna*: Muqātil, *Tafsīr, s.v.* Q. 2:247; Q. 3:37, 40, 47; Q. 5:75; Q. 6:101; Q. 9:30; Q. 10:34; Q. 19:8, 20; Q. 23:89; Q. 29:61; Q. 36:66; Q. 39:6; Q. 40:62, 69; Q. 43:87; Q. 44:13; Q. 47:18; Q. 63:4; Q. 89:23. In the seven remaining occasions, Muqātil provides no gloss at all; see Muqātil, *Tafsīr, s.v.* Q. 2:223, 259; Q. 3:165; Q. 6:95; Q. 10:32; Q. 34:52; Q. 35:3. [Statistics kindly provided by Stephen Burge.]

40 Ḍaḥḥāk, *Tafsīr*, no. 34. This gloss may be theologically significant because of a connection with the discussions about the createdness of the Qur'an: in Q. 43:3, *innā jaʿalnāhu qurʾānan ʿarabiyyan* (*We made it as an Arabic Qur'an*),

the verb *ja'ala* is used rather than *khalaqa*; Ḍaḥḥāk's paraphrase may be intended to underline God's creation of the Qur'an, see Scott C. Lucas, *Constructive Critics, Ḥadīth Literature and the Articulation of Sunnī Islam* (Leiden: Brill, 2004), p. 193.

41 Ḍaḥḥāk, *Tafsīr*, no. 653.

42 Ibid., no. 138; see also Ibn Jurayj, *Tafsīr Ibn Jurayj*, ed. 'Alī Ḥasan 'Abd al-Ghanī (Cairo: Maktabat al-Turāth al-Islāmī, 1992), p. 45, l. 6.

43 *Qisṭ* = *'adl*: Muqātil, *Tafsīr*, vol. 1, p. 412, l. 2; Kalbī, *Tafsīr*, fol. 44r, l. 1; *ghalīẓ* = *shadīd*: Muqātil, *Tafsīr*, vol. 2, p. 287, l. 7; Kalbī, *Tafsīr*, fol. 95v, l. 16.

44 Muqātil, *Tafsīr*, vol. I, p. 286, l. 1; Ḍaḥḥāk, *Tafsīr*, no. 15.

45 Cf. Andrew Rippin, 'Ibn 'Abbās's Gharīb al-Qur'ān', *Bulletin of the School of Oriental and African Studies* 46 (1983), pp. 323–33.

46 Ḍaḥḥāk, *Tafsīr*, no. 653 and 'Abd al-Razzāq al-Ṣan'ānī, *Tafsīr*, ed. Maḥmūd Muḥammad 'Abduh (Beirut: Dār al-Kutub al-'Ilmiyya, 1999), vol. 2, p. 328, l. 4 (← Ibn 'Uyayna ← 'Amr b. Dīnār ← 'Ikrima ← Ibn 'Abbās).

47 Muqātil, *Tafsīr*, vol. 4, p. 752, ll. 9ff.

48 Q. 3:67; Muqātil, *Tafsīr*, vol. 1, p. 288, ll. 5ff.

49 See, for instance, the discussion in Frederick Denny, 'Some Religio-Communal Terms and Concepts in the Qur'ān', *Numen* 24 (1977), pp. 26–59; and in René Dagorn, *La geste d'Ismaël d'après l'onomastique et la tradition arabes* (Geneva: Librairie Droz, 1981), pp. 140–42.

50 Muqātil, *Tafsīr*, vol. 1, p. 573, l. 10; see also Ibn Jurayj, *Tafsīr*, p. 219, l. 13. On the equivalence of *ẓulm* = *shirk*, see Norman Calder, 'Tafsīr from Ṭabarī to Ibn Kathīr: Problems in the Description of a Genre, Illustrated with Reference to the Story of Abraham' in G.R. Hawting and Abdul-Kader A. Shareef, eds, *Approaches to the Qur'ān* (London: Routledge, 1993), pp. 101–40 at pp. 128–9; Cornelia Schöck, *Koranexegese, Grammatik und Logik: Zum Verhältnis von arabischer und aristotelischer Urteils-, Konsequenz- und Schlusslehre* (Leiden: Brill, 2006), pp. 32, 39–42, 52–3, 152–79.

51 There are 106 occurrences of *mubīn*. Of these, sixty-three are glossed with *bayyin* or phrases incorporating *bayyin* (59.4 per cent), for twenty-seven no gloss is provided at all (25.5 per cent), and for sixteen, a different gloss is given (15.1 per cent). The occurrences glossed with *bayyin* or similar phrases can be divided into three categories: (i) those glossed with *bayyin*, although not always '*ya'nī bayyin*'; (ii) instances where *mubīn* is glossed as *ḥujja bayyina* or *al-ni'am bayyina*; and (iii) where the glosses take the verbal form *yabīna*. For the fifty-three occurrences of the gloss *bayyin* (although not always '*ya'nī bayyin*'), see Muqātil, *Tafsīr*, *s.v.* Q. 2:168, 208; Q. 3:164; Q. 5:15, 110; Q. 6:7, 59; Q. 7:184; Q. 10:2, 61, 76; Q. 11:6, 7, 25; Q. 12:1, 5, 8, 30; Q. 14:10; Q. 15:1; Q. 16:35, 82, 103; Q. 22:11, 49; Q. 24:12, 25, 53; Q. 26:2, 30, 115; Q. 27:1, 13, 16, 79; Q. 28:2; Q. 36:24, 60, 69, 77; Q. 38:70; Q. 39:15; Q. 43:2, 15, 29, 40, 62; Q. 44:2, 13; Q. 46:9, 23; Q. 64:12; Q. 71:2. For the eight occurrences in which *mubīn* is glossed as *ḥujja bayyina* or *al-ni'am bayyina*, see ibid., *s.v.* Q. 7:107; Q. 23:35; Q. 27:21; Q. 40:23; Q. 44:19, 33; Q. 51:38; Q. 52:38; and for one occurrence where the gloss takes the verbal form *yabīna*, see Q. 29:18. For the twenty-seven that provide no gloss at all, see ibid., *s.v.* Q. 5:92; Q. 6:74, 142; Q. 7:22, 60; Q. 11:96; Q. 15:79; Q. 16:4; Q. 21:54; Q. 26:97, 195; Q. 28:15, 18, 85; Q. 29:50; Q. 31:11; Q. 34:3, 43; Q. 36:47; Q. 37:113, 156; Q. 44:10; Q. 45:30; Q. 51:50, 51; Q. 64:12; Q. 67:26. The sixteen that

provide a different gloss can be found at Q. 6:16; Q. 15:18, 79; Q. 19:38; Q. 26:32; Q. 34:24; Q. 36:12, 17; Q. 37:15, 106; Q. 39:22; Q. 43:18; Q. 46:7; Q. 61:6; Q. 67:29; Q. 81:23. [Statistics kindly provided by Stephen Burge.]

52 Claude Gilliot, 'The "Collections" of the Meccan Arabic Lectionary' in Boekhoff-van der Voort *et al.*, eds, *The Transmission and Dynamics of the Textual Sources of Islam*, pp. 105–33, at pp. 112–14.

53 Of the sixty-six occurrences of *khālidūna/khalidīna*, the vast majority (72 per cent) are glossed with *lā yamūtūna*: Muqātil, *Tafsīr, s.v.* Q. 2:25, 39, 81, 82, 257, 275; Q. 3:107, 136, 198; Q. 4:13, 57; Q. 5:85, 119; Q. 7:20, 42; Q. 9:17, 22, 68, 89, 100; Q. 10:26, 27; Q. 11:23, 107; Q. 13:5; Q. 14:23; Q. 18:108; Q. 20:76; Q. 21:102; Q. 23:11, 103; Q. 25:16, 76; Q. 29:58; Q. 31:9; Q. 39:72, 73; Q. 40:76; Q. 43:71, 74; Q. 48:5; Q. 57:12; Q. 58:17, 22; Q. 64:9; Q. 72:23; Q. 98:6, 8. There are eighteen instances where a different gloss or no gloss is given: Muqātil, *Tafsīr, s.v.*: Q. 3:88, 116; Q. 4:122, 169; Q. 5:80; Q. 6:128; Q. 7:36; Q. 9:72; Q. 11:108; Q. 16:29; Q. 20:101; Q. 21:8, 34, 99; Q. 33:65; Q. 46:13; Q. 64:10; Q. 65:11. [Statistics kindly provided by Stephen Burge]; Kalbī gives the paraphrase '*dā'imūna lā yamūtūna wa-lā yakhrujūna*' ('everlasting, they do not die and they do not leave') for this word; Kalbī, *Tafsīr*, fol. 3r, l. 11.

54 According to Muḥammad b. Jarīr al-Ṭabarī (*Jāmiʿ al-bayān ʿan taʾwīl āy al-Qurʾān*, 3rd edn [Cairo: Muṣṭafā al-Bābī al-Ḥalabī, 1968], vol. 7, pp. 118–19), Q. 11:107, *staying forever in it as long as the Heavens and the Earth exist* (*khālidīna fīhā mā dāmat al-samawātu wa'l-arḍu*) should be interpreted as an eternal punishment, in accordance with the view of the *ahl al-tawḥīd*, i.e. the Muʿtazilīs. He rejects the view of Ibn Masʿūd (d. 32/652) that ultimately Hell will be emptied of all people and destroyed. For a detailed analysis of theologians' different views on this question, see Binyamin Abrahamov, 'The Creation and Duration of Paradise and Hell', *Der Islam* 79 (2002), pp. 87–102.

55 Abrahamov, 'The Creation and Duration of Paradise and Hell', pp. 93, 99.

56 I owe this suggestion to Reza Shah-Kazemi.

57 See Wansbrough, *Quranic Studies*, pp. 208–11.

58 See Muqātil, *Tafsīr*, on Q. 2:230; Q. 7:171; Q. 9:118; Q. 10:22, 24; Q. 12:42, 110; Q. 18:53; Q. 21:87; Q. 24:12; Q. 28:39; Q. 38:24; Q. 41:22, 23, 48; Q. 48:12 (twice); Q. 59:2 (twice); Q. 69:20; Q. 72:5, 7 (twice), 12; Q. 84:14. [Statistics kindly provided by Stephen Burge.]

59 Zayd b. ʿAlī, *Tafsīr gharīb al-Qurʾān*, ed. Ḥasan Muḥammad Taqī al-Ḥakīm (Beirut: al-Dār al-ʿĀlamiyya, 1992), p. 81, l. 14.

60 Ḍaḥḥāk, *Tafsīr*, no. 2687.

61 See Kees Versteegh, 'Zayd ibn ʿAlī's Commentary on the *Qurʾān*' in Yasir Suleiman, ed., *Arabic Grammar and Linguistics* (London: Curzon Press, 1999), pp. 9–29, at pp. 21–3.

62 Zayd b. ʿAlī, *Tafsīr*, p. 85, l. 3.

63 On colour terminology in Arabic, see Wolfdietrich Fischer, *Farb- und Formbezeichnungen in der Sprache der altarabischen Dichtung: Untersuchungen zur Wortbedeutung und zur Wortbildung* (Wiesbaden: Otto Harrassowitz, 1965), specifically on the colour 'yellow', see p. 365.

64 See Versteegh, 'Zayd ibn ʿAlī's Commentary on the *Qurʾān*', pp. 21–3. *Aṣfar* as a *ḍidd* occurs, for instance, in Abū Bakr Ibn al-Anbārī, *Kitāb al-Aḍdād*, ed. Muḥammad Abū'l-Faḍl Ibrāhīm (Kuwait: Dā'irat al-Maṭbūʿāt wa'l-Nashr,

1960), pp. 160–62; see Hans Kofler, 'Das *Kitāb aḍdād* von Abū ʿAlī Muḥammad Quṭrub ibn al-Mustanīr, herausgegeben und mit erklärenden Anmerkungen versehen', *Islamica* 5 (1931–32), pp. 241–84, 385–461, 493–544; specifically on *aṣfar* as a *ḍidd*, see pp. 445–7.

65 On the place of *aḍdād* in the Arabic lexicographical tradition, see Lidia Bettini, '*Ḍidd*' in *EALL*, vol. 1, pp. 626–9.

66 Régis Blachère, 'Origine de la théorie des *aḍdād*' in Jacques Berque and Jean-Paul Charnay, eds, *L'ambivalence dans la culture arabe* (Paris: Editions Anthropos, 1967), pp. 397–403.

67 Ḍaḥḥāk, *Tafsīr*, no. 1596.

68 For a discussion of these passages, see Richard Martin, 'Anthropomorphism', *EQ*, vol. 1, pp. 103–7.

69 Muqātil, *Tafsīr*, vol. 4, p. 409, l. 3.

70 The classic treatment of Muʿtazilī exegesis is Ignaz Goldziher, *Die Richtungen der islamischen Koranauslegung* (Leiden: Brill, 1970), pp. 99–147; see also John Wansbrough, '*Majāz al-Qur'ān*: Periphrastic Exegesis', *Bulletin of the School of Oriental and African Studies* 33 (1970), pp. 247–66; Wolfhart Heinrichs, 'On the Genesis of the *Ḥaqīqa-Majāz* Dichotomy', *Studia Islamica* 59 (1984), pp. 111–40.

71 ʿAbd al-Razzāq, *Tafsīr*, vol. 2, p. 345. Ibn ʿAbbās's reading *ḥamiʾatin* also plays a role in a discussion between him and the Umayyad caliph Muʿāwiya (r. 40/661–60/680), see Tayeb El-Hibri, 'The Redemption of Umayyad Memory by the ʿAbbāsids', *Journal of Near Eastern Studies* 61, no. 4 (2002), pp. 241–65, at pp. 264–5.

72 Ibn Jurayj, *Tafsīr*, p. 35; Labīd is also quoted on p. 181 in the story about his brother Irbid.

73 Ibid., p. 73.

74 Ḍaḥḥāk, *Tafsīr*, no. 1197.

75 For the terminological debate about what constitutes wine, see John Burton, *Abū ʿUbaid al-Qāsim b. Sallām's* K. al-Nāsikh wa-l-mansūkh *(MS Istanbul, Topkapı, Ahmet III A 143), edited with a commentary* (Bury St. Edmunds: St. Edmundsbury Press, 1987), pp. 154–6.

76 On the debate about the presence of foreign loanwords in the Qur'an, see Lothar Kopf, 'Religious Influences on Medieval Arabic Philology', *Studia Islamica* 5 (1956), pp. 33–59; etymologies by early lexicographers based on the resemblance between Semitic languages are dealt with by Ramzi Baalbaki, 'Early Arab Lexicographers and the Use of Semitic Languages', *Berytus* 31 (1983), pp. 117–27; the latest synthesis from a linguistic point of view is Federico Corriente, 'Some Notes on the Qur'ānic *lisānun mubīn* and its Loanwords' in Juan Pedro Monferrer-Sala and Urbán Ángel, eds, *Sacred Text: Explorations in Lexicography* (Frankfurt am Main: P. Lang, 2009), pp. 31–46. On Hebrew and Aramaic loanwords in the Qur'an see also Catherine Pennacchio, *Les emprunts à l'hébreu et au judéo-araméen dans le Coran* (Paris: Maisonneuve, 2014).

77 Mujāhid b. Jabr, *Tafsīr*, ed. ʿAbd al-Raḥmān al-Ṭāhir al-Sūratī (Islamabad, n.d.), vol. 2, p. 560, l. 3; and Muqātil, *Tafsīr*, vol. 3, p. 765, l. 11.

78 Mujāhid, *Tafsīr*, vol. 2, p. 699, l. 5.

79 Sufyān al-Thawrī, *Tafsīr al-Qur'ān al-karīm*, ed. Imtiyāz ʿAlī ʿArshī (Beirut: Dār al-Kutub al-ʿIlmiyya, 1983), p. 47, l. 9.

80 See Rippin, 'Ibn 'Abbās's *Gharīb al-Qur'ān*'.

81 Ignaz Goldziher, *Muhammedanische Studien* (Halle, Max Niemeyer, 1888; repr., Hildesheim: G. Olms, 1971), vol. 1, pp. 195–200.

82 Abū 'Ubayda, *Majāz al-Qur'ān*, ed. Fū'ād Sazgīn [Fuat Sezgin] (Cairo: Muḥammad Sāmī Amīn al-Khānjī, 1954–62), vol. 1, p. 17, ll. 5ff.

83 Ibn Fāris, *al-Ṣāḥibī fī fiqh al-lugha*, ed. Moustafa Chouémi (Beirut: A. Badran, 1964), pp. 28–30. On Ibn Fāris' views about the superior nature of Arabic, see Travis Zadeh, *The Vernacular Qur'an: Translation and the Rise of Persian Exegesis* (Oxford: Oxford University Press in association with the Institute of Ismaili Studies, 2012), pp. 193–8.

84 Muqātil, *Tafsīr*, vol. 3, p. 337, l. 7; it is unknown what Muqātil's source was, but the Coptic words are more or less recognisable: *mow*, *maw*, *mū* – 'water'; and *she*, *shē* – 'wood'.

85 Ibid., vol. 2, p. 621, l. 5; cf. Q. 19:2–15.

86 Ibid., vol. 3, p. 53; the commentator does not mention his source, but the story has a parallel in Genesis 25:26.

87 On the genre of the *isrā'īliyyāt*, see Roberto Tottoli, 'Origin and Use of the Term *Isrā'īliyyāt* in Muslim Literature', *Arabica* 46 (1999), pp. 193–210.

88 Suddī, *Tafsīr*, p. 105; the same etymology is given by Muqātil, *Tafsīr*, vol. 3, p. 653, l. 13 and by Zayd b. 'Alī, *Tafsīr*, p. 81, l. 1.

89 'Abd al-Razzāq, *Tafsīr*, vol. 2, p. 378, ll. 1–2 on the authority of Sufyān al-Thawrī and eventually from Ibn 'Abbās.

90 Mohammad-Nauman Khan, *Die exegetischen Teile des* Kitāb al-'Ayn: *Zur ältesten philologischen Koranexegese* (Berlin: K. Schwarz, 1994), pp. 38ff.

91 See Jalāl al-Dīn al-Suyūṭī, *Bughyat al-wu'āt fī ṭabaqāt al-lughawiyyīn wa'l-nuḥāt*, ed. Muḥammad Abū'l-Faḍl Ibrāhīm (Cairo: Maṭba'at 'Īsā al-Ḥalabī, 1964–5), vol. 2, p. 212.

3

Lexicological Hadith and the 'School' of Ibn ʿAbbās

HERBERT BERG

Introduction

ʿAbd Allāh ibn ʿAbbās (d. ca. 68/687), cousin of Muhammad and ancestor of the Abbasid caliphs, came to be seen as the single most authoritative and prolific early *mufassir* in Sunni Islam. Credited with both a large number of students and a specific methodology, Ibn ʿAbbās appears as the founder of an exegetical school. He and his students display an interest in most exegetical techniques, including lexicology. Sezgin certainly speaks of formal students who perpetuated his exegetical techniques.[1] By examining the exegesis of three passages of the Qur'an by Ibn ʿAbbās and by a number of his 'students', I will argue that there may have been such a school, but Ibn ʿAbbās served only as the mythic and paradigmatic symbol of its origins, not as its founder or even exemplar of its purported methodology.

Ibn ʿAbbās was only ten (or thirteen or fifteen) years old when Muhammad died in 10/632.[2] If he remained with his father in Mecca until 8/630, when his father made his hijra, then it seems that he was unlikely to have had much significant exegetical instruction from Muhammad in these remaining two years. As a young man he participated in several campaigns during the reigns of the caliphs ʿUmar b. al-Khaṭṭāb (r. 13–23/634–44) and ʿUthmān b. ʿAffān (r. 24–36/644–56). Appointed by ʿUthmān to lead the hajj in 35/656, Ibn ʿAbbās was rather conveniently absent from Medina when the caliph was assassinated. He pledged allegiance to his successor, ʿAlī b. Abī Ṭālib (r. 36–40/656–61), and served as a commander to some of the fourth caliph's troops at both the battles of the Camel and Ṣiffin. Later he served as ʿAlī's governor in Basra but retired to Mecca after a financial dispute with ʿAlī. After the fourth caliph's death in 40/661, he chose the unsuccessful side by supporting ʿAlī's son al-Ḥasan, and yet managed to protect both his life and wealth when Muʿāwiya b. Abī Sufyān (r. 41–60/661–80) secured the caliphate. Apart from participating in the campaign against Constantinople in 49–50/669–70, Ibn ʿAbbās withdrew from political life for two decades until ʿAbd Allāh b. al-Zubayr established his caliphate in Mecca in 63/683. Though imprisoned for refusing to acknowledge this rival caliph, he was rescued and spent the last four years of his life in al-Ṭāʾif.

Presumably, it was during the last quarter century of his life that Ibn ʿAbbās focused on his many scholarly interests. According to the later biographical literature, he transmitted information from thirty people, including Muhammad and the first four caliphs, and transmitted this knowledge and his own teachings to over eighty-five others, including major exegetes such as ʿIkrima (d. ca. 107/725–6), Saʿīd Ibn Jubayr (d. ca. 95/713), Qatāda b. Diʿāma (d. 118/736) and Mujāhid b. Jabr (d. 104/722–3).[3] His prominence in *tafsīr* is not mere happenstance; Ibn Saʿd (d. 230/845) reports several traditions in which Muhammad called on God to give Ibn ʿAbbās *al-ḥikma* ('wisdom' or 'the wisdom'),[4] teach him the interpretation of the Book (*taʾwīl al-kitāb*) and instruct him in the religion (*al-dīn*).[5] Another report describes the second caliph, ʿUmar, listening to the Companions who had fought at Badr in 2/624, which Ibn ʿAbbās – being at most seven years of age at the time – obviously had not. After Ibn ʿAbbās answered, ʿUmar said to the others, 'How can you reproach me about him after what you have [just] seen?'[6] Another such report has ʿUmar and ʿUthmān taking his counsel along with those Companions who had fought at Badr, with Ibn ʿAbbās giving legal rulings (*yuftī*) during their reigns.[7] These two reports may reflect later attempts to negate the widely reported presence of his father, al-ʿAbbās, among the captives of Muhammad's Meccan opponents at the Battle of Badr in 2/624. Abbasid propagandists expended much effort in obviating the embarrassing implications of this purported incident. The mention of Badr in both these reports suggests that they are a product of similarly motivated efforts.[8] Yet other reports focus on his reputation as an exegete. ʿAbd Allāh Ibn Masʿūd (d. 32 or 33/652–4) called him the interpreter (*turjumān*) of the Qur'an. When Ibn ʿAbbās died, Muḥammad b. al-Ḥanafiyya stated, 'Today the master (*rabbanī*) of this community has died.'[9] Moreover, to Ibn ʿAbbās is attributed the following methodology:

> Ibn ʿAbbās, when he was asked about some matter, if it was in the Qur'an, he reported that; if it was not in the Qur'an but was from the Messenger of God, he reported that; if it was not in the Qur'an nor from the Messenger of God but was from Abū Bakr and ʿUmar, he reported that; and if there was nothing from that, he formulated his [own] opinion (*ijtahada ra'yahu*).[10]

In other words, in what appears to be rather anachronistically supporting much later exegetical procedures, his authorities were the Qur'an, the Sunna and the precedents of the two most prominent Sunni Companions, and only in the absence of guidance from these sources would he rely on his own *ra'y*.[11] Nevertheless, with the prophetic imprimatur, the thousands of exegetical interpretations ascribed to him, his impressive lists of students who in turn became major exegetes, and a paradigmatic exegetical methodology, the existence of a school of Ibn ʿAbbās seems a certainty.

But was there such a school? One way to test the 'school of Ibn ʿAbbās' hypothesis is to compare exegeses ascribed to him with exegeses ascribed to his students. Presumably, in a school, the teacher has some influence over his students, and they would be inclined in many, if not most, cases to cite their teacher, especially if he had expressed his interpretation of a particular word or verse. One would also expect a significant degree of agreement between the various students. To facilitate such a comparison, I have selected three passages on which Ibn ʿAbbās and his alleged students comment: Q. 1:7, Q. 50:5 and Q. 15:89–92. None of these passages is particularly theologically controversial, nor do they have dogmatic importance, lest their exegesis be tendentially shaped. Ibn ʿAbbās, of course, is renowned for his lexicographical aptitude. Therefore, each of the aforementioned verses has been selected because it contains a lexical ambiguity, thus allowing me to further refine this 'test'.

Qur'an 1:7

The last verse of the first sura contains the phrases, *Not* [*the path*] *of those on whom is* [*your*] *anger nor of those who go astray* (*ghayr al-maghḍūb ʿalay-him wa-lā al-ḍāllīn*). Muḥammad b. Jarīr al-Ṭabarī (d. 310/923) provides fourteen hadiths that identify the recipients of the anger as the Jews, three of which cite Ibn ʿAbbās (via al-Ḍaḥḥāk b. Muzāḥim [d. ca. 106/724], Abū Ṣāliḥ Bādhām [or Bādhān, a client of Umm Hāniʾ, d. unknown], and Ibn Jurayj [d. 150/767]). Muhammad himself is cited seven times, as are other commentators including Ibn Jurayj, Rabīʿ b. Anas (d. 139 or 140/756–8), ʿAbd al-Raḥmān Ibn Zayd (d. 182/798), and the latter's father. For the second phrase, once again there are fourteen hadiths identifying them as Christians, with three from Ibn ʿAbbās via the same students. Again, seven come from Muhammad and the other four from Mujāhid, Rabīʿ, Ibn Zayd and his father. Several of these exegetes are listed as students of Ibn ʿAbbās. There are no dissenting views among the suspiciously numerically and numerologically parallel set of hadiths.[12]

The consistency is remarkable and seems to support the existence of a school. However, it might also serve as evidence for an alternative interpretation proposed by Harris Birkeland and John Wansbrough. Birkeland had suggested that Ibn ʿAbbās was a 'sociological fact' – that is, his exegetical opinions represented Muslim consensus at the end of the second/eighth century. He uses the example of the family *isnād* of Ibn Saʿd, who like his contemporaries, had no sound traditions to support the Qur'anic interpretations for which groups had reached consensus (*ijmāʿ*). So, convinced that what Ibn Saʿd had learned from his father must derive from Ibn ʿAbbās, Birkeland argues that 'The authority of Ibn ʿAbbās gives expression to the *sociological* fact of the *matn* as a representation of a common opinion', though the *isnād*, especially the older portion, is 'fictitious and spurious'.[13] Wansbrough generalised Birkeland's more specific assertion by stating that Ibn ʿAbbās was the 'personification of consensus (*ijmāʿ*)'[14] sometime prior to the beginning of the third/ninth century.

Qur'an 50:5

Q. 50:5 reads, *Rather, they deny the truth when it comes to them; thus they are in a 'confused' state* (*fa-hum fī amr marīj*). This verse is neither particularly prominent nor controversial. Even so, the exegesis of *marīj* illustrates some noteworthy features about Ibn ʿAbbās-hadiths. This word, tentatively translated 'confused', itself caused some confusion. Ṭabarī includes three Ibn ʿAbbās-hadiths, which explain that: (1) '*marīj* is something detestable (*al-shayʾ al-munkar*)'; (2) it means 'disagreeing' (*mukhtalif*); and (3) 'they are in a state of error (*amr ḍalāla*)'. Obviously, these three Ibn ʿAbbās-hadiths are not identical. Moreover, three of Ibn ʿAbbās's most prominent students, Ibn Jubayr, Mujāhid and Qatāda, along with Maʿmar b. Rāshid (d. 153/770), who elsewhere transmits Ibn ʿAbbās-hadiths via earlier exegetes, favour the explanation of 'confused' (*multabis*), while Ibn Zayd prefers the synonym 'mixed up' (*mukhallaṭ*). The five interpretations were recognised by Ṭabarī as divergent, for he separated them and introduced each by saying that the exegetes 'differed'.[15] He, however, attempted to obscure these differences:[16]

> These explanations, though their formulation differed (*ikhtalafat*), come close to each other in meaning because something [that] is disagreeing (*mukhtalif*) [and] confused (*multabis*) means it is vague (*mushkil*). And if it is like that [i.e. vague], it is detestable (*munkar*), because that which is good (*maʿrūf*) is patently obvious. And if it was not that which is good, it was undoubtedly an error (*ḍalāla*), because the Guidance is obvious, in which there is no confusion (*labs*).[17]

Claude Gilliot, too, has recognised that the exegeses attributed to Ibn ʿAbbās for any one passage of the Qur'an often disagreed among themselves. He has therefore likened the figure of Ibn ʿAbbās to a mirror: he reflected the exegetical controversies for which consensus had *not* been achieved. His was a 'living tradition' in which individual hadiths could be revised as needed.[18] Ṭabarī's material for Q. 50:5 appears to be more in accord with Gilliot's suggestion that Ibn ʿAbbās reflected the acceptable range of diversity within the community than with Wansbrough's earlier assertion that he represents a portion of the Muslim community's consensus. The consensus, such as it was, is entirely a product of Ṭabarī's own efforts to harmonise the exegesis attributed to Ibn ʿAbbās. In other words, the diversity evident in the independent Ibn ʿAbbās-hadiths disappears by the time Ṭabarī has finished harmonising them in his *Tafsīr.* In any case, the exegesis of Q. 50:5 belies the existence of a school of Ibn ʿAbbās, unless the founder of that school was extremely inconsistent and failed to follow his own methodology.

It may be worth noting that Gregor Schoeler has argued that early teachers and transmitters of hadiths relied on both oral and written transmission simultaneously. As a result, not only might different students transmit one teaching of their teacher in significantly different ways, but even that teaching might differ each time the teacher transmits it. This could explain at least several of these similar interpretations of Q. 50:5 by different students of Ibn ʿAbbās. Thus, according to Schoeler, all of these variations or recensions should be considered authentic.[19] Whereas Ṭabarī uses linguistic arguments, Schoeler uses arguments on the nature of transmission to ameliorate what both recognise as problematic exegetical differences. However, at most, the differences introduced in this mixed form of transmission would likely be restricted to wording, such as synonyms, glosses, and paraphrases. It is less likely to explain differences in interpretation that are mutually exclusive, and much less the methodological differences between students.

Qur'an 15:89–92[20]

Q. 15:89–92 reads *And say, 'I am the clear warner.' Just as We sent down* (*anzalnā*) *on the partitioners* (*muqtasimīn*) *who made the Qur'an into fragments* (*ʿiḍīn*). *By your Lord, we will question them, all of them.* The first and last sentences are clear enough, but not the middle one: Who are the partitioners? What did they partition? And, what is the nature of the Qur'an's fragmentation?

The material in Ṭabarī's *Tafsīr* makes it clear that early Muslim scholars disagreed over what these verses meant even more markedly than they did with Q. 50:5. In particular, the identity of the *muqtasimīn* and the meaning of *'iḍīn*, tentatively translated here as 'fragments', were ambiguous. The exegesis of this passage focuses on these two key terms, and Ṭabarī presents three distinct and mutually exclusive themes of interpretations. The most common and well-attested theme identifies the *muqtasimīn* as People of the Book or Jews and Christians. Many of the reports cite as their authority Ibn 'Abbās, and if not him, then one of his purported students. The act of partitioning is generally said to consist of believing in some (*ba'ḍ*) and disbelieving in some. However, they disagree about the antecedent of 'some'. Some thought it referred to specific suras of the Qur'an, and others to the Book or their books, presumably the Torah and the Gospel. The second theme identifies the *muqtasimīn* instead as the disbelievers among the prophet Ṣāliḥ's community. A third theme of interpretation identifies the *muqtasimīn* as non-Muslim Qurashīs who slander the Qur'an. Table 1, drawn from a range of early sources, outlines these three themes and the key phrases and concepts associated with them.[21]

The hadiths of Theme 1 are fairly consistent, but with some minor variations in pronouns, particles and the tenses of the verbs. Analysing this theme using Harald Motzki's *isnād-cum-matn* method produces few noteworthy results, except to show that, despite the termination of most of the *isnād*s with Ibn 'Abbās, the *matn*s almost certainly did not originate with him but with the common link in the *isnād*s, Sulaymān b. Mihrān al-A'mash (d. 146/765–6) or perhaps Abū Ẓaybān (d. between 89/708 and 96/714–15).[22] Muqātil b. Sulaymān also favours Theme 1, though he characteristically presents the material in a narrative form:

> They partitioned (*iqtasmū*) the Book: the Jews believed in the Torah and disbelieved in the Gospel and the Qur'an; the Christians believed in the Gospel and disbelieved in the Qur'an and the Torah. They partitioned it by believing some of what was revealed to them of the Book and disbelieving in some. Then [God] described the Jews and Christians [as] *those who made the*

Table 1: Key phrases and concepts

Theme	The Partitioners (*muqtasimīn*)	How they made a *qur'ān* pieces (*ʿiḍīn*)
1	'Jews and the Christians' (Ṭabarī, Sufyān, Bukhārī, Muqātil) 'People of the Book' (Ṭabarī, Bukhārī, Mujāhid) 'Jews and the Christians from among People of the Book' (Ṭabarī)	'They believed in some and they disbelieved in some' (Ṭabarī, Sufyān, Bukhārī, Ibn Wahb) 'They partitioned it (*jazza'ū*)' (Ṭabarī, Bukhārī) 'They made it into many pieces (*jaʿalū aʿḍā*) like the parts of a slaughtered camel/sheep' (Ṭabarī, Muqātil) They used to mock, this one saying, '*Sūrat al-Baqara* is for me', and this one saying, '*Sūrat Āl ʿImrān* is for me' (Ṭabarī) 'They divided (*qasamū*) their Book' (Ṭabarī) The Jews believed in the Torah and disbelieved in the Gospel and the Qur'an; the Christians believed in the Gospel and disbelieved in the Qur'an and the Torah. They partitioned it by believing some of what was revealed to them of the Book and disbelieving in some. Then [God] described the Jews and Christians '*alladhīna jaʿalū'l-Qur'ān ʿiḍīn*': they made the Qur'an into pieces like the pieces of a slaughtered camel. They separated the Book and did not agree on the belief in all of the Book. (Muqātil) They separated it: • *farraqū* • *farraqūhu'l-kitāb* • *firaqan* • *farraqū'l-Qur'ān* (Ṭabarī, Mujāhid) And they altered/divided it (*baddalū/ baddadū*) (Ṭabarī) 'They cut it up into books, each party with that which they pleased (*taqaṭṭaʿūhu zuburan kullu ḥizbin bi-mā ladayhim fariḥūn*)' (Ṭabarī)

2	Those who made a mutual oath against Ṣāliḥ and God (*alladhīna taqāsamū bi-Ṣāliḥ* . . . [Q. 27:48] . . . *taqāsamū bi'llāh ḥattā balagha'l-āya*) (Ṭabarī)	'The singular of *ʿiḍīn* is *ʿiḍw* and it is inferred from their saying *ʿaḍḍayta al-shay' taʿḍiyatan* if you separate it just as Ru'ba said, "the religion of God is not *muʿaḍḍā*" [and] means "separated". Likewise another [poet] said, "the tribe of 'Awf *ʿaḍḍā*; as for their enemy, he satisfied [them]; as for their might, it changed". By *ʿaḍḍā* he means "captured them and cut them into pieces".'[23] (Ṭabarī)
3	A group of five Qurashīs (*raht khamsa min Quraysh*) (Ṭabarī)	They slandered the Qur'an • *ʿaḍḍahū'l-Qur'ān* • *ʿaḍḍahū kitāb Allāh* • *ʿaḍahūhu wa bahatūhu* (Ṭabarī, Mujāhid)
	A number of Quraysh (*nafar min Quraysh*) (Ibn Hishām) The Quraysh (Ṭabarī) al-Walīd b. al-Mughīra (Ibn Hishām, Ibn Isḥāq)	They said it is magic, poetry, soothsaying, ancient fables, and/or the product of madness, that is, someone possessed by jinn • *siḥran* • *al-ʿaḍh al-siḥr bi-lisān Quraysh, taqūlu li-sāḥira: innahā'l-ʿāḍiha* • *wa'l-ʿiḍīn bi-lisāni Quraysh al-siḥr* • *yuqālu li'l-sāḥira al-ʿāḍiha; siḥran aʿḍā' al-kutub kulluhā* • *wa Quraysh faraqū'l-Qur'ān, qālū: huwa siḥr* • *hādhā siḥr wa shiʿr* • *fa-qāla baʿḍuhum: sāhir, wa qāla baʿḍuhum: shāʿir. wa qāla baʿḍuhum: majnūn. fa-dhālika'l-ʿiḍūn* • *zaʿama baʿḍuhum annahu siḥr, wa zaʿama baʿḍuhum annahu shiʿr, wa zaʿama baʿḍuhum annahu kāhin* (Ṭabarī, 'Abd al-Razzāq, Ibn Hishām, Ibn Isḥāq)
		They interdicted the roads during the fair (Ṭabarī, Ibn Hishām, Ibn Isḥāq)

> *Qur'an into pieces* (*ʿalladhīna jaʿalū'l-Qur'ān ʿiḍīn*): they made the Qur'an into pieces (*aʿḍā'*) like the pieces of a slaughtered camel. They separated (*faraqū*) the Book and did not agree on believing in all of the Book.[24]

The phrase 'pieces like the pieces of a slaughtered camel' is significant, for it indicates the lexicographical interests of this theme, as we will see.

Theme 2 identifies the Qur'anic verses with the Thamūd, the people whom the Arabian prophet Ṣāliḥ attempted to reform but who demanded a miracle involving a pregnant camel as proof of his prophethood. When God provided the miracle, some members still refused to believe and killed the camel, for which they were punished. The Ṣāliḥ material is completely independent and unique, and thus little analysis can be done of the Yūnus b. ʿAbd al-Aʿla (d. 264/877) ← ʿAbd Allāh Ibn Wahb (d. 197/812) ← Ibn Zayd transmission, though Ṭabarī frequently cites material from this source. The *muqtasimīn* are identified in the hadith as those who made an oath to oppose the prophet Ṣāliḥ.[25] As I will show, Theme 2 also depends on lexical manoeuvers.

Theme 3 is more problematic when one examines the *isnāds*. Various bits and pieces of it come from ʿIkrima, one of the prominent students of Ibn ʿAbbās, and not too surprisingly his teacher is also credited as the source for this theme. That Ibn ʿAbbās is seen as the source of such significant contradictory material again belies the existence of a school. This time, not even Ṭabarī could harmonise the divergent themes. Motzki agrees with me, however, that ʿIkrima (or, for Motzki, more likely Maʿmar) is responsible for reading *ʿiḍīn* as the plural of 'sorcery' and Qatāda for reading the word as the plural for 'slander'[26] – with 'sorcery' along with 'soothsaying', 'poetry' and 'ancient tales' being among the various slanders, which Motzki therefore sees as not a real, but only a 'superficial contradiction' (which is a bit reminiscent of Ṭabarī's harmonisation of *marīj*). In any case, both 'sorcery' and 'slander' have the same root (i.e. *ʿ-ḍ-h*), and this suggests a lexical significance.

All this variety tells us more than just that early generations of Muslim scholars did not know what these verses meant. As suggested above, closer analysis of this example shows that most of the interpretations have lexicographical bases, or more accurately, seem to be largely based on lexically informed guesses. For example, *anzalnā* (if understood as revelation) implies for some exegetes that the *muqtasimīn* had received a scripture. The displeasure of God implies that it must refer to non-Muslims, and the People of the Book are the obvious choice. The object of their partitioning could be either the Qur'an or their own versions of the Book, namely, the

Gospel and the Torah, since the term *qur'ān* as used within the Qur'an is multivalent enough to permit such a reading.[27] Theme 2 is more obviously lexical in origin. The Ibn Zayd hadith (see Table 1, Theme 2) explicitly connects the Form VIII verb *iqtasama*, meaning 'to divide' (via the plural of its active participle) with the Form VI verb *taqāsama*, meaning 'to make an oath'. The *muqtasimīn* become 'oath takers' (in this case, an oath against Ṣālih and Allah). Such a convoluted lexical explanation seems prompted on the common understanding of *'iḍīn* as the pieces of the camel. Abū Zakariyyā' Yaḥyā al-Farrā' (d. 207/822) provides some justification for this understanding of *'iḍīn*:

> It is said: *'aḍḍawhu*, that is, *farraqū* ('they divided it'), just as sheep and the slaughter camel are *ta'aḍḍaw*. The singular of *al-'iḍīn* is *'iḍa*, its nominative is *'iḍūn*, and its accusative and genitive are *'iḍīn*. And among the Arabs are those who put the letter *yā'* in all cases and vocalise the letter *nūn*.[28]

In Ṭabarī's *Tafsīr*, *'iḍīn* appears in hadiths connected to Theme 1 as meaning 'fragments of a slaughtered camel'. In any case, the Theme 2 explanation of *muqtasimīn* is creative, if not particularly convincing. Theme 3, surprisingly, has a similar but more complex origin. *'Iḍīn* is seen not as parts of a camel, but more oddly as an obscure variation of 'slanders' generally, or 'sorcery' or 'sorcery and poetry' more specifically. This variation is itself suspicious. The former is odd because it involves dropping one of the letters in an unusual way that prompts Ṭabarī to provide lexicographical justification:

> Others said instead that it [*'iḍīn*] is the plural of *'iḍa* and the plural *'iḍin* is like the plurals of *bura*, *burin*, and of *'iza*, *'izin*. If one accepts this interpretation, then the basis of this word is *'iḍaha* (slander). The 'h' of the word has been dropped just as the 'h' has from *shifa* (lips) which is based on *shafaha* and the 'h' from *sha* (sheep) which is based on *shaha*. These original bases are demonstrated by their diminutives (*taṣghīr*): *shufayha* and *shuwayha*. The 'h' which has been dropped in the non-diminutive situation (*ghayr ḥāl al-taṣghīr ilayhā*) returns in the diminutive. When one says: 'I *'aḍahtu* the man', one says I slander

him and defame him with slander. Thus, those who slandered (*ʿaḍḍahū*) the Qur'an are saying: 'It is sorcery, or it is poetry, or similar things, as was related by Qatāda.'[29]

To interpret the word *ʿiḍīn* as related to sorcery is also odd and requires an equally unconvincing lexicographical explanation from Farrāʾ and Ṭabarī that makes *ʿāḍih* a singular Qurashī-ism for 'sorcerer'; Farrāʾ concisely argues:

> *Who made the Qur'an into ʿiḍīn*: they divided (*farraqū*) it. That is, they maintained that it was sorcery, a lie and ancient tales. And *al-ʿidūna* in the speech of the Arabs is none other than 'sorcery'.[30]

Ṭabarī is far more elaborate and relies on hadiths:

> A group of the interpreters (*jamāʿa min ahl al-taʾwīl*) said that *ʿaḍh* in this passage is related to 'sorcery' specifically, without any allusion to disparagement [that is, slander]. Just as the poet said, 'The water of Zamzam is magical (*ʿiḍathunna*)', meaning magical (*siḥrhunna*). Those who say this [are the following]:
>
> - Aḥmad b. Ishaq ← Abū Aḥmad ← Ibn ʿUyayna ← ʿUmar ← ʿIkrima [concerning] *those who made the Qur'an ʿiḍīn*, that he said: '[It is] sorcery.'
> - Muḥammad b. ʿAbd al-Aʿlā ← Muḥammad b. Thawr ← Maʿmar ← Qatāda: [Concerning] "*ʿiḍīn*' that he said: 'They slandered (*ʿaḍahū*) it and defamed (*bahatū*) it.'
> - Ibn ʿAbd al-Aʿlā ← Muḥammad b. Thawr ← Maʿmar ← ʿIkrima: "*aḍh* is "sorcery" in the language of the Quraysh. A female sorcerer (*sāḥira*) is called *ʿāḍaha*.'
> - Muḥammad b. ʿUmar ← Abū ʿĀṣim ← ʿIsā; al-Ḥasan ← Waraqāʾ; al-Muthannā ← Abū Hudayfa ← Shibl; and al-Muthannā ← Isḥāq ← ʿAbd Allāh ← Waraqāʾ ← Ibn Abī Najīḥ ← Mujāhid: [Concerning] His statement *those who made the Qur'an ʿiḍīn*: 'Sorcery. The fragments of the Book, all of them, and the Quraysh said the Qur'an is sorcery.'[31]

Again, the partitioning here has nothing to do with fragmenting the Qur'an, but refers to something else – in this case, the act of interdicting or blocking the roads to Mecca by various Qurayshīs (i.e. Theme 3) and is closely related to a story in the *Sīra* by Ibn Isḥāq (d. 150/767).[32] According to this story, a notorious opponent of Muhammad, al-Walīd b. al-Mughīra, plots with a small group of fellow Qurashīs to discredit Muhammad. Just before the time of the annual pagan hajj in Mecca, he and his co-conspirators consider the various accusations that can be levelled at Muhammad in the hope of discouraging the visitors from taking his message seriously. Of all of these accusations including sorcery, soothsaying, poetry and possession, he deems the charge of sorcery to be most applicable, even though they admit that there has been 'neither spitting nor knots' – an apparent allusion to the *secret blowing on knots* mentioned in Q. 113:4. Afterwards, they intercept visitors on the roads to Mecca and spread their accusation. God, it is said, then revealed Q. 74:11–16 concerning al-Walīd b. al-Mughīra. This passage states that God will deal with him whom He created and gave wealth, sons and comfort, but who nevertheless rejected God's signs. Then He revealed one of our verses, Q. 15:90, concerning the men with him. This tale obviously corresponds to the concepts of Theme 3 in Table 1. In the *Kitāb al-Siyar wa'l-maghāzī*, Ibn Isḥāq's story is provided with an *isnād* that ends with Ibn Jubayr or 'Ikrima citing Ibn 'Abbās. Were one to trust this *isnād*, the views ascribed to Ibn 'Abbās could not be reconciled. Even if one were not to trust this *isnād*, but trusted those recorded by Ṭabarī, one would be perplexed at the prospect of Ibn 'Abbās being so unfamiliar with the biography of Muhammad that he thought the passage referred to Jews and Christians.

As pointed out above, the hadiths in Ṭabarī's *Tafsīr* are falsely ascribed to Ibn 'Abbās, and this story is likewise fairly late, and it turns out to be contemporary with the other false ascriptions. Motzki argues that the most likely source of the story is Muḥammad b. Abī Muḥammad (d. unknown, but active in the late first/seventh century), who passed it on to Ibn Isḥāq.[33] The Qur'an declares over twenty times that Muhammad is not a soothsayer, sorcerer, possessed or a poet.[34] It is possible that this minor incident with al-Walīd b. al-Mughīra provoked a profound and prolonged response in the Qur'an, and so one could see in the story evidence of Muhammad's biography elucidating the Qur'an, and the Qur'an referring to historical events in his life.[35] But there are problems with such a view. For example, if one accepts any of the traditional or Western chronologies of the Qur'an, the story is suspect because of the three suras referred to in this story: Q. 74 and Q. 113 are very early Meccan suras (the former is thought to be one of the first five and the latter some fifteen suras later), perhaps before opposition emerged, whereas Q. 15 is late Meccan, perhaps the fifty-fourth or fifty-seventh sura. These verses were not revealed at the same time, and at least some were either significantly before or after this supposed event with al-Walīd b. al-Mughīra is said to have occurred (at least according to classical chronologies). Nor are they usually connected with al-Walīd b. al-Mughīra. Belying the historicity of this event even more is the version of this story recorded by Muqātil, which connects the story to Q. 15:95, Q. 16:24 and Q. 16:30.[36] It seems, therefore, that the origin of the story need not be a real historical event, but could be merely a metonymy of 'challenge stories' or narrative exegesis of the twenty or so verses that suggest the Qur'an is not a product of revelation, as had first been suggested by Wansbrough.[37] The various verses of the Qur'an certainly seem to be later interjections, with different verses being interjected by different transmitters. While it is not impossible that such an event may have occurred, this story – as it is transmitted by Muḥammad b. Abī Muḥammad – hinges entirely on a lexical interpretation: reading *ʿiḍīn* as 'slanders' or 'sorceries'. In that regard, it displays the same lexicographical concerns as the hadiths of Themes 1 and 2, wherein lie its most probable origins.

The example of Q. 15:89–92 does not suggest that Ibn ʿAbbās represents a consensus or even a mirror of acceptable diversity. Motzki likewise concludes that Ibn ʿAbbās is not the source of the opinions ascribed to him. Instead, he argues that the earliest sources of historical opinions are Abū Zaybān, Ibn Jubayr, Ḍaḥḥāk, Mujāhid, Qatāda and Muḥammad b. Abī Muḥammad, who all died between the last decade of the first century AH/seventh century CE and first two decades of the next century. Furthermore, Motzki suggests that later transmitters ascribed their exegesis to Ibn ʿAbbās.[38] Rather, Ibn ʿAbbās is simply being invoked to justify what seem to be various forms of lexical speculation. The school of Ibn ʿAbbās exists only insofar as many later exegetes sought to root their interpretations in him.

Q. 15:89–92, therefore, confirms the results of the analysis of the exegesis of Q. 50:5. However, the first example, the exegesis of Q. 1:7, displays a remarkable degree of uniformity. Its usefulness as an example is not that it definitively demonstrates the existence or non-existence of a lexicographical school of Ibn ʿAbbās; in fact, it could be employed to argue for or against such a claim. However, this ambiguity highlights how influential our preconceptions can be in determining our conclusions. Q. 15:89–92 and Q. 50:5, on the other hand, had no such uniformity. These two examples belie the existence of any influence between the material ascribed to Ibn ʿAbbās and the material ascribed to his so-called students, at least in terms of lexicography. And if one assumes the general trustworthiness of *isnāds*, then these examples also undermine the existence of a school of Ibn ʿAbbās in the normal sense.

A School of Ibn ʿAbbās

It is no surprise that scholars have questioned the authenticity of the prodigious material attributed to Ibn ʿAbbās. Such is the quality and quantity of it that Ibn ʿAbbās was labelled a liar by Aloys Sprenger, and his authoritative status was presumed to be mostly a fiction by Theodor Nöldeke.[39] With Joseph Schacht's work on the legal hadiths, it became possible to envisage wholesale fabrication. His 'backwards growth' of *isnāds*[40] provides a mechanism for Nöldeke's fiction. Tilman Nagel and Rashid Ahmad (Jullandri) separately identified later Abbasid rule as the reason that Ibn ʿAbbās became the main figure in exegesis.[41] Earlier, Birkeland had made a similar though more specific claim: the close association of Muḥammad al-Wāqidī (d. 207/823) with the Abbasids 'may explain the attribution of all generally recognized Koranic interpretations to their ancestor Ibn ʿAbbās'.[42]

In two earlier studies, I attempted to test the proposition that the exegetical opinions ascribed to Ibn ʿAbbās are products of later Muslims in two ways. First, I sought to determine if the main transmission lines including Ibn ʿAbbās contained in Ṭabarī's *Tafsīr* exhibited patterns with respect to the exegetical techniques used. They did not, and this implied that there was no reason to assume the authenticity of Ibn ʿAbbās-hadiths as recorded by Ṭabarī.[43] Second, I examined Ibn ʿAbbās's interpretations in three collections of *tafsīr*, namely those of Ibn Wahb, Bukhārī (d. 256/870)[44] and Ṭabarī. This allowed me to take 'snapshots' of the figure of Ibn ʿAbbās in *tafsīr* over the period of a century.[45] Of Ibn Wahb's 352 exegetical hadiths, less than 7 per cent come from Ibn ʿAbbās, more or less the same amount as the Companion Muḥammad b. Kaʿb al-Quraẓī (d. 117/736) and twice as many as several others. He is prominent but not overly so. By the time of Bukhārī, Ibn ʿAbbās is far more prominent. Of the 500 hadiths in the *Kitāb al-Tafsīr* within his *Ṣaḥīḥ*, 21 per cent come from or through Ibn ʿAbbās. Approximately half as many come from each of Ibn Masʿūd (as they had in Ibn Wahb's *Tafsīr*) and ʿĀʾisha bt. Abī Bakr. When one eliminates those hadiths in which they act as merely transmitters of the interpretations of others, Ibn ʿAbbās is the authority in almost 15 per cent of the hadiths, whereas Ibn Masʿūd and ʿĀʾisha are the authorities in merely 4 per cent and 3 per cent respectively. In the half century between Ibn Wahb and Bukhārī, Ibn ʿAbbās became far more prominent. In the next half century, as evidenced by Ṭabarī, this trend seems to level out significantly. Of his 38,397 hadiths, 15 per cent are attributed to Ibn ʿAbbās. Although this may appear to be a decrease in prominence, it is only because Ṭabarī is willing to cite later, non-Companion exegetes in large numbers. If the latter are overlooked, Ibn ʿAbbās's prominence again increases. Moreover, in absolute terms Ibn Wahb cites twenty-four Ibn ʿAbbās-hadiths, Bukhārī cites 105, and Ṭabarī a staggering 5,835.

All this indicates that the status of Ibn ʿAbbās in Qurʾanic exegesis developed over time, the zenith of which corresponds with that of the early Abbasid caliphs' political power. That is to say, Ibn ʿAbbās's growing reputation as Islam's greatest *mufassir* is suspiciously correlated to the onset of Abbasid propaganda and their later patronage of some scholars. Were an exegetical opinion to be ascribed to Ibn ʿAbbās that fell within the acceptable range of opinions, it would be in (almost) no one's interest to question it. This propaganda is also evident with historians such as Sayf b. ʿUmar (d. ca. 180/796), Wāqidī, Ibn Hishām (d. 218/833) and al-Balādhurī (d. ca. 279/892), who were obviously catering to Abbasid sensibilities or perhaps even spreading pro-Abbasid propaganda when writing about Ibn ʿAbbās's father. As I have argued elsewhere, because very early sources depicted ʿAbbās as a very late convert, later historians were restricted to embellishing his personal importance to Muhammad and, occasionally, omitting more problematic details. Despite these attempts, it was impossible to recast ʿAbbās as one who could compete with ʿAlī for religious authority. Within Abbasid propaganda, that role was projected onto his son, Ibn ʿAbbās, whereas his father was used in the Abbasid Shiʿi propaganda battle for the legal 'inheritance'. This role, I contend, is the origin of the mythic image of Ibn ʿAbbās as a *mufassir* commissioned by Muhammad himself.[46] However, the proliferation of these deutero-Ibn ʿAbbās hadiths had, by Ṭabarī's time, forced the compiler into the awkward need to reconcile conflicting opinions and, every now and then, to disagree with him. By then, the Abbasids had ruled for 150 years and their propagandist needs were considerably less urgent; but Ibn ʿAbbās was then no longer just the property of his descendants, but of the whole community, having become the embodiment of both its consensus and a reflection of its exegetical disagreements.[47] Unfortunately, the sources do not permit one to peer prior to the rise of the Abbasids. And so, it is difficult to tell what, if any, reputation Ibn ʿAbbās had as an exegete is based in reality. However, it is clear that the basis of Ibn ʿAbbās's reputation as an exegete and founder of a school – the thousands of hadiths ascribed to him – is suspect. Moreover, his purported methodology is equally suspect; the report cited at the beginning of this chapter contended that Ibn ʿAbbās first consulted the Qur'an, and if that failed him, reports from Muhammad, and then those from Abū Bakr and ʿUmar – all before relying on his own opinion. However, none of the Ibn ʿAbbās-hadiths discussed in this chapter cite other verses in the Qur'an, nor Muhammad, Abū Bakr or ʿUmar – even, it seems, when prophetic hadith were in circulation. According to the reports, all he used was his own opinion! This methodological report, therefore, also casts Ibn ʿAbbās as the idealised, mythic authority.

Thus, if there is a 'school of Ibn ʿAbbās' in the sense that certain methodologies or specific interpretations were shared by hadiths ascribed to Ibn ʿAbbās and to his 'students' such as Mujāhid, Ibn Jubayr and ʿIkrima, that school was not formed by the aforementioned exegetes learning at the feet of Ibn ʿAbbās. Nevertheless, in at least three senses there was a 'school of thought' for which Ibn ʿAbbās was a mythic ideal. First and most obviously, later exegetes or their transmitters adopted a myth of origins – a myth that included an ideal, if mostly unimplemented, methodology and that envisioned Qur'anic exegesis as originating with Companion founder-teachers, the most prominent of which was Ibn ʿAbbās. The exegesis of Q. 15:89–92 demonstrates this most clearly, though that of Q. 1:7 may as well. There was simply a consensus about the interpretation of the latter. Second, as the exegesis of Q. 50:5 demonstrates, scholars such as Ṭabarī wrestled with the legacy that this myth of origins had produced. He felt the need to impose, where he could, a consensus and the appearance of consistency on the material. Third, the multivalent interpretations of Q. 15:89–92 seems to indicate that the earliest exegetes of the Qur'an already displayed strong (if not particularly sophisticated) lexicographical interests.

NOTES

1 Fuat Sezgin, *Geschichte des arabischen Schrifttums* (Leiden: Brill, 1967–84), vol. 1, p. 26.

2 Aḥmad Ibn Ḥajar al-ʿAsqalānī, *Tahdhīb al-tahdhīb*, ed. Muṣṭafā ʿAbd al-Qādir ʿAṭā (Beirut: Dār al-Kutub al-ʿIlmiyya, 1994), vol. 5, p. 248.

3 Ibn Ḥajar, *Tahdhīb*, vol. 5, pp. 245–7.

4 In the Qur'an, *al-ḥikma* is used in ways that suggest it may be the name of a text (e.g. Q. 2:151 and Q. 3:48). It is not clear what the report is claiming. Is it claiming that God has bestowed on Ibn ʿAbbās that which is generally reserved for prophets?

5 Muḥammad Ibn Saʿd, *Kitāb al-Ṭabaqāt al-kubrā*, Foreword by Iḥsān ʿAbbās on the basis of the edition by Eduard Sachau *et al.* (Beirut: Dār Ṣādir, 1960–68), vol. 2, p. 365; see also Ibn Ḥajar, *Tahdhīb*, vol. 5, p. 247.

6 Ibn Saʿd, *al-Ṭabaqāt*, vol. 2, p. 365.

7 Ibid., pp. 365–6.

8 See Herbert Berg, "Abbasid Historians' Portrayals of al-ʿAbbās b. ʿAbd al-Muttalib' in John Nawas, ed., *Abbasid Studies II: Occasional Papers of the*

School of Abbasid Studies, Leuven, 28 June – 1 July 2004 (Leuven: Peeters Publishers, 2010), pp. 13–38.

9 Ibn Ḥajar, *Tahdhīb*, vol. 5, p. 247.

10 Ibn Sa'd, *al-Ṭabaqāt*, vol. 2, p. 366.

11 Claude Gilliot also argues that this hadith reflects a much later debate; see his 'Portrait "mythique" d'Ibn 'Abbās', *Arabica* 32 (1985), pp. 127–84, at pp. 156–77.

12 Muqātil also identifies the referents as Jews and Christians, though he adds that monkeys and pigs were fashioned from the former. See Muqātil b. Sulaymān, *Tafsīr Muqātil b. Sulaymān*, ed. 'Abd Allāh Maḥmūd Shiḥāta (Cairo: al-Hay'a al-Miṣriyya al-'Āmma li'l-Kitāb, 1979–89), vol. 1, p. 36. Thus, others also explained this verse in the same way, without reference to Ibn 'Abbās.

13 Harris Birkeland, *Old Muslim Opposition against Interpretation of the Koran* (Oslo: Jacob Dybwad, 1955), p. 37.

14 John Wansbrough, *Quranic Studies: Sources and Methods of Scriptural Interpretation* (Oxford: Oxford University Press, 1977), p. 158.

15 Muḥammad b. Jarīr al-Ṭabarī, *Tafsīr al-Ṭabarī al-musammā Jāmi' al-bayān fī ta'wīl al-Qur'ān* (Beirut: Dār al-Kutub al-'Ilmiyya, 1992), vol. 11, p. 408.

16 For another example of Ṭabarī's efforts to dismiss differences as irrelevant, see S.R. Burge, 'The Angels in *Sūrat al-Malā'ika*: Exegeses of Q. 35.1', *Journal of Qur'anic Studies* 10 (2008), pp. 50–70, at p. 51.

17 Ṭabarī, *Tafsīr*, vol. 11, p. 409. Once again Muqātil is in 'agreement' with Ibn 'Abbās, or more accurately Ṭabarī, for he too uses the gloss, '*mukhtalif multabis*'. See Muqātil, *Tafsīr*, vol. 4, p. 110.

18 Gilliot, 'Portrait "mythique" d'Ibn 'Abbās', pp. 177–84.

19 Gregor Schoeler, 'Die Frage der schriftlichen oder mündlichen Überlieferung der Wissenschaften im frühen Islam', *Der Islam* 62 (1985), pp. 201–30.

20 This example was previously used in Herbert Berg, 'Competing Paradigms in the Study of Islamic Origins: Qur'ān 15:89–91 and the Value of *Isnāds*' in idem, ed., *Method and Theory in the Study of Islamic Origins* (Leiden: Brill, 2003), pp. 259–90. Motzki also re-analyses this example using his *isnād-cum-matn* method, because my earlier one was 'too superficial and . . . not accurate and sophisticated enough'; see Harald Motzki, 'The Origins of Muslim Exegesis. A Debate' in Harald Motzki with Nicolet Boekhoff-van der Voort and Sean W. Anthony, *Analysing Muslim Traditions: Studies in Legal, Exegetical and Maghāzī Ḥadīth* (Leiden: Brill, 2010), pp. 231–303, with the quotation from p. 232.

21 The material in this table is drawn from Ṭabarī, *Tafsīr*, vol. 7, pp. 543–7; Sufyān al-Thawrī, *Tafsīr Sufyān al-Thawrī*, ed. Imtiyāz 'Alī 'Arshī (Beirut: Dār al-Kutub al-'Ilmiyya, 1403/1983), pp. 161–2; al-Bukhārī, *Ṣaḥīḥ al-Bukhārī*, ed. Qāsim al-Shammā'ī al-Rifā'ī (Beirut: Dār al-Qalam, 1987), vol. 6, p. 431; Mujāhid b. Jabr, *Tafsīr Mujāhid*, ed. 'Abd al-Raḥmān al-Ṭāhir al-Sūratī (Beirut: al-Manshūrāt al-'Ilmiyya, n.d.), vol. 1, p. 419; Muqātil b. Sulaymān, *Tafsīr*, vol. 2, pp. 436–7; 'Abd al-Razzāq al-Ṣan'ānī, *al-Muṣannaf*, ed. Ḥabīb al-Raḥmān al-A'ẓamī (Beirut: al-Maktab al-Islāmī, 1983), vol. 5, p. 361; 'Abd al-Malik Ibn Hishām, *al-Sīra al-nabawiyya*, ed. Muṣṭafā al-Saqqā, Ibrāhīm al-Abyādī and 'Abd al-Ḥāfiẓ Shalabī (Beirut: Dār al-Ma'rifa, n.d.), vol. 1, pp. 270–72; and Muḥammad Ibn Isḥāq, *Kitāb al-Siyar wa'l-maghāzī*, ed. Suhayl Zakkār (Beirut: Dār al-Fikr, 1978), pp. 150–52.

22 Motzki, 'The Origins of Muslim Exegesis. A Debate', pp. 238–41.

23 This hadith begins with: 'they made it fragments (*a'ḍa'*) just as sheep are fragmented. Some of them said, "Soothsaying." Some of them said, "Sorcery." Some of them said, "Poetry." And, some of them said, "Old fables which he has written for himself [Q. 25:5]."' (*qāla ba'ḍuhum: kihāna, wa qāla ba'ḍuhum: huwa siḥr, wa qāla ba'ḍuhum: shi'r, wa qala ba'ḍuhum: asāṭīr al-awwalīna iktatabahā*). The first sentence seems more akin to Theme 1, the second to Theme 3, and the remaining lexical explanation given in the table is not obviously connected to Ṣaliḥ. Ṭabarī, *Tafsīr*, vol. 7, p. 546.

24 Muqātil, *Tafsīr*, vol. 2, pp. 436–7. Motzki points out that Muqātil also has the story that lies behind Theme 3, though Muqātil has attached it to his exegesis of Q. 15:95. Motzki, 'The Origins of Muslim Exegesis. A Debate', pp. 274–6.

25 When discussing *'iḍīn*, however, Ibn Zayd (as reported in Ṭabarī) seems to employ expressions found in Muqātil and elsewhere ascribed to Ibn 'Abbās when *muqtasimīn* is understood to refer to Jews and Christians and *'iḍīn* to parts of a slaughtered camel. Motzki, in his analysis of this material, states, 'Ṭabarī gives two traditions with the *isnād* Yūnus ← Ibn Wahb, one with Ibn Zayd, and another one with Yazīd as Ibn Wahb's informant. Berg obviously either read Yazīd as Zayd and overlooked the fact that in that case *ibn* would be missing, or he thought that the name Yazīd must be an error of transmission and that it should have been Ibn Zayd and emendated it in silence.' Motzki, 'The Origins of Muslim Exegesis. A Debate', p. 268. Unfortunately, the error, if there is one, belongs to the editor of this edition of the *Tafsīr*, which has both *isnāds* ending with Ibn Zayd. Ṭabarī, *Tafsīr*, vol. 7, p. 546.

26 Motzki, 'The Origins of Muslim Exegesis. A Debate', pp. 254–61. Compare Berg, 'Competing Paradigms in the Study of Islamic Origins', p. 274.

27 See Herbert Berg, 'Tabarī's Exegesis of the Qur'ānic Term *al-kitāb*', *Journal of the American Academy of Religion* 63, no. 4 (1995), pp. 761–74.

28 Abū Zakariyyā' Yaḥyā b. Ziyād al-Farrā', *Ma'ānī al-Qur'ān*, ed. Aḥmad Yūsuf Najātī and Muḥammad 'Alī al-Najjār (Cairo: Maṭba'at Dār al-Kutub al-Miṣriyya, 1955), vol. 2, pp. 91–2.

29 Ṭabarī, *Tafsīr*, vol. 7, p. 546.

30 Farrā', *Ma'anī al-Qur'ān*, vol. 2, pp. 91–2. Farrā' then continues with the previously cited passage that suggests *'iḍīn* refers to the parts of a slaughtered camel.

31 Ṭabarī, *Tafsīr*, vol. 7, pp. 546–7.

32 Despite providing evidence for Theme 2, Farrā' favours Theme 3: '*I am the clear warner. Just as We sent down on the muqtasimīn*. He is saying: I warned of what I sent down upon the *muqtasimīn*. The *muqtasimīn* are men from the people of Mecca. The people of Mecca sent them to the paths [to the city] during the days of the hajj. They said, "If the people ask you about the Prophet, say, 'He is a soothsayer.'" They said to some of them, "Say, 'He is a sorcerer'", to some, "He is divided between the two", and to some, "Say, 'He is possessed by jinn [i.e. crazy].'" God sent down a punishment upon them. They died, or five of them had an evil death. They are called *muqtasimīn* because they partitioned the roads of Mecca'; see Farrā', *Ma'ānī al-Qur'ān*, vol. 2, pp. 91–2.

33 Motzki, 'The Origins of Muslim Exegesis. A Debate', pp. 264–7.

34 References to one or more of these accusations occur in Q. 6:7; Q. 11:7; Q. 15:6; Q. 21:5; Q. 26:27, 224; Q. 34:43; Q. 37:15, 36; Q. 43:30; Q. 44:14; Q. 46:7; Q. 51:39, 52; Q. 52:29–30; Q. 54:2, 9; Q. 68:2, 51; Q. 69:41–2; Q. 74:24; Q. 81:22.

35 For example, W. Montgomery Watt, *Muhammad at Mecca* (Oxford: Oxford University Press, 1953), pp. 127–9.

36 Muqātil, *Tafsīr,* vol. 2, pp. 437–8. See also Motzki, 'The Origins of Muslim Exegesis. A Debate', pp. 274–6.

37 'The narrative is parabolic ... by means of which the ... scriptural terms were endowed with specific history.' See John Wansbrough, *The Sectarian Milieu: Content and Composition of Islamic Salvation History* (Oxford: Oxford University Press, 1978), p. 11. In this regard, Motzki and I also agree. He writes: 'It is obvious that the stories do not describe a specific event that really happened. Rather, using qur'ānic notions, they attempt to give an idea of what happened in Mecca at the time of the Prophet.' Motzki, 'The Origins of Muslim Exegesis. A Debate', p. 276. Compare Berg, 'Competing Paradigms in the Study of Islamic Origins', pp. 279–80.

38 Motzki, 'The Origins of Muslim Exegesis. A Debate', p. 271. Motzki, responding to my earlier analysis of Q. 15:90–91, argues that the earliest authorities for the exegesis of the passage are 'Abū Ẓabyān, Saʿīd ibn Jubayr, al-Ḍaḥḥāk, Mujāhid, Qatāda, and Muḥammad ibn Abī Muḥammad and *not* Ibn ʿAbbās as Berg claims. They all died in the last decade of the first/seventh or the first two decades of the second/eighth centuries. Most of them (Saʿīd ibn Jubayr, al-Ḍaḥḥāk, Mujāhid, Qatāda) did *not* ascribe their opinions to Ibn ʿAbbās. Only some transmitters *from* them did so. That happened in the second quarter of the second/eighth century and later. Yet, a few early scholars seem to have (probably falsely) ascribed their exegesis to Ibn ʿAbbās as early as the turn of the first/seventh century (Muḥammad ibn Abī Muḥammad, perhaps also Abū Ẓabyān).' He also suggests that the exegetical narratives of Muqātil, Kalbī and Ibn Isḥāq 'derive from a common source that can be approximately dated to the turn of the first/seventh century'. Ibid., pp. 297–8. In other words, Motzki's analysis broadly supports my conclusions here about the 'school' of Ibn ʿAbbās.

39 Aloys Sprenger, 'Notes on Alfred von Kremer's Edition of Wakidy's Campaigns', *Journal of the Asiatic Society of Bengal* 25 (1856), pp. 53–74 and 199–220, at p. 72; and Theodor Nöldeke *et al.*, *Geschichte des Qorāns*, 2nd rev. edn (Leipzig: Dieterich, 1909–38), vol. 2, p. 266.

40 Joseph Schacht, *The Origins of Muhammadan Jurisprudence*, 3rd rev. edn (Oxford: Clarendon Press, 1959), pp. 138–49.

41 Tilman Nagel, '*Die Qiṣāṣ-al-anbiyaʿ*: Ein Beitrag zur arabischen Literaturgeschichte' (Bonn, Rheinische Friedrich-Wilhelms-Universität, 1967), p. 57; and Rashid Ahmad (Jullandri), 'Qur'ānic Exegesis and Classical Tafsīr', *Islamic Quarterly* 12 (1968), pp. 71–119, at p. 79.

42 Birkeland, *Old Muslim Opposition against Interpretation of the Koran*, p. 41.

43 Herbert Berg, *The Development of Exegesis in Early Islam: The Authenticity of Muslim Literature from the Formative Period* (Richmond, Surrey: Curzon, 2000). The question of whether my conclusion can be generalised to other Ibn ʿAbbās-hadiths (such as those in Ṭabarī's history) remains unanswered. G.H.A. Juynboll argues, for example, that legal and historical hadiths must be treated differently. Unfortunately, Juynboll does not discuss *tafsīr.* See

G.H.A. Juynboll, 'Some Thoughts on Early Muslim Historiography', *Bibliotheca Orientalis* 49 (1992), pp. 685–91. In my study, I noticed no difference in terms of genres. Lexical hadiths could not be distinguished from other genres of hadiths based on their *isnāds*, suggesting that they should not be singled out as being any more (or less) authentic than the others.

44 R. Marston Speight has argued that the *mufassir*, such as Ṭabarī, and the *muḥaddith*, such as Bukhārī, had different concerns. The former was concerned with elucidating the text of the Qur'an and could draw on many sources, including the Sunna. The latter was concerned with the Sunna of Muhammad, and so included sections devoted to *tafsīr* in his compilations. As my example shows, the Ibn ʿAbbās reports recorded by Ibn Wahb cite Muhammad a little under 30 per cent of the time; in those recorded by Bukhārī a little under 60 per cent; and in those recorded by Ṭabarī approximately 16 per cent. Although Bukhārī was clearly more concerned with prophetic *tafsīr*, it was hardly his sole criteria in his chapter on *tafsīr*. Moreover, the issue that I am addressing is the relative prominence of Ibn ʿAbbās when compared with other Companion exegetes, all of whom cite Muhammad more frequently in the hadiths collected by Bukhārī. R. Marston Speight, 'The Function of *ḥadith* as Commentary on the Qur'ān, as Seen in the Six Authoritative Collections' in Andrew Rippin, ed., *Approaches to the History of the Interpretation of the Qur'ān* (Oxford: Clarendon Press, 1988), pp. 63–81.

45 Muranyi has argued that Ibn Wahb's *Tafsīr* contains exegesis from the first decades of the second/eighth century and perhaps some material stretching into the end of the first/seventh century. He is on firmer ground when he argues that Ibn Wahb's work was likely disseminated after 191/806–7 but only in written form a few decades later. ʿAbd Allāh Ibn Wahb, *al-Jāmiʿ: Tafsīr al-Qurʿān (Die Koranexegese)*, ed. Miklos Muranyi (Wiesbaden: Otto Harrassowitz, 1993), pp. xxi and 9. Similar questions about the exact date when the extant works of Bukhārī and Ṭabarī achieved their present form have been raised. See the discussions in Jonathan Brown, *The Canonization of al-Bukhārī and Muslim: The Formation and Function of the Sunnī Ḥadīth Canon* (Leiden: Brill, 2007), pp. 385–6; and Berg, *The Development of Exegesis in Early Islam*, pp. 122–4.

46 Berg, "Abbasid Historians' Portrayals of al-ʿAbbās b. ʿAbd al-Muttalib', pp. 13–38.

47 Herbert Berg, 'Ibn ʿAbbās in ʿAbbāsid-Era *Tafsīr*' in James E. Montgomery, ed., *Abbasid Studies: Occasional Papers of the School of Abbasid Studies, Cambridge, 6–10 July 2002* (Leuven: Peeters Publishers, 2004), pp. 129–46.

4

The Interpretation of Three Qur'anic Terms (*Siyāḥa*, *Ḥikma* and *Ṣiddīq*) of Special Interest to the Early Renunciants

CHRISTOPHER MELCHERT

THIS ARTICLE was commissioned, first of all, to test the usefulness of lexicographical sources for the interpretation of the Qur'an. The Qur'an is a difficult text to understand, and Qur'anic commentary (*tafsīr*) has been a major concern since the beginning of Islamic religious writing outside the Qur'an itself. The Qur'an was also a major concern of the early grammarians, who copiously quote it to illustrate good Arabic usage.[1] The comprehensive quality of the *tafsīr* genre has recently and rightly been celebrated, starting with Norman Calder and continuing with Walid Saleh.[2] *Tafsīr* does seem to comprehend the lexicographic genre – my undergraduate students are always surprised, at first, to see the discussion of a verse begin with grammatical explanations. Still, it is a point worth testing: whether the *tafsīr* genre is so comprehensive that it is superfluous to consult lexicographical works, besides.

My principal research interest is presently renunciant piety before Sufism, the mystical tradition of Islam. Modern Western scholars have agreed with medieval Muslims that Sufism evolved in the third/ninth century out of earlier renunciant piety, which stressed self-denial but not communion with God, the hallmark of mysticism. Louis Massignon is especially associated with a lexicographical argument: that the technical terminology of the Islamic mystical tradition is so thoroughly Qur'anic that the mystical tradition must have been primarily endogenous.[3] Express glosses on the

Qur'an are fairly common in the early literature of renunciation, but, in line with my lexicographical commission, I here examine how renunciants used three Qur'anic terms: *siyāḥa*, *ḥikma* and *ṣiddīq*. The first came to my attention when I was investigating the piety of third/ninth-century traditionalists – Sunnis who considered that law and theology should be inferred directly from Hadith, with as little resort to reason and figurative interpretation as could be managed. Aḥmad Ibn Ḥanbal (d. 241/855), their leading figure, said, '*Siyāḥa* has nothing to do with Islam.'[4] Yet I observed that normally Qur'anic commentaries glossed *siyāḥa* in the Qur'an as 'fasting', which has a lot to do with Islam. In renunciant literature, I later observed, *siyāḥa* is normally used for 'roaming'. For some reason, Aḥmad and the renunciants on the one hand and Qur'anic commentaries on the other interpreted *siyāḥa* very differently. The other two terms, *ḥikma* and *ṣiddīq*, also came up in Qur'anic commentaries on suras that I was teaching, where they likewise seemed to be glossed otherwise than as I was used to seeing them in renunciant literature. But the way they are used in renunciant literature seems entirely compatible with the context of their occurrences in the Qur'an. Renunciant concepts and practices seem to have aroused opposition from the nascent Sunni party late in the second/eighth century.[5] My hypothesis is that the Qur'anic commentary tradition reflects that opposition in avoiding the suggestion that the Qur'an endorses such concepts and practices. My method is to look up each of these three terms in, by turn, Qur'anic commentaries, Hadith (a convenient control, since it overlaps with both Qur'anic commentary and renunciation), medieval Arabic dictionaries and renunciant literature.

Siyāḥa in the Qur'an, Qur'anic Commentaries and Renunciant Literature

The first term I will take up is *siyāḥa*. The Qur'an uses the active participles *sā'iḥūn* and *sā'iḥāt*, meaning on the face of it 'persons who wander about'. The Islamic renunciant tradition naturally took up the term, applying it to persons who wandered from place to place, worshipping. But the commentary tradition is evidently distrustful of wandering and makes out that Qur'anic *siyāḥa* is something else than what it appears to mean.

The Qur'an once uses the verb *sāḥa*, at Q. 9:2, where it plainly means what one would expect: *Travel freely* (*sīḥū*) *in the land.*[6] *Sā'iḥūn* are numbered with other pious persons in Q. 9:112: *Those who turn in repentance, those who serve, those who praise, those who travel* (*al-sā'iḥūn*) (*for God*), *those who bow, those who prostrate themselves, those who enjoin what is considered right and who forbid what is considered wrong, those who keep God's limits.* And in Q. 66:5, ideal new wives are described as *women who have surrendered, believing, obedient, devout, travelling* (*sā'iḥāt*) (*for God*), *married or virgin.*

Siyāḥa in Hadith

In prophetic Hadith, as it appears in famous collections, *siyāḥa* means just what it looks like: 'roaming'. In one example, widely reported, the Prophet declares, 'God has angels who travel the Earth (*sayyāḥīn fī'l-arḍ*) transmitting peace to me from my community.'[7] The Kufan Sufyān al-Thawrī (d. 161/777?) is the common link in all these versions.[8] Abū Dāwūd al-Sijistānī (d. 275/889) reports discouragement of *siyāḥa*: that a man said, 'O Messenger of God, permit me (to engage in) *siyāḥa*', to which the Prophet replied, 'The *siyāḥa* of my community is jihad in the path of God (mighty and glorious is He).'[9] Abū Umāma is the Companion who reports this; the *isnād* is solidly Damascene. The rhetorical form of this hadith has many parallels; for example, 'Every prophet has a *rahbāniyya*. The *rahbāniyya* of this community is jihad in the path of God.'[10] Here is discouragement, but whatever *siyāḥa* means, it is plainly not 'fasting', as the commentary tradition usually maintains.

Siyāḥa in the commentary tradition

There is nothing on Q. 9:112 in the commentaries of Sufyān al-Thawrī or 'Abd al-Razzāq al-Ṣan'ānī (d. 211/827), nor, likewise, in the early Twelver Shi'i commentary of 'Alī b. Ibrāhīm al-Qummī (fl. mid-fourth/tenth century). At Q. 9:112, Muḥammad b. Jarīr Ṭabarī (d. 310/923) declares at the start, 'As for his saying *al-sā'iḥūn*, they are the *ṣāʾimūn* ('those who fast')'. As evidence, he cites two prophetic hadith reports. The first goes back (through, oddly, Sufyān al-Thawrī) to a Meccan preacher (*qāṣṣ*), the Follower ʿUbayd Ibn ʿUmayr (d. 68/687–88): 'The Prophet was asked about *al-sāʾiḥūn*. He said, "They are the fasters."' The second goes back to an Abū Hārūn, presumably a mistake for the prolific Companion Abū Hurayra, who quotes the Prophet as saying, 'The *sāʾiḥūn* are the fasters.'[11] This is obviously the source for 'those who fast' in modern translations.

The following are also cited by Ṭabarī:

al-Ḥasan (d. 110/728), Basran, sometimes specifying those who fast in Ramadan;
the Prophet (Kufan *isnād*);
ʿAbd Allāh (Ibn Masʿūd, d. 32/652–3; Kufan *isnād*);
Abū ʿAbd al-Raḥmān (al-Sulamī, Kufan, d. after 70/689–90)
Ibn ʿAbbās (d. 68/687–8); Kufan *isnād*);
Saʿīd b. Jubayr (Kufan, d. 96/714–15?);
Mujāhid (Meccan, d. 103/721–22?);
Abū ʿAmr al-ʿAbdī (unidentified);[12]
al-Ḍaḥḥāk (Khurasani, d. after 100/718–19);
ʿAṭāʾ (Meccan, d. 114/732–33?)
Qatāda (b. Diʿāma, d. 117/735–6?)

In commenting on a story from Wahb b. Munabbih (d. 113/731–2?) about an Israelite *sāʾiḥ*, Ṭabarī quotes the Kufan Sufyān Ibn ʿUyayna (d. Mecca, 198/814) as explaining, 'Whoever leaves food, drink and women is a *sāʾiḥ*.'[13]

Abūʾl-Ḥasan al-Māwardī (d. 450/1058) tells us rather that there are four interpretations of *al-sāʾiḥūn*.[14] One is that it means *al-mujāhidūn* ('those who fight on the path of God'). He quotes the hadith report through Abū Umāma by which the Prophet declared, 'The *siyāḥa* of my nation is the jihad in the path of God.' The second interpretation is that it means *al-ṣāʾimūn* ('those who fast'), which he says is the position of Ibn Masʿūd and Ibn ʿAbbās; he then quotes the hadith report through Abū Hurayra that Ṭabarī had quoted before. The third, he says, is that it means *al-muhājirūn* ('those who emigrate'), which he identifies as the position of ʿAbd al-Raḥmān

Ibn Zayd, a client of Medina (d. 182/798–99) often cited by Ṭabarī. The fourth interpretation, finally, is that the *sā'iḥūn* are seekers of knowledge, the position of the Medinese ʿIkrima (d. 107/725–6?), himself one of the most travelled of the Followers.[15] The first two obviously defer to Hadith, the second two respect the literal meaning of *sā'iḥūn*.

The later commentary of the Twelver al-Faḍl b. al-Ḥasan al-Ṭabrisī (d. 548/1153–4?) is similar. In a section on linguistic problems, he states that the *sā'iḥ* is one who travels the earth, persisting in motion, but that a derived meaning is one who fasts, persisting in obedience as he leaves what is desired.[16] In his section of verse-by-verse commentary, Ṭabrisī stresses the interpretation of *al-sā'iḥūn* as *al-ṣā'imūn* ('those who fast'), which he attributes to Ibn ʿAbbās and Ibn Masʿūd, as well as to al-Ḥasan al-Baṣrī, Saʿīd b. Jubayr and Mujāhid (all on Ṭabarī's list). He also says that they are reportedly seekers of knowledge who wander the earth in quest of it, attributing this view to ʿIkrima. But he also does admit that they are reportedly those who wander the earth, seeking the marvels of God. He mentions 'fasters' as the meaning of *sā'iḥāt* in Q. 66:5, now attributing this interpretation to Ibn ʿAbbās, Qatāda and Ḍaḥḥāk (all, again, on Ṭabarī's list), and also the alternative meaning as 'emigrants', which interpretation he attributes to Ibn Zayd (with Māwardī), his father Zayd b. Aslam, a Medinese client (d. 136/754), and Abū ʿAlī Muḥammad al-Jubbā'ī (d. 303/915–16), the famous Muʿtazilī.[17]

Muḥammad b. Aḥmad al-Qurṭubī (d. 671/1273?) likewise attributes the interpretation of *sā'iḥūn* as 'those who fast' to Ibn Masʿūd and Ibn ʿAbbās. First, he quotes Ibn ʿUyayna: 'The one who fasts is called a *sā'iḥ* because he leaves all pleasures by way of food, drink and sex.' This is almost identical to Ṭabarī's quotation of Ibn ʿUyayna. Qurṭubī quotes ʿĀ'isha, and also Abū Hurayra, as saying that the *siyāḥa* of this community is fasting. According to the Baghdadi grammarian Ibrāhīm b. al-Sarī al-Zajjāj (d. 311/923), it was the opinion of al-Ḥasan al-Baṣrī that it meant those who observe the required fast, although it is also said that it means those who fast continuously. ʿAṭā' is quoted as saying that the *sā'iḥūn* are the *mujāhidūn*, followed by the prophetic hadith report through

Abū Umāma quoted by Abū Dāwūd and Māwardī (this in contradiction to Ṭabarī, who quotes ʿAṭāʾ for the interpretation '*ṣāʾimūn*'). Ibn Zayd is quoted again as calling them *muhājirūn*, ʿIkrima as those who travel in quest of Hadith and knowledge. Then Qurṭubī offers a new interpretation: according to the Baghdadi Qur'an commentator Muḥammad b. al-Ḥasan al-Naqqāsh (d. 351/962), the *sāʾiḥūn* are those who roam with their thoughts as to pronouncing God one, in contemplation of God's kingdom and creation, looking for signs of His oneness. He concludes with a linguistic argument, that the basic meaning of the root *s-y-ḥ* is 'going on the face of the earth as water flows'. The one who continuously fasts in obedience leaves such food and other things as he does and so may be called a wanderer, similarly those who meditate, their minds (*qulūb*) wandering as they bring different things to remembrance.[18]

Translators of the Qur'an into English have usually followed the commentary tradition that *sāʾiḥūn* are actually fasters, not wanderers. M.M. Khatib at least halfway acknowledges that this is not the plain meaning: 'The Arabic word for fasting is al sāʾiḥūn, which literally means travelling in pursuit of knowledge or a sacred cause. In this connection, the Prophet said, "The travelling of my nation is fasting."'[19] Of course, 'pursuit of knowledge or a sacred cause' has no part of the literal meaning. Students of fasting in Islam have likewise complacently accepted the commentary tradition on this point. Kees Wagtendonk argues not philologically but by what he perceives as the Prophet's intentions: 'Mohammed can not have considered this itinerant existence in complete poverty and privation desirable for his wives. Therefore, *sāḥa* is to be translated as *fasting* in 66^{5} . . . And so *sāḥa* in $9^{112(113)}$ must also mean *fasting*.'[20]

Siyāḥa in the lexicographic tradition

The dictionaries go even further than the commentary tradition in identifying *siyāḥa* with fasting, not wandering. Edward William Lane quotes *al-Qāmūs al-muḥīṭ* by Muḥammad b. Yaʿqūb al-Fīrūzabādī (d. 817/1415) as defining *sāʾiḥ* as '*a faster who keeps to the mosques*'. From *Tāj al-ʿarūs*, by Murtaḍā al-Zabīdī (d. 1205/1791), is quoted this explanation: 'The faster is said to be thus called because he who journeys as a devotee does so without having any provision with him, and eats only when he finds provision: therefore the faster is likened to him.' *Al-sāʾiḥūn* in Q. 9:113 is said to mean '*the fasters*' by the Qur'an commentators ʿAbd Allāh b. ʿUmar al-Bayḍāwī (d. 685/1286–7?), and Jalāl al-Dīn al-Maḥallī (d. 864/1459) and Jalāl al-Dīn al-Suyūṭī (d. 911/1505), and in *Tāj al-ʿarūs*. This is also the source of the further specification, 'or *those who observe the obligatory fasts*; or *those who fast constantly*'. Acknowledgements of the plain meaning of the word are quoted only from counter-consensual commentaries, not dictionaries: 'a man *going*, or *journeying*, [*as a devotee, or otherwise*] through the land or earth' is quoted from *al-Asās* by Maḥmūd b. ʿUmar al-Zamakhsharī (d. 538/1144).[21]

Siyāḥa in the renunciant tradition

A number of stories of *sāʾiḥūn* are attributed to Wahb b. Munabbih, a Yemeni of Persian descent.[22] A man described as one of the *sāʾiḥūn* prayed for three days, until someone saw him and remarked that he looked as if he had already been burnt by Hellfire. He said, 'This is what fear of Hellfire has achieved, so what if I had entered it?'[23] An Israelite who *sāḥa* (wandered, presumably) for forty years customarily saw a sign of acceptance (*ʿalāmat al-qabūl*), but a certain bastard did this without seeing such a sign. He prayed to God, 'My lord, my parents did wrong, but what is my sin?', whereupon he saw the usual sign.[24] Two reported dialogues between a worshipping *sāʾiḥ* and Satan reveal the wiles of the latter as well as how to resist them.[25] A *sāʾiḥ* disdained to run from a lion lying in wait by the way, explaining that he dreaded only God.[26] A *sāʾiḥ* and his companion wondered why they had not received their usual provision until the younger remembered turning away a beggar. After they repented, their usual provision reappeared.[27] What is common to these stories is that the *sāʾiḥūn* are anonymous. In most, the *sāʾiḥ* is plainly associated with the outdoors, but wandering is essential to only one of them, so that the term seems to be on its way to becoming a general designation of a renunciant, like *qāriʾ* (lit. a reciter of the Qur'an). Still, the verb may be used literally. There are many stories of wandering on the part of the Egyptian Dhū'l-Nūn (d. 245/860?) in which he encounters some mysterious wise person. He usually uses the verb *sāra* or a related noun for 'wandering', but at least once rather *siyāḥa*, plainly as a synonym.[28]

Although Aḥmad's collection *al-Zuhd* includes several approving stories of *sā'iḥūn*, he opposed *siyāḥa*. '*Siyāḥa* has nothing to do with Islam', he said, as has been noted.[29] He plainly had no idea that *siyāḥa* meant 'fasting'. His opposition was of a piece with his rejection of other renunciant practices that tended to create a specialist caste of the pious. (There is a contemporary Christian parallel in Byzantine opposition to eremitism as opposed to cenobitism, but here the concern was not to avoid having a specialist caste of the pious – that would not come until Protestantism – but to keep the religious under the control of the ecclesiastical hierarchy, easier with groups of religious than solitaries.[30]) In sum, in the literary tradition of renunciation, as in that of Hadith, *siyāḥa* kept its evident meaning of 'wandering'.[31] In the literary tradition of Qur'anic commentary, however, its evident meaning was denied in favour of the Sunni consensus calling for bourgeois propriety and an ethical model within reach of the average believer, which ruled out wandering. The lexicographical tradition evidently follows the commentary.

Ḥikma in the Qur'an, Qur'anic Commentaries and Renunciant Literature

The basic meaning of *ḥikma* is 'wisdom'. It occurs often in the Qur'an. In the chronologically earliest suras (as identified by present consensus[32]), it plainly means 'wisdom', and calls for no comment here. In later suras, however, it is often juxtaposed with *kitāb* ('book'), suggesting that it represents another body of divine direction, perhaps a second canon of revealed texts. In the Qur'anic commentary tradition, the legal tradition predominates, by which *ḥikma* is identified with *sunna*, the second source of the law.[33] In the renunciant tradition, however, it is often mentioned as the source of wise sayings, evidently on a level with Jewish and Christian scriptures, that is, similarly to later Qur'anic usage. Here, the renunciant tradition seems to preserve the outlook of a time when Muslims were more pleased than at later times to see themselves as part of a large monotheistic tradition, and less concerned to stress the novelty and uniqueness of Islam *vis à vis* other religions.

Ḥikma in the commentary tradition

Even concerning its early appearances, where *ḥikma* most plainly seems to mean just what it looks like, 'wisdom', the Qur'anic commentary tradition seems anxious to make it specifically Islamic.[34] Q. 54:4–5 reads, *The news that has come to them contains a deterrent—Eloquent wisdom.* Ṭabarī says this means 'this Qur'an', no authority cited (i.e. it is his own opinion). Of David, Q. 38:20 says, *We strengthened his kingdom, and We gave him wisdom and decisive speech.* Ṭabarī says, 'The people of interpretation have disagreed over the meaning of *ḥikma* in this place. Some say "prophecy" (*nubuwwa*) is meant by it': he goes on to quote the Kufan Ismā'īl b. 'Abd al-Raḥmān al-Suddī (d. 127/744–45). 'Others say it means knowledge of the binding precedents (*sunan*)': for this Ṭabarī quotes, with an *isnād*, the Basran Qatāda.[35] At Q. 43:63, the Qur'an says, *When Jesus came with the clear proofs, he said, 'I have come to you with wisdom and to make clear to you some of that about which you differ. Fear God and obey me.'* Ṭabarī says, 'It is said that in this place *al-ḥikma* means prophecy.' He goes on to quote Qatāda again as glossing *bayyināt* (lit. 'clear proofs') as 'the Gospel' (Injīl), then Suddī as equating *ḥikma* with *nubuwwa*.

We gave Luqman wisdom, saying, "Give thanks to God", according to Q. 31:12. Ṭabarī goes on to a discussion of whether Luqmān was a prophet. Qatāda is quoted as saying that *ḥikma* means 'discernment concerning Islam'. He is also quoted as denying that Luqmān was a prophet, receiving inspiration (*lam yūḥa ilayh*). There follow other characterisations of Luqmān as Egyptian or Ethiopian. Mujāhid is quoted as saying that '*Al-ḥikma* is *al-ṣawāb* (what is correct).' Someone other than Abū Bishr is quoted as saying it means '*al-ṣawāb* short of prophecy'. Then Mujāhid is quoted again, by an implicitly less reliable *isnād*,[36] as explaining that *ḥikma* means the Qur'an, then by yet a third *isnād* as saying *al-ḥikma* means *al-amāna* ('reliability'). 'Others say he was a prophet', Ṭabarī concludes, citing the Medinese 'Ikrima as an example.

Whenever the term is directed to Muhammad, Ṭabarī takes *ḥikma* to mean the Qur'an (Q. 54:5, Q. 17:39, Q. 16:125) unless it is next to a reference to the Book, in which case he takes it to mean *sunan* (Q. 2:151, 231) or explanation of what the Book means (Q. 4:113). But even when it is not directed to Muhammad, the Qur'an and Sunna seem to be strong possibilities. Abraham is quoted at Q. 2:129: *'Our Lord, raise up among them a messenger,* [*who is one*] *of themselves, who will recite Your signs to them and will teach them the Scripture and the Wisdom and will purify them.'* 'The Scripture' means the Qur'an, according to Ibn Zayd. Interpreters (*ahl al-ta'wīl*) disagree over the meaning of 'the Wisdom'. Some say it is the Sunna, for which opinion Ṭabarī quotes Qatāda. But then Ibn Zayd is quoted again for a sense something like 'supernaturally-acquired wisdom': '*Al-Ḥikma* is the faith that they do not know save by means of Him . . ., which He teaches them. *Ḥikma* is reason concerning the faith.' This seems to be Ṭabarī's own preference, for he ends the discussion by saying,

> It [i.e. *ḥikma*] is knowledge of the ordinances of God, knowledge of which is not obtained save by the explanation of the Messenger of God and knowing by their means. What distinguishes this from things like it is that, in my opinion, it is derived from *al-ḥukm*, which means separating between truth and falsehood, as *jilsa* and *qi'da* are from *julūs* and *qu'ūd* [. . .] The verse means [. . .], 'Detail Your judgements and ordinances, which You will teach him.'

Thus he directs our attention to the law (reaffirmed *ad* Q. 2:151).

In the last occurrences of *ḥikma* chronologically, the Qur'an comes closest to suggesting that it refers to supplementary scripture at Q. 4:54, *In the past We gave the family of Abraham the Scripture and the Wisdom and We gave them a mighty kingdom.* Ṭabarī's interpretation is '*Al-kitāb* means the book that He gave them by inspiration, like the scrolls (*ṣuḥuf*) of Ibrāhīm and Moses and the Book of Psalms (*zabūr*), along with the rest of what he brought them by way of books. As for *al-ḥikma*, it is what he gave them by inspiration that is not a recited book.' Of the Messiah (al-Masīḥ), Q. 3:48 says, '*He* [i.e. God] *will teach him the Scripture and the Wisdom and the* ***Torah*** *and the* ***Gospel***.' Ṭabarī paraphrases,

> He will teach him the *kitāb*, which is the writing he writes by hand. The *ḥikma* is the Sunna that We will inspire him with without writing. The *tawrāh* is the Torah that was sent down onto Moses. It was among them from the time of Moses. The *injīl* is the Gospel of Jesus, which was not before him, rather God informed Mary before the creation of Jesus that he would inspire him with it.

Here, he resists making Jesus a bearer of the same Qur'an as Muhammad, although allowing him to have the same book as Moses alongside his own. Ṭabarī's interpretations of Q. 4:54 and Q. 3:48 both suggest awareness of distinct oral and written Torahs, although it seems that the Hebrew term *ḥokhmah* cannot be firmly identified with the oral Torah in rabbinic texts of the first millennium.[37]

In the Twelver Shiʿi tradition, Qummī quotes Jaʿfar al-Ṣādiq apropos of Q. 4:54 as glossing *al-kitāb* as 'prophethood', *al-ḥikma* as 'understanding and effectuation' (*al-fahm wa'l-qaḍā'*), thus pointing away from scripture altogether.[38] Ṭabrisī quotes the same, then offers an alternative, by which *al-kitāb* means the Torah and *al-ḥikma* what the prophets were brought by way of *ʿilm*, meaning 'knowledge', especially Hadith. He attributes this view to the Sunni authorities al-Ḥasan al-Baṣrī, Qatāda and Ibn Jurayj, a Medinese client (d. 151/768–9?).

Ṭabarī does allow *ḥikma* to indicate a body of writing in his chronicle. Raif Georges Khoury has remarked that he quotes someone as saying he read something 'in the book (*majalla*) of Luqmān, meaning his *ḥikma*'.[39]

Ḥikma in the lexicographic tradition

The dictionaries naturally offer general definitions of 'wisdom'. For example, Lane quotes *al-Mughrib* by the Ḥanafi Muʿtazilī *littérateur* Nāṣir b. ʿAbd al-Sayyid Muṭarrizī (d. 610/1213) as telling us *ḥikma* 'signifies *What prevents, or restrains, from ignorant behaviour*'. There are some specific references to the Qur'an, though, some acknowledging a body of writing as well as an unwritten tradition. *Tāj al-ʿarūs* says of Q. 31:12, in Lane's summary, 'by the *ḥikma* given by God to Luḳmān, is meant *the evidence of the intellect in accordance with the statutes of the law*', thus something neither inspired nor written. Presumably, Zabīdī preferred the tradition by which Luqmān was said to be a wise man but no prophet. Of Q. 2:225, Q. 3:48 and Q. 38:20, however, dictionaries say,

> . . . it means—*The Book of the Psalms* [of David]: or, as some say, *any saying*, or *discourse, agreeable with the truth*: (*al-Mughrib*:) and it also means [in other instances] the *Book of the Law of Moses*: (*Tāj al-ʿarūs*:) and the *Gospel*: and the *Ḳur-án*: (*al-Qāmūs*:) because each of these comprises what is termed *al-ḥikma al-manṭūq bi-hā*, i.e. *the secrets of the sciences of the law and of the course of conduct*; and *al-ḥikma al-maskūt ʿan-hā*, i.e. *the secrets of the science of the Divine Essence*.[40]

The renunciant literature often uses *ḥikma* in this way to indicate a body of written tradition additional to the Qur'an, the Gospel, the Torah and the Psalms actually named in the Qur'an.

Ḥikma in the renunciant tradition

Glosses of the Qur'an are not a rare feature of the renunciant literature (e.g. about 6 per cent of Ibn al-Mubārak's *Zuhd*). For example, the Kufan Muḥammad b. Kaʿb (d. 120/737–38?) glosses Q. 11:114 (*Perform prayer at the two ends of the day* [*ṭarafay al-nahār*] *and the early parts of the night* [*zulafan min al-layl*]) as alluding to the five required prayers, *ṭarafay al-nahār* being the dawn, noon and mid-afternoon prayers, *zulafan min al-layl* being the sunset and evening prayers.[41] This does not contradict what is found in the commentaries, where they quote the more usual authorities (e.g. in Qurṭubī's treatment of this passage, Mujāhid, Ibn ʿAbbās and al-Ḥasan al-Baṣrī are cited, besides the later commentators Ṭabarī, Māwardī and Ibn ʿAṭiyya). Sometimes, Qur'anic glosses in the renunciant literature more or less echo glosses reported in the commentary literature. Of

Q. 31:12, *We gave Luqman wisdom, saying, 'Give thanks to God'*, Mujāhid is quoted in Aḥmad's *Zuhd* as saying, 'Discernment and accuracy of speech (*al-iṣāba fī'l-qawl*) short of prophecy.'[42] Ṭabarī attributes the same gloss to Qatāda. Another renunciant collection quotes Mujāhid as saying rather 'Correctness' (*al-ṣawāb*), which agrees with Ṭabarī's quotation.[43]

Also not rare, however, are quotations of extra-Qur'anic scriptures. For example, Qatāda is quoted as saying, 'It is written in the Torah, "O son of Adam, you mention Me with your tongue but forget Me; you pray to Me but flee from Me; I provide for you but you worship other than Me."'[44] The Yemeni ʿAbd al-Raḥmān b. Būdhawayh (fl. first half of the second/eighth century) quoted from the psalms of the family of David (*zabūr āl Dāwūd*): 'Blessed is he who has not taken the path of the sinners. Blessed is he who has not accepted the command of the oppressors. And blessed is he who has not sat with the idlers.'[45] The Kufan Follower Kurdūs al-Thaʿlabī is quoted as saying, 'I used to find in the Gospel, when I read in it, that God likes to afflict his servant with what he dislikes.'[46] As David Vishanoff says of a somewhat later period, such pseudo-Biblical quotations are not mainly about inter-religious polemic (Muslims against Jews and Christians) but rather sustain 'an intramural argument . . . against alternative visions of the religious life, and against the general spiritual negligence of the largely Muslim societies in which they lived'.[47]

Often, it appears that among the extra-Qur'anic scriptures is *al-ḥikma*. The Basran Mālik b. Dīnār (d. 130/747–8?) is quoted as saying, 'I have found in part of the *Ḥikma*, "There is no good for you in learning what you do not know when you do not practise what you have already learnt. The like of that is a man who gathers firewood and bundles it. Then he goes to lift it and cannot, so he ties another bundle to it."'[48] Another Basran, Abū'l-Jald (fl. late first/early eighth century), is typically quoted as saying, 'I have read in the *Ḥikma* that whoever has a warner in himself has a guardian from God . . .'[49] Sometimes, the words of the *Ḥikma* echo the Bible. For example, Qatāda is quoted as saying, 'It is written in the *Ḥikma*, "Drink and you will be satisfied, desire and you will find, fear and you will be protected [reading *tūqā* for printed *tuwaqqah*]."'[50]

Compare Matthew 7:7, 'Ask, and it shall be given you; seek, and ye shall find; knock, and it shall be opened unto you.'[51] In one quotation, by my observation, *ḥikma* is apparently personified (perhaps as in the Wisdom of Solomon 8–11) and speaks to mankind: 'O Son of Man, you will touch me as you find me in two particles (*ḥarfayn*) – doing good so far as you know and leaving off evil so far as you know.'[52] Thus the renunciant literature maintains one interpretation of the Qur'anic *ḥikma* that the Qur'anic commentary literature itself avoids, namely that it refers to a body of revelation alongside the Torah, Gospel and Psalms.

Sometimes *ḥikma* appears to be interchangeable with *tawrāh*. Three third/ninth-century sources quote the Medinese 'Urwa Ibn al-Zubayr (d. ca. 94/712–13) as saying, 'It is written in the *Ḥikma*, "Let your face be gay (*basṭ*) and your word good, and the people will like you better than someone who gives them something."'[53] A fourth, however, quotes 'Urwa as introducing the same advice with 'It is written in the Torah'.[54] 'Urwa is also quoted as saying, 'It is written in the *Ḥikma*, "Do not betray the betrayer. Let his betrayal suffice him."'[55] But, with a Kufan *isnād*, we are also told, 'It is written in the Torah, "Do not betray the betrayer. His treachery is enough for you."'[56] Uncertainty as between *Ḥikma* and Torah is expressly acknowledged in another quotation of 'Urwa: 'It is written in the *Ḥikma*' or 'in the Torah that kindness (*rifq*) is the beginning of wisdom.'[57] Here the renunciant literature agrees with the lexicographical tradition, using *ḥikma* as an additional name for the Torah, Gospel and Psalms.

Ṣiddīq in the Qur'an, Qur'anic Commentaries and Renunciant Literature

Ṣiddīq appears five times in the Qur'an (sometimes in the plural). Once, in its earliest appearance, in Q. 57:19, it apparently designates all believers: *Those who believe in God and his messengers—they are* ***the loyal ones*** *and the witnesses with their Lord*. They are contrasted in the same verse with *those who do not believe and deny the truth of Our signs*. (*Shuhadā'* is here interpreted in its non-technical meaning of 'witnesses' rather than, as later, 'martyrs', and likewise apparently refers to all believers.) More often, however, *ṣiddīq* designates a very high spiritual rank. Of Abraham, the Qur'an says, *He was a* ***true friend*** *of God, a prophet* (*ṣiddīqan nabiyyan*, Q. 19:41). Shortly afterwards, it says the same of Idrīs: *He was a* ***true friend*** *of God, a prophet* (*ṣiddīqan nabiyyan*, Q. 19:56). In the story of Joseph, the king says, *Joseph, you* ***man of truth****, give me your opinion about seven fat cows* . . . (Q. 12:46). Finally, the *ṣiddiqīn* are enumerated among the blessed: *the prophets and* ***the loyal ones*** *and the witnesses and the righteous* (Q. 4:69). Once, there appears the feminine form *ṣiddīqa*, used to characterise Mary: *his mother was an* ***honest woman*** (Q. 5:75). Arthur Jeffery observes of *ṣiddīq* that,

> As used in the Qur'ān . . . it seems to have a technical sense, being used in the sing. only of Biblical characters, and in the plu. as 'the righteous' . . . In the O.T., *ṣadīq* means *just, righteous* . . . In the Rabbinic *ṣadīqa* the sense of piety becomes even more prominent and it is used in a technical sense for *the pious*, as in *Succa*, 45, b. It is precisely in this sense that Joseph, Abraham, and Idrīs are called *ṣadīq* and the Virgin Mary *ṣadīqa* in the Qur'ān.[58]

'Righteous' or 'pious', as Jeffery suggests, would apparently be a better translation from context – in common with other translators, Alan Jones has been influenced here by the commentary tradition.

Ṣiddīq in Hadith

In prophetic Hadith, as it appears in famous collections, *ṣiddīq* is prominent in two *matn* clusters, that is, similar texts with similar chains of transmitters. The first may be represented here by Bukhārī: ← Muḥammad b. Bashshār ← Yaḥyā ← Sa'īd ← Qatāda ← Anas b. Mālik: 'The Prophet ascended [Mount] Uḥud along with Abū Bakr, 'Umar and 'Uthmān. It shook them, so he said, "Be still, Uḥud, for on you are a prophet, a *ṣiddīq* and two martyrs."'[59] Here *ṣiddīq* obviously refers to Abū Bakr and a rank between 'prophet' and 'martyr', which agrees with a natural reading of Qur'anic references to *ṣiddīq*s (as well as the Sunni dogma that the first caliphs reigned in the precise order of their virtue). A more famous version substitutes Ḥirā' for Uḥud and the ten who were promised Paradise for the first three caliphs. Juynboll ascribes the version with three caliphs to Saʿīd b. Abī ʿArūba (Basran, d. 157/773–4?), the version with the ten to Qutayba b. Saʿīd (Khurasani, d. 240/854).[60]

The second *matn* cluster may also be represented by Bukhārī's version: ← ʿUthmān Ibn Abī Shayba ← Jarīr ← Manṣūr ← Abū Wāʾil ← ʿAbd Allāh (Ibn Masʿūd) ← the Prophet: 'Truthfulness leads to piety (*birr*) and piety to Paradise. A man tells the truth until he becomes a *ṣiddīq*.'[61] The hadith goes on to contrast the *ṣiddīq* with the man who continually lies until he is registered as a liar (*kadhdhāb*). This cluster obviously reduces the stature of *ṣiddīq* in accordance with a presumed Arabic etymology, i.e. *fiʿʿīl* with the meaning of *fāʿil*, meaning 'telling the truth'.

Ṣiddīq in the commentary tradition

Apropos of Q. 4:69, Ṭabarī says,

> There is disagreement over the meaning of *ṣiddīqīn*. Some say the *ṣiddīqūn* are the followers of the prophets who believe them (*ṣaddaqūhum*) and follow their ways after them until they catch up to them. It is as if *ṣiddīq* is [the pattern] *fiʿʿīl* . . . coming from *ṣidq*, as a man is said to be *sikkīr* ('given to drunkenness') from *sukr* ('drunkenness'), if he is given to that; likewise *shirrīb* ('given to drink') and *khimmīr* ('given to wine').

Others, says Ṭabarī, relate *ṣiddīq* to *ṣadaqa* ('alms'), but he cites no one, going on rather to relate a hadith report by which the Prophet says expressly, 'The *ṣiddīqīn* are the *muṣaddiqūn*', meaning 'those who believe'. As for Ṭabarī's own opinion, he admits to having doubts about the *isnād* but thinks its most probable meaning is 'one who ascribes truth to someone's word by his actions'. He may allude to a major theological controversy of his time, namely whether faith (*īmān*) comprises works, specifically the ritual prayer, as well as profession and belief. The Murjiʾa were the theological party that held faith to be indivisible: whoever declared sincerely, *There is no god but God and Muhammad is the Messenger of God*, was a believer. They were opposed by people who called themselves Ahl al-Sunna and held that faith comprised both profession and works (*qawl wa 'amal*), that there were degrees of faith, some having more than others, and that someone who failed to perform the ritual prayer was not just inobservant but an unbeliever.[62] Ṭabarī took just the Sunni position on this point, that faith comprised both profession and works and that there were degrees of faith, some people having more than others. Contrast the position of Ṭabarī's Ḥanafi contemporary Abū Jaʿfar al-Ṭaḥāwī (d. 321/933), a professed adherent of Ahl al-Sunna but whose creed declares minimally that 'Faith is confessing with the tongue and counting true with the heart . . .'[63] Of course, the more Ṭabarī connected the term *ṣiddīq* with the boundary between believers and unbelievers, the further it was from denoting any unusual degree of righteousness.

In the Twelver tradition, Qummī shows no interest in the term *ṣiddīq*. Ṭabrisī says that in Q. 19:41, where Abraham is called a *ṣiddīq*, it means 'has much *taṣdīq* (ascribing truthfulness) concerning matters of faith', an opinion he attributes to Jubbāʾī. He also relates that it has been derived from *ṣādiqan*, 'going to an extreme in *ṣidq* (telling the truth) concerning what he says of God', an opinion he attributes to an Abū Muslim.[64] At Q. 4:69, he says,

> it is said that the meaning of *ṣiddīq* is that he [a person] believes all that God has ordered and in His prophets, not admitting any doubt about that. This is strengthened by His saying, *Those who believe in God and his messengers – they are ṣiddīqūn and shuhadāʾ* [Q. 57:19], meaning those killed in jihad.[65]

Ṭabrisī goes on to justify using 'witnesses' to designate those who die in the jihad. Notice that his approach to *ṣiddīq* is exactly the opposite of his approach to *shahīd*: in the first case, he uses an early, non-technical occurrence to fend off the suggestion of a technical meaning related to the Christian tradition (OT *ṣadīq* = 'righteous'), whereas in the second case, it is precisely the later, technical meaning related to the Christian tradition ('witness' = 'one who has died violently for the faith') that he imposes on the early, non-technical occurrence. The Ismaili jurisprudent al-Qāḍī al-Nuʿmān quotes the Prophet as saying, 'Every believer of my community is a *ṣiddīq* and a *shahīd*', then quoting Q. 57:19. This is a plausible interpretation of this early Qur'anic passage, but by putting it in the section on what is desirable in the holy war (*dhikr al-raghāʾib fīʾl-jihād*), he implies of course that *shahīd* has its later, technical meaning of 'martyr'.[66]

Ṣiddīq in the lexicographic tradition

Lane quotes no dictionary that departs from finding a weak, Arabic-etymological understanding of *ṣiddīq*. 'One who *speaks, says, utters*, or *tells, truth*, or *truly*, or *veraciously, much*, or *often*', he begins. It may also mean 'one *who accepts*, or *admits, the truth of what is said*, or *who verifies*, &c.' No definition is reported that departs from the sense of truth-telling, as to denote a saint more generally.[67] For example, *Lisān al-ʿarab* says, 'A *ṣiddīq* is someone who believes (*muṣaddiq*). In the revelation is "His mother was a *ṣiddīqa*" [Q. 5:75]; that is, going to an extreme in truthfulness and believing true' (*s.v. ṣ-d-q*).

Ṣiddīq in the renunciant tradition

In the renunciant literature, *ṣiddīq* sometimes designates a high spiritual rank, as in the Qur'an. Louis Massignon points to an appeal by the Basran ʿAbd al-Wāḥid b. Zayd (d. 177/793–4?): 'Perhaps your thirst will be quenched in the Dwellings of Holiness, with the best of the ancients and companions by way of the prophets, *ṣiddīqīn*, martyrs and pious ones, they being the best company.'[68] Unsurprisingly, this usage continued into the Sufi period; for example, when the Egyptian Dhū'l-Nūn is quoted as referring to 'the prayer of the prophets, the messengers and the *ṣiḍḍīqīn*'.[69]

More often, *ṣiddīq* is used in a lightened sense as 'saint'. The Companion Kaʿb al-Aḥbār (d. 34/654–5?) is quoted as saying, 'While the Children of Israel were praying in Jerusalem, there came two men. One of them entered while the other did not, standing outside the doors of the mosque. He said, "That I should enter the house of God – the like of me does not enter the house of God, when I have done such and such." He began to weep and did not enter. The next day, it was recorded that he was a *ṣiddīq*.'[70] Muṭarrif b. al-Shikhkhīr (Basran, d. 95/713–14) is quoted as saying, 'I have found the neglect that God has thrown in the hearts of the *ṣiddīqīn* of His creation to be a mercy He has shown to them. If He threw fear in their hearts in proportion to their knowledge, life would give them no pleasure (*mā hanna'ahum al-'aysh*).'[71] Abū'l-Jald is credited with several sayings involving the *ṣiddīqīn* in the sense of 'saints' such as his audience aspired to be. 'I read in the *Ḥikma* that God (be He exalted) says, "O my servants the *ṣiddīqīn*, enjoy worshipping Me in the world and by this means you will enjoy Paradise."'[72] 'God (be He blessed and exalted) told David by inspiration, "O David, warn My servants the *ṣiddīqīn* not to be pleased with themselves nor to rely on their works . . . Give the good news to the sinners that there is no sin too great for Me to forgive and overlook."'[73] References to the *Ḥikma* and the prophet David associate Abū'l-Jald's usage with the Rabbinic literature referred to by Jeffery. Mālik b. Dīnār (Basran, d. 130/747–8?) said, 'A man does not reach the state of the *ṣiddīqīn* until he leaves his wife like a widow and takes refuge with dogs in refuse heaps.'[74] Again associating the term with the Jewish tradition, Mālik is also quoted as saying, 'I read in the Torah, "'Umar b. 'Abd al-'Azīz is a *ṣiddīq*."'[75] This is surely to use the word to designate more than someone who is habitually truthful. In another quotation, Mālik does connect the *ṣiddīqīn* with *ṣidq*, truthfulness, while maintaining the primary meaning of 'saint': 'When the Qur'an is recited to the *ṣiddīqīn*, their hearts are moved (so that they think of) the Afterlife. He (God) says . . . "Listen to what the *ṣādiq* (truthteller) says" from above His throne.'[76] This is not so exalted as the Qur'anic rank, but it seems to respect the Qur'anic association with the outstandingly righteous better than half the Hadith and almost all of the commentary and lexicographical traditions.

In an early Twelver account, *ṣiddīq* designates all the believers (i.e. all the Imāmiyya), but so does *shahīd* (similarly to how the words work in Q. 57:19). Al-Ḥusayn b. 'Alī told Zayd b. Arqam (d. 66/685–6) that every one of his party (*shī'a*) was either a *ṣiddīq* or a *shahīd*. Zayd said, 'May I be made your ransom – how can that be, when most of them die in their beds?' He said, 'Do you not read in the Book of God, in [*Sūrat*] *al-Ḥadīd*, *Those who believe in God and his messengers—they are* ***the loyal ones*** *and* ***the witnesses*** *with their Lord* [Q. 57:19]' – which can alternatively be translated, of course, as 'the saints and the martyrs in the view of their Lord'. Zayd said, 'It is as if I had never before read this verse of the Book of God.' Al-Ḥusayn commented, 'If the martyrs were only as you said, then the martyrs would be few.'[77] As 'martyr' here has displaced 'witness' as the sense of *shahīd*, *ṣiddīq* seems to be ignored, as indeed it is in the following four reports, in which loyal Shiʿa are defined as martyrs.[78]

Conclusion

My principal conclusion is simple. However comprehensive may be the genre of Qur'anic commentary, it does not include all the interpretation proposed by early Muslims. I am continually approached by beginning graduate students who want to study this or that legal question and assume that *tafsīr* is the place to start. I tell them actually it is the literature of *fiqh* (jurisprudence). I have them look up some problem in an extensive exposition of rules and in a Qur'anic commentary and they see what I mean – the fuller discussion is almost invariably to be found in the legal work. But this is mainly a question of the length at which issues are treated. Some problems are evidently discussed entirely outside the commentary literature. I point for one example to a recent study of mine of God's creation of Adam in his image, a controversial proposition that comes up in Hadith but not in Qur'anic commentaries.[79] With these three words, *siyāḥa*, *ḥikma* and *ṣiddīq*, the Qur'anic commentary tradition plainly faces away from some natural interpretations of the Qur'an. These interpretations are taken up instead in the literature of Hadith and (especially) of renunciant piety. In explaining all three of these words, the lexicographical literature is plainly beholden to the commentary, scarcely venturing beyond it (*ḥikma* is the partial exception). This is fitting, inasmuch as the study of the Qur'an has always been principally a part of the tradition of *adab* (*belles lettres*). To know what Muslims thought about something that comes up in the Qur'an, it is not enough to read only Qur'anic commentaries.

This survey of usage may also document the waxing and waning of different sorts of piety. Renunciant piety seems to have been fairly pervasive in the early period of Islamic history. Fred Donner, sketching the piety of first-/seventh-century Muslims on the basis of dated inscriptions, finds that pleas for divine forgiveness and express hopes for entry into Paradise are so predominant that virtually no other features of the new religion can be made out.[80] Another indication that the renunciant piety we read of goes back very far is the lack of regional variations, suggesting a common origin. Early Islamic law, by contrast, is riddled with regional variations, suggesting substantial development after the Muslims had settled in different places.[81] Concern that outward renunciation should mask inward self-indulgence and greed is evidently as old as renunciation, but distrust of austerity itself seems to date to the later second/eighth century, to judge mainly by scattered notices in the biographical and renunciant literature; for example, when Sufyān al-Thawrī is quoted as saying, 'Renunciation (*zuhd*) is shortness of hope, not eating poorly or wearing the *'abā'*.'[82] Inasmuch as the third/ninth-century renunciant literature preserves expressions of both admiration for austerities and distrust of them, it apparently documents the pieties of different times. Inasmuch as third/ninth-century and later Qur'anic commentary literature documents only distrust of austerity (by relating only forced interpretations of *siyāḥa* and *ṣiddīq*), it shows itself to be more selective.

The question is, which of the literary genres *tafsīr*, *fiqh*, Hadith and *zuhd* is the earliest; that is, in which do the extant sources, beginning not earlier than the late second/eighth century, preserve the most genuinely early discussions as opposed to later back-projections? An apparently primitive feature of *tafsīr* is heavy dependence on the sayings of Companions and Followers, as if the genre was frozen before back-projection to the Prophet had advanced so far as it did in the literature of *fiqh*. For example, scarcely one-tenth of the hadith in the famous *Ṣaḥīḥ* collection of al-Bukhārī (d. 256/870) go back to later Muslims than the Prophet, in contrast with almost a third of the hadith in the long book of *tafsīr* within the *Ṣaḥīḥ*. Ibn Abī Ḥātim (d. 327/938) was a major hadith critic, but of items in his massive collection of hadith explicating the Qur'an, only 3 per cent go back to the Prophet, 29 per cent to Companions, 50 per cent to Followers, and 18 per cent to men of subsequent generations.[83] To the contrary, however, hadith and renunciant literature appear to preserve older interpretations of the terms *siyāḥa*, *ḥikma* and *ṣiddīq* than *tafsīr*. Either *tafsīr* is in fact less primitive than it has seemed or we must consider it strictly selective in what it recalls and what it ignores of late first-/early eighth-century Islam. I should guess that it is a little more willing than hadith literature to suppress indications of what seemed to the commentators an outdated piety because of its stronger association with *adab*.

NOTES

1 It is even argued that Qur'anic exegesis was the principal reason for the earliest development of Arabic grammar by C.H.M. [Kees] Versteegh, *Arabic Grammar and Qur'ānic Exegesis in Early Islam* (Leiden: Brill, 1993).

2 Norman Calder, 'Tafsīr From Ṭabarī to Ibn Kathīr: Problems in the Description of a Genre, Illustrated with Reference to the Story of Abraham' in G.R. Hawting and Abdul-Kader A. Shareef, eds, *Approaches to the Qur'ān* (London: Routledge, 1993), pp. 101–40; Walid A. Saleh, 'Preliminary Remarks on the Historiography of *tafsīr* in Arabic', *Journal of Qur'anic Studies* 12 (2010), pp. 6–40.

3 Louis Massignon, *Essay on the Origins of the Technical Language of Islamic Mysticism*, tr. Benjamin Clark (Notre Dame, IN: University of Notre Dame Press, 1997), especially chapters 1–3. Actually, *zuhd* (the usual word for renunciation of the world, lit. 'indifference') might be a calque on Greek *apátheia*, while Greek *askētēs* corresponds precisely to *mujtahid* (lit. 'one who exerts himself'), used in the Islamic renunciant tradition to designate someone who spends extraordinary amounts of time in ritual worship. Borrowings from Greek do not discredit the hypothesis of endogenous development inasmuch as they point away from Indian influence, normally stressed by those who hold Sufism to be exogenous; most notoriously R.C. Zaehner, 'Abū Yazīd of Bisṭām: A Turning Point in Islamic Mysticism', *Indo-Iranian Journal* 1 (1957), pp. 286–301.

4 Ibn Hāni' al-Naysābūrī, *Masā'il al-imām Aḥmad ibn Ḥanbal*, ed. Zuhayr al-Shāwīsh (Beirut: al-Maktab al-Islāmī, 1400), vol. 2, p. 176. See also Christopher Melchert, 'The Piety of the Hadith Folk', *International Journal of Middle East Studies* 34 (2002), pp. 425–39, esp. pp. 428–32.

5 'Sunni' has even been used with the primary sense of legal-minded opposition to Sufism: Marshall G.S. Hodgson, *The Venture of Islam* (Chicago, IL: University of Chicago Press, 1974), vol. 1, p. 278, n. 18. For early examples of opposition, see Christopher Melchert, 'Early Renunciants as *Ḥadīth* Transmitters', *The Muslim World* 92 (2002), pp. 407–18, at pp. 411–14. See also idem, 'Baṣran Origins of Classical Sufism', *Der Islam* 82 (2005), pp. 221–40, esp. pp. 229–30.

6 Unless otherwise noted, translations of the Qur'an are from *The Qur'ān*, tr. Alan Jones ([Cambridge:] Gibb Memorial Trust, 2007).

7 With some minor variation, mostly alternation between *min* and *'an*, in Nasā'ī, *al-Sunan al-kubrā*, *Kitāb ṣifat al-ṣalāt* 81, *al-taslīm 'alā'l-nabī*; al-Dārimī,

al-Sunan (Damascus: Maṭbaʿat al-Iʿtidāl, 1349), vol. 2, p. 317; Aḥmad Ibn Ḥanbal, *al-Musnad* (Cairo: al-Maṭbaʿa al-Maymaniyya, 1313/1895), vol. 1, pp. 387, 441, 452 = ed. Shuʿayb al-Arnaʾūṭ *et al.* (Beirut: Muʾassasat al-Risāla, 1413–21/1993–2001), vol. 6, p. 183; vol. 7, pp. 260, 343; ʿAbd al-Razzāq, *al-Muṣannaf*, ed. Ḥabīb al-Raḥmān al-Aʿẓamī (Johannesburg: al-Majlis al-ʿIlmī, 1390–92/1970–72), vol. 2, p. 215; and elsewhere.

8 When the sources report more than one date, which is not rare for the early period, I present one of them followed by a question mark. The sources also sometimes report approximate dates, e.g. 'He died in (1)67 or thereabouts'; I present such a date with 'ca.' before it.

9 Abū Dāwūd, *al-Sunan, Kitāb al-Jihād 7, bāb fī'l-nahy ʿan al-siyāḥa*, no. 2486. Similarly, Ibn al-Mubārak, *al-Zuhd wa'l-raqāʾiq*, ed. Ḥabīb al-Raḥmān al-Aʿẓamī (Malegaon: Majlis Iḥyāʾ al-Maʿārif, 1386; repr., with different pagination, Beirut: Dār al-Kutub al-ʿIlmiyya, 1419/1998), no. 845.

10 Aḥmad, *Musnad* (1313/1895), vol. 3, p. 266; (1413–21/1993–2001), vol. 21, p. 317; also Ibn al-Mubārak, *Kitāb al-Jihād*, ed. Nazīh Ḥammād (Beirut: Dār al-Nūr, 1391/1971), p. 35 = (Beirut: al-Maktaba al-ʿAṣriyya, 1409/1988), p. 16. Quoted from Ibn al-Mubārak by Sara Sviri, '*Wa-rahbāniyyatan ibtadaʿūhā*', *Jerusalem Studies in Arabic and Islam* 13 (1990), pp. 195–208, at p. 200.

11 This saying is so quoted, as from Abū Hurayra, by Muḥammad b. Aḥmad al-Qurṭubī, *al-Jāmiʿ li-aḥkām al-Qurʾān*, ed. ʿAbd al-Razzāq al-Mahdī (Beirut: Dār al-Kitāb al-ʿArabī, 1418/1997), vol. 8, p. 245, *ad* Q. 9:112. I have used several editions of Ṭabarī's commentary, most often *Jāmiʿ al-bayān ʿan taʾwīl āy al-Qurʾān*, ed. Maḥmūd Shākir, rev. ʿAlī ʿĀshūr (Beirut: Dār Iḥyāʾ al-Turāth al-ʿArabī, 1421/2001). There are so many editions of this commentary about, none of them entitled by its manuscript basis to be considered standard, I dislike to cite any by volume and page number. I hope, rather, that my citations will be easily traceable across editions by sura and verse number.

12 Bukhārī mentions two persons by this name, both apparently Kufan Followers: Bukhārī, *Kitāb al-Taʾrīkh al-kabīr* (Hyderabad: Maṭbaʿat Jamʿiyyat Dāʾirat al-Maʿārif al-ʿUthmāniyya, 1360–64; repr. 1377/1958; repr. Beirut: Dār al-Kutub al-ʿIlmiyya, n.d.), vol. 8, p. 54.

13 Variant through Sufyān *apud* Abū Nuʿaym al-Iṣfahānī, *Ḥilyat al-awliyāʾ wa ṭabaqāt al-aṣfiyāʾ* (Cairo: Maktabat al-Khānjī, 1352–7/1932–8), vol. 4, p. 51; also, using the general *taʿabbada* ('gave himself to worship') rather than *sāḥa* and not through Sufyān, Aḥmad Ibn Ḥanbal, *al-Zuhd*, ed. ʿAbd al-Raḥmān b. Qāsim (Mecca: Maṭbaʿat Umm al-Qurā, 1357/1938), pp. 46–7 = (repr. Beirut: Dār al-Kutub al-ʿIlmiyya, 1403/1983), p. 60.

14 Abū'l-Ḥasan al-Māwardī, *al-Nukat wa'l-ʿuyūn*, *ad* Q. 9:112; ed. al-Sayyid b. ʿAbd al-Maqṣūd b. ʿAbd al-Raḥīm (Beirut: Dār al-Kutub al-ʿIlmiyya and Muʾassasat al-Kutub al-Thaqāfiyya, n.d.), vol. 2, p. 407.

15 For this opinion with an *isnād* back to ʿIkrima, see Abū Nuʿaym, *Ḥilya*, vol. 3, p. 335.

16 al-Faḍl b. al-Ḥasan al-Ṭabrisī, *Majmaʿ al-bayān fī tafsīr al-Qurʾān* (Sidon: Maṭbaʿat al-ʿIrfān, 1333–56), vol. 3, p. 74.

17 Ibid., vol. 10. p. 316.

18 Qurṭubī, *Jāmiʿ*, vol. 8, pp. 245–6, *ad* Q. 9:112.

19 *The Bounteous Koran*, tr. M.M. Khatib (London: Macmillan, 1986), p. 261fn.

20 K. Wagtendonk, *Fasting in the Koran* (Leiden: Brill, 1968), p. 130.
21 Edward William Lane, *An Arabic-English Lexicon* (London: Williams and Norgate, 1863–93), vol. 1, p. 1482.
22 On Wahb b. Munabbih, see Tilman Nagel, '*Die Qiṣaṣ al-anbiyā'*: Ein Beitrag zur arabischen Literaturgeschichte' (Bonn: Rheinische Friedrich-Wilhelms-Universität, 1967), pp. 61–5; Raif Georges Khoury, *Wahb b. Munabbih.* Volume 1: *Der Heidelberger Papyrus PSR Heid Arab 23*, Codices arabici antiqui (Wiesbaden: Otto Harrassowitz, 1972); Josef van Ess, *Theologie und Gesellschaft im 2. und 3. Jahrhundert Hidschra. Eine Geschichte des religiösen Denkens im Frühen Islam* (Berlin: Walter de Gruyter, 1991–5), vol. 2, pp. 702–6; Michael Pregill, 'Isrā'īliyyāt, Myth, and Pseudepigraphy: Wahb b. Munabbih and the Early Islamic Version of the Fall of Adam and Eve', *Jerusalem Studies in Arabic and Islam* 34 (2008), pp. 215–84, and Alfred-Louis de Prémare, 'Wahb b. Munabbih, une figure singulière du premier Islam', *Annales. Histoire, Sciences Sociales* 60 (2005), pp. 531–49.
23 Abū Nu'aym, *Ḥilya*, vol. 4, p. 32.
24 Aḥmad, *Zuhd* (1357/1938–39), pp. 46–7; (1403/1983), p. 60; Abū Nu'aym, *Ḥilya*, vol. 4, p. 51.
25 Abū Nu'aym, *Ḥilya*, vol. 4, pp. 52–3 and 55.
26 Aḥmad, *Zuhd* (1357/1938–39), p. 101; (1403/1983), p. 126; Abū Nu'aym, *Ḥilya*, vol. 4, p. 57.
27 Aḥmad, *Zuhd* (1357/1938–39), pp. 101–2; (1403/1983), pp. 126–7; Abū Nu'aym, *Ḥilya*, vol. 4, p. 57.
28 Abū Nu'aym, *Ḥilya*, vol. 9, pp. 340 (*sāra*), 341 (*masīr*), 344 (*sā'ir*), 345 (*sāra*), 348 (*sāra, tayh*), 354 (*sā'ir*), 355 (*sā'ir*), 360 (*siyāḥa*), 368 (*tayh*), 391 (*tayh*).
29 See this chapter, n. 4.
30 For more on this see, for example, Daniel Caner, *Wandering, Begging Monks: Spiritual Authority and the Promotion of Monasticism in Late Antiquity* (Berkeley, CA: University of California Press, 2002).
31 Some time after the writing of this article, my attention was drawn to Houari Touati, *Islam et voyage au Moyen Âge: histoire et anthropologie d'une pratique lettrée* (Paris: Seuil, 2000), also available as *Islam and Travel in the Middle Ages*, tr. Lydia G. Cochrane (Chicago, IL: University of Chicago Press, 2010). Although proceeding in a different direction from there, Chapter 5 on Sufi travel begins with the observation that the commentators resisted the obvious interpretation of the Qur'anic terms *sā'iḥūn* and *sā'iḥāt* as having to do with roving, probably related to the eremitical monastic model, whereas the Sufis and their ascetical forbears embraced it.
32 As for the chronology of the suras of the Qur'an, I follow Neal Robinson, *Discovering the Qur'an: A Contemporary Approach to a Veiled Text*, 2nd edn (London: SCM Press, 2003), Part 2, esp. pp. 87–91.
33 For one history of the equation, see Joseph E. Lowry, 'Early Islamic Exegesis as Legal Theory: How Qur'ānic Wisdom (*Ḥikma*) Became the Sunna of the Prophet' in Natalie B. Dohrmann and David Stern, eds, *Jewish Biblical Interpretation and Cultural Exchange* (Philadelphia, PA: University of Pennsylvania Press, 2008), pp. 139–60, 286–95; idem, *Early Islamic Legal Theory: The Risāla of Muḥammad ibn Idrīs al-Shāfi'ī* (Leiden: Brill, 2007), pp. 170–83.

34 I align myself with those who think that, just as some time passed before Christians considered themselves other than Jews, so some time passed before Muslims considered themselves other than generic monotheists in substantial continuity with a larger tradition. For an overstated version of the case, see Fred M. Donner, *Muhammad and the Believers: At the Origins of Islam* (Cambridge, MA: Belknap Press of Harvard University Press, 2010).

35 Lowry infers that the equation of Qur'anic *ḥikma* with *sunna* goes back to Basra in the mid-second/eighth century, since Ibn Taymiyya attributes it to al-Shāfiʿī, Qatāda and Yaḥyā b. Abī Kathīr (Basran, d. 132/749–50?): see Lowry, 'Early Islamic Exegesis', p. 152. Ṭabarī here confirms that Qatāda was interested in the term, whereas glosses of it are not quoted of other second/eighth-century exegetes, but not that he straitly identified it with the *sunna*.

36 The second quotation from Mujāhid comes later in Ṭabarī's discussion, and there is some express disagreement about both the wording and the *isnād*.

37 Lowry, 'Early Islamic Exegesis', p. 154.

38 ʿAlī b. Ibrāhīm al-Qummī, *Tafsīr al-Qummī*, ed. Ṭayyib al-Mūsawī al-Jazā'irī ([Najaf]: Maṭbaʿat al-Najaf, 1386–7/1967), vol. 1, p. 140.

39 Khoury, *Wahb b. Munabbih*, p. 265, citing Muḥammad b. Jarīr al-Ṭabarī, *Ta'rīkh al-rusul wa'l-mulūk*, ed. M.J. de Goeje *et al.* as *Annales quos scripsit Abu Djafar Mohammed ibn Djarir at-Tabari* (Leiden: Brill, 1879–1901), vol. 1, p. 1208 = *Ta'rīkh al-Ṭabarī*, ed. Muḥammad Abū'l-Faḍl Ibrāhīm (Cairo: Dār al-Maʿārif, 1960–69), vol. 2, p. 352.

40 Lane, *Arabic-English Lexicon*, vol. 1, p. 617.

41 Ibn al-Mubārak, *Zuhd*, no. 905.

42 Aḥmad, *Zuhd* (1357/1938–9), pp. 48–9; (1403/1983), p. 64.

43 Abū ʿUbayd al-Qāsim b. Sallām, *al-Khuṭab wa'l-mawāʿiẓ*, ed. Ramaḍān ʿAbd al-Tawwāb (Cairo: Maktabat al-Thaqāfa al-Dīniyya, 1406/1986), p. 173.

44 Aḥmad, *Zuhd* (1357/1938–9), p. 106; (1403/1983), p. 132; a similar hadith ← al-Ḥasan al-Baṣrī ← 'a certain book', *apud* Ibn al-Mubārak, *Zuhd*, no. 210.

45 Aḥmad, *Zuhd* (1357/1938–9), p. 72; (1403/1983), p. 91.

46 Abū Nuʿaym, *Ḥilya*, vol. 4, p. 180.

47 David R. Vishanoff, 'An Imagined Book Gets a New Text: Psalms of the Muslim David', *Islam and Christian–Muslim Relations* 23 (2011), pp. 85–99, at p. 95. Other outstandingly good treatments of extra-Qur'anic scriptures in the Islamic tradition are Khoury, *Wahb b. Munabbih*; idem, 'Quelques réflexions sur les citations de la Bible dans les premières générations islamiques', *Bulletin d'études orientales* 29 (1977), pp. 269–78; J. Sadan, 'Some Literary Problems Concerning Judaism and Jewry in Medieval Arabic Sources' in M. Sharon, ed., *Studies in Islamic History and Civilization in Honour of Professor David Ayalon* (Jerusalem and Leiden: 1986), pp. 353–98; and Omar Alí-de-Unzaga, 'The Conversation between Moses and God (*munāǧāt Musā*) in the *Epistles* of the Pure Brethren' in Daniel De Smet, Godefroid de Callataÿ and Jan van Reeth, eds, *Al-Kitāb: La sacralité du texte dans le monde de l'Islam. Actes du Symposium international tenu à Leuven et Louvain-la-Neuve du 29 mai au 1 juin 2002* (Brussels: Société Belge d'Etudes Orientales, 2004), pp. 371–87. I attempt to review such quotations specifically in relation to the renunciant tradition in 'Quotations of Extra-Qur'anic Scripture in Early Renunciant Literature' in Agostino Cilardo, ed., *Islam and Globalisation: Historical*

and Contemporary Perspectives. Proceedings of the 25th Congress of L'Union Européenne des Arabisants et Islamisants (Leuven, Peeters, 2013), pp. 97–107.

48 Aḥmad, *Zuhd* (1357/1938–9), p. 50; (1403/1983), p. 65.

49 Aḥmad, *Zuhd* (1357/1938–9), p. 105; (1403/1983), p. 130.

50 Abū 'Ubayd, *Khuṭab*, pp. 179–80.

51 Translation taken from the King James Version.

52 Aḥmad, *Zuhd* (1357/1938–9), p. 105; (1403/1983), p. 130 (addition from 'Abd Allāh), Syrian *isnād*.

53 Abū 'Ubayd, *Khuṭab*, p. 179; Ibn al-Mubārak, *Zuhd*, no. 1058 (addition from al-Ḥusayn b. al-Ḥasan al-Marwazī); Aḥmad, *Zuhd* (1357/1938–9), p. 50; (1403/1983), p. 65. (addition from 'Abd Allāh).

54 Ibn Abī Shayba, *Muṣannaf, al-adab* 2, *mā dhukira fī ḥusn al-khuluq*; ed. Ḥamad b. 'Abd Allāh al-Jum'a and Muḥammad b. Ibrāhīm al-Luḥaydān (Riyadh: Maktabat al-Rushd, 1425/2004), vol. 8, p. 379.

55 Aḥmad, *Zuhd* (1357/1938–9), p. 106; (1403/1983), p. 132.

56 Ibn Abī Shayba, *Muṣannaf, al-buyū' wa'l-aqḍiya* 441, *fī'l-rajul yakūnu lahu 'alā'l-rajul al-dayn fa-yajḥaduh*, vol. 7, p. 707.

57 Aḥmad, *Zuhd* (1357/1938–9), p. 49; (1403/1983), p. 65.

58 Arthur Jeffery, *The Foreign Vocabulary of the Qur'ān* (Baroda: Oriental Institute, 1938; repr. Lahore: al-Biruni, 1977), p. 195.

59 al-Bukhārī, *al-Ṣaḥīḥ* 62, *Kitāb faḍā'il aṣḥāb al-nabī* 5, *bāb qawl al-nabī law kuntu muttakhidhan khalīlan*, no. 3675 (numbering after Muḥammad Fu'ād 'Abd al-Bāqī). Almost identical texts in idem, *Kitāb faḍā'il al-aṣḥāb al-nabī* 6, *bāb manāqib 'Umar b. al-Khaṭṭāb*, no. 3686, and *Kitāb faḍā'il aṣḥāb al-nabī* 7, *bāb manāqib 'Uthmān ibn 'Affān*, no. 3697. A similar hadith, Abū Dāwūd, *Sunan* 39, *Kitāb al-sunna* 8, *bāb fī'l-khulafā'*, no. 4651 (numbering after Muḥammad Muḥyī'l-Dīn 'Abd al-Ḥamīd). A similar hadith, Tirmidhī, *al-Jāmi'* 46, *Kitāb al-manāqib* 18, *manāqib 'Uthmān*, no. 3697 (numbering of Kamāl Yūsuf al-Ḥūt, continuing that of 'Abd al-Bāqī).

60 G.H.A. Juynboll, *Encyclopedia of Canonical Ḥadīth* (Leiden: Brill, 2007), pp. 452–3, 459–60.

61 Bukhārī, *Ṣaḥīḥ* 78, *Kitāb al-adab* 69 (untitled), no. 6094. A similar hadith, Muslim, *Ṣaḥīḥ* 45, *Kitāb al-birr* 29, *bāb qubḥ al-kadhib*, no. 2607 (numbering of 'Abd al-Bāqī). A similar hadith, Abū Dāwūd, *Sunan* 80, *bāb fī'l-tashdīd fī'l-kadhib*, no. 4989. A similar hadith — Tirmidhī, *Jāmi'* 25, *Kitāb al-birr* 46, *bāb mā jā'a fī'l-ṣidq wa'l-kadhib*, no. 1971. Tirmidhī comments, 'On the same topic [are reports] from Abū Bakr, 'Umar, 'Abd Allāh b. al-Shikhkhīr and Ibn 'Umar.'

62 See W. Madelung, 'Murdji'a', EI^2, vol. 7, pp. 605–7.

63 For Ṭabarī, see idem, *Ṣarīḥ al-sunna*, in Dominique Sourdel, 'Une profession de foi de l'historien al-Ṭabarī', *Revue des études islamiques* 36 (1968), pp. 177–99, at pp. 190–91 (Fr.) = 197 (Ar.). For Ṭaḥāwī, see E.E. Elder, 'Al-Ṭaḥāwī's "Bayān al-sunna wa'l-jamā'a"' in *The Macdonald Presentation Volume* (Princeton, NJ: Princeton University Press, 1933), pp. 131–44, p. 139; alternatively *Islamic Creeds*, tr. W. Montgomery Watt (Edinburgh: Edinburgh University Press, 1994), pp. 48–56, at p. 52 (whence the translation above); also Ṭaḥāwī, *Bayān i'tiqād ahl al-sunna wa'l-jamā'a*, appended to Aḥmad Ibn Ḥanbal (attrib.), *Kitāb al-Wara'*, ed. Zaynab Ibrāhīm al-Qārūṭ (Beirut: Dār al-Kutub al-'Ilmiyya, 1403/1983), pp. 198–205, at p. 202.

64 Ṭabrisī, *Majma'*, vol. 3, p. 516.
65 Ibid., vol. 1, p. 72.
66 al-Qāḍī al-Nu'mān, *Da'ā'im al-islām*, ed. 'Āṣif b. 'Alī Aṣghar Fayḍī [Asaf A.A. Fyzee], 3rd edn (Cairo: Dār al-Ma'ārif, 1969; repr. Beirut: al-Manāra, n.d.), vol. 1, p. 351.
67 Lane, *Arabic-English Lexicon*, vol. 2, p. 1668.
68 Massignon, *Essay on the Origins of the Technical Language of Islamic Mysticism*, p. 148, citing Abū Nu'aym, *Ḥilya*, vol. 6, p. 161 (translation modified by me). Massignon seems to be careless in asserting of *al-ṣiddīqīn*, 'This is one of the oldest mentions of this term.' Admittedly, however, he wrote when much less early renunciant literature was available in print.
69 Abū Nu'aym, *Ḥilya*, vol. 9, p. 354; vol. 10, p. 242.
70 Ibn al-Mubārak, *Zuhd*, no. 478.
71 Abū Nu'aym, *Ḥilya*, vol. 2, p. 210.
72 Abū 'Ubayd, *Khuṭab*, pp. 180–81.
73 Aḥmad, *Zuhd* (1357/1938–9), pp. 72–3; (1403/1983), p. 92.
74 Abū Nu'aym, *Ḥilya*, vol. 2, p. 359.
75 Ibid., vol. 5, p.339. Also called a *ṣiddīq* by a monk, ibid., vol. 6, p. 328.
76 Ibid., vol. 2, p. 358.
77 al-Barqī, *Kitāb al-Maḥāsin*, ed. Jalāl al-Dīn al-Ḥusaynī (Tehran: Dār al-Kutub al-Islāmiyya, 1370; repr. Najaf: al-Maṭba'a al-Ḥaydariyya, 1384/1964), p. 123. There is a question, of course, whether this book is rightly classified with renunciant literature. Forty-odd books are attributed to Barqī in Muḥammad b. al-Ḥasan al-Ṭūsī (Shaykh al-Ṭā'ifa), *al-Fihrist*, ed. Muḥammad Ṣādiq Āl Baḥr al-'Ulūm (Najaf: al-Maṭba'a al-Ḥaydariyya, 1937; repr. 1960), pp. 20–21, of which nine appear to make up the extant *Kitāb al-Maḥāsin*. Another attribution is *Kitāb al-Fiqh*, regrettably not extant; but many items in *al-Maḥāsin* have close parallels in Sunni renunciant literature, renunciation of the world apparently being a major theme of Imāmi literature in this early–middle period (third century AH/ninth and early tenth centuries CE).
78 Barqī, *Maḥāsin*, p. 124.
79 Christopher Melchert, '"God Created Adam in His Image"', *Journal of Qur'anic Studies* 13 (2011), pp. 113–24.
80 Fred M. Donner, *Narratives of Islamic Origins: The Beginnings of Islamic Historical Writing* (Princeton, NJ: Darwin Press, 1998), Chapter 2. Donner's view was anticipated by Solange Ory, 'Aspects religieux des texts épigraphiques du début de l'Islam' in Alfred-Louis de Prémare, ed., *Les premières écritures islamiques* (Aix-en-Provence: Édisud, 1990), pp. 30–39, and confirmed by Leor Halevi, 'The Paradox of Islamization: Tombstone Inscriptions, Qur'ānic Recitations, and the Problem of Religious Change', *History of Religions* 44 (2004–5), pp. 120–52.
81 An early attempt to make out regional patterns is Kāmil Muṣṭafā al-Shaybī, *al-Fikr al-shī'ī wa'l-naza'āt al-ṣūfiyya* (Baghdad: Maktabat al-Nahḍa, 1386/1966) and idem, *al-Ṣila bayna'l-taṣawwuf wa'l-tashayyu'* (Baghdad: Maṭba'at al-Zahrā', 1382–3/1963–4).
82 Wakī', *al-Zuhd*, ed. 'Abd al-Raḥmān 'Abd al-Jabbār al-Faryawā'ī (Medina: Maktabat al-Dār, 1404/1984; repr. Riyadh: Dār al-Ṣumay'ī, 1415/1994), vol. 1, p. 222; Ibn Abī'l-Dunyā, *al-Zuhd*, ed. Yāsīn Muḥammad al-Sawwās (Damascus:

Dār Ibn Kathīr, 1420/1999), p. 63; Abū Nuʿaym, *Ḥilya*, vol. 6, p. 386. Wakīʿ and Abū Nuʿaym represent the overlapping cultures of Hadith and renunciation, but Ibn Abīʾl-Dunyā (d. 281/894) represents, rather, overlapping *adab* and renunciation.

83 Based on a sample of 170 items from Ibn Abī Ḥātim, *Tafsīr al-Qurʾān al-ʿaẓīm*, ed. Asʿad Muḥammad al-Tayyib (Mecca: Maktabat Nizār Muṣṭafā al-Bāz, 1419/1999).

SECTION II

Lexical Methodologies in Action: Four Case Studies

5

The Use of Lexicography in the Great Qur'anic Commentary of al-Wāḥidī (d. 468/1076)

CLAUDE GILLIOT

I Introduction

THE PURPOSE of this study is to present the main features of the recourse to lexicography by the exegete al-Wāḥidī (Abū'l-Ḥasan ʿAlī b. Aḥmad al-Naysābūrī, d. 468/1076) in his Great Commentary of the Qur'an, *al-Tafsīr al-basīṭ*, within a historical perspective. For that reason we begin, in section II, with a brief presentation of the first steps of Islamic exegesis in the linguistic field. Then, in section III, we deal conversely with an ancient Arabic dictionary attributed to al-Khalīl b. Aḥmad (d. 175/792, 170/786 or other dates), the *Kitāb al-ʿAyn*, which contains exegetical elements. In section IV we focus Wāḥidī's training in lexicography, and more generally in the linguistic disciplines, although only to the extent useful to our present purposes. Section V is dedicated to the evolution of exegesis, in relation to lexicography, from Ṭabarī (d. 310/923) to Wāḥidī. In section VI we have tried to gain an insight into the evolution of the lexicological practice of Wāḥidī in comparison with Ṭabarī's practice; this has been done through ten lexicological case studies taken from Wāḥidī's *al-Tafsīr al-basīṭ*.[1] The influence on Wāḥidī's exegesis of the dictionary by Abū Manṣūr al-Azharī (d. Rabīʿ II 370/October 980), entitled *Tahdhīb al-lugha*, is especially emphasised.

II The Introduction of Linguistic Elements in Qur'anic Exegesis

The recourse to what in later Islamic scholarship was called the 'sciences of language' (*'ulūm al-lugha*), above all lexicography and grammar, was made gradually in Qur'anic exegesis. Given the position of the Qur'an in Islam, there was also 'a close professional relationship between philology and the religious disciplines'.[2] As for lexicography, it was practised *in nuce* in a primitive way at the very beginnings of Qur'anic exegesis, for instance by explaining a Qur'anic word by giving another word, Qur'anic or non-Qur'anic; or by quoting poetic verses, as in *Masā'il Nāfi' b. al-Azraq 'an 'Abd Allāh Ibn 'Abbās*.[3] There can also be found a kind of 'periphrastic exegesis',[4] an expression that we have borrowed from the late John Wansbrough.[5] This kind of exegesis was used by, among others, Mujāhid b. Jabr (d. 104/722–3)[6] and Muqātil b. Sulaymān (d. 150/767–8).[7] It also has a prominent place in the *Majāz al-Qur'ān* by Abū 'Ubayda Ma'mar b. al-Muthannā (d. 206/821–2 or other dates),[8] *majāz* here meaning: 'what it is possible to say', that is, what is usual (in the Arabic language), because 'the Arabs say so'.[9]

Indeed, Abū 'Ubayda's *Majāz al-Qur'ān*, also called *Gharīb al-Qur'ān*, was an important step for the introduction of lexicological elements into Qur'anic exegesis, but conversely also for the 'Qur'anisation' of subsequent Arabic–Islamic lexicography, by introducing to it odd Qur'anic words and expressions which did not pertain to the system of Arabic. According to the Sevillian traditionist Ibn Khayr (d. 575/1179), this work was 'the first book collected on the uncommon (or rare) words (or expressions) of the Qur'an and their significations'.[10]

The recension of Abū 'Ubayda's *Majāz al-Qur'ān* used by Wāḥidī was perhaps the same for which his master Tha'labī (d. 427/1035) had been given a licence of transmission (*ijāza*), that of Abū Ghassān Rufay' b. Salama Muslim (*leg.* Salama b. Muṣallam)[11] b. Rufay' al-'Abdī al-Baṣrī, called Damādh,[12] Abū 'Ubayda's pupil and copyist (*kātib*, *apud* Yāqūt; *warrāq*, *apud* Maymanī), who also audited his lessons on *akhbār* and genealogy.[13]

III The *Kitāb al-ʿAyn*: Elements of Qur'anic Exegesis in an Early Dictionary

In contrast to Abū ʿUbayda, who deals only with a partial corpus (*Teilkorpus*) relating to the exegesis of the Qur'an, in the *Kitāb al-ʿAyn* attributed to al-Khalīl b. Aḥmad we have 'an abundant and a many-facetted "old" Qur'anic commentary'.[14] The question remains open as to at what stage of development of the Khalīlī lemmata the single elements of this commentary entered the *Kitāb al-ʿAyn*.[15] We know that several sources attribute a role to Khalīl's friend (and/or student) al-Layth b. al-Muẓaffar b. Naṣr (or al-Layth b. Naṣr b. Sayyār, d. ca. 190/805–6) in the composition of this work.[16] Azharī was perhaps one of the first important scholars to put in doubt the attribution of *Kitāb al-ʿAyn* to Khalīl, as he noted that the text always says: *qāla'l-Layth* ('Layth said').[17] It should be noted here that Azharī, in his *Tahdhīb al-lugha*, and Wāḥidī in his *Basīṭ*, refer to Layth very often, but not so much to Khalīl. Whatever the case may be, the *Kitāb al-ʿAyn* was already in circulation at the end of the second/eighth century.[18] Rafael Talmon, who has concentrated his study on the grammatical matters and terminology found in the *Kitāb al-ʿAyn*,[19] argues that 'the assessment of its place in the general grammatical theory of the pre-Sībawayhian era' brings together data from two poles: 'the available details of the "Old Iraqi School" and Ḫalīl's putative innovations'.[20] However, Mohammad-Nauman Khan, who has dealt with the *materia exegetica* in the *Kitāb al-ʿAyn*, has evidence showing that it uses 'the large spectrum of the observed techniques and aspects of the Baṣrian tradition'.[21] Furthermore, many words treated in the lemmata of the *Kitāb al-ʿAyn* are also found in Abū ʿUbayda's *Majāz al-Qur'ān*.[22] Although Abū ʿUbayda is sometimes presented as a colleague of Khalīl, we are not quite sure that such was the case.[23]

Already by the end of the third/ninth century, some scholars had expressed very critical judgements concerning the *Kitāb al-ʿAyn*. For example, the grammarian Thaʿlab (d. 291/904), on being asked about its value by Abū'l-Faḍl al-Mundhirī al-Harawī (Muḥammad b. Abī Jaʿfar, d. Rajab 329/April 941), a lexicographer, grammarian and master of Azharī, answered: 'This book is filled with bubonic pieces (*malā ghudad* [sic]).' This was the expression of Abū'l-ʿAbbās (i.e. Thaʿlab) according to al-Mundhirī al-Harawī, but 'the correct expression for the grammarians (*wa ḥaqquhu ʿinda'l-naḥwiyyīn*) is: *mal'ān ghudadan*; however, Abū'l-ʿAbbās addressed common people according to their capacity of understanding (*wa lākinna Abā'l-ʿAbbāsi yukhāṭibu ʿawāmma'l-nāsi ʿalā qadri afhāmihim*)'.[24] Having quoted Thaʿlab's judgement, Azharī gives an interesting statement on the way in which he dealt with the *materia* of *Kitāb al-ʿAyn*. He states that he read it several times systematically, and carefully noted down the mistakes and the modifications in it (*wa ʿunītu bi-tatabbuʿi mā ṣuḥḥifa wa ghuyyira minhu*), and that, subsequently, he indicated what is correct and what is erroneous (in *Kitāb al-ʿAyn*) in his own book (i.e. *Tahdhīb al-lugha*).[25]

IV Wāḥidī's Linguistic Formation

The main subject of this contribution is the important exegete Wāḥidī.[26] It will be sufficient here to provide an outline of the most important aspects concerning his linguistic formation, primarily based on his 'intellectual autobiography', which he wrote in the introduction to *al-Tafsīr al-basīṭ*.[27]

According to Wāḥidī, his master in prosody, poetry and language, particularly in lexicography, was 'al-Shaykh Aḥmad b. Muḥammad b. ʿAbd Allāh b. Yūsuf al-ʿArūḍī'.[28] However, one of Wāḥidī's students, ʿAbd al-Ghāfir al-Fārisī Abū'l-Ḥasan al-Naysābūrī (d. 529/1134–5),[29] gives the following name: Abū'l-Faḍl Aḥmad b. Muḥammad b. ʿAbd Allāh b. Yūsuf b. Muḥammad b. Malik (or Mālik) al-Sahlī al-Adīb al-Naysābūrī al-ʿArūḍī[30] al-Ṣaffār al-Shāfiʿī (d. after 416/1025–6), 'the master in *adab* (*belles-lettres*) in his time'.[31] This same name is taken up by Qifṭī who adds 'al-Sahlakī' to the name,[32] which is given by Dhahabī as 'al-Sahlī'.[33] The *nomen relativum* 'al-Sahlī' is replaced in the *Talkhīṣ akhbār al-naḥwiyyīn* by Ibn Maktūm (d. 749/1348) with 'al-Sahlakī',[34] the *kāf* being a diminutive in Persian: 'Sahl/Sahlak'. According to the same Ibn Maktūm, his name was: Aḥmad b. Muḥammad b. ʿAbd Allāh b. Sahlak al-Sahlakī.[35] Suyūṭī (or a copyist) reads 'al-Nahshalī', but this is erroneous.[36]

Al-ʿArūḍī al-Sahlakī was one of the most important pupils of Azharī,[37] the author, among other works, of *Kitāb al-Taqrīb fī'l-tafsīr,*[38] or *Kitāb al-Tafsīr,*[39] *Tahdhīb al-lugha* and *Maʿānī al-qirā'āt,*[40] whom Wāḥidī quotes very often in his *Wasīṭ*. It should be noted that, according to Wāḥidī himself, ʿArūḍī not only followed the lessons of Azharī, but also transmitted his *Tahdhīb al-lugha*.[41]

V Lexicography and Exegesis from Ṭabarī to Wāḥidī

Among the most important concerns of Ṭabarī in writing his commentary we can count: 1. *al-qirā'a al-mutawātira* (or *al-qirā'a al-mustafīḍa*), that is, the so-called uninterrupted (authentic) reading, also called the 'reading of the people of the cities' (*qirā'at ahl al-amṣār*), that is, the cities of Medina, Mecca, Kufa, Basra and Damascus. 2. That the interpretation should not contradict the interpretation of the 'majority' consensus (*ijmāʿ*, or *mā ajmaʿa ʿalayhi . . .*) of the (early) exegetes (*ahl al-tafsīr* or *ahl al-ta'wīl*). 3. Added to this second principle is a third axiom: that it is not permitted to interpret the Qur'an according to one's own opinion (*bi-ra'yihi*). 4. A corollary of the second and third axioms is that the Qur'an cannot be interpreted according to one's own opinion, basing oneself on the practice of the language of the Arabs (*bi-ra'yihi ʿalā madhhabi kalāmi'l-ʿarabi*).[42] Particularly the readings (*qirā'āt*), and, above all, the reading according to the so-called ʿUthmānic codex, was still a crucial issue in some areas during Ṭabarī's time, for instance in Baghdad. However, by Wāḥidī's time, particularly in Nishapur, the situation concerning the readings had changed. Of course they were still studied and used in Qur'anic exegesis and elsewhere, but they no longer challenged the ʿUthmānic codex. As for the early exegetes, their opinions were generally accepted, but since they had so many different interpretations, the 'consensus' of the early exegetes remained a fiction as before!

As for lexicography at the time of Wāḥidī, the situation had also changed. Ṭabarī could have had the *Kitāb al-ʿAyn* at his disposal,[43] but he does not refer to it, probably both because he did not consider it a *corpus exegeticum* and because it was a controversial work. He knew Abū ʿUbayd's *al-Gharīb al-muṣannaf* and *Gharīb al-Ḥadith*,[44] and he used Abū ʿUbayda's *Majāz al-Qurʾān*. Wāḥidī had access to the same works,[45] but he also often quotes Layth (i.e. *Kitāb al-ʿAyn*), and other lexicographical works such as *Jamharat al-lugha* by Ibn Durayd (Abū Bakr Muḥammad b. al-Ḥasan al-Azdī al-Baṣrī, d. 19 Shaʿbān 321/14 August 933),[46] the first dictionary preserved after *al-Gharīb al-muṣannaf*;[47] *Iṣlāh al-manṭiq* by Ibn al-Sikkīt (d. 244/858–9 or other dates); *Maʿānī al-Qurʾān* by Abū Isḥāq al-Zajjāj (d. 311/923) which contains much lexical material, even if the basis of the exegetical comments for this book (*fīʾl-tafsīr*, meaning the early exegetes) is the *Kitāb al-Tafsīr* by Ibn Ḥanbal (d. 241/855).[48] Above all, he also had at his disposal Azharī's *Tahdhīb al-lugha* – one of his most quoted sources – which was organised like the *Kitāb al-ʿAyn*. Wāḥidī often quotes a source indirectly, through *Tahdhīb al-lugha*.[49] Of course we have taken into account here only the works concerned with lexicography, and not the works on the 'meanings' (*maʿānī*) of the Qur'an, such as those by al-Kisāʾī (d. 189/804), al-Farrāʾ (Abū Zakariyyāʾ, d. 207/822) and al-Akhfash al-Awsaṭ (Abūʾl-Ḥasan Saʿīd b. Masʿada, d. 215/830), or the lexicological material contained in earlier Qur'anic commentaries, such as those by Muqātil, al-Kalbī (Abūʾl-Naḍr Muḥammad b. al-Sāʾib al-Kūfī, d. 146/763), Ṭabarī and Thaʿlabī.

Thus, we can understand why the lexicological matter *ut sic* is more abundant in Wāḥidī's *al-Basīṭ* than in Ṭabarī's Commentary. But there is also a more personal reason which has to do with Wāḥidī's interests and training. As Walid Saleh has rightly written: 'there is no denying that the study of philology shaped him intellectually'.[50] Or according to the same: 'The poignancy of al-Wāḥidī's life is that it started with a failed attempt to write poetry and ended instead with a commentary on the most admired of Arab poets [al-Mutanabbī].'[51]

VI Wāḥidī at Work on Lexicography: A Comparison with Ṭabarī and other Exegetes

A comprehensive study of Wāḥidī's recourse to lexicography would require a whole thesis or book. Therefore, for this chapter we have chosen to examine ten representative case studies of this exegete's lexicological treatment of Qur'anic words. As shall be seen, most of Wāḥidī's lexicographical choices are conditioned by a theological or juridic pre-comprehension of the Qur'anic text, and sometimes by both.

1. Q. 4:78 – *burūj mushayyada*

Aynamā takūnū yudrikkumu'l-mawtu wa law kuntum fī burūjin mushayyadatin wa-in tuṣibhum ḥasanatun yaqūlū hādhihi min 'indi'llahi wa-in tuṣibhum sayyi'atun yaqūlū hādhihi min 'indika qul kullun min 'indi'llahi famāli hā'ulā'i'l-qawmi lā yakādūna yafqahūna ḥadīthan.

Arberry: *Wherever you may be, death will overtake you, though you should be in raised-up towers. And if a good thing visits them, they say, 'This is from God'; but if an evil thing visits them, they say, 'This is from thee.' Say: 'Everything is from God.' How is it with this people? They scarcely understand any tiding.*[52]

Other possible translations of *burūj mushayyada* include: *lofty towers* (Pickthall); *towers built up strong and high* (A. Yusuf Ali)

This verse refers to the fact that death will reach even those who are *fī burūjin mushayyadatin* ('*in raised-up towers*'). Ṭabarī begins his treatment of the phrase by discussing the different treatments of *mushayyada*: 'The Arabs disagree about the meaning of *mushayyada*. Some of the Basrans say regarding it: *al-mushayyadatu* [means] tall (*muṭawwal*). As for the word *mashīdu* (without the doubling [*bi'l-takhfīf*]), it [means] adorned (*muzayyan*).' (*Wa'khtalafa ahlu'l-arabiyyati fī ma'nā'l-mushayyadati fa-qāla ba'ḍu ahli'l-Baṣrati minhā al-mushayyadatu al-ṭawīlatu wa ammā'l-mashīdu bi'l-takhfīfi fa-innahu'l-muzayyanu.*)[53] This interpretation is also found in Abū 'Ubayda, who defines the word in this way: '*mushayyada* [means] tall, and *mashīd* means adorned'.[54] Ṭabarī then quotes the point of view of a Kufan, also without naming him,[55] who is Farrā'.[56]

Wāḥidī's discussion of the word is very similar to that of Ṭabarī: 'Abū 'Ubayda and Ibn Qutayba [d. 276/889] said: *al-mushayyada* means the tall ones (*al-muṭawwala*).'[57] He also quotes Farrā', but before Abū ʿUbayda, saying: 'he said in the *Maʿānī*'.[58] Wāḥidī, then, uses the same material; he presents it in a different order, but cites his sources more clearly.

2. Q. 18:52 – *mawbiqan*

Wa yawma yaqūlu nādū shurakāʾīʾlladhīna zaʿamtum fa-daʿwhum fa-lam yastajībū lahum wa jaʿalnā baynahum mawbiqan.

Arberry: *And on the day He shall say, 'Call on My associates whom you asserted'; and then they shall call on them, but they will not answer them, and We shall set a gulf between them.*

Other possible translations of *mawbiqan* include: *a gulf of doom* (Pickthall), *a place of common perdition* (A. Yusuf Ali), *un abîme* (Blachère), *einen Abgrund* (Paret), *eine grause Kluft* (Fr. Rückert).

The word *mawbiq* is a *crux interpretum*. The embarrassment of the exegetes appears in almost all commentaries,[59] but especially in that of Burhān al-Dīn al-Biqāʿī (d. 17 Rajab 885/22 September 1480).[60] As is often the case when exegetes do not know what a word means, they find a pseudo-solution; for example, the unknown word '*al-kawthar*' (Q. 108:1) came to be interpreted as a river in Hell, Paradise or elsewhere.

What interests Ṭabarī, above all, is the interpretations of the early exegetes, and he builds his own opinion upon them.[61] He gives the interpretation of Ibn ʿAbbās (ʿAbd Allāh, d. 69/688 or other dates), Qatāda (b. Diʿāma al-Sadūsī al-Baṣrī Abūʾl-Khaṭṭāb, d. 118/736) and others, who gloss the word *mawbiq* with *mahlik* ('place of destruction'), or *mahlak* ('perdition, destruction'). Al-Ḥasan al-Baṣrī (d. 110/728) refers to 'the enmity between them on the Day of Resurrection' (*jaʿalnā baynahum ʿadāwatan yawmaʾl-qiyāmati*),[62] in other words, between the 'associators' and 'the associated' (the idols). ʿAbd Allāh b. ʿAmr (b. al-ʿĀṣ, d. 63/682 or 66) or his pupil Nawf b. Faḍāla al-Bikālī (d. 101/719) states that it is a deep river,[63] separating 'the people of error' (*ahl al-ḍalāla*) from 'the people of right guidance' (*ahl al-hudā*), or separating the people of Paradise from the people of Hell.[64] Ṭabarī then gives evidence from the 'language of the Arabs':

I have caused somebody to perish (*wa qad awbaqtu fulānan*), if I have destroyed him (*idhā ahlaktuhu*), and in the words of God, *or he causes them to perish for what they have earned* (*aw yūbiqhunna bimā kasabū* [Q. 42:34]); with the meaning of 'he destroys them' (*yuhlikuhunna*). And it is said of the one who was destroyed: someone has been destroyed (*wa qad wabiqa fulānun*), and he destroys (*fa-huwa yawbaqu wabaqan*). According to the manner of speech (*lugha*) of the Banū 'Āmir [it is]: *yābiqu* (without *hamza*); and according to the Banū Tamīm: *yaybiqu* (*apud* Wāḥidī: *yabiqu*) [and other forms, or alleged forms, in the dialects]. According to Kisā'ī, it is said: *wabaqa, yabiqu, wubūqan.*[65]

Ṭabarī then presents the opinion of Abū 'Ubayda:

There are some people with knowledge of the speech of the Arabs from Basra who say: *mawbiq* means promise (*al-maw'id*) and this is attested (*wa yatashhid*) in the words of the poet:

Wa ḥāda[66] *Sharawrā*[67] *fa'l-Sitāri fa-lam yada'*
Ti'āran lahu wa'l-wādiyayni bi-mawbiqi.

He [or it] avoided Sharawrā and Sitār and he did not let
Ti'ār and the two wadis become for him a place of
appointment.

There are some variants of this line of poetry in other sources. Azharī includes the following version in his *Tahdhīb al-lugha*:

Wa jāda Sharawrā fa'l-Sitāri fa-lam yada'
Ya'āran[68] *lahu wa'l-wādiyayni bi-mawbiqi.*

An abundant rain fell on Sharawrā and Sitār, and it did not let
Ya'ār and the two wadis become for him a place of
appointment.[69]

Azharī also includes another similar verse attibuted to Khufāf b. Nudba (or Nadba, both forms being attested: Abū Khurāsha Khufāf b. 'Umayr b. al-Ḥārith, d. between 13/634 and 23/644, of the Banū Sulaym [Qays]):[70]

Fa-jāda Sharawrā fa'l-Sitāri fa-aṣbaḥat
Ya'āru lahu wa'l-wādiyayni bi-mawdiqi.

> An abundant rain fell on Sharawrā and al-Sitār; in the morning
> Yaʿār and the two rivers also were raining places.[71]

Azharī comments: 'And he [Abū 'Ubayda] interprets it as a [perilous] "place of appointment" (*mawʿid*)'. Ṭabarī does not give his own opinion on this interpretation of Abū 'Ubayda, but he obviously does not favour it; rather, he seems to prefer the interpretation of the Kufan linguists (he quoted Kisāʾī earlier), and we know that Farrāʾ (whom he does not mention here) said: '*wa jaʿalnā baynahum mawbiqan*. It is said: we have set their constant union together (*tawāṣulahum*) a *mawbiq*, that is, "a place of perdition" (*mahlikan*) (or "perdition")[72] to them in this world, and it is said that it is a river in Hell.'[73]

Turning now to Wāḥidī,[74] he begins his commentary of this verse by giving the interpretations of the early exegetes, but contrary to Ṭabarī, with no chains of authorities. For Anas b. Mālik (d. 91/709 or 93, etc.), *mawbiq* consists of 'a river of pus (*qayḥ*) and blood in Hell',[75] which is also the interpretation of Mujāhid and 'Abd Allāh b. 'Amr (b. al-'Āṣ). He also gives the interpretation of Nawf b. Faḍāla al-Bikālī: 'a river which separates the misled people from the people of faith'.[76] As we have seen, many of the same interpretations were quoted by Ṭabarī with the chains of authorities.

Wāḥidī next refers to one of the interpretations given from Ibn 'Abbās, but not quoted by Ṭabarī: 'this means an impediment separating (*yurīdu ḥijāzan ḥājizan*)'.[77] Then he focuses on the explanation of the linguists, remarking that the interpretation of Ibn 'Abbās (*ḥājiz*) has its equivalent given by the Kufan Ibn al-Aʿrābī (Muḥammad b. Ziyād, d. 231/846), and in this case the indirect expression (*kināya*) *baynahum* refers to both groups, the believers and the unbelievers, but it is not known whether *mawbiq* could have the meaning of *ḥājiz* with that derivation (*wa laysa yuʿrafu li'l-mawbiqi bi-maʿnā'l-ḥājizi'shtiqāqun*). He also refers to the interpretation of Farrāʾ, for whom *baynahum mawbiq* refers to the union of the associators and the associated. God has set their mutual union (*tawāṣulahum*) in this world as a *mawqit*, in other words, their perdition (*mahlikan lahum*) in the other world, but this concerns only the associators.[78]

Then Wāḥidī quotes Abū Isḥāq al-Zajjāj (Ibrāhīm b. Muḥammad b. al-Sarī, d. 19 Jumādā II 311/3 October 923, or 310 or 316): 'We have set between them a chastisement which *yūqitbuhum*, that is, destroys them (*yuhliluhum*), as if it was said: we have set between them a destruction.'[79] He also quotes Farrā''s *al-Maṣādir* (*al-Maṣādir fī'l-Qur'ān*).

Wāḥidī gives two further interpretations for *mawbiq*, but says that 'no basis is known to support them' (*lā yudrā lahumā aṣlun*).[80] The first one is an explanation of the interpretation of al-Ḥasan al-Baṣrī which we have seen above: 'He has set between them enmity on the Day of Resurrection'; some of the specialists of the meanings (*ahl al-maʿānī*) said [it means]: 'a destructive enmity' (*ʿadāwatan muhlikatan*),[81] which for Wāḥidī is absurd (*baʿīd*). The second one is the interpretation of Abū 'Ubayda, with the poetic verse that we encountered above. Wāḥidī considers this interpretation an error (*hādhā'l-qawlu fāsidun*) from the point of view of the word and of its meaning. He remarks that al-Akhfash al-Awsaṭ said that *mawbiq* is similar to *mawʿid*; he could have meant this either morphologically (*yurīdu dhālika fī'l-lafẓi*), or regarding the interpretation (*fī'l-tafsīri*).[82]

3. Q. 18:96 – *bayna'l-ṣadafayni* and *qiṭran*

> *Ātūnī zubara'l-ḥadīdi ḥattā idhā sāwā bayna'l-ṣadafayni qāla'nfakhū ḥattā idhā jaʿalahu nāran qāla ātūnī ufrigh ʿalayhi qiṭaran.*
>
> Arberry: *'Bring me ingots of iron!' Until, when he had made all level between the two cliffs, he said: 'Blow!' Until, when he had made a fire, he said: 'Bring me, that I may pour molten brass on it.'*
>
> Other possible translations of *bayna'l-ṣadafayni* include: (*the gap*) *between the cliffs* (Pickthall); between *the two steep mountain-sides* (A. Yusuf Ali).
>
> Other possible translations of *qiṭran* include: *molten copper* (Pickthall); *molten lead* (A. Yusuf Ali).

The two greatest problems in this verse are the meanings of *bayna'l-ṣadafayni* and *qiṭran*. Ṭabarī begins by explaining that *bayna'l-ṣadafayni* is: 'what is between the two sides of the two mountains and their two summits' and he supports this reading with a quotation of a *rajaz* verse, which is also in Abū ʿUbayda's *Majāz al-Qurʾān*, although Ṭabarī does not mention this:

Qad akhadhat mā bayna ʿarḍiʾl-ṣudfayni
nāḥiyatayhā wa aʿālīʾl-ruknaynī.

And they [i.e. a group of people] took from that which was
between the sides of the two mountains
its two areas and two tall pillars.[83]

Then he gives the interpretation of the early exegetes: '*al-ṣadafāni*, that is, *al-jabalāni* (the two mountains)'. He also mentions the three readings *al-ṣadaf* (the majority of the readers of Medina and Kufa), *al-ṣuduf* (Basra) and *al-ṣudf* (some readers of Mecca and Kufa). His own choice is the first reading.

On *qiṭr*, Ṭabarī begins by giving the interpretation of the early exegetes, which is 'brass' (*nuḥās*).[84] Then he gives the interpretation of 'somebody from amongst the people of knowledge on the language of the Arabs, of the people of Basra' (i.e. Abū ʿUbayda): '*al-qiṭr* [means] molten iron (*al-ḥadīd al-madhāb*)'. He illustrates this with a verse of poetry:

Ḥusāman ka-lawniʾl-milḥi ṣāfin ḥadīduhu
jurāzan[85] *min aqṭāriʾl-ḥadīdiʾl-munaʿʿati.*

A sword, coloured like salt dried on a rock, its iron
made sharp by the dripping of generous molten bronze.[86]

Wāḥidī remarks that *al-ṣadafān* is interpreted by all the exegetes as 'the two mountains' (*al-jabalayn*).[87] Then he gives the interpretation of Abū ʿUbayda; 'the two sides of the mountain' (*jānibāʾl-jabal*); he adds that that is also Zajjāj's interpretation. But his main source is Azharī: '*al-ṣadaf waʾl-ṣuduf*: the side and the part (*al-jānib waʾl-nāḥiyya*)'. In Azharī's *Tahdhīb al-lugha*, the full statement is as follows:

> The side of two mountains which are opposite each other is called *ṣuduf* or *ṣadaf*. The two sides are called *ṣudufānī* or *ṣadafānī* when they are joined together or encounter, that is when this side encounters the opposite side. What is between is a way between two mountains or a ravine or a valley; and so, from

this it is said: I joined someone (*ṣādaftu fulān*), meaning 'met him'.[88]

The following hadith quoted by Wāḥidī is also taken over from Azharī: 'When he [Muhammad] passed by something high inclined (*bi-ṣadafin* [or *bi-ṣudufin*] *mā'ilin*), he used to hasten.'[89] Wāḥidī also gives the three readings, taken over from Azharī who took them from Farrā'; but Wāḥidī does not mention Farrā'.[90] As for *qiṭr*, Wāḥidī explains it as 'molten brass' (*al-nuḥās al-dhā'ib*); he bases this on the fact that the root *q-ṭ-r* means 'to fall in drops', and when brass is molten it falls in drops like water.

4. Q. 69:35–7 – *ghislīn*

Fa-laysa lahu'l-yawma hāhunā ḥamīmun wa lā ṭa'āmun illā min ghislīnin lā ya'kuluhu illā'l-khāṭi'ūna.

Arberry: *Therefore he today has not here one loyal friend, neither any food saving foul pus, that none excepting the sinners eat.*

Other possible translations of *ghislīn* include: *filth* (Pickthall); *the corruption from the washing of wounds* (A. Yusuf Ali)

Ṭabarī declares that *ghislīn* is 'the pus which seeps out of the people of Hell' (*mā yasīlu min ṣadīdi ahli'l-nāri*),[91] then he quotes 'a scholar in Arabic from Basra', i.e. Abū 'Ubayda: 'Every wound (*jurh*) you have washed (*ghasaltahu*), something comes out of it, that is, *ghislīn* [following the pattern] *fi'līn*, after having washed a wound or hairs (*mina'l-ghasli min al-jirāḥi wa'l-wabari*)'.[92] Ṭabarī adds to the explanation of Abū 'Ubayda: 'a *yā'* and a *nūn* has been added to it [i.e. to *gh-s-l*], as in the case of '*ifirrīn*'. This has been taken from Akhfash who adds "*ifirrīn: kifirrīn*'.[93] Then Ṭabarī gives interpretations by early exegetes, like 'the pus of the people of Hell'; or 'what comes out of their flesh' (both from Ibn 'Abbās); 'the worst, most foul and most disgusting food' (Qatāda); or 'nobody knows what *al-ghislīn* and *al-zaqqūm* are' (Ibn Wahb, i.e. 'Abd Allāh Ibn Wahb al-Fihrī al-Miṣrī, d. 197/813; Ibn Zayd, i.e. the exegete 'Abd al-Raḥmān Ibn Zayd b. Aslam al-Madanī, d. 182/798).

Wāḥidī mentions first of all the interpretations of the early exegetes;[94] 'Ikrima ← Ibn 'Abbās: 'I do not know what *al-ghislīn* is';[95]

'Aṭā' ← Ibn 'Abbās: 'the pus of the people of Hell';[96] Kalbī: 'the pus (*qayḥ*), blood and filth (*ṣadīd*) which seeps out of the people of Hell when they are tormented (*idhā 'udhibū*)'.[97] Then he quotes Abū 'Ubayda, like Ṭabarī (only up to *fi'līn*); then he cites the two grammarians Akhfash, who was also an exegete, and al-Mubarrad (Abū'l-'Abbās Muḥammad b. Yazīd al-Baṣrī, d. 285/898), but in an abridged way,[98] and Zajjāj: 'Its meaning is the pus of people of Hell. Its derivation comes from what spills from their bodies (*wa'shtiqāquhu mimmā yanghasilu min abdānihim*)'.[99] Finally, Wāḥidī summarises the interpretations of the *ahl al-ma'ānī*: '*al-ghislīn* is the pus which flows from the people of Hell (*yasīlu min ahli'l-nārī*).[100] It has been called *ghislīn* because it flows (*li-sayālānihi*) from their bodies, as if it spilled from them (*ka-annahu yanghasilu minhum*).'[101]

5. Q. 16:94 – *fa-tazilla qadamun*

Wa lā tattakhidhū aymānakum dakhalan baynakum fa-tazilla qadamun ba'da thubūtihā wa tadhūqū'l-sūwā'a bi-mā ṣadadtum 'an sabīli'llahi wa lakum 'adhābun 'aẓīmun.

Arberry: *Take not your oaths as mere mutual deceit, lest any foot should slip after it has stood firm, and you should taste evil, for that you barred from the way of God, and lest there should await you a mighty chastisement.*

Other possible translations of *fa-tazilla qadamun* include: *lest a foot should slip* (Pickthall); *with the result that someone's foot may slip* (A. Yusuf Ali).

Tabarī comments:

> So you perish after you were safe from perdition. And that is like a parable (*mathalun*)[102] for everybody put to the test (*mubtalan*) after well-being (*'āfiyya*), or falling into difficulty (*warṭa*) after safety (*salāma*). It is said (in Arabic): *zallat qadamuhu* (his foot has slipped).

The second part of this explanation ('And that is like a parable . . .') is copied from Abū 'Ubayda, although Ṭabarī includes a poetic verse which is not in the edition of *Majāz al-Qur'ān*.

Sa-yumnaʿu minka'l-sabqu in kunta sābiqan
wa tulṭaʿu in zallat bika'l-naʿlāni.

And he forbids you before you arrive
and you are hit so that your sandals slip.[103]

Wāḥidī quotes and names Abū ʿUbayda,[104] as well as mentioning Ṭabarī and his poetic verse (*anshada'bnu Jarīrin*). However, it should be noted that he does not refer to his master Thaʿlabī, although the latter copied the interpretation and the poetic verse from Ṭabarī, without naming him.[105]

6. Q. 18:56 – *li-yudḥiḍū*

Wa mā nursilu'l-mursalīna illā mubashirīna wa mundhirīna wa yujādilu alladhīna kafarū bi'l-bāṭili li-yudḥiḍū bihi'l-ḥaqqa wa'ttakhadhū āyātī wa mā undhirū huzuwan.

Arberry: *And We send not the Envoys, but good tidings to bear, and warning. Yet do the unbelievers dispute with falsehood, that they may rebut thereby the truth. They have taken My signs, and what they are warned of, in mockery.*[106]

Other possible translations of *li-yudḥiḍū* include: *in order to refute* (Pickthall); *in order therewith to weaken* (A. Yusuf Ali).[107]

Ṭabarī interprets this as meaning:

that they may invalidate thereby the truth, eliminate it and remove it (*li-yubṭilū bihi'l-ḥaqqa wa yuzīlūhu wa yadhhabū bihi*). In this sense one says something *daḥaḍa* if it withdraws and goes away (*idhā zāla wa dhahaba*). And it is said: that is a *daḥḍun* place, that is, slippery and sliding (*muzillun muzliqun*) where no shoe, hoof or foot remains firm (*lam yathbut fīhi khuffun wa ḥāfirun wa qadamun*), for instance in the verse of the poet:

Radītu wa najjā [in Abū ʿUbayda: *waradtu wa naḥḥā*]
'l-Yashkuriyya ḥidhāruhu
wa hāda kamā ḥāda'l-ba'īru ʿani'l-daḥḍi.
I tumbled down, but his own cautiousness saved al-Yashkurī
he moved slowly, like a camel to avoid slipping.[108]

This verse was probably in Abū ʿUbayda's *Kitāb Ashʿār al-qabāʾil*, which was still extant in Aleppo during the seventh/thirteenth century.[109]

Wāḥidī begins by giving an interpretation from Ibn ʿAbbās: 'that they may invalidate thereby what is delivered by Muhammad' (*li-yubṭilū mā jāʾa bihi Muḥammad*).[110] This was the interpretation given by Ṭabarī and Thaʿlabī, but Wāḥidī gives no attribution to either. His explanations on the meaning of the word are taken partly from Azharī[111] and partly from Thaʿlabī, whom he does not name. He then quotes part of a tradition concerning Muhammad: 'He [i.e. Muhammad] used to pray the first [prayer] when the sun began to wane' (*annahu kāna yuṣalli'l-ūlā ḥīna tadḥaḍu'l-shamsu*).[112]

7. Q. 8:11 – *wa yuthabbita bihi'l-aqdāma*

Idh yughashīkumu'l-nuʿāsa amanatan minhu wa yunazzilu ʿalaykum mina'l-samāʾi māʾan li-yuṭahhirakum bihi wa yudhhiba ʿankum rijza'l-shayṭāni wa li-yarbiṭa ʿalā qulūbikum wa yuthabbita bihi'l-aqdāma.

Arberry: *When He was causing slumber to overcome you as a security from Him,*[113] *and sending down on you water from heaven, to purify you thereby, and to put away from you the defilement of Satan, and to strengthen your hearts, and to confirm your feet.*

A. Yusuf Ali: *Remember He covered you with a sort of drowsiness, to give you calm as from Himself, and he caused rain to descend on you from heaven, to clean you therewith, to remove from you the stain of Satan, to strengthen your hearts, and to plant your feet firmly therewith.*

Here, the problem is with the phrase *wa yuthabbita bihi'l-aqdāma*. This is not, in reality, a lexicological problem, but the issue has to do with the interpretation of the expression. Abū ʿUbayda explains it figuratively: 'He pours and brings down on them endurance, so that they should be firm against the enemy' (*yufrighu ʿalayhimi'l-ṣabra wa yunazaziluhu ʿalayhim fa-yathbutūna li-ʿaduwwihim*).[114] Ṭabarī rejects that interpretation absolutely,[115] 'because it is not in accordance with that of the exegetes among the Companions and Followers who were exegetes (*qawlun khilāfun li-qawli jamīʿi ahli al-taʾwīli mina ṣaḥābati wa'l-tābiʿīna*)'.[116] So, here, Ṭabarī refuses to accept this figurative sense over the proper sense given by these early exegetes: by sending rain, God has made it possible for the rain and sand to adhere together (*talbīd*), so that the feet of the Muslims and those of their mounts would not sink in the sand (*ḥattā lā tasūkha fīhi aqdāmuhum*).[117]

As for Wāḥidī, he does not quote Abū ʿUbayda's intepretation at all,[118] but only declares that the exegetes (*mufassirūn*) explain that the believers had settled on a sandhill (*kathīb*) and that their feet sank in the sand; the rain made the sand compact (*labbadahu'l-maṭaru*), so that their feet became firm.[119] It should be noted that al-Māturīdī (d. 333/944) takes into consideration both possibilities: the proper sense: 'the feet were rendered firm' (*ḥaqīqat tathbīt al-aqdām*) and the figurative sense: their 'perseverance' in what they had to do (*al-thabāt ʿalā mā hum ʿalayhi*).[120]

8. Q. 12:49 – *fīhi yughāthu'l-nāsu*

> *Thumma yaʾtī min baʿdi dhālika ʿāmun fīhi yughāthu'l-nāsu wa fīhi yaʿṣirūna.*
>
> Arberry: *Then thereafter there shall come a year wherein the people will be succoured and press in season.*
>
> Other possible translations of *fīhi yughāthu'l-nāsu* include: *the people will have plenteous crops* (Pickthall); *the people will have abundant water* (A. Yusuf Ali).

This verse is part of the dream of Pharaoh interpreted by Joseph. Abdullah Yusuf Ali, summarising and historicising the traditional interpretations of the early exegetes, comments:

> This is a symbol of a very abundant year, following the seven years of drought. The Nile must have brought abundant fertilising waters and silt from its upper reaches, and there was probably some rain also in Lower Egypt. The vine and the olive trees, which must have suffered in the drought, now revived, and yielded their juice and their oil; among the annuals, also, the oil seeds, such as linseed, sesame, and the castor oil plant, must have been grown, as there was irrigated land to spare from the

> abundant grain crops. And the people's spirits revived, to enjoy the finer products of the earth, when their absolute necessities had been more than met in their grain crops.[121]

Ṭabarī, first of all, as usual, gives the interpretations of the early exegetes: '*fīhi yughāthu'l-nāsu* [means] with water and rain (*bi'l-maṭari wa'l-ghaythi*)'. Ibn Kathīr (d. 774/1373) understood this in the sense of 'water [or rain] came to them' (*ya'tīhimi'l-ghaythu*);[122] but here there is an ambiguity between *ghātha, yaghūthu* (to aid, to succour) and *ghātha yaghīthu* (to water), and this ambiguity is not taken into consideration by Ibn Kathīr, Ibn Abī Ḥātim al-Rāzī (d. 327/938) or Ṭabarī, who quotes four exegetical traditions in that sense.[123]

As for Wāḥidī, he does not give the early exegetes' interpretation of this expression, because he supposes that it is known and evident in a context of drought (*jadb*), refering only to Muqātil b. Sulaymān.[124] However, he quotes the philologian and lexicographer Ibn al-Sikkīt (d. 244/858, or Rajab 243, 246):[125]

> God watered the country [or: countries] with rain (*ghātha'llāhu'l-bilāda*),[126] *yurīthuhā ghaythan*, and it [refers to] when water/rain (*ghaythu*) falls upon it.[127] So the land was watered with rain, and it is watered (*wa qad ghītati'l-arḍu tughāthu ghaythan*[128]), and it is a land watered with rain (*wa hiya arḍun maghīthatun wa maghyūthatun*).[129]

Then Wāḥidī adds:

> According to this, *yughāthu'l-nāsu* has the meaning: 'They are showered with rain (*yumṭarūna*)'. But it is possible that the sentence *aghātha'llāhu* could have the [following] meaning: 'When He saves it [i.e. the country] from a distress or affliction (*idhā anqadhahu min karbin aw ghammin*)'; because He saves the people by it from the affliction of drought.'[130]

This second interpretation does not come from Ibn al-Sikkīt directly; he only quotes the saying: 'Somebody demanded succour from me, and I succoured him (*istaghāthanī fulānun fa-aghathtuhu*).'[131] In Azharī, the whole quotation is introduced by the following chain of authorities: al-Ḥarrānī on the authority of (*'an*) Ibn al-Sikkīt. We know from Azharī himself[132] that he obtained a licence of transmission for *Iṣlāḥ al-manṭiq* and other works by Ibn al-Sikkīt from Abū'l-Faḍl al-Mundhirī (d. Rajab 329/941)[133] 'save what he [al-Mundhirī] failed to transmit (*illā mā fātahu minha*)', which he got from Abū Shu'ayb al-Ḥarrānī (d. Dhū'l-Ḥijja 295/908).[134]

9. Q. 12:49 – *wa fīhi ya'ṣirūna*

Other possible translations of *wa fīhi ya'ṣirūna* include: *they will press* (*wine and oil*) (Pickthall and A. Yusuf Ali).

As for the phrase *wa fīhi ya'ṣirūna*, the issue is more complex. First of all, Ṭabarī gives two interpretations.[135] The first is that they press out grapes, or grease of sesame, oilseeds, etc.; this interpretation is given by Ibn 'Abbās, Mujāhid, al-Ḍaḥḥāk b. Muzāḥim (al-Hilālī al-Balkhī, d. 106/724 or other dates) and Qatāda. The second is that they milk (*yaḥlibūna*, 'they pull out milk', or *yaḥlubūna*, 'they milk'); this interpretation is given by Ibn 'Abbās. There are variant readings for *yā'ṣirūna*: Ibn 'Abbās reads *ta'ṣirūna* ('you press'), i.e. *taḥtalibūna* ('you pull out milk'); *ya'ṣirūna* is the reading of readers (*qurrā'*) of Medina, Basra and Kufa; *ta'ṣirūn* ('you press') is the reading of the majority of the Kufans (and Ibn 'Abbās, according to Ṭabarī); some read *yu'ṣarūna* ('they are watered with rain'), like Ja'far b. Muḥammad (al-Ṣādiq, d. 148/765), al-A'raj ('Abd al-Raḥmān b. Hurmuz al-Madanī, d. 117/735), 'Īsā b. 'Umar (al-Hamdānī al-Kūfī, d. 156/772) and Sa'īd b. Jubayr (al-Asadī al-Kūfī, d. ca. 95/713); and lastly there is also the reading *tu'ṣarūn* ('you were watered with rain'), given by 'Īsā b. 'Umar.[136] Of these five variant readings, Ṭabarī permits *ta'ṣirūna* and *ta'ṣirūn* because they are received among the metropolitan readers, and both give the same meaning, even if their pronunciation is diffferent (*li-annahumā qirā'atāni mustafīḍatāni fi qara'ati'l-amṣāri bi-ttifāqi'l-ma'nā, wa ini'khtalafati'l-alfāẓū bi-himā*). However, he rejects the third reading (*yu'ṣarūna*) entirely, because it is in opposition to that of the metropolitan readers (*wa hādhihi'l-qirā'atu lā astajīzu'l-qirā'ata bihā*).[137] We know that the Basran grammarian and exegete Quṭrub (d. 206/821)[138] understood it as *yumṭarūna* ('they are watered with rain').

Ṭabarī then gives two semantic possibilities: 'If you want, you can infer it from (*akhadhtahu min*) *al-ʿuṣra* and *al-ʿaṣar* ("a refuge, a place of safety"),[139] for rescue and salvation (*li-manjāt*, with *tāʾ marbūṭa*); but if you want, you can infer it from *ʿaṣarati'l-saḥābu māʾan ʿalayhim* ("the clouds expressed water on them").'[140] But there is another Basran who is a cause of wrath for Ṭabarī, who declares:

> Somebody who has no knowledge of what the early exegetes have said and who interprets the Qur'an with his own opinion, basing himself on the practice of the language of the Arabs, links the meaning of *wa fīhi yaʿṣirūna* to [the phrase] 'in it they are rescued from drought and famine by the rain' (*fīhi yanjawnā mina'l-jadbi wa'l-qaḥṭi bi'l-ghaythi*), and he alleges that this word comes from *al-ʿaṣar* and *al-ʿuṣra*, the meaning of which is 'rescue' (*al-najāt*), as in the verse of Abū Zubayd al-Ṭāʾī:[141]
>
> *Ṣādiyan yastaghīthu ghayra mughātin*
> *wa laqad kāna ʿuṣrata'l-manjūdi.*
>
> He appeals for help a thirsty [person] who cannot help,
> This was the rescue of the distressed (or vanquished).[142]

Ṭabarī concludes that this interpretation of the Qur'anic word is 'sufficient evidence of his mistake' (*wa dhālika'l-taʾwīlu yakfī mina'l-shāhidati ʿalā khaṭaʾih*). Of course, this unnamed Basran is Abū ʿUbayda.[143]

As for Wāḥidī, concerning *fīhī yaʿṣirūna*, he mentions, with no details, the interpretations of 'most of the exegetes',[144] among whom are Ibn ʿAbbās, Mujāhid and Qatāda. Then he quotes Abū ʿUbayda with the second hemistich of Abū Zubayd's verse cited by Ṭabarī, as well as a verse by Labīd, as found in Abū ʿUbayda. He also adds a verse by ʿAdī b. Zayd, which he could have taken from either Zajjāj[145] or from Azharī.[146] Indeed Wāḥidī refers to 'Abū Isḥāq', i.e. Zajjāj, who mentions this interpretation, and similarly to that of Abū ʿUbayda. But Zajjāj gives the line of poetry before, rather than after, the interpretation of the exegetes.[147]

Wāḥidī then quotes Abū ʿUbayd: '*yaʿṣirūn* [means] they "reach what they like and they take what they desire"', and a verse of Ibn Aḥmar,[148] quoted by Abū ʿUbayd.[149] We note that Wāḥidī has no reaction against the interpretation of Abū ʿUbayda, contrary to Ṭabarī's strong criticism. The reason is that he had already given the interpretation of Q. 12:36, '*I dreamed that I was pressing wine*' (*innī arānī aʿṣiru khamran*),[150] quoting first of all, as he often does in his *Basīṭ* (and as too does Azharī), Layth (b. Muẓaffar): 'One says: *ʿaṣartu'l-ʿinaba wa ʿaṣartuhu*, if you press it for yourself; and *iʿtaṣartu*, if it is pressed for you; and *al-ʿuṣāra* (expressed juice, or the like)[151] is what is expressed from a thing in squeezing it (*mā yuḥlabu ʿani'l-shay'i bi-ʿaṣrihi*).' Then Wāḥidī says that the exegetes and the *ahl al-maʿānī* have given three interpretations for this: firstly, what has been pressed is the grape whose juice produces wine; secondly, the Arabs called a thing by the name of the produce which is derived from it, for instance they say somebody 'cooks bricks', meaning by this, unburnt bricks (*fulānu yaṭbakhu'l-ājurra yaʿnūna'l-labina*), so they use the name of the derivate (*al-faʿrʿ*) for that of the root (*al-aṣl*).[152] We could say that this is a kind of metonymy. Lastly, among the Arabs some call grapes, wine.[153] The Qurashīs used this manner of speech, and for that reason 'God mentioned it in His Book'.[154] Or according to Ḍaḥḥāk, 'The Qur'an has been revealed in every language (*lisān*), and in the manner of speech of some of them, grape is called *khamr*'.[155] Fakhr al-Dīn al-Rāzī (d. 606/1209), who quotes Wāḥidī often, gives the same three possibilities of interpretation when discussing this phrase and probably took them from Wāḥidī, although he does not quote him here.[156]

10. Q. 2:3 – *īmān*

Alladhīna yu'minūna bi'l-ghaybi wa yuqīmūna'l-ṣalata wa mimmā razaqnāhum yunfiqūna.

Arberry, Pickthall and A. Yusuf Ali: *Who believe in the unseen, and perform the prayer, and expend of that We have provided them;*

For both Ṭabarī and Wāḥidī *īmān* means assent (*taṣdīq*; German: *Fürwahrhalten*), but Ṭabarī is more concerned with refuting those for whom the essence of *īmān*, *per se*, is the formal profession of faith, consisting in word, as we have shown in our book on Ṭabarī.[157]

Of course, as Sunnis, Ṭabarī and Wāḥidī agree that *īmān* consists in word and act, and that is in the formal profession of belief and in the fulfilment of the duties prescribed by law. But Wāḥidī realised that the Qur'an has introduced a new meaning of *īmān*: 'the meaning of assent cannot be known by the way of language, save through examination and reflection', an expression by Abū'l-Qāsim al-Zajjājī which Wāḥidī appreciates, as we will see below.

Wāḥidī refers first of all to Azharī: 'The scholars agree (*ittafaqa'l-'ulamā'u*) that *īmān* means 'assent', for instance: *wa-mā anta bi-mu'min lanā* (Q. 12:17), that is, "you do not believe our saying", or, "you do not accept it as true" (*ay muṣaddiqun*).'[158] Wāḥidī continues:

> And the meaning of assent (*taṣdīq*) is that he who hears believes the truthfulness of the informant in what he informs (*huwa 'tiqādu'l-sāmi'i ṣidqa'l-mukhbiri*). Its basis in the language is a state of quietness towards a thing (*al-ṭuma'nīna ilā'l-shay'*). Therefore they say: *amina, ya'manu, amnan* when one becomes quiet and fear leaves him (*idhā'ṭma'anna wa zāla'l-khawfu 'anhu*). [You say]: I render somebody secure (or safe; *āmantu fulānan*),[159] if you cause him to be quiet and calm. [And you say]: He believes in (*āmana bi-*) God and His Messenger, if he gives his assent to them, being confident and quiet with it (*ṣaddaqahumā wāthiqan bi-dhālika muṭma'innan ilayhi*).[160]

Then Wāḥidī[161] quotes a poetic verse recited by Ibn al-Anbārī (Abū Bakr Muḥammad b. al-Qāsim, d. 328/940),[162] followed by a declaration by Abū 'Alī al-Fārisī (d. 377/987):[163]

> It is possible from the point of view of linguistic analogy[164] that *āmana*, 'he got trustiness' (*ṣāra dhā amānatin*), is similar to *ajdaba* and *a'āha*, that is, he got a defect (*'āha*) in his property, and so *āmana*, he got security for himself and his property in expressing the two testimonies (*bi-iẓhāri'l-shahādayni*), as you say *aslama*, that is, he got peace (*ṣāra dhā salamin*),[165] he ceased to be at war (*kharaja 'an an yakūna ḥarban*, i.e. he ceased to be considered an enemy of Islam), one whose life and property can be lawfully taken (*mustaḥill al-dami wa'l-māli*).[166]

For Wāḥidī, Azharī's explanation of the meaning of *īmān* is the better one, but he considers Zajjājī's[167] to be clearer (*bimā huwa aẓharu mimmā dhakarahu'l-Azhariyyu*):

> The meaning of assent cannot be known by the way of language, save through examination and reflection (*min ṭarīqi'l-lughati illā bi'l-iʿtibāri wa'l-naẓari*), because its proper sense is not that of assent. Indeed, if you give assent to somebody concerning what he informs you, you do not say *āmantu bihi* ('I believe in him'); but if you consider the expression of the construction of this word and examine its morphology well, [its meaning] can become clear to you from its inner meaning, which refers to the assent (*lākinnaka idhā naẓarta ilā mawḍūʿi hādhihi'l-kalimati wa ṣarrafta ḥaqqa'l-taṣrifī, ẓahara laka min bāṭinihā maʿnan yarjiʿu ilā'l-taṣdīqi*).[168]

In other words: the proper sense of *īmān* is not solely assent, but assent can be one of its meanings.

It will be useful to give some background to discussions about the meaning of *īmān* in Arabic, as it generated much discussion, which can help us to understand Wāḥidī's position. The idea that a *mu'min* was, above all, before the advent of Islam, a person who grants *amān*, i.e. security, safe conduct, etc., is supported by 'an unusual and most interesting discussion on *mu'min*',[169] concerning one of the names (*ṣifāt*) of God, given by the Qarmaṭī (Ismaili) *dāʿī* and scholar Abū Ḥātim al-Rāzī (Aḥmad b. Ḥamdān b. Aḥmad al-Warsāmī al-Laythī, d. 322/933–4).[170] We know little about him and his intellectual environment, save that he had been in contact with the grammarian Thaʿlab (d. 291/904) and the physician, philosopher and alchemist Abū Bakr al-Rāzī Muḥammad b. Zakariyyā' (d. 313/925 or 323/935).

We must emphasise here that the Ismaili Abū Ḥātim al-Rāzī called particular attention to the fact that Islam introduced new words or new significations for existing words in the Arabic language.[171] So too did Ibn Fāris (d. 395/1004) who was also from Rayy, in his well-known book on *fiqh al-lugha*.[172] For Abū Ḥātim al-Rāzī, the root of *al-mu'min* is *'-m-n*, i.e. security, safety, protection, 'as if God gives His servants security, against treating them injuriously (*ka-annahu āmana*

ʿibādahu an yaẓlimahum)'.[173] According to Rāzī, it is said in Arabic: *āmana'l-amīru fulānan*, i.e. 'the *amīr* gave so-and-so security, that is, he granted him security'; this means that this man does not have to fear injustice (*ʿādiyatahu*), violence (*baṭshahu*) or attack (*saṭwatahu*) from the *amīr*. We are, of course here, in a context of tribal relations which marks the proper sense of *īmān* before Islam and in its beginnings, for instance, in the Constitution of Medina.

Abū Ḥātim al-Rāzī quotes Q. 6:82, *Those who have guaranteed security* (*alladhīna āmanū*) *and have not confused their security-guaranteeing* (*īmānahum*) *with injurious actions*.[174] God is called *mu'min*, and the servant/worshipper is as well, because the *amān* is between both God and the worshipper. This relation of *amān* also exists between the *mu'minūn*. Rāzī understands the original sense of *mu'min* as someone who accords physical security. This sense is also preserved in some prophetic traditions, such as: 'He will not enter Paradise whose neighbour is not secure (*man lā ya'manu jārahu*) from his wrongful conduct.'[175] Or more clearly: 'He does not believe until his neighbour is secure from his wrongful conduct (*lā yu'minu ḥattā ya'mana jāruhu bawā'iqahu*).'[176] Or in Abū Ḥātim al-Rāzī's version: 'Who is the *mu'min*? [The Prophet] said: The one whose neighbour is secure from his wrongful conduct (*man amina jāruhu bawā'iqahu*).'[177] Rāzī comments: 'The root of *īmān* comes from *amān* (security, safety).'

VII Conclusion

At the beginning of this chapter we emphasised the importance of the introduction of grammar and lexicography at different stages of Qur'anic exegesis and also the progressive Qur'anisation of Arabic lexicography. At the time of Azharī (d. 370/980), himself an exegete and a lexicographer, the Qur'anisation of lexicography arrived at its summits. As seen in the case studies, the exegesis and lexicography of Azharī had a great influence on Wāḥidī. However, Wāḥidī's formation in poetry and lexicography contributed to a certain tension in him between the exegete and the lexicographer. He could not be unaware of the very peculiar language and style of the Qur'an, often not pertaining to the system of the Arabic language, even if both language and style of this Book was, in his theological representation, 'inimitable'. Theodor Nöldeke (d. 1930) who, of course, did not believe in this dogma, could write: 'It is important that the healthy linguistic sense of the Arabs prevented them almost completely from imitating the oddities and weaknesses of the language of the Koran.'[178] This tension or this embarrassment between the *sensus linguae* and the dogma of the inimitability (*iʿjāz*) of the Qur'an is often discernible among those of the exegetes who had an excellent formation in Arabic, as was the case with Wāḥidī.

As for Ṭabarī, he was also a good grammarian of the 'Kufan' tradition, and also well-versed in lexicography, but, writing a century and a half earlier, he was above all concerned with affirming the superiority of the interpretations of the recognised ancient exegetes, so that the language of the Qur'an should not be submitted to the criteria of other manners of speaking (*lughāt*); this was one of the results of the dogma of the Qur'an's inimitability, which developed in the fourth/tenth century.[179]

NOTES

1 al-Wāḥidī, *al-Tafsīr al-basīṭ*, ed. Muḥammad Ṣāliḥ b. ʿAbd Allāh al-Fawzān *et al.* (Riyadh: Jāmiʿat al-Imām Muḥammad b. Suʿūd, 1430/2010).

2 Lothar Kopf, 'Religious Influences on Medieval Arabic Philology', *Studia Islamica* 5 (1956), pp. 33–59, at p. 33; reprinted in Moshe H. Goshen-Gottstein, ed., *Studies in Arabic and Hebrew Lexicography* (Jerusalem: The Hebrew University, 1976), pp. 19–45, at p. 19; Bernard George Weiss, 'Language in Orthodox Muslim Thought. A Study of "*Wadʿ al-lughah*" and its Development' (Unpublished PhD dissertation, Princeton University, 1966), pp. 20–35. See, however, Ramzi Baalbaki, 'Early Arab Lexicographers and the Use of Semitic Languages', *Berytus* 31 (1983), pp. 117–27, with examples of grammarians of Jewish, Syriac or 'Nabatean' origin (pp. 122–3).

3 Ibn ʿAbbās (attrib.), *Masāʾil Nāfiʿ b. al-Azraq ʿan ʿAbd Allāh Ibn ʿAbbās* (MS Ẓāhiriyya; recension of Abū Bakr ʿAbd Allāh b. Jaʿfar al-Khuttalī, d. 365/975), ed. Muḥammad A. al-Dālī (Limassol: al-Jaffān wa'l-Jābī, 1992); idem, *Masāʾil al-Imām al-Ṭastī ʿan asʾilat Nāfiʿ b. al-Azraq wa ajwibat ʿAbd Allāh Ibn ʿAbbās*, ed. ʿAbd al-Raḥmān ʿUmayra (Cairo: Dār al-Iʿtiṣām, n.d.); Angelika Neuwirth, 'Die *Masāʾil Nāfiʿ b. al-Azraq*. Éléments des "Portrait mythique d'Ibn ʿAbbās" oder ein Stück realer Literatur? Rückschlüsse aus einer bisher unbeachteten Handschrift', *Zeitschrift für Arabische Linguistik* 25 (1993), pp. 233–50.

4 In German: *umschreibende Tafsīr*. See Claude Gilliot, 'Kontinuität und Wandel in der "klassischen" islamischen Koranauslegung', *Der Islam* 85 (2010), pp. 1–155, at pp. 7ff.

5 Claude Gilliot, 'Exegesis of the Qur'ān: Classical and Medieval', *EQ*, vol. 2, p. 105.

6 On Mujāhid, see Claude Gilliot, 'Mujāhid's Exegesis: Origins, Paths of Transmission and Development of a Meccan Exegetical Tradition in its Human, Spiritual and Theological Environment' in Andreas Görke and Johanna Pink, eds, *Tafsīr and Islamic Intellectual History: Exploring the Boundaries of a Genre* (Oxford: Oxford University Press in association with the Institute of Ismaili Studies, 2014), pp. 63–111.

7 Claude Gilliot, 'Muqātil, grand exégète, traditionniste et théologien maudit', *Journal Asiatique* 279 (1991), pp. 39–92; Mehmet Akif Koç, 'A Comparison of the References to Muqātil b. Sulaymān (150/767) in the Exegesis of al-Thaʿlabī (427/1036) with Muqātil's Own Exegesis', *Journal of Semitic Studies* 53 (2008), pp. 69–101.

8 Abū ʿUbayda, *Majāz al-Qur'ān*, ed. Fū'ād Sazgīn [Fuat Sezgin] (Beirut: Mu'assasat al-Risāla, 1401/1981; orig. pub. Cairo: Muḥammad Sāmī Amīn al-Khānjī, 1954–62); John Wansbrough, '*Majāz al-Qur'ān*: Periphrastic Exegesis', *Bulletin of the School of Oriental and African Studies* 33 (1970), pp. 247–66; Claude Gilliot, *Exégèse, langue et théologie en islam: L'exégèse coranique de Tabari* (Paris: Vrin, 1990), pp. 96–7.

9 For the discussions on the meaning of *majāz* in Abū ʿUbayda among modern scholars, see Salvador Peña Martín, *Corán, palabra y verdad: Ibn al-Sid y el humanismo en al-Ándalus* (Madrid: Consejo Superior de Investigaciones Científicas, 2007), pp. 227–35; Wolfhart Heinrichs, 'On the Genesis of the *Ḥaqīqa-Majāz* Dichotomy', *Studia Islamica* 59 (1984), pp. 111–40; idem, 'Contacts between Scriptural Hermeneutics and Literary Theory in Islam: The Case of *Majāz*', *Zeitschrift für Geschichte der arabisch-islamischen Wissenschaften* 7 (1991–92), pp. 253–84; Gilliot, *Exégèse, langue et théologie en islam*, pp. 96–7.

10 Ibn Khayr, *Fahrasa mā rawāhu ʿan shuyūkhihi . . . [Index librorum de diversis scientiarum . . .*], ed. Fransciso Codera and Julián Ribera y Tarragó (Caesaraugustae [Saragossa]: n.p., 1894–95), pp. 59–60 and 134: *awwalu kitābin jumiʿa fī gharībi'l-Qur'āni wa maʿānīhi kitābu Abī ʿUbaydata Maʿmari'bni'l-Muthannā wa huwa Majāzu'l-Qur'āni*; cf. Abū ʿUbayda, *Majāz al-Qur'ān*, Introduction, vol. 1, pp. 19–20; al-Thaʿlabī, *al-Kashf wa'l-bayān ʿan tafsīr al-Qur'ān*, tr. and ed. Isaiah Goldfeld as *Qur'ānic Commentary in the Eastern Islamic Tradition of the First Four Centuries of the Hijra: An Annotated Edition of the Preface to al-Thaʿlabī's 'Kitāb al-Kashf wa'l-Bayān an Tafsīr al-Qur'ān'* (Acre: Srugy, 1984), pp. 56–7.

11 *Apud* Maymanī (see n. 13): 'Muṣallam', but without vocalisation.

12 Meaning 'palm shoot' (*fasīla*), according to Yāqūt al-Rūmī, *Muʿjam al-udabā' aw Irshād al-arīb ilā maʿrifat al-adīb*, ed. Iḥsān ʿAbbās (Beirut: Dār al-Gharb al-Islāmī, 1993), vol. 3, pp. 1307–8, no. 489.

13 His most complete name is given by ʿAbd al-ʿAzīz al-Maymanī in his edition of Abū ʿUbayd al-Bakrī, *Simṭ al-la'ālī fī sharḥ Amāli al-Qālī* (Cairo: Lajnat al-Ta'līf wa'l-Tarjama wa'l-Nashr, 1936), vol. 3, p. 87. On Damādh, see al-Zubaydī, *Ṭabaqāt al-naḥwiyyīn wa'l-lughawiyyīn*, ed. Muḥammad Abū'l-Faḍl Ibrāhīm (Cairo: M. Sāmī Amīn al-Khanjī, 1373/1954), p. 198; al-Qifṭī, *Inbāh al-ruwāt ʿalā anbāh al-nuḥāt*, ed. Muḥammad Abū'l-Faḍl Ibrāhīm (Cairo: Dār al-Fikr

al-ʿArabī, 1950–73), vol. 2, pp. 5–6, no. 249; Ibn Qutayba, *Kitāb ʿUyūn al-akhbār*, ed. A. Zakī al-ʿAdwī (Cairo: Dār al-Kutub, 1925–30), vol. 2, pp. 156–7; Abū'l-Faraj al-Iṣfahānī, *Kitāb al-Aghānī* (Cairo: Dār al-Kutub, 1927–74), vol. 13, p. 351 (*Akhbār al-Shamardal*); Qālī (Abū ʿAlī), *Kitāb Dhayl al-Amālī* (Cairo: Dār al-Kutub al-Miṣriyya, 1344/1926), vol. 1, pp. 17, 107 and 186. In Isaiah Goldfeld's edition of Thaʿlabī's introduction to his Qur'anic commentary, 'Salama b. Rufayʿ' should be corrected to 'Rufayʿ b. Salama'; Thaʿlabī–Goldfeld, *Qur'anic Commentary in the Eastern Islamic Tradition*, p. 57.

14 Mohammad-Nauman Khan, *Die exegetischen Teile des* Kitāb al-ʿAyn: *Zur ältesten philologischen Koranexegese* (Berlin: Klaus Schwarz Verlag, 1994), p. 83: '[. . .] daß uns mit dem exegetischen Teilkorpus des *Kitāb al-ʿAyn* ein reichhaltiger und facettenreicher "alter" Korankommentar vorliegt'.

15 Ibid.

16 Rafael Talmon, *Arabic Grammar in its Formative Age:* Kitāb al-ʿAyn *and its attribution to Ḫalīl b. Aḥmad* (Leiden: Brill, 1997), pp. 28, 97–9, 102–8 and 113–16.

17 al-Azharī, *Tahdhīb al-lugha*, ed. ʿAbd al-Ḥalīm al-Najjār *et al.* (Cairo: al-Mu'assasa al-Miṣriyya al-ʿĀmma li'l-Ta'līf, 1964–7), vol. 1, pp. 28 and 30; cf. ʿAbd Allāh Darwīsh, 'Muʿjam Tahdhīb al-lugha li-Abī Manṣūr al-Azharī', *Revue de l'Académie Arabe de Damas* (*RAAD*) 18 (1968), pp. 71–8.

18 Fuat Sezgin, *Geschichte des arabischen Schrifttums* [*GAS*] (Leiden: Brill, 1967–84), vol. 8, p. 159 (notice on Layth).

19 Talmon treats lexicography partly in *Arabic Grammar in its Formative Age*, Chapter 2, pp. 113–16.

20 Ibid., p. 280.

21 Khan, *Die exegetischen Teile des* Kitāb al-ʿAyn, p. 83.

22 Ibid., pp. 71–3.

23 Talmon, *Arabic Grammar in its Formative Age*, p. 23.

24 Azharī, *Tahdhīb al-lugha*, vol. 1, p. 29. With a slightly different wording *apud* Yāqūt, *Muʿjam al-udabā'*, vol. 6, pp. 2471–2, no. 1015, on Abū'l-Faḍl al-Harawī (d. 329/941), one of the pupils of Thaʿlab and Mubarrad, and one of the masters of Ḥarawī who quotes him very often; the answer of Thaʿlab is also quoted in idem, *Muʿjam al-udabā'*, vol. 5, p. 2254.

25 Azharī, *Tahdhīb al-lugha*, vol. 1, p. 29.

26 Claude Gilliot, 'Textes arabes anciens édités en Égypte au cours des années 1996 à 1999', *Mélanges de l'Institut dominicain d'études orientales du Caire* (*MIDEO*) 24 (2000), pp. 115–346, at pp. 183–7; idem, 'Textes arabes anciens édités en Égypte au cours des années 1999 à 2002', *Mélanges de l'Institut dominicain d'études orientales du Caire* (*MIDEO*) 25–26 (2004), pp. 193–475, at p. 199 (an addendum to *MIDEO* 24, no. 66); Jūda Muḥammad Muḥammad Mahdī, *al-Wāḥidī wa manhajuhu fī'l-tafsīr* (Cairo: Wizārat al-Awqāf, 1978); al-Bāriqī (ʿAbd al-Raḥmān b. Ḥasan b. ʿAbduh), *al-Naḥw fī'l-Tafsīr al-wasīṭ li'l-Wāḥidī* (Mecca: University of Umm al-Qurā, 1426–7/2005–6); Walid A. Saleh, 'The Last of the Nishapuri School of *Tafsīr*: Al-Wāḥidī (d. 468/1076) and His Significance in the History of Qur'anic Exegesis', *Journal of the American Oriental Society* 126 (2006), pp. 223–43.

27 Wāḥidī, *Basīṭ*, vol. 1, pp. 391–429 (introduction of the editor al-Fawzān). The whole intellectual autobiography of Wāḥidī can be found in his introduction to *al-Basīṭ*, vol. 1, pp. 391–429. A part of it has been copied by Yāqūt, *Muʿjam*

al-udabā', vol. 4, pp. 1661–4. See Walid A. Saleh, 'The Introduction of Wāḥidī's *al-Basīṭ*: An Edition, Translation and Commentary' in Karen Bauer, ed., *Aims, Methods and Contexts of Qur'anic Exegesis (2nd/8th–9th/15th c.)* (Oxford: Oxford University Press in association with the Institute of Ismaili Studies, 2013), pp. 67–100.

28 Wāḥidī, *Basīṭ*, vol. 1, p. 417; about him, pp. 417–19; Yāqūt, *Muʿjam al-udabā'*, vol. 4, pp. 1661–2; cf. Saleh, 'The Last of the Nishapuri School of *Tafsīr*', pp. 229–30.

29 Dhahabī, *Siyar aʿlām al-nubalā'*, ed. Shuʿayb al-Arna'ūṭ *et al.* (Beirut: Mu'assasat al-Risāla, 1401–9/1981–8), vol. 20, pp. 16–17, d. 529/1134–5, and not 539/1135 as written in Saleh, 'The Last of the Nishapuri School of *Tafsīr*', p. 229.

30 After correction of the edition of al-Ṣarīfīnī, *al-Muntakhab* (see n. 31) which has 'al-Arūnī'.

31 According to al-Ṣarīfīnī, *al-Muntakhab min al-siyāq li-ta'rīkh Naysābūr* (Beirut: Dār al-Kutub al-ʿIlmiyya, 1989), p. 85, no. 186. This date is given because al-Ḥaskānī said that he attended his lessons in 416; al-Ḥaskānī (Ibn al-Ḥadhdhā'ī Abū'l-Qāsim ʿUbayd Allāh b. ʿAbd Allāh b. Aḥmad b. Muḥammad al-Qurāshī al-ʿĀmirī al-Naysābūrī al-Ḥanafī, d. after 474/1081–2, or ca. 480/1087–8); Dhahabī, *Siyar*, vol. 18, pp. 268–9; Ibn Abī'l-Wafā' al-Qurashī, *al-Jawāhir al-muḍiyya fī ṭabaqāt al-ḥanafiyya*, ed. ʿAbd al-Fattāḥ Muḥammad al-Ḥulw (Cairo and Riyadh: n.p. 1978–88; 2nd edn. Cairo: Hajar, 1993), vol. 2, pp. 496–7, no. 897.

32 Qifṭī, *Inbāh al-ruwāt*, vol. 1, p. 154, no. 58

33 Dhahabī, *Ta'rīkh al-islām wa ṭabaqāt al-mashāhīr wa'l-aʿlām*, ed. Bashshār ʿAwwād Maʿrūf (Beirut: Dār al-Gharb al-Islāmī, 1424/2003), vol. 9, pp. 326–7; idem, *Siyar*, vol. 17, p. 389.

34 Ibn Maktūm (Tāj al-Dīn Abū Muḥammad ʿAbd Allāh b. ʿAbd al-Qādir b. ʿAbd Allāh b. Maktūm al-Qaysī al-Ḥanafī, born in Cairo, Dhū'l-Ḥijja 682/1284, d. 749/1348): Kahh (ʿUmar Riḍā Kaḥḥāla), *Muʿjam al-mu'allifīn* (Damascus: al-Maktaba al-ʿArabiyya, 1957–61; repr. Beirut: al-Muthannā and Dār Iḥyā' al-Turāth al-ʿArabī, n.d.), vol. 1, pp. 278–9; Carl Brockelmann, *Geschichte der arabischen Litteratur* (*GAL*). (Leiden: Brill, 1943–9), vol. 2, p. 110; *GAL-S* vol. 2, p. 137; Ibn Maktūm, *Talkhīṣ akhbār al-naḥwiyyīn*, MS 3069, *Ta'rīkh Taymūr* (Cairo: Dār al-Kutub), fol. 18, used by Abū'l-Faḍl Ibrāhīm in his edition of Qifṭī, *Inbāh al-ruwāt*, vol. 4, p. 418.

35 Cf. Qifṭī, *Inbāh al-ruwāt*, vol. 1, p. 154.

36 al-Suyūṭī, *Bughyat al-wuʿāt fī ṭabaqāt al-lughawiyyīn wa'l-nuḥāt*, ed. Muḥammad Abū'l-Faḍl Ibrāhīm (Cairo: Maṭbaʿat ʿĪsā al-Ḥalabī, 1964–5), vol. 1, p. 369, no. 720.

37 Abū Manṣūr Muḥammad b. Aḥmad b. Ṭalḥa b. Nūḥ b. al-Azhar (or Muḥammad b. Aḥmad b. al-Azhar b. Ṭalḥa b. Nūḥ) al-Harawī al-Shāfiʿī; R. Blachère, 'al-Azharī', *EI²*, vol. 1, p. 845 (French edn); Ibn Khallikān, *Wafayāt al-aʿyān wa anbā' abnā' al-zamān*, ed. Iḥsān ʿAbbās (Beirut: Dār Ṣādir, 1968–77), vol. 4, pp. 334–6, no. 639; Qifṭī, *Inbāh al-ruwāt*, vol. 4, pp. 177–81, no. 953; Yaqūt, *Muʿjam al-udabā'*, vol. 5, pp. 2321–2, no. 965; Dhahabī, *Siyar*, vol. 16, pp. 315–17; al-Subkī, *Ṭabaqāt al-shāfiʿiyya al-kubrā*, ed. Maḥmūd Muḥammad al-Ṭināḥī and ʿAbd al-Fattāḥ al-Ḥulw (Cairo: ʿIsā al-Bābī al-Ḥalabī, 1964–76), vol. 3, pp. 63–8, no. 107; Suyūṭī, *Bughyat al-wuʿāt*, vol. 1, pp. 19–20, no. 29; al-Dāwūdī,

Ṭabaqāt al-mufassirīn, ed. ʿAlī Muḥammad ʿUmar (Cairo: Maktabat Wahba, 1392/1972), vol. 2, pp. 61–3; repr. 2008, vol. 2, pp. 53–5, no. 431.

38 Yaqūt, *Muʿjam al-udabāʾ*, vol. 5, p. 2322; Subkī, *Ṭabaqāt*, vol. 3, p. 64; Suyūṭī, *Bughyat al-wuʿāt*, vol. 1, p. 30; Dāwūdī, *Ṭabaqāt al-mufassirīn* (1972), vol. 2, p. 62; ibid. (2008), vol. 2, p. 54; Ḥājjī Khalīfa, *Kashf al-ẓunūn ʿan asāmī'l-kutub wa'l-funūn*, ed. and tr. Gustav Flügel as *Lexicon Bibliographicum et Encyclopaedicum* (Leipzig: Oriental Translation Fund of Great Britain and Ireland, 1835–58), vol. 2, p. 389, no. 3473.

39 Ibn Khallikān, *Wafayāt al-aʿyān*, vol. 4, p. 335; Qifṭī, *Inbāh al-ruwāt*, vol. 4, p. 181; Dhahabī, *Siyar*, vol. 16, p. 316.

40 al-Azharī, *Maʿānī al-qirāʾāt*, ed. Muṣṭafā Darwīsh and ʿAwaḍ b. Ḥamad al-Qawzī (Cairo: Maṭābiʿ Dār al-Maʿārif, 1991–3).

41 Wāḥidī, *Basīṭ*, vol. 1, p. 427. Azharī, *Tahdhīb al-lugha* was read in the presence of the author by the best scholars of Harāt, like Abū ʿUbayd al-Harawī (Aḥmad b. Muḥammad al-Bāshānī/al-Fāshānī al-Shāfiʿī al-Muʾaddib, d. 6 Rajab 401/13 February 1011; *GAL*, vol. 1, p. 130; *GAL-S*, vol. 1, p. 200; Dhahabī, *Siyar*, vol. 17, pp. 146–7), the author of *Kitāb al-Gharibayn*, and also one the transmitters of *Tahdhīb al-lugha*; Qifṭī, *Inbāh al-ruwāt*, vol. 4, p. 179; cf. Abū ʿUbayd al-Harawī, *Kitāb al-Gharībayn*, ed. Maḥmūd Muḥammad al-Tinaḥī (Cairo: Lajnat Iḥyāʾ al-Turāth al-Islāmī, 1970).

42 On the axioms in Ṭabarī's Commentary, see Gilliot, *Exégèse, langue et théologie en islam*, pp. 140–45, 175, 183–4, 202, *et passim*.

43 Jörg Kraemer, 'Studien zur altarabischen Lexicographie nach istanbuler und berliner Handschriften', *Oriens* 6 (1953), pp. 201–38, at pp. 207–8; Stefan Wild, 'Arabische Lexicographie' in Helmut Gätje, ed., *Grundriss der arabischen Philologie: II - Literaturwissenschaft* (Wiesbaden: Ludwig Reichert, 1987), pp. 136–47, at pp. 139–40; Amidu Sanni, 'The Arabic Science of Lexicography: State of the Art', *Islamic Studies* 31, no. 2 (1992), pp. 141–68, at pp. 145–9; Ḥusayn Naṣṣār, *al-Muʿjam al-ʿarabī: nashaʾtuhu wa taṭawwuruhu* (Cairo: Dār Miṣr li'l-Ṭibāʿa, 1965; repr. 1968), pp. 218–312.

44 Kraemer, 'Studien', pp. 209–10; Ramaḍān ʿAbd al-Tawwāb, *Das Kitāb al-Gharīb al-muṣannaf von Abū ʿUbaid und seine Bedeutung für die nationalarabische Lexikographie* (Munich: Heppenheim, 1962); Claude Gilliot, 'Textes arabes anciens édités en Égypte au cours des années 1987 à 1990', *Mélanges de l'Institut dominicain d'études orientales du Caire* (*MIDEO*) 20 (1991), pp. 301–504, no. 6 (*al-Gharīb al-muṣannaf*); idem, 'Textes arabes anciens publiés en Égypte au cours des années 1992 à 1994', *Mélanges de l'Institut dominicain d'études orientales du Caire* (*MIDEO*) 22 (1992), pp. 271–412, no. 72 (*Gharīb al-ḥadīth*, the only good and complete edn); see also idem, 'Textes arabes anciens édités en Égypte au cours des années 1996 à 1999', no. 88; Naṣṣār, *al-Muʿjam al-ʿarabī*, pp. 55–8, *et passim*, see index. On the transmission of Abū ʿUbayd's works to Azharī, see Azharī, *Tahdhīb al-lugha*, vol. 1, pp. 19–20.

45 For Wāḥidī's sources in his *Basīṭ*, see the introduction of the editor Muḥammad. b. Ṣāliḥ b. ʿAbd Allāh al-Fawzān, in *Basīṭ*, vol. 1, pp. 140–262.

46 Sezgin, *GAS*, vol. 8, pp. 101–5; vol. 9, pp. 85–6; al-Khaṭīb al-Baghdādi, *Taʾrīkh Baghdād*, ed. Muḥammad Saʿīd al-ʿUrfī (Cairo: Maṭbaʿat al-Saʿāda and Maktabat Amīn al-Khānjī, 1931–49; repr. Beirut: Dār al-Kitāb al-ʿArabī, 1970–80), vol. 2, pp. 195–7, no. 621; Dhahabī, *Siyar*, vol. 15, pp. 96–7; Kraemer, 'Studien',

pp. 210–12; Naṣṣār, *al-Muʿjam al-ʿarabī*, pp. 83–5 *et passim*; Ramaḍān ʿAbd al-Tawwāb, in his introduction to *al-Gharīb al-muṣannaf* (Cairo: Maktabat al-Thaqāfa al-Dīniyya, 1989), vol. 1, pp. 186–7; Sanni, 'The Arabic Science of Lexicography', pp. 140–50.

47 Kraemer, 'Studien', pp. 210–12; Naṣṣār, *al-Muʿjam al-ʿarabī*, pp. 332–59, *et passim*; ʿAbd al-Tawwāb, in *al-Gharīb al-muṣannaf*, vol. 1, pp. 189–91; Sanni, 'The Arabic Science of Lexicography', p. 151.

48 As for Azharī, he declares that what he borrows from Zajjāj in exegetical matters comes from his *Maʿānī al-Qurʾān* (*wa mā waqaʿa fī kitābī lahu min tafsīr al-Qurʾān fa-huwa min kitābihi*); *Tahdhīb al-lugha*, vol. 1, p. 27.

49 See the introduction by the editor al-Fawzān, in *Basīṭ*, vol. 1.

50 Saleh, 'The Last of the Nishapuri School of *Tafsīr*', p. 231.

51 Ibid., p. 243.

52 A.J. Arberry, tr., *The Koran Interpreted* (New York: Macmillan Publishing Company, 1955). In this chapter, translations from the Qur'an are taken from Arberry unless otherwise stated. Other translations referred to are Pickthall, tr., *The Meaning of the Glorious Koran: An Explanatory Translation* (New York and London: A.A. Knopf, 1930); Abdullah Yusuf Ali, tr., *The Holy Qur'an: Translation and Commentary* (Lahore: 1934–37); Régis Blachère, tr., *Le Coran, Traduit de l'arabe par Régis Blachère* (Paris: Maisonneuve-Besson, 1957; orig. pub. 1949–50); Rudi Paret, tr., *Der Koran* (Stuttgart: Kohlhammer, 1962) and Friedrich Rückert, tr., *Der Koran*, ed. Hartmut Bobzin, 3rd edn. (Würzburg: Ergon, 2000; orig. pub. Frankfurt am Main: 1888).

53 Muḥammad b. Jarīr al-Ṭabarī, *Jāmiʿ al-bayān ʿan taʾwīl āy al-Qurʾān* [*Tasfīr*], ed. Maḥmūd Muḥammad Shākir and Aḥmad Muḥammad Shākir (Cairo: Dār al-Maʿārif, 1374–89/1954–69), vol. 8, p. 554; cf. al-Badr (Badr b. Nāṣir b. Badr), *Aqwāl Abī ʿUbayda fī Tafsīr al-Ṭabarī wa mawqifuhu minhā* (Riyadh: Jāmiʿat al-Imām Muḥammad b. Suʿūd, 1428/2007), p. 48, no. 1.

54 Abū ʿUbayda, *Majāz al-Qurʾān*, vol. 1, p. 132.

55 Ṭabarī, *Tafsīr*, ed. Shākir, vol. 8, pp. 554–5.

56 al-Farrāʾ (Abū Zakariyyāʾ Yaḥyā b. Ziyād al-Kūfī), *Maʿānī al-Qurʾān*, ed. Aḥmad Najātī and Muḥammad ʿAlī al-Najjār (Cairo: Maṭbaʿat Dār al-Kutub al-Miṣriyya, then al-Hayʾa al-Miṣriyya al-ʿĀmma li'l-Kitāb, 1955–73, repr. Beirut: ʿĀlam al-Kutub, 1980), vol. 1, p. 277.

57 Ibn Qutayba, *Tafsīr gharīb al-Qurʾān*, ed. al-Sayyid Aḥmad Ṣaqr (Beirut: Dār al-Kutub al-ʿIlmiyya, 1398/1978), p. 130.

58 Wāḥidī, *Basīṭ*, vol. 6, p. 612.

59 Rudi Paret, *Der Koran: Kommentar und Konkordanz*, repr. (Stuttgart: Kohlhammer, 1980), p. 315.

60 al-Biqāʿī, *Naẓm al-durar fī tanāsub al-āyāt wa'l-suwar*, ed. ʿAbd al-Razzāq Ghālib al-Mahdī (Beirut: Dār al-Kutub al-ʿIlmiyya, 1415/1995), vol. 4, pp. 477–80.

61 Muḥammad b. Jarīr al-Ṭabarī, *Jāmiʿ al-bayān ʿan taʾwīl āy al-Qurʾān* [*Tasfīr*], ed. Muṣṭafā al-Saqqā *et al.* (Cairo: Muṣṭafā al-Bābī al-Ḥalabī, 1373–7/1954–7), vol. 15, p. 265; cf. Badr, *Aqwāl Abī ʿUbayda*, pp. 47–8, no. 2.

62 Ṭabarī, *Tafsīr*, ed. Saqqā, vol. 15, p. 264.

63 Cf. Muqātil b. Sulaymān, *Tafsīr Muqātil b. Sulaymān*, ed. ʿAbd Allāh Maḥmūd Shiḥāta (Cairo: Muʾassasat al-Ḥalabī, 1967; repr. Cairo: al-Hayʾa al-Miṣriyya al-ʿĀmma li'l-Kitāb, 1979–89), vol. 2, p. 590: *yaʿnī wādiyan ʿamiqan fī jahannam.*

64 Ṭabarī, *Tafsīr*, ed. Saqqā, vol. 15, p. 264.
65 Ibn Manẓūr, *Lisān al-ʿArab* (Cairo: Dār al-Maʿārif, 1400–1/1979–80), vol. 6, p. 4755a: *wabiqa, yabiqu, wabqan* and *wuqūban*; and *wabiqa, wabqan*, and *istawbaqa: halaka*. And there are also other manners of speech (*lughāt*): *wabaqa, yawbiqu, wabaqan: awbaqahu: ahlakahu*. Cf. al-Zabīdī, *Tāj al-ʿarūs min jawāhir al-qāmūs*, ed. ʿAbd al-Sattār Aḥmad Farāj *et al.* (Kuwait: al-Majlis al-Waṭanī li'l-Thaqāfa wa'l-Funūn wa'l-Ādāb, 1385–1422/1965–2001), vol. 26, p. 448b: three manners of speech: *wabqan ka-waʿdin, wuqūban*, and *wabaqan ka-wajalin*, according to Jawharī. Then he adds *mawbiqan ka-mawʿidin: halaka ka-stawbaqa*, according to Ibn Sīda. Then he says (p. 449a): *wa'l-mawbiqu ka'l-majlisi: al-mahlik*. Arberry's translation of Q. 42:34 is slightly modified here.
66 Abū ʿUbayda, *Majāz al-Qur'ān*, vol. 1, p. 406, also: *wa ḥāda*; in Wāḥidī, *Basīṭ*, vol. 14, p. 55: *wa jāda*.
67 A mountain dominating Tābūk or in the territory of the Banū Sulaym; Yāqūt al-Rūmī, *Muʿjam al-buldān*, published as *Jacut's Geographisches Wörterbuch*, ed. Ferdinand Wüstenfeld (Leipzig: F.A. Brockhaus, 1866–73; repr. 1924), vol. 3, p. 282.
68 Ya'āru is said to be a mountain in the territory of the Banū Sulaym; ibid., vol. 4, p. 1031; Zabīdī, *Tāj al-ʿarūs*, vol. 14, p. 477a.
69 Azharī, *Tahdhīb al-lugha*, vol. 9, p. 355a.
70 Zabīdī, *Tāj al-ʿarūs*, vol. 4, p. 256b: Nudba or Nadba was the name of Khufāf's mother; Sezgin, *GAS*, vol. 2, pp. 243–4, has only Nadba. He is called by Abū ʿUbayda, *Majāz al-Qur'ān*, vol. 1, p. 28: Khufāf b. Nudba/Nadba al-Sulamī.
71 al-Aṣmaʿī (ʿAbd al-Malik b. Qurayb), *Dīwān al-Aṣmaʿiyyāt*, ed. Muḥammad Nabīl Ṭarīfī, repr. (Beirut: Dār Ṣādir, 1425/2005; orig. pub. 1423/2002), p. 30, verse 36.
72 *Mawbiqan* could be either 'a place of perdition' or simply 'perdition' because it can be seen as a *nomen loci* or a *maṣdar*; in the same way *baynahum* can be a *ẓarf* or *complemens agentis*, the last in the sense of: *wa ṣayyarnā waṣlahum ihlākan lahum*; see Abū'l-Baqā' al-ʿUkbarī, *Imlā' mā manna bihi al-Raḥmān min wujūh al-iʿrāb wa'l-qirā'āt fī jamīʿ al-Qur'ān*, ed. Ibrāhīm ʿAṭwa ʿAwaḍ (Cairo: Dār al-Ḥadīth, 1992; orig. pub. Cairo: Muṣṭafā al-Bābī al-Ḥalabī, 1380/1961; also pub. Beirut: Dār al-Kutub al-ʿIlmiyya, 1399/1979, without the name of the editor); the same work is also published with the title *al-Tibyān fī iʿrāb al-Qur'ān*, ed. ʿAlī Muḥammad al-Bijāwī (Cairo: ʿĪsā al-Bābī al-Ḥalabī, 1396/1976), vol. 2, p. 851.
73 Farrā', *Maʿānī al-Qur'ān*, vol. 2, p. 147. cf. al-Māturīdī (Abū Manṣūr), *Ta'wīlāt al-Qur'ān*, ed. Ahmet Vanlioğlu *et al.* (Istanbul: Mizan Yayinevi, Imam Ebû Hanîfe ve Imam Mâtürîdî Arastirma Vakfi, 2005–8), vol. 9, p. 73: 'Somebody has said: We have set their union (*waṣlahum*) in this world, the one which was between the associators and the idols *mawbiqan*, i.e. a place of perdition (*mahlikan*)'.
74 Wāḥidī, *Basīṭ*, vol. 14, pp. 52–5.
75 According to Ibn Abī Ḥātim, quoting Kaʿb: there are four rivers in Hell in which God torments its inhabitants: *ghalīẓ, mawbis, athām* and *ghayy*. Suyūṭī, *al-Durr al-manthūr fī'l-tafsīr al-ma'thūr*, ed. ʿAbd Allāh ʿAbd al-Muḥsin al-Turkī (Cairo: Dār Hajr, 1424/2003), vol. 9, p. 572 (not present *ad loc.* in the published commentary of Ibn Abī Ḥātim).

76 This last interpretation is also given by Ṭabarī, without the mention of pus and blood.

77 Cf. al-Qurṭubī, *al-Jāmiʿ li-aḥkām al-Qurʾān*, ed. Aḥmad al-Bardūnī *et al.*, 2nd edn (Cairo: al-Hayʾa al-Miṣriyya al-ʿĀmma liʾl-Kitāb, 1952–67), vol. 11, p. 2: *ay wa jaʿalnā baynaʾl-muʾminīn waʾl-kāfirīn ḥājizan.* Or: *wādiyan fīʾl-nār, wa jaʿalnā mā baynahum minaʾl-waṣlī waʾl-waddi fīʾl-dunyā mawbiqan mahlikan fīʾl-ākhirati*; Fīrūzābādī (attrib.; a commentary in a partly Karrāmī transmission), *Tanwīr al-miqbās min tafsīr Ibn ʿAbbās*, with, in the margin, Suyūṭī, *Kitāb Lubāb al-nuqūl fī asbāb al-nuzūl*, and Ibn Ḥazm, *Kitāb Fī maʿrifat al-nāsikh waʾl-mansūkh* (Cairo: Muṣṭafā al-Bābī al-Ḥalabī, 1370/1951), p. 186.

78 Wāḥidī, *Basīṭ*, vol. 14, p. 53.

79 Abū Isḥāq al-Zajjāj, *Maʿānī al-Qurʾān wa iʿrābuhu*, ed. ʿAbd al-Jalīl ʿAbduh Shalabī (Beirut: ʿĀlam al-Kutub, 1408/1988), vol. 3, p. 295.

80 Wāḥidī, *Basīṭ*, vol. 14, p. 54.

81 We could not find who gave this explanation. A much latter exegete says: 'an enmity which is destructive because of its violence'; Fakhr al-Dīn al-Rāzī, *Mafātīḥ al-ghayb* [*Tafsīr*], ed. Muḥammad Muḥyīʾl-Dīn ʿAbd al-Ḥamīd, ʿAlī Ibrāhīm al-Ṣāwī *et al.* (Cairo: al-Maṭbaʿat al-Bahiyya al-Miṣriyya, 1933–62), vol. 21, p. 139. We suggest that this explanation of Ḥasan's interpretation circulated among the Muʿtazilīs. We find it in the exegesis of Abū Jaʿfar al-Ṭūsī (d. 22 Muḥarram 460/2 December 1067), commenting on Ḥasan's interpertation: *wa ka-annahu qāla ʿadawatan muhlikatan*; al-Tūsī, *Tafsīr* [*al-Tibyān fī tafsīr al-Qurʾān*] repr. (Beirut: Dār Iḥyāʾ al-Turāth al-ʿArabī, n.d.; reprint of Najaf: al-Maṭbaʿa al-ʿIlmiyya, 1367–83/1957–63), vol. 7, p. 58; cf. al-Ṭabrisī (or Ṭabarsī, Amīn al-Dīn), *Tafsīr* [*Majmaʿ al-bayān fī tafsīr al-Qurʾān*] (Beirut: Dār Maktabat al-Ḥayāt, n. d.; reprint of Beirut: 1380/1961), vol. 15, p. 172. On him, see Bruce Fudge, *Qurʾānic Hermeneutics: Al-Ṭabrisī and the Craft of Commentary* (Abingdon and New York: Routledge, 2011).

82 Wāḥidī, *Basīṭ*, vol. 14, p. 55. Cf. al-Akhfash al-Awsaṭ, *Maʿānī al-Qurʾān*, ed. Fāʾiz Fāris, repr. (al-Ṣafāt, Kuwait: n.p., 1981; orig. pub. 1979), vol. 2, p. 397.

83 Abū ʿUbayda, *Majāz al-Qurʾān*, vol. 1, p. 414; Ṭabarī, *Tafsīr*, ed. Saqqā, vol. 16, p. 24; Ṭūsī, *Tafsīr*, vol. 7, p. 93.

84 Ṭabarī, *Tafsīr*, ed. Saqqā, vol. 16, pp. 25–6.

85 *Jurāzan* means 'sharp and cutting'.

86 Ṭabarī, *Tafsīr*, ed. Saqqā, vol. 16, p. 26.

87 Wāḥidī, *Basīṭ*, vol. 14, pp. 149–50.

88 *Yuqālu li-jānibiʾl-jabalayni idhā taḥādhayā: ṣudufāni wa ṣadafāni li-taṣādufihimā ay talāqihimā yulāqī hādhāʾl-jānibuʾl-jāniba lladhī yulāqīhi* (*wa mā baynahumā fajjun aw shiʿbum aw wādin*)*; wa min hādhā yuqālu: ṣādaftu fulānan, ay lāqītuhu.* Azharī, *Tahdhīb al-lugha*, vol. 12, p. 146 b; Wāḥidī, *Basīṭ*, vol. 14, p. 149. The part between brackets is not in Wāḥidī (in the translation: ['What is . . . valley']. Also, the text is slightly different in Wāḥidī.

89 Ibn al-Athīr (Majd al-Dīn), *al-Nihāya fī gharīb al-ḥadīth*, ed. Ṭāhir Aḥmad al-Zāwī and Maḥmūd Muḥammad al-Ṭināḥī (Cairo: ʿĪsā al-Bābī al-Ḥalabī, 1383–4/1963–4; repr. Beirut: Dār Iḥyāʾ al-Turāth al-ʿArabī, n.d.), vol. 3, p. 17; Qurṭubī, *al-Jāmiʿ*, p. 61; Abū ʿUbayd al-Qāsim b. Sallām, *Gharīb al-ḥadīth*, vol. 1, p. 208, no. 44: *innahu kāna idhā marra bi-hadafin* [a height] *māʾilin aw ṣadafin māʾilin asraʿaʾl-mashī*; Ibn Ḥanbal, *al-Musnad*, ed. Muḥammad al-Zuhrī al-Ghamrāwī

(Cairo: al-Maṭbaʿa al-Maymaniyya, 1313/1895), vol. 2, p. 256/ed. Aḥmad Muḥammad Shākir, Ḥamza A. al-Zayn *et al.* (Cairo: Dār al-Ḥadīth, 1416/1995), vol. 7, p. 282, no. 8651, according to Abū Hurayra: *marra bi-jidārin aw ḥāʾiṭin māʾilin fa-asraʿaʾl-mashī, wa qāla: innī akrahu mawtaʾl-fawāti.*

90 Wāḥidī, *Basīṭ*, vol. 14, pp. 149–50; Azharī, *Tahdhīb al-lugha*, vol. 12, p. 146b; Farrāʾ, *Maʿānī al-Qurʾān*, vol. 2, pp. 159–60.

91 Ṭabarī, *Tafsīr*, ed. Saqqā, vol. 29, p. 65.

92 We follow the reading of Sezgin, in Abū ʿUbayda, *Majāz al-Qurʾān*, vol. 2, p. 268; the edition of Ṭabarī, *Tafsīr*, ed. Saqqā, vol. 29, p. 65, has: *al-dabar* (with *fatḥa*) which is the plural of *dabara*, i.e. wounds on the the back of a camel; Zabīdī, *Tāj al-ʿarūs*, vol. 11, p. 256; cf. Badr, *Aqwāl Abī ʿUbayda*, p. 49.

93 Akhfash, *Maʿānī al-Qurʾān*, vol. 2, pp. 506–7; the edition by ʿAbd al-Amīr Muḥammad Amīn al-Ward (Beirut: ʿĀlam al-Kutub, 1405/1985), vol. 2, p. 713, has the erroneous vocalisation: *ʿufrīn*. It is said: *ʿifirrīn kifirrīn*, i.e. a wicked devil (*ʿifrīt khabīth*).

94 Wāḥidī, *Basīṭ*, vol. 22, pp. 182–5.

95 In Ibn Abī Ḥātim al-Rāzī, *Tafsīr al-Qurʾān al-ʿaẓīm*, ed. Asʿad Muḥammad al-Ṭayyib (Mecca and Riyadh: al-Maktaba al-ʿArabiyya al-Saʿūdiyya, 1417/1997), vol. 10, p. 3372, no. 18976: 'I do not know what *al-ghislīn* is, but I think it is *al-zaqqūm*', without a chain of authorities; ibid. no. 18978: [. . .] Khuṣayf ← Mujāhid ← Ibn ʿAbbās, 'I do not know what *al-ghislīn* is, but I think it is *al-zaqqūm*', taken over from Ibn Abī Ḥātim by Ibn Kathīr, *Tafsīr al-Qurʾān al-ʿaẓīm*, ed. ʿAbd al-ʿAzīz Ghunaym, Muḥammad A. ʿĀshūr and Muḥammad Ibrāhīm al-Bannā (Cairo: Dār al-Shaʿb, 1390/1971), vol. 8, p. 244.

96 Wāḥidī, *Basīṭ*, vol. 22, p. 183.

97 Quoted also from Kalbī by Fakhr al-Dīn al-Rāzī, *Tafsīr*, vol. 30, p. 116.

98 Wāḥidī, *Basīṭ*, vol. 22, p. 184; cf. Mubarrad, *al-Kāmil*, ed. Muḥammad A. al-Dālī (Beirut: Muʾassasat al-Risāla, 1406/1986), vol. 2, p. 634; also ed. William Wright as *The Kamil of El-Mubarrad* (Leipzig: F.A. Brockhaus, 1864–92), p. 292.

99 Zajjāj, *Maʿānī al-Qurʾān*, vol. 5, p. 218; taken over by Azharī, *Tahdhīb al-lugha*, vol. 8, p. 35b, who also gives the interpretation of Farrāʾ, *Maʿānī al-Qurʾān*, vol. 3, p. 183: *innahu mā yasilu min ṣadīdi ahliʾl-nāri.*

100 Cf. Farrāʾ, *Maʿānī al-Qurʾān*, vol. 3, p. 183.

101 Wāḥidī, *Basīṭ*, vol. 22, p. 184.

102 In Abū ʿUbayda, *Majāz al-Qurʾān*, vol. 1, p. 367: *mathalun yuqālu li-kulli mubtalan . . .*

103 Ṭabarī, *Tafsīr*, ed. Saqqā, vol. 14, p. 169.

104 Wāḥidī, *Basīṭ*, vol. 13, p. 185.

105 Thaʿlabī, *al-Kashf waʾl-bayān ʿan tafsīr al-Qurʾān*, ed. Abū Muḥammad b. ʿĀshūr, revised by Naẓīr al-Saʿidī (Beirut: Dār Iḥyāʾ al-Turāth al-ʿArabī, 2002), vol. 6, p. 39, both (Wāḥidī and Thaʿlabī) with a variant of two words.

106 Arberry has obviously taken over this translation from Edward William Lane, *An Arabic-English Lexicon* (Cambridge: Islamic Texts Society, 1984), vol. 2, p. 108c.

107 Elsaid M. Badawi and Muhammad Abdel-Haleem, *Arabic-English Dictionary of Qurʾanic Usage* (Leiden: Brill, 2008), p. 299: *adḥaḍa*: to refute, to invalidate, to argue down; Martin R. Zammit, *A Comparative Lexical Study of Qurʾānic Arabic* (Leiden: Brill, 2002), p. 172: to weaken, nullify, condemn.

108 Ṭabarī, *Tafsīr*, ed. Saqqā, vol. 15, pp. 267–8; Abū ʿUbayda, *Majāz al-Qurʾān*, vol. 1, p. 408; cf. Badr, *Aqwāl Abī ʿUbayda*, p. 50. Ṭabarī gives no attribution for the verse, but Abū ʿUbayda attributes it to Ṭarafa. Cf. Ibn Manẓūr, *Lisān al-ʿarab*, *sv. d-ḥ-ḍ*; al-Zamakhsharī, *Asās al-balāgha* (Beirut: Dār Ṣādir, 1979), p. 184a. There is another version in Thaʿlabī, *al-Kashf*, vol. 6, p. 178 (after our corrections): *Abā Mundhirin rumtaʾl-wafāʾa* [*apud* Ibn ʿĀdil: *wa*] *fa-hibtahu / wa ḥidta kamā ḥādaʾl-baʿīru minaʾl-daḥḍi*; Shawkānī, *Fatḥ al-qadīr al-jāmiʿ bayna fannayʾl-riwāya waʾl-dirāya fī ʿilm al-tafsīr* (Cairo: Muṣṭafā al-Bābī al-Ḥalabī, 1349/1930; repr. Beirut: Dār al-Fikr, 1973), vol. 3, p. 296; Ṭabrisī, *Tafsīr*, vol. 23, p. 83 (only the second hemistich); Ibn ʿĀdil, *al-Lubāb fī ʿulūm al-Kitāb*, ed. ʿĀdil Aḥmad ʿAbd al-Mawjūd and ʿAlī Muḥammad Muʿawwaḍ (Beirut: Dār al-Kutub al-ʿIlmiyya, 1419/1998), vol. 12, p. 516, has two different versions of the first hemistich: no. 3539: *Abā Mundhirin rumtaʾl-wafāʾa wa hibtahu*, and no. 3540: *waradtu wa najjāʾl-yashkuriyya ḥidhāruhu*; Ibn ʿAṭiyya al-Andalusī, *al-Muḥarrir al-wajīz*, ed. ʿAbd al-Salām ʿAbd al-Shāfī Muḥammad (Beirut: Dār al-Kutub al-ʿIlmiyya, 1413/1993), vol. 3, p. 525: *waradtu wa najjāʾl-yashkuriyyanakhāʾuhu* (without attribution); Qurṭubī, *al-Jāmiʿ*, vol. 9, p. 6: *Abā Mundhirin rumtaʾl-wafāʾa fa-hibtahu / wa ḥidta kamā ḥādaʾl-baʿīru minaʾl-daḥḍi* (without attribution). Abū Mundhir is ʿAmr b. al-Mundhir, called ʿAmr b. Hind Abū Hind, the prince of Ḥīra; called by Ṭarafa 'Abūʾl-Mundhir'; see A.J. Wensinck, "Amr b. Hind', *EI*[2], vol. 1, pp. 464–5 (French edn)/vol. 1, pp. 451–2 (English edn); Gustav Rothstein, *Die Dynastie der Laḥmiden in al-Ḥīra* (Berlin: Verlag von Reuther & Reichard, 1899), pp. 94–9.

109 Sezgin, *GAS*, vol. 2, p. 42.

110 Wāḥidī, *Basīṭ*, vol. 14, pp. 60–61.

111 Azharī, *Tahdhīb al-lugha*, vol. 4, p. 198.

112 Cf. Bukhārī, *Ṣaḥīḥ*, 9 (*Kitāb Mawāqīt al-ṣalāt*), *bāb* 11, in Ibn Ḥajar al-ʿAsqalānī, *Fatḥ al-bārī fī Ṣaḥīḥ al-Bukhārī*, ed. ʿAbd al-ʿAzīz b. Bāz *et al.*, numeration of the traditions by Muḥammad Fuʾād ʿAbd al-Bāqī, under the direction of Muḥibb al-Dīn al-Khaṭīb (Cairo: al-Maṭbaʿa al-Salafiyya, 1379–90/1960–70; repr. Beirut: al-Maʿrifa, n.d. [ca. 1980]), vol. 2, p. 22, no. 541 (*idhā zālatiʾl-shamsu*); tr. Octave Houdas and William Marçais as el-Bokhâri, *Les Traditions islamiques* (Paris: Adrien Maisonneuve, 1977; orig. pub. 1903–14), vol. 1, p. 191; Ibn Ḥanbal, *Musnad*, vol. 4, p. 450/vol. 15, p. 30, no. 19655: *kāna yuṣallīʾl-hajīru wa hiya llatī tadʿūnahuʾl-ūlā ḥina tadḥaḍuʾl-shamsu*. Lexicographers and exegetes also quote the following tradition to explain *d-ḥ-ḍ*: 'Under the bridge of Hell there is a way which is slippery and sliding (... *dhā daḥḍin wa mazallatin*)'; Ibn Ḥanbal, *Musnad*, vol. 5, p. 158/ vol. 15, p. 519, no. 21310; cf. Abū ʿUbayd, *Gharīb al-ḥadīth*, vol. 5 p. 48, no. 738.

113 Cf. Q. 3:154: *Then He sent down upon you, after grief, security – a slumber overcoming a party of you* ... (*thumma anzala ʿalaykum min baʿdiʾl-ghammi amanatan nuʿāsan yaghshā* ...).

114 Abū ʿUbayda, *Majāz al-Qurʾān*, vol. 1, p. 242.

115 Ṭabarī, *Tafsīr*, ed. Shākir, vol. 13, pp. 427–8.

116 These exegetical traditions have been given by Ṭabarī before; Ṭabarī, *Tafsīr*, ed. Shākir, vol. 13, pp. 422–7. For a summary of the traditional interpretations, see

Paret, *Der Koran: Kommentar und Konkordanz*, p. 8; Richard Bell, *A Commentary on the Qur'ān*, ed. Clifford Edmund Bosworth and Mervin Edwin John Richardson (Manchester: University of Manchester Press, 1991), vol. 1, p. 272.

117 Ṭabarī, *Tafsīr*, ed. Shākir, vol. 13, p. 428.

118 Wāḥidī, *Basīṭ*, vol. 10, pp. 49–52.

119 Ibid., vol. 10, p. 51.

120 Māturīdī, *Ta'wīlāt al-Qur'ān*, vol. 6, p. 181.

121 Abdullah Yusuf Ali, *The Holy Qur'an*, published as *The Meaning of the Glorious Qur'an. Text, Translation and Commentary*, pdf downloaded from http://www.islamicbulletin.org, p. 149, commentary no. 1706.

122 Ibn Kathīr, *Tafsīr*, vol. 4, p. 318. As in Ibn Abī Ḥātim al-Rāzī, *Tafsīr*, vol. 7, p. 2154, no. 11677, according to a version attributed to Ibn ʿAbbās: *yuṣībuhum fīhi ghaythun*.

123 Ṭabarī, *Tafsīr*, ed. Shākir, vol. 15, pp. 128–9, nos 1578–82.

124 Muqātil b. Sulaymān, *Tafsīr*, vol. 2, p. 338: *yaʿnī baʿda'l-sinīna'l-mujdibāti . . . yaʿni ahla Miṣra bi'l-maṭari*.

125 Ibn al-Sikkīt (Abū Yūsuf Yaʿqūb b. Isḥāq al-Baghdādī); Sezgin, *GAS*, vol. 8, pp. 129–36; vol. 9, pp. 137–8; Dhahabī, *Siyar*, vol. 12, pp. 16–19; Qifṭī, *Inbāh al-ruwāt*, vol. 4, pp. 56–63, no. 826.

126 *Apud* Ibn al-Sikkīt, *Iṣlāḥ al-manṭiq*, ed. Aḥmad Muḥammad Shākir and ʿAbd al-Salām Muḥammad Hārūn (Cairo: Dār al-Maʿārif, 1970; orig. pub. 1949; also reprinted 1987), p. 255: *wa qad ghātha . . .*; taken over by Azharī, *Tahdhīb al-lugha*, vol. 8, p. 176b: al-Ḥarrānī *ʿan* Ibn al-Sikkīt.

127 *Apud* Ibn al-Sikkīt: *idhā anzala bihā'l-ghaytha*.

128 *Ghaythan* is an addition by Wāḥidī.

129 Wāḥidī, *Basīṭ*, vol. 12, p. 139. This is also cited in Lane, *Arabic-English Lexicon*, vol. 2, p. 2314a–b, without the name of Ibn al-Sikkīt. Ibn al-Sikkīt, *Iṣlāḥ al-manṭiq*, p. 255, adds a tradition: al-Aṣmaʿī ← 'Īsā b. ʿUmar al-Thaqāfī and Abū ʿAmr Ibn al-ʿAlā', quoting Dhū'l-Rumma, who asked a woman of a tribe who answered in pure language: 'How was rain by you?' 'We were showered with the rain that we wanted (*ghithnā mā shi'nā*).'

130 Wāḥidī, *Basīṭ*, vol. 12, p. 139.

131 Ibn al-Sikkīt, *Iṣlāḥ al-manṭiq*, p. 255; Azharī, *Tahdhīb al-lugha*, vol. 8, p. 176b.

132 Azharī, *Tahdhīb al-lugha*, vol. 1, p. 23.

133 Muḥammad b. Abī Jaʿfar al-Ustādh Abū'l-Faḍl al-Mundhirī al-Harawī al-Lughawī al-Adīb, one of the pupils of Thaʿlab and Mubarrad; *GAL-S*, vol. 1, p. 189; al-Ṣafadī, *al-Wāfī bi'l-wafayāt* [*Das biographische Lexicon des Ṣalāḥaddin Ḫalīl Ibn Aibak aṣ-Ṣafadī*], ed. Helmut Ritter *et al.* (Istanbul, then Beirut: Deutsche Morgenländische Gesellschaft, Wiesbaden, then Stuttgart, 1931–2004), vol. 2, p. 297, no. 732; Yāqūt, *Muʿjam al-udabā'*, vol. 6, pp. 2471–2, no. 1015, with a list of his works.

134 ʿAbū Shuʿayb ʿAbd Allāh b. al-Ḥasan b. Abī Shuʿayb ʿAbd Allāh b. al-Ḥasan al-Umawī (*mawlā*) al-Ḥarrānī al-Baghdādī al-Mu'addib; al-Khaṭīb al-Baghdādī, *Ta'rīkh Baghdād*, vol. 9, pp. 435–7, no. 5052; Dhahabī, *Siyar*, vol. 13, pp. 536–7.

135 Ṭabarī, *Tafsīr*, ed. Shākir, vol. 16, pp. 129–30.

136 It should be noted that there are around thirteen different readings for this articulation (*ḥarf*); Abū'l-Baqā' al-ʿUkbarī, *Iʿrāb al-qirā'āt al-shawādhdh*, ed. Muḥammad al-Sayyid A. ʿAzzūz (Beirut: ʿĀlam al-Kutub, 1417/1996), vol. 1,

pp. 707–9: ʿAbd al-Laṭīf Muḥammad Khaṭīb, *Muʿjam al-qirāʾāt* (Damascus: Dār Saʿd al-Dīn li'l-Ṭibāʿa wa'l-Nashr wa'l-Tawzīʿ, 2002), vol. 4, pp. 280–82.

137 Some justify this reading by refering to Q. 78:14: *wa anzalnā mina'l-muʿṣirāti māʾan thajjājan*; Abū'l-Baqāʾ al-ʿUkbarī, *Iʿrāb al-qirāʾāt al-shawādhdh*, p. 708.

138 Abū ʿAlī Muḥammad b. al-Mustanīr Quṭrub; See Sezgin, *GAS*, vol. 8, pp. 61–7; and vol. 9, pp. 64–5.

139 Lane, *Arabic-English Lexicon*, vol. 1, pp. 2062c and 2061a, for *ʿaṣara*, to squeeze, but also *ʿaṣarahu*: he saved or preserved him.

140 Ibn Jinnī (Abū'l-Fatḥ ʿUthmān), *al-Muḥtasib fī tabyīn wujūh shawādhdh al-qirāʾāt*, ed. ʿAlī al-Najdī Nāṣif *et al.* (Cairo: al-Majlis al-Aʿlā, 1386–1415/1966–94), vol. 1, p. 345 with the verse by Abū Zubayd al-Ṭāʾī.

141 Abū Zubayd al-Ṭāʾī Ḥarmala b. al-Mundhir; Sezgin, *GAS*, vol. 2, pp. 161–2, in his *marthiyya* for his nephew al-Lajlāj. This verse is in al-Qurashī (Abū Zayd Muḥammad b. Abī'l-Khaṭṭāb), *Jamharat ashʿār al-ʿArab*, ed. ʿAlī Muḥammad al-Bijāwī, repr. (Cairo: Dār Nahḍat Miṣr, 1981; orig. pub. 1967), p. 583, v9; Luwīs Shaykhū [Louis Cheikho], *Shuʿarāʾ al-naṣrāniyya*, repr. (Beirut: Dār al-Mashriq, 1986; orig. pub. 1901), vol. 2, p. 87, l. 1.

142 Abū ʿUbayda quotes also a verse of Labīd, as too does Ṭabarī.

143 Abū ʿUbayda, *Majāz al-Qurʾān*, vol. 1, pp. 313–14.

144 Wāḥidī, *Basīṭ*, vol. 12, pp. 139–40.

145 Zajjāj, *Maʿānī al-Qurʾān*, vol. 3, p. 114.

146 Azharī, *Tahdhīb al-lugha*, vol. 2, pp. 15–16.

147 Zajjāj usually has the expression: *fī'l-tafsīri* (in the interpretation of the exegetes). He writes: 'Most of the exegesis which I have transmitted in this book comes from the book of exegesis transmitted from Aḥmad Ibn Ḥanbal' (*aktharu mā rawaytu fī hadhā'l-kitābi mina'l-tafsīr fa-huwa min kitābi'l-tafsīri ʿan Aḥmadi'bni Ḥanbalin*); Zajjāj, *Maʿānī al-Qurʾān*, vol. 4, p. 166. On Ibn Ḥanbal's *Tafsīr*, see Gilliot, 'Kontinuität und Wandel in der "klassichen" islamischen Koranauslegung', pp. 27–30, nos 28–9.

148 ʿAmr Ibn Aḥmar al-Bāhilī; Sezgin, *GAS*, vol. 2, pp. 195–6.

149 Abū ʿUbayd, *Gharīb al-ḥadīth*, vol. 5, p. 496; idem, *al-Gharīb al-muṣannaf*, ed. Muḥammad al-Mukhtār al-ʿUbaydī, repr. (Tunis: n.p., 1416/1996), vol. 1, p. 355; cf. Azharī, *Tahdhīb al-lugha*, vol. 2, p. 18b.

150 Wāḥidī, *Basīṭ*, vol. 12, pp. 113–14.

151 Lane, *Arabic-English Lexicon*, vol. 2, pp. 2002–3.

152 For this, Wāḥidī, *Basīṭ*, vol. 12, p. 113 refers to Zajjāj (*Maʿānī al-Qurʾān*, vol. 3, p. 109) and to Abū Bakr al-Anbārī (neither the editor of the *Basīṭ* nor I have been able to find this interpretation in the works of Abū Bakr Ibn al-Anbārī).

153 Zajjāj, *Maʿānī al-Qurʾān*, vol. 3, p. 109: a manner of speech in ʿUmān (*lughat ʿUmān*).

154 The Qur'an is supposed to be in the manner of speech of Quraysh.

155 Wāḥidī, *Basīṭ*, vol. 12, p. 114. Cf. Ṭabarī, *Tafsīr*, ed. Shākir, vol. 16, p. 97, nos 19274–5; It should be noted that the reading of Ibn Masʿūd is: *aʿṣiru ʿinaban*; Ṭabarī, *Tafsīr*, ed. Shākir, vol. 16, pp. 96–7.

156 Fakhr al-Dīn al-Rāzī, *Tafsīr*, vol. 18, p. 134; he also refers to Ḍaḥḥāk.

157 Gilliot, *Exégèse, langue et théologie en islam*, pp. 210–21.

158 Wāḥidī, *Basīṭ*, vol. 2, p. 59; Azharī, *Tahdhīb al-lugha*, vol. 15, p. 513, has: *wa'ttafaqa ahlu'l-ʿilmi min al-lughawiyyīn wa ghayruhum anna'l-īmāna maʿnāhu'l-taṣdīqu*, with reference to Q. 49:14.

159 Cf. Robert Bertram Serjeant, 'The "Constitution of Medina"', *Islamic Quarterly* 8 (1964), pp. 3–16, at p. 11; idem, 'The Sunnah Jāmiʿah, Pacts with the Yathrib Jews, and the Taḥrīm of Yathrib: Analysis and Translation of the Documents Comprised in the so called "Constitution of Medina"', *Bulletin of the School of Oriental and African Studies* 41 (1978), pp. 1–42, at p. 11: the meaning of *mu'min* includes the sense of 'giving security'; Meir Max Bravmann, *The Spiritual Background of Early Islam: Studies in Ancient Arab Concepts* (Leiden: Brill, 1972), pp. 26ff.: 'feeling secure', 'being given security'; Michael Lecker, *The 'Constitution of Medina': Muḥammad's First Legal Document* (Princeton, NJ: Darwin Press, 2004), p. 143: '*muwādaʿa* and *amān* are near-synonyms'.

160 Cf. al-Māturīdī, *Kitāb al-Tawḥīd*, ed. Bekir Topaloğlu and M. Aruçi (Ankara: Türkiye Diyanet Vakfi [Isam], 2003), p. 612; Toshihiko Izutsu, *The Concept of Belief in Islamic Theology: A Semantic Analysis of* Īmān *and* Islām (Tokyo: Keio Institute of Cultural and Linguistic Studies, 1965), p. 130.

161 Wāḥidī, *Basīṭ*, vol. 2, p. 60; (Ibn) al-Anbārī, *al-Zāhir fī maʿānī kalimāt al-nās*, ed. Ḥātim Ṣāliḥ al-Ḍāmin (Baghdad: Dār al-Rashīd, 1979), vol. 1, p. 203.

162 Abū Bakr Muḥammad b. al-Qāsim b. Bashshār al-Muqri' al-Naḥwī, died during the night of *al-aḍḥā*, 10 Dhū'l-Ḥijja 328/16 September 940.

163 Abū ʿAlī al-Fārisī al-Ḥasan b. Aḥmad b. ʿAbd al-Ghaffār al-Fasawī, d. 17 Rabīʿ I 377/17 July 987.

164 *Min ḥaythu qiyāsi'l-lughati* is an addition of Wāḥidī to the edited text of Azharī.

165 Or: *ṣāra silman wa kharaja ʿan an yakūna ḥarban*; Abū ʿAlī al-Fārisī, *al-Ḥujja fī'l-qurrā' al-sabʿa*, ed. Badr al-Dīn al-Qahwajī, Bashīr Juwayjātī *et al.* (Damascus: Dār al-Ma'mūn li'l-Turāth, 1404–19/1984–99), vol. 3, p. 177, at Q. 4:94.

166 Wāḥidī, *Basīṭ*, vol. 2, pp. 60–61; al-Fārisī, *al-Ḥujja*, vol. 1, p. 220; see also ed. ʿAlī al-Najdī Nāṣif *et al.* (Cairo: al-Hay'a al-Miṣriyya, 1403/1983), vol. 1, pp. 164–5.

167 Abū'l-Qāsim ʿAbd al-Raḥmān b. Isḥāq al-Zajjājī al-Baghdādī, d. Ramaḍan 340/952, in Tiberias, or Rajab 339/950 (according to Ibn ʿAsākir, *Ta'rīkh madīnat Dimashq*, ed. Muḥibb al-Dīn al-ʿAmrawī and ʿAlī Shīrī (Beirut: Dār al-Fikr, 1995–2001), vol. 34, p. 204 ult.: *ra'aytu fī kitābin ʿatikin*); Sezgin, *GAS*, vol. 8, pp. 105–6; and vol. 9, pp. 88–95; Dhahabī, *Siyar*, vol. 15, p. 4756; Ibn ʿAsākir, *Ta'rīkh madīnat Dimashq*, vol. 34, pp. 202–4, no. 3756. The editor of Wāḥidī's *Basīṭ* could not find this explanation in one of the edited works of Zajjājī. We have checked in his *Ishtiqāq asmā' Allāh*, ed. ʿAbd al-Ḥusayn al-Mubārak, repr. (Beirut: Mu'assasat al-Risāla, 1406/1986), pp. 221–7, *sub*: *al-mu'min* (one of God's names), but could not find this quotation, only some elements which are near to Zajjājī's argumentation, as given by Wāḥidī.

168 Wāḥidī, *Basīṭ*, vol. 2, pp. 61–2.

169 Serjeant, 'The Sunnah Jāmiʿah, Pacts with the Yathrib Jews, and the Taḥrīm of Yathrib', p. 13.

170 Kahh, *Muʿjam al-muʾallifīn*, vol. 1, pp. 210–11; Ibn Ḥajar, *Lisān al-mīzān*, ed. Amīr Ḥasan al-Nuʿmānī *et al.* (Hyderabad: Dāʾirat al-Maʿārif al-Niẓāmiyya, 1330–31/1912–13; repr. Beirut: Muʾassasat al-Aʿlamī, 1986), vol. 1, p. 164, no. 523. Above all, see Farhad Daftary, *Ismaili Literature: A Bibliography of Sources and Studies* (London: I.B. Tauris in association with the Institute of Ismaili Studies, 2004), pp. 147–8, and index.

171 Abū Ḥātim al-Rāzī, *Kitāb al-Zīna fīʾl-kalimāt al-islāmiyya al-ʿarabiyya*, ed. Ḥusayn b. Fayḍ Allāh al-Hamdānī al-Yaʿburī al-Ḥarrāzī (Cairo: Maṭbaʿat al-Risāla, 1957–8), vol. 1, pp. 127–8.

172 Ibn Fāris, *al-Ṣāḥibī fī fiqh al-lugha*, ed. Moustafa Chouémi (Beirut: A. Badran, 1964), pp. 778–81 and pp. 788–93.

173 Abū Ḥātim al-Rāzī, *Kitāb al-Zīna*, vol. 2, p. 70; cf. Daniel Gimaret, *Les noms divins en Islam* (Paris: Le Cerf, 1988), pp. 359–61.

174 Translation from Serjeant, 'The Sunnah Jāmiʿah, Pacts with the Yathrib Jews, and the Taḥrīm of Yathrib', p. 14.

175 al-Bukhārī, *al-Adab al-mufrad*, ed. Samīr b. Amīn al-Zuhayrī (Riyadh: Maktabat al-Maʿārif, 1419/1998), vol. 1, ch. 66, no. 121, p. 65.

176 Ibn Ḥanbal, *Musnad*, vol. 1, p. 387/vol. 3, p. 539, no. 3672; cf. A.J. Wensinck, ed., *Concordance et indices de la tradition musulmane* (Leiden: Brill, 1936–88), vol. 1, p. 232a.

177 Abū Ḥātim al-Rāzī, *Kitāb al-Zīna*, p. 71, ll. 12–13; cf. Ibn Ḥanbal, *Musnad*, vol. 4, p. 31/vol. 12, p. 537, no. 16324, according to Abū Shurayḥ al-Khuzāʿī: 'By God, he does not believe (three times). They said: Who is that, Messenger of God? He said: The neighbour who does not secure his neighbour from his *bawāʾiq* (wrongful conduct). They said: What are his *bawāʾiq*? He said: His mischief (*sharruhu*).' More versions are given in *Musnad*, vol. 7, pp. 520–21, no. 7865, in the long note of Aḥmad Muḥammad Shākir; Bukhārī, *Ṣaḥīḥ*, 78 (*Adāb*), 29, ed. Ludolf Krehl (Leiden: Brill, 1862–1908), vol. 4, p. 118; in Ibn Ḥajar, *Fāth al-bārī*, vol. 10, p. 443, no. 6016; cf. Lane, *Arabic-English Lexicon*, vol 1, p. 273c.

178 In the original German language: 'Wichtig is nun, daß der gesunde Sprachsinn der Araber sie fast ganz davor bewahrt hat, die eigentlichen Seltsamkeiten und Schwächen der Koransprache nachzuahmen.' Theodor Nöldeke, 'Zur Sprache des Korāns' in idem, *Neue Beiträge zur semitischen Sprachwissenschaft* (Strassburg: K.J. Trübner, 1910), pp. 1–30, at p. 22; translated into French by G.-H. Bousquet as *Remarques critiques sur le style et la syntaxe du Coran* (Paris: Maisonneuve, 1953), p. 34. The English translation here is taken from Ibn Warraq, tr., 'On the Language of the Koran' in Ibn Warraq, ed., *Which Koran? Variants, Manuscripts, Linguistics* (Amherst, NY, Prometheus Books, 2011), pp. 85–129, at p. 107.

179 See Gilliot, *Exégèse, langue et théologie*, pp. 138–45 (on Ṭabarī's axioms on the *variae lectiones* in the Qur'an), *et passim*.

6

Authority and the Defence of Readings in Medieval Qur'anic Exegesis: Lexicology and the Case of *Falaq* (Q. 113:1)*

S.R. BURGE

THE NOUN *falaq*, after which the penultimate chapter of the Qur'an, *Sūrat al-Falaq*, is most often named, is a fairly innocuous word. It is a *hapax legomenon*, although other cognates are used in the Qur'anic text.[1] It is often seen as a 'difficult' (*gharīb*) word, appearing in medieval works that explain such words, and is not particularly frequent in the hadith corpus or in poetry.[2] *Falaq* is interpreted in three main ways: with the meaning of 'dawn'; as a generic reference to Hell, or to a specific place in Hell; or referring to 'creation' (*khalq*) in general. The base meaning of the root *f-l-q* is 'to divide', and all three readings ('dawn', 'Hell' and 'creation') can be traced back to this base meaning, albeit in rather circuitous ways. 'Dawn' is the moment that divides night and day, or the moment when day 'breaks'. 'Hell' as a reading for *falaq* is not usually described as being a place 'divided' from heaven, but stems from a more complex idea of separation: two mountain peaks are divided or separated from each other with a valley in-between, and the *falaq* is this depression between the two mountains; in other words, an idea of depth, where Hell is a pit or an abyss.[3] For the idea of 'creation', there are other roots used in the Qur'an (e.g. *f-ṭ-r*) that

* I would like to thank Asma Hilali for her detailed comments on this article, and for comments I received at the American Oriental Society Annual Meeting in Boston, March 2011, where I first presented these ideas.

show that 'splitting' or 'dividing' is often a generative creative action.[4] So all three of the glosses can be related to the base meaning of the root, but, each gloss ('dawn', 'Hell' and 'creation') operates in markedly different semantic fields.

The most commonly held view in all periods of interpretation, both medieval and modern, is that the word refers to 'dawn', and this is the gloss most often found in contemporary English translations of the Qur'an, although more often in the form 'daybreak'.[5] The difficulty with trying to find the precise meaning of a word like *falaq* is that all three are feasible, and none has much potential for generating theological controversy. The word appears in the opening oath: *Say: 'I take refuge with the Lord of the falaq* (*aʿūdh bi-rabbi'l-falaq*)' (Q. 113:1). This is both an imperative and an oath, both typical features of the 'early Meccan' period.[6] The epithet '*rabb al-falaq*' is clearly an attribute of God, but whether it means 'Lord of Hell', 'Lord of Creation' or 'Lord of the Dawn' is largely immaterial: Qur'anic theology presumes all of these, so the different glosses do not compete on a theological level. This is not the case, of course, with all Qur'anic lexica; the interpretations of *qadar* are a prime example, such as its use in Q. 54:49: *Surely We have created everything in measure* (*qadar*). Here, the meaning of *qadar* is dependent on the theological leanings of the exegetes to the extent that 'the very same Qur'anic words are taken as proof texts for totally opposed stances'.[7]

In other contexts, some words have been the focus of debate for very different reasons. For example, the divine epithet *al-ṣamad* (Q. 112:2) received much attention because some modern Western scholars saw the title as potentially referring to a pre-Islamic 'High God',[8] but it drew considerably much less debate of any kind in the Muslim sources themselves.[9] In the Muslim sources, the discussion of the epithet *al-ṣamad* is linked to notions of divine unicity (*tawḥīd*) raised in the previous and subsequent verses of the sura: *Say: 'He is God, One . . .'* (Q. 112:1) and . . . *who has not begotten, and has not been begotten* . . . (Q. 112:3).[10] In this case, the focus of the Muslim exegetes is on situating the meaning of the word within the context of its theological surroundings. In contrast, 'orientalist' scholars focus on reading this verse in light of its pre-Islamic religious context, with the result that the interpretation of *ṣamad* becomes linked to ideas and theories concerning the historical and religious milieu of pre-Islamic Arabia, particularly the 'High God theory' of Montgomery Watt.[11]

The selection of *falaq* for this study is precisely because it is not contentious: the word is not the focus of a theological dispute (nor could it ever really be so), and it has not been the subject of any detailed comparative philological analysis by scholars. This means that *falaq* is almost entirely 'neutral'. The focus of this article is not necessarily on what the word *falaq* actually means, but to analyse how exegetes interpret *falaq*; how they come to make lexical decisions; and how they defend them. The neutrality of *falaq* provides a basis from which it is possible to see how medieval exegetes approach the task of lexicology on a theologically level field. The first part of this chapter presents a chronological study of exegeses that deal with *falaq*, followed by a short discussion of the treatment of the word in medieval Arabic lexicographical works and their relation to Qur'anic exegesis. The second part draws out two main themes that influence the way in which exegetes defend their lexical readings: firstly, a discussion of the importance of notions and sources of authority in the formation and defence of lexical readings; and secondly, the influence of Islamic philosophies of language on some exegetes.

The Meaning of *Falaq*: An Exegetical Survey

The survey that follows will be largely chronological, and the aim is to show various exegetes in the context of other exegetical works written around the same time. It is, then, possible to gain some understanding of the general trends that developed over time, particularly in the methodological approaches that different exegetes took when dealing with lexicological problems.[12] *Falaq* appears in one of the two suras known as the *muʿawwidhatān* ('the suras of protection'). According to traditional accounts, these two suras, *Surāt al-Falaq* and *Sūrat al-Nās* (Q. 113–14), were revealed after Muhammad was bewitched by a Jew called Labīd b. al-Aʿṣam.[13]

As it will be seen, not all commentators necessarily make very much of this context in their interpretation of *falaq*, but some do interpret the word in light of the bewitchment.

Early exegeses

The debate about *falaq* can be seen in two very early exegeses. I have excluded the exegetical comments and *tafsīr*s attributed to *muḥaddith*s such as ʿAbd Allāh Ibn ʿAbbās (d. ca. 68/687) and Wahb b. Munnabih (d. 110/728 or 114/732), on account of some concerns about their historical reliability.[14] However, I have included the exegeses of Zayd b. ʿAlī (d. 120/738),[15] and the Murjiʾī theologian and traditionist Muqātil b. Sulaymān (150/767), whose works are often seen as being authentic works. Indeed Muqātil's *tafsīr* is widely held to be the earliest extant exegesis of the Qur'an.[16]

Muqātil begins his exegesis with a reference to the *asbāb al-nuzūl* ('occasions of revelation') literature, which includes the story of Muhammad being bewitched by a Jew named Labīd b. al-Aʿṣam, although he makes no specific link between *falaq* and the bewitchment.[17] Muqātil's exegesis tends to supply only undefended glosses of complicated words in the text,[18] and on *falaq*, Muqātil simply states: '*falaq* meaning, [seek protection] with the Lord of Creation (*yaʿnī bi-rabbi'l-khalq*)'.[19] As will be seen in the following analysis, this interpretation is found in other exegeses, but it is not the most common gloss found for the word. However, without any defence of his lexical reading being provided it is difficult to make any judgements about how Muqātil came to gloss *falaq* in this way, and, more importantly, whether he knew of other glosses.

If Zayd b. ʿAlī's exegesis, *Tafsīr gharīb al-Qurʾān*, is accepted as being authentic, a much more detailed, contemporaneous explication of *falaq* can be seen:

> . . . *bi-rabbi'l-falaq*, its meaning is: 'with the Lord of the Dawn' (*maʿnāhu bi-rabbi'l-ṣubḥ*). It is said: *al-falaq* is a valley in Hell (*wādin fī Jahannam*); and it is [also said]: *al-falaq* is the path between two mountains (*al-ṭarīq bayn al-ṣuddayn*); and it is said: *al-falaq* is creation (*al-khalq*). Thus God, Most High, commands his Prophet to seek refuge from that evil.[20]

Such a full and lengthy treatment of the meaning of *falaq* may raise some concerns about its authenticity;[21] but, nevertheless, it raises some important issues. Firstly, Zayd appears to favour the gloss 'dawn', by mentioning it first and introducing it with a definitive *maʿnā* ('meaning'), as opposed to the slightly further removed *yuqālu* ('it is said'). Secondly, he makes it quite clear that the theological importance of the verse is in the apotropaic use of the sura to combat evil; for Zayd, it does not really appear to matter what *falaq* actually means. Perhaps this is why he includes the whole gamut of available options – the focus shifts from the meaning of the word *falaq* to the role of the phrase '*aʿūdhu bi-rabbi'l-falaq*' in seeking divine protection. In this case, the *sabab* of Labīd's bewitchment of Muhammad does not come to influence the actual lexical reading of the word *falaq*, but moves any significance *falaq* might have in itself to the significance of the phrase to combat magic. This is seen even more clearly in the exegesis of the early Shiʿi exegete Furāt b. Furāt al-Kūfī (fl. late third/ninth century), who provides no explanation of the word *falaq* whatsoever (nor of any other word in the sura), simply providing an account of Muhammad's bewitchment.[22] Lastly, Zayd, like Muqātil, provides no evidence or defence for his preferred lexical reading, nor indeed for any of his readings.

The formative period

It is in the exegeses of Sahl al-Tustarī (d. 283/896) and Muḥammad b. Jarīr al-Ṭabarī (d. 310/923) that a more systematic approach to the process of exegesis can be seen, and, in terms of lexical discussion, exegetes begin to provide evidence to support their lexical decisions. This is seen most commonly in their use of hadith. Ṭabarī begins his exegesis of this verse with the statement, 'The Most High said to his Prophet Muhammad: "Muhammad, Say: Protection is sought (*ustujīza*) *with the Lord of the falaq from the evil of what He has created* in creation (*min al-khalq*)". However, the interpreters (*ahl al-ta'wīl*) disagree on the meaning of *falaq*.'[23] As with Zayd b. ʿAlī's exegesis, there is a slight move away from the importance of *falaq* as a word in and of itself: the subsequent discussion of *falaq* is framed within the context of the statement that 'protection is sought *with the Lord of the falaq*'. Ṭabarī goes on to provide a detailed analysis of the possible interpretations, all supplied with supporting hadith, with both full and partial *isnāds* (see Table 1).

Table 1: A summary of Ṭabarī's glosses on *falaq*

Reading	No.	Specific gloss	Authority
Hell	1	prison (*sijn*) in Hell	Ibn ʿAbbās
	2	prison (*sijn*) in Hell	Ibn ʿAbbās
	3	house (*bayt*) in Hell	al-Jawlānī
	4	pit (*jubb*) in Hell	al-Suddī
	5	pit (*jubb*) in Hell	al-Suddī
	6	pit (*jubb*) in Hell	al-Suddī
	7	covered (*mughaṭa*) pit in Hell	Abū Hurayra
	8	house (*bayt*) in Hell	Kaʿb
	9	name (*hiya jahannam*)	Khaytham b. ʿAbd Allāh
dawn	10	dawn (*ṣubḥ*)	Ibn ʿAbbās
	11	dawn (*ṣubḥ*)	al-Ḥasan
	12	dawn (*ṣubḥ*)	Saʿīd b. Jubayr
	13	dawn (*ṣubḥ*)	Saʿīd b. Jubayr
	14	dawn (*ṣubḥ*)	Saʿīd b. Jubayr
	15	dawn (*ṣubḥ*)	Jābir
	16	dawn (*ṣubḥ*)	Jābir
	17	the splitter of the dawn (*fāliq al-ṣubḥ*)	al-Qurẓī; Q. 6:96
	18	dawn (*ṣubḥ*)	Mujāhid; Q. 6:96
	19	break of day (*falaq al-nahār*)	Qatāda
	20	break of dawn (*falaq al-ṣubḥ*)	Qatāda
	21	break of dawn (*falaq al-ṣubḥ*)	Ibn Zayd; Q. 6:96
creation	22	creation (*khalq*)	Ibn ʿAbbās

Ṭabarī concludes the discussion with a personal opinion, stating:

> The answer to the statements is this; it is said: God commanded his Prophet Muhammad, saying: '*Take refuge with the Lord of the falaq*. And *falaq* in the speech of the Arabs (*bī kalām al-'arab*) is the breaking of the dawn (*falaq al-subḥ*). The Arab says: 'It is clearer than the break of dawn'; and [the Arab also says: 'clearer] than the break (*faraq*) of dawn'. It is [also] possible that it is the name of a prison in Hell.[24]

This last statement is incredibly important because it makes it possible to look at Ṭabarī's presentation of the hadith concerning *falaq* in light of his own personal opinion. It is clear that Ṭabarī believed, *pace* Muqātil, that *falaq* means either 'dawn' or 'a prison in Hell'. Given, then, that there is a fairly even distribution between the 'hell'-glosses and the 'dawn'-glosses, why is 'dawn' more likely?

It would take an extremely thorough examination of Ṭabarī's use of lexical glosses to come to any firm conclusions about his methodology, but the following features of Ṭabarī's presentation of the material regarding *falaq* appear to be significant. Firstly, despite thinking that 'dawn' is the most likely gloss, the 'hell'-glosses appear first: this means that it cannot be assumed that whatever comes first in Ṭabarī's *tafsīr* is preferred by him. (Although, of the 'hell'-glosses, the preferred reading [*sijn fī Jahannam*, nos 1–2] is put first.) Secondly, despite including more hadiths for 'a pit in Hell' (*jubb fī Jahannam*, nos 4–7), the 'hell'-gloss that Ṭabarī believes could be acceptable is 'a prison in Hell'. Quantity, then, is also not necessarily an important factor (although, there are more glosses for 'dawn' than 'Hell'). Thirdly, the only glosses to be supported by a Qur'anic proof text are the 'dawn'-glosses (nos 17, 18 and 21), which adds strength to the interpretation 'dawn'. Fourthly, the fact that Ibn 'Abbās is given as an authority for all three readings does not present a problem for Ṭabarī (nos 1, 2, 10 and 22), but it may be significant that Ibn 'Abbās is an authority for only one version of each of the three glosses. To provide a comparison, the exegete Tustarī, writing slightly before Ṭabarī, cites Ibn 'Abbās as the authority of only one gloss ('dawn').[25] Lastly, the 'creation'-gloss, favoured by Muqātil, is only given the support of one hadith, making it a much weaker reading. The fact that Ṭabarī ignores this reading in his final comments suggests that he did not accept it as likely at all. Tustarī is similarly dismissive of the 'creation'-gloss, concluding his short discussion of *falaq* by stating, 'It has also been said that He intended by it all people (*jamīʿ al-khalq*). Or it has been said that it refers to the rock from which water springs forth.'[26] Neither of these two interpretations is supported with hadith.

Both Ṭabarī and Tustarī appear to prefer a reading of 'dawn', admit the possibility that it refers to somewhere in Hell (most likely a prison), and discount the idea of it referring to creation as a whole. It is of note, therefore, that ʿAlī b. Ibrāhīm al-Qummī (fl. mid-fourth/tenth century),[27] another exegete working in roughly the same period, focuses entirely on the 'Hell'-glosses.[28] He does not provide any evidence by way of hadith for his readings, but he does provide an explanation:

> *Al-falaq* is a pit in Hell (*jubb fī Jahannam*). The inhabitants of the Fire seek protection from the intensity of its heat, and so ask God that He may give them permission to have a break from it. [God] gives them permission to have a break from it, and Hell is set on fire. He [Qummī] said: The pit is a box (*ṣundūq*) of fire, and the people of the pit seek protection from the flames of that box. It is a chest (*tābūt*) and in that chest are six people . . .[29]

Qummī is one of the few exegetes to give an extended exposition of the 'Hell'-gloss. Zayd b. ʿAlī, Ṭabarī and Tustarī simply list it amongst other possible options. The six people or groups of people in the chest (*tābūt*) of fire are given by Qummī as being Cain, Nimrod, Pharaoh, al-Sāmirī,[30] the Christians[31] and the Khārijites, with the murderer of ʿAlī b. Abī Ṭālib, Ibn Muljam, being singled out specifically.[32] Qummī uses this verse to introduce some fierce Shiʿi polemic. The six people in what is 'the worst place' in Hell are those who have, in a sense, the greatest guilt and who have committed the worst crimes: murder (Cain), rejecting a prophet (Nimrod and Pharaoh), committing *shirk* (al-Sāmirī and the Christians) and murdering an imam (Ibn Muljam). A similar consignment of the 'worst' sinners to punishment in Hell can be seen in Jewish and Christian apocalyptic literature, in which visionaries often see their persecutors in Hell,[33] a theme that also became a staple of *miʿrāj* literature in Islam.[34] In Zayd b. ʿAlī's exegesis there is a hint that the meaning of *falaq* does not much matter, rather the focus is on the apotropaic power of the oath; whereas in Qummī's treatment of the word, the interpretation of *falaq* is driven by polemical discourse. It is not surprising, therefore, to see Qummī provide no source for his interpretation: it would simply distract from the main thrust of the argument that he is making. The text is no longer concerned with explaining the meaning of *falaq*, but it serves as a basis for polemical attack.

In subsequent exegeses largely considered part of the 'formative' period, increasingly more sophisticated and nuanced defences of lexical readings can be found. There is a sense that exegetes felt the need to make their lexicological interpretations on stronger bases. Abū'l-Layth al-Samarqandī (d. 375/985–6), for example, makes use of the method of interpreting the Qur'an *qua* Qur'an (interpreting the Qur'an through the Qur'an), using Q. 6:95–6 as a means of defending a 'dawn'-gloss.[35] Although Samarqandī appears to favour the reading 'dawn', he opens his interpretation by referring to 'creation'. This appears to be something of finesse between the two different readings. He writes:

> . . . meaning: Say, Muhammad: 'I seek shelter (*aʿtaṣimu*), I seek protection (*astaʿīdhu*), and I seek help (*astaʿīnu*) in the Creator of Creation (*bi-khāliq al-khalq*)'; and *falaq* is 'creation' (*khalq*). Creation (*khalq*) is referred to by the term *falaq* because creation [contains things] separated from their fathers and their mothers. It is said: '*I take refuge with the Lord of the falaq*' – meaning in the Creator of the Dawn (*khāliq al-ṣubḥ*). It is said: the splitter (*fāliq*) of the grain and the date-stone, as God, Most High, says: *It is God who splits (fāliq) the grain and the date-stone . . .* (Q. 6:95); and He says: *He splits the sky into dawn* (*fāliqu'l-aṣbāḥ*; Q. 6:96).[36]

Samarqandī's opening statement that *falaq* means 'creation' (following Muqātil) is then subsumed into the 'dawn'-gloss. This link between the 'creation'-gloss and the 'dawn'-gloss can also be seen, perhaps, in Ṭabarī's inclusion of the 'creation'-gloss between the hadith given in support of the 'dawn'-glosses and his final statement in preference for such a reading. Samarqandī also gives a selection of the 'Hell'-glosses, some of which are supported by hadith, but these are weaker as they are provided without full *isnād*s: a valley in Hell (no authority given); a pit in Hell (on the authority of the Prophet); and a well in Hell (Kaʿb).[37] Of these three readings, the reading supported by a prophetic hadith (a pit in Hell) is undoubtedly the strongest.

Abū'l-Ḥasan al-Māwardī (d. 450/1058) provides six options for the meaning of *falaq*. Like Samarqandī, he does not provide *isnād*s for each reading, but he does provide an authority. The six interpretations given are: a prison in Hell (Ibn ʿAbbās); one of the names of Hell (Abū ʿAbd al-Raḥmān); all of creation (al-Ḍaḥḥāk); the breaking (*falaq*) of the dawn (Jābir b. ʿAbd Allāh); the splitting of mountains and rock by water (no authority given); anything that is split (al-Ḥasan).[38] From the exegetes' point of view, of these six options it is possible to discount the opinion given without any authority as being a weak lexical reading. Of the others, only 'the breaking of the dawn' is supported further, with a line of poetry.[39] Māwardī's recourse to poetry, as well as Ṭabarī's reference to 'the speech of the Arabs' (*bi-kalām al-ʿarab*) shows an increasing reliance on external linguistic evidence to interpret the Arabic of the Qur'an.

In this formative period it is possible to see a development in the ways in which exegetes approached the lexical meaning of *falaq*. Whilst early exegeses tend to give a simple reading, often without any support or proof text, a hundred years or so later a number of elements to lexical readings have changed. Firstly there is a move to include all of the readings that are available, which can be seen in the three main glosses of the word ('dawn', 'Hell' and 'creation'), but also in the wide range of 'Hell'-glosses. The use of hadith to provide support to a lexical reading is also introduced, although in a slightly inconsistent way: few include full *isnād*s, but authorities are given for each of the lexical readings. Lastly, as time progresses it is possible to see more sophisticated responses to the problems presented by the meaning of *falaq*: particularly the use of arguments focused on the strength or soundness of lexical hadith; the use of other Qur'anic verses in support of a lexical reading; and the citation of poetry or unsourced references to 'Arabic'.[40]

Later exegeses

The rise of philosophical exegesis sees a new methodology of dealing with lexical material in the Qur'an emerging, namely the application of linguistic reasoning. This is not to say that linguistic reasoning is not found in earlier exegetes. Indeed, Ṭabarī frequently employs linguistic reason to varying degrees throughout his exegesis. However, those exegetes who composed 'philosophical' *tafsīr*s employ linguistic reasoning in a different manner. For these exegetes, the application of rules of Arabic grammar, discussions of the derivation of words (*ishtiqāq*) and so on, is the main focus of the approach to lexicology. In earlier authors, such as Ṭabarī, any linguistic reasoning is one element amongst many others in establishing a word's meaning, whereas the philosophical exegetes use it as their main and, most often, only method of interpreting words' meanings. Maḥmūd b. ʿUmar al-Zamakhsharī (d. 538/1144), Fakhr al-Dīn al-Rāzī (d. 606/1209) and ʿAbd Allāh b. ʿUmar al-Bayḍāwī (d. 685/1286) are the most commonly cited examples, but their methods can also be found elsewhere.[41]

Zamakhsharī, famed for his Muʿtazilism,[42] eschews any references to hadith in his discussion of the meaning of *falaq*; yet, underlying this, there are a number of elements in his treatment of *falaq* that clearly exhibit a debt to earlier exegetical treatments of the word based on the transmission of hadith. Zamakhsharī writes:

> *Falaq* and *faraq* [both mean] the dawn, because night is split (*yufliqu*) from it, and it is divided (*yufraqu*). The form *faʿal* [i.e. *falaq*] carries the meaning of the passive participle (*mafʿūl*). A proverb says [both]: 'It is clearer (*abyan*) than the *falaq* of the dawn', and '[it is clearer] than the *faraq* of the dawn'.[43]

The link between *falaq* and *faraq* has already been encountered in Ṭabarī's discussion of the word, and was used by Ṭabarī to lend support to his view that *falaq* referred to the dawn.[44] The introduction of specific linguistic terminology, particularly the argument that *falaq* is the passive participle of *falaqa*, is innovative.[45] It serves as a shibboleth for this type of exegesis, since, alongside the absence of hadiths, interpretative and linguistic authority is moved from the Prophet and the early exegetes to pure linguistic analysis. Zamakhsharī includes further interpretation of the word, stating: 'It is everything that God divides: the earth from the grass; and the mountains from the wells, the clouds from the rain, the parent from progeny, the grain (*ḥabb*) and the date-stone (*nawāt*), and other things.'[46] These final two are a clear reference to Q. 6:95–6, which we have already encountered. Again, these interpretations are a continuation of the exegetical material that Zamakhsharī inherited. Although there is no reference to other exegeses, or to the hadith material on which these interpretations are based, it would seem safe to assume that most of those reading this material would be fully aware of these interpretations and their origins. Although Zamakhsharī is, in some respects, moving away from the body of exegesis that preceded him, it leaves its traces on his reformulation of the material. Zamakhsharī does not simply create a list of possible options, as Ṭabarī and other exegetes did; but the idea that *falaq* refers to all kinds of splitting seeks to reinforce his interpretation of 'dawn' as a moment of 'splitting'. This also provides Zamakhsharī with an opportunity to bring the 'creation'-gloss, seen in many other exegeses, into the sphere of the 'dawn'-glosses more easily.[47] Zamakhsharī does also include the 'Hell'-gloss:

> It is a well in Hell, or a pit (*jubb*), and it [a *jubb*] is, according to the speech [of the Arabs], a depression in the earth.[48] The plural of *falaq* is *falqān*. [A hadith is given] on the authority of one of the Companions, that when he came to Syria, he saw the monasteries of the protected people (*ahl al-dhimma*), and [the evil things] that happened within them that should have shortened their life, but whose lives had not been shortened by the depravity. He said to them: 'It is fine by me! Surely their reward will be *falaq*!' Someone said (*fa-qīla*): 'What is *falaq*?' He said: 'It is a house in Hell. When it is opened, all of the inhabitants of Hell cry out because of its intense heat.'[49]

This discussion of the 'Hell'-gloss is in complete contrast to the analysis of *falaq* in light of the 'dawn'-gloss, where the reading is supported with linguistic and theological reasoning. The 'Hell'-gloss has none and its inclusion seems purely to be out of deference to earlier exegetical material, and that his exegesis would be startling with its omission.

Rāzī provides a much more extensive treatment of *falaq*. His discussion, which raises seven different readings of *falaq*, echoes Zamakhsharī's in its approach, particularly the rejection of hadith and the primacy of linguistic reasoning. Indeed, the first line establishing the link between *falaq* and *faraq* is given almost verbatim as it appears in Zamakhsharī – although Rāzī attributes it to Ibrāhīm b. al-Sarī al-Zajjāj (d. 311/923) and states that the 'dawn'-gloss is the majority reading (*wa-huwa qawl al-aktharīn*).[50] Rāzī is one of the few to develop an argument in support of his reading of *falaq* with an interpretation of the verse as a whole, referring to both the oath in which the word appears and the wider context of Labīd's bewitchment of the Prophet. He provides a lengthy analysis of why the reading of 'dawn' is theologically compatible with its use in an apotropaic oath:

> Its use (*takhṣīṣ*) in the act of seeking protection is [understood] for different reasons: (i) He [God] is the one who is able (*al-qādir*) to remove this intense darkness (*ẓulumāt*) from all of this universe, and He also wills that it will also drive from the one who seeks protection (*al-ʿāʾidh*) everything that frightens him and scares him.[51]

This is a reference to *the evil of what He has created, from the evil of darkness (ghāsiq) when it gathers* (Q. 113:2–3). The second and third arguments relate to human experience of the dawn as something that dispels fear, and thus become a useful metaphor for God's action in seeking protection from magic. The fourth continues the reading of 'dawn', but is related to a story about Joseph. The fifth states that it is related to the time of day at which protection is required, and Rāzī states that it is as if the verse were to read: 'Take protection with the Lord of the Time (*bi-rabbiʾl-waqt*) at which you need delivering from every distress (*mahmūm*).'[52] The sixth relates the term to eschatology, and the seventh relates it to the time of prayer. This last argument is supported further by references such as Q. 83:6, *a day when mankind shall stand before the Lord of all*

Being, and Q. 68:42, *Upon the day when the leg shall be bared, and they shall be summoned to bow themselves . . .*[53] However, the act of prayer is linked to the prayers performed by the faithful on the Last Day. Although the root *f-l-q* is not used in any of the eschatological descriptions in the Qur'an concerning the splitting of the heavens on the Last Day, the root is associated with divine action: God's splitting the grain and date-stone (Q. 6:95–6) and Moses's splitting of the Red Sea (Q. 26:63). In the last two interpretations, Rāzī skilfully links the idea of *falaq* as the dawn with the obvious eschatological idea of the 'splitting of the heavens' on the Last Day.

This leads into Rāzī's discussions of the two other readings ('creation' and 'Hell'). Rāzī states that the second reading is that *falaq* is 'a way of expressing (*'ibāra*) everything which God divides (*yafliquhu*), such as the earth from the plants'.[54] Rāzī follows Zamakhsharī almost verbatim, but, as before, adds some extra material; here, he interpolates some Qur'anic proof texts (Q. 6:95 and Q. 2:74).[55] Rāzī's discussion of the 'Hell'-gloss is substantially shorter than those of both the 'dawn' and 'creation'-glosses. As before, he draws heavily on Zamakhsharī.[56] Rāzī is one of only a few exegetes to defend his readings so extensively; this is important, since none of his readings is 'unorthodox' and Rāzī is clearly following the majority of exegetes in interpreting *falaq* as 'dawn', 'creation' or 'Hell'. Rāzī provides an elegant and sophisticated harmony between the usual meaning of *falaq* and its actual use in that particular instance; not only does he establish its lexical meaning through reason (as Zamakhsharī does), he also contextualises the meaning to make such a reading theologically credible, as well as providing a great number of Qur'anic proof texts.

Having seen extensive discussions of *falaq* in Zamakhsharī and Rāzī, Bayḍāwī's treatment is noticeably more concise, but it includes largely similar material.[57] Bayḍāwī, Zamakhsharī and Rāzī, through their methodologies, may appear to be moving exegesis away from the earlier exegetical tradition, but their exegeses are clearly heavily reliant upon it: their answers to lexical questions are the same as those of earlier exegetes; they simply differ in the ways in which they support them. This shift towards a defence by reason rather than through hadith delineates scholastic lines concerning authority,[58] where the defence of lexical readings cannot be justified simply with recourse to hadith, but needs to have linguistic basis.

It would, however, be misleading to suggest that Zamakhsharī and Rāzī were typical of this period. The Andalusian exegete Muḥammad b. Aḥmad al-Qurṭubī (d. 671/1272), a contemporary of Zamakhsharī's interpreter Bayḍāwī, is a good example of a scholar continuing the method of exegesis exemplified by Ṭabarī. Qurṭubī's discussion of *falaq* is clearly modelled on that of earlier exegetes,[59] as can be seen in Table 2.[60]

Qurṭubī cites two Qur'anic verses (Q. 6:95–6) in defence of the reading 'dawn', as well as a particularly high number of lines of poetry that also support the reading of 'dawn'; he includes many more lines of poetry than Ṭabarī and, notably, none is quoted in

Table 2: Qurṭubī's glosses of *falaq*

Reading	Specific gloss	Authority
Hell	prison (*sijn*) in Hell	Ibn ʿAbbās
	house (*bayt*) in Hell	Ubayy b. Kaʿb
	a name of Hell (*ism min asmāʾ Jahannam*)	al-Ḥubalī (Abū ʿAbd al-Raḥmān)
	a valley in Hell	al-Kalbī
	a tree in Hell	ʿAbd Allāh b. ʿUmar
	a pit (*jubb*) in Hell	Saʿīd b. Jubayr
	a pit (*jubb*) in Hell	al-Naḥḥās
dawn	dawn (*al-ṣubḥ*)	Jābir b. ʿAbd Allāh
	dawn (*al-ṣubḥ*)	al-Ḥasan
	dawn (*al-ṣubḥ*)	Saʿīd b. Jubayr
	dawn (*al-ṣubḥ*)	Mujāhid
	dawn (*al-ṣubḥ*)	Qatāda
	dawn (*al-ṣubḥ*)	al-Qurẓī
	dawn (*al-ṣubḥ*)	Ibn Zayd
	falaq–faraq	Ibn ʿAbbās; Q. 6:95–6

support of 'Hell'. Qurṭubī also includes the 'creation'-gloss, with a line of poetry.[61] Other authors, particularly Ṭabarī, do interpret *falaq* in light of other occurrences of the roots in the Qur'an (i.e. interpretation of the Qur'an through the Qur'an), namely Q. 6:95–6, where such analysis is being used as a proof text. Qurṭubī, however, is distinctive by being explicit in his treatment of the word's derivation: 'I say: This statement bears witness to its derivation – *al-falaq* is "the splitting" (*al-shaqq*). "I have *falaq*-ed something" (*falaqtu al-shay'a falaqan*) means I split it (*shaqaqtuhu*).'[62] It is after this statement that Qurṭubī uses Q. 6:95–6 to support his reading. Such open linguistic reasoning highlights the advances in exegetical analysis. Qurṭubī shows much dependence on exegeses such as that of Ṭabarī, but also reveals knowledge of Zamakhsharī and Rāzī. Qurṭubī includes the further definition of *jubb* as a depression in the earth;[63] this is, among those works included in the present sample, only found in Zamakhsharī and Rāzī.[64] It is, then, possible to see Qurṭubī interacting with the methodologies both of exegetes like Ṭabarī and of the philosophical exegeses. The introduction of linguistic reasoning into a work that is highly reliant on hadith as the source of meaning indicates the increased sophistication seen in later exegeses. Indeed, Qurṭubī utilises the whole range of available tools to interpret and defend his readings of *falaq*: the Qur'an, hadith, poetry and also reason.

Exegeses after Qurṭubī, such as *al-Tafsīr al-kabīr* by Ismā'īl b. 'Umar Ibn Kathīr (d. 774/1374), the *Tafsīr al-Jalālayn* by Jalāl al-Dīn al-Maḥallī (d. 864/1459) and Jalāl al-Dīn al-Suyūṭī (d. 911/1505), and Suyūṭī's *al-Durr al-manthūr* rehearse the same arguments, but poetry largely falls out of use.[65] However, one line of poetry is included in Suyūṭī's treatment of *falaq* in his *al-Durr al-manthūr*:

> al-Ṭastī [d. 346/957–8] [related] on the authority of Ibn 'Abbās that Nāfi' b. al-Azraq said to him: 'Tell me about the words of God *qul a'ūdhu bi-rabbi'l-falaq*'. He said: '*I take refuge with the Lord* of the Dawn, when it [the sun] splits the darkness of the night.' He said: 'Do you know if it is an Arabic word?' He said: 'Yes. I heard Zuhayr Ibn Abī Sulmā say:

'Praise God, the one who can split a single piece of twine from a rope,
Just as the dawn splits the veil of darkness.'[66]

Ibn Taymiyya (d. 728/1328) made a famous call to interpret the Qur'an through the Qur'an,[67] and there does appear to have been a move away from using poetry and reason, back towards hadith after this. However, it must be remembered that in earlier exegeses poetry is used sparingly and for specific reasons, so this does not mark a definitive break from the past. It is also necessary to acknowledge that exegetes in this period did not necessarily subscribe to Ibn Taymiyya's views on exegesis, but the effects of Ibn Taymiyya's hermeneutics (and approach to hadith and concepts of authority) undoubtedly came to affect the discipline.

This can be seen in the paucity of formal linguistic reasoning in late-Mamluk exegesis, even though linguistics was a present and well-established part of Mamluk scholarship.[68] Suyūṭī is a prime example: linguistic reasoning is absent from his *al-Durr al-manthūr* because he chose to compile an exegesis purely based on hadith; yet his other works show that he was well aware of the importance of linguistic reasoning in studying the Qur'an.[69] Although the *Tafsīr al-Jalālayn* does not include lexical discussions *per se*, it can be used to indicate Suyūṭī's 'preferred' reading, or, at the least, the 'most common' reading. For example, for '*fāṭir*' in Q. 35:1, *Tafsīr al-Jalālayn* gives '*khāliq*' ('creator'), which is the predominant reading in the exegeses.[70] One can either make the assumption that the absence of linguistic reasoning in *al-Durr al-manthūr* means that Suyūṭī specifically excluded it from his exegetical methodology or, perhaps more likely, posit that such linguistic reasoning lies behind the text of the *al-Durr al-manthūr* and came to influence the interpretation and the presentation of the material. This could have been done subconsciously, but it would seem more likely that an exegete such as Suyūṭī, being so immersed in the exegetical literature that preceded him, would have been influenced by the various linguistic debates and reasoning seen in earlier exegeses. Indeed, Suyūṭī refers to Zamakhsharī, Rāzī and Qurṭubī in his other works, and he was evidently well acquainted with them.[71] It is necessary, then, to see these later, largely hadith-based exegeses as continuing to engage with those exegeses that preceded them, but that such an engagement may not be being made openly.

Lexicographical Works and *Tafsīr*

To place the lexicology of the exegetical tradition in the wider context of medieval Arabic scholarship, it is beneficial to consider briefly the more formal works of lexicography, and to examine the extent to which the exegetical interpretations found in the *tafsīr*s reflect lexicographical studies and vice versa. Lexicography is, by its nature, a different discipline to exegetical lexicology: lexicography examines a word in the context of the totality of its uses, rather than in the specific context of a word in the Qur'an as discussed by exegetes.[72] The Qur'an undoubtedly exerted an influence on lexicography, but the extent of this influence is difficult to ascertain. The methodologies of different lexicographers naturally varied, and some relied on the Qur'an, *tafsīr* and hadith frequently, such as Abū Manṣūr al-Azharī (d. 370/980) in his *Tahdhīb al-lugha*, but others less so.[73]

The earliest formal work of lexicography is usually considered to be the *Kitāb al-'Ayn* by al-Khalīl b. Aḥmad (d. ca. 175/791–2),[74] although there is some debate (both modern and medieval) about whether this is the authentic work of Khalīl.[75] Regardless of the attribution, it remains an early work of lexicography that provides fairly extensive entries for each root, and the work contains an entry for *f-l-q*:

> *falaq*: the daybreak (*fajr*), and His words *Say: 'I take refuge with the Lord of the falaq'* (Q. 113:1); it is the dawn (*al-ṣubḥ*), since God *falaq*-ed it, meaning he made it manifest (*awḍaḥahu*) and created it, so that it became split (*fa'nfalaqa*). God split (*yufliqu*) the grain, so that it becomes separated (*fa-yanfaliqu*) from its shoot.[76]

This entry is enlightening in a number of ways, since it echoes some of the treatments of *falaq* seen in the exegeses, but also includes other interpretations. Whilst the gloss *ṣubḥ* is found in almost every exegesis of *falaq*, the gloss *fajr* is not. Why does Khalīl opt for *fajr*? The reason may be a result of the base meanings of *fajr* and *ṣubḥ*, which both refer to the 'dawn', but in different ways. The verb *ṣabaḥa* carries connotations of drinking, with *ṣabaḥa* meaning 'he gave him to drink a morning-draught, or what is termed *ṣabūḥ*';[77] and by extension the root came to refer to the early part of the morning (i.e. dawn as a period of time). In contrast, *fajara* means 'he clave [a thing]; cut, or divided, [it] lengthwise: this is the primary signification, whence several others . . . derived';[78] and has a more specific meaning (i.e. the physical moment of dawn/daybreak, the 'crack' of dawn). *Fajr*, then, with its association with 'splitting', has much more in common with the noun *falaq*, as they both have similar base meanings.

It seems significant that Khalīl gives a meaning of *falaq* that is not found in the exegeses, and one that is, in many respects, a closer translation; indeed, the reference to Q. 113:1 forces Khalīl into a fairly roundabout definition. The other interpretations of *falaq* ('Hell' or 'creation') are notably absent, and similarly the synonym *faraq* is also omitted.[79] This suggests that whilst Khalīl was aware of the exegetical material regarding *falaq*, the text is not subservient to *tafsīr*, and does not include all the interpretations found in works of *tafsīr*. The same pattern can be seen in other lexicographical works, such as *al-Qāmūs al-muḥīṭ* by Muḥammad b. Yaʿqūb al-Fīrūzabādī (d. 817/1415). Fīrūzabādī avoids direct reference to the Qur'an in his entry for *falaq*, giving pre-eminence to the gloss *shaqqa* – a synonym of *fajara* and *falaqa*.[80]

In contrast, a group of lexicographical works were tied to the Qur'anic text and the genre of *tafsīr*, and a number of works were written that explained 'rare' (*gharīb*) words or grammatical forms found in the Qur'an.[81] These works emerged in the third/ninth century when more non-Arabic speaking people converted to Islam, but also when the Arabic spoken by the majority in the early Abbasid period had developed and many native Arabic speakers were also confronted in the Qur'an with Arabic that was not easily understood. The *Majāz al-Qur'ān* (also known as *Gharīb al-Qur'ān*) by Abū 'Ubayda Maʿmar b. al-Muthannā (d. between 207/822 and 213/828) is a prime example, operating in both linguistic and exegetical spheres whilst being neither *tafsīr* nor linguistics (*'ilm al-lugha*) in their technical senses as academic genres.[82] John Wansbrough describes the *Majāz al-Qur'ān* genre as being a type of exegesis,[83] but such works are only exegetical in so far as they elicit meaning from the Qur'anic text; they are not *tafsīr stricto sensu*, since the works are focused solely on the linguistic meaning of a limited number of specific cases. There is a wider concern at hand here: can a work that simply looks at lexical meaning be considered exegetical, or does the process of exegesis require different approaches to the text of the Qur'an? The lists of fields included within the *'ulūm al-Qur'an* (sciences of the Qur'an) suggest that whilst particular sciences can be applied to the Qur'an individually, the genre of *tafsīr* employs a number of the 'sciences' in order to comprehend the meaning of the Qur'an. This distinction can, perhaps, be seen in the case of Suyūṭī, who wrote works which he called *tafsīr*s, and works devoted to the *'ulūm al-Qur'ān*.[84] Nevertheless, this close link between the *majāz al-Qur'ān* literature and the *tafsīr* literature can be seen in Abū 'Ubayda's very brief gloss of *falaq*. His entry simply states: '*falaq* [means] dawn (*ṣubḥ*)'.[85] Here Abū 'Ubayda does not give any information on the semantic field of *falaq*, there is no defence or proof text for the reading, and he merely gives its exegetical interpretation. The idea that *falaq* refers to the notion of dividing or splitting is not mentioned at all. The reliance of the *gharīb* genre on *tafsīr* can be seen in Abū'l-Ḥayyān al-Gharnāṭī's (d. 745/1344) *gharīb* work, which states: '*al-falaq* [means] dawn (*ṣubḥ*), and it is said [that it means] a valley in Hell',[86] despite glossing *fāliq* (Q. 6:96) as *shāqq* ('divider').

The lexicographical works encountered thus far reveal two main methodologies in the medieval lexicographic tradition: one which is closely identified with *tafsīr*, and the other which attempts to distance itself from it, albeit rarely completely. The first position glosses *falaq* with dawn (*ṣubḥ*), and the second with more synonymous glosses (*fajara / shaqqa*). There are, however, a number of works that are situated in between these two poles, particularly the two most widely used Arabic lexicons, the *Lisān al-'Arab* by Muḥammad b. Mukarram Ibn Manẓūr (d. 711/1311–12), and the *Tāj al-'arūs* by Murtaḍā al-Zabīdī (d. 1205/1791). In the *Lisān al-ʿArab*, Ibn Manẓūr gives the meaning of *falaqa* / *falq* with the gloss *al-shaqq* (the 'act of splitting'), as Fīrūzabādī does; but he gives a more specific, exegetical treatment of *falaq*.[87] Ibn Manẓūr gives all three exegetical readings found in the *tafsīr* tradition, presents all the Qur'anic references, and the readings are supported with both hadith and poetry, as is found in many of the exegeses. Zabīdī takes a similar approach,[88] as does Abū Bakr Muḥammad b. al-Ḥasan Ibn Durayd (d. 321/933) in his *Jamahara*.[89]

The lexicographical tradition, therefore, does not always undergo a process of Qur'anisation, although some works were closely identified with it. Lexicographers were, understandably and quite naturally, aware of the Qur'an and integrated elements of *tafsīr* into their lexicographical works. However, in the case of *falaq*, some incorporate the *tafsīr* tradition in its entirety (Ibn Manẓūr, Zabīdī); others make reference to the Qur'an and *tafsīr* in passing, whilst stressing the meaning of the root as a whole (al-Khalīl b. Aḥmad, Fīrūzabādī). In these cases, the Qur'an and its interpretation provide one example amongst many others to explain the meaning of an individual word.

Lexicology, Interpretation and Authority

The idea with the most impact on Arabic exegetical lexicology is the relationship between definition and authority. This works on two levels: (i) an exegete's general and overarching hermeneutic approaches to the Qur'an; and (ii) an exegete's articulation of lexicological preferences in specific cases (here *falaq*). There is a distinct difference between the general hermeneutic approaches of early exegetes (such as Muqātil), exegetes in the early tradition (such as Ṭabarī), philosophical exegetes (such as Rāzī), exegetes working in the late Mamluk period after Ibn Taymiyya, and lexicographers. Each of these has a different methodology, i.e. a process of exegesis, but, more importantly, different hermeneutics, that is, theological and religious values or expectations. These come to have an impact on the way in which the exegetes deal with individual words like *falaq*. Crucially, the interpretations of *falaq* are relatively constant through the medieval period, and nearly all of the exegetes include its three principal glosses ('dawn', 'Hell' and 'creation'), with the vast majority giving prominence to the 'dawn'-gloss. It is only in the ways in which they present the material and defend the lexical reading that differences between the exegetes can be seen.

Many of these differences can be viewed as being rooted in notions of authority. Muqātil, for example, provides simple explications of meaning. There is no deference to a wider notion of 'authority' and his lexical readings are undefended. It would seem unlikely that Muqātil was unaware of competing interpretations and meanings of words, but Muqātil saw no need to cite them. Muqātil is not necessarily basing authority in himself as a scholar, but is, more likely, passing on an interpretation that was prevalent or was a reading with which he agreed. The exegesis of Zayd b. ʿAlī is more sophisticated, which may indicate that it is not authentically dated to this period, or it may indicate an early move to a summative approach to lexicology, seen and developed by Ṭabarī, where evidence to support particular readings starts to emerge in increasingly complex ways.

In Ṭabarī's exegesis, lexical readings are articulated more clearly and more openly. However, as seen in the case of *falaq*, Ṭabarī still gives his own judgement, based on his own reflection on the text. Ṭabarī's lexical methodology is based on a two-stage process. Firstly, he admits a range of interpretations as being admissible in his exegetical 'court'; evidence which is admitted on the grounds that they have been given authority through some means, usually through early interpreters or directly from the Prophet (i.e. hadith). This is why Ṭabarī allows all three readings of 'dawn', 'Hell' and 'creation' into his exegesis of this word; at a basic level they are all authoritative, because they are all transmitted through hadith, and Ṭabarī does not present himself as having the authority to disregard them. However, once a number of readings have entered his exegetical 'court', Ṭabarī assesses the lexical readings, and gives preference to some readings over others. In the case of *falaq*, Ṭabarī prefers the reading of 'dawn', which is supported by other external evidence (the 'language of the Arabs') and a cognate (*faraq*), whereas the other readings have little or no external support. Ṭabarī's methodology is to establish lexical meanings through this two-stage process: first by detailing the hadith available, and then, through the use of external proof texts (the Qur'an, 'Arab language', poetry, linguistic reasoning, etc.),[90] he creates an argument for the correct reading. The fact that these types of sources are only used as proof texts, and not as primary sources for defining words, is revealing. The 'language of the Arabs' (taken in a vague, non-specific, un-sourced sense) or Arabic poetry cannot stand alone to defend a lexical reading, they never act as a 'primary' source for a word's meaning, and they can only support or give credence to a lexical reading already found in the hadith. The hadith are authoritative in and of themselves, but Ṭabarī critiques them and they need to be 'tested'. This is not as controversial as it may at first sound, since lexical hadith, and indeed many hadith used in *tafsīr* works, are the views of the early exegetes, and not of the Prophet: for Ṭabarī or any exegete, a figure, even one as influential as Ibn ʿAbbās, does not have religious authority in the same way as the Qur'an or a prophetic hadith does.[91]

The citation of poetry in defence of lexical readings has generated some discussion in the secondary literature. John Wansbrough argued in his *Quranic Studies* that the use of poetry in lexicological debates appeared relatively late in the development of *tafsīr*. He maintained that the

> most flagrantly intrusive of the explicative elements found in haggadic exegesis is poetry adduced to explain Quranic lexica [. . .] That method of interpretation belonged to the masorah and was intimately related to the contemporary development of techniques for the transmission of poetic texts.[92]

Wansbrough is certainly correct in that the use of poetic citations does not become dominant in the *tafsīr* process until later, as this survey has shown. However, Issa Boullata has argued that whilst works such as Ibn ʿAbbās's *Masāʾil Nāfiʿ b. al-Azraq* appear to have grown over time, this does not necessarily mean that the use of poetic citations to illustrate lexical meaning was not unknown in the early period of the development of *tafsīr*, and some of the verses purportedly cited by Ibn ʿAbbās may be authentic.[93] For those interested in uncovering the development of exegesis, the problem lies in determining which of these are authentic, which is largely impossible, as Boullata comments:

> One cannot determine what of these materials is authentic and what is not, but everything points to the possibility that there existed a smaller core of materials which was most likely preserved in a tradition of oral transmission for several generations before it was put down in writing with enlargements.'[94]

However, it is necessary to highlight the fact that Boullata and Wansbrough are discussing the question of the authenticity of the quotation of verses by Ibn ʿAbbās. Regardless of the authenticity of these citations, what is clear is that they did become a means to authenticate lexical meanings in the Qur'an, but, importantly, they only formed a part of the process of defining words, and one that was subservient and secondary to the definition of lexica through hadith.

This method is in direct contrast to works of medieval Arabic linguistics, in which, according to Adrian Gully, hadith are rarely cited as evidence in debates about grammar. For medieval grammarians, hadith were too variable to provide any firm proof text for a particular grammatical problem or usage. It was not until Ibn Mālik (d. 672/1274) that using hadith as grammatical proof texts became more common: even after the canonisation of the hadith collections by al-Bukhārī (d. 256/870) and Muslim (d. 261/875), when the wording of hadith began to stabilise,[95] grammarians remained 'persistent in their reluctance to use Ḥadīth as textual evidence on the grounds that the transmission of material might have incurred some inaccuracies during the two centuries or so after the death of the Prophet Muḥammad'.[96] The Arabic lexicographical tradition sits somewhere between these two poles: hadith are used to substantiate lexical meaning, but, generally, only as part of a wide range of different sources.

These vastly divergent views on hadith stem from the different tasks and aims of the grammarians and exegetes. The grammarian is attempting to find a 'standardised' Arabic grammar, using reliable data in order to establish the function and meaning of, for example, specific particles (*mā*, *lā*, *li-* etc.). Medieval grammarians were not interested in garnering any religious authority for grammatical phenomena, but sought linguistic authority, seen in the practical use of Arabic poetry, 'Bedouin' Arabic and the Qur'an (taken as an example of 'pure' Arabic, rather than solely a religious authority). The *mufassirūn* are undertaking a different enterprise, using grammar and, in this study, lexicology, as part of a wider exegetical process. Indeed, as Gully puts it, 'exegesis was often carried out by its own band of scholars, *mufassirūn*, who would not necessarily be classed as grammarians'.[97] Any lexical discussions are not distinct from the wider theological, legal or ritual interpretations of a given verse. The analysis is inherently religious: it is an attempt to find the meaning of a verse of the Qur'an (and not the meaning of a word), and as such it requires religious not linguistic authority.[98] In the case of Ṭabarī, and many other exegetes (especially Qurṭubī), hadith provide the religious authority, and through a process of testing with vehicles bearing linguistic authority, a preferred option is given. The strongest option in the case of *falaq* is the one that has both religious and linguistic authority, but the linguistic is subservient to the religious.[99] Later exegeses, such as Suyūṭī's *al-Durr al-manthūr*, move authority firmly back towards hadith, but there must still have been some awareness of the linguistic issues raised by a verse of the Qur'an in other exegetical works.[100]

Not all exegetes subscribed to such a view of authority, and the philosophical exegeses of Zamakhsharī and Rāzī provide a veritable foil to the model of authority seen most often in the earlier exegetical tradition. Despite their apparent move away from this earlier tradition of exegesis, Zamakhsharī and Rāzī follow almost exactly the arguments found in exegeses that preceded them concerning *falaq*. They differ, however, in the ways in which their lexical readings are defended, relying on linguistic reasoning as the ultimate arbiter in meanings of *falaq*. Their recourse to etymology (*ishtiqāq*) and linguistic analysis illustrates this prioritisation of reason over the acceptance of hadith. This, naturally, fits in with their general hermeneutic approaches to the Qur'an. There is, however, slightly more to this position, since, by defending lexical readings through theory rather than practical examples, there is also an assumption being made about the origin of semantic meaning. For Ṭabarī, meaning is generated through its use and practice. A word means what it does because it was used in a particular way: in the case of *falaq*, the 'Hell'-gloss is rejected, because the 'dawn'-gloss has support in Arab linguistic practice. For Rāzī and Zamakhshārī, there is the implication that words have an innate meaning: the triliteral base has a meaning which is immutable, and nuances in a root's meanings are found in the different linguistic patterns and inflexions. Much of Zamakhsharī's and Rāzī's linguistic arguments centre on the linguistic pattern of a root, and the meaning of that pattern (i.e. *taṣrīf*). *Falaq* means what it does because the root *f-l-q* has a meaning, and the form *faʿal* is a specific form of the root with a specific meaning.[101]

It is also necessary to read Zamakhsharī's and Rāzī's linguistic analysis in light of debates about the philosophy of language in the medieval period; indeed Zamakhsharī, and others such as ʿAlī b. ʿĪsā al-Rummānī (d. 384/994), operated in the fields of linguistics, theology and exegesis.[102] Debates about the philosophical meaning of words stemmed from considerations about the nature of God's speech (*kalām*),[103] which is why they were of interest to figures like Zamakhsharī. For Muʿtazilīs, such as Zamakhsharī, language was of human origin, arising out of a process of convention (*iṣṭilāḥ*). A word is a collection of sounds (e.g. *fa-la-q*^{un}) that, after a process of general agreement, came to signify a specific idea or concept.[104] As an exegete, Zamakhsharī encounters this series of sounds and attempts to establish what they signify. It is noteworthy that, as we have seen, Zamakhsharī defends the reading of 'dawn' by deferring not to hadith, but to a definition founded on its base meaning of 'to split': '*falaq* and *faraq* [both mean] the dawn, because night is split from it, and it is divided. The form *faʿal* carries the meaning of the passive participle'.

Ṭabarī and other exegetes also make the connection between *falaq* and *faraq*, as well as the relation of 'dawn' to the action of splitting (*yufliqa*), but only Zamakhsharī defends this link with grammatical analysis. For Zamakhsharī, the agreed human signifiers of the form *faʿal* (i.e. *falaq*) indicate the passive participle, or if not the passive participle specifically, something that resembles or is understood as a passive participle. *Falaq*, then, means the 'broken' or 'divided' [thing]. The readings 'dawn', 'Hell' and 'creation' are then interpreted in light of their meaning and relationship to the concept of being a 'divided thing'.

Although as an Ashʿarī, al-Rāzī believed that language was revealed by God, rather than developing through a process of general agreement, he still draws much material from Zamakhsharī's Muʿtazilī *Kashshāf.* Rāzī may not have held a rigidly revelationist view of language, since, in his *al-Maḥṣūl*, he provides detailed critiques of both the conventionalist and revelationist views.[105] The most important concept behind Rāzī's lexicology is the fact that the words in the Qur'an are linked to the divine.[106] Rāzī frames his discussion of *falaq* in the context of the verse's apotropaic theology as a whole, making the meaning of *falaq* consonant with it; he also supplies a great many Qur'anic proof texts. For Rāzī, words have specific meanings because the (divine) origin of language has created fixed meanings for each phoneme, but each word also has a context in the 'Word of God' as a whole.

These discussions do not have a direct bearing on the meaning of *falaq*, and are only pertinent inasmuch as they form the theological and theoretical basis from which exegetes approached lexicology in general. The detailed explications in these exegeses regarding what *falaq* means and the relation of its form (i.e. *faʿal*) to its meaning verify the wider understanding of the theoretical relationship between words (*alfāẓ*) and what they signify (*maʿānī*).[107] The analysis of grammatical and syntactical structures can be found in Ṭabarī's *tafsīr*, but such analysis is always subservient to hadith, particularly in the case of lexicology. This is because the hadith provide the religious authority for the interpretation, and any linguistic analysis is a means of making sense of often contradictory interpretations given by the hadith. For philosophical exegetes, the linguistic patterns of words are the products of a logical grammatical system, arising out of agreement between human speakers of a language, or given directly by God. Authority, in this case, stems from the language itself: words only have meaning through language, and they must be defined through linguistic analysis.

Conclusions

In the survey of different exegetes' treatments of *falaq* above, the lexicological approach of an exegete mirrors each exegete's approach to exegesis as whole. The methodology by which Muqātil, Ṭabarī, Rāzī or Suyūṭī define Qur'anic lexica is much the same as the way in which they define and interpret legal passages, theological opinions, questions of grammar and syntax and so on. This is not unexpected and it would be surprising had an exegete provided a radically different method in the case of lexicology. The many exegetes included in this case study approach the word in different ways: some read *falaq* in the context of the related *sabab* for the sura (the bewitching of the Prophet by Labīd), others interpret the word in light of early exegesis, and others look to linguistic analysis.

Throughout the *tafsīr* tradition, there is, however, a strong reliance on hadith for providing the meanings of words; and even the exegeses of Zamakhsharī and Rāzī, although eschewing hadith, are clearly reliant on the glosses of *falaq* found in the hadith and analyse *falaq* in light of them, nor do they introduce any new definitions of the word. As a general rule, although undoubtedly with some exceptions, hadith form the main basis of lexical readings, rather than poetry or 'Bedouin' Arabic. However, verses from poetry and references to 'Bedouin' Arabic (either specifically or in a vague notion of 'Arabic') are used to promote certain readings over others. This is essentially a blending of two main strands of early Muslim intellectual thought: firstly, the established practice or interpretation of the Prophet, or, more likely, the early exegetes, alongside the perceived purity, excellence and dominance of Arabic as a language. Exegetes such as Ṭabarī incorporate both of these strands together in a two-stage process: hadith provide the possible solutions to a lexical problem, and linguistic analysis (incorporating notions of 'Arabic') is used to distinguish and support the final exegetical choice that is made.

This is quite distinct to other areas of Arabic linguistics. In morphology and grammar, for example, figures such as Abū Bishr Sībawayhi (d. ca. 180/796) interacted with 'Bedouins' (whoever are meant by the term),[108] but the use of hadith is found significantly later.[109] For medieval Arabic linguists, hadith proved too fluid to provide any basis on which to establish a grammar. Likewise, lexicographers use the Qur'an and the hadith as a source for determining meaning, but often incorporate them as one source amongst many others. In this sense the Qur'an and the hadith are not as 'authoritative' as they are in the *tafsīr* tradition. A different task is also being undertaken by linguists, lexicographers and exegetes. Linguists and lexicographers seek to define terms or linguistic forms in Arabic taken as a whole; exegetes are looking at specific cases and uses of a term or word in a single instance, and are necessarily bound to come to slightly different conclusions about a word's meaning.

That is not to say, however, that there was no cross-over between the disciplines of exegesis, linguistics and lexicography. Many exegetes engage with the Arabic linguistic tradition, but *tafsīr* is not generally characterised by being fully immersed in contemporary linguistic scholarship and debate, and, as Michael Carter has argued, the linguists and the exegetes were, to some extent, rivals in the scholarly world.[110] Exegetes needed to engage with and understand grammatical forms and phenomena, but they are not necessarily grammarians. Similarly, exegetes engage with lexicology, but not lexicography: exegetes have as their main aim the interpretation of the Qur'an, which necessitates an explication and explanation of Qur'anic lexical material, but not a general survey of a word's meaning. For exegetes, grammar and lexicography are 'sciences' (i.e. *ʿulūm al-Qur'ān*) that are a means to an end; they are not studied in and of themselves, but, rather, have a utility for explaining the Qur'anic text.

In the majority of the exegeses, the exegete finds it necessary to find a proof text to support his lexical reading. For many exegetes, grammar and lexicography cannot provide any religious authority to the interpretation of the Qur'an. Such religious authority needs to be garnered from elsewhere, most often the hadith. Verses from the Qur'an, pre-Islamic poetry and 'Bedouin' Arabic are used to distinguish and analyse readings found in hadith, rather than providing definitions on their own. Hadith are certainly predominant, but they are only used in conjunction with other types of sources and proof texts.

Those who do not use hadith to substantiate and defend their lexical readings look to other sources of authority. For 'philosophical' exegetes, such as Rāzī and Zamakhsharī, authority can be found in the Arabic language itself and through an analysis of its forms and structures. For others, such as Qummī, the interpretation of *falaq* is not defended *per se*, but is used as a vehicle for polemic, which provides a more abstract discourse of authority. The polemic, by itself, provides both the authority and the interpretation, and is founded on Shiʿi theology derived from the imams. Sufism also provides another means of exploring lexical meaning that operates in a completely different way, finding and articulating meaning through mystical experience.[111]

The vast majority of the exegetes in this survey provide all three of the possible interpretations of *falaq*; however, the ways in which the exegetes defend their lexical readings vary to a great extent. The differences between each of the defences reveal exegetes' diverging sources of authority: for some hadith, for others linguistic reasoning, even polemic. These differences are also revealed by comparing different genres: lexicographers utilise a range of sources as proof texts, whereas exegetes are focused on the Qur'an and the occurrences of words in a Qur'anic, rather than wider Arabic, context. This should not be unexpected, since an author will have ideas about where authority should be garnered before exploring the Qur'an and writing an exegesis, lexicon or grammatical work. Above all, *falaq* may have a consistent, rigid meaning in the exegetical tradition, but the ways in which lexical glosses are defended and the places in which authority is sought for such defences, is constantly fluid, changing from one author to another.

NOTES

1 Muḥammad Fu'ād ʿAbd al-Bāqī, *al-Muʿjam al-mufahras li-alfāẓ al-Qur'ān al-karīm*, repr. (Riyadh: Dār al-Ḥadīth, 1417/1996), pp. 636–7. The other forms are: *infalaqa* (Q. 26:63) and *fāliq* (Q. 6:95 and 96).

2 Cf. A.J. Wensinck, ed., *Concordance et indices de la tradition musulmane* (Leiden: Brill, 1936–88), vol. 5, pp. 197–8; and Albert Arazi and Salmā Maṣāliḥa, *al-ʿIqd al-thamīn fī diwāwīn al-shuʿarā' al-sitta al-jāhilliyyīn* (Jerusalem: al-Jāmiʿa al-ʿIbriyya fī Ūrushalayim, 1999), p. 845 [of seven verses using the root *f-l-q*, only one contains the word *falaq*]. For more on *gharīb* works, see Andrew Rippin, 'Lexicographical Texts and the Qur'ān' in idem, ed., *Approaches*

to the History of the Interpretation of the Qur'ān (Oxford: Oxford University Press, 1988), pp. 158–74, esp. pp. 165–7.

3 See Edward William Lane, *An Arabic-English Lexicon*, repr. (Cambridge: Islamic Texts Society, 1984), p. 2442; cf. Thomas O'Shaughnessy, 'The Seven Names for Hell in the Qur'ān', *Bulletin of the School of Oriental and African Studies* 24 (1961), pp. 444–69, at pp. 449–51. Although the Arabic name for Hell, Gehenna, ultimately derives from the Hebrew for the 'valley of Gehinnom' (see 2 Chronicles 28:3 and Jeremiah 7:31), it is difficult to ascertain whether the definition of *falaq* as a place in Hell, through its meaning of a 'valley', is an intentional reference or a coincidence; however, the lexicons do not make this explicit connection.

4 See S.R. Burge, 'The Angels in *Sūrat al-Malāʾika*: Exegeses of Q. 35:1', *Journal of Qur'anic Studies* 10 (2009), pp. 50–70, at pp. 54–8.

5 E.g. 'daybreak': M.A.S. Abdel Haleem, tr., *The Qur'an: A New Translation* (Oxford: Oxford University Press, 2004), p. 445; Arthur J. Arberry, tr., *The Koran Interpreted*, repr. (Oxford: Oxford University Press, 1998), p. 668; J.M. Rodwell, tr., *The Koran*, repr. (London: Everyman, 1994), p. 430; George Sale, tr., *The Korân*, repr. (London: Frederick Warne & Co., n.d.), p. 596; and 'dawn': Abdullah Yusuf Ali, tr., *The Holy Qur'ān*, repr. (London: Wordsworth, 2000), p. 561; Tarif Khalidi, tr., *The Qur'ān* (London: Penguin, 2008), p. 525. See also Afnan H. Fatani, 'The Lexical Transfer of Arabic Non-core Lexicon: Sura 113 of the Qur'an — *al-Falaq* (The Splitting)', *Journal of Qur'anic Studies* 4 (2002), pp. 61–81.

6 Cf. Neal Robinson, *Discovering the Qur'an: A Contemporary Approach to a Veiled Text* (London: SCM Press, 1996), pp. 100–3.

7 Feras Hamza and Sajjad Rizvi with Farhana Mayer, eds, *An Anthology of Qur'anic Commentaries. Volume 1: On the Nature of the Divine* (Oxford: Oxford University Press in association with the Institute of Ismaili Studies, 2008), p. 456.

8 Cf. R. Köbert, 'Das Gottesepitheon *aṣ-Ṣamad* in Sure 112, 2', *Orientalia* 30 (1961), pp. 204–5; Rudi Paret, 'Der Ausdruck *ṣamad* in Sure 112, 2', *Der Islam* 56 (1979), pp. 294–5; Uri Rubin, '*al-Ṣamad* and the High God - an Interpretation of Sura CXII', *Der Islam* 61 (1984), pp. 197–217.

9 Another similar debate is that of the Satanic verses, which received remarkably little interest in Muslim scholarship, but became an important focus in debates about the development of Islam; cf. John Burton, '"Those are High Flying Cranes"', *Journal of Semitic Studies* 15 (1970), pp. 246–65; Shahab Ahmed, 'Ibn Taymiyya and the Satanic Verses', *Studia Islamica* 87 (1998), pp. 67–124; W. Montgomery Watt, 'Belief in a "High God" in Pre-Islamic Mecca', *Journal of Semitic Studies* 16 (1971), pp. 35–40, at pp. 37–8.

10 See Hamza *et al.*, *On the Nature of the Divine*, pp. 491–575.

11 Watt, 'Belief in a "High God" in Pre-Islamic Mecca'; and idem, 'The Qur'ān and a Belief in a "High God"', *Der Islam* 56 (1979), pp. 205–11. Cf. idem, 'Ḥanīf', *EI*^{2}, vol. 3, pp. 165–6.

12 There is also a study of the interpretation of this sura, focusing on the narrative of the bewitching of the Prophet; see David Cook, 'The Prophet Muḥammad, Labīd al-Yahūdī and the Commentaries to *Sūra* 113', *Journal of Semitic Studies* 45 (2000), pp. 323–45.

13 See Cook, 'The Prophet Muḥammad, Labīd al-Yahūdī and the Commentaries to *Sūra* 113'; and S.R. Burge, 'Jalāl al-Dīn al-Suyūṭī, the *Muʿawwidhatān* and

the Modes of Exegesis' in Karen Bauer, ed., *Aims, Methods and Contexts of Qur'anic Exegesis (2nd/8th–9th/15th c.)* (Oxford, Oxford University Press in association with the Institute of Ismaili Studies, 2013), pp. 277–307.

14 See A. Rippin, 'Al-Zuhrī, *Naskh al-Qur'ān* and the Problem of Early *Tafsīr* Texts', *Bulletin of the School of Oriental and African Studies* 47 (1984), pp. 22–43.

15 See Kees Versteegh, 'Zayd ibn ʿAlī's Commentary on the Qur'ān' in Yasir Suleiman, ed., *Arabic Grammar and Linguistics*, repr. (London: RoutledgeCurzon, 2003), pp. 9–29. Some have doubted its authenticity, e.g. Rudolf Strothmann, 'Das Problem der literarischen Persönlichkeit Zaid ibn ʿAlī', *Der Islam* 10 (1923), pp. 1–52; see also Harald Motzki, 'The Origins of Muslim Exegesis. A Debate' in Harald Motzki with Nicolet Boekhoff-van der Voort and Sean W. Anthony, *Analysing Muslim Traditions: Studies in Legal, Exegetical and Maghāzī Ḥadīth* (Leiden: Brill, 2010), pp. 231–304, at pp. 281–5.

16 Cf. Hamza *et al.*, *On the Nature of the Divine*, pp. 21–3.

17 See Cook, 'The Prophet Muḥammad, Labīd al-Yahūdī and the Commentaries to *Sūra* 113'; and Burge, 'Jalāl al-Dīn al-Suyūṭī, the *Muʿawwidhatān* and the Modes of Exegesis'.

18 Wansbrough makes the link between *gharīb al-Qur'ān* and periphrastic exegesis; see John Wansbrough, *Quranic Studies: Sources and Methods of Scriptural Interpretation*, new edn (Amherst, NY: Prometheus Books, 2004), pp. 218–27; see also Rippin, 'Lexicographical Texts and the Qur'ān'.

19 Muqātil b. Sulaymān, *Tafsīr Muqātil b. Sulaymān*, ed. ʿAbd Allāh Maḥmūd Shiḥāta (Cairo: al-Hay'a al-Miṣriyya al-ʿĀmma li'l-Kitāb, 1979–89), vol. 4, p. 924.

20 This interpretation incorporates some of the verse that follows (Q. 113:2): *from the evil of what He has created (min shirr mā khalaqa)*. Zayd b. ʿAlī, *Tafsīr gharīb al-Qur'ān*, ed. Muḥammad Jawād al-Ḥusaynī al-Jalālī (Tehran: Markaz al-Nashr al-Tibāʿ li-Maktabat al-Iʿlām al-Islāmī, 1376 Sh./1418/1997).

21 Cf. Herbert Berg, *The Development of Exegesis in Early Islam: The Authenticity of Muslim Literature from the Formative Period* (Richmond, Surrey: Curzon, 2000), pp. 14–15.

22 Furāt b. Furāt al-Kūfī, *Tafsīr Furāt al-Kūfī*, ed. Muḥammad al-Kāẓim (Tehran: Mu'assasat al-Ṭabʿ wa'l-Nashr, Wizārat al-Thaqāfa wa'l-Irshād al-Islāmī, 1416/1995), vol. 2, pp. 259–60.

23 Muḥammad b. Jarīr al-Ṭabarī, *Jāmiʿ al-bayān ʿan ta'wīl al-Qur'ān* (Cairo: Būlāq, 1905–12), vol. 30, p. 349.

24 Ibid., p. 351.

25 'According to Ibn ʿAbbās, *al-falaq* means the morning (*ṣubḥ*), while according to al-Ḍaḥḥāk it refers to a valley in the Hellfire. [On the other hand], according to Wuhayb it refers to a chamber in Hell, and according to Ḥasan it refers to a well in Hell.' Sahl al-Tustarī, *Tafsīr*, tr. Annabel Keeler and Ali Keeler as *Tafsīr al-Tustarī* (Louisville, KY: Fons Vitae / Royal Aal al-Bayt Institute for Islamic Thought, 2011), p. 318.

26 Tustarī, *Tafsīr*, p. 318; lit. 'rocks split (*tunfalaqu*) by water'. Also, *jamīʿ al-khalq*, may properly refer to 'all of creation' not just 'all people'.

27 Cf. Hamza *et al.*, *On the Nature of the Divine*, pp. 24–5; and Meir M. Bar-Asher, *Scripture and Exegesis in Early Imāmī Shiism* (Leiden: Brill, and Jerusalem: The Magnes Press, 1999), pp. 33–56.

28 ʿAlī b. Ibrāhīm al-Qummī, *Tafsīr al-Qummī*, ed. Ṭayyib al-Mūsawī al-Jazāʾirī (Najaf: Maṭbaʿat al-Najaf, 1387/1967), vol. 2, p. 449.

29 Ibid.

30 Al-Sāmirī is the name given to the man who induced the Israelites to worship the golden calf (Q. 2:85, 87); see Ismail Albayrak, 'The Qur'anic Narratives of the Golden Calf Episode', *Journal of Qur'anic Studies* 3 (2001), pp. 47–69.

31 For early Islamic anti-Christian polemic, both Sunni and Shiʿi, see David Thomas, *Anti-Christian Polemic in Early Islam: Abī ʿĪsā al-Warrāq's "Against the Trinity"* (Cambridge: Cambridge University Press, 1992), pp. 31–50.

32 See L. Veccia Vaglieri, 'Ibn Muldjam', *EI*^{2}, vol. 3, pp. 887–90.

33 Martha Himmelfarb, *Tours of Hell: An Apocalyptic Form in Jewish and Christian Literature* (Philadelphia, PA: University of Pennsylvania Press, 1983).

34 Brooke Olson Vuckovic, *Heavenly Journeys, Earthly Concerns: The Legacy of the* Miʿrāj *in the Formation of Islam* (London: Routledge, 2005), p. 120; Roberto Tottoli, 'Tours of Hell and Punishment of Sinners in *Miʿrāj* Narratives: Use and Meaning of Eschatology in Muḥammad's Ascension' in Christiane J. Gruber and Frederick S. Colby, *The Prophet's Ascension: Cross-Cultural Encounters with the Islamic* Miʿrāj *Tales* (Bloomington, IN: University of Indiana Press, 2010), pp. 11–26.

35 Abū'l-Layth al-Samarqandī, *Tafsīr*, ed. ʿAbd al-Raḥmān al-Zaqqa (Baghdad: Maṭbaʿat al-Irshād, 1985–6).

36 Ibid.

37 Ibid.

38 Abū'l-Ḥasan al-Māwardī, *Tafsīr al-Māwardī*, published with *Muṣḥaf al-tahajjud* (Cairo: Dār al-Ṣafwā li'l-Ṭibāʿa wa'l-Nashr, 1413/1993), vol. 4, p. 570.

39 Ibid., vol. 4, p. 570: *yā laylatan lam anamhā bittu / arʿā'l-nujūm ilā an nawwara'l-falaqu* ('Night! May I not be separated from the flock remaining in the field / the stars are set to pasture until the *falaq* brings light'). For the use of poetry in exegesis, see the discussion below, and also Issa J. Boullata, 'Poetry Citation as Interpretive Illustration in Qurʾān Exegesis: *Masāʾil Nāfiʿ ibn al-Azraq*', reprinted in Mustafa Shah, ed., *Tafsīr – Interpreting the Qurʾān: Critical Concepts in Islamic Studies* (London: Routledge, 2013), vol. 2, pp. 65–77.

40 See Johann Fück, *Arabiyya: Untersuchungen zur arabischen Sprach- und Stilgeschichte* (Berlin: Akademie Vorlage, 1958).

41 Cf. Alena Kulinich, 'Representing "a Blameworthy *Tafsīr*": Muʿtazilite Exegetical Tradition in *al-Jāmiʿ fī tafsīr al-Qurʾān* of ʿAlī ibn ʿĪsā al-Rummānī (d. 384/994)' (Unpublished PhD Dissertation, School of Oriental and African Studies, University of London, 2011).

42 See Andrew J. Lane, *A Traditional Muʿtazilite Qurʾān Commentary: The* Kashshāf *of Jār Allāh al-Zamakhsharī (d. 538/1144)* (Leiden: Brill, 2006).

43 Maḥmūd b. ʿUmar al-Zamakhsharī, *al-Kashshāf ʿan ḥaqāʾiq al-tanzīl wa-ʿuyūn al-aqāwīl fī wujūh al-taʾwīl* (Beirut: Dār al-Maʿrifa, 1987), vol. 4, pp. 300–1.

44 Cf. Ṭabarī, *Jāmiʿ al-bayān*, vol. 30, p. 351.

45 Cf. Maḥmūd b. ʿUmar al-Zamakhsharī, *Nukat al-aʿrāb fī gharīb al-iʿrāb fī'l-Qurʾān al-karīm*, ed. Muḥammad Abū'l-Fatūḥ Sharīf (Cairo: Dār al-Maʿārif, 1986), pp. 164–5.

46 Zamakhsharī, *al-Kashshāf*, vol. 4, p. 300.

47 Cf. Samarqandī's interpretation of *falaq*; see this chapter, pp. 165–6.

48 *Iṭmaʾanna*: a Form IV quadraliteral, which can be used to refer to depressions in land; see Lane, *Arabic-English Lexicon*, p. 1882.
49 Zamakhsharī, *al-Kashshāf*, vol. 4, p. 300.
50 Zamakhsharī leaves this unattributed. For Rāzī's citations of Zamakhsharī, see Michel Lagarde, *Index du Grande Commentaire de Faḫr al-Dīn al-Rāzī* (Leiden: Brill, 1996), p. 84 and pp. 98–9.
51 Fakhr al-Dīn al-Rāzī, *al-Tafsīr al-kabīr* (Tehran: Dār al-Kutub al-ʿIlmiyya, n.d.), vol. 32, p. 191.
52 Ibid., pp. 191–2.
53 Rāzī also cites Q. 42:12; Q. 68:42; Q. 45:28; Q. 17:78 and Q. 3:17; ibid., vol. 32, pp. 191–2.
54 Ibid., p. 192.
55 Ibid., pp. 192–3; Lagarde notes a strong reliance on Zamakhsharī in the spheres of grammar and lexicology, see Lagarde, *Index du Grande Commentaire de Faḫr al-Dīn al-Rāzī*, p. 3.
56 Rāzī, *al-Tafsīr al-kabīr*, p. 193.
57 ʿAbd Allāh b. ʿUmar al-Bayḍāwī, *Anwār al-tanzīl wa asrār al-taʾwīl* (Cairo: Muṣṭafā al-Bābī al-Ḥalabī, 1968), vol. 3, pp. 582–3. For a discussion of Bayḍāwī's approach to exegesis, see Y. Rahman, 'Hermeneutics of al-Baydawi in his Anwar al-Tanzil wa Asrar al-Ta'wil', *Islamic Culture* 71 (1997), pp. 1–14.
58 Lane, *A Traditional Muʿtazilite Qurʾān Commentary*, pp. 104–13.
59 The structure of Qurṭubī's argument appears to be heavily reliant on Ṭabarī.
60 Muḥammad b. Aḥmad al-Qurṭubī, *al-Jāmiʿ li-aḥkām al-Qurʾān* (Cairo: Dār al-Kutub al-ʿArabī, 1387/1967), vol. 20, pp. 254–5.
61 Ṭabarī does not cite any poetry in his treatment of *falaq*, but he frequently cites verses in his exegesis; see Muḥammad al-Mālikī, *Juhūd al-Ṭabarī fī dirāsāt al-shawāhid al-shaʿriyya fī 'Jāmiʿ al-bayān ʿan taʾwīl al-Qurʾān': Dirāsa lughawiyya adabiyya fī tafsīr al-Qurʾān al-karīm* (Ribat: Maṭbaʿat al-Maʿārif al-Jadīda, 1994).
62 Qurṭubī, *al-Jāmiʿ li-aḥkām al-Qurʾān*, vol. 20, pp. 254–5.
63 Ibid., p. 255.
64 Zamakhsharī, *al-Kashshāf*, vol. 4, p. 300; Rāzī, *al-Tafsīr al-kabīr*, vol. 32, p. 193.
65 Ismāʿīl b. ʿUmar Ibn Kathīr, *Tafsīr al-Qurʾān al-karīm* (Cairo: Dār al-Fikr, n.d.), vol. 4, p. 573; and Jalāl al-Dīn al-Maḥallī and Jalāl al-Dīn al-Suyūṭī, *Tafsīr al-Jalālayn* (Damascus: Maṭbaʿat al-Mallāḥ, 1389/1969), p. 815.
66 Jalal al-Dīn al-Suyūṭī, *al-Durr al-manthūr fī'l-tafsīr bi'l-maʾthūr* (Cairo: Dār al-Maʿarifa, 1978), vol. 6, p. 417.
67 Ibn Taymiyya, *Muqaddima fī uṣūl al-tafsīr*, ed. ʿAdnān Zarzūr (Kuwait: Dār al-Qurʾān al-Karīm, 1971); see also Walid A. Saleh, 'Ibn Taymiyya and the Rise of Radical Hermeneutics: An Analysis of *An Introduction to the Foundation of Qurʾānic Exegesis*' in Yossef Rapoport and Shahab Ahmed, eds, *Ibn Taymiyya and his Times* (Lahore: Oxford University Press, 2010), pp. 123–62.
68 Cf. Jalāl al-Dīn al-Suyūṭī, *al-Muzhīr fī ʿulūm al-lugha wa anwāʾihā* (Cairo: ʿĪsā al-Bābī al-Halabī, 1954–7).
69 Cf. Jalāl al-Dīn al-Suyūṭī, *[Kitāb] al-Itqān fī ʿulūm al-Qurʾān* (Beirut: Dār al-Fikr, 1423/2003), vol. 1, pp. 160–290 [nos 36–42].
70 See S.R. Burge, 'The Angels in *Sūrat al-Malāʾika*, pp. 50–70. For more on lexicology in the *Tafsīr al-Jalālayn*, see Feras Hamza, tr., *Tafsīr al-Jalālayn: An*

Annotated English Translation of the Commentary of the Two Jalāls (Louisville, KY: Fons Vitae, 2008), pp. xii–xiv.

71 See S.R. Burge, 'Scattered Pearls: Exploring al-Suyūṭī's Hermeneutics and Use of Sources in *al-Durr al-manthūr fī'l-tafsīr bi'l-ma'thūr*', *Journal of the Royal Asiatic Society* 24, no. 2 (2014), pp. 251–96.

72 See Rippin, 'Lexicographical Texts and the Qur'ān', pp. 158–63.

73 See John A. Haywood, 'The Entry in Medieval Arabic Monolingual Dictionaries: Some Aspects of Arrangement and Context' in Reinhard R.K. Hartmann, ed., *The History of Lexicography: Papers from the Dictionary Research Centre Seminar at Exeter, March 1986* (Amsterdam: J. Benjamins, 1986), pp. 107–13.

74 Ḥusayn Naṣṣār, *al-Muʿjam al-ʿarabī: nasha'tuhu wa taṭawwuruhu* (Cairo: Dār Miṣr li'l-Ṭibāʿa, n.d.); and Stefan Wild, *Das Kitab al-ʿAin und die arabische Lexikographie* (Wiesbaden: Otto Harrassowitz, 1965).

75 See Rafael Talmon, *Arabic Grammar in its Formative Age:* Kitāb al-ʿAyn *and its Attribution to Ḫalīl b. Aḥmad* (Leiden: Brill 1997), p. 96; Naṣṣār, *al-Muʿjam al-ʿarabī*, vol. 1, pp. 218–313. For a discussion of the problems with dating early lexicographical works, see Jaako Hämeen-Antilla, 'Al-Aṣmāʿī, Early Lexicography and *Kutub al-Farq*', *Zeitschrift für Geschichte der arabisch-islamischen Wissenschaften* 16 (2004–5), pp. 141–8.

76 al-Khalīl b. Aḥmad, *Kitāb al-ʿAyn* (Beirut: Dār Iḥyā' al-Turāth al-ʿArabī, 2001), p. 754.

77 Lane, *Arabic-English Lexicon*, p. 1640.

78 Ibid., p. 2340.

79 Haywood notes four main ways of defining *lemmata* in medieval Arabic lexicons: (i) antonyms, (ii) synonyms, (iii) a phrase explaining the term; and (iv) meanings given through implications; see Haywood, 'The Entry in Medieval Arabic Monolingual Dictionaries', p. 110.

80 Muḥammad b. Yaʿqūb al-Fīrūzabādī, *al-Qāmūs al-muḥīṭ* (India: n.p., n.d.), vol. 4, p. 133; see also Naṣṣār, *al-Muʿjam al-ʿarabī*, vol. 2, pp. 575–638.

81 Works also emerged that discussed similar problems in hadith (*gharīb al-ḥadīth*); see T. Seidensticker, 'Lexicography: Classical Arabic', *EALL*, vol. 3, pp. 30–37; see also Naṣṣār, *al-Muʿjam al-ʿarabī*, vol. 1, pp. 39–50.

82 Karen Bauer has stressed the need to think of *tafsīr* in terms of genre; see Karen Bauer, 'Introduction' in eadem, ed., *Aims, Methods and Contexts of Qur'anic Exegesis*, pp. 1–16.

83 John Wansbrough, '*Majāz al-Qur'ān:* Periphrastic Exegesis', *Bulletin of the School of Oriental and African Studies* 33 (1970), pp. 247–66; and idem, *Quranic Studies*, pp. 217–20. See also Wolfhart Heinrichs, 'Contacts between Scriptural Hermeneutics and Literary Theory in Islam: The Case of *Majāz*', *Zeitschrift für Geschichte der arabisch-islamischen Wissenschaften* 7 (1992), pp. 253–84.

84 Cf. Suyūṭī, *al-Itqān*; idem, *Lubāb al-nuqūl fī asbāb al-nuzūl* (Tunis: Dār al-Tūnisiya, 1981); idem, *Asrār tartīb al-Qur'ān*, ed. Muḥammad Abū'l-Faḍl Ibrāhīm (Cairo: Dār al-Iʿtiṣād, 1376/1976); idem, *al-Mutawakkilī*, ed. and tr. William Y. Bell as *The Mutawakkilī of as-Suyūṭī* (Cairo: Nile Mission Press, 1924); and idem, *al-Muhadhdhab fī-mā waqaʿa fī'l-Qur'ān min al-muʿarrab* (Beirut: Dār al-Kutub al-ʿIlmiyya, 1988); Maḥallī and Suyūṭī, *Tafsīr al-Jalālayn*.

See also Jane Dammen McAuliffe, 'Exegetical Sciences' in Andrew Rippin, ed., *The Blackwell Companion to the Qur'ān* (London: Blackwell, 2006), pp. 403–19.

85 Abū 'Ubayda, *Majāz al-Qur'ān*, ed. Aḥmad Farīd al-Mazīdī (Beirut: Dār al-Kutub al-'Ilmiyya, 2006), p. 298.

86 Athīr al-Dīn Abū'l-Ḥayyān al-Andalūsī [al-Ghanāṭī], *Tuḥfat al-arīb bi-mā fi'l-Qur'ān min al-gharīb*, ed. Aḥmad Maṭlūb and Khadīja al-Ḥadīthī (Baghdad: Maṭba'at al-'Ānī, 1397/1977), pp. 209–10.

87 Ibn Manẓūr, *Lisān al-'Arab*, ed. Amīn Muḥammad 'Abd al-Wahhāb and Muḥammad al-Ṣādiq al-'Ubaydī (Beirut: Dār Iḥyā' al-Turāth al-'Arabī, 1999), vol. 10, pp. 320–22; see also Naṣṣār, *al-Mu'jam al-'arabī*, vol. 2, pp. 544–74.

88 Murtaḍā al-Zabīdī, *Tāj al-'arūs min jawāhir al-qāmūs*, ed. 'Abd al-Sattār Aḥmad Farāj *et al.* (Kuwait: Maṭaba'at Ḥukūmāt al-Kuwayt, 1965–2001), vol. 26, pp. 308–16; see also Naṣṣār, *al-Mu'jam al-'arabī*, vol. 2, pp. 639–79.

89 Abū Bakr Muḥammad b. al-Ḥasan Ibn Durayd, *Kitāb Jamaharat al-lugha*, repr. (Baghdad: al-Muthanna Library, n.d.), vol. 3, p. 154.

90 Since this chapter has focused on one word, it has not been possible to tell whether Ṭabarī arranges these external proof texts into any sort of hierarchy. For example, would a line of poetry trump a vague notion of 'Arab language' or linguistic reasoning?

91 Cf. 'I (Suyūṭī) say: "The second part refers to the Qur'ān; the first is the *Sunna*, according to the reports that Gabriel would bring down the *Sunna* the same way He would bring down the Qur'ān."' Jalāl al-Dīn al-Suyūṭī, *al-Itqān fī 'ulūm al-Qur'ān*, tr. Ḥamid Algar, Michael Schub and Ayman Abdel Ḥaleem as *The Perfect Guide to the Sciences of the Qur'ān: al-Itqān fī 'ulūm al-Qur'ān* (Reading: Garnet, 2011), p. 101; Suyūṭī, *al-Itqān*, vol. 1., p. 63.

92 Wansbrough, *Quranic Studies*, p. 142; see also pp. 216–18 and Andrew Rippin, 'Ibn 'Abbās's *Lughāt fī'l-Qur'ān*', *Bulletin of the School of Oriental and African Studies* 44, no. 1 (1981), pp. 15–25, at pp. 15–16.

93 Boullata, 'Poetry Citation as Interpretative Illustration in Qur'ān Exegesis', pp. 74–5.

94 Ibid., p. 75.

95 See Jonathan Brown, *The Canonization of al-Bukhārī and Muslim: The Formation and Function of the Sunnī Ḥadīth Canon* (Leiden: Brill, 2007).

96 Adrian Gully, *Grammar and Semantics in Medieval Arabic: A Study of Ibn-Hishām's* 'Mughni l-Labīb' (Richmond, Surrey: Curzon Press, 1995), pp. 89–90.

97 Gully, *Grammar and Semantics in Medieval Arabic*, p. 84.

98 There is a similar division between exegetes and *muḥaddiths*, who often include sections on '*tafsīr*'; their agenda are completely different and the shape and content of each of their *tafsīrs* are radically different; see R. Marston Speight, 'The Function of *ḥadīth* as Commentary on the Qur'ān, as Seen in the Six Authoritative Collections' in Andrew Rippin, ed., *Approaches to the History of the Interpretation of the Qur'ān* (Oxford: Clarendon Press, 1988), pp. 63–81, at p. 80.

99 Arabic grammar was often regarded as a 'low' science; see Gully, *Grammar and Semantics in Medieval Arabic*, pp. 73–4; and Michael G. Carter, 'Language Control as People Control', *al-Abḥath* 31 (1983), pp. 65–84.

100 See Burge, 'Scattered Pearls'.
101 Cf. George Bohas and Jean-Patrick Guillaume, *Étude des theories des grammairiens arabes. I. Morphologie et phonologie* (Damascus: Institut Française de Damas, 1984), pp. 25–31.
102 Rummānī is, perhaps, the best example of a scholar operating in all three of these disciplines; see Kulinich, 'Representing "a Blameworthy *Tafsīr*" '.
103 See J.R.T.M. Peters, 'La théologie musulmane et l'étude du langage', *Histoire Épistémologie Langage* 2 (1980), pp. 9–19; Andrzej Czapkiewicz, *The Views of the Medieval Arab Philologists on Language and Its Origins in Light of 'As-Suyūṭī's* "al-Muzhir' (Krakow: Naktadem Uniweisytetu Jagiellońskiego, 1988); and for other instances of theological ideas that had an impact on Rāzī's exegesis, see Yasin Ceylan, *Theology and Tafsīr in the Major Works of Fakhr al-Dīn al-Rāzī* (Kuala Lumpur: International Institute of Islamic Thought and Civilization, 1996), pp. 17–23.
104 Peters, 'La théologie muslumane et l'étude du langage', p. 15; see also Bernard Weiss, 'Medieval Discussions of the Origin of Language', *Zeitschrift der Deutschen Morgenländischen Gesellschaft* 124 (1974), pp. 33–41; and Mustafa Shah, 'Classical Islamic Discourse on the Origins of Language: Cultural Memory and the Defense of Orthodoxy', *Numen* 58 (2011), pp. 314–43.
105 See Czapkiewicz, *The Views of the Medieval Arab Philologists*, pp. 51–7; Weiss, 'Medieval Discussions of the Origin of Language', pp. 34–5.
106 See Lagarde, *Index du Grande Commentaire de Faḫr al-Dīn al-Rāzī*, p. 3.
107 Debates about this relationship also move into the field of logic; see Cornelis H.M. [Kees] Versteegh, 'Logique et grammaire au dixième siècle', *Histoire Épistémologie Langage* 2 (1980), pp. 39–52; Jacques Langhade, 'Grammaire, logique, études linguistiques chez al-Farabi', *Historiographica Linguistica* 8 (1981), pp. 365–77; and Shukri B. Ahmed, *Aristotelian Logic and the Arabic Language in Alfārābī* (Albany, NY: State University of New York Press, 1991).
108 See Joshua Blau, 'The Role of the Bedouins as Arbiters in Linguistic Questions and the *Mas'ala az-Zunburiyya*,' *Journal of Semitic Studies* 8, no. 1 (1963), pp. 42–51.
109 See Gully, *Grammar and Semantics in Medieval Arabic*, pp. 88–90.
110 Carter, 'Language Control as People Control', p. 84.
111 Cf. Toby Mayer's contribution in this volume, Chapter 8.

7

Poetic Licence and the Qur'anic Names of Hell: The Treatment of Cognate Substitution in al-Rāghib al-Iṣfahānī's Qur'anic Lexicon

DEVIN STEWART

Many Qur'anic passages exhibit poetic licence, in which deviations from ordinary grammar, morphology and usage occur for the sake of verse-final rhyme, and this poses a basic lexicographical problem.[1] One such type of deviation, the focus of this study, may be termed cognate substitution: the substitution, for the sake of rhyme, of a cognate word containing the same root consonants as an underlying term but following a different morphological pattern from the word one would have expected in the context, such as *amīn* ('trustworthy') for an expected *āmin* ('safe') in Q. 95:3. The new word has the advantage of creating satisfactory end-rhyme, but may be unknown, rare or ordinarily take a meaning somewhat different from what it is required to convey in the context in question. In essence, the issue of poetic licence places any interpreter or translator of the text, including the Arabic lexicographer, on the horns of a dilemma: should he or she admit that poetic licence has occurred, reporting the meaning as it would have been without the rhyme-occasioned deviation, or rather adhere to the text as it is, choosing not to recognise that a deviation has occurred and explaining the apparently odd or incongruous form as specifically intended and meaningful in accordance with ordinary grammatical and stylistic rules? In order to assess one prominent medieval lexicographer's awareness of, and reaction to, instances of poetic licence in the Qur'anic text, this essay examines verse-final words that have been identified by the modern German scholar Friedrun Müller, in her 1969 work *Untersuchungen zur Reimprosa im Koran*,[2] as examples of cognate substitution and analyses their interpretation in the well-known Qur'anic lexicon *Mufradāt alfāẓ al-Qur'ān* of al-Rāghib al-Iṣfahānī (d. 422/1031).[3] This analysis is extended to a group of words that Müller points out but does not address: the distinctive names given to Hell in the Qur'an.

As the primary text of Islamic civilisation, the Qur'an has played a central role in the history of Arabic lexicography. This has meant not only that medieval Arabic dictionaries tend to devote entries to the lexical items included in the Qur'an but also that they are caught up with a host of other issues that arose in the history of interpretation of the sacred text. Lexicography has thus been affected by theological controversy and specific points of dogma: that the Qur'an is miraculous, that it is unlike any text produced by humans, that it is not poetry, that its language is purely Arabic, and so on. In addition, the definitions of Qur'anic vocabulary provided in Arabic lexica are inevitably tied to their particular contexts and coloured by the particular rhetorical figures and patterns in conjunction with which they occur. This can lead to odd or misleading results when the lexicographer – or the entire lexicographical tradition – ignores the rhetoric of particular passages in which a lexical item from the Qur'an is ensconced. It is the task of modern scholars to rectify some of these interpretations by pointing out the origin of the lexical definitions in question, retrieving the rhetorical sense of the passages and providing a more careful assessment of the terms' meanings.

An example of this phenomenon may be seen in the definition of the Form II verb *bashshara, yubashshiru* given in Lane's *Arabic–English Lexicon*, which draws on the major classical Arabic dictionaries:

> *bashsharahu*: . . . *He announced to him an event which produced a change in his basharah* (or complexion): and hence, . . . *he announced to him an event which rejoiced him* . . . [or *he rejoiced him by an annunciation*:] and *he announced to him an event which grieved him*: [or *he grieved him by an annunciation*:] both these significations are proper.[4]

Lane reports that the verb *bashshara* means to convey either good news or bad news; both senses are correct. To current native speakers of Arabic, this is counter-intuitive and quite surprising, for *bashshara* ordinarily means to convey good news exclusively; the cognates *bushrā* and *bishāra* also mean 'glad tidings' and never the opposite. A survey of literature, whether modern or medieval, confirms the truth of this in general. Then why do the dictionaries record that *bashshara* means also 'to convey bad news', including this sense that violates common usage?

This claim derives ultimately from several verses of the Qur'an in which the verb *bashshara, yubashshiru* is used in connection with the complement *ʿadhāb alīm* ('a painful punishment'). Translated somewhat over-literally, with the key imperative *bashshir* rendered in a neutral fashion, the phrases in question read as follows:

> *fa-bashshirhu bi-ʿadhābin alīm* (*So announce to him a painful punishment*, Q. 31:7; Q. 45:8)
>
> *fa-bashshirhum bi-ʿadhābin alīm* (*So announce to them a painful punishment*, Q. 3:21; Q. 9:34; Q. 84:24)
>
> *bashshiri'l-munāfiqīna bi-anna lahum ʿadhāban alīmā* (*Announce to the Hypocrites that they will have a painful punishment*, Q. 4:138)
>
> *wa bashshiri'lladhīna kafarū bi-ʿadhābin alīm* (*And announce to those who have rejected belief a painful torment*, Q. 9:3)

From these verses, lexicographers concluded that the verb *bashshara, yubashshiru* may refer to evil tidings, the future punishment announced here, as well as glad tidings, such as the angel's annunciation to Abraham that he would have a son (Q. 11:71; Q. 15:53; Q. 51:28; Q. 37:101, 112). While this follows from a flat reading of the texts above, it does not withstand scrutiny. In the Qur'an itself, *bashshara* is mainly a positive term. The cognate *bushrā* refers exclusively to good news.[5] The cognates *bashīr* and *mubashshir* denote exclusively someone who brings glad tidings, and they are used often in merisms together with their negative counterparts *nadhīr* and *mundhir* (both 'warner').[6] The Qur'anic text frequently applies these positive and negative terms to prophets in order to convey the complementary facets of their function: to convey both the promise of paradise for believers and the threat of damnation for unbelievers. The several passages where the imperative *bashshir* is used in conjunction with the phrase *bi-ʿadhābin alīm* thus seem to deviate from the conventional meaning of words of the triconsonantal root *b-sh-r* elsewhere in the Qur'an.

An understanding of the rhetorical features of prophetic discourse in general and Qur'anic discourse in particular, especially that of address to the unbelievers, suggests that the phrase *fa-bashshirhum bi-ʿadhābin alīm* is a case of ironic antiphrasis. The tone of many Qur'anic passages like those just mentioned that address the unbelievers is one of challenge and taunt rather than simple condemnation. The verb *bashshara* means to convey glad tidings, but the text is indulging in ironic or sarcastic humour: 'Give them the *glad tidings* of a painful punishment.' The verb does not ordinarily refer to bad news, but here the positive verb is used with a negative predicate in an ironic inversion for rhetorical effect, taunting the unbelievers and suggesting that they will receive their just deserts, a fitting reward for their sinful actions. Lexicographers then interpreted the passage too literally, with the result that Arabic dictionaries included, and have continued to include, the definition 'to convey evil tidings' among the meanings of *bashshara*.

Ironic inversions of this type occur frequently in the Qur'an in similar taunts directed at the unbelievers. Another similar antiphrasis, again in reference to punishment in Hell, occurs in Q. 9:35: *yawma yuḥmā ʿalayhā fī nāri Jahannama fa-tukwā bihā jibāhuhum wa junūbuhum wa ẓuhūruhum: hādhā mā kanaztum li-anfusikum fa-dhūqū mā kuntum taknizūn* (*On the day when the fire of Hell is stoked, and their foreheads, flanks, and backs are seared thereby: 'This is what you have hoarded as a treasure for yourselves, so taste what you used to hoard!'*).[7] Here the verb *kanaza, yaknizu* ('to store up treasure') is used in a pejorative manner. It is suggestive that this follows immediately after Q. 9:34, one of the verses in which the phrase *fa-bashshirhum bi-ʿadhābin alīm* appears. One may point to yet another ironic and biting address to the unbeliever suffering the torments of Hell, in Q. 44:43–50:

inna shajarata'l-zaqqūm
ṭaʿāmu'l-athīm
ka'l-muhli yaghlī fī'l-buṭūn
ka-ghalyi'l-ḥamīm
khudhūhu fa-ʿtilūhu ilā sawā'i'l-jaḥīm
thumma ṣubbū fawqa ra'sihi min ʿadhābi'l-ḥamīm
dhuq innaka anta'l-ʿazīzu'l-karīm
inna hādhā mā kuntum bihī tamtarūn

The tree of Zaqqum
Is the food of the sinner.
Like molten copper it seethes in their bellies,
Just as boiling water seethes.
Take him and lift him up to the surface of Hell.
Then pour upon his head the torment of scalding water.
'Taste! For you are the powerful and noble one.
This is what ye used to doubt.'

The phrase *innaka anta'l-ʿazīzu'l-karīm* (*'For you are the powerful and noble one!'*) is patently ironic since it refers to the debased and tortured denizen of hell, even more so because it mimics exactly the form of the Qur'anic tag phrases that frequently apply paired positive epithets to God, expressing high reverence for the Deity.[8] These examples show that ironic inversion is a regular feature of Qur'anic rhetoric, and they corroborate the interpretation of *fa-bashshirhum bi-ʿadhābin alīm* as just such an inversion. This being the case, *bashshara* means to convey good news, as one would expect, and the other meaning assigned to the verb results from an over-literal reading that fails to note the text's irony.

Analysis of the Qur'an's Poetic Features

Rhyme-words, like ironic inversions, pose lexical difficulties for the interpreter of the Qur'an. Rhyme and rhythm play crucial roles in the sacred text: in their prosodic structure, many Qur'anic passages resemble *sajʿ*, usually translated as 'rhyming prose' but perhaps better characterised as a type of accent poetry. End-rhyme is a particularly strong feature of the Qur'an: 86 per cent of its verses exhibit end-rhyme, and end-rhyme often influences the forms of verse-final words, the choice of verse-final words and the structure of entire verses or significant parts thereof.[9] However, commentators on the Qur'an have usually suppressed the analysis of the Qur'an's poetic features in an effort to dissociate the Qur'an from Arabic poetry and the pre-Islamic *saj*ʿ of pagan soothsayers and religious specialists. Both the need to defend the Prophet from the accusations that he was a poet or soothsayer and the doctrine of *iʿjāz al-Qurʾān*, according to which the Qur'an is a miraculous text, categorically different from all texts produced by humans, led to the downplaying of rhyme and rhythm. To suppress such considerations completely was simply impossible, for rhyme is crucially important to the text for such basic procedures as counting the number of verses in each sura or determining where each verse ends and the next begins. In order to avoid using terms such as *qāfiya* ('rhyme' or the 'rhyme word'), an alternative set of terms was developed. The terms *fāṣila* ('divider') and *raʾs āya* ('end of a verse') were used to designate verse-final words – in the majority of cases rhyme-words – without referring directly to rhyme.

Some medieval scholars, particularly experts in rhetoric, admitted more freely the existence of the Qur'an's poetic features, including rhyme and rhythm. These include Abū Hilāl al-ʿAskarī (d. after 395/1005), Ḍiyāʾ al-Dīn Ibn al-Athīr (d. 637/1239), Sulaymān b. ʿAbd al-Qawī al-Ṭūfī (d. 716/1316), al-Qalqashandī (d. 821/1418) and Ibn Ḥijja al-Ḥamawī (d. 837/1434), all of whom admitted that the Qur'an contained substantial passages of *saj*ʿ or rhyming and rhythmical prose. Other scholars of rhetoric and the Qur'anic sciences such as Jalāl al-Dīn al-Suyūṭī (d. 911/1505) held that while the Qur'an should not be termed *saj*ʿ, it contained passages that were *saj*ʿ-like, or conformed to the rules that governed the production of *saj*ʿ in other texts. Both groups described the features and types of *saj*ʿ composition using Qur'anic examples nearly exclusively.[10] Some medieval Muslim rhetoricians such as Ibn al-Ṣāʾigh al-Ḥanafī (d. 776/1375), who will be discussed below, recognised the existence of poetic licence in the Qur'an, terming it *riʿāyat al-fāṣila* ('taking into account the verse-final word' or 'maintaining similar verse-final words').[11] Yet, despite its usefulness, the concept of poetic licence does not appear to have played a major role in Qur'anic commentary. Even investigators of the text whom one would expect to have had some sensitivity to issues of rhyme and rhythm, such as Maḥmūd b. ʿUmar al-Zamakhsharī (d. 538/1144), seem to have avoided resort to poetic licence as a possible hermeneutic device on ideological grounds and simply interpreted the affected words as conforming to ordinary Arabic lexicon, grammar and style.

An obvious example of an odd lexical item produced by the exigencies of verse-final rhyme is *Ṭūr Sīnīn* (Q. 95:2), which appears in verse-final position in *Sūrat al-Tīn*, the verses of which rhyme throughout in *–īn/-ūn/-īm*. The term is manifestly equivalent to *Ṭūr Sīnāʾ* or *Saynāʾ*, which denotes Mount Sinai in Q. 23:20: *wa shajaratan takhruju min Ṭūri Saynāʾa tunbitu biʾl-duhni wa ṣibghin liʾl-ākilīn* (*and a tree that comes forth from Mount Sinai which grows oil and relish for the eaters*). The ending of *Sīnāʾ/Saynāʾ* is modified to *Sīnīn* in Q. 95:2 for the sake of rhyme.[12] The change is quite radical, so that the resulting form looks quite different and might even be taken for a different word were it not for the accompanying *ṭūr* ('mountain'), which is related to the Aramaic or Syriac word for mountain, *ṭōr*, and occurs in the Qur'an only in reference to Mount Sinai (Q. 2:63, 93; Q. 4:154; Q. 19:52; Q. 20:80; Q. 23:20; Q. 28:29, 46; Q. 52:1; Q. 95:2), while other mountains are designated by the common Arabic word for mountain (*jabal*, pl. *jibāl*, e.g. Q. 2:260; Q. 7:74). In his *Mufradāt*, al-Rāghib merely gives an entry on *Saynāʾ* or *Sīnāʾ*, the usual form, adding, *wa qīla ayḍan Ṭūr Sīnīn* ('and it has also been said: the Mount of *Sīnīn*').[13] In other words, he recognises that *Sīnīn* and *Saynāʾ* or *Sīnāʾ* are alternative forms of the same word, but he neither mentions poetic licence nor recognises that the form *Sīnīn* requires explanation.

Analysis of Examples of Cognate Substitution in Müller's *Reimprosa*

Many unusual forms occurring as verse-final words in the Qur'an result from cognate substitution, the use of a cognate of different morphological pattern in place of the word that would ordinarily have occurred. In general, its use is apparent because the resulting pattern is either rare or non-existent outside this occurrence or, if interpreted strictly literally according to the semantic rules governing morphological patterns, would convey a meaning that is inappropriate for the context. The phenomenon, well known in Arabic in general, is termed *ʿadl* ('modification') or, less commonly, *naql* ('transfer'). Thus, for example, Arab grammarians identify the male given name *ʿUmar* as a 'modified' form derived from an original *ʿĀmir*, *Juḥā* as a 'modified' form of *Jāḥin*, *ukhar* as a 'modified' form of *ākharūn*, and so on.[14] Discussion of this phenomenon forms a large part of Müller's work, which treats various changes that occur in the Qur'an for the sake of rhyme, though she did not use the term cognate substitution, referring instead to verse-final words subject to morphological variation, change or modification.[15] A typical example discussed by Müller is *amīn*, which would ordinarily mean 'trustworthy' but is used in Q. 95:3 to refer to the holy sanctuary in Mecca to describe it as 'safe', which would ordinarily be *āmin* instead. This is corroborated by passages where the word appears but not in verse-final position; then it is *āmin* ('safe'), as one would expect (Q. 2:126; Q. 14:35; Q. 28:57; Q. 29:67). Müller identifies nineteen cases of such morphological changes (twenty-one instances in all, because two occur twice; See Table 1: Müller's examples of morphological change).

While not all of Müller's interpretations are valid – and they are discussed in more detail below – most represent clear cases of the use of one particular morphological pattern to convey the meaning of what would ordinarily be a different pattern.

The question arises, then, to what extent medieval Muslim authors were aware of the phenomenon of cognate substitution and to what extent they referred to cognate substitution, poetic licence, rhyme or rhythm in their analyses of the Qur'anic text. Müller showed no awareness that medieval authors touched on the topic or used a specific technical term to describe it. Nevertheless, some medieval Muslim authors treated cognate substitution to some extent, yet voiced their views on the topic in a guarded fashion. Several pre-modern rhetoricians, including Abū Hilāl al-ʿAskarī, Ibn al-Athīr, Ṭūfī and Ibn Ḥijja were certainly aware of the phenomenon, for they report that the Prophet Muhammad

Table 1: Müller's examples of morphological change

No.	Phrase	Verse	Müller's Interpretation	Pages in Müller	English translation
1	*bi'l-sāhira*	Q. 79:14	*sāhirūn*	13–16	'awake, wakeful'
2	*bi'l-ṭāghiya*	Q. 69:5	*bi-ṭughyānihim*	16–20	'in recompense for their tyranny'
3	*kādhiba*	Q. 56:2	*kadhib*	20–24	'lies, act of lying'
4	*lāghiya*	Q. 88:11	*laghw*	24–6	'idle talk'
5	*bāqiya*	Q. 69:8	*baqiyya*	26–8	'remnant'
6	*kāshifa*	Q. 53:58	*kashf*	29–30	'uncovering'
7	*al-rājifa*	Q. 79:6	*al-rajfa*	30–33	'quake'
8	*akhdhatan rābiya*	Q. 69:10	*akhdhan . . .*	33–8	*rābiya* = 'growing, tremendous'
9	*bi-rīḥin ṣarṣarin ʿātiya*	Q. 69:6	*bi-rīḥin ṣarṣarin . . .*	38–41	*ʿātiya* = 'rebellious'
10	*kidhdhābā*	Q. 78:28	*takdhībā*	41–3	'rejection'
11	*kidhdhābā*	Q. 78:35	*kadhibā*	44–6	'lies'
12	*taḍlīl*	Q. 105:2	*ḍalāl*	46–50	'error, being astray'
13	*dhū'l-ikrām*	Q. 55:27, 78	*dhū'l-karāma*	50–54	'possessing dignity'
14	*amīn*	Q. 44:51; Q. 95:3	*āmin*	54–9	'safe'
15	*dīnu'l-qayyima*	Q. 98:5	*al-dīn al-qayyim*	59–62	'the straight religion'
16	*al-rujʿā*	Q. 96:8	*al-rajʿ* or *al-rujūʿ*	62–4	'return'
17	*bi-ṭaghwāhā*	Q. 91:11	*bi-ṭughyānihā*	64–8	'in recompense for their tyranny'
18	*dhikrāhā*	Q. 79:43	*dhikrihā*	68–72	'recounting it'
19	*fa'ntaṣir*	Q. 54:10	*fa'nṣurnī*	73–8	'make me victorious'

used this sort of modification of pattern in rhyming contexts in his own speech. Ibn al-Athīr's discussion in particular shows signs of self-censorship or guarded presentation in this regard. Though he gives examples of cognate substitution in the speech of the Prophet Muhammad, he does not cite any from the Qur'an, even though his discussion of *saj*ʿ focuses strongly on Islam's sacred text. This suggests that he is omitting Qur'anic examples on purpose, perhaps to avoid negative criticism on ideological grounds. Ṭūfī gives one example of cognate substitution in the Qur'an, but it is a minor case of verse-internal rhyme.[16]

The most perceptive analysis of poetic licence in the Qur'an in pre-modern Islamic letters known to date is *Iḥkām al-rāy fī aḥkām al-āy* ('Sound opinion on the rules governing verses') by the eighth/fourteenth-century rhetorician, jurist and Qur'anic expert Ibn al-Ṣā'igh al-Ḥanafī. This work, which is preserved only in an abridgement, presents forty types of deviation, occurring in the Qur'an for the sake of end-rhyme, from the ordinary rules of Arabic grammar and style evident from other passages of the Qur'an and from the classical grammatical tradition. The text provides a number of examples that merit consideration as instances of cognate substitution, such as the use of an active participle when a passive participle would ordinarily be required and vice versa. Thus, he points out that the phrase *ʿīshatin rāḍiya* (*an approving life*, Q. 69:21; 101:7) is used to convey the meaning of *ʿīshatin marḍiyya* ('a life approved of', or 'an agreeable life') and that *mā'in dāfiq* (*pouring water*, Q. 86:6) is used to express *mā'in madfūq* ('poured water'). Similarly, he claims that *ḥijāban mastūrā* (*a covered barrier*, Q. 17:45) is used for *ḥijāban sātirā* ('a covering barrier') and that *kāna waʿduhu ma'tiyyā* (*His promise will be arrived at*, Q. 19:61) means *ātiyā* ('will come'), all for the sake of rhyme.[17] He also identifies cases in which an emphatic form has been substituted for its non-emphatic counterpart, or for another emphatic form, such as the use of *qadīr* (Q. *passim*) many times in verse-final position, as opposed to the expected form *al-qādir*, which appears in *huwa'l-qādir* (*He is the powerful One*, Q. 6:65); *ʿalīm* (*knowing*, Q. *passim*) as opposed to *ʿālimu'l-ghayb* (*Knower of the Unseen*, Q. *passim*); *mā kāna rabbuka nasiyyā* (*Thy Lord was not forgetful*, Q. 19:64) for *nāsiyā* ('forgetful');

and *inna hādhā la-shay'un 'ujāb* (*This is indeed an astounding thing*, Q. 38:5) for *'ajīb* (*amazing*, Q. 11:72; Q. 50:2).[18] While Ibn al-Ṣā'igh al-Ḥanafī does not present an overarching category corresponding to cognate substitution, these examples show that he was aware of its occurrence in the Qur'an.

Cognate substitution posed a problem for lexicographers, who were faced with a dilemma. For example, in Q. 2:87, the well-known verse . . . *a-fa-kullamā jā'akum rasūlun bimā lā tahwā anfusukum istakbartum fa-farīqan kadhdhabtum wa farīqan taqtulūn* (. . . *Is it ever so, that, whenever there came to you a messenger with that which you desire not, you grew arrogant, and one group you denied, and another group you kill*), does *taqtulūn* mean 'you kill' in the present tense – matching the normal meaning of the form actually used – or does it mean 'you killed', ordinarily expressed as *qataltum*, as suggested by parallelism with *kadhdhabtum*, for that appears to be the form required were it not for the exigencies of end-rhyme?[19] A literal translation or definition risks misrepresenting the actual sense of the verse, while a translation or definition that presents the intended or underlying rather than the formal meaning risks redefining the meanings of words radically according to context or, worse, coining entirely new forms to fit particular passages. A cursory survey of lexica and commentaries on the Qur'an would suggest that rhyme, rhythm, poetic licence and particularly the modification of the morphological pattern of a word for the sake of end-rhyme are regularly, although not completely, ignored.

In what follows, I examine Müller's examples, assessing whether they indeed merit consideration as cases of cognate substitution. In addition, al-Rāghib al-Iṣfahānī's entries relevant to the passages that Müller identified as cases of morphological distortion are examined, in order to determine how al-Rāghib treats these examples.

Category I: Forms ignored by al-Rāghib al-Iṣfahānī

Four of the forms cited by Müller as examples are completely ignored by al-Rāghib al-Iṣfahānī, including some that are clear cases of cognate substitution. The form *amīn* [no. 14] occurs twice in rhyme position (Q. 44:51; Q. 95:3), in both cases referring to the sanctity of the city of Mecca, the site of the shrine of the Kaʿba. Müller argues convincingly that *amīn* in these cases is modified from *āmin* ('safe'), which occurs in other verses in non-rhyme position.[20] The adjective *āmin* ('safe') is applied to Mecca many times (Q. 2:126; Q. 14:35; Q. 28:57; Q. 29:67) and *amīn* ('trustworthy') is applied to prophets many times (Q. 7:68; Q. 26:107, 125, 143, 162, 178, 193; Q. 44:18). Al-Rāghib's entry on the triconsonantal root *ʾ-m-n* presents examples of *āmin* but not *amīn*.[21] One supposes that he did not see that the examples of *amīn* required any special explanation. Similarly, the examples of *ʿātiya* ('rebellious', Q. 69:6) [no. 9];[22] *kidhdhābā* ('rejection', Q. 78:28) [no. 10], which Müller interprets as a modified form of *takdhībā* ('rejection');[23] and *kāshifa* ('revealing', Q. 53:58) [no. 6], which she interprets as a modified form of *kashf* ('revelation'),[24] are not addressed by al-Rāghib at all.[25]

The form *ʿātiya* [no. 9] does not merit consideration as a case of cognate substitution even though it may be considered a product of poetic licence. A feminine adjective, *ʿātiya*, is applied to the feminine noun *rīḥ* ('a wind') in Q. 69:6: *wa-ammā ʿĀdun fa-uhlikū bi-rīḥin ṣarṣarin ʿātiya* (*And as for ʿĀd, they were destroyed by a rebellious, screeching wind*). Müller apparently considers it a case of morphological change because the form *fāʿila* is required by the rhyme context and the adjective *ʿātiya*, which would ordinarily mean 'rebellious' or 'intransigent', usually applies to people and not to winds. Even though this is true, one cannot consider this a case of cognate substitution, because it is the expected pattern for the meaning and not a replacement for an underlying cognate form.

The term *kāshifa* [no 6], however, is a proper instance of cognate substitution. It is clearly conditioned by the rhyme context, but I would argue that the expected form would be *kāshif* and not *kashf*, as Müller claims, for the intended meaning is that the only agent who has knowledge of the Hour and can disclose it is God, and the active participle would convey this idea. The passage in question reads, ... *azifati'l-āzifa laysa lahā min dūni'llāhi kāshifa* (... *The approaching one has drawn near. It has no revealer other than God*, Q. 53:57–8). Similar examples addressed in the *Mufradāt* suggest that al-Rāghib would not have recognised it as a modified form but would have instead interpreted it as an adjective modifying a suppressed noun, as in *fiʿla kāshifa* ('an uncovering act').

In my view, Müller's argument that *kidhdhāb* in Q. 78:28 [no. 10] is an altered form of *takdhīb* is correct on the grounds that *kidhdhābā* is not the common, expected form in this context. In the phrase in question, *wa kadhdhabū bi-āyātinā kidhdhābā* (*They rejected our signs decisively*, Q. 78:28), it is clear that *kidhdhābā* is a verbal noun of the Form II verb *kadhdhaba*, serving as a cognate accusative of *kadhdhabū*. This would ordinarily be *takdhībā*, but *fiʿʿāl* is one of the recognised morphological patterns of the verbal noun of Form II verbs, along with *tafʿīl*, *tafʿila*, *tafʿāl* and *tifʿāl*.[26] This particular pattern therefore occurs here with its expected meaning, but it is quite rare, and so may be considered a case of cognate substitution.

Two of the forms cited by Müller as examples are mentioned by al-Rāghib without any particular comment. Müller interprets the adjective *rābiya* in *fa-ʿaṣaw rasūla rabbihim fa-akhadhahum akhdhatan rābiya* (*Then they disobeyed the messenger of their Lord, so He grasped them with an increasing grasp*, Q. 69:10) [no. 8] as a morphologically modified form from *r-b-w*, used with *akhdhatan* in the feminine to replace some other phrase such as *akhdhan shadīdan* or *akhdhan rābiyan* ('a strong grasping') for the sake of rhyme.[27] Al-Rāghib cites the phrase that occurs in Q. 69:10 along with other instances of the tri-consonantal root *r-b-w*, but does not make any particular comment.[28] Similarly, Müller argues that the verse-final word *al-rājifa* (Q. 79:6) [no. 7] is a modified form of *al-rajfa* ('tremor', 'quake'),[29] in the phrase *yawma tarjufu'l-rājifa* (*On the day when the tremor will quake*). This makes sense, for the verb *yarjufu* and the cognate *al-rajfa* occur several times in the Qur'an in similar contexts, such as Q. 73:14: *yawma tarjufu'l-arḍu wa'l-jibālu . . .* (*On the day when the earth and the mountains will quake . . .*) and, with slight variants, in Q. 7:78, 91, 155 and Q. 29:37: *fa-akhadhathumu'l-rajfatu fa-aṣbaḥū fī dārihim jāthimīn* (*So the earthquake seized them, and morning found them prostrate in their dwelling-place*). Al-Rāghib cites verses with *al-rajfa* and *al-rājifa*, but makes no comment on the form *al-rājifa* in particular.[30]

Category II: Interpretation as a different but nevertheless cognate term

Müller interprets the verse-final word *sāhira*, a feminine singular adjective, in *idhā hum bi'l-sāhira* (Q. 79:14) [no. 1] as altered from an underlying sound masculine plural adjective *sāhirūn*, meaning that on the Day of Resurrection 'they' – the dead who are brought forth from their graves – will stay awake.[31] It is by no means certain that this is a correct interpretation, although it is plausible. The passage (Q. 79:10–14) is admittedly a difficult one:

yaqūlūna innā la-mardūdūna fī'l-ḥāfira
idhā kunnā ʿiẓāman nakhira
qālū tilka idhan karratun khāsira
fa-innamā hiya zajratun wāḥida
fa-idhā hum bi'l-sāhira

They will say: Shall we really be restored to the ḥāfira?
When we are crumbled bones?
That would be a futile step.
Rather it will require only one shout,
And lo and behold: They will be in the sāhira.

No other instance of the tri-consonantal root *s-h-r* occurs in the Qur'an. Müller interprets *al-sāhira* as an adjective referring to the unbelievers on the Day of Resurrection. Pickthall's translation agrees with this assessment: . . . *they will be awakened*. Müller interprets the *bi-* as a superfluous preposition introducing the predicate of a nominal sentence,[32] something quite odd in this case, because the preposition *bi-* serves to introduce a predicate only in negative constructions, with *laysa bi-* or *mā bi-*, and not in positive constructions. There are many instances of this usage in negative constructions in the Qur'an, as in . . . *wa-mā naḥnu bi-mabʿūthīn* (*and we shall not be resurrected*, Q. 6:29; Q. 23:37), but none in the positive: a typical positive statement is *idhā hiya thuʿbānun mubīn* (*Lo! It was a serpent manifest*, Q. 7:107; Q. 26:32). Alternatively, one might interpret *al-sāhira* as a noun: 'they [the unbelievers] will be in the wakeful state'.

However, it appears from the passage that *al-sāhira* is parallel with *al-ḥāfira*, suggesting that it refers to a place, and that *idhā hum bi'l-sāhira* means that they will be *in the sāhira*, whatever the exact sense of the word is. A number of commentaries report that *al-sāhira* means 'land' in the expressions *laḥm sāhira* ('meat from land animals') or *ṣayd sāhira* ('land game'), as opposed to *laḥm baḥr* ('meat from the sea') or *laḥm bāḥira* ('sea game'). Also in keeping with the interpretation of *al-sāhira* as a place, Arthur Jeffery suggests that it might derive from Aramaic or Syriac *saḥartā* ('environs'). This seems quite unlikely because of the required sound change *ḥ* > *h*, and Jeffery admits that *sāhira* might be the ordinary Arabic word meaning 'awake'.[33]

The fact that the meaning of *al-ḥāfira* is also ambiguous makes it difficult to use parallelism to determine the meaning *of al-sāhira*, but if it refers to Hell, this might help resolve the problem of interpretation. *Al-ḥāfira* may be a cognate substitute for *al-ḥufra* ('hole, pit'), and could refer to Hell itself. The latter meaning is suggested by the one Qur'anic occurrence of the noun *al-ḥufra* in Q. 3:103: *wa'dhkurū niʿmata'llāhi ʿalaykum idh ... kuntum ʿalā shafā ḥufratin mina'l-nār fa-anqadhakum minhā ...* (*And remember God's favour to you since . . . you were on the brink of a pit of fire, and He saved you from it* . . .). Here the text reminds the believers that God's favour has saved them from burning in Hell, described as a pit of fire (*ḥufra mina'l-nār*). Other interpretations associate *al-ḥāfira* with *al-arḍ al-maḥfūra* ('excavated ground') and understand it to refer to the graves or graveyards of the dead,[34] in which case the verse would mean that they will be brought up to the surface of their graveyards.

Interpreters have found it difficult to understand the narrative sequence into which these short descriptions fit. In Q. 79:10 the dead who are about to be raised, or have just been resurrected, express chagrin at being resurrected from their graves only to be thrown into Hell. In my view, both v. 10 and v. 14 refer to the unbelievers' being thrown into Hell after the Judgement, rather than to two separate events in the narrative. The chronological leap from rotting in the grave to consignment to Hell has confused commentators, who think the text should refer to the gathering of mankind on the face of the earth prior to Judgement. Many early authorities therefore understood *al-ḥāfira* to mean 'life' or 'rebirth', in order to contrast with the ensuing verses.[35] This interpretation finds some support from context and from parallel passages – the dead are being raised in this passage, and descriptions of the bodily resurrection abound in the Qur'an. However, there is no etymological corroboration: the tri-consonantal root *ḥ-f-r* is associated with digging or animals' hooves, but not with life. It makes more sense to interpret *al-ḥāfira* as 'the Pit (of fire)' or Hell. The feminine adjective *al-sāhira* ('waking') also refers to Hell: it should be construed as modifying the suppressed noun *al-Nār* ('the Fire') and meaning 'the ever-waking' or 'that which does not sleep', i.e. Hell-fire that gives the unbelievers no respite. This interpretation finds corroboration in verses that insist that the flames of Hell never die down (e.g. Q. 17:97). A similar statement occurs in the Gospels regarding Gehenna (Mark 9:43). Moreover, according to Muḥammad b. Jarīr al-Ṭabarī (d. 310/923), ʿAbd Allāh Ibn Wahb (d. 197/813) interpreted both *al-ḥāfira* and *al-sāhira* as two of the many names of Hell.[36] In this case, Müller's interpretation is improbable and Ibn Wahb's seems more likely.

Al-Rāghib does not interpret the adjectival form *al-sāhira* as a reference to mankind on the Day of Resurrection or as a reference to Hell. Rather, he reports that *al-sāhira* has been defined as the surface of the earth or as the earth on the Day of Resurrection. He then explains that since the ground will be heavily trodden on the Day of Resurrection, it is as if the earth were kept awake by this tremendous activity. He interprets the preposition *bi-* as a locative: 'They are on the wakeful ground', understanding the adjective as modifying a suppressed noun, *al-arḍ*.[37]

A second example is the verse-final word *bi'l-ṭāghiya* in *fa-ammā Thamūdu fa-uhlikū bi'l-ṭāghiya* (Q. 69:5) [no. 2], which Müller interprets as an altered form from an original *bi-ṭughyānihim*: accordingly, the verse would mean ('And as for Thamūd, they were destroyed on account of their rebellion').[38] She is drawing here on other Qur'anic uses of the verb *ṭaghā, yaṭghā* to mean rebellion against God or tyrannical behaviour (Q. 11:112; Q. 20:81; Q. 79:37; Q. 96:6), especially on the part of Pharaoh (Q. 20:24, 43; Q. 79:17;

Q. 89:11). The adjectival form *ṭāghūn* (Q. 37:30; Q. 38:55; Q. 51:53; Q. 52:32; Q. 68:31; Q. 78:22), the comparative *aṭghā* (Q. 53:52) and the verbal noun *ṭughyān* (Q. 2:15; Q. 5:64, 68; Q. 6:110; Q. 7:186; Q. 10:11; Q. 17:60; Q. 18:80; Q. 23:75) all occur with related meanings. Al-Rāghib, in contrast, interprets *al-ṭāghiya* as referring to the calamity by means of which Thamūd were annihilated. He writes, 'They were destroyed by the *ṭāghiya*'. This is a reference to the flood (*ṭūfān*) described in Q. 69:11: (*When the water overflowed* [*ṭaghā*] . . .).[39] In other words, *al-ṭāghiya* means 'that which overflowed' and refers to a flood. Again, there is a difference in the interpretations of the preposition *bi-*: for Müller, it indicates cause, but for al-Rāghib, it indicates instrument. One potential problem with al-Rāghib's interpretation is that while the two verses occur in the same sura, *Sūrat al-Ḥāqqa*, they refer to different destructions. Q. 69:5, with *bi'l-ṭāghiya*, refers to the destruction of Thamūd, but Q. 69:11, with the verb *ṭaghā*, refers to the destruction of Noah's people. Moreover, Thamūd, who are portrayed as inhabiting a desert valley with rocky walls out of which they carved their buildings, are reported elsewhere in the Qur'an to have met their destruction in other ways, and never through a flood. The instrument of their destruction is described using various terms: *rajfa* (*earthquake*, Q. 7:78), *ṣayḥa* (*shout*, Q. 11:67; Q. 54:31) and *ṣā'iqa* (*thunderbolt*, Q. 41:14; Q. 51:44).

However, it appears that Müller's interpretation here is flawed and al-Rāghib's better founded. Parallelism in the sura itself requires that *al-ṭāghiya* be the instrument of Thamūd's destruction, because the next verse describes 'Ād's destruction by a wind (Q. 69:6), and later verses describe the destruction of Pharaoh and the Overturned Cities (*al-Mu'tafikāt*, i.e. Sodom and Gomorrah) by God's grasp (Q. 69:9–10). Al-Rāghib's interpretation of *al-ṭāghiya* as a flood, however, is not appropriate to the narrative of the destruction of Thamūd; the term should rather be understood as a cataclysmic event: 'the overpowering (blow)'. This would be in keeping with the many feminine adjectives used to describe calamities in similar contexts. Although *ṭūfān* ('flood') is masculine, the term *ṭāghiya* is apparently a feminine form because it refers to a particular, one-time calamity. Such a phenomenon, in which feminine adjectival forms take on such meanings, is quite common in Arabic from pre-Islamic times until the present, so that, for example, the feminine form *muṣība* ('hitting the mark') means 'disaster',[40] *dāhiya* ('befalling') means 'calamity', *ḥāditha* ('befalling') means 'accident', and so on.

The interpretation of *al-ṭāghiya* as the calamity that will befall is corroborated by other Qur'anic verses relating to punishment stories in which wayward peoples of the past have denied the future cataclysmic events by which they will be punished, using the verb *kadhdhaba* with the preposition *bi-*. This is the case with Q. 91:11: *kadhdhabat Thamūd bi-ṭaghwāhā* (*Thamūd denied its overwhelming blow*) [no. 17], discussed under Category III, although al-Rāghib interprets the two verses quite differently. Q. 69:5 is immediately preceded by the verse *kadhdhabat Thamūdu wa 'Ādun bi'l-qāri'a* (*Thamūd and 'Ād denied the knocking blow*, Q. 69:4), a clear reference to an impending punishment, since *al-qāri'a* appears exclusively as a future catastrophe in the Qur'an (Q. 13:31; Q. 101:1–3).

Al-Rāghib does not interpret these last two examples as cases of cognate substitution, but rather claims that they refer to something else entirely. He interprets both terms, of the pattern *al-fā'ila* (i.e. feminine active participles), as adjectives modifying suppressed nouns, *al-sāhira* referring to the earth (*arḍ*) and meaning 'the wakeful ground'; and *al-ṭāghiya* referring to a flood.

Category III: Interpretations that address the morphological pattern

A number of al-Rāghib's interpretations include some attempt to explain or justify an odd or unexpected morphological form. This represents recognition on his part that there is some problem or at least oddity in the text as it stands. Müller interprets *bāqiya* (lit. 'remaining', Q. 69:8) [no. 5], as a modified form of *baqiyya* ('remnant').[41] This reading makes sense in context. The verse, again in *Sūrat al-Ḥāqqa*, asks a rhetorical question after recounting the destruction of Thamūd: *fa-hal tarā lahum min bāqiya* (*'Do you* [*O Muhammad*] *see any remnant of them?'*). In contrast, al-Rāghib interprets *bāqiya* as an adjective applied to a suppressed feminine noun: in his view it means *jamā'a bāqiya* ('a remaining group'), or *fi'la lahum bāqiya* ('a deed of theirs that remains').[42] He then mentions an alternative interpretation: *wa qīla ma'nāhu baqiyya* ('It has also been said that it means "remainder"').[43] The latter interpretation amounts to a direct admission that *bāqiya* is a cognate substitution for *baqiyya*, but al-Rāghib favours the former, suggesting that the cognate substitution is difficult for him to justify. He remarks, 'Some verbal nouns take the pattern *fā'il* or *maf'ūl*, but the first interpretation is more correct.'[44] In other words, he considers it remotely possible, but unlikely in this case, that a form *fā'ila* could serve as a verbal noun. He clearly does not wish to admit the possibility that the active participle, *fā'ila*, may be used on an ad hoc basis to convey the meaning of the verbal noun *fa'īla*.

Müller interprets *dhikrāhā* (Q. 79:43) [no. 18] as a modified form of *dhikr*.[45] This verse occurs in a passage (Q. 79:42–6) that rhymes in *-āhā* and discusses the Hour, or the end of time:

yas'alūnaka 'ani'l-sā'ati ayyāna mursāhā
fīma anta min dhikrāhā
ilā rabbika muntahāhā
innamā anta mundhiru man yakhshāhā
ka'annahum yawma yarawnahā lam yalbathū illā 'ashiyyatan aw ḍuḥāhā

They ask you about the Hour: when will it come to port?
What do you have to do with telling thereof?
Unto your Lord belongs the term thereof.
You are but a warner to him who fears it
On the day when they behold it, it will be as if they had tarried but for an evening or the morning thereof.

Müller's point is that *dhikr* is more fitting here on the grounds that it means 'telling' or 'recounting', which fits the context, as in Q. 18:83, where it refers to the recounting of the tale of Dhū'l-Qarnayn (usually identified as Alexander the Great). Usually *dhikrā*, in contrast, means 'warning'. This interpretation is corroborated by other passages which stress that the Prophet does not know when the Hour will come, and that only God knows (e.g. Q. 7:187). While one may agree with Müller that *dhikrā* represents an underlying form *dhikr*, it is also possible that the precise sense of *dhikr* here is 'knowledge', for *ʿilm* ('knowledge') appears several times in closely parallel passages (Q. 7:187; Q. 41:47; Q. 43:61, 85).

Al-Rāghib likewise connects *dhikrā* with *dhikr*, but argues that it is simply an emphatic synonym: '*al-dhikrā* is an abundance of *dhikr*, and it is more emphatic than *dhikr*'.[46] The form *dhikrā* occurs twenty-two times in the Qur'an, three times in verse-final position in contexts that require a rhyme in -*ā* (Q. 80:4; Q. 87:9; Q. 89:23) but also eighteen times in non-rhyme position (Q. 6:68, 69, 90; Q. 7:2; Q. 11:114, 120; Q. 21:84; Q. 26:209; Q. 29:51; Q. 38:43, 46; Q. 39:21; Q. 40:54; Q. 44:13; Q. 50:8, 37; Q. 51:55; Q. 74:31). Its cognate *dhikr* occurs seventy times in the Qur'an, and the cognates *tadhkira* (Q. 20:3; Q. 56:73; Q. 69:12, 48; Q. 73:19; Q. 74:49, 54; Q. 76:29; Q. 80:11) and *tadhkīr* (Q. 10:71) also occur. In most cases, *dhikrā*, *tadhkira* and *tadhkīr* refer to warnings or prophetical sermons that remind the audience of God's power and unity, of their approaching demise and judgement, and of their obligations to their Creator. Al-Rāghib's reading is not convincing here, because *dhikrā* is not merely an emphatic form of *dhikr* but in this verse takes on one particular sense of *dhikr* that *dhikrā* does not ordinarily convey.

Müller interprets the unusual form *rujʿā* in *inna ilā rabbika'l-rujʿā* (*Indeed to your Lord is the return*, Q. 96:8) [no. 16] as a modified form from *rajʿ* or *rujūʿ*.[47] The form *fuʿlā* is recorded as one of the many possible patterns of verbal nouns of the Form I verb, and it occurs in *bushrā* ('glad tidings'), for example, but *rujʿā* is certainly a rare form, *rujūʿ* being the most common verbal noun of the verb *rajaʿa, yarjiʿu* ('to return'), while *rajʿ* and *marjiʿ* occur somewhat less frequently. *Rujʿā* occurs here in verse-final position in a passage with verses rhyming in -*ā* (Q. 96:6–14), so it is likely that this conditioned the form's occurrence. Al-Rāghib cites *al-rujʿā* along with *marjiʿ*, which occurs in similar phrases: *ilā llāhi marjiʿukum* (*to God is your return*, Q. 5:48, 105; Q. 11:4) and *thumma ilā rabbikum marjiʿukum* (*Then to your Lord is your return*, Q. 6:164; Q. 39:7). He comments that one may interpret these as deriving either from the intransitive *rujūʿ* ('returning'), as in God's word, *thumma ilayhi tarjiʿūn* (*Then you will return to Him*), or from the transitive *rajʿ*

('returning something'), as in, for example, Q. 30:11: *thumma ilayhi turjaʿūn* (*Then you will be returned to Him*).[48] That is, both *rujʿā* and *marjiʿ* may be construed as referring either to 'your returning' or to 'your being sent back or brought back' to God. Al-Rāghib thus admits that *al-rujʿā* is related to more common cognate forms, but presents it as an alternative form acceptable according to ordinary morphological rules, and not an actual cognate substitute.

Müller interprets *taḍlīl* (lit. 'sending astray', Q. 105:2) [no. 12] as a modified form of *ḍalāl* ('being astray').[49] *Taḍlīl* is not an alternative verbal noun of the first form *ḍalla, yaḍillu* ('to go astray'), but rather a verbal noun from *ḍallala, yuḍallilu* ('to cause to go astray'). Together with the verb *jaʿala* ('to render') in the same phrase – *fa-jaʿala kaydahum fī taḍlīl* (lit. 'and rendered their plot in leading astray', Q 105:2) – it would imply that God is causing their plot to send some third party astray, when it is clear from the context that He is merely causing their plot to go awry. Müller's interpretation is corroborated by the frequent occurrence in similar passages of the phrases *fī ḍalāl* (Q. 13:14; Q. 40:25, 50) and *fī ḍalālin mubīn* (Q. 3:164; Q. 6:74; Q. 7:60; Q. 12:8, 30; Q. 19:38; Q. 21:54; Q. 26:97; Q. 28:85; Q. 31:11; Q. 34:24; Q. 36:24, 47; Q. 43:40; Q. 46:32; Q. 62:2; Q. 67:29), while *taḍlīl* occurs only in this instance, in a passage with end-rhyme in *-īl/-ūl*. The case that *taḍlīl* is a cognate substitute is therefore strong, but al-Rāghib avoids stating that *taḍlīl* here is the result of cognate substitution for *ḍalāl*, and instead attempts to explain the semantic nuance required by the form in some fashion. He explains the meaning of *taḍlīl* as follows:

> God's word *kaydahum fī taḍlīl* means 'their plot comes to naught (*bāṭil*)' and 'sends themselves astray' (*iḍlāl li-anfusihim*). 'Sending astray' (*iḍlāl*) is of two types. In one of these, sending astray is caused by being astray. It has two sub-categories. Either something of yours goes missing (*yaḍilla ʿanka*), as when you say 'I have misplaced (*aḍlaltu*) the camel', meaning 'it has gone missing from me', or you judge it to be lost. In both cases, something's being lost (*ḍalāl*) has caused the misplacement (*iḍlāl*). In the second type, sending astray (*iḍlāl*) causes being astray (*ḍalāl*). In this type, that which is worthless is made to seem favourable to a

> person so that he then goes astray, as in God's word, . . . *a party of them would have resolved to mislead you* (*an yuḍillūka*), *but they will mislead* (*yuḍillūna*) *only themselves*, Q. 4:113). That is, they purposefully undertake deeds intending thereby that you go astray, but their acts result only in their going astray themselves.[50]

Al-Rāghib interprets *taḍlīl* in Q. 105:2 as an example not of the second type, which would be the ordinary, causative sense, but rather of the first type. He argues, in effect, that what looks like a causative has a different relationship to the Form I verb. His explanation is based on the recognition that *taḍlīl* is ordinarily causative, for he equates it with *iḍlāl*, but he clearly recognises that the causative requires additional explanation and that it is not the expected form given the context. It is worth noting that he replaces the Form II verbal noun *taḍlīl* with the Form IV verbal noun *iḍlāl* and corresponding verbal forms *aḍlalta, yuḍillu* without any explanation, confirming both that *taḍlīl* is ordinarily causative and that it is an unusual form. His pairing of the causative *iḍlāl* with *bāṭil* ('error', 'futility'), which derives from the Form I intransitive verb *baṭala, yabṭulu*, suggests a realisation on his part that *taḍlīl* has a surprisingly intransitive sense here, and his use of the reflexive construction *iḍlāl li-anfusihim* strengthens this hypothesis. However, he seems compelled to explain that a causative is appropriate for this passage in one of its ordinary senses, and does not entertain the possibility that *taḍlīl* here is simply substituted for *ḍalāl* and has an essentially equivalent meaning. Al-Rāghib's analysis is less than satisfactory because the verse does not indicate that God considered the plotters to have gone astray, or that He misplaced them. The other verses in the sura make it clear that God actively foiled their machinations, and the verb *jaʿala* ('render') in Q. 105:2 already conveys God's active role. The interpretation of *taḍlīl* as a cognate substitute for *ḍalāl* conditioned by the end-rhyme in adjacent verses is more convincing semantically.

Müller interprets *ṭaghwāhā* in *kadhdhabat Thamūdu bi-ṭaghwāhā* (Q. 91:11) [no. 17] as a modified form from *ṭughyānihā* ('their rebellion'), a reference to Thamūd's rebellion against God.[51] Al-Rāghib identifies *ṭaghwā* as a verbal noun from the verb *ṭaghawtu* or *ṭaghaytu*, in addition to the more common verbal nouns *ṭaghawān* and *ṭughyān*, and reports them to mean 'extreme rebellion' or 'extreme disobedience'. He states that the verse announces that they did not believe when they were threatened with the punishment for their disobedience.[52] He thus interprets it as a metonymy, in which their disobedience stands in for the punishment they are destined to receive for that disobedience. As in the case of *al-ṭāghiya* discussed above [no. 2], I believe that Müller and al-Rāghib are both mistaken here. While the verb *ṭaghā* refers to disobedience or tyrannical behaviour in many instances in the Qur'an, it was clear in Q. 69:5 that *al-ṭāghiya* referred to the calamity that would befall Thamūd as divine punishment, and this is probably the case here as well. The phrase *kadhdhabat Thamūdu bi-ṭaghwāhā* means 'Thamūd denied their overwhelming calamity', a reference to the disaster that was going to befall them. Again, they are denying the instrument of their impending doom; the verse is not identifying their rebellion as its cause. This interpretation is corroborated by the fact that the preposition *bi-* in the verbal idiom *kadhdhaba bi-* in the Qur'an serves consistently to indicate not the reason for rejection but rather what is rejected. Common items rejected with this verbal idiom include God's signs (*āyāt*: Q. 2:39; Q. 3:11; Q. 5:10, 86; Q. 6:21, 39, 49, 66, 150; etc.), God's gifts (*ālā'*: Q. 55, *passim*) or the truth (*al-ḥaqq*: Q. 6:5; Q. 50:5), but many complements have to do with the future or the afterlife: the meeting with God (*liqā' Allāh*: Q. 6:31; Q. 10:45), the Day of Judgement (*Yawm al-Dīn*: Q. 83:11; *Yawm al-Faṣl*: Q. 37:21; *al-Sā'a*: Q. 25:11) and Hell (*Jahannam*: Q. 55:43; *al-Nār*: Q. 52:14). In several cases, the denial is of God's warnings (*al-nudhur*), and the context is similar since the deniers identified are 'Ād, Thamūd and the Folk of Lot (Q. 54:23, 33; Q. 69:4). Al-Rāghib's explanation is thus half-correct: he recognises that the term *ṭaghwāhā* refers to their eventual punishment, but he connects it with the meaning 'rebellion' by characterising it as the punishment for their disobedience. It is nevertheless a case of cognate substitution, for *ṭaghwāhā* is substituted for what would presumably have been *al-ṭāghiya* had it not been for the exigencies of rhyme.

The phrase *dīnu'l-qayyima* (Q. 98:5) [no. 15] occurs only once in the Qur'an, and the pattern of the final word parallels that of the adjacent rhyme-word *bayyina* (Q. 98:4), *-m-* rhyming with *-n-* both in Arabic poetry and in the Qur'an. Müller considers this a modified form from *al-dīn al-qayyim* ('the right religion'), which occurs in other passages (Q. 9:36; Q. 12:40; Q. 30:30, 43). In Müller's view, this odd modification of a noun–adjective phrase to the same noun in construct with a definite feminine form of the same adjective is an example of morphological modification conditioned by rhyme.[53] Al-Rāghib, in contrast, interprets *al-qayyima* as an adjectival form modifying a suppressed noun *al-umma* ('nation' or 'community'). He adds that the nation in question is thereby identified as *al-qā'ima bi'l-qisṭ* ('that which upholds fairness') – evidently understanding *qā'ima* and *qayyima* to be equivalent. He also claims that this is the same nation referred to in Q. 3:110: *kuntum khayra ummatin ukhrijat li'l-nās* ... (*You are the best nation that has been brought forth for mankind* . . .) and, again citing a cognate of *qayyima*, in Q. 4:135: *kūnū qawwāmīna bi'l-qisṭi shuhadā'a li'llāh* ... (*Be staunch upholders of justice, witnesses for God* . . . [54] In other words, he does not recognise that the phrase *dīn al-qayyima* is simply a modified form of *al-dīn al-qayyim*, which seems to be the most logical explanation, given that the phrase *dhālika dīnu'l-qayyima* (Q. 98:5) matches *dhālika'l-dīnu'l-qayyim* (*That is the right religion* . . .) in Q. 9:36, Q. 12:40 and Q. 30:30, but nevertheless recognises the connection of *al-qayyima* with other cognate forms.

Müller interprets *kādhiba* ('lying' [adj.]) in the verse *laysa li-waqʿatihā kādhiba* (*There is no denying that it will befall*, Q. 56:2) [no. 3] as a modified form of *kadhib* ('lies, the act of lying') adopted for the sake of rhyme.[55] Al-Rāghib argues instead that this is an adjective modifying a suppressed noun and describes their lying act, as when one says 'a truthful act' (*fiʿla ṣādiqa*) or 'a lying act' (*fiʿla kādhiba*).[56] In this instance, it makes more sense to understand *kādhiba* as a cognate substitute for *takdhīb* ('denial'): the meaning required by the context is that 'there is no denying that it will befall', and *takdhīb* rather than *kadhib* would ordinarily convey that sense. Müller reports the meaning *takdhīb* as well, citing

Zamakhsharī's *al-Kashshāf 'an ḥaqā'iq al-tanzīl*, but appears to favour *kadhib*.[57]

The paired divine epithet *dhū'l-jalāli wa'l-ikrām* (lit. 'possessed of majesty and the capacity to honour') [no. 13] occurs in the Qur'an twice, both times in verse-final position (Q. 55:27, 78). Since the seventy-eight verses of *Sūrat al-Raḥmān* (Q. 55) rhyme nearly entirely in *-ān*/*-ām*, a relatively infrequent rhyme in the Qur'an, it is very likely that this form is conditioned by end-rhyme. Müller interprets this as a modified version of an underlying form *dhū'l-karāma* ('possessed of dignity, venerability').[58] In part since neither the epithet *dhū'l-karāma* nor the noun *karāma* ('dignity') occurs in the Qur'an, *dhū'l-ikrām* is more likely a cognate substitute for *karīm* ('generous, noble'), which occurs several times as a divine epithet (Q. 27:40; Q. 82:6).[59] However, one would ordinarily expect the term *dhū'l-karam* ('possessed of generosity') as an equivalent of *karīm* ('generous' or 'noble'). Al-Rāghib takes some pains to explain the term *ikrām*, stating:

> *Ikrām* and *takrīm* mean that there be conveyed to a person an honour (*ikrām*), that is, a benefit untarnished by any ill effect, or that he consider that which comes to him an 'honourable' (*karīm*) thing, meaning 'noble' (*sharīf*). God said, *Have you heard the story of the honoured guests of Abraham* (*ḍayfi Ibrāhīma'l-mukramīn*, Q. 51:24)?' and *Rather, honoured worshippers* (*bal 'ibādun mukramūn*, Q. 21:26). That is to say, God made them noble (*kirām*). God also said, *Noble scribes* (*kirāman kātibīn*, Q. 82:11); and *In the hands of scribes, noble* (*kirām*) *and reverent* (Q. 80:16); and *And He made me one of those honoured* (*al-mukramīn*, Q. 36:27). God's word *dhū'l-jalāli wa'l-ikrām* contains both of these meanings.[60]

Here al-Rāghib takes pains to show that the forms derived from Form IV of the verb – *ikrām* ('honouring') and *mukram* ('honoured') – are close in meaning to *karīm* ('noble'). It remains the case, however, that one would expect the adjectives *jalīl wa karīm* as the simplest wording to convey the meaning of *dhū'l-jalāli wa'l-ikrām*. It appears that *ikrām* occurs primarily to provide the proper end-rhyme and that *al-jalāl* occurs for the sake of parallelism with *ikrām*, as it is also a verbal noun with a long -*ā*- in the final syllable. The fact that it occurs as *al-jalāl*, a verbal noun of the Form I verb *jalla* ('to be magnificent'), and not as *al-ijlāl*, the verbal noun of the Form IV verb *ajalla* ('to honour' or 'to exalt'), which would match the pattern of *al-ikrām* exactly, tends to confirm that *al-ikrām* is not the expected form.

Müller interprets *kidhdhābā* in Q. 78:35 [no. 11], describing the conversation of 'the residents of Paradise' – *lā yasmaʿūna fīhā laghwan wa-lā kidhdhābā* (*They hear therein neither idle talk nor lies*) – as a modified form of *kadhib*.[61] This is a clear instance of cognate substitution, for the form *kidhdhāb*, as we have seen, is a rare alternative form for the verbal noun *takdhīb* ('denying', 'calling a liar', 'rejecting as a lie'), but the context requires *kadhib* ('lies, lying'). Al-Rāghib does not recognise this as a possibility, but rather attempts to explain the form as derived from either Form II of the verb (*kadhdhaba, yukadhdhibu*) or, somewhat less strongly, Form III of the verb (*kādhaba, yukādhibu*). He writes:

> *Kidhdhāb* is 'to give the lie to someone', and the meaning of the passage is that they do not call one another liars. Denying the occurrence of accusations of lying in a place necessarily entails denying that lying occurs there. *Kidhdhāb* has also been read *kidhāb*, from *mukādhaba* ('addressing lies to someone'). The meaning would be 'They do not address lies to one another as people do in this world' (*lā yatakādhabūna takādhuba'l-nās fī'l-dunyā*).[62]

Here, al-Rāghib first interprets *kidhdhāb* as an equivalent of *takdhīb*, the verbal noun of the Form II verb. He then stresses that if accusations of lying are not heard in Paradise, this would necessarily imply that lying itself does not occur there either, a backhanded admission that one would ordinarily expect *kadhib* in this particular context rather than *takdhīb*. Al-Rāghib's second interpretation depends on the variant reading *kidhāb* for *kidhdhāb*. The form *fiʿāl* can serve as a verbal noun of the Form III verb, as in *qitāl* (*fighting*, Q. 2:216, 217, 246; etc.), so *kidhāb* could be a verbal noun from *kādhaba, yukādhibu* ('to address lies to s.o.'). He then uses the reflexive Form VI verb *yatakādhabūna* ('to lie to each other') in his explanation. Neither interpretation is very convincing; it makes more sense to interpret *kidhdhāb* as a cognate substitution for *kadhib*.

Müller interprets *lāghiya* in *fī jannatin ʿāliya lā tasmaʿu fīhā lāghiya* (*In a high garden. In which they do not hear idle speech*, Q. 88:10–11) [no. 4] as a modified form from an underlying *laghw* ('idle talk'), which occurs nine times outside of verse-final position elsewhere in the Qur'an (Q. 2:225; Q. 5:89; Q. 19:62; Q. 23:3; Q. 25:72; Q. 28:55; Q. 52:23; Q. 56:25; Q. 78:35).[63] Al-Rāghib recognises the connection with *laghw*, but interprets *lāghiya* as an adjectival form describing their speech (*kalām*). Since *kalām* is masculine and *lāghiya* is not, one must supply a feminine noun that is related in meaning such as *kalima* ('word, phrase, statement') or a noun of instance such as *qawla* ('statement, saying'). Al-Rāghib compares it with the form *kādhiba* ('lying') in Q. 56:2 [no. 3], which he interpreted in a similar fashion.[64] It makes more sense to interpret this as a case of cognate substitution, and this is corroborated by the parallel texts in which *laghw* appears.

Müller argues convincingly that the imperative in Noah's prayer to God, *annī maghlūbun fa'ntaṣir* (*I am defeated, so be victorious!*, Q. 54:10) [no. 19], is a modified form conveying the underlying meaning *fa'nṣurnī* ('So champion me' or 'So make me victorious').[65] This interpretation is corroborated by the use of the imperative *unṣurnī* ('champion me') in similar contexts three times in the Qur'an: *qāla rabbi'nṣurnī bimā kadhdhabūn* (*He said: My Lord, champion me, since they have denied me*, Q. 23:26, 39) and *qāla rabbi'nṣurnī ʿalā'l-qawmi'l-mufsidīn* (*He said: My Lord, champion me against the corrupting people*, Q. 29:30). In each of these cases, a prophet is entreating God: Noah (Q. 23:26), Lot (Q. 29:30) and an anonymous prophet in Q. 23:39. Al-Rāghib does not entertain this possibility, and he takes some pains to explain the form as it is. He comments, '[The Prophet Noah] said *fa'ntaṣir* [in Q. 54:10], and did not say *unṣur*, as an indication that that which befalls me will befall You, since I came to the [unbelievers] by Your command, so that if You make me victorious You will be gaining victory for Yourself'.[66] It is evident here that even though al-Rāghib attempts to explain the exact meaning conveyed by the form *fa'ntaṣir*, he nevertheless admits that the reader would have expected the first form *unṣur*, a confirmation of sorts that *fa'ntaṣir* is indeed a cognate substitute. Al-Rāghib's interpretation is not entirely convincing, for it would involve a blasphemy on Noah's part, attempting to convince God to do something on the grounds that it would be beneficial for God Himself. Al-Rāghib does not mention the distinct rhyme of *Sūrat al-Qamar*: *-ar/-ur/-ir* throughout its fifty-five verses. A postulated *fa'nṣur* ('So champion') without the attached pronoun *-nī* ('me') would also match this rhyme in the last syllable, but *fa'ntaṣir* fits better as it matches the rhythmical pattern of the other rhyme-words in the final two syllables, which are of the form *CvCvr* throughout. The verse-final rhyming feet in the immediate context are: *wa'zdujir, fa'ntaṣir, munhamir, qad qudir, wa dusur, kāna kufir, muddakir* (Q. 54:9–15). These are not all exactly parallel in syllabic quantity, for some are –⏑–, and some are ⏑⏑–, but all end in *CvCvr*. In this case, it seems evident that *fa'ntaṣir* is a case of cognate substitution for the sake of rhyme and metrical parallelism.

Assessment of Müller's Analysis

In my assessment, most of Müller's examples merit consideration as *bona fide* cases of cognate substitution. Of her nineteen examples, I accept thirteen more or less as she interprets them. I reject four of her examples as being instances of cognate substitution. In my view, *bi'l-sāhira* (Q. 79:14) [no. 1] is not a cognate substitute for *sāhirūn* ('awake'), referring to the unbelievers on the Day of Resurrection, but rather an adjective in the expected form modifying a suppressed noun, *al-Nār*, referring to the constant flames of Hell. The adjectives *'ātiya* (69:6) [no. 9] and *rābiya* (Q. 69:10) [no. 8] appear in odd phrases that are certainly conditioned by the rhyme context and merit consideration as cases of poetic licence of some type, but they should not be considered substitutes for some other cognate form. The phrase *bi'l-ṭāghiya* (Q. 69:5) [no. 2] is a feminine adjective of the form *fā'ila* that typically occurs in the Qur'an in reference to future calamities. It does not refer to Thamūd's rebellious behaviour and is not a substitute for the cognate *bi-ṭughyānihim*. In two further cases, analysis confirms that Müller's examples are indeed cases of cognate substitution, but I identify alternative underlying cognates or alternative senses. While she views *dhū'l-ikrām* (Q. 55:27, 78) [no. 13] as a cognate substitute for an underlying *dhū'l-karāma* ('possessed of dignity'), I argue that the underlying term is *al-karīm* ('generous' or 'noble') instead. While she argues that *bi-ṭaghwāhā* [no. 17] refers to Thamūd's rebellious behaviour and is a cognate substitute for *bi-ṭughyānihim*, I argue that it refers to the impending catastrophe that will befall them and is instead a cognate substitute for *bi'l-ṭāghiya*.

This discussion by no means exhausts the instances of cognate substitution that occur in the Qur'an. Analysis of *al-sāhira* (Q. 79:14) [no. 1] above suggested that the term *al-ḥāfira* (Q. 79:10) in the same sura is actually a cognate substitute for *ḥufra* ('pit'). I have argued elsewhere that *taqwīm* (Q. 95:4) is a cognate substitute for *qawām* ('form').[67] A number of other instances of cognate substitution may be identified in the works of both Müller and Ibn al-Ṣā'igh al-Ḥanafī. Some of the terms in Müller's section on the use of rare words might be considered cognate substitutes, such as *ghislīn* (Q. 69:36) for *ghusāla*.[68] Al-Rāghib treats this directly as a cognate, reporting that it is *ghusālat abdān al-kuffār fī'l-nār* ('The wash-water of the bodies of the unbelievers in the Fire').[69] While his entry does not provide any explanation for the use of this unusual form, he accepts the connection between the terms, implying that one has been substituted for the other. Similar is the word *kubbārā*, also included by Müller in her list of rare words that occur for the sake of rhyme, which appears in the verse *wa makarū makran kubbārā* (lit. *they have plotted a mighty plotting*, Q. 71:22) following the rhyme-word *khasārā* in the preceding verse (Q. 71:21).[70] *Kubbārā* occurs as an adjective modifying *makran* in a cognate accusative construction, and while Müller does not identify it as having been morphologically altered, to interpret it as a cognate substitute for *kabīrā* ('great') is certainly plausible. One might compare this phrase with similar cognate accusative constructions in Q. 17:4: . . . *wa-la-ta'lunna 'uluwwan kabīrā* (*you will engage in great arrogance*); Q. 25:21: . . . *wa 'ataw 'utuwwan kabīrā* (. . . *and they were extremely refractory*); and Q. 33:68: . . *wa'l'anhum la'nan kabīrā* (. . . *and curse them mightily*). Al-Rāghib connects *kubbārā* with *kabīr*, observing that *kubār* is an emphatic form of *kabīr* and that *kubbār* is even more emphatic than *kubār*.[71]

Additional Examples of Cognate Substitution Addressed by Ibn al-Ṣā'igh al-Ḥanafī

Ibn al-Ṣā'igh al-Ḥanafī identifies several cognate substitutions that do not appear in Müller's list. One group of examples includes active participles substituted for passive participles and vice versa.[72] He explains that the phrase *ʿīshatin rāḍiya* (*an approving life*, Q. 69:21; Q. 101:7) is used to convey the meaning of *ʿīshatin marḍiyya* ('a life approved of' or 'an agreeable life'). Al-Rāghib does not address this form in his entry on the tri-consonantal root combination *r-ḍ-w*.[73] Ibn al-Ṣā'igh al-Ḥanafī writes that *mā'un dāfiq* (*pouring water*, Q. 86:6) is used to express *mā'un madfūq* ('poured water'). Al-Rāghib mentions the phrase, but merely defines it as *sā'il bi-surʿa* ('flowing quickly') and obviously saw no reason to explain or justify the form in any detail.[74] One might argue that this interpretation is not necessary: as in English, water or rain gushing down may be described as 'pouring'. In other words, 'to pour' can act as an intransitive as well as a transitive verb. In Ibn al-Ṣā'igh al-Ḥanafī's view, *ḥijāban mastūrā* (*a covered barrier*, Q. 17:45) occurs as a replacement for *ḥijāban sātirā* ('a covering barrier'), but al-Rāghib makes no special comment about this form, even though he cites the phrase.[75]

Al-Rāghib generally ignores the cruxes of this type addressed by Ibn al-Ṣā'igh al-Ḥanafī, but Q. 19:61 is an exception. Ibn al-Ṣā'igh al-Ḥanafī reports that *kāna waʿduhu ma'tiyyā* (*His promise will be arrived at*, Q. 19:61) means *kāna waʿduhu ātiyā* ('His promise will come'). Al-Rāghib addresses this issue directly, writing:

> God's word '*ma'tiyyā*' is the passive participle from the verb *ataytuhu* ('I came to him'). One authority said that *ma'tiyyā* means *ātiyā* ('coming') and rendered the passive participle an active participle, but this is not the case. Rather, one says *ataytu'l-amra* ('I came to the matter') and *atānī'l-amru* ('the matter came to me').[76]

Here al-Rāghib recognises that one Qur'anic exegete, identified only as *baʿḍuhum* ('a certain one of them'), interpreted *ma'tiyyā* as a substitute for *ātiyā*, but he rejects this interpretation. Rather, he argues that the verb *atā, ya'tī* ('to come') may be used in a bivalent manner, describing not only the action of an event that happens to someone but also the action of someone to whom an event occurs. The explanation is strained and unconvincing. This is one of the very few cases in which al-Rāghib unambiguously reports an interpretation based on cognate substitution, and he rejects the possibility, avoiding the use of cognate substitution as a hermeneutic principle. It is also worth noting that he does not refer to the rhyme context, which might explain the need for the form *ma'tiyyā* in the first place.

Similar are cases that Ibn al-Ṣā'igh al-Ḥanafī identifies as involving the substitution of an emphatic for an ordinary form.[77] These include *qadīr* (Q. *passim*) many times in verse-final position, as opposed to the expected form *al-qādir*, which appears in *huwa'l-qādir* (*He is the powerful One*, Q. 6:65). Al-Rāghib reports that *qadīr* means the one who does what He wills to the amount required by wisdom, no more and no less. It cannot properly be applied to anyone other than God.[78] The divine epithet *ʿalīm* (*knowing*, Q. *passim*) occurs, in Ibn al-Ṣā'igh al-Ḥanafī's estimation, for *ʿālim* (*knower*), as in *ʿālimu'l-ghayb* (*Knower of the Unseen*, Q. *passim*). Al-Rāghib identifies *ʿalīm* as an emphatic form, but does not suggest that it is a substitute for *ʿālim*.[79] Ibn al-Ṣā'igh al-Ḥanafī also identifies *nasiyyā* in *mā kāna rabbuka nasiyyā* (*Thy Lord was not forgetful*, Q. 19:64) as a substitute for *nāsiyā* ('forgetful'). Al-Rāghib's entry on the root *n-s-y* does not address this form at all.[80] According to Ibn al-Ṣā'igh al-Ḥanafī, the form *ʿujāb* in *inna hādhā la-shay'un ʿujāb* (*This is indeed an astounding thing*, Q. 38:5) is a replacement for *ʿajīb* (*amazing*, Q. 11:72; Q. 50:2). Al-Rāghib's entry on the root *ʿ-j-b* includes Q. 38:5 as an example, but does not give any special explanation of the particular form, and actually omits any example of *ʿajīb*.[81]

Ibn al-Ṣā'igh al-Ḥanafī devotes another category in his work to rare synonyms that have been substituted for more common words.[82] Among these is the adjective *ḍīzā* in the phrase *qismatun ḍīzā* (*a ḍīzā division*, Q. 53:22), which, he states, is an uncommon synonym of *jāʾira* ('unjust', 'oppressive') used in place of the latter for the sake of rhyme. Al-Rāghib states in his entry on *ḍ-y-z* that *ḍīzā* means *nāqiṣa* ('deficient') instead of 'unjust', noting that it is of the pattern *fuʿlā* but that the *-u-* vowel is assimilated to the following consonantal *-y-*. He adds, 'It has been said that *fuʿlā* does not occur in their speech.'[83] This cannot mean that the pattern *fuʿlā* does not occur in Arabic, for it is fairly common in the Qur'an (e.g. *kubrā*, *ḥusnā*, *muthlā*, etc.).[84] Al-Rāghib apparently intends that the pattern *fuʿlā* is not ordinarily used with this particular tri-consonantal root in the speech of the Arabs, an admission that *ḍīzā* is an extremely rare or odd form. It seems likely that *ḍīzā* is a product of cognate substitution, but it is difficult to justify this interpretation without corroborating evidence.

The Eight Names of Hell in the Qur'an

While the preceding discussion is not a comprehensive treatment of cognate substitution in the Qur'an, it covers nearly all the cases evident in the analyses of Müller and Ibn al-Ṣāʾigh al-Ḥanafī. Missing is one category of terms that Ibn al-Ṣāʾigh al-Ḥanafī addresses and that Müller points out without any further analysis: the distinctive names of Hell that occur in the Qur'an. This section examines the eight main names applied to Hell in the Qur'an in order to assess the connection between their forms and rhyme, rhythm and cognate substitution, as well as al-Rāghib al-Iṣfahānī's treatment of these matters in his lexicon.[85] In a 1961 study, Thomas O'Shaughnessy discussed seven names of Hell, omitting one of the most common names, *al-Nār*, apparently on the grounds that it is not a proper noun but rather an ordinary noun used in a descriptive manner. He provides a chart showing the occurrence of the seven names according to Theodor Nöldeke's four periods of Qur'anic chronology and an appendix providing the texts of the verses in which they appear.[86] It was a mistake for O'Shaughnessy to omit *al-Nār*, since that is actually the most common name for Hell in the Qur'an; it is used as a proper noun – 'the Fire' – and it is also the primary counterpart of the main term for Paradise, *al-Janna* ('the

Garden'). A cursory examination of the occurrence of the names of Hell in the sacred text suggests that their use is conditioned to a large extent by rhyme.

At the end of her study on rhymed prose in the Qur'an, Müller observes that words like *al-Ḥuṭama* (Q. 104:4–5), which she states is difficult to understand and untranslatable, represent another class of forms created on account of the exigencies of end-rhyme, remarking that one might devote an entire separate work to such terms.[87] The term *al-Ḥuṭama* is one of the eight main names for Hell in the Qur'an, the variety of which has engendered comment both in medieval exegesis and in modern scholarship: *Jaḥīm/al-Jaḥīm*, *Jahannam*, *al-Ḥuṭama*, *Saʿīr/al-Saʿīr*, *Saqar*, *Laẓā*, *al-Nār* and *Hāwiya*. Ibn al-Ṣāʾigh al-Ḥanafī recognised that some of these names were unusual, and while he did not indicate that they resulted from cognate substitution, he reasoned that their appearance was conditioned by end-rhyme. His seventeenth out of forty categories of deviation from ordinary grammatical and stylistic rules for the sake of rhyme reads as follows:

> XVII. Preferring the rarer of two [synonymous] terms, as in *qismatan ḍīzā* (*a ḍīzā division*, Q. 53:22), where God did not say *jāʾira* ('unjust'), and *la-yunbadhanna fī'l-ḥuṭama* (*He will certainly be flung into the Ḥuṭama*, Q. 104:4), where He did not say *Jahannam* ('Gehenna, Hell') or *al-Nār* ('the Fire'). God said in *Sūrat al-Muddaththir*, *sa-aṣlīhi saqar* (*I will cause him to roast in Saqar*, Q. 74:26), in *Sūrat Saʾala*, *innahā laẓā* (*It is Laẓā*, Q. 70:15), and in *Sūrat al-Qāriʿah*, *fa-ummuhu hāwiya* (*Then his mother will be Hāwiya*, Q. 101:9) to match the verse-final words of those suras.[88]

Ibn al-Ṣāʾigh al-Ḥanafī suggests that the terms for Hell *al-Ḥuṭama*, *Saqar*, *Laẓā* and *Hāwiya*, in addition to the odd adjectival form *ḍīzā*, were all rare forms that appeared for the sake of rhyme in the verses cited here as replacements for other, more common forms. The following remarks examine each name of Hell in detail, assessing whether it may be considered a product of cognate substitution and then assessing al-Rāghib's analysis of the term.

1. *al-Nār*

The term *al-Nār*, meaning literally 'the Fire', is the most obvious name of Hell and needs no explanation. 'The fire' is also associated with Hell, or Gehenna, in the Gospels (e.g. Matthew 5:22; 18:9; Mark 9:43). The term is feminine because the noun *nār*, like *ḥarb* ('war'), *arḍ* ('earth'), *shams* ('sun'), and so on, is feminine despite its morphological form, which is ordinarily taken by masculine nouns.[89] *Nār/al-Nār* appears 146 times in the Qur'an. It refers to ordinary fire in a number of these instances (Q. 2:17, 226; Q. 3:183; Q. 4:10; Q. 5:64; Q. 7:12; Q. 15:27; Q. 18:96; Q. 21:69; Q. 24:35; Q. 29:34; Q. 36:80; Q. 38:76; Q. 55:15), to the fire of the Burning Bush (Q. 20:10; Q. 27:7–8; Q. 28:29) and to the fire from which Abraham escaped unscathed (Q. 21:69; Q. 29:24). Even when it is indefinite, though, it refers to Hell in many passages, for example, in Q. 18:29: *innā aʿtadnā li'l-kāfirīna nāran aḥāṭa bihim surādiquhā* (*We have prepared for the unbelievers a fire the tent of which surrounds them*). The term appears in conjunction with other names of Hell, in which instances it is clear that *al-nār* is not a proper noun: *Jahannam* (Q. 9:35, 63, 68, 81, 109; Q. 35:36; Q. 40:49; Q. 52:13; Q. 72:23; Q. 98:6), *Saqar* (Q. 54:48), *Hāwiya* (Q. 101:11) and *al-Ḥuṭama* (Q. 104:6). It occurs in a number of passages in verse-final position, rhyming with adjacent verses (Q. 2:167, 175, 201; Q. 3:10, 16, 191; Q. 13:35; Q. 38:27, 59, 61, 64; Q. 39:8, 19; Q. 40:6, 41, 43, 47). *Al-Nār* seems to be the fundamental term for Hell in the Qur'an, as it is paired with *al-Janna*, the most common term for Paradise, in several passages (Q. 2:221; Q. 3:195; Q. 5:72; Q. 7:44, 50; Q. 59:20).

2. *Jahannam*

Jahannam is the next most frequent term for Hell, occurring seventy-seven times. It derives from the Hebrew toponym *Gehinnom* ('the Valley of Hinnom') a contraction of *Gei Ben-Hinnom* ('The Valley of the Son of Hinnom'), which originally designated a place just outside Jerusalem where the Canaanites sacrificed children in fire to the god Moloch (2 Chronicles 28:3, 33:6; Jeremiah 7:31, 19:2–6). The term came to be used for Hell in Judaism, and the related term *Gehenna* appears in the speech of Jesus in the Gospels with this meaning (e.g. Matthew 5:22, Mark 9:42, etc.). The Arabic form could not have been borrowed directly from Greek *Geenna* or Syriac/Aramaic *Gēhannā*, because they lack the final *-m* found in *Jahannam*. Nöldeke, and Jeffery following him, argued that the likely immediate source is the Ethiopic *gähännäm* or *gähannäm*.[90] *Jahannam* is a proper noun and never appears with the definite article. It is feminine despite the fact that Hebrew *gei* ('valley') is masculine. In fact, all the names of Hell are feminine in the Qur'an, even when their morphological pattern is not inherently feminine, apparently on the grounds that *al-Nār* is feminine, thus giving another indication that *al-Nār* is the fundamental term for Hell. For example, denizens of *Jahannam* are described as *khālidīna fīhā* ('residing in it eternally') with the feminine pronominal suffix *-hā*. In one passage, *Jahannam* is personified and addressed in the feminine singular: *yawma naqūlu li-Jahannama hal imtala'ti wa taqūlu hal min mazīd* (*On the day when We will ask Jahannam, 'Are you* [fem.] *full?' And she will ask, 'Is there any more?'*, Q. 50:30). *Jahannam* never occurs in verse-final position, evidently because its unusual form precludes a satisfying rhyming and metrical close to a verse. When it occurs near the end of a verse, it is followed by a short tag that forms a satisfactory rhyming and rhythmical clausula such as . . . *wa bi'sa'l-mihād* (. . . *and what an evil resting-place it is!* Q. 3:197; Q. 13:18; Q. 38:56), . . . *wa bi'sa'l-maṣīr* (. . . *and what an evil journey's end it is!* Q. 8:16; Q. 58:8; Q. 66:9; Q. 67:6), . . . *wa sā'at maṣīrā* (. . . *and how horrid that is as a journey's end!* e.g. Q. 4:97; Q. 48:6).

Al-Rāghib states that *Jahannam* is 'A name of God's lighted Fire. It has been said that its origin is Persian, the word *J-h-nām*, but God knows best.'[91] Other Persian writers also support this etymology: 'Alī Akbar Dihkhuda reports that the term *Jahannām*, *Juhannām* or *Jihannām* means a bottomless pit, citing the dictionaries *Muntahā al-arab fī lughat al-'arab* by 'Abd al-Raḥīm b. 'Abd al-Karīm Ṣafīpūrī (d. 1267/1850) and *Muhadhdhab al-asmā' fī murattab al-ḥurūf wa'l-ashyā'* by Maḥmūd b. 'Umar al-Zanjī al-Sinjārī (fl. eighth/fifteenth century). The latter identifies the word as the origin of *Jahannam*.[92] It appears likely that these words derive from *Jahannam* rather than the other way around, given that the origin of *Jahannam* is certainly Hebrew and not Persian. In my view, al-Rāghib or his sources may have interpreted the reported Persian antecedents of *Jahannam* as compound terms with the suffix *-nām*, meaning 'name' or 'reputation', and the first element derived from *chāh*, meaning 'well' or 'pit': *chāh-nām* or *chahnām* ('reputed to be an abyss'). In any case, the Persian etymology is unfounded, and this claim shows al-Rāghib's familiarity with Persian and limited knowledge of Biblical tradition.

3. *al-Jaḥīm / Jaḥīm*

This term occurs twenty-six times in the Qur'an, twenty-three times as *al-Jaḥīm*, with the definite article, and three times as *Jaḥīm*, without the definite article (Q. 56:94; Q. 73:12; Q. 82:14). It occurs in rhyme position, or verse-final position, twenty-one times and outside verse-final position five times (Q. 26:91; Q. 69:31; Q. 79:36, 39; Q. 81:12). It is a feminine noun, as is evident from such verses as *fa-inna'l-jaḥīma hiya'l-ma'wā* (*For al-Jaḥīm is the refuge*, Q. 79:39) in which *al-Jaḥīm* is the antecedent of the feminine pronoun *hiya*, and as well from the feminine verb forms in *burrizati'l-Jaḥīmu li-man yarā* (*Al-Jaḥīm will be made to stand forth to him who can see*, Q. 79:36) and *wa-idhā'l-Jaḥīmu su''irat* (*And when al-Jaḥīm is stoked*, Q. 81:12). The fact that it is used in the indefinite suggests that it is understood to mean 'flames', 'fire' or 'a pit of fire': *inna ladaynā ankālan wa jaḥīmā* (*Heavy fetters and a raging fire are our lot*, Q. 73:12). O'Shaughnessy is of the opinion that *al-Jaḥīm* derives from a syncopated version of Ethiopic *Gahannam*.[93] This is not convincing, particularly since it would require a radical sound change, from *-h-* in *Gahannam* to *-ḥ-* in *al-Jaḥīm*. *Al-Jaḥīm* does not always refer to Hell in the Qur'an. The fact that it refers to the fire of Nimrod in Q. 37:97 suggests that it is understood as a general term for a flaming or blazing fire.

Regarding this term, al-Rāghib observes, '*Jaḥma* refers to the intense flaming of fire, and from this meaning derives *al-Jaḥīm*'.[94] He thus recognises a connection between the term *Jaḥīm* and the root-consonant combination *j-ḥ-m*, with its characteristic meaning 'the flaring up of fire'.[95] However, he does not attempt to explain the morphological pattern *fa'īl* or the specific literal sense of *Jaḥīm*. The form *fa'īl* is often used as an equivalent of *fā'il* or *maf'ūl*, that is, either an active or passive participle, and, as we will see, al-Rāghib identifies *al-Sa'īr* as taking the pattern *fa'īl* with the meaning of the passive participle *maf'ūl*. One might, therefore, suppose that he would understand *al-Jaḥīm* in this manner as well, but if the Form I verb *jaḥama, yajḥumu* is intransitive, meaning 'to flare up', it is perhaps preferable to consider *jaḥīm* as conveying the meaning of the active participle *fā'il*, meaning *jāḥima* ('that which flares up').

4. *al-Ḥuṭama*

The term *al-Ḥuṭama* occurs only twice in the Qur'an, in one passage in *Sūrat al-Humaza* (Q. 104:4–5). Both occurrences are in verse-final position in a passage rhyming in *-a*, and more specifically with rhyme words of the form *CvCvCa*. *Al-Ḥuṭama* is clearly feminine on account of its form, and it appears both times with the definite article. The two instances of *al-Ḥuṭama* are embedded in a *mā adrāka* construction: *kallā la-yunbadhanna fi'l-ḥuṭama wa-mā adrāka ma'l-ḥuṭama nāru'llāhi'l-mūqada* (*Nay, he will be flung into the Ḥuṭama. And what will convey to you what the Ḥuṭama is? The kindled fire of God . . .*, Q. 104:4–6). In this pre-Islamic oracular form, which usually follows the pattern *X, mā X, wa-mā adrāka mā X, Y*, an obscure or ambiguous term *X* is presented, followed by the question 'What is *X*?', followed by the question 'And what makes you know what *X* is?', followed by the answer *Y*, an explanation of *X* in other terms.[96] This suggests that the meaning of *al-Ḥuṭama*, like those of *Saqar* and *Hāwiya*, which also appear in this construction, is not immediately evident to the audience and requires clarification. In the one occurrence in the Qur'an of a cognate, the Form I verb *ḥaṭama, yaḥṭimu* ('to crush'), one ant warns others of King Solomon's approaching army: . . . *udkhulū masākinakum lā yaḥṭimannakum Sulaymānu wa junūduhu* (. . . *Enter your dwellings, lest Solomon and his troops crush you!* Q. 27:18). It appears likely that *al-Ḥuṭama* is a cognate substitute for an underlying form such as *al-Ḥāṭima* or *al-Ḥaṭṭāma* ('the Crusher').

Al-Rāghib states that *al-Jaḥīm* was called *Ḥuṭama*, which he presents without the definite article despite the fact that it only occurs in the Qur'an with the definite article.[97] He adds that one calls a glutton a *ḥuṭama*, drawing comparison between him and Hell, because his belly consumes a tremendous amount, as a furnace does.[98] In other words, although *al-Ḥuṭama* is clearly related to the verb 'to crush', al-Rāghib understands by this 'crushing' the action of a furnace that consumes fuel rapidly and in great quantities. He does not take the rhyme context into account, discuss the particular meaning conveyed by the pattern *fuʿala* or suggest that *al-Ḥuṭama* has replaced another underlying form, but he understands *al-Ḥuṭama* to be related to the verb *yaḥṭimu*.

5. *al-Saʿīr / Saʿīr*

The term *al-Saʿīr/Saʿīr* occurs sixteen times in the Qur'an, eight times with the definite article *al-* (Q. 22:4; Q. 31:21; Q. 34:12; Q. 35:6; Q. 42:7; Q. 67:5, 10, 11) and eight times without (Q. 4:10, 55; Q. 17:97; Q. 25:11; Q. 33:64; Q. 48:13; Q. 76:4; Q. 84:12). In all sixteen instances, it occurs in verse-final position, and the eight instances that lack the definite article are all accusatives, producing the rhyme form *saʿīrā*. When definite, *al-Saʿīr* is a proper noun. It is evidently feminine. In the verses *inna'llāha laʿana'l-kāfirīna wa aʿadda lahum saʿīrā. khālidīna fīhā abadan lā yajidūna waliyyan wa-lā naṣīrā* (*God cursed the unbelievers and prepared for them a burning. They will remain therein forever, and will find neither an ally nor a champion*, Q. 33:64–5), *Saʿīr* is the antecedent of the feminine pronominal suffix in *fīhā*. *Saʿīr* without the definite article, however, is not a proper noun, for it describes an aspect of *Jahannam*, another name of Hell, in . . . *wa kafā bi-Jahannama saʿīrā* (. . . *Gehenna is sufficient as a burning* [*for them*], Q. 4:55) and in *ma'wāhum Jahannamu kullamā khabat zidnāhum saʿīrā* (*Their refuge is Gehenna: whenever it abates, we increase the blazing for them*, Q. 17:97). The fact that *saʿīrā* occurs as an accusative of specification after *kafā* and *zidnā* shows that it is a noun rather than an adjective, indefinite, and not a proper noun.

A verb cognate with *Saʿīr/al-Saʿīr* occurs once in the Qur'an, also in connection with Hell, but with the name *al-Jaḥīm* in particular:

wa-idhā'l-Jaḥīmu suʿʿirat (*And when the Flames are set ablaze*, Q. 81:12). Al-Rāghib also reports the Form I variant, *suʿirat*. The cognate noun *suʿur* occurs twice in the Qur'an (Q. 54:24, 47), both times in verse-final position in *Sūrat al-Qamar*, which rhymes throughout in *CvCvr*, and both times in the phrase *fī ḍalālin wa suʿur*. While Q. 54:47 is followed by an explicit mention of Hell, Q. 54:24 is not: in it, the Thamūd tribe said, . . . *a-basharan minnā wāḥidan nattabiʿuhu innā idhan la-fī ḍalālin wa suʿur* (*Is it a mortal man alone among us, that we are to follow? Then indeed we would fall into error and madness*). Since this verse addresses not eternal punishment for one's sins but rather the consequences of actions in this world, *suʿur* probably refers to madness rather than Hell or fire. *Suʿur* is evidently singular, parallel to *ḍalāl*, and likely a variant of *suʿr* ('madness', 'frenzy').

Al-Rāghib cites many cognates in his explanation of *saʿīr*, including many that do not appear in the Qur'an: *masʿūr* ('rabid'), *suʿār* ('rabies'), *saʿr* ('the flaring up of fire'), the verbs *saʿara*, *saʿʿara* and *asʿara* ('to cause fire to flare up'); *istaʿara* ('to be lit [of fire]'); *saʿura* ('to get hot, be overcome by heat'). It is clear, therefore, that he connects the particular form *al-Saʿīr* strongly with its cognates. He explains the form *al-Saʿīr* as a *faʿīl* pattern conveying the meaning of a passive participle (*mafʿūl*),[99] meaning 'set ablaze', 'stoked', 'caused to rage'.

6. *Saqar*

The term *Saqar* occurs four times in the Qur'an, three times in verse-final position in passages rhyming in *-ar*. One of these occurs in *Sūrat al-Qamar*: *yawma yusḥabūna fī'l-nāri ʿalā wujūhihim dhūqū massa Saqar* (*On the day when they are dragged into the Fire upon their faces: 'Feel the touch of Saqar!'*, Q. 54:48). The two other instances occur in a *mā adrāka* construction, which, as mentioned above, ordinarily introduces ambiguous terms. Thus, in Q. 74:26–30:

sa-uṣlīhi Saqar
wa-mā adrāka mā Saqar
lā tubqī wa-lā tadhar

lawwāḥatun li'l-bashar
ʿalayhā tisʿata ʿashar

I shall roast him in Saqar.
And what will inform you what Saqar is?
It leaves nothing, and it spares nothing.
It scorches mankind.
Above it are nineteen.

In the fourth case (Q. 74:42), *Saqar* occurs in a passage rhyming in *-ūn/-īn* (Q. 74:39–41, 43–9). This passage drew the attention of earlier scholars, who suggested that *Saqar* has been substituted here for *al-Jaḥīm*, which would have rhymed with the adjacent verses. O'Shaughnessy argues that this occurred because the Prophet was seeking to abandon the term *al-Jaḥīm* at this point in his mission, supposedly because of criticism based on the fact that it was a corrupt borrowing from Ethiopic *gahannam*.[100] Although this argument about the Ethiopic borrowing is weak, not least because *al-Jaḥīm* is probably not related to *Jahannam*, the interruption of the rhyme scheme is striking, and it seems plausible that an instance of *al-Jaḥīm* has been replaced with *Saqar*. *Saqar* may have been inserted here in order to echo the occurrences of *Saqar* earlier in the sura (Q. 74:26–7). The passage Q. 74:38–49 is as follows:

kullu nafsin bimā kasabat rahīnah
illā aṣḥābu'l-yamīn
fī jannātin yatasāʾalūn
ʿani'l-mujrimīn
mā salakakum fī Saqar
qālū lam naku min al-muṣallīn
wa-lam naku nuṭʿimu'l-miskīn
wa-kunnā nakhūḍu maʿa'l-khāʾiḍīn
wa-kunnā nukadhdhibu bi-yawmi'l-dīn
ḥattā atānā'l-yaqīn
fa-mā tanfaʿuhum shafāʿatu'l-shāfiʿīn
fa-mā lahum ʿani'l-tadhkirati muʿriḍīn

Every soul is a pledge for its own deeds.
Save those of the right hand.

In gardens they will ask one another
Concerning the sinners:
What led you into Saqar?
They will answer: We were not among those who prayed,
Nor did we feed the wretched.
We used to plunge into sinful behaviour along with others who did the same.
And we used to deny the Day of Judgement
Till the inevitable came to us.
The intercession of those who intercede will not avail them then.
So why do they turn away from the Admonishment?

Saqar is evidently a proper noun; it never occurs with the definite article. In Q. 74:26–30, the feminine verbs *tubqī* and *tadhar*, the feminine adjective *lawwāḥah* and the feminine pronominal suffix in *ʿalayhā* show that it is a feminine noun. No cognates of *Saqar* occur in the Qur'an.

Al-Rāghib reports that *Saqar* was rendered a proper name for *Jahannam*. He also connects *Saqar* with the cognate verb *saqara, yasqaru, saqran* in *saqarat-hu'l-shamsu* (*the Sun scorched it*; also *ṣaqarat-hu*, with *ṣād*), meaning *lawwaḥat-hu wa adhābat-hu* ('scorched it and caused it to melt').[101] Given this meaning of the verb *saqara*, it is reasonable to interpret *Saqar* as a cognate substitute for an underlying verbal noun such as *al-saqr* ('scorching'). Al-Rāghib does not suggest this directly but nevertheless recognises the connection of *Saqar* with the cognate verb.

7. *Laẓā*

Laẓā occurs only once in the Qur'an, in verse-final position, in a context that requires end-rhyme in *-ā*. The passage in which it appears (Q. 70:15–18) is:

kallā innahā Laẓā
nazzāʿatan li'l-shawā
tadʿū man adbara wa tawallā
wa jamaʿa fa-awʿā

Nay! It is Laẓā.
Eager to roast.
It calls him who turned his back and fled.
And hoarded and withheld.

It is feminine, as indicated by the attached pronoun in *innahā*, the feminine adjective *nazzāʿa*, and the feminine third person verb *tadʿū*. It is a proper noun, definite without the article *al-*. Al-Rāghib states that *Laẓā* is a name of *Jahannam*, i.e. a proper noun, and that it is not declined. He also reports that *al-laẓā* means pure flames, and that it derives from the verbs *laẓiyat al-nār* or *talaẓẓat al-nār* ('the fire flamed, or flared up').[102] He thus recognises that the name *Laẓā* is related to these cognate verbs. One may interpret it as the verbal noun *laẓā* from *laẓiya* or a collective noun 'flames'. This may not be an actual case of cognate substitution, as the name derives from the ordinary form of the verbal noun, but it is certainly a case in which the rhyme context has affected the choice of the word for Hell.

8. *Hāwiya*

Hāwiya occurs only once in the Qur'an, in verse-final position in a context requiring the rhyme *CāCiya: fa-ummuhu hāwiya* (Q. 101:10). It occurs in an oracular text focused on the Day of Judgement, and it is part of a *mā adrāka* construction, which, as in the cases of *al-Ḥuṭama* and *Saqar*, suggests that it is a mysterious or ambiguous term, the meaning of which is not immediately evident. Its pattern, *fāʿila*, is a form commonly encountered in cognate substitution, as with *kādhiba*, *lāghiya*, *bāqiya*, *kāshifa* and *rājifa*, mentioned above [nos 3–7], and also in other oracular texts: *al-qāriʿa* (Q. 101:1–3), *al-wāqiʿa* (Q. 56:1), *al-ḥāqqa* (Q. 69:1–3), and so on. Jeffery has interpreted the term as a borrowing from Ethiopic *ḥewaye* ('the fiery red glow of the evening sky') or *ḥäwe* ('fire', 'burning coal'), and O'Shaughnessy endorses this opinion.[103] However, this interpretation is highly unlikely because it would involve a rare sound change of *-ḥ-* to *-h-*.

Comparison with *Laẓā* and *Saqar* suggests that *Hāwiya* is a proper noun even though it lacks the definite article. Like *al-Ḥuṭama*, it is feminine in form. As I have argued elsewhere, *Hāwiya* is likely a cognate substitute for an underlying term such as *huwwa* or *mahwāh* ('abyss').[104] Al-Rāghib reports two main interpretations of the verse, which has been subject to some controversy. One is that *hāwiya* is a predicate adjective to *umm*, and that the phrase *fa-ummuhu hāwiya* derives from the idiom *hawat ummuhu* (lit. 'His mother fell' but idiomatically, 'His mother became bereft of children', i.e. 'mourned his loss'). The verse would then mean, 'His mother will be bereft of him' or perhaps a curse in the optative, 'May his mother be bereft of him', i.e. 'may he die'. According to the second interpretation, *al-Hāwiya* – and al-Rāghib supplies the definite article *al-* – means Hell, and the verse means *maqarruhu al-nār* ('His settling-place will be the Fire'). Al-Rāghib begins the entry by citing several cognates, including *al-hawā* ('longing' or 'desire'), *yuhwī* ('to cause to plummet from a height'), and *al-huwiyy* ('the act of plummeting from a height'). He connects the noun *al-hawā* with these other cognates, and also with *al-Hāwiya*: 'It was called this because it causes its possessor to be cast down in this world to every calamity, and in the next world to *al-Hāwiya*.'[105] It thus seems evident that he favours the interpretation that *Hāwiya* is Hell in this verse, and he connects it with cognate forms, but he does not explain the significance of its morphological pattern.

Lexical Analysis and the Qur'anic Portrayal of Hell

This examination of the eight names of Hell suggests that three – *al-Ḥuṭama*, *Saqar* and *Hāwiya* – should be considered cases of cognate substitution. *Al-Ḥuṭama* is a substitute for a postulated adjectival form such as *al-Ḥāṭima* or *al-Ḥaṭṭāma* ('the Crusher') or perhaps ('that which consumes'). *Saqar* is a cognate substitute for a form such as *al-saqr* ('the scorching'). *Hāwiya* is a cognate substitute for the noun *huwwa* ('abyss') or the nouns of place *mahwā* or *mahwāh* ('abyss'). *Laẓā*, although its occurrence is clearly conditioned by the rhyme, takes the ordinary form of the verbal noun from the verb *laẓiya, yalẓā* ('to flame') and so means 'the Flaming' without, however, meriting consideration as a case of cognate substitution. The terms *al-Jaḥīm* and *al-Sa'īr* are clearly chosen as names of Hell on account of the denotations of their tri-consonantal roots. However, they are not to be considered cases of cognate substitution, because the forms that they take are not extraordinary in context. *Al-Jaḥīm* and *al-Saʿīr* can be interpreted as uses of the form *faʿīl* to convey the meaning of the passive participle *mafʿūl* – so *al-Saʿīr* would mean 'that which is stoked' or 'that which is brought to a blaze' – or of the active participle *fāʿil* – so *al-Jaḥīm* would mean 'that which flares up'. With the exception of *Jahannam* and *al-Nār*, it is clear that use of the names of Hell is strongly conditioned by the rhyme context, both in oracular passages that present mysterious or ambiguous terms and in more prosaic passages in which certain forms are required to conform to common Qur'anic end-rhymes such as *-ūn/-īn/-ūm/-īm*.

What does this reveal about the nature of Hell? Paradise and Hell as portrayed in the Qur'an are in a relationship of symmetrical opposition. Torment corresponds to pleasure. Beautiful, pleasant surroundings in the Garden of Paradise correspond to miserable, unbearable surroundings in Hell. The wonderful food and drink of the inhabitants of Paradise are mirrored by the terrible food and drink of the inhabitants of Hell. Bunches of grapes and dates in the Garden of Paradise correspond to the grotesque fruit of the Zaqqūm tree, which consists of demons' heads (Q. 37:62–6; Q. 44:43–6). Hell is evidently a prison, for the inmates are burdened with chains and fetters (Q. 13:5; Q. 34:33; Q. 36:8; Q. 76:4) and are guarded over by nineteen angels who serve as wardens (Q. 66:6; Q. 74:30). Both Paradise and Hell have gates (Q. 15:44; Q. 16:29; Q. 38:50; Q. 39:71–3; Q. 40:76), but while the Qur'an sets the number of Hell's gates at seven (Q. 15:44), it does not specify the number of the gates of Paradise. Later tradition sets the number of Paradise's gates at eight,[106] perhaps for symmetry's sake, or perhaps simply to stress its superiority.

Later Islamic tradition, already attested in a hadith included in *al-Musnad* of Aḥmad Ibn Ḥanbal (d. 241/855), connects the various names of Hell with its topography, assigning each name to a different level of Hell, according to the following scheme:

1. *Jahannam*, for grave sinners among the Muslims;
2. *al-Laẓā*, for the Jews;

3. *al-Ḥuṭama*, for the Christians;
4. *al-Saʿīr*, for the Sabaeans;
5. *al-Saqar*, for the Zoroastrians;
6. *al-Jaḥīm*, for the idolaters;
7. *al-Hāwiya*, for the hypocrites.[107]

Hell in the Qur'an, like Paradise, appears to have a particular structure or topography. Hell is portrayed in the Qur'an as fire stoked in a pit; this is explicit in the phrase *ʿalā shafā ḥufratin mina'l-nār* (*on the brink of a pit of fire*) in Q. 3:103. Several passages in the Qur'an suggest that Hell has topographical differentiation, including levels. For example, the Zaqqūm tree is said to sprout from the 'root' or 'bottom' (*aṣl*) of Hell (Q. 37:64); the floor of the pit evidently slopes downward to a low point in the middle. The hypocrites are reported to inhabit the lowest level (*al-darak al-asfal*) of the Fire (Q. 15:44), which implies the existence of several additional, higher levels.

However, al-Rāghib's lexicon contains no hint that the various names of Hell refer to its levels, and the evidence of the Qur'an suggests that the hierarchical scheme is an imaginative invention. We have seen that use of Hell's various names is strongly conditioned by the requirements of end-rhyme. Their existence does not, therefore, reflect an intention to distinguish between particular parts or sections of Hell, for the names of Hell all refer to the same entity, but occur instead in order to fit the rhyme-context in different passages. Nevertheless, the names certainly stress distinct aspects of Hell. *Jahannam* differs from the other names in that it is in origin a proper name that designates Hell without referring to any particular physical aspect, at least in an obvious or etymological manner. *Hāwiya* ('Abyss' or 'the Abyss') stresses the identification of Hell as an immense pit. The other terms for Hell are all semantically connected with fire and are thus equivalent replacements for the term *al-Nār* ('the Fire'). *Saqar* emphasises the scorching effect of the fire. *Laẓā* refers to the flames themselves. *Saʿīr* refers to the process of being kindled, or stoked, while *al-Jaḥīm* refers to the blazing of the fire. *Al-Ḥuṭama* may refer to the fire's rapid consumption of fuel. There is no indication that these appellations are meant to be placed in a hierarchy of intensity or value or assigned to particular sections of Hell.

Other Terms Related to Hell and to Paradise

It was suggested above that the terms *al-Sāhira* and *al-Ḥāfira* may also refer to Hell and that *al-Ḥāfira* may be a cognate substitute for *al-Ḥufra* ('the Pit'). Another term that commentators have erroneously interpreted as a reference to Hell is *Sijjīn*, which occurs twice in the Qur'an. Both occurrences are in rhyme position, embedded in a *mā adrāka* construction in Q. 83:7–9:

inna kitāba'l-fujjāra la-fī Sijjīn
wa-mā adrāka mā Sijjīn?
kitābun marqūm

The record of the sinners is in Sijjīn.
And what will inform you what Sijjīn is?
An engraved book.

Al-Rāghib interprets *Sijjīn* as a name of Hell, a counterpart to *'Illiyyūn* (Q. 83:18, 19), supposedly a name for Paradise, adding that the patterns of both words have been augmented in order to reflect an additional meaning (*zīda lafẓuhu tanbīhan 'alā ziyādati ma'nāhu*).[108] In the entry on *'Illiyyūn*, which is discussed below, he states that, just as *'Illiyyūn* refers to the best, most elevated part of Paradise, so does *Sijjīn* refer to the worst part of Hell.[109] Some have claimed, he adds, that *Sijjīn* is a name for 'the seventh earth' (*al-arḍ al-sābi'a*), or the lowest level of earth below ground.[110] Other commentaries state that *Sijjīn* is a boulder or black tree in the seventh level of earth below ground.[111] While the meaning 'Hell' may be suggested by the reference to sinners (*fujjār*) and their fate, the fact that the verses do not report that the sinners themselves are in *Sijjīn*, but rather that their 'book' or 'record' (*kitāb*) is in *Sijjīn*, calls this interpretation into question. It seems more likely that *Sijjīn* is the name of the book in which their sins or fates are recorded. This is corroborated by the conclusion of the *mā adrāka* construction, which defines *Sijjīn* as *kitābun marqūm* ('an engraved book'). The alternative interpretation of *Sijjīn* as a book was well known among pre-modern commentators.[112] Zamakhsharī defines it as follows: '*Sijjīn* is a comprehensive book (*kitāb jāmiʿ*), the Register of Evil in which God recorded the deeds of demons and the deeds of unbelievers and sinners, both genies and humans . . .'[113]

Although al-Rāghib presents *Sijjīn* in the entry on the tri-consonantal root *s-j-n*, along with the noun *sijn* ('prison', Q. 12:35) and the verb *la-yusjananna* (*he will indeed be imprisoned*, Q. 12:32), he does not connect the word with those meanings, and it appears that he considers it unrelated to them. His remark that the form has been augmented presumably refers to the ending *-īn*, and one is tempted to see in this term a distorted ending similar to those found in *Ilyāsīn* ('Elias', Q. 37:130) and *Sīnīn* ('Sinai', Q. 95:2).[114] It is not a sound masculine plural ending, because the form *Sijjīn* occurs in the nominative case as well as the genitive, unlike *ʿIlliyyūn*. One might suggest connecting *Sijjīn* with *sijill* ('scroll', 'register', 'edict') and interpreting it as a distorted form that refers to a recorded document.[115] Zamakhsharī, on the other hand, connects the term explicitly with *sijn* ('prison') and states that it is the emphatic pattern *fiʿʿīl* derived from *sijn*.[116]

A number of other descriptive terms related to Hell appear to have been created ad hoc in the Qur'an and may have been formed by cognate substitution. The drink of the denizens of Hell is *ḥamīm* ('scalding water'), as in: . . . *lahum sharābun min ḥamīm* (*They will have a drink of ḥamīm*, Q. 6:70), *thumma ṣubbū fawqa ra'sihi min ʿadhābi'l-ḥamīm* (*Then pour on his head some of the punishment of ḥamīm*, Q. 44:48), and so on (Q. 6:70; Q. 10:4; Q. 22:19; Q. 37:67; Q. 38:57; Q. 40:72; Q. 44:46; Q. 55:44; Q. 56:43, 54, 93; Q. 47:15; Q. 78:25), which clearly derives from the tri-consonantal root *ḥ-m-m* ('to heat'). Since *ḥamīm* is clearly of the common pattern *faʿīl* with the meaning of the passive participle *mafʿūl*, meaning 'that which is heated', one should not consider it a case of cognate substitution. From the same tri-consonantal root is *yaḥmūm* (Q. 56:43), of the relatively rare pattern *yafʿūl*, which is described as the substance of their shades or canopies, and is often translated as 'black smoke'.[117] This interpretation of *yaḥmūm* is derived from the context and has little etymological support. This is a better candidate for consideration as a case of cognate substitution since it clearly refers to something that is hot, like the 'tent' (*surādiq*) of fire mentioned in Q. 18:29.

Several terms designate the food of the denizens of Hell. These include *ghislīn* (Q. 69:36), discussed earlier, which may be interpreted as a cognate substitute for *ghusāla* ('filth' or 'dirty wash-water'). Their food is also supposed to be the fruit of the Zaqqūm tree, which grows up from the bottom of the pit of *al-Jaḥīm* and bears fruit like demons' heads (Q. 37:62; Q. 44:43; Q. 56:52). It is difficult to connect this with the verb *zaqama, yazqumu, zaqman* ('to swallow' or 'to gobble up'), which apparently formed a pair with *laqama* ('to eat a morsel') and had the positive meaning, 'to eat dates with butter'. The term *al-zaqqūm* is also reported as meaning 'a certain food in which are dates and fresh butter'.[118] Al-Rāghib does not explain the origin of *zaqqūm*, but rather states that it is the origin of one sense of the verb *zaqama* or *tazaqqama* ('to swallow something vile').[119] One might connect it instead with the tri-consonantal root *z-q-q*: the verb *zaqqa, yazuqqu*, said of a bird, means either to drop dung or to feed its young by ejecting food from its beak.[120]

While Ibn Wahb expressed wonder at the large number of Qur'anic terms for Hell,[121] fewer distinct terms apply to Paradise. Among the many terms for Paradise in the Qur'an, few are mysterious words or require explanation. The most common term is *al-Janna* ('the Garden'), which occurs in the plural *jannāt* ('gardens') as well. The main term for Paradise in the Qur'an, it serves as the counterpart of *al-Nār* (Q. 7:44–50; Q. 59:20). *Janna* occurs in construct with a number of terms such as *Jannat al-khuld* ('the Garden of Eternity', Q. 25:15), *Jannat al-na'īm* or *Jannāt al-na'īm* (*the Gardens of Bliss*, Q. 10:9; Q. 22:56; Q. 31:8; Q. 56:12, 89; Q. 68:34; Q. 70:38), *Jannāt al-ma'wā* (*the Gardens of Refuge*, Q. 32:19; Q. 37:43), and so on. Other terms refer to Paradise as an abode or station: *Dār al-muqāma* (*Abode of Residence*, Q. 35:35), *Dār al-salām* (*Abode of Peace*, Q. 10:25), *Dār al-ākhira* (*Abode of the Next World*, Q. 2:94; Q. 6:32; Q. 7:169). The term *Jannāt 'Adn*, used often to refer to Paradise (Q. 9:72; Q. 13:23; Q. 16:31; Q. 18:31; Q. 19:61; Q. 20:76; Q. 35:33; Q. 38:50; Q. 40:8; Q. 61:12; Q. 98:8), derives from the

Biblical Garden of Eden.[122] Likewise, *Firdaws* ('Paradise'), by itself or in the construct *Jannāt al-Firdaws* (*the Gardens of Paradise*, Q. 18:107; Q. 23:11), derives from the Biblical tradition, though the word comes ultimately from Avestan *pairidaeza* ('circular enclosure', 'park', 'garden') through Greek *paradeisos*.[123]

Nevertheless, *'Illiyyūn* (Q. 83:18–19), often understood to refer to Paradise, resembles the names of Hell in its oddity. It is a sound masculine plural, for it occurs in the genitive as *'Illiyyīn*, and it is a proper noun, definite without the definite article. Jeffery, following Siegmund Fraenkel, claims that *'Illiyyūn* derives from Hebrew *'Elyōn*, an appellation of God, meaning 'higher' or 'upper', or 'heavenly' as opposed to 'earthly'.[124] This identification is not convincing. The form corresponding to Hebrew *'Elyōn* in Arabic would be *'Ilyān*, *'Ilwān*, *'Ulwān* or a similar form, rather than *'Illiyyūn*. In addition, the text of *Sūrat al-Muṭaffifīn* (Q. 83) makes it clear that *'Illiyyūn*, like *Sijjīn*, with which it is parallel in that passage, is not the place where people on the Day of Judgement are going to be sent, but rather the name of the book in which their fate or deeds are recorded, for the passage in which it occurs describes that book: *kallā inna kitāba'l-abrāri la-fī 'Illiyyīn wa-mā adrāka mā 'Illiyyūn kitābun marqūm yashhaduhu'l-muqarrabūn*' (*Nay, but the record of the righteous is in 'Illiyyūn. And what will convey to you what 'Illiyyūn is? An engraved book. Attested to by those who are brought near*, Q. 83:18–21). It is the positive counterpart of the book *Sijjīn*. Al-Rāghib, however, reports two explanations. One, which we have mentioned above, is that *'Illiyyūn* is the name of the highest part of the gardens of Paradise, just as *Sijjīn* is the name of the worst of the fires of Hell; the other is that it is a plural form referring to the inhabitants of Paradise. The meaning of the passage is that the righteous will be among those exalted and honoured individuals.[125] Neither of these explanations is entirely convincing, since the parallelism between the two books of fate – that which contains the names of those who merit Hell, and that which contains the names of those who merit Paradise – is obvious. Nevertheless, it is clear that the term *'Illiyyūn* has been formed, or coined, from the triconsonantal root *'-l-w* meaning 'high', 'lofty', and that the unusual pattern of the word, which fits the rhyme context, is the result of cognate substitution. It is possible to understand the name of this book of fate as an adjective referring to those who are chosen to enter Paradise, meaning that the book is called 'the Lofty Ones', which would explain the sound masculine plural form and grant some credit to al-Rāghib's second interpretation. There is little to suggest that the term could be an epithet of God.

Several additional terms are related, or have been interpreted as being related, to Paradise. *Tasnīm* is a name, a proper noun without the definite article, for a spring in Paradise that is mentioned once in the Qur'an, in verse-final position: *wa mizājuhu min Tasnīm ʿaynan yashrabu bihā'l-muqarrabūn* (*It will be mixed with water from Tasnīm. A spring from which those who are brought near will drink*, Q. 83:27–8). No other instances of the tri-consonantal root *s-n-m* occur in the Qur'an, and it does not appear to be related to words from that root such as *sanām* ('camel's hump') or *tasannama* ('to ascend, mount'). One might entertain the possibility that the final *-m* in *Tasnīm* has been added for the sake of rhyme, as the ending *-īn* is added in *wa Ṭūri Sīnīn* (Q. 95:2). If this is so, one might propose to connect *Tasnīm* with another tri-consonantal root such as *s-n-y* ('to shine' or 'to be brilliant') instead of *s-n-m*. Al-Rāghib's analysis does not shed much light on the original meaning of the word, for he merely reports that *Tasnīm* is a spring of exalted status in Paradise.[126] Another spring in Paradise is termed *Salsabīl* (Q. 76:18). It also occurs in verse-final position as *Salsabīlā*, in the accusative, despite the fact that it would ordinarily follow the weak declension (*Salsabīla*), and it rhymes with *zanjabīlā* (Q. 76:17) in the previous verse. Though it is a rare quinqueliteral, one is tempted to connect the name with the tri-consonantal root *s-l-s*, one of the meanings of which is 'flowing', *salsal* ('fresh water'), *tasalsala* ('to drip, trickle'), and so on. Al-Rāghib does not include the word in his lexicon.

Conclusion

The results of this investigation are in one sense negative. Overall, al-Rāghib al-Iṣfahānī, like many other commentators, shows either limited awareness or a determined reluctance to admit that cognate substitution is a feature of Qur'anic style, aiming instead to explain the meanings of Qur'anic terms in ways that do not point to apparent violations of ordinary grammatical or stylistic rules and do not invoke rhyme or poetic licence. He does not interpret any of the instances discussed as cases of cognate substitution, nor does he use any of the terms that he might conceivably have used to refer to it, such as *'adl*, or other periphrastic discussions of the morphological form (*wazn* or *ṣīgha*) involved. Examination of al-Rāghib's interpretations of the cases of cognate substitution that Müller has pointed out, those found in Ibn al-Ṣā'igh al-Ḥanafī's work, and the Qur'anic names of Hell show that he addressed the cruxes involved in three main ways overall. The first is neglect: al-Rāghib omits some examples from his lexicon or else merely presents them without any special explanation. In the second, he treats the word as related in some way to the tri-consonantal root in question, but interprets it as referring to something other than what is expected according to the usual semantics of Arabic morphological patterns. In the third, he attempts to explain that the apparently unusual form actually conveys the correct meaning for the context. For the analysis of cognate substitution as a phenomenon in the Qur'an, the last tactic is the most interesting, because it shows an awareness both that the word is related to other cognates that impinge on its meaning and that the particular form present in the text seems out of place and begs an explanation. Al-Rāghib most often endeavours to get out of the interpretive impasse by suggesting that the form in question is an alternative, but perhaps rare, form, or by interpreting the form in question as modifying a suppressed word in an elliptical construction, especially with adjectival forms.

Several of al-Rāghib's analyses give strained or implausible interpretations that fall short of convincing the contemporary scholar of the Qur'an and, while doing so, suggest that the forms in question have been produced by cognate substitution. In a few cases, such as those of *bāqiya* [no. 5] and *ma'tiyyā*, al-Rāghib's analysis shows an awareness of the possibility of cognate substitution, but in both cases he rejects this alternative, suggesting that he was unwilling to admit it in general. This is corroborated by other instances such as his analyses of *taḍlīl* [no. 12], *kidhdhābā* [no. 11] and *dhū'l-ikrām* [no. 13], complex attempts to avoid admitting that the form presented in the text must have a meaning that that particular form does not ordinarily convey. Telling is his use of the turn of phrase *iḍlāl li-anfusihim* ('sending astray of themselves') with a reflexive that does not occur in the Qur'anic verse in his attempt to explain how the ordinarily causative form *taḍlīl* takes on a transitive sense. This is perhaps the most blatant example of the tension created by endeavouring to explicate the term without invoking cognate substitution. The traditional organisation of Arabic dictionaries by tri-consonantal roots forces him to recognise the connection between cognate terms, but he is reluctant to suggest that morphological patterns are altered for the sake of rhyme. His explanations regularly ignore the rhyme context and do not call attention to the rhyme words in adjacent verses. One would not expect his analyses to use the technical terms for rhyme (*qāfiya*) or poetic licence (*ḍarūra*) in poetry, but nor does he refer to rhymed prose (*saj*ʿ), the verse-final word (*fāṣila* or *ra's al-āya*), homoioteleuton or the maintenance of similar verse-final words (*riʿāyat al-fāṣila*).

Part of the reluctance to use rhyme as a hermeneutic device evidently stemmed from anxiety over treating the Qur'an as poetry, but this was not the only concern. Recognition of the phenomenon of cognate substitution risked implying that God coined new forms on an ad hoc basis for particular texts in the Qur'an or that God could say one word while intending another, both of which bordered on blasphemy. Exegetes therefore argued that every difference in form implied a difference in meaning. Badr al-Dīn al-Zarkashī (d. 794/1392), for example, argued that if an augmented morphological pattern were used, it must contain an aspect of meaning that would not have been conveyed by the cognate un-augmented form.[127] This same tension arose with regard to a number of other hermeneutical topics, including apparent grammatical errors in the Qur'an and lexical borrowings from other languages such as Hebrew, Aramaic, Ethiopic, Greek or Persian.[128] Medieval exegetes and rhetoricians used the concept of *iltifāt* ('grammatical shift'), a well-known feature of Qur'anic Arabic and the Arabic of pre-Islamic poetry, in order to explain apparent grammatical anomalies in the text.[129] They also stressed the different shades of meaning conveyed by near-synonymous or apparently synonymous but nevertheless distinct phrases in the Qur'an, which they called *ashbāh wa naẓā'ir* or *wujūh wa naẓā'ir* ('similar cases and parallels').[130] In modern studies of the Qur'an, one of the most systematic presentations of this view is that of Bint al-Shāṭi' (d. 1999) in her *I'jāz al-Qur'ān al-bayānī*, in which she seeks to refute the claims of Ibn al-Athīr and other medieval rhetoricians that *saj'* plays a crucial role in the text of the Qur'an and that the Qur'anic text exhibits examples of poetic licence.[131]

Preliminary examination of the commentarial tradition suggests that the three manners in which al-Rāghib al-Iṣfahānī treated cases of cognate substitution, and cases of poetic licence in general, were widespread and that further investigation would turn up many additional examples of similar explications. While scholars such as Abū Hilāl al-'Askarī, Ibn al-Athīr and Ibn al-Ṣā'igh al-Ḥanafī were aware of the phenomenon of cognate substitution in the Qur'an, their insights were either little known or regularly ignored or suppressed by the majority of commentators on the Qur'an. Discussion of the Qur'an as a rhyming and rhythmical text does occur in the medieval Islamic patrimony of scholarship on the text of the Qur'an, but dedicated, explicit and extensive discussions appear to be limited to a small number of authors, mainly scholars of rhetoric like Ibn al-Athīr who were not writing in the genre of *tafsīr*, and even those appear to have been hampered because of dogmatic pressures of the environment in which they wrote. One may hope for the discovery of new material such as Ṭūfī's lost work *Bughyat al-wāṣil ilā ma'rifat al-fawāṣil* or similar works that may be extant in manuscript but have yet to be identified. Failing that, one may hope to retrieve significant material from short comments and asides scattered throughout the vast literature of exegesis, rhetoric, lexica and other genres of Qur'anic scholarship.

NOTES

1 It is admittedly difficult to determine what 'ordinary' grammar and usage are in the Qur'an, since Arabic grammar developed as a science long after the Qur'an was compiled, and the Arabic language obviously changed from one period to the next. The best procedure is to derive general grammatical and stylistic rules through examination of the Qur'anic text in passages that are not

influenced by considerations of rhyme. Nevertheless, it is difficult to prevent one's ideas of the norms of Arabic grammar and style from being influenced by later Arabic, whether grammatical texts or otherwise.

2 Friedrun R. Müller, *Untersuchungen zur Reimprosa im Koran* [Investigations on Rhymed Prose in the Qur'an] (Bonn: Selbstverlag des Orientalischen Seminars der Universität, 1969).

3 Al-Rāghib's death date was long unknown to modern scholars. The date 502/1108–9 was often given, but research suggested that he had died earlier, in the first half of the fifth/eleventh century. Recently there came to light a note on a manuscript copy of the *Mufradāt* that states that al-Rāghib was born in Rajab 343/October–November 954 and died in Rabīʿ II 422/March–April 1031. On al-Rāghib al-Iṣfahānī in general, see E.K. Rowson, 'al-Rāghib al-Iṣfahānī', *EI²*, vol. 8, pp. 389–90; Muḥammad ʿAdnān Jawharjī, 'Raʾy fī taḥdīd ʿaṣr al-Rāghib al-Iṣfahānī', *Majallat Majmaʿ al-Lugha al-ʿArabiyya fī Dimashq* 61, no. 1 (1986), pp. 191–200; Yasien Mohamed, 'The Ethical Philosophy of al-Rāghib al-Iṣfahānī', *Journal of Islamic Studies* 6, no. 1 (1995), pp. 51–75; idem, 'Knowledge and Purification of the Soul: An Annotated Translation of Iṣfahānī's *Kitāb al-Dharīʿa ilā Makārim al-Sharīʿa* (58–76; 89–92)', *Journal of Islamic Studies* 9, no. 1 (1998), pp. 1–34; Sayyid ʿAlī Mīr Lawḥī, *Rāghib-i Iṣfahānī: zindigī va āthār-i ū* (Isfahan: Sāzimān-i Farhangī-yi Tafrīḥī-yi Shahrdārī-yi Iṣfahān, 2008); Alexander Key, 'A Linguistic Frame of Mind: al-Rāghib al-Iṣfahānī and What it Meant to be Ambiguous' (Unpublished PhD Dissertation, Harvard University, 2012). The edition of al-Rāghib's Qur'anic dictionary used in this chapter is Abū'l-Qāsim al-Ḥusayn b. Muḥammad al-Rāghib al-Iṣfahānī, *al-Mufradāt fī gharīb al-Qur'ān*, ed. Muḥammad Sayyid Kīlānī (Beirut: Dār al-Maʿrifa, 1961).

4 Edward William Lane, *An Arabic-English Lexicon* (London: Williams & Norgate, 1863), vol. 1, p. 207.

5 Q. 2:97; Q. 3:126; Q. 8:10; Q. 10:64; Q. 11:69, 74; Q. 12:19; Q. 16:89, 102; Q. 25:22; Q. 27:2; Q. 29:31; Q. 39:17; Q. 46:12; Q. 57:12.

6 *Bashīr*: Q. 2:119; Q. 5:19; Q. 7:188; Q. 11:2; Q. 12:96; Q. 34:28; Q. 35:24; Q. 41:4; *mubashshir*: Q. 2:213; Q. 4:165; Q. 6:48; Q. 17:105; Q. 18:56; Q. 25:56; Q. 33:45; Q. 48:8; Q. 61:6.

7 Translations of Qur'anic passages in this study are based to some extent on the translation of Marmaduke William Pickthall in *The Meaning of the Glorious Quran: Text and Explanatory Translation* (Elmhurst, NY: Tahrike Tarsile Qur'an, 1999) but have been modified and in some cases translated in an overly-literal fashion in order to render particular lexical and rhetorical points clearer to the reader.

8 Hundreds of these tag-phrases or clausulae containing paired divine epithets occur in the Qur'an, but the exact pair of *ʿazīz* and *karīm* is not applied to God. The epithet *ʿazīz* is most frequently paired with *ḥakīm*, as in *innaka anta'l-ʿazīzu'l-hakīm* (Q. 40:8), and somewhat less frequently with *raḥīm* ('Merciful').

9 Müller, *Reimprosa*; Angelika Neuwirth, *Studien zur Komposition der mekkanische Suren* (Berlin: Walter de Gruyter, 1981), pp. 65–116; Muḥammad al-Ḥasnāwī, *al-Fāṣila fī'l-Qur'ān* (Beirut: al-Maktab al-Islāmī, 1986); Devin J. Stewart, '*Sajʿ* in the Qur'ān: Prosody and Structure', *Journal of Arabic Literature* 21 (1990), pp. 101–39; idem, 'Rhymed Prose', *EQ*, vol. 4, pp. 476–84;

idem, 'Poetic License in the Qur'an: Ibn al-Ṣā'igh al-Ḥanafī's *Iḥkām al-rāy fī aḥkām al-āy*', *Journal of Qur'anic Studies* 11, no. 1 (2009), pp. 1–54; idem, 'Divine Epithets and the *Dibacchius*: *Clausulae* and Qur'ānic Rhythm', *Journal of Qur'anic Studies* 15, no. 2 (2013), pp. 22–64.

10 Stewart, '*Saj*ʿ in the Qur'ān'.

11 Stewart, 'Poetic License', where I discuss the work of Ibn al-Ṣā'igh al-Ḥanafī especially.

12 See Stewart, 'Poetic License', pp. 39 and 41; Müller, *Reimprosa*, p. 137.

13 al-Rāghib, *Mufradāt*, p. 251.

14 Stewart, 'Poetic License', pp. 20–22.

15 On this work, see John Wansbrough, 'Review: Friedrun Müller, *Unterzuchungen zur Reimprosa im Koran*', *Bulletin of the School of Oriental and African Studies* 33 (1970), pp. 389–91; idem, *Quranic Studies: Sources and Methods of Scriptural Interpretation* (Oxford: Oxford University Press, 1977), pp. 25 and 116–17; Neuwirth, *Studien*, pp. 75 and 173; Stewart, 'Poetic License', pp. 4–5 and 21–3.

16 Stewart, 'Poetic License', pp. 23–8.

17 Ibid., pp. 22–3 and 38.

18 Ibid., pp. 37–8.

19 This was noted by Ibn al-Ṣā'igh al-Ḥanafī and al-Zarkashī, among other medieval scholars. See Theodor Nöldeke, *Geschichte des Qorans*, ed. Friedrich Schwally, Gotthelf Bergsträsser and Otto Pretzl, 2nd edn (Leipzig: Dieterich, 1909–38; repr. Hildesheim: G. Olms, 1961), vol. 1, pp. 40–41; Müller, *Reimprosa*, pp. 129–30; Stewart, 'Poetic License', pp. 39 and 46.

20 Müller, *Reimprosa*, pp. 54–9.

21 al-Rāghib, *Mufradāt*, pp. 25–6.

22 Müller, *Reimprosa*, pp. 38–41.

23 Ibid., pp. 41–3.

24 Ibid., pp. 29–30.

25 al-Rāghib, *Mufradāt*, pp. 321–2, 427–8 and 432.

26 W. Wright, *A Grammar of the Arabic Language*, 3rd edn (Cambridge: Cambridge University Press, 1981), vol. 1, p. 115.

27 Müller, *Reimprosa*, pp. 33–8.

28 al-Rāghib, *Mufradāt*, p. 187.

29 Müller, *Reimprosa*, pp. 30–3.

30 al-Rāghib, *Mufradāt*, p. 189.

31 Müller, *Reimprosa*, pp. 13–16.

32 On the use of the preposition *bi-* to indicate the relationship between topic and predicate, see Wright, *A Grammar of the Arabic Language*, vol. 2, pp. 158–9.

33 Arthur Jeffery, *The Foreign Vocabulary of the Qur'ān* (Baroda: Oriental Institute, 1938), pp. 159–60.

34 See, e.g. Muḥammad b. Jarīr al-Ṭabarī, *Jāmiʿ al-bayān ʿan ta'wīl āy al-Qur'ān*, ed. Muṣṭafā al-Saqqā *et al.* (Cairo: Muṣṭafā al-Bābī al-Ḥalabī, 1373–7/1954–7).

35 Ibid., vol. 30, pp. 33–4.

36 Ibid., p. 34.

37 al-Rāghib, *Mufradāt*, p. 557.

38 Müller, *Reimprosa*, pp. 16–20.

39 al-Rāghib, *Mufradāt*, p. 304.

40 Q. 2:156; Q. 3:165; Q. 4.62, 72; Q. 5:106; Q. 9:50; Q. 28:47; Q. 42:30; Q. 57:22; Q. 64:11.
41 Müller, *Reimprosa*, pp. 26–8.
42 al-Rāghib, *Mufradāt*, p. 57.
43 Ibid.
44 Ibid.
45 Müller, *Reimprosa*, pp. 68–72.
46 al-Rāghib, *Mufradāt*, pp. 179–80.
47 Müller, *Reimprosa*, pp. 62–4.
48 al-Rāghib, *Mufradāt*, p. 189.
49 Müller, *Reimprosa*, pp. 46–50.
50 al-Rāghib, *Mufradāt*, p. 298.
51 Müller, *Reimprosa*, pp. 64–8.
52 al-Rāghib, *Mufradāt*, p. 304.
53 Müller, *Reimprosa*, pp. 59–62.
54 al-Rāghib, *Mufradāt*, p. 417.
55 Müller, *Reimprosa*, pp. 20–24.
56 al-Rāghib, *Mufradāt*, p. 427.
57 Müller, *Reimprosa*, p. 21.
58 Ibid., pp. 50–54.
59 In addition, the cognate superlative adjective *al-akram* ('the most generous' or 'the most noble') occurs as a divine epithet once (Q. 96:3).
60 al-Rāghib, *Mufradāt*, p. 429.
61 Müller, *Reimprosa*, pp. 44–6.
62 al-Rāghib, *Mufradāt*, p. 427.
63 Müller, *Reimprosa*, pp. 24–6.
64 al-Rāghib, *Mufradāt*, pp. 451–2.
65 Müller, *Reimprosa*, pp. 73–8.
66 al-Rāghib, *Mufradāt*, p. 495.
67 Stewart, 'Poetic License', pp. 21–2.
68 Müller, *Reimprosa*, p. 138.
69 al-Rāghib, *Mufradāt*, p. 361.
70 Müller, *Reimprosa*, pp. 144–4.
71 al-Rāghib, *Mufradāt*, p. 423.
72 Stewart, 'Poetic License', pp. 22–3 and 38.
73 al-Rāghib, *Mufradāt*, p. 197.
74 Ibid., p. 170.
75 Ibid., p. 223.
76 Ibid., p. 9.
77 Stewart, 'Poetic License', pp. 37–8.
78 al-Rāghib, *Mufradāt*, p. 394.
79 Ibid., p. 344.
80 Ibid., pp. 491–2.
81 Ibid., p. 322.
82 Stewart, 'Poetic License', pp. 35–6.
83 al-Rāghib, *Mufradāt*, p. 300.
84 *Kubrā*: Q. 20:23; Q. 44:16; Q. 53:18; Q. 79:20; Q. 87:12; *ḥusnā*: Q. 4:95; Q. 7:137, 180; etc.; *muthlā*: Q. 20:63.

85 On Islamic Hell in general, see Jonas Meyer, *Die Hölle im Islam* (Basel: Universitäts-Buchdrucherei, 1901); James Robson, 'Is the Moslem Hell Eternal?' *Muslim World* 28 (1938), pp. 386–96; Thomas O'Shaughnessy, 'The Seven Names for Hell in the Qur'ān', *Bulletin of the School of Oriental and African Studies* 24 (1961), pp. 444–69, esp. pp. 447–9 and 466–9; Jane I. Smith and Yvonne Y. Haddad, *The Islamic Understanding of Death and Resurrection* (Albany, NY: State University of New York Press, 1981); Nerina Rustomji, *The Garden and the Fire: Heaven and Hell in Islamic Culture* (New York: Columbia University Press, 2009); Rosalind W. Gwynne, 'Hell and Hellfire', *EQ*, vol. 2, pp. 414–20; Einar Thomassen, 'Islamic Hell', *Numen* 56 (2009), pp. 401–16.

86 O'Shaughnessy, 'The Seven Names for Hell', pp. 447–9 and 466–9; Rustomji, *The Garden and the Fire*; Gwynne, 'Hell and Hellfire'. For an excellent overview of attempts to fix the Qur'an's chronology, including that of Nöldeke, see Gerhard Böwering, 'Chronology and the Qur'ān', *EQ*, vol. 1, pp. 316–35.

87 Müller, *Reimprosa*, p. 145; Stewart, 'Poetic License', p. 21.

88 See Stewart, 'Poetic License', pp. 23 and 35–6. I have here modified the translation given in that work, rendering some Qur'anic phrases in an over-literal fashion in order to reflect the indeterminate meaning of some of the terms for Hell.

89 Hebrew *esh* ('fire') is similarly feminine despite the masculine form.

90 Jeffery, *Foreign Vocabulary*, pp. 105–6.

91 al-Rāghib, *Mufradāt*, p. 102.

92 'Alī Akbar Dihkhudā *et al.*, *Lughatnāma* (Tehran: Dānishgāh-i Tihrān, 1946–), vol. 2 [*jīm*], p. 181.

93 O'Shaughnessy, 'The Seven Names for Hell', p. 452.

94 al-Rāghib, *Mufradāt*, p. 88.

95 Lane, *Arabic-English Lexicon*, vol. 1, p. 384.

96 See Devin J. Stewart, 'Pit', *EQ*, vol. 4, pp. 100–4; idem, 'The Mysterious Letters and Other Formal Features of the Qur'ān in Light of Greek and Babylonian Oracular Texts' in Gabriel Said Reynolds, ed., *New Perspectives on the Qur'ān: The Qur'ān in Its Historical Context 2* (London: Routledge, 2011), pp. 321–46, esp. pp. 325–7.

97 Al-Rāghib could intend that this be a proper noun of the weak declension, serving as a name of Hell, or an ordinary noun – 'a *ḥuṭama*' – taking the strong declension. The former seems more likely, because he mentions giving a name in the immediate context and because other names for Hell occur both with the definite article and without it.

98 al-Rāghib, *Mufradāt*, p. 123.

99 Ibid., p. 233.

100 Frantz Buhl, 'Koran', *EI*, vol. 2, p. 1128; O'Shaughnessy, 'The Seven Names for Hell', p. 454.

101 al-Rāghib, *Mufradāt*, p. 235; see also Lane, *Arabic-English Lexicon*, vol. 1, p. 1379.

102 al-Rāghib, *Mufradāt*, p. 450.

103 Jeffery, *Foreign Vocabulary*, pp. 285–6.

104 Stewart, 'Pit'.

105 al-Rāghib, *Mufradāt*, p. 548.

106 ʿAbd al-Razzāq al-Ṣanʿānī, *al-Muṣannaf*, ed. Ḥabīb al-Raḥmān Aʿẓamī (Beirut: al-Maktab al-Islāmī, 1983), vol. 1, p. 46; Ibn Abī Shayba, *Kitāb al-Muṣannaf fi'l-aḥādīth wa'l-āthār*, ed. Muḥammad ʿAbd al-Salām Shāhīn (Beirut: Dār al-Kutub al-ʿIlmiyya, 1995), vol. 1, p. 13, vol. 6, p. 113.

107 Thomassen, 'Islamic Hell', esp. p. 408.

108 al-Rāghib, *Mufradāt*, p. 225.

109 Ibid., p. 346.

110 Ibid., p. 225. The 'seventh earth', mentioned in a number of hadith reports, refers to the lowest level of the world, the terrestrial counterpart of the seventh or highest heaven. One such hadith report reads, 'The Bearers of the Throne [of God] have their feet planted in the Seventh Earth, while their heads rise above the Seventh Heaven, and they have horns as tall as they are, upon which rests the Throne.' Abū Nuʿaym al-Iṣfahānī, *Ḥilyat al-awliyā' wa ṭabaqāt al-aṣfiyā'* (Beirut: Dār al-Kutub al-ʿIlmiyya, 1988), vol. 6, p. 75; al-Majlisī, *Biḥār al-anwār* (Tehran: al-Maktaba al-Islāmiyya, 1956–72), vol. 55, p. 4.

111 Aḥmad al-Thaʿlabī, *al-Kashf wa'l-bayān ʿan tafsīr al-Qur'ān* (Beirut: Dār Iḥyā' al-Turāth al-ʿArabī, 2002), vol. 10, pp. 151–3.

112 The identification of *sijjīn* with Lat. *sigillum* ('seal') has been suggested by O'Shaughnessy, 'The Seven Names for Hell', p. 444. See also S.R. Burge, *Angels in Islam: Jalāl al-Dīn al-Suyūṭī's* al-Ḥabā'ik fī akhbār al-malā'ik (London: Routledge, 2012), p. 164.

113 Maḥmūd b. ʿUmar al-Zamakhsharī, *al-Kashshāf ʿan ḥaqā'iq al-tanzīl* (Cairo: Dār ʿĀlam al-Maʿrifa, n.d.), vol. 4, p. 195.

114 Müller, *Reimprosa*, pp. 136–8.

115 One could explain the particular form of *Sijjīn* as deriving from *Sijill* through a hypothetical form such as *Sijlīn*, parallel with *ghislīn* from e.g. *ghusālah*, and then, by assimilation of *-jl-* to *jj*, to *Sijjīn*. On Lat. *sigillum* > Gr. *sigillon*, see Jeffery, *Foreign Vocabulary*, pp. 163–4.

116 Zamakhsharī, *al-Kashshāf*, vol. 4, p. 195.

117 al-Rāghib, *Mufradāt*, p. 130.

118 Lane, *Arabic-English Lexicon*, vol. 1, pp. 1238–9.

119 al-Rāghib, *Mufradāt*, p. 213.

120 Lane, *Arabic-English Lexicon*, vol. 1, p. 1238.

121 Ṭabarī, *Jāmiʿ al-bayān*, vol. 30, p. 34.

122 Jeffery, *Foreign Vocabulary*, pp. 212–13.

123 Ibid., pp. 223–4.

124 Ibid., pp. 215–16. The term *ʿElyōn* occurs several times in the Hebrew Bible as a divine epithet in the alliterative pair *El ʿElyōn*, usually rendered 'God Most High'. See Genesis 14:18–20, 22; Psalms 78:35.

125 al-Rāghib, *Mufradāt*, p. 346.

126 Ibid., p. 245.

127 Stewart, 'Poetic License', pp. 47–8.

128 John Burton, 'Linguistic Errors in the Qur'an', *Journal of Semitic Studies* 33, no. 2 (1988), pp. 181–96; Jeffery, *Foreign Vocabulary*, pp. 1–41; Andrew Rippin, 'Foreign Vocabulary', *EQ*, vol. 2, pp. 226–37; idem, 'Syriac in the Qur'ān: Classical Muslim Theories' in Gabriel Said Reynolds, ed., *The Qur'ān in Its Historical Context* (London: Routledge, 2008), pp. 249–61.

129 M. Abdel Haleem, 'Grammatical Shift for Rhetorical Purposes: *Iltifāt* and Related Features in the Qur'ān', *Bulletin of the School of Oriental and African Studies* 55, no. 3 (1992), pp. 407–32.

130 Hārūn b. Mūsā al-Qāri' al-A'war, *al-Wujūh wa'l-naẓā'ir fī'l-Qur'ān al-karīm*, ed. Ḥātim Ṣāliḥ al-Ḍāmin (Baghdad: Wizārat al-Thaqāfa, 1988).

131 'Ā'isha 'Abd al-Raḥmān 'Bint al-Shāṭi'', *al-I'jāz al-bayānī li'l-Qur'ān wa Masā'il Ibn al-Azraq* (Cairo: Dār al-Ma'ārif, 1971), pp. 235–58.

8

Paradoxes in al-Shahrastānī's Lexicological Methodology

TOBY MAYER

Introduction and Problematic

EVEN THE cursory reader of the Qur'an commentary by Muḥammad b. ʿAbd al-Karīm al-Shahrastānī (d. 548/1153), entitled *Mafātīḥ al-asrār* ('Keys to the Arcana'),[1] notes its steady concern with the linguistic and semantic analysis of the text. That this was the author's prime lens on the scripture is also clear from the rather triumphal terms in which he introduces his commentary:

> I transcribed recitation, grammar, lexicology, exegesis and Qur'anic semantics from their exponents, as they quoted it in books, by pure authentic transcription, without taking any liberty therein by adding or subtracting, except in elaborating what was summary or abridging what was prolix. I commented on each verse using what I heard about it consisting in arcana, I examined them carefully through the allusions of the godly (*min ishārāti'l-abrār*), and I prefaced the investigation of them with sections on the science of the Qur'an which are the 'Keys of the Criterion',[2] expounding twelve chapters by way of which other commentaries have become redundant.[3]

The parting boast promotes the book for a coming readership and, if ill-sounding now, was then an accepted (even expected) authorial posture.[4] It has an irony in retrospect: Shahrastānī's work was almost lost, just surviving as a unicum.[5] Yet the author's claim was not mere bombast, for the scope of the project (sadly, never completed) is indeed sweeping. True to his word, Shahrastānī quotes a mass of pre-existing linguistic data in his book. His commentary on each verse, phrase and even on individual words, is carefully split up under a string of rubrics: lexicology (*lugha*), semantics (*maʿānī*), grammar (*naḥw*), regular exegesis (*tafsīr*), harmonious order (*naẓm*), secrets or 'arcana' (*asrār*) – and according to need, other rubrics too, such as orthography (*kitāba*) and law (*fiqh*).

The documentation of earlier traditions (some, unattributed) of understanding the Qur'an's language seems one of the work's two main interests. The other is the penetrating system which Shahrastānī uses in the 'arcana' – arguably the core of his project and what marks it out in the genre. However, to square the two sides is a conundrum: a fierce tension lurks in their premises. The premise of his understanding of lexicology is that words have developed out of other words, that the Arabic of the Qur'an can be analysed in terms of its emergence from common usage, historical borrowings, elisions, euphony and etymological derivation (*ishtiqāq*). Shahrastānī transmits these kinds of analysis faithfully and finds intrinsic scholarly interest in them. They seem, however, at odds with his own deeper teaching on the Qur'an and its language, the premise of the arcana sections. It here becomes clear that Shahrastānī views the Qur'an as substantially identical with God's Command (*amr Allāh*). He sees the scripture as the direct epiphany of the realm of the Logos–Command (*ʿālam al-amr*), which is distinct from the created realm (*ʿālam al-khalq*) and the very means by which it has been – rather, is being – projected into existence by the Creator.[6]

In view of this deep-seated standpoint, it seems unfounded for Shahrastānī elsewhere to treat the Qur'an's language as etymologically derivative (*mushtaqq*) and traceable to earlier forms. That said, as will come out in the following, a kind of 'esoteric lexicology' is, according to him, viable and indeed necessary in fathoming the Qur'an. He speaks, for instance, of the 'mystery of its phonetic composition' (*sirr tarkībi ḥurūfihi*). Such elements recur in the arcana sections of his commentary. In them he analyses the scripture's words in terms of their perceived deeper rationale, without there being any suggestion of a linguistic development. The probing is ahistorical and takes the text to be beyond not only human history but even the whole time-bound realm of creation.

Any treatment of Shahrastānī's lexicology must broach this problem. Given the discipline's manifestly historical, even evolutionary, footing, a clash in premises is glaring in this aspect of his commentary. In terms of *kalām* linguistic theories, a conventionalist theory (*iṣṭilāḥ/muwāḍaʿa*) is arguably implicit in these sections. Such a theory of the roots of language in general (*aṣl al-lugha*), and of Arabic in particular, formed against the more pietistic, revelationist theory of the emergence of language (*tawqīf al-lugha*). It is significant that the stricter backers of the revelationist theory, like ʿAlī b. Aḥmad Ibn Ḥazm (d. 456/1064) and other members of the Ẓāhiriyya, simply denied that *ishtiqāq* was a viable means to look into the Arabic language at all, precisely because it implied its development, historicity and relativity. They suppressed *ishtiqāq* altogether. Abū'l-Ḥasan al-Ashʿarī (d. 324/935), founder of the *kalām* school with which Shahrastānī's repute was widely linked, was also an arch-revelationist (as reported in Ibn Fūrak's *Mujarrad maqālāt al-Shaykh Abi'l-Ḥasan al-Ashʿarī*), while it was Muʿtazilī thinkers who tended to conventionalism, starting with the major Muʿtazilī, Abū Hāshim al-Jubbāʾī (d. 321/933) – credited with first devising the theory of *iṣṭilāḥ*.[7]

Shahrastānī's scholarly inquisitiveness made him keenly interested in the history of the Qur'an's language and the history of the Qur'anic text in general; but his underlying intellectual orientations, expressed in his religious philosophy (ultimately a form of Ismailism), compelled him to renounce or transcend his scholarly historicism on the Qur'an. In fact, this retreat follows equally from either a more exoteric, Ashʿarī, view of Shahrastānī's underpinnings or a more esoteric, Ismaili, view of them, as will come out, for both teachings ascribed a highly exalted metaphysical status to God's Word.

There are many further cases of the clash in premises in the commentary. A circumspectly historical consciousness informs much of Shahrastānī's introduction, as seen, say, in his detailed interest in *qirāʾāt* lineages[8] and his inclusion of variant lists of the right ordering of suras.[9] He notes that some authorities included things subsequently omitted, such as Ubayy b. Kaʿb (d. 21/642) who included the so-called *Sūrat al-Ḥafd* and *Sūrat al-Khalʿ* (recited in the *qunūt* prayer),[10] while others omitted things subsequently included, such as ʿAbd Allāh Ibn Masʿūd (d. 32/652) who left out *Sūrat al-Falaq* (Q. 113) and *Sūrat al-Nās* (Q. 114) and who even left *Sūrat al-Fātiḥa* (Q. 1) itself out of the Qur'an, as did Ibn Wāqid (d. 157/774) in his list of chapters as presented in our text.[11] If such data are on hand in some other medieval Qur'an commentaries, rarer is Shahrastānī's outspoken treatment of the canonisation of the Qur'an in chapter 2 of his introduction, entitled 'On the Collection of the Qur'an' (*fī jamʿi'l-Qur'ān*). His urge to probe is seen here at its starkest, with our author risking unusual views on the dawn of the *textus receptus* (*al-muṣḥaf al-ʿUthmānī*).[12] This is no place to detail the controversial discussion but suffice to say, Shahrastānī airs reports that suggest that the text may partly result from human contingencies, not escaping their impact in its form. He mentions as a view from towering Sunni authorities like ʿĀ'isha bt. Abī Bakr (d. 58/678), ʿUthmān b. ʿAffān (r. 24–36/644–56) and ʿAbd Allāh Ibn ʿAbbās (d. ca. 68/687), that it bears the trace of vernacular solecisms (*alḥān*) and scribal slips.[13] Moreover, in the case of one or two statements in the course of his treatment, Shahrastānī even hints at a syndrome of intentional omission (i.e. *kitmān* rather than *taḥrīf*)[14] akin to the one to which the two testaments of the Bible were widely viewed in Islam as having been prey.[15] At the same time, he puts forward reports from Shiʿi sources that the supposed apograph of the revelations, namely the *muṣḥaf ʿAlī*, was shunned by the earliest community.[16] All this minimally adds up to some sense of the ʿUthmanic version's historical contingency and relativity.

Cases of Shahrastānī's regular method from the *lugha* (lexicology) sections are put forward in the first, thetic stage of the following discussion mainly using his commentary on the *Fātiḥa* (Q. 1). Of note are analyses where a conventionalist stance seems overt. In the next, antithetic stage, Shahrastānī's 'esoteric lexicology' and interpretations evoking the Qur'an's special status as the uncreated Logos are sampled from the *asrār* sections. A synthesis is lastly sought and I consider how Shahrastānī himself may have wed these rival stances on the text within his total theory of scripture and his theology of the Qur'an. He himself arguably saw no mismatch in his methodologies, given his over-arching doctrine on the Word.

Thesis: Historical Analysis

While matters headed 'arcana' tend to be last in our scholar's systematic unfolding of a verse, lexicology is first – the bedrock for all to come. Lexicology, he states, is basic to the methodology of *tafsīr*, and is mainly for turning the language of scripture to one intended signification amongst other possible significations (*wujūh al-lugha*).[17] He stresses, however, that it is not enough on its own. The vital complement is material reliably transmitted from religious authorities, whether this takes the form of prophetic traditions or non-prophetic reports.[18] Such guidance, accessible through the respected (*sunan* and *ṣaḥīḥ*) compendia, is necessary either to disambiguate what is equivocal (*mushtarak*) in the scripture, or else to particularise what is general (*ʿāmm*) in it.[19] With the two comprehensive instruments of lexicology and reliable transmissions, the sense of the outward text can be stabilised and determined by the would-be commentator.

Lexicology's key role is clear in Shahrastānī's habit of defining words as they arise, through etymologies – his first step is to formulate lexical definitions. This is even true when he first broaches *tafsīr* (exegesis) itself, as a project set apart from *ta'wīl* (hermeneutics). His comments on *ta'wīl* link it, in the standard way, to *awwal* ('first' or 'origin'), *awl* ('returning') and *āla* ('to go back'). Oddly for a lexical definition, Shahrastānī notes that this etymology can be traced to the high authority of the imams. As he says: 'one of the great ones of the imams (may God be pleased with them) said: "*Ta'wīl* is returning something to its beginning (*awwaluhu*), just as *ta'khīr* is pushing it through to its end (*ākhiruhu*)."' He goes on: 'This is a powerful pronouncement whose style is that of prophetic pronouncements (*uslūbuhu kalāmu'l-nubuwwa*). Since the final end of everything is its beginning, it is said that it is the *ta'wīl* of it . . .'[20]

Rightly or not, Shahrastānī here takes the imam's likening of *ta'khīr* to *ta'wīl* to be about more than the terms' forms. Rather, it supposedly concerns a convergence in their very meanings: tracing a thing to its conclusion, *mutatis mutandis*, is tracing it to its origin. The dictum points, he says, to cyclicality and the unity of ends and beginnings. With regard to the Qur'an, then, *ta'wīl* could just as well be seen as *ta'khīr.* Hermeneutics pursues the scripture to its trans-temporal reality, *from* which it emerged and *with* which it will merge. Shahrastānī finds such truths hinted in this lexical definition because it is, he believes, on the imamate's authority and 'prophetic' in quality.[21] There is also, one suspects, a 'systemic' motive for him to claim this high pedigree for it. Though, in passing, Shahrastānī airs the view that *ta'wīl* rests on the use of intellect,[22] it seems that this is not his own stance. He stresses that his own *ta'wīl* (found in the arcana sections) stands on the authority of the Prophet and imams, not reason. It would jar with this, then, for him to define it initially through free reason. This may be why Shahrastānī calls attention to the fact that the well-known lexical definition of *ta'wīl* can in reality be traced to an imam, in the style of a 'prophetic dictum', as he puts it. On the other hand, on the word *tafsīr* he says:

> The lexicologists say: *tafsīr* is the second form *maṣdar* of the verb *fasara* which means to make something apparent and to explain it. It is said 'I disclosed (*fasartu*) the thing', 'I am disclosing (*afsiru*), (with the vowel 'i'), with a disclosure (*fasr*) – if I make it evident.' Then if it is intense in difficulty it is said: 'he commented (*fassara* [with gemination, i.e. Form II]) on it with a commentary (*tafsīr* [Form II *maṣdar*])'. Some of them [the lexicologists] said: It is not farfetched that the idea of disclosure (*fasr*) goes back to the idea of unveiling (*sifr*). It is said: 'The lady unveiled (*safarat*)', when she bared her face. Then *safara* and *fasara* would fall under the category of the metathetic (*min bābi'l-maqlūb*), like *jadhaba* ('he attracted') and *jabadha* ('he pulled').[23]

In the last part of this quotation it may be noted what Shahrastānī is *not* doing. Metathesis/consonant transposition (*qalb*) is a method sometimes used in mystical hermeneutics in Islam, as in the mystical hermeneutics of other scripture-based faiths. Through it some unforeseen, intuitive link is found between words, thus also between their underlying meanings or referents. Though at times

Shahrastānī himself does use metathesis to draw out secret links of this kind,[24] it is surely not what he aims at by invoking it here. He invokes this method more or less as it is used now in historical phonology, as one of the possible ways that words are explained through changes in their articulation over time – hence Shahrastānī's talk of X going back to (*kāna rāji'an ilā*) Y (he also uses such phrases as *ukhidha min* ['it is obtained from'] such and such other word).

Various levels of etymology were acknowledged in medieval Arabic lexicography. Above the simplest method, known as minor etymology (*al-ishtiqāq al-ṣaghīr*) in which words were explained through their underlying triliteral roots, with the identical sequence of radicals, lay the method of major etymology (*al-ishtiqāq al-kabīr*) in which the sequence of the same radicals might actually change, in other words, metathesis.[25] The etymology of Shahrastānī's day did thus acknowledge the possibility of metathesis, as a shift in how a particular word was actually spoken over time. Perhaps Shahrastānī's quasi-historical framework adds to the force of his very evocative explanation of the word *tafsīr*: a process of unveiling the face (*tasfīr*) of scripture to our gaze. The same parallel is later, more boldly, pursued in Rūmī's *Fīhi mā fīhi*, where the great Sufi poet likens the Qur'an to a bride who must be served patiently until she unveils herself to her devotee.[26]

This leads to a (tentative) generalisation: in his lexicology sections, when Shahrastānī quotes others' etymologies or he himself etymologises, he is on a literal search for etymons. A line is drawn in current scholarship between linguistic or historical etymologies and semantic or hermeneutic etymologies, marking a growth in understanding of the medieval traditions in question.[27] An earlier orientalist trend was to treat all unhistorical etymologies as folk etymologies, that is, as fanciful ones. This nomenclature betrayed an ignorance of the consciously associative and intuitive basis of semantic etymologies which have been widely used in religious and mystical texts all over the world (e.g. *nirukti* in Sanskrit literature, which is quite distinct from Paninian analysis).

Although in medieval Islamic texts *ishtiqāq* was the generic term for both exercises, this does not mean that thinkers were blind to their contrast. The medieval thinker who put forward a semantic etymology arguably understood that what he was doing was didactic or even playful in intent, and that he was unleashing the spiritual resonances of words, not literally tracing etymons. Semantic or hermeneutic etymologies often rest on the likeness in words' sounds (i.e. homonymy), word-plays and suchlike. The fact that a single writer could give such explanations for words at the same time as giving reputable historical etymologies for the same words, suggests that semantic etymology was engaged in as a conscious exercise.

A good case of this which I encountered recently, is from the Sufi theorist ʿAbd al-Karīm al-Jīlī (d. ca. 832/1428). In his *Perfect Man* (*Al-Insān al-kāmil*), Jīlī gives both a historical and a semantic etymology for *anniyya* ('that-ness', or 'quoddity'), the metaphysical complement of *māhiyya* ('essence', or 'quiddity'). He thus gives the objective, historical derivation of this abstract noun as being from the conjunction *anna* ('that'), but he also relates it hermeneutically to the first person pronoun *anā* ('I') – emphasising the role of egoity and ego-consciousness in our 'ontological alienation', in generating our being as something seemingly apart from the divine.[28] Grammatically, this is strictly unlikely (the abstract noun from *anā* ought to be *anāʾiyya* not *anniyya*). Yet to fault Jīlī as un-factual here is to miss his subtle point.[29]

With Shahrastānī too, this is so. One example from a choice springs to mind. Later in his commentary (notably, in the section on Q. 2:185 headed *Tafsīr*) when he gives views on the derivation of the word '*qurʾān*', he includes authorities (e.g. Muḥammad b. al-Mustanīr Quṭrub, d. 206/821) for the historically factual derivation of the word from the triliteral root *q–r–ʾ*, ('to recite').[30] However, earlier in the text he has urged its alternate derivation from *qarina* ('to yoke or join together', 'to combine', etc.).[31] This etymology rests on compelling semantic concerns. In Shahrastānī's doxology-*cum*-preface, he alludes in passing to two of his key interpretive concepts, the dyad of contrariety (*taḍādd*) and hierarchy (*tarattub*). Shahrastānī views these as two principles which deeply inform creation and also the realm of the Command with which the Qur'an is unfathomably one. In line with both the dyad's elements, the scripture of Islam is marked by a disjunctive and conjunctive function. This dual function, says Shahrastānī, is clear in its revealed names. It is because the scripture expresses the principle of contrariety – separating conflictive groupings, ethical categories, opposed cosmological phenomena, etc. – that it is called *al-Furqān*, based on the triliteral root *f-r-q* ('to differentiate'). And it is because it also, in contrast, expresses the principle of hierarchy – co-ordinating things and combining them as a unitary, but ranked, community of realities – that it is called *al-Qur'ān*. The noteworthy point here is that the semantic etymology of *qur'ān* from *qarina* ('to join together'), is explicitly what is in the author's mind. Shahrastānī's own statement of all this seals his analysis with the talisman of a single Qur'anic citation which unusually refers to the scripture with words from both triliteral roots:

> [God] called the scripture *Qur'ān*, gathering together the things ordered hierarchically within it (*jam'an bayna'l-mutarattibāti fīhi*), and *Furqān*, distinguishing between contraries. For He said (mighty is the recollection of Him): *It is a Qur'an which We divided up* (*faraqnāhu*) *so that you might recite it to people at intervals, and We send it down in steps.* [Q. 17:106][32]

Despite sure signs of grasping that hermeneutic and historical etymologies were not the same, the methods were not marked out clearly, as today. The force of some hermeneutic etymologies even sprang from their historical plausibility, their seeming rootedness in linguistic facts. Thus Shahrastānī (as earlier Arabic lexicologists) may have backed the derivation of *Qur'ān* from *qarina* because this made such an elegant contrast with its coupled epithet *furqān*. If the two names formed a true complementarity, *Qur'ān* should have an antonymous sense – specifically contrasting with the idea of the scripture's dividing function. Shahrastānī also had weighty authorities like 'Abd Allāh Ibn Kathīr (d. 120/737–8) and Muḥammad b. Idrīs al-Shāfi'ī (d. 204/820) for the view that the original, correct pronunciation of *Qur'ān* omitted the glottal stop or *hamza*, that is, *qurān*, again suggesting that the word was better drawn from the *q-r-n* root than the *q-r-'* root.[33] In short, the split categories of semantic or hermeneutic etymology, and linguistic or historical etymology, were diverging trends, not free-standing methods.

Unhistorical, if ingenious, etymologies are sometimes put forward in earnest as would-be facts in the *lugha* sections on verses. One such is the Basran tradition, favoured by Shahrastānī, that *ism* ('name', appearing in the *basmala*-formula) is derived from *samuw* ('height'). This is said to be because '[a name] rises above (*yasmu ʿalā*) the meaning and it manifests the meaning'.[34] He also cites the view that it is from *sima*, 'which means "sign" (*ʿalāma*), [which in turn is so called] because it descends upon (*ʿalā*) the thing named'.[35] The word *ʿalāma* ('sign' or 'emblem') is of course also brought up by Shahrastānī in the lexicology of Q. 1:2, with its key phrase *rabb al-ʿālamīn* (*The Lord of the worlds*). The analysis in question hints at how loaded lexical discussions can be when they concern key terms in a sacred text: no lexicology is neutral here. One view, which Shahrastānī credits to the major lexicologist Ibn Fāris (d. 395/1004) in his *Kitāb al-Maqāyīs*, draws the word *ʿālam* ('world') from *ʿalam* ('sign') or *ʿalāma* ('emblem'). This, we are told, is because '[the worlds] are an indication of the Creator' (*fa-innahā dalālatun ʿala'l-khāliq*).[36] Philosophical vistas thus hide in the lexeme. To spell out the embedded claim: condensed in the very Qur'anic term for 'world' is the proposition that the universe demonstrates God's existence via a cosmological argument. Ibn Fāris, again, and Abū Naṣr Ismāʿīl al-Jawharī (d. ca. 397/1006) are quoted for an alternate view that *ʿālam* in the plural signifies created beings (*khalāʾiq*) or the kinds of created being (*aṣnāf al-khalq*). This may be put with what Shahrastānī reports on the word *rabb* ('Lord'), for he leavens the usual connotations of rulership and ownership with interpretations from ʿAbd al-Malik b. Qurayb al-Aṣmaʿī (d. 213/828 or 216/831), Jawharī and others, which accent the deep pedagogic and nurturing role implied by the word. Hence, Shahrastānī notes, *rabbā* means 'he instructed', *al-murabbī* means 'the educator', and *tarbiya*, 'education'. The snag in the theory is of course that such words have *yāʾ* as their third radical. They must come, then, from a quite different root, *r-b-y*, not *r-b-b*, and the gemination of the middle radical of the former root in line with the Form II does not hide this. That said, this should not keep us from seeing that the lexical configuration of the phrase *rabb al-ʿālamīn* to mean something paternal or even maternal, 'the teacher of all beings', is theologically virtuosic. It may also just fall within the bounds of Arabic lexicology as framed at the time.[37]

In step with a reductionism marking even modern philology, in his lexicological method Shahrastānī typically traces a conceptually laden Qur'anic term to a simpler word or workaday usage, referring to some basic, even domestic, activity. For instance, the word *ḍalāl* in relation to *nor those who go astray* (*wa-la'l-ḍāllīn*) in Q. 1:7, is linked by Shahrastānī to the absorption of water into milk when blended: '*Ḍalāl* in lexicology means "disappearing" (*ghaybūba*). It might be said, "the water went astray (*ḍalla*) in the milk" when it disappeared . . .'[38] Again, the word *mālik* (or *malik*) in the divine epithet from Q. 1:4, *mālik yawmi'l-dīn* (*The Ruler of the Day of Judgement*), in passing is linked by Shahrastānī to a primitive sense, 'to knead', of the root *m-l-k*, as in the action of mixing up dough for baking bread. Shahrastānī says: '. . . The *mālik* of something is whoever binds it to himself; and the *malik* of a people is whoever occupies himself with them and controls their affair. From this is [the expression] "I kneaded the dough" (*wa minhu malaktu'l-'ajīn*).'[39]

Again, such lexical minutiae may hint at theological enormities. In the lexicology of *ihdinā* in Q. 1:6, *ihdina'l-ṣirāṭa'l-mustaqīm* (*Guide us on the straight path*), Shahrastānī observes that the verb *hadā* can connote the act of physically conveying or supporting something: 'the origin (*aṣl*) of *hidāya* (guiding) is *ihāla* (conveying from A to B). It is said: "I conveyed (*hadaytu*) the bride to the house of her husband with a conveying (*hady*)"; "I conducted (*ahdaytu*) her with a conducting (*ihdā'*)" . . .'[40] Shahrastānī goes on to quote a tradition according to which

> the Prophet (may God bless him and his family) came out during his illness in the course of which he died, 'being supported (*yuhādī*) between two men', i.e. he was propped up by them because of his weakness and his staggering along. The [action of the] verb [derived] from it extends to two objects, it extending to the second simply through one of the two prepositions, *ilā* (to) and *li-* (to). And the preposition might be ellipted, so it is said *hadaytuhu'l-ṭarīq* ('I guided him to the way'), this being idiomatically purer (*afṣah*).[41]

The implications of tracing the Qur'anic term for guidance to primitive senses of 'conveying' and 'propping up', are radical theologically. These lexical views hint that divine guidance is about more than gesturing the way to go – they indicate the guide actually taking those guided to their goal. A like sense that the guide is deeply present in the *being* guided of those guided, is found in an earlier lexical comment by Shahrastānī where he points out that *hādī*, as well as meaning 'guide', can mean 'neck': '. . . everything ahead is called *hādī*, even if it is not ahead for pointing out [which way to go] – thus the neck (*'unuq*) is called *hādī*'.[42] This seems to link guide and guided in a yet deeper unity, moving in a common direction as a single body, though one is active, the other passive.

However pregnant conceptually, a reductive spirit in such explanations is clear. Lexemes are explained through – that is, traced back to – their most primitive denotation. Though a historical, evolutionary frame is not overt, it becomes so at some points of Shahrastānī's discussion. For example, in explaining the orthography (*kitāba*) of the *Basmala* formula, he presents explanations for the idiosyncrasy that the *bā'* is written with its first stroke lengthened, which is never otherwise the case:

> As for the lengthening of the *bā'*, it has been made comparable to the *alif* [in length] because of two things. The first of them is that they only wanted to start God's Speech and His Scripture with a visually emphatic and lengthened letter. The second is that since they dropped the *alif* from the formula, they gave back the length of the *alif* to the *bā'* – only omitting the *alif* from [the orthography of] *ism* due to the frequency of its use, abbreviating (*wa innamā hadhafū'l-alifa mina'l-ismi li-kathrati isti'mālihā ṭalaban li'l-khiffa*).[43]

Such an explanation is notable for invoking not only the role of human agency (*they* wanted, *they* omitted, etc.), but even an orthographic development over time – so, for instance, from the impact of frequent transcription (*kathrat al-isti'māl*) of *ism* in the *Basmala*-formula, the *alif* in it came to be left out, with the compensatory reflex of lengthening the first stroke of the *bā'*.

There are even more glaring explanations of the kind in the text, as when Shahrastānī gives views on how God's *nomen proprium* has itself developed – the history of the word *'Allāh'*. He quotes Jawharī as saying that the original form of the name was *ilāh* (deity). This was, he argued, a passive participle on the pattern of *fi'āl*. The notion that divinity was first framed less as an agent, more as a patient (i.e. the one acted upon), is itself boldly counter-intuitive. Shahrastānī even quotes Jawharī as saying: 'He is [as it were] "made God" (*ma'lūh*) in the sense of "is worshipped" (*ma'būd*) – like our saying [of someone], *imām* in the sense of the passive participle, since his example is followed (*mu'tamm bihi*).'[44] Alternatively, the view of Basran scholars like al-Khalīl b. Aḥmad (d. ca. 175/791) and Sībawayhi (d. ca. 180/796) is quoted, according to which the name's etymon was (again) *ilāh* (deity), to which the definite article *al-* was added 'to give emphasis and glorification' (*tafkhīman wa ta'ẓīman*), hence became *al-ilāh* ('the god'). Then the *kasra* (i) of the original word *ilāh* was modified into a *fatha* (a), making *al-'alāh*. Next: 'the original *hamza* was omitted [completely] by way of abbreviation due to its frequent repetition in speech (*li-kathratihi fi'l-kalām*), so it became *al-lāh*'. Finally the two *lāms* were completely assimilated to produce the familiar form of the word, *Allāh*.[45] Shahrastānī relays similar analyses from the Kūfan lexicologists, and others. As can be seen, such explanations are explicitly framed in terms of euphonic processes of elision, etc., and a historical chronology: the original root (*aṣl*) was X; next (*thumma*) they did such and such; then they did such and such.

Antithesis: Esoteric Analysis

Such historical etymologies of the divine *nomen proprium* clash hard with Shahrastānī's own 'theology of the Qur'an'. Ever the doxographer, anthologist and transmitter of other's views, he likes keeping firmly to the background when airing teachings, but he surely identifies with the group now quoted under the heading 'arcana', 'those who magnify God's names' (*al-mu'aẓẓimūn li-asmā'i'llāh*). This group shuns any notion that the word is etymologically derivative (*mushtaqq*) – for 'how could there be an etymology for it (*kayfa ishtiqāquhu*)?!'[46] Yet, having distanced themselves from the premise of any 'horizontal', historical development which explains the name, these scholars fully accept that it can nevertheless be analysed in terms of an esoteric significance and deeper rationale. As Shahrastānī puts it: 'you should not fail to give attention to an arcanum in the composition of its letters (*lā taghfulu min sirrin fī tarkībi ḥurūfihi*) and that the root of the word and its construction (*binā'uhā*) is from the *alif*, the *lām* and the *hā*''.[47]

Shahrastānī dives here into a remarkable analysis of the Islamic *nomen divinis*, an analysis which uncovers profound theological truths hidden in it. He says:

> the letters which are the basis of the word ['*Allāh*'] point to what it is obligatory to know and is made known to be obligatory. No letter of any of the names of existents (*asmā' al-mawjūdāt*) points to any part or attribute of the thing [here] named, but only this highest name. For each letter of it points out something special and, taken as a whole, they point to the entirety of gnosis (*majmū'uhā yadullu 'alā kulli'l-ma'rifa*)![48]

From more than one viewpoint, this declaration is weighty. It states that each of the name's individual letters contains a particular secret and that buried within the Arabic word is a unique comprehension of God. Moreover, Shahrastānī includes the unobtrusive but vital detail that this is because all other names are of things which fall within existence (*asmā' al-mawjūdāt*). This surely has an implication – easily missed – that God is per se *beyond existence*, which was of course one of the leitmotifs of medieval Ismaili teaching, and a deep trait of Shahrastānī's higher thought.[49]

His interpretation of the structure of the name is, then, as follows. The seed-phoneme of the name is *huwa*, the Arabic third person singular masculine pronoun ('He'). This is supposedly implicit in the final *hā'* of the name *Allāh*, which fully vowelled in the nominative is *Allāhu. Huwa* simply results from this final *ḍamma* through adding the consonantal consort (*qarīna*) of the vowel 'u', that is, 'w'. This basic element of the divine name, claims Shahrastānī, acknowledges that the deity is a reality – it declares its 'thingness' (*shay'iyya*), or as we might say, it reifies God. He states, by way of detail, that *huwa* relates to God's majesty or transcendence (*jalāl*). It implies that only God's quoddity, the fact that He is, is knowable, and not His intrinsic identity.

Next, connected to this core phoneme and the meaning that it enshrines, is the *lām*, identified by Shahrastānī using the stock grammatical term *lām al-tamlīk*, the '*lām* of possession' (i.e. *li-*). In addition to possession, *li-* may also designate the author or originator of something. Thus, prefixed to the basic *–hu* to produce *la-hu*, this generates the meaning 'His' or perhaps 'due to Him'. Our author explains that, just as the *–hu* bespeaks the inscrutable majesty of God, this phonemic expansion through the *lām* of possession relates to the bounty or largesse of God (*ikrām*). The duality of fundamental divine qualities, majesty and bounty, is of course derived from Q. 55:26–7: *All that is in* [*earth and heaven*] *will pass away, and your Lord's face alone will endure in its majesty and bounty* (*dhu'l-jalāli wa'l-ikrām*). The complete form of the divine name then involves its prefixion by *al-*, the article of grammatical definition or *taʿrīf* in Arabic (lit. 'making known'). According to Shahrastānī, the meaning of *taʿrīf* in relation to God is to affirm that God is 'more known' (*aʿraf*) than anything else. This relates to the dictum of ʿAlī b. Abī Ṭālib, which Shahrastānī quotes here: 'God is too mighty to be seen, yet too evident (*aẓhar*) to be hidden.'[50] In sum, the beauty of this lexical analysis, taken as a whole, is that it combines the paradoxical truths that God is both wholly hidden from our comprehension and wholly manifest to it also, via the name's phonemic limits *–hu* and *al-*; it also articulates through its middle phoneme, the possessive *lām*, how this is not really paradoxical at all: the godhead is unknowable in itself, but undeniable as the proprietor/originator of the universe. In Shahrastānī's words: 'Insofar as He is He (*huwa*), He is ungraspable and insofar as all belongs to Him (*la-hu*), He is undeniable.'[51] Lastly, Shahrastānī's analysis bears out a principle that inner meanings relate to outward forms through inversion and chiasmus. The phonemic meanings that he finds encoded in the divine name run in the direction opposite to its outward form and articulation (*hu*, *lah*, *al* versus *al*, *lah*, *hu*).

This then falls under what may be termed Shahrastānī's esoteric lexicology, and typifies the arcana sections of the commentary. The whole frame of reference of this lexicology has shifted. *Ishtiqāq* literally means division into halves or splitting up, and connotes the derivation of cognate words from a common etymon. *Ishtiqāq* of a kind is, arguably, also at work here in the arcana but not through one word emerging laterally or historically from another more basic word. Tracing up has in effect replaced tracing back; that is, the word is now derived via its phonemic structures from higher principles and truths. In some discussions, the letters indeed turn out themselves to constitute the metaphysical principles. Shahrastānī formulates a full-blown doctrine of phonic *principia* in discussing the 'disjointed letters' (*muqaṭṭaʿāt*) which open *Sūrat al-Baqara* (Q. 2:1).[52] At any rate, etymology seems an unspoken model for this exercise of tracing the word up through higher levels and stages to transcendental roots.

Another example of Shahrastānī's 'esoteric lexicology' is in the following mysterious comment on Q. 1:5, *iyyāka naʿbudu wa iyyāka nastaʿīn* (*it is You we worship and it is You we ask for help*). Shahrastānī says:

> The *kāf* and the *nūn* are interconnected in the two words. The *kāf* entails direct witnessing (*mushāhada*) since it is a second person pronoun which only belongs to someone present, and the *nūn* entails [our] exertion (*mujāhada*), since it is a verbatim quotation from someone with capacity and power. Just as beings receive light by contact with the *kāf* and the *nūn* upon origination and existentiation, likewise hearts receive light by contact with the *kāf* and the *nūn* upon obedience and unreserved acceptance (*taslīm*).[53]

Lexicology and grammar stir in the potent mysticism of this typically concise analysis. To unpack it as far as possible: Shahrastānī takes it that Q. 1:5 is the declaration par excellence of *taslīm* (acceptance of, or self-submission to, God). This spiritual act triggers light in the human annunciator's heart, a light which evokes an earlier one from the time of his projection into existence. *Kāf* and *nūn*, the Arabic letters, catalyse both photic events – the phonic sparks the photic. It is as if these letters are resumed by the creature in time present, in response to their use by God beyond time. In the case of the creature's first creation, what is clearly meant by *kāf* and *nūn* here is the existentialising imperative *kun* ('Be!'), in line with verses like Q. 16:40, *Our word unto a thing when We will it is only that We say to it "Be!"* (*kun*) *and it is.* On the other hand, in the case of the creature's subsequent act of self-submission through Q. 1:5, the *kāf* and the *nūn* correspond with: (1) the second person singular pronominal suffix *-ka*, in *it is You* (*iyyāka*) *we worship and it is You we ask for help*, called the *kāf al-khiṭāb* (the 'k' of direct address) in the Arabic grammatical tradition because it implies the actual presence of the addressee to the speaker; (2) the first person plural inflexion of the imperfect, *na-*, of *we are worshipping* (*naʿbudu*) and *we are asking for help* (*nastaʿīnu*), acknowledging our creaturely self-determination and freedom in the actions of worship and seeking aid. The criteria of *taslīm* are thus fulfilled by the *kāf* and the *nūn* of verse 5, which explains their catalytic function for the 'cardiac light' referred to by Shahrastānī.

In such analyses the arcana sometimes share tools with the lexicology sections, but are otherwise remote. They mainly use quite separate, highly specific means to decipher the text: an elaborate lattice of dyadic concepts (the 'keys' [*mafātīḥ*] of the whole work's title), as presented in chapters 9 and 10 of Shahrastānī's introduction. Using these keys, he uncovers a buried semantic logic in the Qur'anic plaintext, virtually amounting to a philosophical system on the level of its deeper meanings.[54] His 'esoteric lexicology' instead works on the level of verbal minutiae in the text. There are even cases where Shahrastānī finds great meanings in the shape of its graphemes.[55]

Resolution: Shahrastānī's Theology of the Qur'an

How, then, might a scholar who unmistakably acknowledged the plaintext's historicity and aired the boldest thoughts on the development of its written form, its language and its compilation, also view it with such awe that its every detail was fraught with arcane meanings? It should not be taken that Shahrastānī was merely intellectually conflicted and methodologically inconsistent, for he gives clues enough in his oeuvre to resolve the paradox. The gist of his solution is hidden in the scripture's broadly bi-dimensional character, as voiced throughout the tradition, and even written into a stock concept of Qur'anic hermeneutics like *asbāb al-nuzūl* (the occasioning causes of the descent of the revelation). The phrase is so routine in the commentarial lexicon as to go almost unscrutinised. It refers, of course, to the contextual, biographical events in the Prophet's career, in view of which this or that verse of the Qur'an first emerged. Yet the innocuous terminology already gives voice to the idea of the text's twin dimensions: firstly, a vertical, metaphysical one assumed in its descent (*nuzūl*) from origins *in divinis*; secondly, its piecemeal promulgation according to this or that contingency or occasion (*sabab*), that is, a horizontal, historical dimension. In his commentary, then, Shahrastānī simply draws the fullest consequences from such seeds. In his scriptural analysis, he seems to have pursued an uncompromising inquiry into *both* dimensions of the text, the vertical and the horizontal, his *asrār* sections corresponding with the reality of the former, and his *lugha* sections, his radical discussion of the ʿUthmānic compilation of the *textus receptus*, etc., corresponding with the reality of the latter.

One place to seek to unriddle Shahrastānī's hermeneutic paradox and bridge his outwardly incongruent methods is his *Nihāyat al-aqdām fī ʿilm al-kalām*. In this work, his major theological treatise, are full discussions of a set of germane subjects: that God speaks with an eternal speech, that the reality of the said speech is absolutely unitary, on the clash of conventionalist and revelationist theories of language, and on 'psychic utterance' (*al-nuṭq al-nafsānī*, an Ashʿarī model for divine speech). Though the *Nihāya* is a considered defence of Neo-Ashʿarite orthodoxy, it is by no means unlinked to the Qur'an commentary with its Ismaili background. Close reading shows that the *Nihāya* shares ideas with Shahrastānī's Ismaili texts, such that we are forced to think of his total teachings as marked by some continuity, despite the cleft between esoteric Ismaili and exoteric, Sunni–Ashʿarī, teachings – the split starker in some areas than others.

So it is that, in his *Nihāya*, Shahrastānī (as expected) spurns the Muʿtazilī conventionalist teaching which holds that speech is at one with its outward, human forms that vary so widely, both historically and geographically. He pleads that although external speech is indeed variable and subject to human convention (*yakhtalifu dhālika bi-ḥasabi'l-iṣṭilāḥ wa'l-muwāḍa'a*), it yet devolves on 'psychic utterance', that is, speech internal to the self, which is a reality that is generic, invariant, and divinely revealed to humanity in its first origin. It alone is strictly 'speech', he rules, while the external kind is so called in a derivative and even metaphorical sense.[56] He here seems, at bottom, to take speech as its inmost semantic content rather than its physical manifestations. His teaching thus clings to the claim that speech *sensu stricto* is a unified reality, first conferred by God, though it ingeniously allows that speech as commonly understood is multifarious and does rest on human convention, thereby naturalising linguistic conventionalism within a paradigm of linguistic revelationism – matching his subtle stance on holy scripture.

An allied discussion delves into the epiphany of the Archangel Gabriel, or alternatively 'God's Spirit', to the Virgin Mary and others (as in Q. 19:17: *We sent unto her Our Spirit and it appeared* [or: 'was configured', *tamaththala*] *to her in the likeness of a mortal*). Weighing the terminology of *tamaththul* in the Qur'an, Shahrastānī denies that the process of X appearing as Y can involve the annihilation of X as Y comes into being, for this is no longer X appearing through Y; neither can it be that X makes use of a pre-existing person, Y, for this is not rightly termed *tamaththul* but *tanāsukh* (metempsychosis, a kind of spirit possession). X and Y are thus commutable in a true identity relation, yet have enough distinction to account for the temporal contingency, variation, etc., of the epiphany as against the epiphanised. The analogy given is of clothing (*libās*), so Shahrastānī says: 'That which clothed Gabriel changes, but his reality, by reason of which he is Gabriel, is unchangeable.'[57] It is, he goes on, just the same with God's Word. 'The clothing of God's pre-eternal Word changes, but its reality does not change' (*libās al-kalāmi al-azalī yatabaddalu wa lā tatabaddalu ḥaqīqatuhu*).[58] How else could the eternal Command appear now as Arabic, now as Syriac, etc., yet stay one thing?[59] Shahrastānī rules that in identifying the Qur'an, as in identifying

Gabriel, the epiphanised subject (*muẓhir*) must be accented over the epiphanic form (*ẓuhūr*/*maẓhar*).[60]

Shahrastānī also brings forward human experience. The mind, say, may grasp the solution of a complex question in an instant, yet a day is not enough for the tongue to detail it, nor a single volume for the pen to go over the insight.[61] Likewise, communications gained in visionary dreams 'take more than a day to describe though they were perceived in less than a moment'.[62] Analogously, God's Word is a synthetic unity, communicated analytically by many expressions spread through time. When God's Word is spoken of, the real reference is to the former, not the latter. This is urged by Shahrastānī through a simple example: when we observe that someone's statement is right or wrong, this judgement plainly relates to the statement's meaning, not the rightness or otherwise of its wording or grammar.[63] At the end of this discussion, Shahrastānī actually chides Ashʿarī for having left consensus and the pious ancestors' stance, when in the case of the Qur'an he drew too firm a distinction between the thing expressed and its expression, and said that what we recite is only the speech of God metaphorically (*majāzan lā ḥaqīqatan*).[64] The immanent scriptural epiphany and the transcendent Word are a single, albeit biform, reality.

Though drawn from a Sunni *kalām* context, all this goes towards understanding how Shahrastānī himself may have thought to undo the antinomy in his hermeneutics. There are also clues on its resolution in the Qur'an commentary itself – allusions which have the added interest of drawing on the, at bottom, Ismaili system used there. A noteworthy case is a statement which closes Shahrastānī's discussion in *Mafātīḥ al-asrār* (already referred to earlier) of the difference between *tafsīr* (exegetical commentary) and *ta'wīl* (hermeneutic interpretation). He ends this discussion by bringing in key conceptual dyads from his Ismaili system – hierarchy (*tarattub*) and contrariety (*taḍādd*), and more importantly, the accomplished (*mafrūgh*) and the inchoate (*musta'naf*). There is no scope here to explore these rich concepts, but suffice to say that, according to Shahrastānī, both the realm of creation, that is, the external universe, and the realm of the Command, with which the Qur'an must be ultimately identified, are characterised by an unfolding or inchoate aspect as well as an ever-accomplished aspect. The accomplished dimension and the unfolding dimension must always be co-affirmed, for both hold true on their given level. Shahrastānī now makes clear that he ties the subordinate inquiry on the revealed text, *tafsīr*, to the Qur'an's inchoate level, while he ties the superordinate inquiry, *ta'wīl*, to its eternally accomplished level. Thus he says:

> In the Qur'an are rulings of the 'accomplished', [and] rulings of the 'inchoative', mutually opposed rulings on the basis of contrariety, and rulings differing in superiority on the basis of hierarchy. So viewing the 'inchoative' is the literal, the sending down [of the Qur'an], and exegesis (*tafsīr*); and viewing the principle of the 'accomplished' is the esoteric, hermeneutics (*ta'wīl*), the meaning and the inner reality (*al-ma'nā wa'l-ḥaqīqa*). *And those firm-rooted in knowledge say 'we believe in it, all is from our Lord'. And only those possessed of minds pay heed!* [Q. 3:7][65]

In sum: on one side, Shahrastānī viewed his etymology, regular lexicology and other historical treatments of the text as addressing the Qur'an *qua* inchoate, as manifest within the conditions of human history. On the other side, he viewed the arcana sections with their items of 'esoteric lexicology' and their unlocking of the text's latent semantic system through the dyadic keys as addressing the scripture *qua* eternally accomplished. Through the scripture's own radically dual nature, Shahrastānī saw his oddly paired methodologies as working together, in an ultimate, synergic kind of hermeneutics.

NOTES

1 Muḥammad b. 'Abd al-Karīm al-Shahrastānī, *Mafātīḥ al-asrār wa maṣābīḥ al-abrār*, tr. Toby Mayer as *Keys to the Arcana: Shahrastānī's Esoteric Commentary on the Qur'an* (Oxford: Oxford University Press in association with the Institute of Ismaili Studies, 2009), p. 66.
2 *Mafātīḥ al-Furqān*, the title of his introduction.
3 Shahrastānī, *Keys to the Arcana*, p. 66 (slightly amended translation).
4 Traditions of literary boasting and 'auto-encomia' are explained by the dynamics of medieval patronage in Islam and had roots extending back to pre-Islamic Arab culture. See e.g. B. Farès, '*Mufākhara*', *EI*², vol. 7, pp. 308–10.

5 Muḥammad b. ʿAbd al-Karīm al-Shahrastānī, *Mafātīḥ al-asrār wa maṣābīḥ al-abrār*, MS 8086/B78, Library of the Islamic Consultative Assembly in Tehran.

6 For more on the notions of creation and the command in Ismaili philosophy, see Paul E. Walker, *Early Philosophical Shiʿism: The Ismaili Neoplatonism of Abu Yaʿqub al-Sijistani* (Cambridge: Cambridge University Press, 1993), pp. 81–6.

7 These alignments are partly explained by the strongly variant theologies of Ashʿarism and Muʿtazilism. In Ashʿarism there was a trend to identify the divine names with the One Named (hence the dictum *al-ismu huwa'l-musammā*), and to view God's attributes as real hypostatic entities. A revelationist theory of the origins of Arabic fitted with this realist theory of divine predication. However, in Muʿtazilism there was a trend, in the interests of preserving divine unity and transcendence, to nominalism, i.e. to reduce or even negate such factors in relation to God. The conventionalist theory fitted with this reduction. Mustafa Shah, 'The Philological Endeavours of the Early Arabic Linguists: Theological Implications of the *tawqīf-iṣṭilāḥ* Antithesis and the *majāz* Controversy – Part I', *Journal of Qur'anic Studies* 1, no. 1 (1999), pp. 27–46; and Part II, *Journal of Qur'anic Studies* 2, no. 1 (2000), pp. 43–66. Also see Bernard Weiss, 'Medieval Muslim Discussions of the Origin of Language', *Zeitschrift der Deutschen Morgenländischen Gesellschaft* 124 (1974), pp. 33–41, and with regards to explaining why select Muʿtazilī figures defended *tawqīf*, Cornelis [Kees] H.M. Versteegh, 'Linguistic Attitudes and the Origin of Speech in the Arab World' in Alaa Elgibali, ed., *Understanding Arabic: Essays in Contemporary Arabic Linguistics in Honor of El-Said Badawi* (Cairo: The American University in Cairo Press, 1996), pp. 15–31. Also, Mustafa Shah, 'Classical Islamic Discourse on the Origins of Language: Cultural Memory and the Defense of Orthodoxy', *Numen* 58 (2011), pp. 314–43.

8 Chapter 4 of Shahrastānī's introduction is dedicated to *qirā'āt* lineages. Shahrastānī, *Keys to the Arcana*, pp. 90–97.

9 Ibid., pp. 79–87.

10 Ibid., pp. 71–2 and 88.

11 Ibid., pp. 71, 72 and 83.

12 For a survey of Sunni accounts of the collection of the Qur'an, see Jalāl al-Dīn al-Suyūṭī, *[Kitāb] al-Itqān fī ʿulūm al-Qur'ān* (Beirut: Dār al-Kutub al-ʿIlmiyya, 1407/1987), vol. 1, pp. 126–41; tr. Ḥamid Algar, Michael Schub and Ayman Abdel Ḥaleem, *The Perfect Guide to the Sciences of the Qur'ān* (Reading: Garnet, 2011), pp. 137–53. See also John Burton, *The Collection of the Qur'ān* (Cambridge: Cambridge University Press, 1977); and Harald Motzki, 'The Collection of the Qur'ān: A Reconsideration of Western Views in Light of Recent Methodological Developments', *Der Islam* 78 (2001), pp. 1–34.

13 Shahrastānī, *Keys to the Arcana*, p. 73.

14 For more on the use of *taḥrīf* in polemical discourse, see Theodore Pulcini, *Exegesis as a Polemical Discourse: Ibn Ḥazm on Jewish and Christian Scriptures* (Atlanta, GA: Scholars Press, 1998); and Martin Whittingham, 'The Value of *taḥrīf maʿnawī* (Corrupt Interpretation) as a Category for Analysing Muslim Views of the Bible: Evidence from *al-Radd al-jamīl* and Ibn Khaldūn', *Islam and Christian–Muslim Relations* 22 (2011), pp. 209–22.

15 E.g. 'Some of the people of learning said: How many verses like [Q. 33:23] did they lose consisting in what referred to the virtues of the People of the [Prophet's] House (peace be upon them)?' Shahrastānī, *Keys to the Arcana*, p. 69. Also see pp. 74–5.
16 Ibid., pp. 73–4.
17 Ibid., p. 105.
18 Ibid., pp. 105 and 123.
19 Ibid., p. 105.
20 Ibid., p. 108.
21 The authority in question appears to be the Fāṭimid caliph-imam, al-Muʿizz li-Dīn Allāh (d. 365/975). The dictum (or part of it) is found in *Taʾwīl al-sharīʿa*, compiled by al-Qāḍī al-Nuʿmān. On this, see Ismail K. Poonawala, *Bibliography of Ismāʿīlī Literature* (Malibu, CA: Undena Publications, 1977), p. 65. My thanks to Faquir Hunzai and Nadia Eboo-Jamal for this attribution. Shahrastānī's respectful quotation of an imam specific to Ismaili Shiʿism is a noteworthy piece of evidence for his hidden affiliation.
22 *Al-taʾwīlu yataʿallaqu ʿalā dirāyati'l-ʿaql*. Shahrastānī, *Keys to the Arcana*, p. 106 (Eng.), p. 48 (Ar.).
23 Shahrastānī, *Keys to the Arcana*, pp. 104–5 (slightly amended translation).
24 E.g. in his Persian sermon, *Majlis-i Maktūb*, Shahrastānī says that the function of angels as conveyors of the *logoi* of the World of the Command to creation is hinted in their very name in Arabic, via metathesis. He says: 'The root of *kalima* ("word") is *k-l-m* and the root of *malak* ("angel") is *m-l-k*; both are a metathetic version of one another' (*aṣl-i kalima kāf-lām-mīm wa aṣl-i malak mīm-lām-kāf; har dū maqlūb-i yakdīgar*). Muḥammad b. ʿAbd al-Karīm Shahrastānī, *Majlis-i Maktūb-i Shahrastānī-i munʿaqid dar Khwārazm*, translated into French by Diane Steigerwald (with Jalālī Nāʾinī's edition of the Persian text) as *Majlis: Discours sur l'ordre et la création* (Saint-Nicolas: Les Presses de l'Université Laval, 1998), p. 83.
25 See H. Fleis, '*Ishtiḳāḳ*', *EI*[2], vol. 4, pp. 122–3.
26 Arthur J. Arberry, tr., *Discourses of Rūmī* (London: John Murray, 1961), pp. 236–7. For the Persian text see Mawlānā Jalāl al-Dīn Muḥammad Mashhūr bi-Mawlawī, *Kitāb Fīhi mā fīhi*, ed. Badīʿ al-Zamān Farūzānfar (Tehran: Muʾassassa-yi Intishār-i Amīr Kabīr, 1362 Sh./1983), p. 229.
27 E.g. Timothy Lubin, 'The Virtuosic Exegesis of the Brahmavadin and the Rabbi', *Numen* 49 (2002), pp. 427–59.
28 ʿAbd al-Karīm b. Ibrāhīm al-Jīlī, *al-Insān al-kāmil fī maʿrifati'l-awākhir wa'l-awāʾil* (Cairo: n.p., 1402/1981), pp. 72 and 98–100.
29 See also, Toby Mayer, 'Anniyya', *EI THREE* (Online).
30 Compare Hebrew *qārāʾ*. See Francis Brown, S.R. Driver and Charles A. Briggs, *Hebrew and English Lexicon of the Old Testament* (Oxford: Clarendon Press, 1968), pp. 894–6.
31 This etymology is also given by Fakhr al-Dīn al-Rāzī, *al-Tafsīr al-kabīr (Mafātīḥ al-Ghayb)* (Tehran: Dār al-Kutub al-ʿIlmiyya, n.d.), vol. 5, p. 86.
32 Shahrastānī, *Keys to the Arcana*, p. 64, amended translation.
33 Muḥammad b. ʿAbd al-Karīm al-Shahrastānī, *Tafsīr al-Shahrastānī al-musammā Mafātīḥ al-asrār wa maṣābīḥ al-abrār*, ed. Muḥammad ʿAlī Ādharshab (Tehran: Mīrās-i Maktūb, 2008), vol. 2, p. 758.

34 Shahrastānī, *Keys to the Arcana*, p. 143.
35 Ibid.
36 Ibid., p. 161.
37 For example, according to the so-called 'hyper-etymology' (*al-ishtiqāq al-akbar*) of Abū'l-Fatḥ 'Uthmān Ibn Jinnī (d. 392/1002), the radical consonants may even differ between the word and its etymon. This should however have the condition that there is *some* reciprocal relation between the two words in the places of articulation. Ibn Jinnī, *[Kitāb] al-Khaṣā'iṣ fī 'ilm uṣūl al-'arabiyya* (Cairo: 1371/1952), vol. 1, pp. 5–17 and (Cairo: 1374/1955), vol. 2, pp. 133–9.
38 Shahrastānī, *Keys to the Arcana*, p. 184.
39 Ibid., p. 166.
40 Ibid., p. 174.
41 Ibid. In other words, the ultra-concise, prepositionless form found in Q. 1:6, *ihdina'l-ṣirāṭa'l-mustaqīm* is more idiomatic than the form *ihdinā ila'l-ṣirāṭi'l-mustaqīm*.
42 Shahrastānī, *Keys to the Arcana*, p. 173.
43 Ibid., p. 142.
44 Ibid., p. 144.
45 Ibid., p. 143.
46 Ibid., p. 144.
47 Ibid.
48 Ibid., p. 145 (slightly amended translation).
49 On this key theme in his higher thought, see Toby Mayer, 'Shahrastānī's Ḥanīf Revelation: A Shi'i Philosophico-Hermeneutical System' in Farhad Daftary and Gurdofarid Miskinzoda, eds, *The Study of Shi'i Islam: History, Theology and Law* (London: I.B. Tauris in association with the Institute of Ismaili Studies, 2014), pp. 563–83, esp. pp. 570–74. Also see Wilferd Madelung, 'Aspects of Ismā'īlī Theology: The Prophetic Chain and the God beyond Being' in S.H. Nasr, ed., *Ismā'īlī Contributions to Islamic Culture* (Tehran: Imperial Academy of Philosophy, 1398/1977), pp. 51–65, esp. pp. 60–62.
50 Compare Muḥammad b. Ya'qūb Kulaynī, *Ṣaḥīḥ al-Kāfī*, ed. 'Alī al-Ghaffārī (Beirut: n.p., 1401/1980), vol. 3, pp. 482–3.
51 Shahrastānī, *Keys to the Arcana*, p. 144.
52 Shahrastānī, *Mafātīḥ al-Asrār*, vol. 1, pp. 119–26.
53 Shahrastānī, *Keys to the Arcana*, pp. 172–3.
54 For more on this hermeneutical system, see translator's introduction to Shahrastānī, *Keys to the Arcana*, pp. 25–35.
55 See for example on the shape of the *alif*, *lām* and *hā'* in the name 'Allāh', Shahrastānī, *Keys to the Arcana*, p. 146, and translator's introduction, pp. 39–40.
56 Muḥammad b. 'Abd al-Karīm Shahrastānī, *Kitāb Nihāyat al-iqdām fī 'ilm al-kalām*, ed. and partially tr. by Alfred Guillaume as *The Summa Philosophiae of al-Shahrastānī* (Oxford: Oxford University Press, 1934), p. 108.
57 Ibid., p. 100.
58 Ibid., p. 300 (Ar.), my translation.
59 Ibid., p. 100.
60 Ibid., p. 104.

61 Ibid., p. 103.
62 Ibid.
63 Ibid., p. 104.
64 Ibid., pp. 104–5 (Ar., p. 313).
65 Shahrastānī, *Keys to the Arcana*, p. 108.

SECTION III

Words, Interpretation and Legal Disputes

9

From Qur'an to *Fiqh*: Sunni and Shi'i *Tafsīr* on the Inheritance Verses and the 'Named Cases' (*al-Masā'il al-Mulaqqaba*)

AGOSTINO CILARDO

STUDIES ON the Islamic law of inheritance are quite numerous, both in the past and more recently.[1] Among these, the work of David S. Powers is worthy of note, since he departs from the 'traditional' doctrine,[2] which assumes a line of continuity from the Qur'an to the legal elaboration of later scholars. According to this view, the Qur'anic rules on inheritance, as we know and read them, constituted the base for the further development of the inheritance system. Powers, however, hypothesises a contrary theory: that of a proto-Islamic law of inheritance, which is quite different from that elaborated by the legal schools. He holds that 'what we know as the Islamic law of inheritance . . . is not identical to the system of inheritance revealed to Muḥammad',[3] and that 'the Muslim community is not in possession of the original reading and understanding of several Qur'anic verses and prophetic *ḥadīth* or of the system of inheritance received by Muḥammad'.[4]

One of my scholarly interests is the investigation of the Islamic inheritance system, both under some specific aspects,[5] and as a whole.[6] Elsewhere I have critiqued Powers's interpretation of early Islamic inheritance law, and reaffirmed the 'traditional' doctrine.[7] This essay aims to confirm the close link between the wording and the reading of the Qur'anic verses on inheritance, as they were revealed to Muhammad, and the final inheritance system elaborated by the legal schools and in force in the Muslim community since then. Furthermore, the divergences existing among the schools of law (*madhāhib*) depend on their different interpretations of those verses.

Arḥām (Q. 8:75), *aqrabūna* (Q. 4:7, 33) and *ʿaṣaba*: 'Relatives' in Sunni and Shiʿi Inheritance Law

In Arabic, different terms are used to designate the different kinds of blood relation. Some of them are specific, like *ibn*, which expressly refers to a male descendant of the first degree, that is, a 'son'; or its correspondent *bint* for a female; or *ʿamm li-ab wa umm*, meaning a 'paternal uncle'; etc. Some other terms have a general meaning, because they designate an unspecified group of blood relatives. This is the case for the term *arḥām*, which generically refers to those people related by a blood tie. The term *aqrabūna*, however, accentuates the quality of proximity of the blood relatives; they are the nearest of kin, or the near kindred. As for the term *ʿaṣaba*, it refers only to the males among the blood relatives.

The inheritance system in force in pagan pre-Islamic times was very simple: it was based on agnatic kinship (*taʿṣīb*), that is, blood ties based exclusively on the male line. The basic principle was proximity: the nearest male excluded the most remote (e.g. a son excluded an uncle), while males with the same degree of kinship inherited on an equal footing (e.g. two or more sons, or two or more full or consanguine brothers, or two or more paternal uncles, etc., received the same share).[8] However, this was kept in force only by some law schools. As a matter of fact, according to the Sunnis (including the Ẓāhirīs), Zaydīs and Ibāḍīs, the Qur'an does not abrogate this customary law, but it overlaps a quota system: firstly, shares are to be attributed to those relatives entitled to receive them; if there is anything left, the remainder is allotted to the agnates according to their proximity to the deceased. This pre-Islamic category of agnates is called *ʿaṣaba bi-nafsihi* (agnates for themselves), that is, agnates *iure proprio*, the true agnates. Shiʿis (other than the Zaydīs), however, reject the combination of the Qur'anic system of fixed shares and the agnatic principle maintained by the Sunni, Ẓāhirī, Zaydī and Ibāḍi law schools.

Amongst the various legal schools (*madhāhib*), the order of proximity of this category of agnates is the matter that is disputed. Ḥanafīs, Ẓāhirīs and Ibāḍīs place the paternal grandfather after the father, and before the full or consanguine brothers, which is closer to the pre-Islamic rule;[9] while Mālikīs, Shāfiʿīs, Ḥanbalīs and Zaydīs prefer to safeguard the right of full and consanguine brothers and sisters who are heirs established in the Qur'an (henceforth referred to as 'Qur'anic heirs'), rather than to follow the pre-Islamic position with regard to the paternal grandfather. The way in which the different legal scholars handle the apportionment of the estate in complex cases can be seen in the 'named cases' (*al-masā'il al-mulaqqaba*), which can be found in various legal works, and which have been collected together in the appendix to this chapter.

Besides the *ʿaṣaba bi-nafsihi*, Sunnis (including the Ẓāhirīs), Zaydīs and Ibāḍīs created specific terminology, present in relatively late sources (fifth/eleventh century), in order to classify two different categories of agnates, which concern the inheritance rights of women. The first category is designated by the term *ʿaṣaba bi-ghayrihi* ('agnates because of another'),[10] a category which is based on interpretations of Q. 4:11 and 176, where it is stated that a son or a brother will have twice the share of his daughter or sister. In contrast to pre-Islamic inheritance law, which only included males, these verses show that women can inherit. However, these schools state that there are restrictions on which women related to the deceased can inherit. According to these schools, there are four types of women who can acquire the quality of agnates due to the presence of males: a full sister is made agnate by her full brother; a consanguine sister by her consanguine brother; a daughter by a son; and a son's daughter by a son's son; in the latter case, female grandchildren *ex filio* (i.e. through the male line) can belong either to the same degree or to a nearer degree with respect to the male descendants. Importantly, these female relatives lose their right to inherit as heirs through the Qur'anic quota system (Q. 4:11, 176), but receive their inheritance as agnates. This means that they can only receive a portion of the inheritance after the division of the estate to those who have fixed shares. The second category of agnation is referred to as *ʿaṣaba maʿa ghayrihi* ('agnates with another'). One or more full or consanguine sisters are considered agnates when one or more daughters, or one or more female grandchildren *ex filio*, are present. Therefore, they are no longer entitled to receive their fixed share, but receive, as agnates, what remains after the allotment of the share to one or more daughters, or to one or more female grandchildren *ex filio*.[11]

The basic feature distinguishing the Twelver and Ismaili inheritance system from the Sunni schools is its rejection of the (pre-Islamic) principle of agnation. This is because the Twelver and Ismaili schools believe that agnates, as well as all other relatives, can only inherit as *dhawū'l-arḥām* (blood relatives), rather than due to any agnatic relationship. The most immediate consequence of this position is that what is left after the attribution of the shares to the heirs by quota is not allotted to the agnates, but is added to the portion of those who have inherited the estate, so that these receive an increased share. This division of the estate can be seen in a number of the 'named cases', such as *Mas'alat al-iltizām*, *al-Kharqā'* and *al-Akdariyya* (discussed in detail in the appendix). Therefore, there are only three ways by which a family member can inherit in the Shi'i system: being an heir by quota (*wārith*); having a blood tie (*qurbā*), such as maternal uncles and aunts, who are neither heirs by quota nor agnates; and having acquired such an entitlement (*asbāb*) through marriage or patronage.

The denial of agnation highlights another rule specific to Shi'i law: the principle of proximity is no longer valid only for agnates, but is instead applied to all blood relatives. The next of kin among the blood relatives (*dhawū'l-arḥām*) is entitled to inherit and is able to exclude other relatives, even if they are agnates. Therefore, the order of proximity among relatives is not based exclusively on family ties based on the male (agnatic) line. As a consequence, this Twelver and Ismaili legal position does not require a list of agnates like the Sunni (including the Ẓāhirī), Zaydī and Ibāḍī schools do. The whole Twelver and Ismaili inheritance system is based on these two principles, that is, the rejection of agnation and the principle of proximity, which lead to the division of the *dhawū'l-arḥām* into three classes. The first class is composed by the direct ascendants (father and mother), by children and any other direct descendant, either a male or a female of any degree. The second class includes ascendants other than the first degree (grandfathers and grandmothers of any degree) and collaterals (*kalāla*) limited to full, consanguine and uterine brothers and sisters, and their descendants. The last class includes the remaining collaterals, namely, paternal and maternal uncles and aunts who are full brothers or sisters of the father or the mother; paternal and maternal uncles and aunts who are consanguine brothers or sisters of the father or the mother; and paternal and maternal uncles and aunts who are uterine brothers or sisters of the father or the mother. If these relatives are not present, their descendants take their place, according to the previous order.

The fundamental divergences between the two systems originate from the interpretation of some Qur'anic verses that deal with inheritance legislation. Early exegeses provide little material on the interpretation of the inheritance verses in the Qur'an, particularly regarding the debates about agnatic inheritance rights. According to the superimposition theory, 'a new system of heirs by quota was superimposed on the pre-Islamic agnatic customary law of inheritance. The ancient system was not abolished, but only modified',[12] so that the Muslim *'aṣaba bi-nafsihi* are identical to the *'aṣaba* of pre-Islamic times. This is the view of the Sunni, Ẓāhirī, Zaydī and Ibāḍī schools. This doctrine is based on the assumption that Q. 4:7, which has only a generic reference to the inheritance rights of the kin (*aqrabūna*), was abrogated by the Qur'anic verses allotting fixed shares to the heirs. Conversely, Twelvers and Ismailis maintain that Q. 4:7 is not abrogated, but argue that it was revealed in order to abolish agnatic rights. In fact, the verse refers to kinsmen, including agnates, and puts men and women on the same footing.

The rejection or acceptance and modification of the pre-Islamic principle of agnation in Islamic inheritance is frequently debated in the exegeses of Q. 4:7. This verse states that, *From what is left by parents and those nearest related there is a share for men and a share for women, whether the property be small or large, – a determinate share.*[13] Sunnis and Shi'is diverge about the reason for the revelation (*sabab al-nuzūl*) of this verse. Ṭabarī stresses that only males were entitled to the inheritance during the *Jāhiliyya* (the 'time of ignorance', i.e. the pre-Islamic period).[14] Subsequently, the Qur'an also included women among the heirs by quota. Sunnis (including the Ẓāhirīs), Zaydīs and Ibāḍīs believe, on the authority of Qatāda b. Di'āma (d. 118/736), 'Abd al-Malik Ibn Jurayj (d. 150/767) and Muḥammad Ibn Zayd, that the reason for this revelation was simply to reform the rule in force during the *Jāhiliyya*.

In contrast, the Twelver Muḥammad b. al-Ḥasan al-Ṭūsī (known as Shaykh al-Ṭā'ifa, d. 460/1067) rejects this interpretation and more broadly states that the reason for the revelation was to affirm two principles: firstly, the right of the prophets and their relatives to inherit from each other (legitimist claim); secondly, the negation of the principle of agnation, because God allotted a fixed share both to males and females.[15] Regarding the latter, Ṭūsī argues that the well-known hadith supporting the right of agnates to the inheritance, 'First allot the fixed shares to heirs by quota; the remainder shall be due to the nearest agnate [of the deceased]'[16] is a *khabar wāḥid* (a tradition or report going back to one single authority), and thus it cannot be taken as a proof.[17]

Moreover, Q. 8:75, *But kindred by blood* (*wa ūlū'l-arḥām*) *have prior rights against each other* (*ba'ḍuhum awlā bi-ba'ḍin*) *in the Book of Allah*, is deemed as being abrogated by Sunnis (including the Ẓāhirīs), Zaydīs and Ibāḍīs, contrary to Twelvers and Ismailis, who believe that this verse remains in force and that the term *ūlū'l-arḥām* refers to blood relatives in general, in other words, cognates from either lineage, rather than only agnates. This last doctrine is supported also by Q. 33:6, where again *ūlū'l-arḥām* are mentioned. However, the Twelver and Ismaili doctrine seems to be contradicted by Q. 4:33, where the term *mawālī* appears. Even if this word is generally interpreted as 'agnates', Twelvers and Ismailis render it as 'heirs' (*al-mawālī . . . hum al-'aṣaba*; . . . *hum al-waratha*).[18] As a consequence of their divergent interpretation of these Qur'anic verses, Twelvers and Ismailis infer that there is no distinction among heirs by kin, 'but relatives must be considered as a whole: cognates and agnates are placed on an equal footing; the only element to be considered is their blood relation both on the paternal and maternal side, and their proximity to a deceased relative'.[19] Based on this principle, heirs are divided into three classes, according to their proximity to the deceased.

As far as the Sunni *tafsīrs* are concerned, the very early work of the Kufan Sufyān al-Thawrī (d. 161/778)[20] has little information fruitful for our concerns. Although in his commentary to *Sūrat al-Nisā'* (Q. 4)[21] he gives a useful interpretation of the term *mawālī* in Q. 4:33 as *'aṣaba*,[22] he does not comment on any other verse relevant to this study. The most important Sunni source to provide information about inheritance law in detail is the *tafsīr* by Muḥammad b. Jarīr al-Ṭabarī (d. 310/923).[23] Subsequent exegetes use the same kind of reasoning, for instance al-Nasafī (d. 710/1310), Ibn Kathīr (d. 774/1373), al-Alūsī (d. 1854) and Muḥammad 'Abduh (d. 1905). As for the Shi'i commentaries, the *tafsīr* of Furāt al-Kūfī (d. ca. 310/922) contains nothing on the Twelver doctrine rejecting the principle of agnation, because the main aim of the author was to comment on verses revealed about the *ahl al-Bayt*. In fact, in his exegesis of *Sūrat al-Nisā'* (Q. 4), Furāt does not refer to inheritance at all.[24] However, in line with his purposes, he stresses that the wording of Q. 8:75 and Q. 33:6 refers to the right of the wives of the Prophet to inherit from him; that is, those verses refer to the *arḥām* of the Prophet, who are the most entitled to his estate (*milk*) and power (*imra*).[25] The most comprehensive *tafsīr* expressing the Twelver point of view is Ṭūsī's *al-Tibyān fī tafsīr al-Qur'ān* whose main intent was both to emphasise the abolition of the principle of agnation and to support the legitimacy of the Family of the Prophet to inherit from him. The diverging interpretations can be seen in discussions of Q. 4:7, 11–12, 33, 176 and Q. 8:75 in particular.

Q. 4:11–12 and the Meaning of *walad* and *ikhwa*

Allah (thus) directs you as regards your children's (inheritance): to the male, a portion equal to that of two females: if only daughters, two or more, their share is two-thirds of the inheritance; if only one, her share is a half. For parents a sixth share of the inheritance to each if the deceased left children; if no children, and the parents are the (only) heirs, the mother has a third; if the deceased left brothers (or sisters), the mother has a sixth. (The distribution in all cases is) after the payment of legacies and debts. Ye know not whether your parents or your children are nearest to you in benefit.

> *These are settled portions ordained by Allah; and Allah is All-Knowing All-Wise.* [11]
>
> *In what your wives leave, your share is a half, if they leave no child; but if they leave a child, ye get a fourth; after payment of legacies and debts. In what ye leave; their share is a fourth, if ye leave no child; but if ye leave a child, they get an eighth; after payment of legacies and debts. If the man or woman whose inheritance is in question, has left neither ascendants nor descendants, but has left a brother or a sister, each one of the two gets a sixth; but if more than two they share in a third; after payment of legacies and debts; so that no loss is caused (to anyone). Thus is it ordained by Allah and Allah is All-Knowing, Most Forbearing.* [12]

The interpretation of the term *walad* has great relevance for the doctrine of agnation in this context. In its linguistic meaning, *walad* refers to a descendant, either a male or a female. If, however, in contrast to its linguistic meaning, the term *walad* is interpreted as including only males (Sunnis, including the Ẓāhirīs, and the Zaydīs and Ibāḍīs), the principle of agnation is stressed, and so agrees with the notion of the inheritance of a male descendant and ascendent (i.e. the father). In fact, if one or more sons, or any other male descendant, and the father are present, the father is considered by these schools only as an heir by quota (1/6), while the remainder is attributed to the sons. In this case, the sons, being the nearest agnates, have precedence over the father. However, if one or more daughters and the father are present, the father, as an agnate, has the advantage over the daughters. In this case, in addition to his Qur'anic share (1/6), the father also receives what remains after the attribution of the share to one or more daughters (1/2 or 2/3), as being the nearest agnate; this means that the father inherits based on two titles, that is, as a quota sharer and an agnate. However, the right of the mother is different; she inherits exclusively as an heir by quota (1/6), whether the descendants are males or females.

Turning to the term *ikhwa*, this refers to three or more siblings in general, both full and consanguine or uterine siblings. If, however, more importance is given to their male tie, only full or consanguine siblings can cause the reduction of the share of the mother from a third to a sixth. Ṭabarī, in his commentary on Q. 4:11,[26] re-affirms the validity of the principle of agnation by quoting the well-known prophetic hadith mentioned in the previous section: 'First allot the fixed shares to heirs by quota; the remainder shall be due to the nearest agnate [of the deceased].'

On his part, Ṭūsī repeats the specific Shi'i principles at Q. 4:11.[27] Firstly, he states that the rule concerning the daughter (*if only daughters, two or more, their share is two-thirds of the inheritance; if only one, her share is a half*) has a general relevance; thus Fāṭima had the right to inherit too. This is a legitimist claim, and it has important theological implications. Secondly, he says that what remains after the attribution of the share to one, two or more daughters should not be attributed to the agnates, because this is based on a weak (*ḍa'īf*) tradition. Thirdly, he reasserts the principle of proximity: any kind of brothers and/or sisters cannot inherit in the presence of the mother (class I), because she is more entitled to the estate than brothers/sisters (class II), since she is nearer by a degree to the deceased. Moreover, at Q. 4:12, Ṭūsī extensively expounds the Twelver system of inheritance based on kinship (*bi'l-qarāba*), which is regulated by two principles: (i) two or more heirs can inherit together only if they have the same entitlements (*asbāb*); (ii) two or more heirs can inherit together only if they are of the same degree (*daraja*).[28] In sum, for the Twelvers and Ismailis (with some exceptions) the principle of proximity plays a key role, both in the classification of heirs (three different classes) and inside each class. Therefore, brothers and/or sisters of any kind (class II) cannot inherit in the presence of descendants and parents (class I). If descendants and parents are not present, brothers and/or sisters and their descendants, grandfathers and grandmothers are the heirs (class II). In their absence, paternal and maternal uncles and aunts and their descendants are the heirs (class III).

Neither Sunni nor Twelver-Shi'i *tafsīr*s mention further disagreements originating from different interpretations of Q. 4:11. However, in the juridical literature, diverging solutions of some cases have further ramifications on the mother's inheritance rights. Sunnis, Zaydīs and Ibāḍīs interpret the term *walad* (descendant) in Q. 4:11 as 'a son or any other son's male descendant', with reference to the father, but as 'a son and a daughter or any other descendant in the male line, be he either a male or a female',[29] with reference to the mother. This, clearly, is an adaptation of the wording of Q. 4:11. In fact, according to these schools, the mother always inherits as an heir by quota and she only bars grandmothers from the inheritance. She has right to a sixth in the presence of direct descendants, either male or female; or in the presence of the descendants of a son of any degree, be they males or females; or in the presence of two or more full or consanguine or uterine brothers/sisters. Conversely, the mother has right to a third if the deceased has left none of these heirs.[30]

The term *ikhwa* is plural in the Qur'an; thus, the rule to be applied to two brothers/sisters would be the same that is valid for one brother/sister. However, the Sunni, Zaydī and Ibāḍī schools interpret it as 'two or more brothers' by analogy with Q. 4:11 (*fawq ithnatayn, two or more daughters*) and Q. 4:176 (*wa-in kānatā ithnatayn, two sisters*).[31] Conversely, based on a tradition from ʿAbd Allāh Ibn ʿAbbās (d. ca. 68/687), the Ẓāhirī school[32] interprets *ikhwa* literally as a plural. As a consequence, the mother has a right to her full share (a third) if the deceased has left one or two brothers, or one or two sisters, or a brother and a sister, and he has left neither a *walad* nor a male *walad* of a male.

Another element connected to the interpretation of Q. 4:11 regards the attribution of the amount detracted from the share of the mother, when she passes from a third to a sixth (partial exclusion) because of the presence of brothers/sisters. The specific case concerns the inheritance of parents and brothers. Who is entitled to receive the difference between a third and a sixth? The doctrine generally agreed on by all, except the Shiʿi schools,[33] is that such difference is given exclusively to the father as an agnate.[34]

The Twelver and Ismaili doctrine on these three points shows a different interpretation of the Qur'anic verses. Firstly, *walad* means a descendant of any degree and any sex, according to the proper sense of the Arabic term. Secondly, the mother (class I) bars brothers and/or sisters of any degree, and their descendants, from inheritance (class II). Although the plural *ikhwa* is interpreted as 'two or more brothers, or a brother and two or more sisters, or four sisters at least', as the other schools do. However, Twelvers and Ismailis state that siblings partially excluding the mother must be full or consanguine siblings. Uterine siblings, whatever their number, can neither inherit nor bar any heir from inheritance when parents are present.[35]

Q. 4:33 and the Meaning of *mawālī*

> *To (benefit) every one We have appointed sharers and heirs to property left by parents and relatives. To those also to whom your right hand was pledged give their due portion: For truly Allah is Witness to all things.*

The term *mawālī* (sg. *mawlā*) is relevant for our purpose because its interpretation centres around the question of the inheritance of agnates. *Mawlā* means both a 'patron' and his 'client', related by a fictive kinship tie deriving from manumission. The patronage (*walā'*) creates a special relationship between a manumitter and his freedman, so that 'the manumitted slave is considered as a member of the manumitter's family and that the manumitter, be that person a male or a female, has the right to inherit in accordance with agnation'.[36] As a result of this, the Qur'anic term *mawlā* is connected to the principle of agnation from the linguistic, historical and juridical points of view. Sufyān al-Thawrī renders *mawālī* as *'aṣaba* (agnates).[37] Ṭabarī repeats that the term *mawālī* is generally interpreted as 'agnates' in this context, for instance the sons of paternal uncles, the brothers and the remaining agnates.[38] This interpretation is supported by some hadiths,[39] which simply state that *mawālī* corresponds to *'aṣaba*, with an interesting specification that 'the agnates (*al-aṣaba*) were the *mawālī* in the *Jāhiliyya*'.[40] In another hadith, *mawālī* are compared to the *awliyā'*,[41] specified as *awliyā' al-ab* (relatives of the father), or *awliyā' al-akh* (relatives of the brother), or *awliyā' ibn al-akh* (relatives of the nephew), or *awliyā'* of the remaining agnates,[42] in other words, all agnates. In the light of his reading, Ṭabarī relates an explicative wording of the Qur'anic verse, on the authority of Abū Ja'far al-Bāqir (d. 114/732), the fifth imam of the Twelvers: '*To (benefit) every one* of you (*wa likullikum*), meaning people (*al-nās*), *We have appointed* agnates (*ja'alnā 'aṣaba*) who will inherit (*yarithūna*) from *property left by parents and heirs* from the estate'.[43] However, Ṭabarī also quotes the opposing (Shi'i) doctrine found in some hadiths,[44] where the term *mawālī* is explicitly rendered as *waratha* or *ahl al-mīrāth* (heirs).

Who, then, are the *mawālī* for the Shi'is? The refutation of agnation by Ṭūsī is incisive here. He is aware that the Sunnis identify the *mawālī* with the agnates, based on the authority of Ibn 'Abbās, Mujāhid b. Jabr (d. 104/722–3), Qatāda and Ibn Zayd, but he agrees with the tradition of Ismā'īl b. 'Abd al-Raḥmān al-Suddī (d. 127/745), who compares the *mawālī* to heirs. The latter interpretation is considered sound by Ṭūsī,[45] as Q. 4:33 says: *To (benefit) every one We have appointed sharers and heirs* (*waratha*) *to property left by parents* (*al-wālidāni*) *and relatives* (*wa'l-aqrabūna*). In discussing the interpretation of the term *mawālī*, medieval scholars also sought to understand how it had been used in the pre-Islamic period. Thus, Ṭabarī refers to the fact that, according to the Bedouins, a son of a paternal uncle, thus an agnate, is called *al-mawlā*, which he supports with a poetic verse.[46] Ṭūsī himself seems to corroborate this explanation.[47] In fact, he expounds the meaning of the term *mawlā* as the one who has a direct *wilāya* (legal power, guardianship, tutorship; the equivalent of Latin '*potestas*') over something. Ṭūsī also cites the poetic verse quoted by Ṭabarī, but he gives *mawlā* a more general meaning. As a matter of fact, according to Ṭūsī, a *mawlā* may be of different kinds, such as a patron, a client, an agnate, a confederate (*ḥalīf*, allied), or a legal guardian; essentially a *mawlā* is someone who is more entitled to something; so, he may also be an heir, who is more entitled to the inheritance.

Thus there is no doubt that Q. 4:33 refers to the heirs in general, but what kind of heir exactly? The subtle difference between the Sunni and Shi'i interpretations of *mawālī* is that the former keeps the original Arabic meaning of the term as *mawālī* = agnates = male heirs, while the latter identifies *mawālī* with Qur'anic heirs, who, for them, are the blood relatives (*dhawū'l-arḥām*). This Shi'i interpretation seems somewhat forced. Yet, the term *mawālī* also appears in Q. 19:5, when Zachariah says: '*Now I fear* (*what*) *my relatives* (*and colleagues*) (*al-mawālā*) (*will do*) *after me* (*min warā'ī*)'. In this context, which is not connected to the law of inheritance, Ṭūsī rightly stresses the pre-Islamic meaning of the term *mawālī* as kinsfolk,[48] and he relates a report comparing them to the *'aṣaba*. According to another report, they are the *awliyā'* (here: relatives). Moreover, Ṭūsī identifies the *mawālī* with the sons of the paternal uncles, based on the same poetic verse quoted above.[49]

Q. 4:176 and the Meaning of *kalāla* and *walad*

> *They ask thee for a legal decision. Say: Allah directs (thus) about those who leave no descendants or ascendants as heirs. If it is a man that dies, leaving a sister but no child, she shall have half the inheritance: if (such a deceased was) a woman, who left no child, her brother takes her inheritance: if there are two sisters, they shall have two-thirds of the inheritance (between them): if there are brothers and sisters, (they share), the male having twice the share of the female. Thus doth Allah make clear to you (His law) lest ye err. And Allah hath knowledge of all things.*

The different interpretations of the term *kalāla* provided by the law schools reflect the different solutions given to the questions about the position of the grandfather in the law of inheritance, particularly in the case of full or consanguine sisters inheriting with the daughters. The literal sense of *kalāla* requires that the grandfather is treated as the father, according to the pre-Islamic agnatic rule, with the consequent exclusion of all siblings. However, some objections emerged concerning: (i) the exclusion of siblings, who are Qur'anic heirs; (ii) the presence of the grandfather, who is not mentioned in the Qur'an, and (iii) the exclusion of the full or consanguine sisters, who are also Qur'anic heirs, because of the presence of the daughters.

Each school gave its own definition of the term *kalāla*, according to the following scheme. As regards the uterine siblings, the Sunni, Ẓāhirī, Zaydī, and Ibāḍī juridical schools define *kalāla* as 'a person who has died leaving neither *walad* nor *wālid* (forefathers)'. In this conception, the *walad* are male descendants of any degree, and daughters and female descendants of male children, and the *wālid* is the father and paternal (or 'true') grandfather (*jadd ṣaḥīḥ*) (all schools).

Concerning full or consanguine siblings, the definition of *kalāla* varies. For Ḥanafīs, Ẓāhirīs, and Ibāḍīs the *kalāla* is 'a person who has died leaving neither *walad* nor *wālid*'. For the Mālikīs, Shāfiʿīs, Ḥanbalīs, and Zaydīs, the *kalāla* is 'a person who has died leaving neither *walad* nor *ab* (father)'. In all cases, the *walad* refers to 'male descendants of any degree alone or together with daughters or female descendants of male children of any degree, when brothers/sisters are excluded from inheritance'. For the Sunnis, Zaydīs and Ibāḍīs, *kalāla* refers to 'male descendants of any degree alone, when one sister or more cannot inherit as an *ʿaṣaba maʿa ghayrihi*, together with one daughter or more'. Lastly, for the Ẓāhirīs *kalāla* is defined as 'daughters or sons' daughters', in which case sisters are considered as *ʿaṣaba* only if there is no one else.[50] The Twelver and Ismaili schools interpret *kalāla* differently, and believe it refers to uterine siblings and full or consanguine siblings. Thus, in this case (Q. 4:176), *kalāla* refers to full or consanguine siblings, when a person has died leaving neither a *walad* nor *wālid*. Here *walad* is understood as male and female descendants of any degree, and *wālid* as both the father and the mother.[51]

In his exegesis, Ṭabarī's main purpose in his treatment of *kalāla* is to support the doctrine of the *ʿaṣaba maʿa ghayrihi*, generally agreed on by the *ahl al-qibla* (i.e. the Sunni community), but which was rejected by Ibn ʿAbbās and ʿUrwa Ibn al-Zubayr (d. ca. 94/712–13).[52] The divergence originates from the interpretation of the terms *walad* and *kalāla*. Such a doctrine cannot be drawn from Q. 4:176, as admitted by Ṭabarī himself. For this he is forced to resort to a convoluted argument to show that there is somehow a connection between the legal doctrine and the Qur'an. Thus, in response to the objection that it is not derived from this Qur'anic verse, Ṭabarī argues that the Qur'anic rule fixing the share of a full or consanguine sister should be applied only when descendants, both male and female, are not present. However, if only a female descendant is present, a sister cannot be included any longer among the heirs, but she is to be considered as an agnate (*ʿaṣaba*).[53]

According to Ṭabarī, the Qur'an does not state that if the deceased does leave a *walad*, the sister cannot claim any right in the inheritance, which the doctrine of Ibn ʿAbbās and Ibn al-Zubayr seems to infer. On the contrary, the actual wording of the Qur'an in Q. 4:176 fixes a determined share in favour of a sister only when she inherits from someone who is an 'indirect heir' (*kalāla*), but the Qur'an omits to mention how much the sister is entitled to receive when she inherits from someone who is not a *kalāla*. However, the doctrine of the *ʿaṣaba maʿa ghayrihi* was strongly established in the prophetic Sunna.[54]

Ṭūsī's commentary on Q. 4:176 is quite different.[55] On the one hand, he stresses the negation of the rule of agnation in general, and repeats that the hadith supporting the principle of agnation is weak and a *khabar wāḥid*. Thus, according to this interpretation, what remains after the attribution of the share to one or more sisters cannot be attributed to the agnates. On the other hand, Ṭūsī rejects the doctrine of the *ʿaṣaba maʿa ghayrihi*, based on linguistic analysis. According to the linguists, a daughter is considered a *walad* in the same manner as a son is. Thus, the mere fact that this Qur'anic verse considers that a sister can only inherit in the absence of a *walad*, excludes any possibility of a sister inheriting in the presence of a daughter, since *walad* is used for both sons and daughters. Moreover, Ṭūsī argues again that the hadith supporting the doctrine of *ʿaṣaba maʿa ghayrihi* is a *khabar wāḥid*, which cannot be used as a legal proof, because it is contrary to an explicit text (*naṣṣ*) of the Qur'an.[56] Ṭūsī also cites the opposing position given on the authority of Ibn ʿAbbās, that the Prophet did not consider sisters as agnates in the presence of daughters.

The earliest Ẓāhirī doctrine corresponds to the Twelver and Ismaili position, as maintained by Dāwūd al-Ẓāhirī (d. 270/884)[57] and attested by ʿAlī b. Aḥmad Ibn Ḥazm (d. 456/1064),[58] rejecting the doctrine of the *ʿaṣaba maʿa ghayrihi*. The literal (*ẓāhir*) interpretation of the Qur'anic verses leads this school to reject the idea that such doctrine is present in the Qur'an. Later on, however, Ibn Ḥazm followed a middle course, distinguishing two hypotheses.[59] Firstly, if a daughter, a sister and an agnate (e.g. a paternal uncle, or a son of a paternal uncle, or a son of a brother, or a patron or his agnate relatives) are present, the remainder, after the attribution to the daughter of her Qur'anic share of a half, is allotted to the agnate, with the exclusion of the sister. Secondly, if, no agnate is present, the remainder is attributed to one or more full or consanguine sisters. It is noteworthy that the Ẓāhirīs ignore the hadith generally used as support of the doctrine of *'aṣaba ma'a ghayrihi*, but they quote the well-known hadith regarding the agnates *iure proprio* (*'aṣaba bi-nafsihi*) encountered in previous sections.

Q. 8:75 and the Meaning of *arḥām*

And those who accept Faith subsequently, and adopt exile, and fight for the Faith in your company – they are of you. But kindred by blood have prior rights against each other in the Book of Allah. Verily Allah is well acquainted with all things.

The interpretation by the Shi'is, consistent with the Arabic language, of the term *arḥām* as blood relatives, allows them to classify the heirs into classes according to their proximity to the deceased; such interpretation excludes the principle of agnation as an element of pre-eminence of certain heirs over the others. For Shi'i jurists, the importance of Q. 8:75 lies in the statement, *But kindred by blood* (*wa ūlū'l-arḥām*) *have prior rights against each other* (*ba'ḍuhum awlā bi-ba'ḍin*) *in the Book of Allah*.

While Ṭabarī relates no specific Sunni doctrine in his commentary on this verse,[60] Ṭūsī repeats that it demonstrates that the next of kin is more entitled to the inheritance, whether or not he is an agnate, and whether or not he is an heir by quota (*tasmiya*).[61] The same rule is repeated by Ṭūsī in his commentary on Q. 33:6, which states:

The Prophet is closer to the Believers than their own selves, and his wives are their mothers. Blood-relations among each other have closer personal ties, in the Decree of Allah, than (*the Brotherhood of*) *Believers and Muhajirs: nevertheless do ye what is just to your closest friends: such is the writing in the Decree* (*of Allah*).

Ṭūsī argues that this verse abrogates the tie of brotherhood and he reaffirms the principle that the next of kin is more entitled to receive the inheritance.[62] The tradition supporting the right of the agnates is, as seen above, a *khabar wāḥid*, and has a problematic use as a source of law, since it contradicts the text of the Qur'an. The evident consequence is that no brother and sister can inherit in the presence of a daughter or the mother (class I), because the latter are closer to the deceased, in the same manner that paternal and maternal uncles and aunts and their descendants (class III) cannot inherit in the presence of a sister (class II).

Inheritance Law, Agnation and the 'Named Cases'

In the different interpretations of the Qur'anic verses examined above, it can be seen that the Shi'is created a coherent system based on general principles. Since the Qur'an provided scriptural authority for the legal judgements regarding law, it is possible to see the ways in which the different legal schools interpret specific words in different ways to accommodate their own interpretation of the inheritance laws. The simplicity of the inheritance law for Twelvers and Ismailis meant that they did not need to puzzle over individual cases as much as can be seen in other legal schools. However, the way in which many law schools developed inheritance laws which overlapped the Qur'anic fixed shares with the pre-Islamic principle of agnation meant that complex cases came into being. Each legal school found it necessary to examine the position of each heir in all possible cases; and out of this a body of cases developed which were given individual names (*al-masā'il al-mulaqqaba*). These cases can be described as casuistic and they developed very complicated solutions to difficult case questions. Analysis of these 'named cases' allows us to highlight the transition from Qur'an to *fiqh* and to point out the substantial effort made by the scholars in the elaboration of the juridical system to answer complex inheritance scenarios. A few observations can be made.

The Sunni (including the Ẓāhirī), Zaydī, and Ibāḍī schools follow no general principles in the inheritance law. Thus they were compelled to adapt Qur'anic provisions, sometimes elaborating new rules. Jurists also gave special names to particular cases. Some cases do not have any particular relationship to the Qur'anic material and do not have any special doctrinal relevance, as in the cases called *al-yatīmatāni* ('the two female orphans'), because the estate is divided into halves; for instance, if the husband and a full or consanguine sister are present, each one of them is allotted one half (see Q. 4:12 and 176); or if the husband and the father, or the husband and a full or consanguine brother, are present, the husband receives one half (see Q. 4:12) and the father, or the brother, is attributed one half as an agnate.[63] Some names reflect the results of the division of the estate, like *umm al-arāmil* ('mother of the widows'), *umm al-furūkh* ('mother of the chicks'), *tisʿīniyyat Zayd* (a case solved by Zayd by having ninety as the denominator), *mukhtaṣarat Zayd* (a case solved by Zayd by reducing the denominator from 108 to 54); somehow they describe the situation resulting from the division of the estate, but they do not have any doctrinal implications. However, in the two cases known as *al-ʿumariyyatāni*, a definite rule of Q. 4:11, that a mother should receive a third of the estate, is changed by the Sunni, Zaydī and Ibāḍī schools. In fact, they interpret the wording of this verse (*. . . if no children, and the parents are the* [*only*] *heirs, the mother has a third . . .*) as: '*. . . if* [there are] *no children, and the parents are the* (*only*) *heirs, the mother has a third* [of what remains after the attribution of the share to the husband/wife] . . .' However, the largest group of cases are related to the reduction of shares (*ʿawl*) and to the inheritance of the paternal grandfather. They show a high level of complexity in the application of the inheritance laws, but each case follows the general interpretations of the Qur'an seen in the discussion above. The Sunni, Zaydī, and Ibāḍī schools maintain the principle of agnation, which is reliant on the interpretations of specific words found in the Qur'an, particularly *walad*, *ikhwa*, *mawālī* and *kalāla*.

The question of proportional reduction was much debated among the earliest scholars because it modifies the Qur'anic order of fixed shares. It is not without relevance that a case was called 'responding with curses' (*mas'alat al-mubāhala*), showing the strong reaction against this principle. In brief, if the estate suffices, each heir receives his own share; if not, a solution needs to be found. If the amount of the shares to be attributed is greater than the estate available (*farīḍa ʿā'ila*), Sunnis, Zaydīs and Ibāḍīs have recourse to the proportional reduction of all the shares, which can be seen in a number of the 'named cases'. The reason that the reduction should be applied to all the heirs is that there is no distinction among them in the Qur'an, being that all of them are heirs by quota alike. Conversely, Ẓāhirīs, Twelvers and Ismailis believe that Qur'anic shares cannot be proportionally reduced. If the amount of the shares to be attributed is greater than the estate available, 'only the juridically weakest heirs – children and full and/or consanguine brothers and/or sisters – must suffer a reduction (*naqṣ*) of their shares'.[64]

Scholars also broadly debated the question of the right of the paternal grandfather since the earliest period of the formation of the Islamic juridical system.[65] A grandfather is not a Qur'anic heir; but how could an agnate like a grandfather, such an authoritative figure in the context of a patriarchal society, be excluded from the inheritance because of the presence of full or consanguine brothers and/or sisters, even if the latter are heirs by quota? The different solutions depend on the interpretation of the Qur'anic verses concerning the father's and brothers'/sisters' inheritance rights. Some legal schools (Ḥanafīs, Ẓāhirīs, Ibāḍīs) give precedence to the agnatic pre-Islamic principle simply comparing the paternal grandfather to the father, when brothers/sisters are present. Some others (Mālikīs, Shāfiʿīs, Ḥanbalīs, Zaydīs) combine the agnatic rule with the Qur'anic provisions, granting the grandfather the right to inherit together with full or consanguine brothers and/or sisters, but in a privileged position with respect to them. Twelvers and Ismailis, however, based on their interpretations of Q. 4:7, Q. 8:75 and Q. 33:6, refer to the principle of proximity, by which they consider the paternal grandfather on the same footing as a full or consanguine brother. The linearity of the doctrine regarding the inheritance of the grandfather elaborated by these two Shiʿi schools and their strict adherence to the wording of the Qur'an did not give rise to complex cases. For this, Twelvers and Ismailis do not know any of complex inheritance cases concerning the paternal grandfather, which is not the case amongst the remaining schools, which created a wide range of names, almost a new terminology, for particular cases.

Although not linked to particular named cases, it is worth noting that some Qur'anic terms were interpreted in different ways by jurists, sometimes contravening their literal meaning. So the word *walad* (Q. 4:11) was rendered by Sunnis, Zaydīs and Ibāḍīs as 'a son or any other son's male descendant', with reference to the father, and as 'a son and a daughter or any other descendant in the male line, be he either a male or a female', with reference to the mother. Moreover, the plural *ikhwa* in Q. 4:11 is considered by all the schools, except the Ẓāhirī school, as also including the dual, contrary to Arabic grammatical rules. Moreover, the doctrine of *'aṣaba ma'a ghayrihi* ('agnation with another'), which constitutes a new and somewhat strange terminology, is justified by the Sunnis, Zaydīs and Ibāḍīs by means of their interpretation of the terms *walad* and *kalāla*, found in Q. 4:176.

The 'named cases' reveal an evolutionary line, starting from the pagan era to the jurisprudential elaboration of later jurists. Pre-Islamic inheritance law was thoroughly reformed in the Qur'an, but two different broad systems emerged which were based on different interpretation of Qur'anic verses: a Sunni system and a Shi'i system. Within the Sunni system, two trends became prominent. One was closer to the pre-Islamic spirit, based on the pre-eminence of agnates, while the other was inspired by the Qur'anic provision of allotted shares. This has resulted in major differences between Sunnis (including the Ẓāhirīs), Zaydīs, and Ibāḍīs on the one hand, and Twelver and Ismaili Shi'is on the other: the first safeguard the right of agnates to the estate, while the latter reject the agnatic rule and consider only the blood ties, according to the principle of proximity.

Appendix: The 'Named Cases' (*al-masāʾil al-mulaqqaba*)

1. *Umm al-arāmil*

The name *umm al-arāmil* ('mother of the widows') is used by the Ḥanbalī Muḥammad b. Aḥmad Ibn Qudāma (d. 620/1223),[66] with reference to the case of two grandmothers, four uterine sisters, eight consanguine sisters and three wives. According to the Sunnis, Zaydīs and Ibāḍīs, grandmothers have right to a sixth, uterine sisters to a third, consanguine sisters to two thirds and the wives to a quarter, giving the following: $\frac{1}{6} + \frac{1}{3} + \frac{2}{3} + \frac{1}{4} = \frac{2}{12} + \frac{4}{12} + \frac{8}{12} + \frac{3}{12} = \frac{17}{12}$. The proportional reduction of the shares is carried out by increasing the denominator to 17. The solution gives rise (*umm*) to a situation where each heir receives a unique share, like widows (*arāmil*).

2. *Umm al-furūkh / Dhāt al-furūkh*

Another case is *umm al-furūkh* or *dhāt al-furūkh* ('mother of the chicks'), so named because of the great proportional reduction of the shares. The typical case of *umm al-furūkh* is the inheritance of the husband, the mother/grandmother, two or more uterine brothers and/or sisters, two full or consanguine sisters (or a full sister and one or more consanguine sisters): $\frac{1}{2} + \frac{1}{6} + \frac{1}{3} + \frac{2}{3} = \frac{3}{6} + \frac{1}{6} + \frac{2}{6} + \frac{4}{6} = \frac{10}{6}$, which needs to become $\frac{10}{10}$. This case is discussed by the Shāfiʿī Abū'l-ʿAbbās Aḥmad b. Muḥammad al-Jurjānī (d. 482/1089),[67] the Ḥanbalī Ibn Qudāma,[68] and the Twelver Ṭūsī, who, however, did not agree with such a solution.[69]

3. *Tisʿīniyyat Zayd*

Two cases are traced back to Zayd b. Thābit (d. 45/666), who was considered an expert jurist in the field of inheritance law, and to whom the Mālikī school often refers. Both cases are examined by Ibn Qudāma, who presumably created them. The first is *tisʿīniyyat Zayd*,[70] so called because the denominator of the fraction is raised to ninety. It concerns the inheritance of the grandfather, the mother/grandmother, a full sister, two consanguine brothers and a consanguine sister. According to Ḥanafīs, Ẓāhirīs and Ibāḍīs, the mother/grandmother has right to a sixth, while the remainder is attributed to the grandfather as the closest agnate (*ʿaṣaba*). However, according to the Mālikīs, Shāfiʿīs and Ḥanbalīs, the mother/grandmother has right to a sixth (= $3/18$), and the grandfather to a third of the remainder ($15/18$) which is $5/18$. The remaining $10/18$ is divided among all the brothers and sisters attributing to a male the equivalent share of two females. Then, part of the amount allotted to the two consanguine brothers and a consanguine sister returns to the full sister to fulfil her Qur'anic share of a half, that is $9/18$ out of the remaining $10/18$. What remains ($1/18$) is divided into five parts between the two consanguine brothers and a consanguine sister, with the male receiving twice the share of the female: $1/18 \div 5 = 1/18 \times 1/5 = 1/90$; thus, $2/90$ to each consanguine brother and $1/90$ to the consanguine sister. Then all the fractions are summed: $3/18 + 5/18 + 9/18 + 5/90 = 15/90 + 25/90 + 45/90 + 5/90 = 90/90$. Thus, the total is $90/90$, of which $15/90$ goes to the mother/grandmother, $25/90$ to the grandfather, $45/90$ to the full sister, $2/90$ to each of the two consanguine brothers and $1/90$ to the consanguine sister.

4. *Mukhtaṣarat Zayd*

The second case attributed to Zayd concerns the inheritance of a grandfather, a mother/grandmother, a full sister, a consanguine brother and a consanguine sister. According to Ḥanafīs, Ẓāhirīs and Ibāḍīs, the mother/grandmother has right to a sixth as a fixed share, while the grandfather receives what remains as the closest agnate.[71] According to the Mālikīs, Shāfiʿīs and Ḥanbalīs, the right of the grandfather to receive his minimum share is guaranteed by two different means, with the result that all the co-heirs have the same amount in both calculations: i) the grandfather may be considered as a brother, or ii) he can claim what remains after the attribution of the shares to the co-heirs. In the first case the mother/grandmother has right to a sixth (= $6/36$). What remains ($5/6 = 30/36$) is divided by six among the remaining heirs, a male having as much as the portion of two females: $10/36$ to the grandfather, $5/36$ to the full sister, $10/36$ to the consanguine brother and $5/36$ to the consanguine sister.

In the second solution, the mother/grandmother has right to a sixth (= $6/36$) and the grandfather to a third of what remains (= $10/36$).

The remainder ($^{20}/_{36}$) is divided into four parts between the full sister ($^{5}/_{36}$), the consanguine brother ($^{10}/_{36}$) and the consanguine sister ($^{5}/_{36}$), attributing to a male the double share of a female. Hereafter the operation follows the same criterion: that is, part of the $^{15}/_{36}$ given to the consanguine brother and the consanguine sister returns to the full sister in order to integrate her Qur'anic share of a half. Therefore, the amount of $^{13}/_{36}$ out of $^{15}/_{36}$ should be added to the share of the full sister: $^{5}/_{36} + ^{13}/_{36} = ^{18}/_{36} = ^{1}/_{2}$, while the remaining $^{2}/_{36}$ is divided between the consanguine brother and the consanguine sister, attributing to a male a double share of a female: $^{2}/_{36} \div 3 = ^{2}/_{36} \text{ x } ^{1}/_{3} = ^{2}/_{108}$; $^{2}/_{108} \text{ x } 3 = ^{6}/_{108}$, of which $^{4}/_{108}$ go to the consanguine brother and $^{2}/_{108}$ to the consanguine sister. Then all the fractions are summed: $^{6}/_{36} + ^{10}/_{36} + ^{18}/_{36} + ^{4}/_{108} + ^{2}/_{108} = ^{18}/_{108} + ^{30}/_{108} + ^{54}/_{108} + ^{4}/_{108} + ^{2}/_{108} = ^{9}/_{54} + ^{15}/_{54} + ^{27}/_{54} + ^{2}/_{54} + ^{1}/_{54} = ^{54}/_{54}$, of which $^{9}/_{54}$ is given to the mother/grandmother, $^{15}/_{54}$ to the grandfather, $^{27}/_{54}$ to the full sister, $^{2}/_{54}$ to the consanguine brother and $^{1}/_{54}$ to the consanguine sister.[72]

5. *'Umariyytāni / Gharrawāni*

Two cases, involving the parents and the husband/wife, lead the Sunni, Zaydī and Ibāḍī schools to change an explicit Qur'anic rule, by which the mother is deprived of her Qur'anic right to receive her share of a third out of the whole estate (Q. 4:11), and she is allotted only a third of what remains after the attribution of the share to the husband/wife. The reason is that the mother would be in a more advantageous position than the father if she received a third of the whole estate.[73] The question is whether the literal wording of Q. 4:11 should be followed, with the result that the mother would receive twice the share of the father (a half to the husband, a third to the mother, and a sixth to the father), or slightly less than the share of the father (a quarter [= $^{3}/_{12}$] to the wife, a third [= $^{4}/_{12}$] to the mother, and $^{5}/_{12}$ to the father). However, another Qur'anic rule, given in Q. 4:11 and 4:176, states that a male has a right to twice the share of a female. In other words, should pre-eminence be given to the position of the father as an agnate, according to the pre-Islamic principle, or should the Qur'anic principles be emphasised?

The solution of the Sunni, Zaydī and Ibāḍī schools is a sort of a compromise between two principles: a male has precedence over a female (pre-Islamic customary law), but his pre-eminence is limited to receiving twice the share of a female (Qur'an). In order to reach such a result, a device is used giving the mother only a third of what remains after the attribution of the share to the husband/wife. When the deceased leaves a husband, father and mother: ½ (= 3/6) is left to the husband, a third of what remains is left to the mother, equivalent to a sixth out of the whole estate, and two sixths to the father.[74]

When the deceased leaves a wife, father and mother: a quarter (= 3/12) is left to the wife, a third of what remains (= 3/12) is left to the mother, corresponding to a quarter of the whole estate, and a half (= 6/12) is left to the father.[75]

The Ẓāhirī school,[76] based on a tradition given on the authority of Ibn ʿAbbās[77] and ʿAlī,[78] attributes to the mother a third of the whole estate in both cases, thus interpreting the provision of the Qur'an literally: the father has right only to the remainder, be it little or much. This is also the linear solution followed by Twelvers and Ismailis.[79]

6. *Mas'alat al-mubāhala*

The denomination means 'responding with curses' (*bāhala*), because of the reaction of Ibn ʿAbbās to the solution of the first case to which the proportional reduction was applied. The case concerns the inheritance of the husband, a full or consanguine sister and the mother.[80] According to the Sunnis, Zaydīs and Ibāḍīs, the husband has right to a half, the sister to a half and the mother to a third: ½ + ½ + ⅓ = 3/6 + 3/6 + 2/6 = 8/6. Applying the proportional reduction to all the shares, the denominator is increased to 8; so the husband receives 3/8, the sister 3/8 and the mother 2/8.[81] Conversely, Dāwūd al-Ẓāhirī[82] (d. 270/884), on the authority of Ibn ʿAbbās,[83] attributes half to the husband and a third to the mother: ½ + ⅓ = 3/6 + 2/6 = 5/6. Thus, only the sister suffers the damage; she can claim the remainder (only 1/6).

Twelvers and Ismailis, following their classification of the heirs into three classes, exclude the sister (class II) from the inheritance because of the presence of the mother (class I). Thus, the husband has right to a half (= 3/6), the mother to a third (= 2/6) as a fixed share and she is also entitled to the remainder (1/6) as *radd* (increase).

7. *Masʾalat al-iltizām*

On at least one occasion, the *madhhab* of Ibn ʿAbbās is forced to have recourse to proportional reduction. This case concerns the husband, the mother and two uterine brothers or sisters. According to the law schools, except the Ẓāhirī and Shiʿi schools, the solution is: half to the husband, a sixth to the mother and a third to the uterine brothers/sisters: 1/2 + 1/6 + 1/3 = 6/6. The shares cover the amount available. However, this cannot be the solution accepted by Ibn ʿAbbās, because, according to one of the doctrines specific to him, two brothers/sisters do not cause the partial reduction of the share of the mother from a third to a sixth. Thus, according to him, the husband has right to a half, the mother to a third and two uterine brothers or sisters to a third: 1/2 + 1/3 + 1/3 = 3/6 + 2/6 + 2/6 = 7/6. Since all the co-heirs are Qur'anic heirs by quota, none of them can be deprived of his full right. Thus the proportional reduction of all the shares is necessarily required in this case.[84]

According to the Ẓāhirī school,[85] only uterine brothers or sisters suffer the reduction of their share, thus receiving only the remaining sixth: a half (= 3/6) to the husband, a third (= 2/6) to the mother, and a sixth to the uterine brothers or sisters.

Twelvers and Ismailis follow their own principles. First of all, two uterine brothers or sisters do not cause the partial reduction of the share of the mother from a third to a sixth. Secondly, the mother bars the brothers from the inheritance. Thirdly, spouses are not entitled to receive the increasing (*radd*) of their shares. Based on these rules, the husband has right to a half (= 3/6) as a fixed share, and the mother to a third (= 2/6) as a determined share; what remains (1/6) is increased exclusively to the mother, as was seen in the case *Masʾalat al-mubāhala* above.[86]

8. *al-Minbariyya* (*al-naḥīla / al-bakhīla*)

The best known case involving proportional reduction is called *al-minbariyya*. The question is said to have been submitted to ʿAlī while he was on the minbar,[87] and he decreased the share of the wife from an eighth to a ninth. The case regards the inheritance of the wife (an eighth), two daughters (two thirds) and parents (a sixth each): $\frac{1}{8} + \frac{2}{3} + \frac{1}{6} + \frac{1}{6} = \frac{3}{24} + \frac{16}{24} + \frac{4}{24} + \frac{4}{24} = \frac{27}{24}$. The estate is not sufficient. Having recourse to the proportional reduction of all the shares, the denominator is increased to 27. Thus the wife receives a ninth ($= \frac{3}{27}$).[88]

The opposite rigid doctrine rejecting the proportional reduction of all the shares, unanimously attributed to Ibn ʿAbbās and followed by Dāwūd al-Ẓāhirī[89] and the Ẓāhirī school,[90] assumes that if God had wanted, He would have given instruction on this subject. Thus Qur'anic provisions must be strictly interpreted and the shares should not be reduced. Since shares must fall in some way within the amount available if the estate is not sufficient for all, the reduction damages only sons and daughters, full or consanguine brothers and sisters.[91] This is the doctrine followed by the Twelvers and Ismailis,[92] who do not consider this tradition of ʿAlī to be sound. Thus they reject the doctrine of the proportional reduction of all the shares and admit that only those heirs who, depending on circumstances, have a right to what remains after the attribution of fixed shares suffer the damage; these are the descendants and the full or consanguine brothers and/or sisters. As a matter of fact, these heirs can sometimes claim a determined share, while at other times they receive what remains after the attribution of the shares to the co-heirs. Thus, according to the Twelvers and Ismailis, the case of the inheritance of the wife, two daughters and parents is solved by allotting an eighth to the wife, and a sixth to each parent: $\frac{1}{8} + \frac{1}{6} + \frac{1}{6} = \frac{3}{24} + \frac{4}{24} + \frac{4}{24} = \frac{11}{24}$. In this case only daughters suffer the reduction of their share, receiving what remains ($\frac{13}{24}$), instead of their full share of two thirds ($= \frac{16}{24}$). Then this remainder ($\frac{13}{24}$) is divided into two parts: $\frac{13}{24} \div 2 = \frac{13}{24} \times \frac{1}{2} = \frac{13}{48}$ to each daughter. All fractions can then be summed: $\frac{3}{24} + \frac{4}{24} + \frac{4}{24} + \frac{13}{48} + \frac{13}{48} = \frac{6}{48} + \frac{8}{48} + \frac{8}{48} + \frac{13}{48} + \frac{13}{48} = \frac{48}{48}$. Thus, the final solution is: $\frac{6}{48}$ to the wife, $\frac{8}{48}$ to the father, $\frac{8}{48}$ to the mother and $\frac{13}{48}$ to each of the two daughters.

9. *al-Kharqāʾ* (*ʿUthmāniyya / muthallatha / ḥajjājiyya / musabbaʿa / musaddasa*)

This case, whose solutions are well attested in very early sources, gave rise to deep divergences among the early scholars. It has various names: *al-kharqāʾ*, *ʿUthmāniyya*, *muthallatha*, *ḥajjājiyya*, *musabbaʿa* and *musaddasa*.[93] The case concerns the inheritance of the paternal grandfather, the mother and a full or consanguine sister.

According to the Ḥanafīs, Ẓāhirīs and Ibāḍīs, on the authority of Ibn ʿAbbās[94] or Abū Bakr,[95] the mother has the right to a third, while the remainder is allotted to the grandfather as agnate. The sister is excluded because of the presence of the grandfather, who is considered to be like the father. Mālikīs, Shāfiʿīs and Ḥanbalīs, on the authority of Zayd b. Thābit, instead, believe that the mother has right to a third (= $3/9$). What remains ($6/9$) is divided between the grandfather ($4/9$) and the sister ($2/9$), attributing to the male twice the share of a female.[96] Lastly, Zaydīs, on the authority of ʿAlī, state that the mother has right to a third (= $2/6$) as a fixed share and the sister to a half (= $3/6$) as a fixed share; the remainder ($1/6$) is given to the grandfather as agnate.[97]

Two solutions are related on the authority of Ibn Masʿūd: (i) a half (= $3/6$) is left to the sister, a sixth ($1/6$) to the mother, and the remainder ($2/6$) goes to the grandfather; or otherwise said, a half (= $3/6$) to the sister, a third of what remains (= $1/6$) to the mother, and the remainder ($2/6$) to the grandfather;[98] (ii) a half (= $2/4$) is left to the sister, while the remainder is divided in half between the mother ($1/4$) and the grandfather ($1/4$).[99] Lastly, on the authority of ʿUthmān, it is related that the estate is divided on an equal footing among the co-heirs: a third to the mother, a third to the sister and a third to the grandfather.[100]

According to the Twelvers and Ismailis, the solution is very simple. The mother (class I) receives the whole estate, because she excludes both the sister and the grandfather (class II) from the inheritance.

10. *al-Akdariyya* (*al-gharrāʾ*)

This case has followed a somewhat unusual fate, because it has been given various names, but is generally known as *al-akdariyya*.[101] It concerns the inheritance of the husband, the paternal grandfather, the mother and a full or consanguine sister. The denomination *akdariyya* is already present in Sufyān al-Thawrī, and thereafter in Muḥammad b. Idrīs al-Shāfiʿī (d. 204/820), ʿAbd al-Razzāq al-Ṣanʿānī (d. 211/827), and in later traditionists and jurists of different schools. This case is also called *al-gharrā'*. However, in one of his works, Ibn Qudāma qualifies a different case as *mas'alat al-gharrā'*: the inheritance of the husband and six sisters of different kinds (two full, two consanguine and two uterine sisters), or its variant: the inheritance of the husband, the mother and three sisters of different kinds (a full, a consanguine and a uterine sister).

Law schools diverged about the solution of *al-akdariyya*. According to the Ḥanafīs, Ẓāhirīs and Ibāḍīs, this case has no particular problems since they exclude brothers and/or sisters because of the presence of the paternal grandfather, based on the principle of agnation; thus the husband has right to a half (= 3/6), the mother to a third (= 2/6) and the grandfather to what remains (1/6). The question was much debated, however, in the other law schools, which depart from some general principles, attributed to Zayd b. Thābit. Firstly, one of his principles is that a proportional reduction of the shares can never be applied in cases involving a grandfather. Secondly, according to Zayd, a full or consanguine sister is not an heir by quota in the presence of the grandfather, but the grandfather and sister share the amount available, giving the grandfather twice the amount of the sister. Thirdly, Zayd deems that the minimum share of a paternal grandfather is a sixth in the presence of heirs by quota.[102]

Since a paternal grandfather does not exclude a full or consanguine sister, any solution contradicts one of these three principles. Firstly, allotting a determined share to each co-heir would require proportional reduction. Secondly, this solution is contrary to Zayd's principle that a sister is not an heir by quota in the presence of the grandfather. However, considering the sister as a residuary heir, nothing remains for her after the attribution of the shares to the heirs by quota: a third (= 2/6) to the mother, half (= 3/6) to the husband, and a sixth to the grandfather (his minimum share); but it is contrary to the letter of the Qur'an (Q. 4:176) that a full or consanguine sister would be excluded from the inheritance. Lastly, if the grandfather and the sister share the remaining sixth, giving him twice the share of the sister, the grandfather would receive less than his minimum share of a sixth.[103]

The solution put forward by the Mālikī, Shāfiʿī, Ḥanbalī and Zaydī schools, which departs from Zayd's principles, is a sort of compromise. On the one hand, the sister is not excluded, but she inherits as an heir by quota and the Qur'anic principle to allot a male twice a share of a female is applied at the same time. On the other hand, the grandfather does not receive less than a sixth. This seems to square the circle. The solution is as follows: considering the sister as an heir by quota, each co-heir is allotted his own share: a half (= $3/6$) to the husband, a third (= $2/6$) to the mother, a sixth (= $1/6$) to the grandfather and a half (= $3/6$) to the sister, giving a total of $9/6$. Then the proportional reduction of all the shares is applied: $3/9$ to the husband, $2/9$ to the mother, $1/9$ to the grandfather, $3/9$ to the sister. However, this solution is also unacceptable, because the grandfather receives less than a sixth out of the whole estate, and because the sister receives more than her male co-heir, the grandfather. In order to avoid this strange consequence, the shares of the grandfather ($1/9$) and the sister ($3/9$) are added together, and the result ($4/9$) is divided among them, attributing to a male the double share of a female: $4/9 \div 3 = 4/9 \times 1/3 = 4/27$; $4/27 \times 3 = 12/27$, of which $8/27$ goes to the grandfather and $4/27$ to the sister. Lastly, all the fractions are summed: $3/9 + 2/9 + 8/27 + 4/27 = 9/27 + 6/27 + 8/27 + 4/27 = 27/27$, of which $9/27$ is left to the husband, $6/27$ to the mother, $8/27$ to the grandfather, $4/27$ to the sister.[104]

For Twelvers and Ismailis, the solution is much more linear: the husband has right to a half as heir by quota, while what remains is due to the mother (class I), a third as an heir by quota and the remainder as *radd*; the grandfather and sister (class II) are excluded by the presence of the mother.[105]

11. *al-Muʿādda*

The case is called *al-Muʿādda* because of the operation made in the attribution of the estate of adding up the number of the co-heirs. If a paternal grandfather, full brothers and/or sisters and consanguine brothers and/or sisters are present, Ḥanafīs, Ẓāhirīs and Ibāḍīs exclude brothers and/or sisters because of the presence of the paternal grandfather, who thus receives the whole estate.

However, the Mālikī, Shāfiʿī and Ḥanbalī schools consider the grandfather as a brother, so both inherit. The course followed by these schools is as such: the number of consanguine brothers and/or sisters is added to the number of full brothers and/or sisters in order to determine the share due to the grandfather. Then consanguine brothers and/or sisters are excluded from the inheritance, and must return their shares to the full brothers and/or sisters. The result is that the amount given to the grandfather is decreased for the benefit of full brothers/sisters. It is clear that these schools give pre-eminence to the brothers/sisters as Qur'anic heirs with respect to the grandfather as agnate. However, the right of the grandfather to receive the best possible share and his right to receive in any scenario his minimum share are assured.[106] This rule admits an exception when there are a unique full sister, grandfather and consanguine brothers and/or sisters. The latter are not excluded in principle. The course is to add up the number of brothers and/or sisters in order to determine the share of the grandfather. If this operation leads to attributing to the sister more than her Qur'anic share of a half, the amount exceeding this quota is attributed to the consanguine brothers and/or sisters.[107] If, however, it is less, any consanguine brothers and/or sisters are excluded.[108] If there are two or more full sisters, obviously nothing remains for the consanguine brothers and/or sisters after the attribution of a third to the grandfather and two thirds to the full sisters.

The solution given by Twelvers and Ismailis is very simple and linear: brothers and sisters and their descendants, as well as paternal and maternal grandfathers and grandmothers of any degree, form the second class of heirs; therefore, they are excluded only by heirs from class I (sons and daughters and their descendants; father and mother). Therefore, the grandfather inherits in the presence of brothers, and he is likened to a brother. A grandfather and brothers/sisters do not exclude each other, but within each category the closest of them excludes the more remote. Moreover, consanguine brothers and sisters are excluded because of the presence of full brothers and sisters.[109] Therefore, if a paternal grandfather, two or more full brothers and sisters, two or more consanguine brothers and sisters, and two or more uterine brothers and sisters are present, according to the Twelvers[110] and Ismailis,[111] uterine brothers and sisters have right to a third, divided among them equally; what remains is divided among the full brothers and sisters and the grandfather, allotting to a male twice the share of a female, while consanguine brothers and sisters are excluded from the inheritance.

12. *Musharraka* (*al-mushtaraka* / *al-tashrīk* / *al-ḥimāriyya*)

This case regards the inheritance of the husband, mother/grandmother, two or more uterine brothers/sisters, and one or more full brothers or one or more full brothers and sisters. Rigidly applying the Qur'anic provisions (Q. 4:11–12), the solution would be: half (= $3/6$) to the husband, a sixth (= $3/6$) to the mother, a third (= $2/6$) to the uterine brothers/sisters, giving a total of $6/6$. Nothing remains for the full brothers (*'aṣaba bi-nafsihi*) or brothers and sisters (*'aṣaba bi-ghayrihi*), who inherit here as agnates. This solution is followed by the Ḥanafīs,[112] Ḥanbalīs[113] and Zaydīs,[114] based on a strict application of the principle of agnation.

One wonders whether such a solution corresponds to the spirit of the Qur'an, being that full brothers and sisters have a stronger family tie than uterine brothers. In order to remedy a harmful outcome for full brothers and sisters, the Mālikīs, Shāfiʿīs and Ibāḍīs prefer a different solution: half (= $3/6$) to the husband, a sixth (= $1/6$) to the mother, a third (= $2/6$) to the uterine brothers/sisters. Then, only based on their common maternal tie, uterine brothers/sisters and full brothers and/or sisters share the third equally among themselves. Precisely for this operation (sharing the same quota), this case is generally called *musharraka*. This denomination is quoted by a very early jurist, Muḥammad b. al-Ḥasan al-Shaybānī (d. 189/805),[115] and repeated in later sources.[116] Mālik b. Anas (d. 179/795) uses the verb *ishtaraka* twice and the verb *sharraka* once in the passive form.[117]

In later sources other names for the case are used, always related to the idea of 'associating' co-heirs and derived from the same root *sh-r-k*. So, Abū Ibrāhīm Ismāʿīl b. Yaḥyā al-Muzanī (d. 264/878),[118] Abū Bakr Aḥmad al-Bayhaqī (d. 458/1066),[119] Ibn Qudāma (d. 620/1223),[120] ʿAbd al-ʿAzīz b. Ibrāhīm al-Muṣʿabī (d. 1808)[121] and al-Aṭfayyish (d. 1914),[122] call it *al-mushtaraka*. Muzanī makes use of the verb *shāraka* too,[123] and Aḥmad b. Muḥammad al-Ṭaḥāwī (d. 321/933) quotes its infinitive, *mushāraka*.[124] Lastly, Muḥammad b. Aḥmad al-Sarakhsī (d. 483/1090)[125] and Aṭfayyish,[126] call it *tashrīk*.

The perspicacity of jurists in creating new names is clearly demonstrated in this case. It is also called *al-ḥimāriyya*, based on a hadith found in Bayhaqī,[127] according to which Zayd b. Thābit would say: 'Suppose their father is a donkey . . .', meaning that the mother is the same for all the brothers/sisters. This *matn*, a little changed, is also related on the authority of ʿUmar and quoted in later sources, like Sarakhsī,[128] Ibn Qudāma,[129] Ibn al-Murtaḍā (d. 840/1437),[130] Muṣʿabī,[131] and Aṭfayyish.[132] Full brothers would say to ʿUmar: 'Suppose our father is a donkey . . .' The denomination *al-ḥimāriyya* appears also in Jurjānī,[133] Khalīl b. Isḥāq (d. 767/1365–6),[134] Muḥammad b. ʿAbd al-Bāqī b. Yūsuf al-Zurqānī (d. 1710),[135] but without the reference to the hadith. The Ibāḍī Aṭfayyish created two new names for the case: *ḥajariyya* and *yammiyya*, not found in any other sources. Adapting the hadith from ʿUmar,[136] brothers would say to him: 'Suppose that our father is a stone (*ḥajar*) thrown into the sea (*yamm*)'. Aṭfayyish also adapted another hadith, in the earliest sources unanimously related on the authority of ʿAlī, but attributed by him to ʿUmar, according to which this case is also denominated *al-minbariyya*. Further denominations are given by the Zaydī jurist Ibn al-Murtaḍā, who names it *al-shurayḥiyya*,[137] because it was submitted at the time of Shurayḥ b. al-Ḥārith b. Qays al-Kindī (d. 78/697), and also *umm al-farrūj* ('mother of chicks'), because of the many divergences existing in its solution.

Although Twelvers and Ismailis know the name *al-mushtaraka*, they reject the solution given by the other law schools. Based on their division of heirs into three classes, a mother (class I) bars the brothers from the inheritance (class II). Therefore, a husband has right to a half and a mother to what remains as heir by quota and by *radd*.[138]

NOTES

1 For a comprehensive bibliography on Islamic inheritance law, see J. Schacht, 'Mirāth', *EI*², vol. 7, pp. 106–111; David Stephan Powers, 'Inheritance' *EQ*, vol. 2, pp. 519–26, and A. Cilardo, 'Inheritance II. Islamic Period', *EIr*, vol. 13, fasc. 2, pp. 131–40.

2 David Stephan Powers, 'The Islamic Law of Inheritance Reconsidered: A New Reading of Q. 4:12b', *Studia Islamica* 55 (1982), pp. 61–94; idem, *Studies in Qur'ān and Ḥadīth: The Formation of the Islamic Law of Inheritance* (Berkeley, CA: University of California Press, 1986); idem, *Muḥammad is Not the Father of Any of Your Men: The Making of the Last Prophet* (Philadelphia, PA: University of Pennsylvania Press, 2009).

3 Powers, *Studies in Qur'ān and Ḥadīth*, p. xi.

4 Ibid., p. xii.

5 See, for instance, Agostino Cilardo, 'The Position of the Grandfather with Regard to the Germane or Consanguine Brothers in the Islamic Law of Inheritance. A Reconsideration' in idem, *Studies of the Islamic Law of Inheritance, Annali dell'Istituto Universitario Orientale di Napoli* 50, Supplement 63 (1990), pp. 1–32; idem, '"The Superimposition Theory" in the Islamic Law of Inheritance' in Alexander Fodor, ed., *Proceedings of the 14th Congress of the Union Européenne des Arabisants et Islamisants: Budapest, 29th August–3rd September 1988* (Budapest: Eötvös Loránd University Chair for Arabic Studies: Csoma de Kőrös Society, Section of Islamic Studies, 1995), pp. 33–41; idem, 'The Position of the Slave in the Islamic Law of Inheritance. A Reconsideration (Conference of the School of Abbasid Studies, University of St Andrews, Scotland, July 31–August 5, 1989)' in *Studies of the Islamic Law of Inheritance*, pp. 43–57; idem, 'Preliminary Notes on the Qur'ānic Term *Kalāla*' in U. Vermeulen and J.M.F. van Reeth, eds, *Law, Christianity and Modernism in Islamic Society. Proceedings of the Eighteenth Congress of the Union Européenne des Arabisants et Islamisants, held at the Katholieke Universiteit Leuven (September 3–September 9, 1996)* (Leuven: Uitgeverij Peeters, 1998), pp. 3–12; idem, 'Some Peculiarities of the Law of Inheritance: The Formation of Imami and Ismaili Law', *Journal of Arabic and Islamic Studies* 3 (2000), pp. 127–37.

6 Agostino Cilardo, *Diritto ereditario islamico delle scuole giuridiche ismailita e imamita. Casistica* (Rome and Naples: Istituto per l'Oriente – Istituto Universitario Orientale, 1993); idem, *Diritto ereditario islamico delle scuole giuridiche sunnite (ḥanafita, mālikita, šāfiʿita e ḥanbalita) e delle scuole giuridiche zaydita, ẓāhirita e ibāḍita. Casistica* (Rome and Naples: Istituto per l'Oriente – Istituto Universitario Orientale, 1994).

7 Agostino Cilardo, *Teorie sulle origini del diritto islamico* (Rome: Istituto per l'Oriente, 1990), pp. 157–94.

8 See Muḥammad b. Jarīr al-Ṭabarī, *Jāmiʿ al-bayān ʿan taʾwīl āy al-Qurʾān*, ed. Maḥmūd Muḥammad Shākir and Aḥmad Muḥammad Shākir (Cairo: Dār al-Maʿārif, 1374–89/1954–69), vol. 8, pp. 265–6, on Q. 4:32.

9 Half siblings are differentiated by their common parent, either the father (consanguine) or the mother (uterine).

10 Khalīl b. Isḥāq, *Mukhtaṣar*, ed. and tr. Ignazio Guidi and David Santillana as *Il 'Mukhtaṣar' o Sommario del diritto malechita* (Milan: Hoepli, 1919), vol. 2,

p. 819; Abū'l-ʿAbbās Aḥmad b. Muḥammad al-Jurjānī, *Kitāb al-Kifāya fī maʿrifat al-farā'iḍ wa qismat al-mawārīth* (MS; see Carl Brockelmann, *Geschichte der Arabischen Litteratur* (*GAL*) (Leiden: Brill, 1943–9), Supplement vol. 1, p. 505, no. 6, fol. 9r; Muḥammad b. Aḥmad Ibn Qudāma, *al-Mughnī* (Cairo: n.p., 1341–8/1922–30), vol. 7, p. 15; idem, *al-Muqniʿ fī fiqh imām al-sunna Aḥmad b. Ḥanbal*, 2nd edn (Cairo: al-Maṭbaʿa al-Salafiyya wa Maktabatuhā, 1382/1962–3), vol. 2, pp. 418–19; idem, *al-Kāfī fī fiqh al-imām Aḥmad Ibn Ḥanbal* (Damascus: n.p., 1964), vol. 2, pp. 545–6; idem, *al-ʿUmda fī fiqh imām al-sunna Aḥmad Ibn Ḥanbal al-Shaybānī* (Cairo: n.p., 1385/1965–6), p. 80; Abū'l-Ḥasan ʿAlī b. Muḥammad al-Basīwī, *al-Mukhtaṣar*, tr. Ignazio Guidi as 'Il diritto ereditario musulmano secondo la dottrina degli arabi ibaditi di Zanzibar e dell'Africa Orientale', *Rivista Coloniale* (1906), pp. 173–96 and 335–87, at p. 356; ʿAbd al-ʿAzīz b. Ibrāhīm al-Muṣʿabī, *Kitāb al-Nīl wa shifā' al-ʿalīl* (Cairo: n.p., 1305/1887–8), vol. 2, p. 384; Muḥammad b. Yūsuf Aṭfayyish, *Sharḥ al-Nīl wa shifā' al-ʿalīl* (Cairo: n.p., 1343/1925), vol. 8, p. 294.

11 Jurjānī, *Kifāya*, fol. 8v; Abū'l-Qāsim al-Khiraqī, *Mukhtaṣar al-Khiraqī ʿalā madhhab al-imām Aḥmad b. Ḥanbal*, in Ibn Qudāma, *al-Mughnī*, vol. 7, pp. 6–7; Basīwī, 'Il diritto ereditario musulmano', p. 356; Muṣʿabī, *Nīl*, vol. 2, p. 381; Aṭfayyish, *Sharḥ al-Nīl*, vol. 8, pp. 293–6.

12 Cilardo, 'The Superimposition Theory', p. 33.

13 *The Holy Qur'ān: Text, Translation and Commentary*, tr. Abdullah Yusuf Ali (Lahore: Shaikh Muhammad Asraf).

14 Ṭabarī, *Jāmiʿ al-bayān*, vol. 7, pp. 597–9.

15 Muḥammad b. al-Ḥasan al-Ṭūsī (Shaykh al-Ṭā'ifa), *al-Tibyān fī tafsīr al-Qur'ān*, ed. Āghā Buzurg al-Ṭihrānī *et al.* (Najaf: al-Maṭbaʿa al-ʿIlmiyya, 1376–83/1957–63), vol. 3, pp. 120–22.

16 See A.J. Wensinck, ed., *Concordance et indices de la tradition musulmane* (Leiden: Brill, 1936–88), vol. 6, p. 99; see also Cilardo, 'The Superimposition Theory', pp. 33–41.

17 Ṭūsī, *Tibyān*, vol. 3, p. 121.

18 See ibid., pp. 185–8.

19 See Cilardo, 'Some Peculiarities of the Law of Inheritance', pp. 127–8; idem, 'Inheritance II. Islamic Period', p. 135.

20 Sufyān al-Thawrī founded a legal *madhhab* which, however, did not have a long life, see Fuat Sezgin, *Geschichte des arabischen Schrifttums* (Leiden: Brill, 1967–84), vol. 1, pp. 518–19, no. 4.

21 Sufyān al-Thawrī, *Tafsīr al-Qur'ān al-karīm*, ed. Imtiyāz ʿAlī ʿArshī (Rāmpūr: n.p., 1385/1965; repr. Beirut: Dār al-Kutub al-ʿIlmiyya, 1403/1983), pp. 43–56.

22 Ibid., p. 51.

23 Ṭabarī, *Jāmiʿ al-bayān*, vol. 7, pp. 597–9; vol. 8, pp. 30–71 and 260–88; vol. 9, pp. 430–46; vol. 14, pp. 77–91 and 347–8.

24 Furāt b. Furāt al-Kūfī, *Tafsīr Furāt al-Kūfī*, ed. Muḥammad al-Kāẓim (Beirut: Mu'assasat al-Nuʿmān, 1412/1992), vol. 1, pp. 101–16.

25 Ibid., pp. 101–16 and 331.

26 Ṭabarī, *Jāmiʿ al-bayān*, vol. 8, pp. 30–33 and 36–8 (in particular).

27 Ṭūsī, *Tibyān*, vol. 3, pp. 127–33.

28 Ibid., pp. 133–9.

29 Aḥmad b. Muḥammad al-Ṭaḥāwī, *Mukhtaṣar*, ed. Abū'l-Wafā' al-Afghānī (Cairo: n.p., 1370/1950), pp. 143 and 146; Muḥammad b. Aḥmad al-Sarakhsī, *Kitāb al-Mabsūṭ* (Cairo: Maṭba'at al-Sa'āda, 1324–31/1906–13), vol. 29, p. 144; Mālik b. Anas, *Kitāb al-Muwaṭṭa'*, with the *Sharḥ Muwaṭṭa'* by Muḥammad b. 'Abd al-Bāqī b. Yūsuf al-Zurqānī (Cairo: n.p., 1373/1954), vol. 3, pp. 103–4, no. 1112; Muḥammad b. Idrīs al-Shāfi'ī, *Kitāb al-Umm* (Cairo: Būlāq, 1321–5/1903–8), vol. 4, p. 6; Abū Ibrāhīm Ismā'īl b. Yaḥyā b. Ismā'īl al-Muzanī, *Mukhtaṣar* on the margins of vols 1–4 of Shāfi'ī, *Umm*, vol. 3, pp. 140 and 143; Abū Zakariyyā' al-Nawawī, *Minhāj al-Ṭālibīn*, ed. and tr. L.W.C. van den Berg as *Le Guide des Zélés Croyants: Manuel de Jurisprudence musulmane selon le rite de Châfi'î* (Batavia: Imprimerie de Gouvernement, 1882–4), vol. 2, p. 233; Ibn Qudāma, *Mughnī*, vol. 7, pp. 16–18.

30 al-Bukhārī, *al-Ṣaḥīḥ*, ed. Muḥammad Muḥammad 'Abd al-Laṭīf. Cairo: n.p., 1351–6/1932–8), *Kitāb al-farā'id*, vol. 23, pp. 152 and 164; Abū Bakr Aḥmad al-Bayhaqī, *al-Sunan al-kubrā* (Hyderabad: n.p., 1354–6/1925–7), vol. 6, pp. 226 and 227; Ṭaḥāwī, *Mukhtaṣar*, p. 143; Abū'l-Layth al-Samarqandī, *Khizānat al-fiqh wa 'Uyūn al-masā'il*, ed. Ṣalāḥ al-Dīn al-Nāhī (Baghdad: Sharikat al-Ṭab' wa'l-Nashr al-Ahliyya, 1385–6/1965–7), vol. 1, pp. 414 and 416; Abū'l-Ḥusayn Aḥmad b. Muḥammad al-Qudūrī, *Mukhtaṣar* (Cairo: n.p., 1367/1948), p. 122; Sarakhsī, *Mabsūṭ*, vol. 29, p. 144; Mālik, *Muwaṭṭa'*, vol. 3, pp. 103–4, no. 1112; Zurqānī, *Sharḥ Muwaṭṭa'*, vol. 3, pp. 103–4; Ibn Abī Zayd al-Qayrawānī, *al-Risāla*, ed. Léon Bercher as *La Risâla ou Epître sur les éléments du dogme et de la loi de l'Islâm selon le rite mâlikite,* 5th edn (Algiers: J. Carbonel, 1960), pp. 274–5; Khalīl, *Mukhtaṣar*, vol. 2, pp. 821–2; Muḥammad b. Muḥammad Ibn 'Āṣim, *Tuḥfat al-ḥukkām*, ed. and tr. Octave Victor Houdas and F. Martel as *Traité de Droit Musulman: La Tohfat d'Ebn Acem. Texte arabe avec traduction française, commentaire juridique et notes philologiques* (Algiers: Gavault Saint-Lager, 1882), pp. 888–9, no. 1677; Muzanī, *Mukhtaṣar*, vol. 3, pp. 140 and 143; Nawawī, *Minhāj al-Ṭālibīn*, vol. 2, p. 233; Khiraqī, *Mukhtaṣar*, vol. 7, p. 16; Ibn Qudāma, *Mughnī*, vol. 7, pp. 16–17; idem, *Muqni'*, vol. 2, p. 408; idem, *Kāfī*, vol. 2, p. 528; idem, *'Umda*, p. 78; Aḥmad b. Yaḥyā Ibn al-Murtaḍā, *Kitāb al-Baḥr al-zakhkhār al-jāmi' li-madhāhib 'ulamā' al-amṣār*, ed. 'Abd Allāh Muḥammad al-Ṣiddīq and 'Abd al-Ḥafīẓ Sa'd 'Aṭiyya (Cairo: Maktabat al-Muthannā, 1366–68/1947–49), vol. 5, p. 344; Basīwī, 'Il diritto ereditario musulmano', pp. 181, 187 and 189; Muṣ'abī, *Nīl*, vol. 2, p. 384; Aṭfayyish, *Sharḥ al-Nīl*, vol. 8, p. 365.

31 Sarakhsī, *Mabsūṭ*, vol. 29, p. 145.

32 Ibid., pp. 144–5; 'Alī b. Aḥmad Ibn Ḥazm, *Kitāb al-Muḥallā*, ed. Aḥmad Muḥammad Shākir (Beirut: al-Maktab al-Tijārī, 1389/1969), vol. 9, pp. 258–60, *mas'ala* no. 1714; idem, *Marātib al-ijmā' fī'l-'ibādāt wa'l-mu'āmalāt wa'l-mu'taqadāt* (Beirut: Dār al-Kutub al-'Ilmiyya, 1978), p. 101.

33 Muḥammad b. al-Ḥasan al-Ṭūsī (Shaykh al-Ṭā'ifa), *al-Istibṣār fī-mā'khtulifa min al-akhbār*, ed. Ḥasan al-Mawsawī al-Khurāsānī, 2nd edn (Najaf: Dār al-Kutub al-Islāmiyya, 1376/1957), vol. 4, pp. 145–6, nos 546–7.

34 Sarakhsī, *Mabsūṭ*, vol. 29, pp. 145–6. On the traditionist grounds of this doctrine, see 'Abd al-Razzāq b. Hammām al-Ṣan'ānī, *al-Muṣannaf*, ed. Ḥabīb al-Raḥmān al-A'ẓamī (Karachi: al-Majlis al-'Ilmī, 1390–92/1970–72), vol. 10, p. 256, no. 19028.

35 Muḥammad b. Yaʿqūb al-Kulaynī, *al-Uṣūl min al-Kāfī. Al-Furūʿ min al-Kāfī. Al-Rawḍa min al-Kāfī*, ed. ʿAlī Akbar al-Ghaffārī (Tehran: Dār al-Kutub al-Islāmiyya, 1388–9/1967–8), vol. 7, pp. 92–3, nos 2–7; 104; Ibn Bābawayh al-Qummī (al-Shaykh al-Ṣadūq), *Kitāb Man lā yaḥḍuruhu'l-faqīh* (Najaf: Dār al-Kutub al-Islāmiyya, 1377–8/1957–9), vol. 4, p. 198, no. 674; Muḥammad b. al-Ḥasan al-Ṭūsī (Shaykh al-Ṭā'ifa), *Kitāb al-Khilāf* (Najaf: Sharikat Dār al-Maʿārif al-Islāmiyya, 1956), vol. 2, p. 265, *mas'ala* nos 31–2; idem, *Istibṣār*, vol. 4, pp. 141–2, nos 524–8; idem, *Tahdhīb al-Aḥkām* (Najaf: Dār al-Kutub al-Islāmiyya, 1377–82/1957–62), vol. 9, p. 280, no. 1013; and p. 281–2, nos 1016–20; Jaʿfar b. al-Ḥasan al-Ḥillī, *Sharā'iʿ al-islām fī masā'il al-ḥalāl wa'l-ḥarām*, ed. ʿAbd al-Ḥusayn Muḥammad ʿAlī (Najaf: Maṭbaʿat al-Ādāb, 1389/1969), vol. 4, p. 19; tr. A. Querry as *Droit Musulman: Recueil de lois concernant les musulmans schyites* (Paris: Imprimerie Nationale, 1871–2), vol. 2, p. 338, nos 95–9; Abū Ḥanīfa al-Nuʿmān (al-Qāḍī al-Nuʿmān), *Kitāb al-Iqtiṣār*, ed. Muḥammad Waḥīd Mīrzā (Damascus: Institut Français de Damas, 1376/1957), p. 133; idem, *Daʿā'im al-islām wa dhikr al-ḥalāl wa'l-ḥarām wa'l-qaḍāyā wa'l-aḥkām ʿan bayt rasūl Allāh*, ed. Āṣif b. ʿAlī Aṣghar Fayḍī [Asif A.A. Fyzee] (Cairo: Dār al-Maʿārif, 1379–83/1960–63), vol. 2, p. 372, no. 1340.

36 Agostino Cilardo, 'The Transmission of the Patronate in Islamic law' in F. de Jong, ed., *Miscellanea Arabica et Islamica. Dissertationes in Academia Ultrajectina prolatae anno MCMXC, Proceedings of the XVth Congress of the U.E.A.I. (Utrecht, September 13–19, 1990)* (Louvain: Uitgeverij Peeters en Departement Oriëntalistiek, 1993), pp. 31–52, at p. 37.

37 Sufyān al-Thawrī, *Tafsīr*, p. 51.

38 Ṭabarī, *Jāmiʿ al-bayān*, vol. 8, pp. 269–72.

39 Ibid., pp. 270–71, nos 9259–60, 9262 and 9265.

40 Ibid., p. 271, no. 9265.

41 Ibid., no. 9261.

42 Ibid., no. 9263.

43 Ibid., p. 272.

44 Ibid., pp. 270–71, nos 9258, 9264 and 9265.

45 Ṭūsī, *Tibyān*, vol. 3, p. 186.

46 Ṭabarī, *Jāmiʿ al-bayān*, vol. 8, pp. 269–70.

47 Ṭūsī, *Tibyān*, vol. 3, pp. 186–7.

48 Ibid., pp. 104–5.

49 Ibid. Ṭūsī also wishes to demonstrate that Q. 19:6 [5] admits a reciprocal inheritance right between Prophets and their relatives. See ibid., vol. 7, pp. 105–7.

50 See Agostino Cilardo, *The Qur'ānic Term* Kalāla: *Studies in the Arabic Language and Poetry,* Ḥadīṯ, Tafsīr, *and* Fiqh. *Notes on the Origin of the Islamic Law* (Edinburgh: Edinburgh University Press, 2005), p. 60.

51 Ibid., p. 76.

52 Ṭabarī, *Jāmiʿ al-bayān*, vol. 9, pp. 443–4.

53 Ibid.

54 Ibid.

55 Ṭūsī, *Tibyān*, vol. 3, pp. 408 and 410. Cf. a broad discussion about the question of the agnation in Ṭūsī, *Khilāf*, vol. 2, pp. 276–81; idem, *Tahdhīb*, vol. 9, pp. 259–68.

56 Ṭūsī, *Tibyān*, vol. 3, p. 411.
57 Muḥammad al-Ṣādiq al-Shaṭṭī, *Risāla fī Masā'il al-imām Dāwūd al-Ẓāhirī* (Damascus: n.p., 1330/1912), p. 19.
58 Ibn Ḥazm, *Muḥallā*, vol. 9, pp. 256–8, *mas'ala* no. 1712.
59 Ibid.
60 Ṭabarī, *Jāmi' al-bayān*, vol. 14, pp. 90–91.
61 Ṭūsī, *Tibyān*, vol. 5, pp. 192–3.
62 Ibid., vol. 8, p. 318.
63 Khalīl, *Mukhtaṣar*, vol. 2, p. 821, n. 81.
64 See Cilardo, 'Inheritance II. Islamic Period', p. 136.
65 Cilardo, 'The Position of the Grandfather', pp. 1–32.
66 Ibn Qudāma, *Kāfī*, vol. 2, p. 541.
67 Jurjānī, *Kifāya*, fol. 7r. The Ḥanafī Sarakhsī (*Mabsūṭ*, vol. 29, p. 164) uses the variant *umm al-firākh* and the denomination *al-shurayḥiyya*, inferred from the name of the jurist to whom the case was submitted, Shurayḥ (d. 78/697).
68 Ibn Qudāma *Mughnī*, vol. 7, pp. 25 and 33; idem, *Muqni'*, vol. 2, p. 420; idem, *Kāfī*, vol. 2, p. 541.
69 Ṭūsī, *Khilāf*, vol. 2, p. 281.
70 Ibn Qudāma, *Mughnī*, vol. 7, p. 80; idem, *Kāfī*, vol. 2, p. 532; idem, *'Umda*, p. 78.
71 Sarakhsī, *Mabsūṭ*, vol. 29, pp. 144 and 179–80; Ibn Ḥazm, *Muḥallā*, vol. 9, p. 282, *mas'ala* no. 1730.
72 Jurjānī, *Kifāya*, fol. 16v; Ibn Qudāma, *Mughnī*, vol. 7, pp. 79–80; idem, *Muqni'*, vol. 2, pp. 407–8; idem, *Kāfī*, vol. 2, p. 532; idem, *'Umda*, p. 78.
73 Sarakhsī, *Mabsūṭ*, vol. 29, pp. 146–7 and 152; Khiraqī, *Mukhtaṣar*, vol. 7, p. 20; Ibn Qudāma, *Mughnī*, vol. 7, pp. 20–21; Ibn Ḥazm, *Muḥallā*, vol. 9, pp. 260–62, *mas'ala* no. 1715; Aṭfayyish, *Sharḥ al-Nīl*, vol. 8, pp. 318–22.
74 Abū Ḥanīfa al-Nu'mān b. Thābit, *Risālat al-farā'iḍ*: see A. Cilardo, ed., 'Un antico documento di diritto ereditario musulmano', *Annali dell'Istituto Orientale di Napoli* 42 (1982), pp. 103–26, pp. 119 and 125, no. 47; Samarqandī, *Khizānat al-fiqh*, vol. 1, p. 416; Sarakhsī, *Mabsūṭ*, vol. 29, pp. 146–7 and 152; Mālik, *Muwaṭṭa'*, vol. 3, pp. 103–4, no. 1112; Zurqānī, *Sharḥ Muwaṭṭa'*, vol. 3, pp. 103–4; Ibn Abī Zayd, *Risâla*, pp. 274–5; Khalīl, *Mukhtaṣar*, vol. 2, p. 821; Ibn 'Āṣim, *Tuḥfa*, pp. 890–91, no. 1679; Muzanī, *Mukhtaṣar*, vol. 3, p. 140; Jurjānī, *Kifāya*, fol. 7r; Nawawī, *Minhāj al-Ṭālibīn*, vol. 2, pp. 233–4; Khiraqī, *Mukhtaṣar*, vol. 7, p. 20; Ibn Qudāma, *Mughnī*, vol. 7, pp. 17 and 20–21; idem, *Muqni'*, vol. 2, pp. 408–9; idem, *Kāfī*, vol. 2, p. 528; idem, *'Umda*, p. 78; Ibn Ḥazm, *Marātib al-ijmā'*, p. 101; Muṣ'abī, *Nīl*, vol. 2, pp. 382 and 384; Aṭfayyish, *Sharḥ al-Nīl*, vol. 8, pp. 318–22. On the traditionist basis of this doctrine, cf. 'Abd al-Razzāq, *Muṣannaf*, vol. 10, pp. 253–4, nos 19019–21; 'Abd Allāh b. 'Abd al-Raḥmān al-Dārimī, *al-Sunan* (also known as *al-Musnad al-jāmi'*), ed. 'Abd Allāh Hāshim Yamānī al-Madanī (Cairo: n.p., 1386/1966), vol. 2, p. 249, nos 2868 and 2873; Bayhaqī, *Sunan*, vol. 6, p. 228; Sufyān al-Thawrī, *Kitāb al-Farā'iḍ*, ed. Hans-Peter Raddatz as 'Frühislamisches Erbrecht nach dem *Kitāb al-Farā'iḍ* des Sufyān al-Thawrī', *Die Welt des Islams* 13 (1971), pp. 26–78, at p. 37.
75 Abū Ḥanīfa, *Risālat al-Farā'iḍ*, p. 116 (Ar.), p. 121 (tr.), no. 17; Samarqandī, *Khizānat al-fiqh*, vol. 1, p. 416; Sarakhsī, *Mabsūṭ*, vol. 29, pp. 146–7 and 152; Mālik, *Muwaṭṭa'*, vol. 3, p. 103, no. 1112; Zurqānī, *Sharḥ Muwaṭṭa'*, vol. 3,

p. 103; Ibn Abī Zayd, *Risâla*, pp. 274–5; Khalīl, *Mukhtaṣar*, vol. 2, p. 821; Ibn ʿĀṣim, *Tuḥfa*, pp. 890–91, no. 1679; Muzanī, *Mukhtaṣar*, vol. 3, p. 140; Jurjānī, *Kifāya*, fol. 7r; Nawawī, *Minhāj al-Ṭālibīn*, vol. 2, pp. 233–4; Khiraqī, *Mukhtaṣar*, vol. 7, p. 20; Ibn Qudāma, *Mughnī*, vol. 7, pp. 17 and 20–21; idem, *Muqniʿ*, vol. 2, pp. 408–9; idem, *Kāfī*, vol. 2, p. 528; idem, *ʿUmda*, p. 78; Ibn Ḥazm, *Marātib al-ijmāʿ*, p. 101; Muṣʿabī, *Nīl*, vol. 2, pp. 382 and 384; Aṭfayyish, *Sharḥ al-Nīl*, vol. 8, pp. 318–22. On the traditionist basis of this doctrine, cf. ʿAbd al-Razzāq, *Muṣannaf*, vol. 10, pp. 252–3, nos 19014–17; Dārimī, *Musnad*, vol. 2, p. 249, nos 2869–72 and 2874; p. 250, nos 2875–6; Bayhaqī, *Sunan*, vol. 6, pp. 227–8; Sufyān al-Thawrī, 'Frühislamisches', pp. 36–7.

76 Ibn Ḥazm, *Muḥallā*, vol. 9, pp. 260–62, *masʾala* no. 1715.

77 ʿAbd al-Razzāq, *Muṣannaf*, vol. 10, p. 253, no. 19018; p. 254, no. 19020; Dārimī, *Musnad*, vol. 2, p. 250, nos 2878–9 and 2881; Abū Ḥanīfa, *Risālat al-Farāʾiḍ*, p. 119 (Ar.), p. 125 (tr.), no. 47; Samarqandī, *Khizānat al-fiqh*, vol. 1, p. 416; Zurqānī, *Sharḥ Muwaṭṭaʾ*, vol. 3, p. 104; Ibn Qudāma, *Mughnī*, vol. 7, p. 21.

78 Dārimī, *Musnad*, vol. 2, p. 250, no. 2880; Abū Ḥanīfa, *Risālat al-Farāʾiḍ*, p. 116 (Ar.), p. 121 (tr.), no. 17.

79 Kulaynī, *Uṣūl*, vol. 7, pp. 98–9, nos 1–5; Ibn Bābawayh, *Kitāb Man lā yaḥḍuruhuʾl-faqīh*, vol. 4, pp. 195–6; Ṭūsī, *Khilāf*, vol. 2, pp. 265–6, *masʾala* nos 33–4; idem, *Istibṣār*, vol. 4, pp. 142–4, nos 529–37; idem, *Tahdhīb*, vol. 9, pp. 284–7, nos 1028–40; Ḥillī, *Sharāʾiʿ*, vol. 4, pp. 21 and 24 (Querry, *Droit Musulman*, vol. 2, p. 340, no. 119; and p. 344, nos 147 and 149); Abū Ḥanīfa al-Nuʿmān (al-Qāḍī al-Nuʿmān), *Mukhtaṣar al-āthār fī-mā ruwiya ʿan al-aʾimma al-aṭhār* (MS; see Brocklemann, *GAL*, vol. 1, p. 576, no. 1), fol. 119v; idem, *Iqtiṣār*, p. 133; idem, *Daʿāʾim*, vol. 2, pp. 373–4, nos 1342–3. For a broad debate on the opposite doctrines, see Sarakhsī, *Mabsūṭ*, vol. 29, pp. 146–7 and 152; Ibn Qudāma, *Mughnī*, vol. 7, p. 21; Ibn Ḥazm, *Muḥallā*, vol. 9, pp. 260–62, *masʾala* no. 1715; Aṭfayyish, *Sharḥ al-Nīl*, vol. 8, pp. 318–22.

80 Ibn Qudāma, *Mughnī*, vol. 7, pp. 26–7 and 32–3; idem, *Kāfī*, vol. 2, pp. 540–41.

81 Sarakhsī, *Mabsūṭ*, vol. 29, p. 161; Khalīl, *Mukhtaṣar*, vol. 2, pp. 832–3; Ibn Qudāma, *Mughnī*, vol. 7, pp. 26–7 and 32–3; idem, *Kāfī*, vol. 2, pp. 540–41.

82 Shaṭṭī, *Risāla*, pp. 19–20.

83 Ibn Qudāma, *Mughnī*, vol. 7, pp. 26–7.

84 Sarakhsī, *Mabsūṭ*, vol. 29, pp. 164–5.

85 Ibn Ḥazm, *Muḥallā*, vol. 9, p. 267.

86 Ṭūsī, *Khilāf*, vol. 2, p. 253, *masʾala* no. 3; p. 306, *masʾala* no. 151; idem, *Istibṣār*, vol. 4, p. 146, no. 548; Abū Ḥanīfa al-Nuʿmān (al-Qāḍī al-Nuʿmān), *Minhāj al-farāʾiḍ*, ed. and tr. Agostino Cilardo as *The Early History of Ismaili Jurisprudence: Law under the Fatimids. A Critical Edition of the Arabic Text and English Translation of al-Qāḍī al-Nuʿmān's* Minhāj al-farāʾiḍ (London: I.B. Tauris in association with the Institute of Ismaili Studies, 2012), pp. 3–4 (Ar.), p. 93 (tr.).

87 Jurists felt free to create other names for this case; e.g. Ibn Qudāma calls it *al-naḥīla* in one of his works (*Kāfī*, vol. 2, p. 541), while in two works he names it *al-bakhīla* (*Mughnī*, vol. 7, p. 35; *Muqniʿ*, vol. 2, p. 424). Both names highlight that the smallest proportional reduction is applied in this case. The name *al-bakhīla* is also found in Aṭfayyish, *Sharḥ al-Nīl*, vol. 8, p. 475. It is remarkable that in a later source the denomination *al-minbariyya* is attributed to a completely different case. The Ibāḍī jurist Aṭfayyish (d. 1332/1914) slightly

improbably says that this is the name used for the inheritance of the husband, mother/grandmother, two or more uterine brothers, one or more full brothers (*Sharḥ al-Nīl*, vol. 8, p. 356). Moreover, imitating the tradition from ʿAlī, Aṭfayyish states that the name derives from the fact that ʿUmar was asked about this case while he was on the minbar. However, it is well known that the latter case is a different one, which is commonly known as *musharraka*.

88 ʿAbd al-Razzāq, *Muṣannaf*, vol. 10, p. 258, no. 19033; ʿAlī b. ʿUmar al-Dāraquṭnī, *al-Sunan*, ed. ʿAbd Allāh Hāshim Yamānī al-Madanī (Medina: n.p., 1386/1966), vol. 4, pp. 68–9, no. 5; Bayhaqī, *Sunan*, vol. 6, p. 253; Abū Ḥanīfa, *Risālat al-farāʾiḍ*, pp. 116–17 (Ar.), p. 122 (tr.), no. 20; Sarakhsī, *Mabsūṭ*, vol. 29, pp. 163–4; Zurqānī, *Sharḥ Muwaṭṭaʾ*, vol. 3, p. 103; Khalīl, *Mukhtaṣar*, vol. 2, p. 829; Jurjānī, *Kifāya*, fol. 7v–8r; Nawawī, *Minhāj al-Ṭālibīn*, vol. 2, p. 251; Ibn Qudāma, *Mughnī*, vol. 7, pp. 35–6; idem, *Muqniʿ*, vol. 2, pp. 423–4; idem, *Kāfī*, vol. 2, p. 541; Basīwī, 'Il diritto ereditario musulmano', p. 366; Muṣʿabī, *Nīl*, vol. 2, p. 392; Aṭfayyish, *Sharḥ al-Nīl*, vol. 8, pp. 474–5.

89 Shaṭṭī, *Risāla*, pp. 19–20.

90 Ibn Ḥazm, *Muḥallā*, vol. 9, pp. 262–7, *masʾala* no. 1717.

91 ʿAbd al-Razzāq, *Muṣannaf*, vol. 10, p. 254, no. 19022; p. 258, no. 19033; and p. 259, no. 19035; Bayhaqī, *Sunan*, vol. 6, p. 253; Dārimī, *Musnad*, vol. 2, p. 287, no. 3166; Sarakhsī, *Mabsūṭ*, vol. 29, p. 161; Ibn Qudāma, *Mughnī*, vol. 7, pp. 24–7.

92 Kulaynī, *Uṣūl*, vol. 7, pp. 79–80, nos 1–3; pp. 80–81, nos 1–7; p. 82, nos 1–4; pp. 101–2, no. 3; and p. 103, no. 5; Ibn Bābawayh, *Kitāb Man lā yaḥḍuruhu'l-faqīh*, vol. 4, pp. 187–90; Ṭūsī, *Khilāf*, vol. 2, pp. 281–4; idem, *Tahdhīb*, vol. 9, pp. 247–59, nos 958–71; Ḥillī, *Sharāʾiʿ*, vol. 4, pp. 11, 18, 20–21, 27, 28 and 59 (Querry, *Droit Musulman*, vol. 2, p. 328, no. 16; pp. 337–8, no. 93; pp. 339–41, nos 110–21; pp. 348–9, no. 183; p. 349, no. 185; and p. 379, no. 378); al-Qāḍī al-Nuʿmān, *Āthār*, fol. 120v–121r; idem, *Iqtiṣār*, p. 135; idem, *Daʿāʾim*, vol. 2, pp. 381–3, nos 1361–3.

93 For the name *al-kharqāʾ*, see Sarakhsī, *Mabsūṭ*, vol. 29, p. 191; Ibn Qudāma, *Mughnī*, vol. 7, p. 78; idem, *Muqniʿ*, vol. 2, p. 406; idem, *Kāfī*, vol. 2, p. 531; idem, *ʿUmda*, p. 78; Ibn Ḥazm, *Muḥallā*, vol. 9, p. 289, *masʾala* no. 1731; for *ʿUthmāniyya* see Sarakhsī, *Mabsūṭ*, vol. 29, p. 191; Ibn al-Murtaḍā, *Baḥr*, vol. 5, pp. 349–50; for the names *muthallatha* and *ḥajjājiyya*, see Sarakhsī, *Mabsūṭ*, vol. 29, p. 191; Ibn Qudāma, *Mughnī*, vol. 7, p. 79; and for the names *musabbaʿa* and *musaddasa*, see Ibn Qudāma, *Mughnī*, vol. 7, p. 79.

94 ʿAbd al-Razzāq, *Muṣannaf*, vol. 10, pp. 269–70, nos 19069–70; Bayhaqī, *Sunan*, vol. 6, p. 252; Sarakhsī, *Mabsūṭ*, vol. 29, pp. 144, 179–80 and 190–91; Ibn Qudāma, *Mughnī*, vol. 7, p. 79; Ibn Ḥazm, *Muḥallā*, vol. 9, p. 282, *masʾala* no. 1730; p. 289, *masʾala* no. 1731; Ibn al-Murtaḍā, *Baḥr*, vol. 5, pp. 349–50; Basīwī, 'Il diritto ereditario musulmano', p. 181.

95 Ibn Qudāma, *Mughnī*, vol. 7, p. 79.

96 ʿAbd al-Razzāq, *Muṣannaf*, vol. 10, pp. 269–70, nos 19069–70; pp. 272–3, no. 19078; Bayhaqī, *Sunan*, vol. 6, p. 252; Sarakhsī, *Mabsūṭ*, vol. 29, p. 190; Shāfiʿī, *Umm*, vol. 7, p. 166; Khiraqī, *Mukhtaṣar*, vol. 7, p. 78; Ibn Qudāma, *Mughnī*, vol. 7, p. 79; idem, *Muqniʿ*, vol. 2, p. 406; idem, *Kāfī*, vol. 2, p. 531; idem, *ʿUmda*, p. 78; Ibn Ḥazm, *Muḥallā*, vol. 9, p. 289, *masʾala* no. 1731; Ibn al-Murtaḍā, *Baḥr*, vol. 5, pp. 349–50.

97 ʿAbd al-Razzāq, *Muṣannaf*, vol. 10, pp. 269–70, nos 19069–70; Bayhaqī, *Sunan*, vol. 6, p. 252; Sarakhsī, *Mabsūṭ*, vol. 29, p. 190; Ibn Qudāma, *Mughnī*, vol. 7, p. 79; Ibn Ḥazm, *Muḥallā*, vol. 9, p. 289, *masʾala* no. 1731; Ibn al-Murtaḍā, *Baḥr*, vol. 5, pp. 349–50.

98 ʿAbd al-Razzāq, *Muṣannaf*, vol. 10, pp. 269–70, nos 19069–70; Bayhaqī, *Sunan*, vol. 6, p. 252; Ibn Qudāma, *Mughnī*, vol. 7, p. 79; Ibn Ḥazm, *Muḥallā*, vol. 9, p. 289, *masʾala* no. 1731. Ibn Ḥazm here attributes this solution to ʿUmar.

99 Ibn Qudāma, *Mughnī*, vol. 7, p. 79.

100 ʿAbd al-Razzāq, *Muṣannaf*, vol. 10, pp. 269–70, nos 19069–70; Bayhaqī, *Sunan*, vol. 6, p. 252; Ibn Qudāma, *Mughnī*, vol. 7, p. 79; Ibn Ḥazm, *Muḥallā*, vol. 9, p. 289, *masʾala* no. 1731.

101 The obscurity of the origin of the term *al-akdariyya* makes clear that its true sense has been lost over time. Relatively late, the Ḥanafī jurist Sarakhsī (*Mabsūṭ*, vol. 29, pp. 183–4) assumed three explanations: a) in this specific case the solution contradicts the principles of the *madhhab* of Zayd concerning the inheritance of the paternal grandfather; b) ʿAbd al-Mālik b. Marwān submitted this case to a *faqīh* named al-Akdar, who issued a *fatwā* wrongly applying a principle of the *madhhab* of Zayd; c) al-Akdar is the name of the deceased who occasioned the case. The first explanation is shared by Sarakhsī's contemporary, Ṭūsī (*Khilāf*, vol. 2, pp. 291–2, *masʾala* no. 107), and by two jurists of a later period, the Ḥanbalī Ibn Qudāma and the Zaydī Ibn al-Murtaḍā (Ibn Qudāma, *Mughnī*, vol. 7, p. 76; Ibn al-Murtaḍā, *Baḥr*, vol. 5, p. 350). The second explanation, which seems the most plausible, is related by the early Sufyān al-Thawrī ('Frühislamisches', p. 36) and by the fifth/eleventh century Jurjānī (*Kifāya*, fol. 15v) and Ibn Qudāma (*Mughnī*, vol. 7, p. 76). Lastly, the denomination deriving from the name of the deceased seems quite unlikely, because no other inheritance case is named after a deceased person.

102 See Ibn Qudāma, *Mughnī*, vol. 7, p. 76.

103 See ibid., pp. 75–7; idem, *ʿUmda*, p. 78.

104 This solution is present in the earliest traditionist sources, such as ʿAbd al-Razzāq, *Muṣannaf*, vol. 10, p. 271, no. 19074; Dārimī, *Musnad*, vol. 2, p. 258, no. 2934; and in Bayhaqī, *Sunan*, vol. 6, pp. 250–51, in the earliest juridical works (such as Sufyān al-Thawrī, 'Frühislamisches', p. 36) and in the works of the different law schools: Sarakhsī, *Mabsūṭ*, vol. 29, pp. 183–4 and 191; Mālik, *Muwaṭṭaʾ*, vol. 3, pp. 108–10, no. 1118; Zurqānī, *Sharḥ Muwaṭṭaʾ*, vol. 3, pp. 108–10; ʿAbd al-Salām b. Saʿīd Saḥnūn, *al-Mudawwana al-kubrā* (Cairo: n.p., 1323–4/1905), vol. 8, p. 90; Ibn Abī Zayd, *Risâla*, pp. 284–7; Khalīl, *Mukhtaṣar*, vol. 2, p. 823; Ibn ʿĀṣim, *Tuḥfa*, pp. 884–7, nos 1669 and 1670; Shāfiʿī, *Umm*, vol. 7, p. 166; Muzanī, *Mukhtaṣar*, vol. 3, pp. 148–9; Nawawī, *Minhāj al-Ṭālibīn*, vol. 2, pp. 242–3; Khiraqī, *Mukhtaṣar*, vol. 7, p. 75; Ibn Qudāma, *Mughnī*, vol. 7, pp. 70 and 75–7; idem, *Muqniʿ*, vol. 2, pp. 404–6; idem, *Kāfī*, vol. 2, pp. 530–31; idem, *ʿUmda*, p. 78; Ibn al-Murtaḍā, *Baḥr*, vol. 5, p. 350.

105 Kulaynī, *Uṣūl*, vol. 7, p. 118; Ṭūsī, *Khilāf*, vol. 2, pp. 291–2, *masʾala* no. 107.

106 ʿAbd al-Razzāq, *Muṣannaf*, vol. 10, p. 267, no. 19063; Bayhaqī, *Sunan*, vol. 6, pp. 251–2; Mālik, *Muwaṭṭaʾ*, vol. 3, p. 110, no. 1118; Zurqānī, *Sharḥ Muwaṭṭaʾ*, vol. 3, p. 110; Ibn Abī Zayd, *Risâla*, pp. 282–5; Khalīl, *Mukhtaṣar*, vol. 2, pp. 822–3; Ibn ʿĀṣim, *Tuḥfa*, pp. 886–7, nos 1671–2; Muzanī, *Mukhtaṣar*,

vol. 3, p. 149; Jurjānī, *Kifāya*, fol. 15v–16v; Nawawī, *Minhāj al-Ṭālibīn*, vol. 2, pp. 241–2; Khiraqī, *Mukhtaṣar*, vol. 7, pp. 70–71; Ibn Qudāma, *Mughnī*, vol. 7, pp. 68 and 71–2; idem, *Muqni'*, vol. 2, p. 406; idem, *Kāfī*, vol. 2, p. 531; idem, *'Umda*, p. 77.

107 The male is allotted twice a share of a female. It should be noted that the surplus could never be more than a sixth, being that the minimum share of the grandfather is a third and the share of a sister is a half.

108 Dāraquṭnī, *Sunan*, vol. 4, pp. 94–5, no. 82; Bayhaqī, *Sunan*, vol. 6, pp. 251–2; Mālik, *Muwaṭṭa'*, vol. 3, p. 110, no. 1118; Zurqānī, *Sharḥ Muwaṭṭa'*, vol. 3, p. 110; Ibn Abī Zayd, *Risâla*, pp. 284–5; Khalīl, *Mukhtaṣar*, vol. 2, pp. 822–3; Muzanī, *Mukhtaṣar*, vol. 3, p. 149; Nawawī, *Minhāj al-Ṭālibīn*, vol. 2, pp. 241–2; Ibn Qudāma, *Mughnī*, vol. 7, p. 68; idem, *Muqni'*, vol. 2, p. 406; idem, *Kāfī*, vol. 2, pp. 531–2; idem, *'Umda*, p. 77.

109 Kulaynī, *Uṣūl*, vol. 7, pp. 109–11, nos 2–10; and p. 115; Ibn Bābawayh, *Kitāb Man lā yaḥḍuruhu'l-faqīh*, vol. 4, pp. 204–11; Ṭūsī, *Khilāf*, vol. 2, pp. 288–91, *mas'ala* nos 97–106; idem, *Istibṣār*, vol. 4, pp. 155–6, no. 583; p. 156, no. 588; p. 157, no. 591; and p. 158, no. 597; idem, *Tahdhīb*, vol. 9, pp. 303–19, nos 1080–144 (inheritance of the grandfather); pp. 319–24, nos 1145–61 (inheritance of brothers and sisters); pp. 324–8, nos 1162–79 (inheritance of paternal and maternal uncles and aunts); Ḥillī, *Sharā'i'*, vol. 4, pp. 17–18, 27 and 28 (Querry, *Droit Musulman*, vol. 2, pp. 336–7, nos 73–84; p. 348, nos 181–2; p. 349, no. 186); al-Qāḍī al-Nu'mān, *Āthār*, fol. 118v–119r; idem, *The Early History of Ismaili Jurisprudence*, pp. 16–17 (Ar.), pp. 103–5 (tr.); idem, *Iqtiṣār*, p. 134; idem, *Da'ā'im*, vol. 2, p. 376, no. 1348.

110 Kulaynī, *Uṣūl*, vol. 7, pp. 111–12, nos 1–7.

111 al-Qāḍī al-Nu'mān, *The Early History of Ismaili Jurisprudence*, pp. 16–17 (Ar.), pp. 103–5 (tr.).

112 Ṭaḥāwī, *Mukhtaṣar*, pp. 145–6; Qudūrī, *Mukhtaṣar*, p. 123; Sarakhsī, *Mabsūṭ*, vol. 29, p. 153.

113 Ibn Qudāma, *Kāfī*, vol. 2, p. 527; idem, *Muqni'*, vol. 2, p. 420.

114 Ibn al-Murtaḍā, *Baḥr*, vol. 5, p. 345.

115 Muḥammad b. al-Ḥasan al-Shaybānī, *al-Ḥujja fī ikhtilāf ahl al-Kūfa wa ahl al-Madīna* (MS), fol. 197r; see *GAL*, vol. 1, p. 180, no. XI; *GAL-S*, vol. 1, p. 291, no. XI; *GAS*, vol. 1, p. 432, no. XII. This work has been partly edited: *Kitāb al-Ḥujja 'alā ahl al-Madīna*, ed. Mahdī Ḥasan al-Kīlānī al-Qādirī (Hyderabad: n.p., 1385/1965).

116 E.g. Bayhaqī, *Sunan*, vol. 6, pp. 255 and 256; Qudūrī, *Mukhtaṣar*, p. 123; Ṭaḥāwī, *Mukhtaṣar*, p. 145; Sarakhsī, *Mabsūṭ*, vol. 29, p. 153; Nawawī, *Minhāj al-Ṭālibīn*, vol. 2, pp. 235–6 and 237; Jurjānī, *Kifāya*, fol. 8r–8v; Ibn al-Murtaḍā, *Baḥr*, vol. 5, p. 345; Aṭfayyish, *Sharḥ al-Nīl*, vol. 8, pp. 355, 356, 359 and 361.

117 Mālik, *Muwaṭṭa'*, vol. 3, p. 106.

118 Muzanī, *Mukhtaṣar*, vol. 3, p. 151.

119 Bayhaqī, *Sunan*, vol. 6, p. 255.

120 Ibn Qudāma, *'Umda*, p. 81.

121 Muṣ'abī, *Nīl*, vol. 2, p. 383.

122 Aṭfayyish, *Sharḥ al-Nīl*, vol. 8, pp. 355, 356, 358, 359, 360, 361 and 362.

123 Muzanī, *Mukhtaṣar*, vol. 3, p. 143.

124 Ṭaḥāwī, *Mukhtaṣar*, p. 145.
125 Sarakhsī, *Mabsūṭ*, vol. 29, pp. 154 and 155.
126 Aṭfayyish, *Sharḥ al-Nīl*, vol. 8, pp. 355, 356, 359 and 361.
127 Bayhaqī, *Sunan*, vol. 6, p. 256.
128 Sarakhsī, *Mabsūṭ*, vol. 29, pp. 154–5.
129 Ibn Qudāma, *Mughnī*, vol. 7, p. 22; idem, *Muqni'*, vol. 2, p. 420; idem, *Kāfī*, vol. 2, p. 527; idem, *'Umda*, p. 81.
130 Ibn al-Murtaḍā, *Baḥr*, vol. 5, p. 345.
131 Muṣ'abī, *Nīl*, vol. 2, p. 383.
132 Aṭfayyish, *Sharḥ al-Nīl*, vol. 8, pp. 355 and 356.
133 Jurjānī, *Kifāya*, fol. 8v.
134 Khalīl, *Mukhtaṣar*, vol. 2, p. 824.
135 Zurqānī, *Sharḥ Muwaṭṭa'*, vol. 3, p. 106.
136 Aṭfayyish, *Sharḥ al-Nīl*, vol. 8, p. 356.
137 Ibn al-Murtaḍā, *Baḥr*, vol. 5, p, 345.
138 Ibn Bābawayh, *Kitāb Man lā yaḥḍuruhu'l-faqīh*, vol. 4, p. 203; Ṭūsī, *Khilāf*, p. 295, *mas'ala* no. 112; idem, *Tahdhīb*, vol. 9, p. 293, no. 1049. For any inheritance where a husband or wife, the mother and any kind of brothers/sisters are present, the latter are excluded by the presence of the mother; see Ṭūsī, *Khilāf*, vol. 2, pp. 266–7, *mas'ala* nos 36–8 and 42–4.

10

Marital Discord in Qur'anic Exegesis: A Lexical Analysis of Husbandly and Wifely *Nushūz* in Q. 4:34 and Q. 4:128

AYESHA S. CHAUDHRY

PRE-MODERN Qur'an commentators, who were often masters of multiple disciplines such as jurisprudence, theology, philology and philosophy, expounded a patriarchal idealised cosmology in their exegesis of the Qur'an. An idealised cosmology describes a perfect and idealised vision of the world; it is a representation of the world as it should be, rather than how it is exactly. Hence, idealised cosmologies are not social and historical snapshots of society, but rather imaginings of what the universe ought to be like. Certainly, the idealised cosmologies of pre-modern exegetes were influenced by their social and historical contexts, as well their personal experiences, religious scriptures, etc., but they did not necessarily reflect these influences in a straightforward manner. It is useful to think of Qur'anic exegesis in this light, because it helps explain the uniform opinions of exegetes on matters such as the contours of an ideal marital relationship, as well as the appropriate way to resolve marital disputes. Such issues do not display the multiplicity of opinions that characterise Qur'anic exegesis in other matters, such as discussions surrounding the rights of neighbours or prisoners of war.

The idealised cosmology of pre-modern exegetes can be gleaned from careful study of exegetical works, with a special focus on lexicology. Since these exegetes deliberately interpreted specific words and technical terms to have precise contextual meanings, it is important to pay attention when they interpreted a term differently based on the context in which it was found. That a technical term could mean something markedly different depending on its context suggests that both the textual and cosmological contexts formed the driving force behind its interpretation. These contexts speak to the presuppositions of the exegete, and can inform the reader about the larger idealised cosmological vision that exegetes brought to bear on their interpretations of the Qur'an.

An excellent example of a technical term that was interpreted in contrasting ways by pre-modern exegetes, which in turn betrayed the supposition of a patriarchal idealised cosmology, is the term *nushūz*. The trilateral root of the verbal noun *nushūz*, *n-sh-z*, is used in its verbal form to describe the behaviour of husbands and wives in separate instances in *Sūrat al-Nisāʾ* (Q. 4). The exegesis of this term in pre-modern Qur'an commentaries is interesting because exegetes generally provided a consistently similar definition for its literal meaning, but they altered its significance and meaning when applying it to the behaviour of wives as opposed to husbands. The different application of this term to husbands and wives, illustrates how exegetes understood the marital relationship as fitting into a larger idealised cosmology.

In the idealised cosmologies of pre-modern exegetes, not all of God's creatures were created equal. Humans ranked above all other animals and, amongst humans, men ranked above women. Social institutions, such as marriage, were designed in conformity with and inextricably connected to the divine ranking of humans. Accepting, fulfilling and submitting to one's cosmological ranking and its social outcomes merited divine reward, whereas resisting, challenging and defying one's ranking resulted in God's wrath. In an idealised cosmology wherein martial roles were divinely ordered, all acts within marriage became subject to divine judgement, resulting in sin or reward.[1] Acts that threatened the divinely sanctioned marital hierarchy, and thereby the larger cosmological order, were especially problematic and attracted a great deal of scholarly attention.

Pre-modern exegetes imagined an ideal marriage as one in which God stands atop the marital hierarchy, followed by husbands and then wives.[2] In this hierarchy, husbands enjoyed a largely unmediated relationship with God, wielding religious, moral, legal and social authority over their wives. The relationship of wives to God was significantly mediated by their husbands. Wives pleased God by properly executing their religious duties, which included pleasing their husbands. Conversely, wives displeased God by displeasing their husbands. This was true to such an extent that wives were discouraged from engaging in supererogatory devotional acts if and when those acts displeased their husbands.[3] The salvation of wives was tied to their relationship with their husbands in a way that husbands were not similarly tied. It is unsurprising, therefore, that pre-modern exegetes interpreted the term *nushūz* to apply differently to husbands and wives, since they saw the roles of the two spouses as fitting differently into their idealised cosmology. Hence, *nushūz* had separate meanings and contrasting implications for each spouse.

In what follows, I will provide an overview of the term '*nushūz*' in the Qur'an, examine the treatment of wifely and husbandly *nushūz* in pre-modern Sunni Qur'anic exegesis,[4] and then conclude with an exposition of the idealised cosmology that can be gleaned from Qur'anic commentaries, in which marriage stands at the nexus of the relationship between God and humans.

Overview of *Nushūz* in the Qur'an

Four forms of the verbal root *n-sh-z* appear in the Qur'an. One conjugation appears in an address to believers, who are advised that when they are asked to *rise up, they should rise up* (*inshuzū fa-nshuzū*, Q. 58:11).[5] It also appears in Q. 2:259 in a parable for resurrection which involves a man and his donkey being brought back to life, after having been dead for a hundred years. The man is brought back to life first and witnesses his donkey's bones becoming clothed with flesh as it, too, is resurrected. The man is told to '*see the bones, how We raise* [*put*] *them together* (*nunshizuhā*)'.[6] Most interestingly for our purposes, the word *nushūz* appears twice in *Sūrat al-Nisā'*, once in Q. 4:34 and once in 4:128, regarding the behaviour of wives (*nushūzahunna*) and husbands (*nushūzan*) respectively. In both cases, marital *nushūz* is a negative quality, something to be 'feared' by the other spouse. The fact that the term *nushūz* is used to refer to the negative behaviour of both husbands and wives in the marital relationship may, at first glance, suggest some parity of the spouses; that they may transgress against one another in a similar manner and may be held to a similar standard of accountability. However, although pre-modern exegetes acknowledge that in both cases the root *n-sh-z* means 'to rise' – most often described in its verbal noun form as 'a hillock' – this rising is interpreted in completely different ways with regard to its application to husbands and wives.

The fact that pre-modern exegetes interpreted wifely and husbandly *nushūz* to have different meanings suggests that they were less concerned with maintaining a cohesive, consistent lexical definition of *nushūz* and were more concerned with interpreting the word *nushūz* to fulfil their vision of an appropriate marital relationship within a larger cosmological framework. In the case of wives, *nushūz* was interpreted to be some form of disobedience and in the case of husbands, it was understood to mean a loss of interest or antipathy toward one's wife.

Exegetical Treatment of Wifely *Nushūz*

The Qur'anic text that discusses wifely *nushūz* is found in Q. 4:34. This verse describes the desirable and despicable characteristics of wives, and advises husbands to take disciplinary action against wives who misbehave. This verse reads:

> *Men are in authority (qawwāmūn) over women, because God has preferred (faḍḍala) some over others and because they spend of their wealth. Righteous (ṣāliḥāt) women are obedient (qānitāt) and guard in [their husbands'] absence what God would have them guard. Concerning those women from whom you* [masc. pl.] *fear nushūz, admonish them (faʿiẓūhunna), and abandon them in bed (wa'hjurūhunna fī'l-maḍājiʿ), and hit them (wa'ḍribūhunna). If they obey you, do not seek a means against them. God is most High, Great.*[7]

Since this verse describes wifely *nushūz* as being worthy of discipline, the exegetical definition of wifely *nushūz* is significant. Whether one interprets *nushūz* expansively or restrictively affects which wifely behaviours require rebuke and which fall outside disciplinary constraints. If, on the one hand, the definition of *nushūz* is narrow and restricted to specific actions, then wives are safeguarded from wanton chastisement. If, on the other hand, the definition of *nushūz* is more ambiguous and general, then husbands' disciplinary power is significantly increased.

Pre-modern exegetes interpreted wifely *nushūz* in Q. 4:34 to have three possible meanings. The 'disobedience' (*ʿiṣyān*) of wives was the primary meaning of *nushūz* in pre-modern exegesis.[8] While many exegetes understood this to be unqualified disobedience, some exegetes limited it to sexual disobedience. An equally widespread interpretation of wifely *nushūz* was her 'rising' (*irtifāʿ*).[9] Finally, wifely *nushūz* was considered to be her hatred/repulsion (*bughḍ*) for her husband. For many exegetes, these interpretations were interconnected and not mutually exclusive.

Exegetes who defined wifely *nushūz* as unqualified 'disobedience', simply replaced '*nushūzahunna*' with '*ʿiṣyānahunna*' in their commentaries.[10] According to these exegetes, the general and unqualified disobedience of wives to their husbands constituted *nushūz*, and was thus deserving of discipline. Sometimes exegetes described specific actions that a wife might take that would qualify as 'disobedience'; at times a wife's disobedience was simply her refusal to obey her husband or her abandonment of his command,[11] but at other times, the definition of disobedience was expanded to include behaviours that did not involve a wife strictly denying her husband's command. For instance, Fakhr al-Dīn al-Rāzī (d. 606/1209) argued that a wife could commit *nushūz* by altering any previously desirable behaviour to something less appealing. Examples of such altered behaviour included if she stood when her husband entered a room or rejoiced when he touched her and then she stopped these practices. Rāzī says:

> Know that the explanation of fear (*khawf*) is the state which enters the heart when he suspects the occurrence of a loathsome

> [or 'disliked'] thing in the future. Al-Shāfiʿī said concerning '*wa'l-lātī takhāfūna nushūzahunna*' that *nushūz* can be in speech and action. Say, for example that she answers his call when he calls her, and is submissive in speech when he addresses her, then she changes. And [it can be] in action, for example that she stands when he enters upon her, or that she hurries to his order and that she hastens to his bed, rejoicing when he touches her, then she changes from all of this. These things are indications of her *nushūz* and her disobedience (*ʿiṣyānuhā*). So then, the suspicion (*ẓanna*) of her *nushūz* and the nascence of these conditions generate the fear of *nushūz*. And *nushūz* is disobedience to the husband and rising against him in opposition, and its [grammatical] root is from people saying something is *nashaza* when it is raised, and from those who say of raised earth: it rose (*nashaza*) and it spread.[12]

This description of *nushūz*, that of a wife altering her behaviour in some way, is intriguing because it does not consider the reasons for why a wife might change her behaviour: is this a reaction to her husband's displeasing behaviour, is she too busy to stand up when he enters a room, too tired at the end of the day to 'rejoice' when he touches her, or is she feeling ill? There are myriad reasons for why a wife might alter her behaviour and the lack of attention to this point in the exegesis of this verse is striking, especially in comparison to the consideration a husband's motivation for *nushūz* receives in Q. 4:128, as will be seen below.

The contrasting treatment of wives and husbands in the discussion of marital *nushūz* is further highlighted in the exegetical definition of wifely *nushūz* as sexual disobedience specifically, as opposed to general disobedience. Sexual disobedience consisted of a wife withholding herself sexually from her husband or refusing herself to him.[13] Muḥammad b. Jarīr al-Ṭabarī (d. 311/923) located the marital bed as a possible site for a wife's disobedience to her husband by including wives' 'rising from their husbands' beds in disobedience to them' in his definition of *nushūz*.[14] As will be seen in the exegesis of Q. 4:128, pre-modern exegetes often defined husbandly *nushūz* as sexual antipathy and devoted a fair amount of energy reflecting on the motivations for husbandly *nushūz*. Thus, whereas a husband's sexual disinterest in his wife was interpreted as sexual antipathy, a wife's sexual disinterest was considered sexual disobedience. A wife's motivation for *nushūz* was rarely considered and her *nushūz* was treated in isolation from any surrounding circumstances. Instead of ascertaining and addressing the cause for wifely *nushūz*, exegetes instead deliberated on the disciplinary measures available to husbands in order to remove wifely *nushūz*.

An equally prevalent definition of wifely *nushūz* in pre-modern *tafsīr* was '*al-irtifāʿ*', which can be translated as 'rebellion', but 'rising' is closer to its literal meaning. Of the Arabic equivalents for *nushūz* offered by pre-modern exegetes, *irtifāʿ* is closest in lexical meaning to *nushūz*. As pre-modern exegetes noted, the basic verbal form of *nushūz*'s trilateral root, *n-sh-z*, means 'to rise'. Sometimes, *istiʿlāʾ* was used as a synonym that denoted the same meaning of 'rising'. For Ṭabarī, the two notions of a wife rising against her husband and rising against him in bed were intertwined. In addition to describing *nushūz* as disobedience, he described it as 'the rising of wives (*istiʿlāʾahunna*) against their husbands, and their rising (*irtifāʿahunna*) from their husbands' beds in disobedience to them'.[15] In this conception, the rising of the wife was figurative and literal, encompassing the definitions of wifely *nushūz* as general and sexual disobedience. Wives rose above their rank in the marital hierarchy when they disobeyed their husbands. They could also rise literally, as in rising from their marital bed in sexual refusal – which counted as sexual disobedience. For many exegetes, such as Rāzī and Muḥammad b. Aḥmad al-Qurṭubī (d. 671/1273), a wife's disobedience to her husband was the same as her rising against him. Qurṭubī explained wifely *nushūz* as wives 'raising themselves (*taʿāliyahunna*) from what God has made obligatory upon them with regard to the obedience of their husbands'. He also noted that a *nāshiza* wife was a wife that was bad for companionship (*al-sayyiʾa liʾl-ʿishra*).[16]

The rising of wives against their husbands carried implications of rising against God as well. This is because the marital hierarchy, with men in a position of authority over women, was considered to be divinely prescribed. When women rose above their station through their disobedience, they also rose against God, who had set up the hierarchy in the first place. Some exegetes expressed this position explicitly, describing a wife's raising herself (*tastaʿlī*) against her husband as 'rising against her nature (*khuluq*)'[17] and rising above the 'rank assigned to them by God' (*ʿan al-rutba allatī aqāmahunna'llāh bihā*).[18] In these descriptions of wifely *nushūz*, exegetes posited marital hierarchy as an essential characteristic of marriage. In this relationship, wives fulfilled their marital obligations and remained in their correct rank within the marriage by being obedient to their husbands, whether sexually or otherwise. Any attempt to rise from their appointed rank in the marital hierarchy was considered to be an act of rebellion requiring discipline.

A final definition offered for wifely *nushūz* was the hatred/repulsion (*bughḍ*) or repugnance (*karāhiyya*) of a wife for her husband.[19] The hatred or repugnance of her husband was either the motivating factor for disobedience and rising, or it was constitutive of *nushūz* itself.[20] Like sexual disobedience, *bughḍ* for one's spouse had the potential for a gender neutral definition of husbandly and wifely *nushūz*. Hatred and repugnance, unlike disobedience, are not hierarchal by definition. One can hate a superior, a subordinate or an equal: Ibrāhīm b. al-Sarī al-Zajjāj (d. 311/923), for instance, interpreted *nushūz* as the repugnance of one spouse for the other (*karāhiyya li-ṣāḥibihi*), as opposed to only a wife's repugnance for her husband or vice versa.[21] However, exegetes interpreted a wife's *bughḍ* as warranting her husband's discipline, while a husband's *bughḍ* was treated as a problem that needed to be resolved between spouses. When hatred was regarded as a motivating factor for wifely *nushūz*, it was treated as an irrational quality that emerged without just cause. Why a wife might hate her husband was not a question that any pre-modern exegete asked, although they did explore in great detail the reasons for why a husband might hate his wife.

Wives who committed *nushūz* were subject to husbandly discipline, according to the exegetes. Husbands were required to correct wifely *nushūz* through three measures: they were to discipline their wives through verbal admonition, sexual withdrawal and refusal, and physical chastisement. Exegetes considered several procedural questions surrounding husbandly discipline, such as whether husbands should follow these three actions simultaneously or consecutively; what exactly they should say to their wives when verbally admonishing them; what 'sexual withdrawal' means and how long it should last; and, finally, how severely or lightly a husband could hit his wife, whether they were permitted to hit with their hands, or whether they were allowed to employ tools such as a whip, sandal or handkerchief. Though pre-modern exegetes generally sought to reduce the possibility for husbands to abuse their power over wives by delimiting their disciplinary power, none questioned the right of husbands to discipline their wives, physically or otherwise.[22]

As seen above, the definitions offered for wifely *nushūz* in pre-modern Qur'an commentaries were hierarchal in nature and they re-instantiated a patriarchal view of marriage. The fact that all of the above definitions of wifely *nushūz* made it a punishable act, that required disciplinary measures from husbands, highlights the asymmetrical relationship between spouses. In this conception, wives ranked below their husbands and owed obedience to them. When wives disobeyed their husbands, they rose above their divinely appointed rank and thus disobeyed God Himself. The hierarchal view of marriage was emphasised in Qur'anic exegesis by the lexical use of the term *nushūz*; when describing the behaviour of wives, it was interpreted in a manner that bolstered the unequal relationship between husbands and wives. When wifely *nushūz* was interpreted as general disobedience, its meaning was distinctly different than that of husbandly *nushūz*. Although in most cases the meanings of wifely and husbandly *nushūz* overlapped, the implications of these actions were altered so that they required discipline in the case of wives and amicable settlement in the case of husbands.

Exegetical Treatment of Husbandly *Nushūz*

The fact that both Q. 4:34 and Q. 4:128 mention the characteristic of spousal *nushūz* suggests an obvious connection between the two verses, and therefore one might expect this overlap to figure prominently in the commentaries of these verses. Yet, in their discussions of each verse, pre-modern exegetes rarely reference the other verse, although some do make brief mention of husbandly *nushūz* in their discussions of wifely *nushūz* in Q. 4:34 and vice versa in Q. 4:128. As a result, the treatment of husbandly *nushūz* is almost exclusively found in the exegesis of Q. 4:128, the text which makes explicit reference to it. Q. 4:128 states:

> *If a wife fears nushūz or desertion (iʿrāḍ) from her husband, there is no blame on them both if they arrange an amicable settlement between themselves. Such amicable settlement (sulḥ) is better,*[23] *even though covetousness lies within the souls. If you do* [masc. pl.] *excellence and are God-fearing, God is acquainted with all that you do.*

The phrasing of Q. 4:34 and Q. 4:128 offer significant differences in the language, tone, context and consequences of husbandly *nushūz*, when compared to wifely *nushūz*. Based on these textual differences, pre-modern exegetes were able to interpret husbandly and wifely *nushūz* in a divergent fashion. Karen Bauer mentions two textual variances between Q. 4:34 and Q. 4:128. First, 'the Qur'anic verse regarding wives' *nushūz* is directly addressed to husbands ('if you fear *nushūz*') whereas the verse regarding the husbands' *nushūz* is impersonal ('if a wife fears *nushūz*')'.[24] Second, the outcome for husbandly *nushūz* is different from that of wifely *nushūz* in the Qur'anic text itself. Whereas Q. 4:34 holds husbands responsible for disciplining wives who commit *nushūz*, Q. 4:128 encourages some sort of settlement between a couple when a husband commits *nushūz*.[25] Additionally, whereas wifely *nushūz* is mentioned as a stand-alone quality in Q. 4:34, Q. 4:128 pairs the quality of husbandly *nushūz* with another term, *iʿrāḍ*. At a basic lexical level, *iʿrāḍ* means 'turning away' and has been historically interpreted to mean a husband's non-performance of his sexual duties to his wife.[26] Pre-modern exegetes listed multiple qualities to describe the *iʿrāḍ* of a husband against his wife, including antipathy, shunning one's wife, not speaking to her, avoiding intimacy with her and generally disliking her.[27] *Iʿrāḍ* was subsumed under the category of husbandly *nushūz* in such a way that many exegetes assumed they were synonymous.[28] These exegetes held that the coupling of *nushūz* with *iʿrāḍ* linked the two, so that the wording of the Qur'anic text itself prevents the reader from treating husbandly *nushūz* in the same manner she would wifely *nushūz*. The addition of *iʿrāḍ* in Q. 4:128 was a sort of proof that husbandly and wifely *nushūz* were discrete concepts with different connotations and consequences.

Pre-modern exegetes employed several interpretive strategies when discussing *nushūz* in the exegesis of Q. 4:128, all of which underscored the substantive difference between wifely and husbandly *nushūz*. Exegetes promoted four definitions of husbandly *nushūz*. One was the lexical definition of *n-sh-z* as a 'rising' (*istiʿlā, irtifāʿ*). The second was the hatred, repugnance or dislike of each spouse for the other (*bughḍ*). The third was a husband's unwillingness or inability to meet the obligations owed to his wife, whether sexual or monetary. The fourth was roughness in speech or action, such as injuring a wife by hitting her (*khushūna*).

The basic lexical meaning of *n-sh-z* as a 'hillock' or 'rising' is mentioned in the exegeses of Q. 4:128, as it was in Q. 4:34. Whereas in the case of wifely *nushūz* exegetes understood the 'rising' of a wife as both metaphorical and literal, in the case of husbandly *nushūz*, they discussed 'rising' only in its literal sense. Husbands might 'rise' from the bed of one wife to the bed of another wife or concubine.[29] However, husbandly 'rising' did not carry metaphorical implications of rebelliousness or disobedience. The non-applicability of the metaphoric sense of 'rising' only makes sense in the context of a marital hierarchy wherein husbands ranked above wives; husbands were owed the obedience of their wives, but they did not owe their wives obedience in return. Pre-modern exegetes offered a potpourri of legitimate reasons for why a husband might commit *nushūz*, thus rising from a wife's bed, such as his preference for another – younger (*shābba*) or more beautiful (*jamīla*) – woman (e.g. *atharatan ʿalayhā*),[30] his repulsion or hatred (*bughḍ*) for this particular wife,[31] his dislike (*kirāha*) for her or for her company,[32] his not loving her (*lā yuḥibbuhā* or *raghaba ʿanhā*),[33] her old age (*ʿajazat* or *kibarihā*),[34] her ugliness/disfigurement (*damāmatihā*),[35] her poverty (*faqrihā*),[36] her bad etiquette (*sūʾ khuluqihā*),[37] her inability to bear children,[38] his being bored by her (*ṭālat ṣuḥbatuhā*)[39] and his general restlessness (*mulāl*).[40] These grounds for a husband's rising from his wife's bed were considered without moral judgement, as legitimate and perfectly reasonable causes for a husband's *nushūz*. This stands in stark contrast to the disapproval exegetes levelled against *nāshiza* wives, as seen above.

The second definition of husbandly *nushūz* is hatred, repugnance or dislike (*bughḍ* or *karāhiyya*).[41] As in the case of wifely *nushūz*, *bughḍ* could function as either a motivation for husbandly *nushūz* or as *nushūz* itself. Again, despite the reciprocal and gender-neutral nature of hatred, pre-modern exegetes interpreted the *bughḍ* or *karāhiyya* of husbands and wives hierarchically. In the case of wives, their repugnance and dislike for husbands was closely linked to their disobedience and rebellion against their husbands. Pre-modern exegetes never discuss what reasons, legitimate or otherwise, might cause a woman to dislike her husband or commit *nushūz* against him. For them, wifely *nushūz* seemed to emerge out of a vacuum, was always unacceptable and husbands were morally obligated to remove their wives' *nushūz* through disciplinary measures. In the case of husbands, though, exegetes placed the blame for husbandly *nushūz* squarely on a deficient wife. Unlike wives, husbands appear to have several reasonable causes for committing *nushūz*, all of which suggest that the wife was unable to keep her husband happy. Exegetes justified the *nushūz* of a husband with some of the same reasons mentioned above, such as a husband's preference for another woman (wife or concubine), her ugliness, old age or bad behaviour.

Thirdly, pre-modern exegetes consider sexual and monetary neglect to be an essential element of husbandly *nushūz*.[42] This neglect included withholding intimacy as well as maintenance (*nafaqa*), thus encompassing a husband's monetary refusal to meet his fiduciary obligations to his wife. In the work of the exegetes under study in this chapter, both of these qualities were considered to be rights of a wife over her husband.[43] Exegetes relied on Q. 30:21, which describes love and mercy (*al-mawadda wa'l-raḥma*) between spouses as an essential quality of marriage and a sign of God, to argue that when love and mercy were lacking in a marriage, this was a failing on the part of husbands. Maḥmūd b. ʿUmar al-Zamakhsharī (d. 538/1143) described husbandly *nushūz* as the absence of *al-mawadda wa'l-raḥma* in marriage. In this context, husbandly *nushūz* occurred when husbands reneged on their duties to their wives; specifically, their obligations to be sexually available on a certain number of nights to each wife and to provide financially for their wives. When they failed to fulfil either of these obligations, they were considered guilty of husbandly *nushūz*.

In contrast to the previous definitions of *nushūz* (i.e. 'rising' and 'hatred'), this interpretation placed a greater emphasis on a husband's deficiency in fulfilling his marital obligations than on a deficient wife who was unable to keep her husband's interest. Nevertheless, exegetes preserved marital hierarchy in their solution to this type of husbandly *nushūz*; wives were encouraged to forgo their rights over their husbands in order to remain married. Some of the rights they could surrender were those of maintenance (*nafaqa*),[44] dowry (*mahr*)[45] and allotted nights (*qism*).[46] While Ismāʿīl b. ʿUmar Ibn Kathīr (d. 774/1374) was more vague about the rights that a wife could give up in order to remain married to her *nāshiz* husband ('forgoing all or some of her rights'), Rāzī was clear that wives could only give up the rights 'that they could demand from their husbands', which specifically were dowry, maintenance and allotment of nights. He believed that wives could not give up sex (*waṭ'*) in this settlement, since husbands 'were not forced to have sex' with their wives, but they were forced to give them dowry, maintenance and allotment of nights.[47] The voluntary relinquishment of wifely rights was understood by exegetes as the 'amicable settlement' (*ṣulḥ*) mentioned in Q. 4:128. Husbands could accept such an abdication of rights from their wives without incurring sin. Interestingly, Qurṭubī reports from Muqātil b. Ḥayyān that if a married man wants to marry a younger woman he should offer to give the older wife wealth in exchange for giving the younger woman more nights and days. If she does not accept this agreement, then he must treat both wives equally. In Qurṭubī's narration of this report, there is no ultimatum of reduced rights or divorce. However, in other reports narrated by Qurṭubī, wives are encouraged to surrender their rights in exchange for remaining married to their husbands. In general, Qurṭubī supported all of these options as legitimate forms of settlements (*ṣulḥ*) recommended in Q. 4:128.[48]

If a wife refused to surrender a portion or all of her rights, then a husband was obligated to either fulfil her rights or divorce her.[49] However, since Q. 4:128 states that *amicable settlement is better*, the exegetes under study assumed that Q. 4:128 meant that it was better for a couple to come to an amicable settlement – which they interpreted as wives relinquishing their marital rights – rather than divorce, continued husbandly *nushūz* or marital disagreement. This point is made well by al-Khāzin al-Baghdādī (d. 721/1321), who defines a man or woman who achieves excellence in faith (*muḥsin* and *muḥsina*) with regard to the reference to 'good/excellence' in '*wa in tuḥsinū*' in Q. 4:128. According to Khāzin,

> [the verse] '*they should make an amicable arrangement* (*baynahumā ṣulḥā*)' refers to the maintenance (*nafaqa*) and allotment of nights (*qism*). When a man says to his wife, 'you have become old and entered old age (*kaburat*), and I plan to marry a beautiful (*jamīla*), youthful (*shābba*) woman, and prefer her over you in the allotment of nights and days. If you are pleased with this, stay with me. If you dislike this, I will be kind to you and let you go your way [i.e. divorce you].' If she is pleased with this, then she is an excellent woman (*muḥsina*) because she does not force her rights [on him]. And if she is not pleased without her rights, it is the husband's obligation to fulfil her rights of maintenance and allotment, or to divorce her with excellence (*iḥsān*). And if he keeps her (*amsikhā*) and fulfils her rights despite his dislike (*kirāha*) for her, then he is an excellent man (*muḥsin*).[50]

The exegetes under study were quite comfortable with the fact that the 'settlement' they were proposing would result in the unequal treatment of wives. In fact, they used their exegesis of Q. 4:128 in order to treat the statement *You will not be able to do justice between your wives* in the following verse (Q. 4:129) as a descriptive statement of fact, rather than an exhortation for husbands to either treat their wives equally or avoid marrying multiple wives.[51]

The contrasting interpretive treatment of husbandly and wifely *nushūz* is also underlined in the moral exhortations of the exegetes under study. Exegetes did not exhort husbands to avoid husbandly *nushūz* as they had exhorted wives to avoid wifely *nushūz* in the exegesis of Q. 4:34. When wives refused their husbands sexually, they disobeyed their husbands and thus transgressed against them by reneging on their marital obligations. In such a situation, husbands were required to reclaim their rights by disciplining their wives. Part of this discipline was verbal; husbands were encouraged to tell their wives, 'Fear God and fulfil my rights which are obligatory on you.'[52] In contrast, when husbands reneged on their marital obligations by shunning their wives, being sexually unavailable or even withholding their maintenance, exegetes did not encourage wives to give similar exhortations to their husbands. Instead of reclaiming their rights, wives were made to bear the burden of their husbands' *nushūz*, since it was assumed that it was likely caused by deficiencies on the part of wives.

Quite the opposite from admonishing husbands for committing *nushūz*, exegetes accepted that husbands might legitimately wish to commit *nushūz* or *iʿrāḍ* in response to a wife who has fallen out of favour. Rather than chide the husbands for their impending *nushūz*, or indeed rather than advocating marital arbitration, exegetes placed the burden on wives to give up rights to maintenance, dowry or allotted nights. By giving up the very rights that their husbands were denying them, wives freed their husbands from fulfilling their marital obligations, as Ibn Kathīr comments:

> If a woman fears aversion/displeasure (*nufūr*) from her husband, or *iʿrāḍ*, she should forgo all or some of her rights, from maintenance and clothing, housing or other rights that she has over him. He should accept these from her. There is no sin on her in surrendering these [rights], and neither on him for accepting this from her.[53]

Husbandly *nushūz* was not removed through disciplinary action; after all, wives ranked lower in the marital hierarchy and therefore did not enjoy disciplinary privileges. Furthermore, wives were encouraged to believe that their husbands' loss of interest might lead to divorce, and were pressured to relinquish their marital rights in order to remain married to their husbands. Al-Khāzin al-Baghdādī reports from Muhammad's wife ʿĀʾisha that she interpreted Q. 4:128 to be about a woman whose husband plans to divorce her to marry another and she pleads with him to 'keep me, don't divorce me' (*amsiknī, lā taṭluqnī*). Instead, she encourages him to marry another woman and sacrifices her rights to maintenance and her allotment of nights.[54] Several exegetes mention the example of Muhammad's wife Sawdā' as being the impetus for the revelation of Q. 4:128.[55] According to these accounts, Sawdā' feared that Muhammad would divorce her because of her old age, so she offered up her nights to 'Ā'isha in order to remain married to him. Muhammad accepted this arrangement, giving such arrangements an air of normativity and acceptability.[56]

Somewhat paradoxically, when husbandly *nushūz* was defined as sexual refusal it consisted of the very action husbands were authorised to undertake in order to discipline their wives when they were guilty of wifely *nushūz*. The paradox is intensified by the fourth definition of husbandly *nushūz* offered by pre-modern exegetes, which is treating a wife roughly (*khushūna*) – 'in words, actions or both',[57] injuring her (*yu'dhīhā*)[58] or hitting her (*ḍarabahā*).[59] According to pre-modern exegetes, a husband could hit his wife in order to correct wifely *nushūz*, but his hitting might also be considered a form of husbandly *nushūz*. It can be argued that although they never explicitly stated it as such, exegetes reckoned that husbandly *nushūz* occurred when husbands withheld sexual intimacy or hit their wives without just cause; that is, apart from rectifying wifely *nushūz*. If wives were guilty of *nushūz*, then husbands would be warranted in withholding sexual intimacy and/or hitting them; but how is a wife to know that her husband's sexual abandonment or hitting are disciplinary measures for her own *nushūz* or constitutive of his *nushūz*? In both cases, the onus was placed on the wife to remove her husband's undesirable behaviour by either changing her behaviour so that she is no longer committing *nushūz* against him, or appeasing him by relinquishing her marital rights. A wife may well be unaware as to exactly why her husband is sexually refusing or hitting her – whether it is because she is committing *nushūz* or because he no longer finds her attractive. This uncertainty helps us see the first disciplinary measure in Q. 4:34 differently; the purpose of verbal admonishment might be to alert a wife to a husband's assessment of wifely *nushūz*, whereas a lack of admonishment might designate a husband's violent behaviour as husbandly *nushūz*.

All of the definitions for husbandly *nushūz* in the pre-modern exegeses analysed here highlight a patriarchal understanding of marriage, where wives were located in a lower and disadvantaged position. According to these exegetes, when wives disobeyed, displeased, rose up against or disliked their husbands, they were subject to disciplinary action at the hands of their husbands and required to correct their behaviour to their husbands' satisfaction. On the other hand, if their husbands reneged on their spousal obligations, it was assumed that this was the result of some deficiency on the part of the wife. In this case, wives were urged to abdicate their limited marital rights in order to remain married to their husbands.[60] In both cases, the vision of this asymmetrical spousal relationship was justified as being divinely ordained. God, the commentators assumed, placed husbands in a higher position than their wives and empowered them to discipline their wives. In this context, wifely *nushūz* consisted of a wife's challenge to her husband's authority in any form and warranted discipline. However, since wives ranked below their husbands, a husband's *nushūz* could not comprise of him challenging his wife's authority. Instead, husbandly *nushūz* comprised his lack of interest in his wife, or a defaulting on his marital duties – whether sexual or monetary – and was resolved by reducing his obligations. This was accomplished by wives voluntarily ceding their marital rights. It stands to reason that if a wife freely gave up her marital rights, then her husband could no longer neglect those obligations. Exegetes bolstered this perspective through recourse to a report of Muhammad's own practice, wherein he accepted a similar arrangement from Sawdā'.

Conclusion

According to pre-modern Sunni Qur'an commentators, both wifely and husbandly *nushūz* were rectified by putting wives in their place in the marital hierarchy. Wifely *nushūz* was to be corrected through disciplinary action by husbands and husbandly *nushūz* was to be ameliorated through a renegotiation of the marital contract, whereby wives gave up their rights in marriage in order to remain married to their husbands. Here, the exegetical interpretations extended the marital hierarchy beyond the Qur'anic text, since the Qur'anic text did not hold wives responsible for their husbands' *nushūz*. Nor did the text call on wives to initiate a settlement with their husbands, but rather encouraged both spouses to find a settlement that would be agreeable to both. In contrast, the varied exegetical definitions of wifely and husbandly *nushūz* re-instantiated and solidified the power of husbands over wives in marriage. A husband had the power to both define and discipline his wife's *nushūz*, while it was a wife's responsibility to ensure that her husband did not commit *nushūz*.

Pre-modern interpretations of both forms of *nushūz*, husbandly and wifely, emphasise the disempowerment of wives by appealing to a cosmological hierarchy within which the marital relationship is subsumed. When a wife commits *nushūz*, she 'rises' from her proper place in the marital hierarchy through disobedience to her husband and thereby disrupts a divinely ordained cosmological hierarchy. A husband is therefore religiously obligated to return her to her place. In contrast, when a husband commits *nushūz*, he does not 'rise' out of his place in the marital hierarchy but rather displaces his wife by depriving her of her legally sanctioned marital rights. In both cases, a woman returns to her correct place in marriage by appeasing her husband and thus maintaining the cosmological order.

Although there is a palpable emphasis on the cosmological order, it is entirely conceivable that exegetes were not just interested in maintaining the marital hierarchy in their interpretation of these two verses, but they were also making sure that a wife had a recognised place in the marital hierarchy both in the case of wifely and husbandly *nushūz*. They did not deny husbands their divinely ordained right to seek pleasure in other women, but rather asked wives to renegotiate their marital rights in order to accommodate their husbands. Pre-modern exegetes may have thought that their attempts to ensure that wives had a place in their marriage, even a diminished one, was in the interest of wives, since a wife who had fallen from her husband's favour due to ugliness, old age, barrenness or other infirmities, would be of depreciated value for other men. If wives were divorced by their husbands because of shortcomings on their end, their prospects for re-marriage, and by extension their social status, might be decreased. It is within this patriarchal worldview that they proposed varied definitions of *nushūz*, both to maintain the cosmological role of husbands over wives, and also to provide a place for undesirable wives.

The interpretation of the same term, *nushūz*, to produce two different meanings, at times reading against the plain-sense meaning of the Qur'anic text, is significant in terms of methodology. It demonstrates that pre-modern exegetes read and interpreted the Qur'an within the context of an idealised cosmology in which a patriarchal marital structure was divinely prescribed. This cosmological order was no doubt influenced by their social, historical and cultural context, and coloured their readings of the text in such a way that the patriarchy inherent in the Qur'anic text was expanded to map onto their own patriarchal context.

NOTES

1 Ayesha S. Chaudhry, *Domestic Violence and the Islamic Tradition: Ethics, Law and the Muslim Discourse of Gender* (Oxford: Oxford University Press, 2013); see especially chapters 1 and 2.

2 Many scholars have written about this phenomenon, see for example, Kecia Ali, *Sexual Ethics in Islam: Feminist Reflections on Qur'an, Hadith and Jurisprudence* (Oxford: Oneworld, 2006); eadem, *Marriage and Slavery in Early Islam* (London: Harvard University Press, 2010); Karen Bauer, 'Room for Interpretation: Qur'ānic Exegesis and Gender' (PhD Dissertation, Princeton University, 2008; published as *Gender Hierarchy in the Qur'an: Medieval Interpretations, Modern Responses* [Cambridge: Cambridge University Press, 2015]), especially pp. 152–81; eadem, '"Traditional" Exegesis of Q 4:34', *Comparative Islamic Studies* 2 (2006), pp. 129–42; eadem, '*The Male Is Not Like The Female* (Q 3:36): The Question of Gender Egalitarianism in the Qur'ān', *Religion Compass* 3, no. 4 (2009), pp. 637–54; Ayesha S. Chaudhry, 'The Problems of Conscience and Hermeneutics: Some Contemporary Muslim Approaches', *Comparative Islamic Studies* 2 (2006), pp. 157–70; Manuela Marín, 'Disciplining Wives: A Historical Reading of Qur'ān 4:34', *Studia Islamica* 97 (2003), pp. 5–40; Sa'diyya Shaikh, 'Exegetical Violence: *Nushūz* in Qur'ānic Gender Ideology', *Journal for Islamic Studies* 17 (1997), pp. 49–73.

3 Kecia Ali, 'Religious Practices: Obedience and Disobedience in Islamic Discourses: Overview' in Suad Joseph, ed., *Encyclopedia of Women & Islamic Cultures* (Leiden: Brill, 2007), vol. 5, pp. 309–13. See also Chaudhry, *Domestic Violence and the Islamic Tradition*, Chapter 2.

4 I will consider the opinions of a representative selection of seventeen exegetes. For a more extensive study of pre-modern approaches to wifely and husbandly *nushūz*, see Bauer, 'Room for Interpretation', pp. 152–81; and Chaudhry, *Domestic Violence and the Islamic Tradition*, Chapter 2.

5 *O believers, when it is said to you 'Make room in the assemblies', then make room, and God will make room for you, and when it is said, 'Move up', move up, and God will raise up in rank those of you who believe and have been given knowledge. And God is aware of the things you do.* Q. 58:11 (translation by Arthur J. Arberry, *The Koran Interpreted* (orig. pub. London: Allen & Unwin, 1955).

6 With the aim of being as literal as possible, I have used my own translations except in a few instances, which are noted. Arberry translates this passage in the following way: *Or such as he who passed by a city that was fallen down upon its turrets; he said, 'How shall God give life to this now it is dead?' So God made him die a hundred years, then He raised him up, saying, 'How long hast thou tarried?' He said, 'I have tarried a day, or part of day.' Said He, 'Nay; thou hast tarried a hundred years. Look at thy food and drink – it has not spoiled; and look at thy ass. So We would make thee a sign for the people. And look at the bones, how We shall set them up, and then clothe them with flesh.' So, when it was made clear to him, he said, 'I know that God is powerful over everything.'* Q. 2:259 (tr. Arberry, *The Koran Interpreted*).

7 This is my translation of the verse; see Chaudhry, 'The Problems of Conscience and Hermeneutics', p. 158.

8 Some exegetes, such as Abū Ḥayyān al-Gharnāṭī (d. 745/1344), explicitly linked their definition of *nushūz* as disobedience to the word *ʿiṣyān*. Abū Ḥayyān wrote, '*if they obey you* suggests that they [wives] become disobedient (*ʿāṣiyāt*) when they commit *nushūz*'. Abū Ḥayyān al-Gharnāṭī, *Tafsīr al-baḥr al-muḥīṭ* (Beirut: Dār al-Kutub al-ʿIlmiyya, 1996), vol. 3, pp. 248–53. Exegetes who offered 'wifely disobedience' as a possible meaning for *nushūz* include Muḥammad b. Jarīr al-Ṭabarī (d. 311/923), *Jāmiʿ al-bayān fī taʾwīl al-Qurʾān* (Beirut: Dār al-Kutub al-ʿIlmiyya, 1999); Ibn Abī Zamanīn (d. 399/1008), *Tafsīr al-Qurʾān al-ʿazīz li-Ibn Abī Zamanīn* (Cairo: al-Fārūq al-Ḥadītha li'l-Ṭibāʿa wa'l-Nashr, 2002), vol. 1, pp. 366–8; Abū'l Ḥasan al-Māwardī (d. 450/1058), *al-Nukat wa'l-ʿuyūn: tafsīr al-Māwardī min rawāʾiʿ al-tafāsīr* (Beirut: Dār al-Kutub al-ʿIlmiyya, 1992), vol. 1, pp. 480–3; Abū'l-Qāsim Maḥmūd al-Zamakhsharī (d. 538/1143), *al-Kashshāf ʿan ḥaqāʾiq al-tanzīl wa ʿuyūn al-aqāwīl fī wujūh al-taʾwīl* (Beirut: Dār al-Kutub al-ʿIlmiyya, 2003), vol. 1, pp. 490–7; Fakhr al-Dīn al-Rāzī (d. 606/1209), *al-Tafsīr al-kabīr* [*Mafātīḥ al-ghayb*] (Beirut: Dār Iḥyāʾ al-Turāth al-ʿArabī, 1997), vol. 4, pp. 70–3; Muḥammad b. Aḥmad al-Qurṭubī (d. 671/1273), *al-Jāmiʿ li-aḥkām al-Qurʾān: Tafsīr al-Qurṭubī* (Beirut: Dār al-Kitāb al-ʿArabī, 1997), vol. 5, pp. 161–7; Abū'l-Barakāt al-Nasafī (d. 710/1310), *Tafsīr al-Nasafī: al-Musammā bi-Madārik al-tanzīl wa ḥaqāʾiq al-taʾwīl* (Beirut: Dār al-Qalam, 1989), vol. 1, pp. 354–5; Ismāʿīl b. ʿUmar Ibn Kathīr (d. 773/1371), *Tafsīr al-ʿaẓīm li-Ibn Kathīr* (Damascus: Dār Ibn Kathīr, 1994), vol. 1, pp. 601–3; Jalāl al-Dīn al-Maḥallī (d. 864/1459) and Jalāl al-Dīn al-Suyūṭī (d. 911/1505), *al-Qurʾān al-karīm: bi'l-rasm al-ʿUthmānī wa bi-hāmishahu tafsīr al-Jalalayn; Mudhayyalan bi-Kitāb Lubāb al-nuqūl fī asbāb al-nuzūl* (Beirut: Dār al-Qalam, 1982),

pp. 105–6 and pp. 179–81. The preponderance of '*nushūzahunna*' as "*iṣyānahunna*' was partly based on the text of Q. 4:34 which states, *If they* [your wives] *obey you, do not find a means against them*. See also Bauer, 'Room for Interpretation', pp. 155–6.

9 Exegetes who gloss *nushūz* as 'rising' by using *al-irtifāʿ* or a conjugation of *ʿalā* include al-Ṭabarī, *Jāmiʿ al-bayān*, vol. 4, pp. 59–72; Māwardī, *al-Nukat wa'l-ʿuyūn*, vol. 1, pp. 480–3; Rāzī, *al-Tafsīr al-kabīr*, vol. 4, pp. 70–3; Qurṭubī, *al-Jāmiʿ*, vol. 5, pp. 161–7; Nasafī, *Madārik al-tanzīl*, vol. 1, pp. 354–5; al-Khāzin al-Baghdādī, *Tafsīr al-Khāzin: al-Musammā Lubāb al-ta'wīl fī maʿānī al-tanzīl* (Baghdad: Maktabat al-Muthannā, 1975), pp. 373–6; Abū Ḥayyān, *al-Baḥr al-muḥīṭ*, vol. 3, pp. 248–53; Ibn Kathīr, *Tafsīr al-ʿaẓīm*, vol. 1, pp. 601–3.

10 Ṭabarī cited a report from Ibn ʿAbbās in which the latter described wifely *nushūz* as a wife 'reneging on her husband's rights' and 'disobeying her husband's commands'. The entire statement of Ibn ʿAbbās on the matter reads: 'she diminishes her husband's rights and disobeys his commands (*wa tastakhiff bi-ḥaqq zawjihā wa-lā tuṭīʿ amrahu*)'. See Ṭabarī, *Jāmiʿ al-bayān*, vol. 4, pp. 59–72. Exegetes who gloss *nushūzahunna* with *iṣyānahunna* include Ibn Abī Zamanīn, *Tafsīr al-Qur'ān*, vol. 1, pp. 366–8; Abū'l-Ḥasan ʿAlī al-Wāḥidī (d. 468/1076), *al-Wajīz fī tafsīr al-Kitāb al-ʿazīz* (Damascus: Dār al-Qalam, 1995), vol. 1, pp. 262–3; Rāzī, *al-Tafsīr al-kabīr*, vol. 4, pp. 70–3; Qurṭubī, *al-Jāmiʿ*, vol. 5, pp. 161–7; Nasafī, *Madārik al-tanzīl*, vol. 1, pp. 354–5; Abū Ḥayyān, *al-Baḥr al-muḥīṭ*, vol. 3, pp. 248–53.

11 Ibn Kathīr, *Tafsīr al-ʿaẓīm*, vol. 1, pp. 601–3.

12 Rāzī, *al-Tafsīr al-kabīr*, vol. 4, pp. 70–3.

13 Exegetes who defined *nushūz* as sexual disobedience included Ṭabarī, *Jāmiʿ al-bayān*, vol. 4, pp. 59–2; Zamakhsharī, *al-Kashshāf*, vol. 1, pp. 490–7; Qurṭubī, *al-Jāmiʿ*, vol. 5, pp. 161–7; Abū Ḥayyān, *al-Baḥr al-muḥīṭ*, vol. 3, pp. 248–53; Ibn Kathīr, *Tafsīr al-ʿaẓīm*, vol. 1, pp. 601–3.

14 Ṭabarī, *Jāmiʿ al-bayān*, vol. 4, pp. 59–72.

15 Ibid.

16 Qurṭubī, *al-Jāmiʿ*, vol. 5, pp. 161–7.

17 Abū Ḥayyān wrote '*nushūz*: that a woman is crooked, and raises her nature and aggrandises herself over her husband' (*wa'l-nushūz: an tataʿawwaj al-mar'a wa yartafiʿ khuluqahā wa tastaʿliya ʿalā zawjihā*); Abū Ḥayyān, *al-Baḥr al-muḥīṭ*, vol. 3, pp. 248–53. This description was later adopted verbatim by ʿAbd al-Raḥmān al-Thaʿālibī (d. 430/1038), *Tafsīr al-Thaʿālibī: al-musammā bi'l-Jawāhir al-ḥisān fī tafsīr al-Qur'ān* (Beirut: Dār Iḥyā' al-Turāth, 1997), vol. 2, pp. 229–31.

18 al-Biqāʿī comments in full, 'as for those [women] from whom you fear *nushūz*: meaning, they rise against you from the rank assigned to them by God, and they disobey you when God has made [their obedience to you] your right. The denotation of *nushūz* is the disturbance caused by rising' (*wa'llātī takhāfūna nushūzahunna ay taraffuʿ ahunna ʿalaykum ʿan al-rutba allatī aqāmahunna'llāhu bihā, wa ʿiyānahunna lakum fī-mā jaʿala'llāhu lakum min al-ḥaqq wa aṣl al-nushūz: al-inziʿāj fī'l-irtifāʿ*). Ibrāhīm b. ʿUmar al-Biqāʿī (d. 885/1480), *Naẓm al-durar fī tanāsub al-āyāt wa'l-suwar* (Hyderabad: Maṭbaʿat Majlis Dā'irat al-Maʿārif al-ʿUthmāniyya, 1972), vol. 5, pp. 269–72.

19 Exegetes who considered either *bughḍ* or *karāhiyya* to be part of their definition of *nushūz* included Ṭabarī, *Jāmiʿ al-bayān*, vol. 4, pp. 59–72; Māwardī, *al-Nukat*

wa'l-'uyūn, vol. 1, pp. 480–3; Abū'l-Faraj Ibn al-Jawzī (d. 597/1200), *Zād al-masīr fī 'ilm al-tafsīr* (Damascus: al-Maktab al-Islāmī li'l-Ṭibā'a wa'l-Nashr, 1964), vol. 2, pp. 73–8; al-Khāzin al-Baghdādī, *Lubāb al-ta'wīl*, pp. 373–6; Ibn Kathīr, *Tafsīr al-'aẓīm*, vol. 1, pp. 601–3.

20 Ṭabarī, 'It [*nushūz*] is their rising against their husbands, rising from their beds in disobedience, challenging their husbands in that which obedience is made obligatory on them, in hatred and aversion to their husbands' (*fa innahu isti'lā'ahunna 'alā azwājihinna, wa irtifā'ahunna 'an furushihim bi'l-ma'ṣiya min-hunna, wa'l-khilāf 'alayhim fī-mā lazimahunna ṭā'atuhum fīhi, bughḍan minhunna wa i'rāḍan 'an-hum*), Ṭabarī, *Jāmi' al-bayān*, vol. 4, pp. 59–72.

21 Ibrāhīm b. al-Sarī al-Zajjāj, *Ma'ānī al-Qur'ān wa i'rābuhu* (Beirut: al-Maktaba al-'Aṣriyya, 1973), vol. 2, pp. 48–9.

22 For more on this, see Chaudhry, *Domestic Violence and the Islamic Tradition*, Chapter 2. See also Bauer, 'Room for Interpretation', pp. 158–61, and Marín, 'Disciplining Wives'.

23 The wording of this verse raises the question of 'better than what?' All the pre-modern exegetes in this study interpreted this to mean 'better than divorce'. Some added: better than both divorce and persistence in husbandly *nushūz*. See, for example, Rāzī, *al-Tafsīr al-kabīr*, vol. 4, p. 236.

24 Bauer, 'Room for Interpretation', p. 156.

25 Ibid.

26 *I'rāḍ* was translated by Yusuf Alī as 'desertion' (Abdullah Yusuf Ali, *The Holy Qur'an*, repr. [London: Wordsworth, 2000], p. 75), and as 'reluctance' by Bauer, 'Room for Interpretation', p. 156; and Kecia Ali, 'Money, Sex, and Power: The Contractual Nature of Marriage in Islamic Jurisprudence' (Unpublished PhD Dissertation, Duke University, 2002), p. 70.

27 See Qurṭubī, *al-Jāmi'*, vol. 5, p. 384; Rāzī, *al-Tafsīr al-kabīr*, vol. 4, p. 235; and Maḥallī and Suyūṭī, *Tafsīr al-Jalālayn*, p. 164.

28 Rāzī wrote, 'The *nushūz* of the man with regard to his woman is that he shuns her (*yu'riḍu 'anhā*) . . .' Rāzī, *al-Tafsīr al-kabīr*, vol. 4, p. 235. See also Ibn Kathīr, *Tafsīr al-'aẓīm*, vol. 1, p. 685; and Zamakhsharī, *al-Kashshāf*, vol. 1, p. 559.

29 Ṭabarī, *al-Jāmi' al-bayān*, vol. 4, p. 304: 'raising himself from [his wife] to someone else'. See also Abū Ḥayyān, *al-Baḥr al-muḥīṭ*, vol. 3, p. 363; Ibn 'Aṭiyya al-Andalusī (d. 541/1147), *al-Muḥarrar al-wajīz fī tafsīr al-Kitāb al-'azīz* (Beirut: Manshūrāt Muḥammad 'Alī Bayḍūn, 2001), vol. 2, p. 119; Ibn Kathīr, *Tafsīr al-'aẓīm*, vol. 1, p. 686; Hūd b. Muḥakkam al-Ḥawwārī (fl. 4th/10th century), *Tafsīr Kitāb Allāh al-'azīz* (Beirut: Dār al-Gharb al-Islāmī, 1990), vol. 1, p. 428; al-Khāzin al-Baghdādī, *Lubāb al-ta'wīl*, vol. 1, p. 436; Muḥammad b. Aḥmad al-Shirbīnī (d. 977/1570), *Tafsīr al-Khaṭīb al-Shirbīnī: al-musammā al-sirāj al-munīr fī'l-i'āna 'alā ma'rifat ba'ḍ ma'ānī kalām Rabbinā al-ḥakīm al-khabīr* (Beirut: Dār al-Kutub al-'Ilmiyya, 2004), vol. 1, p. 389; Maḥallī and Suyūṭī, *Tafsīr al-Jalālayn*, p. 164; Zamakhsharī, *al-Kashshāf*, vol. 1, p. 559; Ibn Abī Zamanīn, *Tafsīr al-Qur'ān*, vol. 1, p. 411.

30 Exegetes described preference for another woman in many ways, including a husband 'turning his eye to a woman other than her'. Nasafī, *Madārik al-tanzīl*, vol. 1, pp. 251–2. See also Abū Ḥayyān, *al-Baḥr al-muḥīṭ*, vol. 3, p. 363; Ibn 'Aṭiyya, *al-Muḥarrar al-wajīz*, vol. 2, p. 119; Ibn al-Jawzī, *Zād al-masīr*, vol. 2, p. 218; Ibn Kathīr, *al-Tafsīr al-'aẓīm*, vol. 1, p. 686; Ḥawwārī, *Tafsīr*, vol. 1,

p. 428; al-Khāzin al-Baghdādī, *Lubāb al-ta'wīl*, vol. 1, p. 436; Shirbīnī, *Tafsīr*, vol. 1, p. 389; Maḥallī and Suyūṭī, *Tafsīr al-Jalālayn*, p. 164; Ṭabarī, *Jāmiʿ al-bayān*, vol. 4, p. 304; Zamakhsharī, *al-Kashshāf*, vol. 1, p. 559; Ibn Abī Zamanīn, *Tafsīr al-Qur'ān*, vol. 1, p. 411.

31 Maḥallī and Suyūṭī, *Tafsīr al-Jalālayn*, p. 164; Ṭabarī, *Jāmiʿ al-bayān*, vol. 4, p. 304.

32 Ibn al-Jawzī, *Zād al-masīr*, vol. 2, p. 218; Shirbīnī, *Tafsīr*, vol. 1, p. 389; Ṭabarī, *Jāmiʿ al-bayān*, vol. 4, p. 304.

33 Ibn ʿAṭiyya, *al-Muḥarrar al-wajīz*, vol. 2, p. 119; Ṭabarī, *Jāmiʿ al-bayān*, vol. 4, p. 305.

34 Abū Ḥayyān, *al-Baḥr al-muḥīṭ*, vol. 3, p. 363; Ibn ʿAṭiyya, *al-Muḥarrar al-wajīz*, vol. 2, p. 119; Ibn Kathīr, *Tafsīr al-ʿaẓīm*, vol. 1, p. 687; Ḥawwārī, *Tafsīr*, vol. 1, p. 428; al-Khāzin al-Baghdādī, *Lubāb al-ta'wīl*, vol. 1, p. 436; Nasafī, *Madārik al-tanzīl*, vol. 1, p. 251; Qurṭubī, *al-Jāmiʿ*, vol. 5, p. 384; Rāzī, *al-Tafsīr al-kabīr*, vol. 4, p. 235; Shirbīnī, *Tafsīr*, vol. 1, p. 389; Ṭabarī, *Jāmiʿ al-bayān*, vol. 4, p. 304; Zamakhsharī, *al-Kashshāf*, vol. 1, p. 559; Ibn Abī Zamanīn, *Tafsīr al-Qur'ān*, vol. 1, p. 411.

35 Abū Ḥayyān, *al-Baḥr al-muḥīṭ*, vol. 3, p. 363; Ibn ʿAṭiyya, *al-Muḥarrar al-wajīz*, vol. 2, p. 119; Ibn Kathīr, *Tafsīr al-ʿaẓīm*, vol. 1, pp. 686–7; Nasafī, *Madārik al-tanzīl*, vol. 1, p. 251; Qurṭubī, *al-Jāmiʿ*, vol. 5, p. 384; Rāzī, *al-Tafsīr al-kabīr*, vol. 4, p. 235; Ṭabarī, *Jāmiʿ al-bayān*, vol. 4, p. 304; Zamakhsharī, *al-Kashshāf*, vol. 1, p. 559.

36 Qurṭubī, *al-Jāmiʿ*, vol. 5, p. 384; Ṭabarī, *Jāmiʿ al-bayān*, vol. 4, p. 305.

37 Ibn Kathīr, *Tafsīr al-ʿaẓīm*, vol. 1, p. 687; Ḥawwārī, *Tafsīr*, vol. 1, p. 428; Nasafī, *Madārik al-tanzīl*, vol. 1, p. 251; Qurṭubī, *al-Jāmiʿ*, vol. 5, p. 384; Ṭabarī, *Jāmiʿ al-bayān*, vol. 4, p. 305; Zamakhsharī, *al-Kashshāf*, vol. 1, p. 559.

38 Ibn al-Jawzī, *Zād al-masīr*, vol. 2, p. 217; Ibn Kathīr, *Tafsīr al-ʿaẓīm*, vol. 1, p. 686; al-Khāzin al-Baghdādī, *Lubāb al-ta'wīl*, vol. 1, p. 436; Ṭabarī, *Jāmiʿ al-bayān*, vol. 4, pp. 305–8; Ibn Abī Zamanīn, *Tafsīr al-Qur'ān*, vol. 1, p. 411.

39 Ṭabarī, *Jāmiʿ al-bayān*, vol. 4, p. 305.

40 Abū Ḥayyān, *al-Baḥr al-muḥīṭ*, vol. 3, p. 363; Nasafī, *Madārik al-tanzīl*, vol. 1, p. 251; Zamakhsharī, *al-Kashshāf*, vol. 1, p. 559.

41 Ḥawwārī, *Tafsīr*, vol. 1, p. 428; al-Khāzin al-Baghdādī, *Lubāb al-ta'wīl*, vol. 1, p. 436; Māwardī, *al-Nukat wa'l-ʿuyūn*, vol. 1, p. 533; Rāzī, *al-Tafsīr al-kabīr*, vol. 4, p. 235; Shirbīnī, *Tafsīr*, vol. 1, p. 389; Maḥallī and Suyūṭī, *Tafsīr al-Jalālayn*, p. 164; Ṭabarī, *Jāmiʿ al-bayān*, vol. 4, pp. 304 and 307; Zamakhsharī, *al-Kashshāf*, vol. 1, p. 559; Ibn Abī Zamanīn, *Tafsīr al-Qur'ān*, vol. 1, p. 411.

42 Abū Ḥayyān, *al-Baḥr al-muḥīṭ*, vol. 3, p. 363; Ibn Kathīr, *Tafsīr al-ʿaẓīm*, vol. 1, p. 687; Nasafī, *Madārik al-tanzīl*, vol. 1, p. 251; Rāzī, *al-Tafsīr al-kabīr*, vol. 4, p. 235; Shirbīnī, *Tafsīr*, vol. 1, p. 389; Wāḥidī, *al-Wajīz*, vol. 1, p. 293; Zamakhsharī, *al-Kashshāf*, vol. 1, p. 559.

43 E.g. al-Khāzin al-Baghdādī, *Lubāb al-ta'wīl*, vol. 1, p. 436; Maḥallī and Suyūṭī, *Tafsīr al-Jalālayn*, p. 164. For a more legal analysis of husbandly *nushūz* in pre-modern sources, see Ali, *Sexual Ethics in Islam*.

44 Abū Ḥayyān, *al-Baḥr al-muḥīṭ*, vol. 3, p. 363; Ibn Juzayy al-Gharnāṭī (d. 735/1334), *Kitāb al-Tashīl li-ʿulūm al-tanzīl* (Beirut: Dār al-Kitāb al-ʿArabī, 1973), vol. 1, p. 285; Nasafī, *Madārik al-tanzīl*, vol. 1, p. 252; Maḥallī and

Suyūṭī, *Tafsīr al-Jalālayn*, p. 164, Ṭabarī, *Jāmiʿ al-bayān*, vol. 4, p. 308; Wāḥidī, *al-Wajīz*, vol. 1, p. 293; Zamakhsharī, *al-Kashshāf*, vol. 1, p. 559.

45 Abū Ḥayyān, *al-Baḥr al-muḥīt*, vol. 3, p. 363; Ibn al-Jawzī, *Zād al-masīr*, vol. 2, p. 218; Ibn Kathīr, *Tafsīr al-ʿaẓīm*, vol. 1, p. 687; Māwardī, *al-Nukat wa'l-ʿuyūn*, vol. 1, p. 533; Nasafī, *Madārik al-tanzīl*, vol. 1, p. 252; Qurṭubī, *al-Jāmiʿ*, vol. 5, p. 384; Ṭabarī, *Jāmiʿ al-bayān*, vol. 4, p. 305; Wāḥidī, *al-Wajīz*, vol. 1, p. 293; Zamakhsharī, *al-Kashshāf*, vol. 1, p. 559.

46 Abū Ḥayyān, *al-Baḥr al-muḥīt*, vol. 3, p. 363; Ibn al-Jawzī, *Zād al-masīr*, vol. 2, p. 218; Ibn Kathīr, *Tafsīr al-ʿaẓīm*, vol. 1, p. 686; Māwardī, *al-Nukat wa'l-ʿuyūn*, vol. 1, p. 533; Nasafī, *Madārik al-tanzīl*, vol. 1, p. 252; Qurṭubī, *al-Jāmiʿ*, vol. 5, p. 384; Maḥallī and Suyūṭī, *Tafsīr al-Jalālayn*, p. 164; Ṭabarī, *Jāmiʿ al-bayān*, vol. 4, p. 304; Wāḥidī, *al-Wajīz*, vol. 1, p. 293; Zamakhsharī, *al-Kashshāf*, vol. 1, p. 559.

47 Rāzī, *al-Tafsīr al-kabīr*, vol. 4, p. 236. Ṭabarī mentions the possibility that a wife might even give her husband some of her own wealth in order to remain married to her husband. Ṭabarī, *Jāmiʿ al-bayān*, vol. 4, p. 305. See also Shirbīnī, *Tafsīr*, vol. 1, p. 389.

48 Qurṭubī, *al-Jāmiʿ*, vol. 5, p. 385. See also Ḥawwārī, *Tafsīr*, vol. 1, p. 428.

49 Maḥallī and Suyūṭī mention that if a wife is not pleased with a reduction of her rights, then her husband must either fulfil her rights (*yuwaffīhā ḥaqqahā*) or divorce her (*yufāriqhā*). Maḥallī and Suyūṭī, *Tafsīr al-Jalālayn*, p. 164. See also Ibn Kathīr, *Tafsīr al-ʿaẓīm*, vol. 1, pp. 687–8; Ṭabarī, *Jāmiʿ al-bayān*, vol. 4, pp. 306–7 and 311; Zamakhsharī, *al-Kashshāf*, vol. 1, p. 559.

50 al-Khāzin al-Baghdādī, *Lubāb al-ta'wīl*, vol. 1, p. 437. See also Abū Ḥayyān, *al-Baḥr al-muḥīṭ*, vol. 3, p. 363; Ibn al-Jawzī, *Zād al-masīr*, vol. 2, p. 218; Ibn Kathīr, *Tafsīr al-ʿaẓīm*, vol. 1, p. 687; Ibn Juzayy, *al-Tashīl li-ʿulūm al-tanzīl*, vol. 1, p. 285; Māwardī, *al-Nukat wa'l-ʿuyūn*, vol. 1, p. 533; Nasafī, *Madārik al-tanzīl*, vol. 1, p. 251; Qurṭubī, *al-Jāmiʿ*, vol. 5, p. 385; Rāzī, al-*Tafsīr al-kabīr*, vol. 4, p. 236; Shirbīnī, *Tafsīr*, vol. 1, p. 389; Maḥallī and Suyūṭī, *Tafsīr al-Jalālayn*, p. 164, Ṭabarī, *Jāmiʿ al-bayān*, vol. 4, p. 307; Wāḥidī, *al-Wajīz*, vol. 1, p. 293; Zamakhsharī, *al-Kashshāf*, vol. 1, p. 559.

51 Modern scholars who promote an egalitarian vision of Islam interpret Q. 4:129 as discouraging husbands from polygyny. They argue that since husbands must treat their wives equally and since Q. 4:129 states that they will never be able to do this, a prohibition against polygyny is implied. See, for example, Amina Wadud, *Qur'an and Woman: Rereading the Sacred Text from a Woman's Perspective* (Oxford: Oxford University Press, 1999), p. 83.

52 See Chaudhry, *Domestic Violence and the Islamic Tradition*, Chapter 2.

53 Ibn Kathīr, *Tafsīr al-ʿaẓīm*, vol. 1, p. 685.

54 al-Khāzin al-Baghdādī, *Lubāb al-ta'wīl*, vol. 1, p. 436. Maḥallī and Suyūṭī, *Tafsīr al-Jalālayn*, p. 164.

55 Others say Q. 4:128 was revealed about Khawla bt. Muḥammad and her husband Rāfiʿ b. Khudayj. In this story, once Khawla became old, Rāfiʿ married a younger woman, whom he favoured over Khawla. Khawla was impatient with this, so Rāfiʿ divorced her. But then he took her back, and she was again unable to be patient with his preference for the younger wife, so he divorced her a second time. Again, he took her back, but when Khawla continued to be impatient with Rāfiʿ's preference for the younger wife, he divorced her a third time.

When the waiting period of the third divorce was about to expire, Rāfi' offered Khawla two choices; either put up with his preference for the younger wife and remain married to him, or be divorced. Khawla opted to remain married despite her diminished status. Exegetes differ about what happened after this; while some mention that she was able to abide by her reduced status, others say that she could not live with the arrangement and in the end was permanently divorced. Abū Ḥayyān, *al-Baḥr al-muḥīṭ*, vol. 3, p. 363; Ibn 'Aṭiyya, *al-Muḥarrar al-wajīz*, vol. 2, p. 119; Ibn al-Jawzī, *Zād al-masīr*, vol. 2, p. 217; Ibn Kathīr, *Tafsīr al-'aẓīm*, vol. 1, p. 687; Qurṭubī, *al-Jāmi'*, vol. 5, p. 384; Ṭabarī, *Jāmi' al-bayān*, vol. 4, pp. 307 and 311. See also Ali, 'Religious Practices', p. 311.

56 Sawdā' is reported to have said, '[Give] my days to 'Ā'isha (*yawmī li-'Ā'isha*)'. Ibn Kathīr mentions several versions of this report. In one, Sawdā' says, 'I have reached old age and you no longer have need for me, but I want to be resurrected amongst your wives on the Day of Judgement.' Ibn Kathīr, *Tafsīr al-'aẓīm*, vol. 1, pp. 685–6. Abū Ḥayyān suggested that 'settlement' meant that 'a wife gives her days to another one of [her husband's] women, as in the [example] of Sawdā''. Abū Ḥayyān, *al-Baḥr al-muḥīṭ*, vol. 3, p. 363. See also Ibn 'Aṭiyya, *al-Muḥarrar al-wajīz*, vol. 2, p. 119; Ibn al-Jawzī, *Zād al-masīr*, vol. 2, p. 216; Ibn Juzayy, *al-Tashīl li-'ulūm al-tanzīl*, vol. 1, p. 285; al-Khāzin al-Baghdādī, *Lubāb al-ta'wīl*, vol. 1, p. 437; Māwardī, *al-Nukat wa'l-'uyūn*, vol. 1, p. 533; Qurṭubī, *al-Jāmi'*, vol. 5, pp. 384–5; Rāzī, *al-Tafsīr al-kabīr*, vol. 4, p. 235; Ṭabarī, *Jāmi' al-bayān*, vol. 4, pp. 308–9 and 310; Zamakhsharī, *al-Kashshāf*, vol. 1, p. 559.

57 Rāzī, *al-Tafsīr al-kabīr*, vol. 4, p. 235.

58 Abū Ḥayyān, *al-Baḥr al-muḥīṭ*, vol. 3, p. 363; Nasafī, *Madārik al-tanzīl*, vol. 1, p. 251; Zamakhsharī, *al-Kashshāf*, vol. 1, p. 559.

59 Abū Ḥayyān, *al-Baḥr al-muḥīṭ*, vol. 3, p. 363; Nasafī, *Madārik al-tanzīl*, vol. 1, p. 251; Zamakhsharī, *al-Kashshāf*, vol. 1, p. 559.

60 Hierarchal interpretations of gender permeated the exegesis of other potentially gender-neutral issues. For instance, in the exegesis of the phrase *covetousness lies within the souls* in Q. 4:128, the exegetes under study interpreted male and female covetousness in light of their varied definitions of wifely and husbandly *nushūz*. Rāzī presents a good example of this, he writes that what is meant by this phrase 'with regard to the woman is that she is covetous as a result of surrendering her portion (*naṣībihā*) and rights (*ḥaqqihā*)'. And in the case where a husband decides to remain married to a wife who refuses to give up her rights, 'the husband is covetous because he must spend his life with her, with her ugliness/disfigurement (*damāmatihā*), her face (*wajhihā*) and her old age (*kibar sinnihā*) and deprivation of deriving sensual delight (*ladhdha*) from her'. Rāzī, *al-Tafsīr al-kabīr*, vol. 4, p. 237. Ṭabarī understands this phrase as primarily describing women, who will covet their husbands' wealth and selves, Ṭabarī, *Jāmi' al-bayān*, vol. 4, p. 309.

11

The Optional Ramadan Fast: Debating Q. 2:184 in the Early Turkish Republic*

M. BRETT WILSON

O believers, prescribed for you is the Fast, even as it was prescribed for those that were before you – haply you will be godfearing – for days numbered; and if any of you be sick, or if he be on a journey, then a number of other days; and for those who are able to fast [ʿalā'lladhīna yutīqūnahu], a redemption by feeding a poor man. Yet better it is for him who volunteers good, and that you should fast is better for you. (Q. 2:184)[1]

IN 1924, during the first Ramadan of the newly established Turkish Republic, a well-known poet in Istanbul ventured into one of the many Islamic debates of the day.[2] Süleyman Nazif (1870–1927) argued, based upon his reading of a recently published translation of the Qur'an, that Q. 2:184 indicates that the Ramadan fast is optional and that one could either fast or feed a poor person. His claim contradicted the dominant view, then and now, that all healthy, non-travelling adult Muslims are required to fast during the month. The Turkish ulama denounced his idea vociferously and decried the translation as a travesty. Nevertheless, the issue that this Qur'an translation and this poet tapped into reopened a debate over Q. 2:184 that stretches back to the early centuries of Islam.

* I would like to thank Stephen Burge, Joseph Lowry, Wadad Qadi, Kevin Reinhart, Shawkat Toorawa and Devin Stewart for their indispensable feedback on and suggestions for this piece. I am grateful to Kenan Tekin for proofreading the Arabic and Turkish transliterations.

As a new style of Qur'anic literature written largely by non-ulama authors, translations of the Qur'an (*tercüme/tarjama*) not only stirred controversy but also faced intense textual criticism in the early years of the Turkish Republic. Turkish language Qur'anic commentaries and interlinear translations had a long and uncontroversial history in the Ottoman Empire, but the publication of modern translations by non-specialists provoked extended public debates in newspapers and journals on the meaning of certain passages. None of the authors of translations published in 1924 were members of the ulama, and some had inadequate knowledge of Arabic or lacked expertise in Qur'anic Studies. Nevertheless, these works brought renewed attention upon and demanded critical examination of difficult passages in the text. In the case of the phrase *'alā'lladhīna yuṭīqūnahu*, these early Turkish renderings of the Qur'an brought a legitimate interpretive issue into the public eye. As we shall see below, renderings of Q. 2:184 published during the first Ramadan of the Turkish Republic caused intense scrutiny of the meaning of the word *yuṭīqūnahu*. In the context of this first post-Ottoman Ramadan, some saw the very requirement to fast as hinging upon the understanding of this word. While the cavalier claim that Ramadan was optional did not persuade many Turkish Muslims, the debate over *yuṭīqūnahu* forced a re-examination of the complexity of Q. 2:184. There is a long history of debate about the verse among Qur'anic commentators, and it is to that history that we now turn. First we will consider the discussions among premodern exegetes and then examine the debate in modern Turkey, which drew upon these earlier sources.

Diversity of Opinion on Q. 2:184

The fasting stipulations contained in *Sūrat al-Baqara* are complex, succinct and, at times, seemingly redundant; Q. 2:184, and more specifically the phrase *'alā'lladhīna yuṭīqūnahu*, is one such instance of this complexity. It has been the subject of much discussion and disagreement among Muslim exegetes over the centuries as is evident in the lengthy treatments it has received in the Qur'anic commentary tradition.[3]

Verses Q. 2:183–5 contain the key provisions for fasting with v. 185 forming the textual basis for the requirement to fast during the month of Ramadan. This cluster of verses stipulates that fasting is required of believers for an unspecified number of days, literally '*numbered days*' (*ayāman maʿdūdātin*, Q. 2:184). Some commentators view this as a reference to a pre-Ramadan fast that Muslims performed upon their arrival in Medina.[4] Others view this as a reference to the Lenten fast or, alternately, to the twenty-nine or thirty days of Ramadan.[5] Two important exemptions immediately follow the mention of the '*numbered days*': those who are sick or travelling are commanded to fast for '*a number of other days*' (*fa-ʿiddatun min ayāmin ukhara*), namely, by postponing their fast until they are healthy or not travelling. The passage then requires that '*those who are able to do it*'[6] or, alternately, '*those who are* not *able to do it*' (*alladhīna yuṭīqūnahu*) are required to offer '*a redemption by feeding a poor man*'. The question of whether this verb signifies ability or lack of ability has guided the interpretive debate.

In parsing the phrase *ʿalā'lladhīna yuṭīqūnahu*, interpreters disagree in several respects. In addition to the debate over whether *yuṭīqūnahu* means to be able or unable, and to whom or to what this ability or inability refers, they hold different opinions regarding the referent of the masculine pronoun suffix – *hu*. The determination of this referent – typically either fasting (*ṣawm*) or paying the recompense (*fidya*) – is crucial to how one interprets the phrase. The *fidya* ('*fidyatun ṭaʿāmu miskīnin*') is the 'ransom' of feeding a poor person required for those who either do not or cannot fast.[7] Secondly, interpreters differ on the question of whether Q. 2:184 is abrogated by Q. 2:185, the verse that proclaims the month of Ramadan as a required period of fasting, '*. . . so let those of you, who are present at the month, fast it . . .*'[8] Whether interpreters choose to abrogate v. 184 or harmonise the two verses, both approaches bring their own particular difficulties.

Many Qur'anic commentaries as well as hadiths from sound collections contain reports that when Muhammad first came to Medina, the Muslims used to fast three days of each month as well as the day of Ashura, which was also Yom Kippur, along with the

Jewish residents.[9] However, they say, Muhammad's community was unaccustomed to the stringency of this kind of fasting and found it arduous. Therefore, according to this narrative, keeping the fast was made optional with the revelation of *wa 'alā'lladhīna yuṭīqūnahu*. Muḥammad b. Jarīr al-Ṭabarī (d. 310/923) reports that 'Some said: "this is what was required of fasting in the beginning. Whoever could do it (*aṭāqahu*) among the residents fasted it if he wished, and, if he wanted, broke it and compensated by feeding a poor person for each day of not fasting."'[10] In this reading, Q. 2:184 provides physically capable Muslims with the option to either fast or feed a poor person.[11] Since the verb *yuṭīqūnahu* is interpreted to mean 'those who can do it' or 'those who have the strength to do it', this choice was offered even to Muslims who were healthy and not on a journey. This optional fast is seen as a temporary provision to ease the transition to new ascetic practices in the spirit of the Qur'anic verses that wish ease, rather than hardship, upon Muslims.[12] According to this understanding, elective fasting continued until the revelation of Q. 2:185, (*. . . so let those of you, who are present at the month, fast it . . .*) which established Ramadan as a required fasting period and abrogated the optional fast in v. 184.

This understanding of the verse reads *yuṭīqūnahu* in the positive sense as meaning 'those who are able'. Since there is no indication of negation, 'ability' or 'capacity' is arguably the most literal, evident meaning of the word. The most common meanings of the trilateral root *ṭ-w-q* in the Form IV verbal noun (i.e. *iṭāqa*) cluster around having strength, ability and capacity.[13] The Qur'an contains no other Form IV usages of *ṭ-w-q* but does have other forms of the root. In Q. 2:286, for instance, *ṭāqa* means 'strength or ability': *Our Lord, do Thou not burden us beyond what we have the strength to bear* (*rabbanā lā tuḥammilnā mā lā ṭāqata lanā bihi*). In Q. 2:249, *ṭāqa* conveys the same meaning: *We have no power today against Goliath and his warriors* (*lā ṭāqata lanā'l-yawm bi-Jālūta wa junūdihi*). In a different sense, Q. 3:180 uses *ṭ-w-q* in Form V (*yuṭawwaqūna*), meaning 'to place a collar around the neck': *That they were niggardly with they shall have hung about their necks* (*sa-yuṭawwaqūna*) *on the Resurrection Day*. While these intra-textual examples give some perspective on resonances of the root, they do not provide any conclusive evidence about the meaning of *yuṭīqūnahu* in the context of Q. 2:184.

However, there is evidence of a different sort that the vast majority of interpreters understood this word, in its most apparent sense, to mean 'ability'. The inventive grammatical and interpretive manoeuvres that have been employed on the passage strongly suggest that commentators were devising ways of changing the most commonly understood meaning. The starkest example of this appears in suggestions by important commentators to change the grammatical form of the word *yuṭīqūnahu*, challenging what became the most widely recognised reading with variants that alter the meaning. Most famously, the important early interpreter ʿAbd Allāh Ibn ʿAbbās (d. 68/687–8) is reported to have read the word as *yuṭawwaqūnahu*,[14] the same form found in Q. 3:180, meaning 'to have a collar placed upon the neck' or, figuratively, 'to bear, to endure, to take on hardship'.[15] Mujāhid b. Jabr (d. 104/722) reports that Ibn ʿAbbās interpreted the passage to refer to those who 'are responsible for fasting but are not able to' and considered this to refer only to the elderly and sick persons who have no chance of recovery.[16] In addition to the reading of Ibn ʿAbbās, other divergent versions of the word appear in the commentary and lexicographic tradition, including *yaṭṭawaqunahu*, *yuṭayyaqūnahu*, *yaṭṭayyaqūnahu* and *yataṭayyaqunahu*.[17]

Ibn ʿAbbās and others who suggested variations appear to have understood the verse to mean 'those who are able', and then sought alternatives that produced a different meaning. Otherwise, it is difficult to explain why they would have suggested multiple readings of the word that contradict the accepted consonantal text and strain the limits of grammatical possibility. By reading the phrase to mean 'those who bear it with hardship', Ibn ʿAbbās could claim that Q. 2:183–4 refers to Ramadan, not to a pre-Ramadan fast from which healthy people could opt out. By virtue of this parsing, he could contend that v. 184 is not abrogated by v. 185. Abrogation is problematic for this verse because it would potentially make the *fidya* obsolete. Ibn ʿAbbās's intervention harmonises the two verses, making the fast non-optional and rescuing the *fidya* from abrogation.

The alternative readings of *yuṭīqūnahu* were not widely accepted by the scholarly community. Ṭabarī, for example, strongly condemned these variations. In reference to Ibn ʿAbbās's reading, he wrote, 'it is not permissible for any of the people of Islam to protest, based on personal opinion, against what has been transmitted clearly and definitively by Muslims as inheritance from their Prophet'.[18] The Andalusian commentator Muḥammad b. Aḥmad al-Qurṭubī (d. 671/1272) called Ibn ʿAbbās's reading 'invalid and preposterous' and the important eighteenth-century Arabic dictionary *Tāj al-ʿarūs* denotes its status among the divergent readings.[19] Ṭabarī and others rejected these readings as textual distortion, but, as we shall see below, the commentators did not abandon Ibn ʿAbbās's attempt to interpret a meaning from Q. 2:184 that differed from the apparent text.

Beyond suggesting a different reading of the verb itself, commentators found other ways to achieve a different understanding of the controversial phrase. Some interpreters argue, for instance, that the phrase means 'those who are able to afford paying a *fidya*'. This reading respects the meaning of the verb but eliminates the possibility of a healthy person opting out of the fast and makes the *fidya* an added requirement for Muslims who postpone their fasts. However, grammatical complications surround this interpretation. The fact that *fidya* is a feminine noun and the pronoun suffix '*hu*' in *yuṭīqūnahu* is masculine presents the most obvious problem: they do not agree. To resolve this dilemma, some suggested that the pronoun could refer to a masculine variant of *fidya*, namely *fidā'*.[20] Though inventive, this opinion did not manage to persuade many commentators. In addition to the problem of gender agreement, the verse exhibits an irregular grammatical structure as the pronoun *hu* precedes the word *fidya* (*yuṭīqūnahu fidyatun*) to which it purportedly refers. Grammatically, this construction is unusual for Arabic, but it is not unknown in the Qur'an. For example, in Q. 20:67, '*fa āwjasa fī nafsi**hi** khīfatan Mūsā*' (*and Moses conceived a fear within him*), the masculine pronoun suffix '*-hi*' comes before its referent *Mūsā*, seemingly to fit the rhyme scheme of the verse. In this instance, there is a strong case for arguing that the unusual syntax is conditioned by the end-rhyme pattern.[21] Devin Stewart has argued that rhyme patterns are often the cause of unusual sentence structure in the Qur'an.[22] However, in Q. 2:184, there is no end-rhyme which could govern the noun/pronoun inversion, so, again, the argument for a *hu–fidya* relationship appears rather weak.

Despite complications, it was none other than the grammarians who favoured these linguistically improbable interpretations. In another grammatical solution to the puzzle, Ṭabarī records that the Arabic linguists from Basra argued that the phrase means 'those who are able to provide food (*ṭaʿām*) for a poor person', since *ṭaʿām* is masculine and agrees with the gender of the pronoun.[23] This approach posits food (*ṭaʿām*) as a specification of the *fidya*. However, Ṭabarī makes it clear that while some of the Basran grammarians favoured this argument, the *'ahl al-ʿilm'* opposed this reading.[24] While *ṭaʿām* solves the gender agreement problem, the pronoun appears before the noun and, again, it is not conditioned by rhyme. Due to these complications, interpretations suggesting ability to provide food have not gained wide acceptance over the centuries. However, they have appeared in popular English translations of the Qur'an. For example, Muhammad Asad renders the passage 'it is incumbent upon those who can afford it',[25] and Marmaduke Pickthall phrases it, 'for those who can afford it there is a ransom'.[26] Differences aside, all of these interpretations read *yuṭīqūnahu* as 'to be able' and construct their solutions around this assumed meaning.

Attempts to harmonise, rather than abrogate, Q. 2:184 may have stemmed partially from practical considerations about the established practice of the *fidya*. Regardless of debates among exegetes, the *fidya* existed as a communal practice, and commentaries and *fiqh* manuals defined what constituted a *fidya*. For instance, Abū Ḥanīfa stipulated that a *fidya* was a 'measure (*ṣāʿ*) of dates or half a measure of wheat', Ibn 'Abbās and Muḥammad b. Idrīs al-Shāfiʿī (d. 204/820) considered it a 'half measure of wheat', and Mālik b. Anas (d. 179/795) understood it to be a measure (*mudd*) of wheat 'according to the measure of the Prophet'.[27] In many Muslim communities, those who had difficulty fasting or for whom fasting posed a health risk could pay the *fidya* as compensation and interpreters identified the elderly, the terminally ill, pregnant women and nursing mothers as those mentioned in Q. 2:184. Therefore, if this verse were abrogated, the existence of the *fidya* would pose a thorny problem.

Ṭabarī records that some commentators did in fact think that the *fidya* was abrogated.[28] If one opts for the abrogation of Q. 2:184, the logic for abrogating the *fidya* is compelling because Q. 2:185, the abrogating verse, repeats the permissions in v. 184 for the sick and the travellers but does not mention the *fidya*. Arguing that v. 184 is completely abrogated eliminates the need for creative readings of *yuṭīqūnahu*, but it makes the existing practice of the *fidya* problematic. Perhaps this dilemma caused commentators to formulate intermediate, partially abrogating positions. Some regard the verse as abrogated but hold that, unlike the optional fast, the *fidya* was not cancelled, but transformed into a practice for the elderly and others.[29]

In fact, descriptions of *fidya* in legal works reflect the confusion over the meaning of *yuṭīqūnahu*. The *Iḥyā ʿulūm al-dīn* by Abū Ḥāmid al-Ghazālī (d. 505/1111), for example, states that the *fidya* 'is obligatory upon pregnant and nursing women' but also requires them to make up for the missed days of the fast.[30] The *fidya* in this case is not compensation or a substitute, but rather an additional requirement. This suggests that *yuṭīqūnahu* could simultaneously mean 'those who are unable to fast and those who are able to pay the *fidya*'. On the other hand, according to Qurṭubī, the elderly should pay the *fidya* because they have no prospect of fasting in the future, so, for them, the *fidya* is a form of compensation.[31] Mālik's *al-Muwaṭṭā'* contains a passage that understands *alladhīna yuṭīqūnahu* to refer to those who had a fasting debt from the previous Ramadan and were 'capable' of performing postponed fasting but had not done so by the arrival of the next Ramadan.[32] At the same time, it conveys a tradition describing the *fidya* as a recommended, but non-obligatory, requirement for the elderly who are 'unable' to fast. Mālik offered the *fidya* when he became old but stated, 'I do not see it as obligatory to do so'.[33] As these examples demonstrate, both meanings – 'ability' and 'inability' – have their place in legal works and affect their descriptions of the *fidya*.

In addition to abrogating approaches, commentators devised several other harmonising solutions to eliminate the need for abrogating the *fidya*. The *Tafsīr al-Jalālayn*, for example, glosses the phrase as 'for those who are, not, able to do it' inserting the negation *lā* before *yuṭīqūnahu* (*'those who are* [*not*] *able to fast'*).[34] It suggests that the Qur'anic text intends to say 'those who are not able', but has left out the word indicating negation. The meaning transforms from ability to inability with the assumed insertion of *lā*. There are other instances in the Qur'an where a negative meaning is assumed: in Q. 4:176 for instance, where *God makes clear to you that you might* [*not*] *go astray* (*yubayyinu'llāhu lakum an taḍillū*). This insertion is occasioned by the assumption that God would not clarify things to people in order to lead them to perdition. Yet such an assumption requires strong contextual indications that, arguably, are not present in Q. 2:184. Others, following Ibn 'Abbās, hold that, even without negation, *yuṭīqūnahu* means 'those who are able to do it with hardship', or 'those who are unable'.[35] They claim that the word conveys the same meaning as *yuṭawwaqūnahu*, as suggested by Ibn 'Abbās. However, since this form of the verb is used in Q. 3:180, it is fair to ask why that word would not also be used in Q. 2:184 if the same meaning were intended. Due to this inconsistency and the unconventional nature of the reading, doubts loom over its linguistic strength as it basically redefines the meaning of the word. Despite these concerns, these two methods of reading the phrase – the insertion of *lā* and the redefinition of *ṭ-w-q* (in Form IV) as 'inability' – both gained acceptance, and both meshed seamlessly with the continued practice of the *fidya*.

Q. 2:184 and the Turkish Republic

In the early years of the Turkish Republic, the regime of Mustafa Kemal Atatürk instigated a series of political and cultural reforms that signalled a profound secularisation of Turkish state and society. On 3 March 1924, immediately preceding the renewed debate over Q. 2:184, the new government abolished the caliphate, administratively subordinated the ulama and closed Islamic courts. Twelve days later, on 15 March, the regime dealt another blow to Islamic institutions when it shut down the madrasas, where many of the late Ottoman ulama worked and earned their livelihoods. In light of these reforms, an air of uncertainty loomed over the future of Islamic tradition in the country, where even basic ritual matters such as fasting could be brought into question and publicly challenged.

Although the new regime based in Ankara had set a decidedly different tone on Islamic matters in the first year of its rule, it was not yet the Turkey that would later become famous in the 1930s for its fervent secularism and high modernism. During Ramadan 1924, Turkish citizens still used the Arabic script, they could still legally wear fezzes and turbans, Islam remained the official religion of the Turkish nation and Sufi orders remained licit. Moreover, although the political power of the ulama had been decimated, the ulama and devout intellectuals still provided a robust critical voice in the public sphere, using newspapers and journal publications to express their opinions about the changes the country was undergoing. During this period of rapid cultural and political change, Qur'anic interpretation took on a sense of urgency as it had the potential to shape the future of Islam in the country. In addition, many saw the genre of translation as the best means to convey the Qur'an to the citizens of the new nation-state and, during Ramadan 1924, several Turkish translations in the Arabic script were published.[36]

One such Qur'anic translation was written by an author and retired state official named Hüseyin Kâzım Kadri (1870–1934). By profession, Kadri was a government official who held several positions in Ottoman state institutions. However, he also pursued writing and lexicography, composing numerous monographs on political and religious subjects, as well as a multivolume Turkic language lexicon with an emphasis on etymology.[37] Influenced by Muslim-modernist intellectual currents, Kadri argued that the translation of the Qur'an into the languages of modern non-Arab Muslim peoples was an essential step in the reform and evolution of Islam. He once wrote that when he saw examples of religious fanaticism among Muslims he reminded himself that 'the Qur'an has not been translated into the languages of the Muslim nations'.[38] In an attempt to remedy this situation, Kadri composed a Turkish translation of the Qur'an titled *Nurü'l-beyan* (*The Light of Explication*) during the last years of the Ottoman Empire, which was published in Ramadan 1924.[39]

In the context of the fasting season, Kadri's rendering of Q. 2:184 sparked a heated controversy.

> *Takatı olduğu halde oruç tutmayanların her gün için fidye vermeleri lazımdır.*

> Those who are capable but do not fast need to give a redemption (*fidye*) for each day.

In opting for this rendering, Kadri preferred the meaning 'ability' (Tr. *takat*) for the disputed phrase. He drew not only upon the Arabic commentaries mentioned earlier, but also on Ottoman Turkish language commentaries published in the nineteenth century, namely İsmail Ferruh's *Mevahib* and Mehmet Antebi's *Tefsir-i Tıbyan*. In the *Mevahib*, Ferruh holds that this phrase means, 'those who have the physical strength but break the fast due to fatigue'.[40] Antebi states in the *Tefsir-i Tıbyan*, 'these are those who, while capable of fasting in their youth, may become incapable of doing so in old age'.[41] This view, present in Qurṭubī, uses ellipsis to frame capacity in the past tense – *alladhīna* [*kāna*] *yuṭīqūnahu* ('those who [were] able').[42] This method respects the evident meaning – 'ability' – while simultaneously extracting the meaning of present 'inability' by specifying that they have subsequently become unable due to old age or infirmity. Additionally, two other Turkish translations by non-ulama writers were published at the same time as that of Kadri, both of which translated the phrase to mean 'those who are physically capable'.[43]

Some of the Turkish intelligentsia interpreted Kadri's translation as meaning that physically able Muslims could opt out of the Ramadan fast by feeding the poor. In newspapers and journals, several writers seized the opportunity to proclaim that the Ramadan fast was optional and that Kadri's recent translation had finally revealed the truth about Q. 2:184, which the ulama had wilfully misinterpreted. A controversial Young Turk partisan and journalist named Mehmet Ubeydullah (1858–1937) wrote a provocative piece on Q. 2:184 championing this view and harmonising traditional opinions in an unconventional manner. Ubeydullah identifies the fast mentioned in Q. 2:183–4 as the Ramadan fast, and therefore as non-abrogated, a common move by interpreters that is usually combined with a definition of *yuṭīqūnahu* as those who cannot fast, i.e. the elderly and terminally ill. However, Ubeydullah argues that *yuṭīqūnahu* clearly means 'to have the strength' and condemns attempts to extract a different meaning from the apparent sense of the text. The unusual combination of these views – seeing the fast in Q. 2:183–4 as the Ramadan fast, as well as defining the word as 'ability' – leads Ubeydullah to the conclusion that the Ramadan fast, not an abrogated pre-Ramadan fast, is optional. For Ubeydullah, the fact that the modern ulama had not acknowledged this meaning was a sign both of their imitation of precedent and of their failure to trust and embrace their own rationality.[44]

Ubeydullah was not alone in his radical appraisal of the verse. The poet Süleyman Nazif penned an intriguing newspaper column that assessed the meaning of this verse within the context of modern Ramadan culture in Istanbul. 'Our rapidly changing social conditions strike one most during the month of Ramadan', he writes. After observing that Ramadan has become a season of sumptuous banquets for Ottoman high society ('What elaborate feasts these eyes of mine have seen'), Nazif expresses the opinion that the month of fasting has lost the spirit of asceticism and simplicity.[45] Given this context, he questions the strong social habit of condemning those who do not fast, suggesting that such disapproval is hypocritical in the context of a Ramadan in which everyone is 'impatient' to have a good time at the evening parties.[46] Moreover, Nazif argues that the Qur'an itself provides a good reason for not harshly judging those who do not fast since Q. 2:184 provides exemptions from the Ramadan fast for sick persons and travellers, as well as for anyone who feeds a poor person. He holds that one can deduce from the verse that someone who pays the *fidya* is not required to fast. The strongest evidence for this, he contends, is the phrase that follows the mention of the *fidya*, *and that you should fast is better for you* (*wa-an taṣūmū khayrun lakum*), which assumes that the *fidya* is a substitute for the fast.[47] In other words, by saying that it would be preferable to fast, it implies that one may legitimately choose not to fast. To formulate his opinion, Nazif studied the Qur'anic commentaries of 'Abd Allāh b. 'Umar al-Bayḍāwī (d. 685/1286) and Maḥmūd b. 'Umar al-Zamakhsharī (d. 538/1144) and concluded that some interpreters have tried, in various ways, to change the apparent meaning of the verse. Nazif announced that he would 'act upon his own *ijtihād*' until the ulama could convince him otherwise.[48]

The implications of Ubeydullah and Nazif's interventions were not lost upon anyone. The call for individual *ijtihād* and the redefinition of a pillar of Islamic ritual practice deeply disturbed the ulama and devout intellectuals in Turkey. Their articles in the press elicited responses from the most influential Islamic intelligentsia in the country, who were genuinely concerned that Turkish citizens would stop fasting and that translations of the Qur'an would become sources of Islamic guidance and authority. Well aware of the changing winds in the country, they feared that the political decline of the ulama and Islamic institutions could be accompanied by a corresponding lapse in Muslim piety. The head of the Directorate of Religious Affairs, Mehmet Rifat Börekçi (1860–1941), issued a public statement that reminded Muslims that fasting was obligatory and denounced Kadri's translation of this passage. Rather than recognise his rendering of *alladhīna yuṭīqūnahu* as a valid interpretation with robust support in the commentary tradition, Börekçi described it as a mistranslation, writing that Kadri had 'knowingly or unknowingly distorted the noble verse 184 of *Sūrat al-Baqara* and confused the thoughts of Muslims'.[49] Seemingly, concern over how this rendering would affect public ritual practice trumped any attempt at acknowledging the diverse array of opinion on this verse. Börekçi argued that the proper interpretation understands *alladhīna yuṭīqūnahu* to mean 'those who cannot fast'. He clarified that they are those who cannot fast due to conditions of old age or infirmity. Unrelenting on this point, Börekçi insisted that this reading of the verse was the only correct interpretation, and that refraining from negating the verb constituted a distortion of the text. Yet the kind of interpretive editing that manages to read *yuṭīqūnahu* as negative evinces the type of illicit scholasticism for which Muslim modernists – Kadri included – criticised the classical *tafsīr* tradition.

An additional barrage of criticism came from another high-profile member of the Directorate of Religious Affairs, Ahmet Hamdi Akseki (1887–1951). Concurring with Börekçi that the translation had confused Muslims, Akseki reported that some Muslims had actually broken their fasts upon reading the translation, while others had sought counsel with the ulama on the matter. Furthermore, Akseki argued that those who do not understand abrogation would think that they could 'give a few cents to a poor man and suppose that they are absolved from the fast'.[50]

In addition to the alleged social confusion caused by this translation, Akseki challenged its linguistic validity, insisting that the true meaning of the verse commands universal fasting and never granted exemption to the healthy. Akseki contended, like many before him, that *yuṭīqūnahu* requires no negation because it contains the meaning 'lack of ability' or 'cessation of capacity'. Citing an array of works on grammar, Qur'anic commentary and abrogation, he argues that the root of the verb *ṭ-w-q* implicitly bears the potential for negation, and, therefore, the presence of a *lā* is unnecessary. Akseki provides a variety of examples in which nouns related to the root *ṭ-w-q* (e.g. *ṭāqa*) mean 'hardship' or the 'cessation of capacity'.[51] In his view, the verse refers to those who can fast but in doing so exhaust themselves or reach the very limits of their strength.[52] Though *yuṭīqūnahu* comes from the same root as the noun *ṭawq* – a collar or heavy yoke that impedes motion, restricts freedom and makes things difficult[53] – that alone does not provide a persuasive argument for the verb to mean 'to be unable'. The vastly different meanings that can be derived from a single Arabic root demonstrate that a shared root is not evidence of shared or similar meaning. Moreover, a similar argument with sound examples could be used to demonstrate the opposite of what Akseki proposes. In Q. 2:249, for instance, *ṭāqa* means power: *We have no power* (*lā ṭāqata lanā*).

Having invested years of work in the translation project, Kadri was stunned by the accusations levelled by Börekçi and Akseki. While he did not claim the translation was perfect, Kadri felt that Börekçi's critique of Q. 2:184 was both unfounded and unfair. In response, he wrote several defences of his rendering that were published in newspapers and in subsequent editions of the text.[54] The appendix to his translation contains a specific defence of his version of Q. 2:184:

> Everyone knows that the text of the Qur'an is — *wa 'alā'lladhīna yuṭīqūnahu* — and the sublime meaning is 'those who are capable but do not fast'. To distort this by making it 'those who do *not* have the capacity to fast' is not for me to do.[55]

Kadri describes Börekçi's negative reading of *yuṭīqūnahu* as a distortion of the text. Like other modernists, Kadri considered such a reading to be linguistically improbable and therefore a violation of the revealed Qur'anic *naẓm*. In his view, reading this verb to mean 'those who are unable' was an example of excessive scholasticism which allowed prevalent opinions and theological dictates to shape interpretation of the text, rather than vice versa. However, Kadri did not base this judgement merely upon the language of the passage. Mustering traditional support, Kadri cites the commentary works by al-Bukhārī (d. 256/870), Ṭabarī, Bayḍāwī, Fakhr al-Dīn al-Rāzī (d. 606/1209) and the Ottoman Shaykh al-Islam Ebu Suud (d. 982/1574), together with the *Tafsīr al-Jalālayn*, as mentioning the opinion that the verse means 'those who are able but do not fast', and that it was later abrogated. He cites Rāzī, for instance, as writing that most commentators understand *alladhīna yuṭīqūnahu* to refer to a 'healthy non-traveller' (*al-muqīm al-ṣaḥīḥ*).[56] The *Tafsīr al-Jalālayn*, he points out, indicates that at the beginning of Islam there was a choice between fasting and providing food for the poor since, in the second year of the Islamic calendar, Muslims were unaccustomed to the fast and this provision was offered as a means of easing their path.[57] Bayḍāwī and Ebu Suud submit that *yuṭīqūnahu* could refer to those who are able to fast, but break it.[58]

Unlike Ubeydullah and Nazif, Kadri did not suggest that the Ramadan fast was optional, nor had he imagined that some would read his translation this way. However, he did want to make the case that his translation was more linguistically accurate than that of the Turkish ulama. Kadri interpreted their refusal to acknowledge the legitimacy of his rendering as evidence that the ulama were intellectually rigid and unduly biased against new interpretations and translations of the Qur'an. Given the abundance of precedent for his interpretation, its linguistic plausibility and the fact that he indicated that the verse had been abrogated, Kadri wondered how Börekçi could accuse him of distorting the Qur'an and confusing Muslims. He concluded that the Islamic establishment intended to undermine the translation regardless of its content.[59]

From the ulama's perspective, the radical responses to Kadri's translation demonstrated that, at this crucial juncture, unrestricted freedom to interpret the Qur'an in the liberal public sphere was dangerous, even potentially devastating, for the future of Islam in modern Turkey. Above all else, they wanted to preserve the Ramadan fast from the ongoing wave of cultural reform and, to this end, they did their utmost to persuade the public and the regime that alternative interpretations of this verse were invalid.

In the wake of the 1924 controversy over fasting, Q. 2:184 continued to receive heightened attention. In the most impressive Turkish language Qur'anic commentary of the twentieth century – *Hak Dini Kur'an Dili* by Elmalılı Muhammed Hamdi Yazır (1878–1942) – the author dedicates significant energy to dealing with the verse, clearly responding to the debates of 1924. One of the most respected Islamic scholars of his time, Elmalılı engaged Q. 2:184 in a more nuanced and thorough fashion than those mentioned above. Whereas his predecessors in the Directorate of Religious Affairs were making public policy with their pronouncements in the press, Elmalılı was composing a scholarly commentary, and he displays a more expansive understanding of debates on the verse. Elmalılı recognises that 'ability'/'capacity' is the most obvious meaning for *itaqa/yuṭīqūnahu*, and acknowledges the diversity of opinion over various aspects of the passage. However, he argues that reading the verse as 'those who have the strength are required to pay a *fidya*' (instead of fasting) presents a logical inconsistency. Since Q. 2:184 provides exemptions for the sick and the travellers in a context of atonement, Elmalılı finds it inconceivable that the passage could then grant an outright exemption for healthy people who would not later be required to make up the fasting days they missed. For the sick to have to make up for days missed and the healthy to simply provide a *fidya* would be a contradiction in the text, an illogical commandment, which, in his view, is impossible. Given the context of atonement and logical inconsistency of such a reading, Elmalılı submits that it is preferable to opt for a less obvious meaning of *yuṭīqūnahu* and makes the case that it means 'to endure with great difficulty', buttressed by the usual references to the *tawq* as a collar, which restricts and impedes.[60] The passage, Elmalılı reasons, must be referring to a different group of people who are neither sick nor travelling (since they have already been mentioned), and who have no prospect of fasting in the future to compensate. This group, for Elmalılı, must be the elderly.[61]

One might reasonably ask: if the intention of the passage is the elderly, then why does it not indicate them in a similar manner as the sick and the travellers? Due to the lack of specification, some early interpretations mentioned by Ṭabarī stipulate the passage as addressing everyone.[62] The conclusion reached by Elmalılı and other interpreters is not obvious from the text alone and, it is possible – though speculative – that communal practice of the *fidya* influenced this outcome as much as, or more than, the letters on the page. Pre-empting potential criticisms of this sort and defending the decisive nature of logic, Elmalılı posits that 'even if this interpretation is metaphorical, it is still necessary'.[63] In sum, Elmalılı acknowledges the linguistic merit of 'those who are able' but rejects it on the basis of incoherence in its textual context. Additionally, invoking intra-textual support, he remarks that the Qur'an does not use *t-w-q* in Form IV in other passages to mean 'ability' but prefers the verb *istaṭāʿa*.[64] Considering the reasoning of various legal schools and commentaries on the verse along the way, Elmalılı provides an extended defence of Ibn ʿAbbās's position and reaches the conclusion that *alladhīna yuṭīqūnahu* does not and, in this context, cannot mean 'those who are able'.

Conclusion

The two opposing interpretations of *yuṭīqūnahu* – 'to be able' or 'to be unable' – have been shaped by linguistic considerations and, possibly, by communal practices of the *fidya* as well. The dictates of Arabic language, as well as the diverse stratagems devised by commentators and grammarians in response to the word, suggest that its most evident meaning is 'to be able'. This opinion has existed since the early days of Qur'anic commentary but, over time, became a minority view. Over the centuries, major legal schools have stipulated the *fidya* for those who lack the physical strength to fast and place themselves (or their children) at a health risk via fasting. This practice either assumes a negative reading of *yuṭīqūnahu* – 'to be unable' – or posits a transformative abrogation in which the purpose of *fidya* changes, after the revelation of Q. 2:185, from elective fasting to compensatory action for the physically vulnerable.

The positive reading – 'to be able' – has been revived via modern renderings of the Qur'an in both Turkish and English. The genre of the modern Qur'an translation has made it possible to unearth and even publicise understandings of the Qur'an that were lesser-known or marginal in the larger commentary tradition. During the first Ramadan of the Turkish Republic, the debate over Q. 2:184 dealt with the question of if and how these excavated meanings could be used in modern Turkish translations. Historical hindsight allows us to appreciate this excavating function of translations, but religious leaders in Turkey in 1924, facing marginalisation and justifiably fearing for the future of Islamic life in the country, viewed Kadri's translation of Q. 2:184 not only as incorrect, but also as dangerous. Accordingly, they disparaged it and insisted that the interpretation favoured by the current Islamic authorities would bear exclusive legitimacy. By revealing the ambiguity over the meaning of the word *yuṭīqūnahu*, the debate over Q. 2:184 in Turkey highlights the importance of political context in the pursuit of meaning in the Qur'an and, methodologically, provides a fascinating case of modern lexicographic analysis, and its limits, in the print-based public sphere.

NOTES

1 Arthur J. Arberry, tr., *The Koran Interpreted* (New York, NY: Macmillan, 1986). Unless otherwise noted, translated verses are taken from Arberry's rendering.

2 In 1924, Ramadan was from 5 April to 4 May.

3 See, for example, the extensive discussion of Q. 2:184 in Muḥammad b. Jarīr al-Ṭabarī's commentary. On issues of fasting in the Qur'an, see K. Wagtendonk, *Fasting in the Koran* (Leiden: Brill, 1968).

4 See Ṭabarī, *Jāmiʿ al-bayān ʿan taʾwīl āy al-Qurʾān*, ed. Maḥmūd Muḥammad Shākir and Aḥmad Muḥammad Shākir (Cairo, Maktabat Ibn Taymiyya, n.d.), vol. 3, p. 414.
5 Ṭabarī, *Jāmiʿ al-bayān*, vol. 3, p. 417. There are many other opinions on the meaning of the *numbered days*.
6 In the translation at the beginning of this chapter, Arberry renders the phrase: 'those who are able to fast', eliminating the ambiguity by assigning – *hu* – to the fast.
7 Gerald R. Hawting, 'Atonement', *EQ*, vol 1, pp. 186–8.
8 Arberry, *The Koran Interpreted*, p. 24.
9 Ṭabarī, *Jāmiʿ al-bayān*, vol. 3, p. 414.
10 Ibid., p. 418. For another early reading in this vein, see Muqātil b. Sulaymān, *Tafsīr Muqātil b. Sulaymān*, ed. ʿAbd Allāh Maḥmūd Shiḥāta (Beirut: Mūʾassasat al-Tārīkh al-ʿArabī, 2002), vol. 1, pp. 160–61.
11 Abū Zakariyyāʾ Yaḥyā b. Ziyād al-Farrāʾ, *Maʿānī al-Qurʾān*, ed. Aḥmad Yūsuf Najātī and Muḥammad ʿAlī al-Najjār (Beirut: ʿĀlam al-Kutub, 1983), vol. 1, p. 112; Ṭabarī, *Jāmiʿ al-bayān*, vol. 3, pp. 418–19.
12 Ibid., p. 419.
13 Edward William Lane, *An Arabic-English Lexicon* (London: Williams and Norgate, 1863–93), vol. 1, pp. 1894–5.
14 Ṭabarī, *Jāmiʿ al-bayān*, vol. 3, p. 418. The reported opinions of Ibn ʿAbbās discussed here are not to be confused with those in the work falsely attributed to Ibn ʿAbbās – *Tanwīr mīn al-miqbās*. This text, in fact, expresses a view on Q. 2:184 that contradicts those reported about Ibn ʿAbbās by most *tafsīr* works. For more on Ibn ʿAbbās, see Herbert Berg's contribution in this volume, Chapter 3.
15 Muḥammad b. Mukarram Ibn Manẓūr, *Lisān al-ʿArab* (Cairo: Bulaq, 1300–8/1883–91), vol. 12, pp. 101–2.
16 Mujāhid b. Jabr, *Tafsīr Mujāhid*, ed. Muḥammad ʿAbd al-Salām Abū Nīl (Cairo: Dār al-Fikr, 1989), pp. 220–21.
17 Murtaḍa al-Zabīdī, *Tāj al-ʿarūs min jawāhir al-qāmūs*, ed. ʿAbd al-Sattār Aḥmad Farāj *et al.* (Kuwait: Maṭbaʿat Ḥukūmat al-Kuwayt, 1385–1422/1965–2001), vol. 16, p. 110.
18 Ṭabarī, *Jāmiʿ al-bayān*, vol. 3, p. 438.
19 Muḥammad b. Aḥmad al-Qurṭubī, *al-Jāmiʿ li-aḥkām al-Qurʾān*, ed. ʿAbd Allāh b. ʿAbd al-Ḥasan al-Turkī and Muḥammad Riḍwān ʿArqusī (Beirut: Muʾassasat al-Risāla, 2006), vol. 3, p. 144; Zabīdī, *Tāj al-ʿarūs*, vol. 16, p. 109.
20 Farrāʾ, *Maʿānī al-Qurʾān*, vol. 1, p. 112.
21 I would like to thank Devin Stewart for pointing out this instance of noun-pronoun inversion conditioned by rhyme.
22 Devin Stewart, 'Poetic License in the Qur'an: Ibn al-Ṣāʾigh al-Ḥanafī's *Iḥkām al-rāy fī aḥkām al-āy*', *Journal of Qur'anic Studies* 11, no. 1 (2009), pp. 1–54, at p. 3. Also see Stewart's contribution in this volume, Chapter 7.
23 Ṭabarī, *Jāmiʿ al-bayān*, vol. 3, p. 438.
24 Ibid., p. 438.
25 Muhammad Asad, *The Message of the Qur'an: Translated and Explained* (Gibraltar: Dar al-Andalus, 1980), at Q. 2:184.

26 Marmaduke Pickthall, *The Meaning of the Glorious Koran: An Explanatory Translation* (New York and London: A.A. Knopf, 1930), at Q. 2:184.
27 Qurṭubī, *al-Jāmiʿ*, vol. 3, p. 147; the Twelver Shiʿi jurist Ayatollah Ali al-Sistani (b. 1930), stipulates that the Ramadan *fidya* consists of 750 grams of wheat per day of missed fasting, see al-Sistani, 'Dialogue on Sawm (fasting)': http://www.sistani.org/english/book/49/2408/ (last accessed 7 October 2012).
28 Ṭabarī, *Jāmiʿ al-bayān*, vol. 3, pp. 422–3.
29 Ibid., p. 422.
30 Abū Ḥāmid al-Ghazālī, *The Mysteries of Fasting – Iḥyā' 'ulūm al-dīn: Kitāb Asrār al-ṣawm*, tr. Nabih Amin Faris (Lahore: SH. Muhammad Ashraf, 1992), p. 20. This position is widely held; see Qurṭubī, *al-Jāmiʿ*, vol. 3, p. 147.
31 Qurṭubī, *al-Jāmiʿ*, vol. 3, p. 147.
32 Mālik b. Anas, *Kitāb al-Muwaṭṭa'*, ed. Ḥasan 'Abd Allāh Sharaf (Cairo: Dār al-Rayyān li'l-Turāth, 1988), vol. 1, p. 204, §49.
33 Ibid., §47.
34 Jalāl al-Dīn al-Maḥallī and Jalāl al-Dīn al-Suyūṭī, *Tafsīr al-Jalālayn: An Annotated English Translation of the Commentary of the Two Jalāls*, tr. Feras Hamza (Amman: Royal Aal al-Bayt Institute for Islamic Thought, 2008), p. 31.
35 Elmalılı Muhammed Hamdi Yazır, *Hak Dini Kur'an Dili: Yeni Mealli Türkçe Tefsir* (Istanbul: Matbaa-i Ebüzziya, 1935), vol. 1, p. 634.
36 For more information on Turkish translations of the period see M. Brett Wilson, *Translating the Qur'an in an Age of Nationalism: Print Culture and Modern Islam in Turkey* (Oxford: Oxford University Press in association with the Institute of Ismaili Studies, 2014); idem, 'The First Translations of the Qur'an in Modern Turkey', *The International Journal of Middle East Studies* 41 (2009), pp. 419–35.
37 Hüseyin Kâzım Kadri, *Meşrutiyet'ten Cumuriyet'e Hatıralarım*, ed. İsmail Kara (Istanbul: İletişim Yayınları, 1991), p. 7; idem, *Türk lûgati; Türk dillerinin iştikakı ve edebi lûgatleri: Uygur, Çağatay, Kazan, Azeri ve Garp Türkçeleriyle, Koybal, Yakut, Altay, Çuvaş, ve Kırgız lehçelerinin lûgatlerini ve Garp Türkçesinde kullanılan Arap ve Acem kelimelerini şevahidi ve emsaliyle havidir* (Istanbul: Devlet Matbaası, 1927).
38 Şeyh Muhsin-i Fani [Hüseyin Kâzım Kadri], *İstikbale Doğru* (Istanbul: Ahmed İhsan ve Şürekası Matbaacılık Osmanlı Şirketi, 1913–14), p. 10. Şeyh Muhsin-i Fani is Kadri's pen name.
39 Şeyh Muhsin-i Fani [Hüseyin Kâzım Kadri], *Nurü'l-Beyan: Kur'an-ı Kerim'in Türkçe Tercümesi* (Istanbul: Matbaa-i Amire, 1924).
40 Mehmet Antebi and İsmail Ferruh, *Tefsir-i Tibyan ve Tefsir-i Mevakib* [published together in one volume] (Dersaadet: Şirket-i Sahafiye-yi Osmaniye, 1902), vol. 1, p. 109.
41 Ibid.
42 Qurṭubī, *al-Jāmiʿ*, vol. 3 p. 146.
43 Cemil Sait [Dikel], *Kur'an-ı Kerim Tercümesi* (Istanbul: Şems Matbaası, 1924); Seyyid Süleyman el-Hüseyni, *Zübdet'ül-Beyan* (Istanbul: Amidi Matbaası, 1924).
44 Mehmet Ubeydullah, 'Cuma Mev'izeleri', *Vatan*, 16 May 1924 (16 Mayıs 1340).

45 Süleyman Nazif, 'Ramazan Musahabesi II', *Resimli Gazete*, 19 April 1924 (19 Nisan 1340), p. 2.
46 Ibid.
47 Ibid.
48 Ibid.
49 Rifat Börekçi, 'Beyan-ı Hakikat Müslümanlara', *Sebilürreşad* 24, no. 599 (1924), p. 8.
50 Ahmet Hamdi Akseki, 'Cevabı Mı? İtirafı Mı?', *Sebilürreşad* 24, no. 600 (1924), pp. 23–6, at p. 25.
51 Ibid., p. 24.
52 Ibid., p. 25.
53 Ibn Manẓūr, *Lisān al-ʿArab*, pp. 101–2; Lane, *Arabic-English Lexicon*, vol. 1, p. 1894.
54 E.g. Şeyh Muhsin-i Fani [Hüseyin Kâzım Kadri], 'Hazret Şeyh'in Sebil'e İlk ve Son Cevabı', *Sebilürreşad* 24, no. 599 (1924), p. 8.
55 Şeyh Muhsin-i Fani [Hüseyin Kâzım Kadri], 'Diyanet İşleri Riyasetinin "Beyan-ı Hakikat" Unvanlı Makalesine Cevap' in *Nurü'l-Beyan*, Appendix, pp. 2–7.
56 Ibid., p. 5.
57 Ibid., p. 6.
58 Ibid.
59 Ibid., p. 7.
60 Elmalılı, *Hak Dini Kur'an Dili*, p. 634.
61 Ibid., p. 638.
62 Ṭabarī, *Jāmiʿ al-bayān*, vol. 3, p. 422.
63 Elmalılı, *Hak Dini Kur'an Dili*, p. 634 [534 in the text is a typo].
64 For example, Q. 2:217; See Elmalılı, *Hak Dini Kur'an Dili*, p. 635.

SECTION IV

The Word in Translation: Medieval and Modern Disputes

12

The *Fātiḥa* of Salmān al-Fārisī and the Modern Controversy over Translating the Qur'an

TRAVIS ZADEH

On 28 March 1936 (5 Muḥarram 1355), the front page of *al-Ahrām*, Egypt's leading newspaper, featured an article by the editor-in-chief of the monthly journal published by al-Azhar University, Muḥammad Farīd Wajdī (d. 1954), arguing for the legitimacy of translating the Qur'an. This is a position that Wajdī, a reformist, had been advancing in the Egyptian press for several years.[1] In this particular article, Wajdī offered as his foremost justification the example of Salmān al-Fārisī, the first Persian convert to Islam. According to Wajdī, the Prophet Muhammad approved a translation of the *Fātiḥa*, the opening sura of the Qur'an; Salmān had composed the translation at the request of recent Persian converts who had written to him seeking something of the Qur'an in Persian, which they could recite during ritual prayer. In Wajdī's view, this historical fact offered prophetic sanction for the production and use of Qur'anic translations.[2]

Needless to say, the authenticity of Salmān's translation of the *Fātiḥa*, and the question of whether or not it received the approval of the Prophet, were matters of serious contention in the controversies over the translation of the Qur'an that raged at the turn of the twentieth century. Wajdī was not the first to draw on the example of Salmān's *Fātiḥa* with this specific juridical end in mind; the appearance of this issue on the front page of a daily newspaper, however, serves as a reminder of how both the medium of debating the matter of translation and of how the audience engaged with this question had radically transformed since the account was first circulated in classical Arabic sources.

I have written elsewhere about the debates over the translatability of the Qur'an, primarily with respect to the early constitution of vernacular piety and the history of Qur'anic hermeneutics.[3] Admittedly, it would be rather cavalier not to address, in some fashion, the ways in which the classical discourses concerning translation, and the concomitant matter of accessing Qur'anic meaning in vehicles other than Arabic, came to inform ideas about and practices of scriptural translation in the modern period. At the heart of this problem are the tensions between meaning and form and their relationship to syntactical and rhetorical structures, categories that generally are expressed in the classical material as *maʿnā*, *lafẓ* and *naẓm*, respectively. Throughout the modern debates, the question of what constitutes a legitimate translation is a matter of primary concern. The extent to which the classical sources of juridical and exegetical authority feature in the early twentieth-century controversies offers insight into a modern process of redefining the purpose and meaning of Qur'anic translation.

One aim of the present article is to develop a fuller genealogy of the issue of Qur'anic translation, as expressed particularly in the controversies in modern Egypt. For, while others have studied this topic,[4] there is much that remains to be done in terms of understanding how these debates relate to earlier juridical and exegetical traditions. Furthermore, I hope to shed light on the discontinuity that at times characterises the modern reception of the classical material on the topic. These moments of rupture illuminate how, often despite contrary appearances, historical and cultural contexts inevitably shape interpretive practices, animating both their production and reception. While there are notable distinctions that separate the diachronic history of Qur'anic translation, the apparent continuity of discursive strategies justifying the translation of the Qur'an also deserves further consideration.

Modern Trajectories

In Cairo, Muḥarram 1355 (March–April 1936) marked not only the coming of the new year but also a renewal of the translation controversy that had cycled in and out of Egyptian public life during the course of the century. The question of translating the Qur'an featured in a series of rather vitriolic debates, reflecting a range of political and religious concerns that extended well beyond the question of scriptural hermeneutics. This particular controversy intersected with the highest echelons of the Egyptian political elite and was a matter that directly related to the king, the prime minister, parliament, the Ministry of Education (Wizārat al-Maʿārif), the religious courts (*al-maḥākim al-sharʿiyya*), the Dār al-Iftāʾ (the state agency for issuing legal decrees) and al-Azhar University. The Egyptian press, in the form of newspapers, journals and pamphlets, offered the print medium for staging these debates, which were often quite acrimonious in tenor.

An important element to the controversy in Egypt were the concomitant developments in Turkey, which was itself in a process of radical political and social transformation. In 1922, the Ottoman sultanate was abolished and by 1924 the caliphate had been dissolved, the symbolism of which had reverberations for Muslims the world over. The publication of a Turkish translation of the Qur'an in 1924 was followed a year later by a state-sponsored translation project, funded by the secular nationalist parliament, to produce an official Turkish translation and commentary of the Qur'an, along with a translation of Bukhārī's canonical hadith collection.[5] Through a programme of modernisation, the government of Kemal Atatürk began to officially promote the use of Turkish in liturgical spheres once reserved for Arabic, such as for the call to prayer, Ramadan recitations and the performance of ritual prayer itself. Writing a year after the legislation of 1932 discouraging the use of Arabic in mosques, Lyman MacCallum, a Canadian missionary and director of the Bible Society in Istanbul, commented that Western law had 'substituted the *Sheriat*',[6] and that the Turks were 'tearing their religious life free from the senseless clutch of the withered hand of Arabia', now they were free from their oppressors to worship in their own language.[7]

Needless to say, many Muslim religious authorities were much less sanguine. Most notably, the Salafī reformist Rashīd Riḍā (d. 1935) stood out as a vocal critic of Qur'anic translation. A student of the Egyptian modernist and reformist Muḥammad ʿAbduh (d. 1905), Riḍā was a stalwart leader of the Salafī movement, who advocated a pan-Islamic reform with Arabic at its centre. Among the sundry topics with which he engaged, Riḍā used his monthly journal *al-Manār*, published in Cairo, as a platform to advance Arabic as the authentic language of Islam and to criticise efforts to translate the Qur'an.[8] Riḍā linked such translations to broader secular and nationalist currents that, in his mind, would result in the further fragmentation and political emaciation of the global community of Muslims.[9]

In 1925, the arrival in Cairo of an English translation of the Qur'an by Mawlānā Muḥammad ʿAlī (d. 1951) of the Lahore Aḥmadiyya also gave occasion for heated debate over the lawfulness of translating the Qur'an. Upon reviewing it, the leadership of al-Azhar issued an order banning the distribution and circulation of the work. Outrage over the sectarian nature of the translation led to the seizure and public burning of copies in the courtyard of al-Azhar mosque.[10] In 1931, this climate of suspicion toward Qur'anic translation greeted the British Muslim convert Marmaduke Pickthall (d. 1936) during his travels in Egypt. Pickthall attributed the resistance he met in Egypt to his translation of the Qur'an to a cultural distinction between Arab and non-Arab Muslims, as he had encountered no such opposition while working on the project in India.[11]

To be sure, opposition even in Egypt was by no means uniform. Arriving from India, Pickthall set out with the aim of working with Shaykh Muḥammad Muṣṭafā al-Marāghī (d. 1945) to improve his English translation.[12] Like Riḍā, Marāghī was also a student of ʿAbduh. In contrast to Riḍā, however, Marāghī was a proponent of establishing an official translation of the Qur'an for the purposes of proselytisation and for Muslims who could not access the meaning of the original Arabic. This translation project fit into his larger efforts toward institutional and curricular reform of al-Azhar. Marāghī's first stint as rector of al-Azhar began in 1928; he immediately proposed the formation of a committee within the university to help revise and review the translation on which Pickthall had been working. However, Marāghī met opposition from King Fu'ād I himself (r. 1917–36), who viewed translating the Qur'an as illicit.[13]

The king had also resisted Marāghī's promotion to the position of Shaykh al-Azhar, preferring instead the Shāfi'ī jurist and royalist Muḥammad al-Aḥmadī al-Ẓawāhirī (d. 1944) for the post. Nominated by the nationalist Prime Minister Muṣṭafā al-Naḥḥās Pashā (d. 1965), Marāghī was only promoted to the position after a ten-month struggle for succession, which pitted the parliament against the king.[14] By the time Pickthall arrived with a letter of introduction to Marāghī, in the middle of November of 1929, the political situation had significantly changed. Just a few weeks earlier, Marāghī had been forced to step down as rector in the face of obstruction from the royalist camp, while his own support had eroded due to a change of leadership in parliament. The king's original choice, Ẓawāhirī, was immediately appointed to head al-Azhar. While Ẓawāhirī ultimately adopted many of the reforms that Marāghī had originally proposed,[15] he stood in opposition to the translation of the Qur'an.[16]

In 1935, Marāghī was reinstated as Shaykh al-Azhar, following a turbulent period for the university, which saw the growing politicisation of the institution. Marāghī returned with a mandate for further reforms. There is much to suggest that attitudes toward the translation of the Qur'an were not entirely static during this period.[17] At the end of the year, Marāghī sent a bill (*mashrū'*) to parliament, co-sponsored by 'Alī 'Allūba Pāshā (d. 1956), the minister of education, seeking governmental approval of and financial support for a project which would see al-Azhar University collaborate with the ministry of education in forming a commission to translate the 'meanings' (*ma'ānī*) of the Qur'an. According to the memoir of 'Alī 'Allūba Pāshā, King Fu'ād I originally resisted Marāghī's proposal; however, after 'Allūba's intervention, the king reversed his position on the matter, a shift apparently occasioned by the proliferation of foreign language translations said to contain errors, often with intentional distortions (*taḥrīf*) aimed at defaming Islam.[18] On 7 April 1936, a *fatwā* in support of the project was signed by the grand mufti, ʿAbd al-Majīd Salīm (d. 1954), head of the Dār al-Iftāʾ; he was joined by several other prominent Egyptian *ʿulamāʾ*, including authorities from al-Azhar and the judiciary.[19] Muḥammad ʿAlī Tawfīq (d. 1955), a prominent member of the royal family, spoke out publicly as a supporter of the bill, defending it as a measure that would benefit Muslims and Islam the world over.[20] On 16 April, the prime minister, ʿAlī Māhir Pāshā (d. 1960), approved the measure with the endorsement of parliament and promised governmental funds for the translation project.[21]

When Marāghī addressed parliament advocating the passage of the measure, he opened his speech by claiming that, 'in both ancient and modern times people have sought to translate the meanings of the Noble Qur'an'.[22] This established tradition of translating the Qur'an served as one of the major justifications for the legitimacy of the entire project. Marāghī argued that these translations, however, were carried out either by those who did not have a full mastery of Arabic, or others who did not have complete command of the target language. The joint commission led by the ministry of education and al-Azhar University sought to make available to the world an accurate and official translation that agreed with the orthodox principles of Islam.[23] In many ways Marāghī's proposal built on earlier translation efforts within al-Azhar. It is also during this period that Wajdī, serving as the editor of the university journal, then titled *Nūr al-Islām*, increased the publication of English language material. This is notably reflected in the serial translation of Bukhārī's hadith collection that the journal began to publish in 1935 during Wajdī's tenure as editor-in-chief.[24]

Despite gaining widespread political backing, Marāghī's proposal met with vocal opposition in the press, both before and after the run-up to the vote in parliament. His opponent, the ousted Ẓawāhirī, was just one of many who challenged the entire measure as an illicit enterprise that ran afoul of convention and religious law.[25] Many of Marāghī's critics were religious lawyers, such as Muḥammad Sulaymān (d. 1936), a judge of the Supreme Court of Religious Law in Cairo, and Muḥammad Muṣṭafā al-Shāṭir, a provincial judge in the religious court of Shibīn al-Kūm, in the Nile Delta, both of whom published denouncements of the translation project as the case made its way through parliament.[26] On 12 June, a faction of lawyers from the religious courts (*al-maḥākim al-sharʿiyya*) issued an opinion claiming that it was unlawful to translate either the Qur'an or its meanings, as it would cause harm to religion, language and nation (*al-dīn wa'l-lugha wa'l-waṭan*) – a turn of phrase that at once highlights the intersection between Arabic, nationalism and religious identity.[27]

Despite these vocal objections, parliament continued its commitment to the project and funds were allocated in the autumn for a commission to oversee the translation. This commission included such members as the grand mufti ʿAbd al-Majīd Salīm and Maḥmūd Shaltūt, a lecturer in the faculty of religious law, who would ultimately become rector of al-Azhar after Marāghī's death in 1945.[28] The commission was charged with first concisely paraphrasing in Arabic the *maʿānī* (meanings) of the Qur'anic text; this was then to serve as the basis for further foreign language translation.[29] However, evidently due to a parliamentary budget crisis which soon followed, funding was ultimately cut, putting an end to the entire project.[30] While the translation never materialised, Marāghī's success before parliament and within al-Azhar played a role in changing public opinion over the nature and form of Qur'anic translation.[31] The entire episode gave public expression to translation as an exegetical enterprise that sought to communicate the meaning of the Qur'an but not to actually replace the Arabic text itself.[32]

The Shibboleth of Salmān's Persian Translation of the *Fātiḥa*

Throughout this controversy, Salmān's Persian translation of the *Fātiḥa* served as a site of contestation. For the proponents of Marāghī's project, the account offered a *sunna* of the early community that had the sanction of the Prophet.[33] Newspapers presented one of the most prominent staging grounds for this issue.

At stake in the back and forth of the arguments was not only a political struggle. As the competing sides of the controversy made repeatedly clear, at the heart of this debate was the contested relationship between Arabic and vernacular languages in the fields of religious knowledge for Muslims the world over.

In March 1936, at the height of the controversy, Wajdī published his article in *al-Ahrām*, opening with the account of Salmān's *Fātiḥa*, as a rebuttal to the judge Sulaymān, who had earlier attacked Marāghī's proposal to the parliament in the same newspaper, calling it a repugnant innovation.[34] Quoting the Khwārazmī polymath Abū'l-Rayḥān al-Bīrūnī (d. 440/1048), Sulaymān had argued that the religion (*dīn*) and the state (*dawla*) of Islam are by their very nature Arabic, 'one is lifted up by divine power, the other by a heavenly hand';[35] Sulaymān further claimed that for over twelve centuries no Muslim has ever thought of translating the Qur'an.[36] As far as the historical record is concerned, the notion that Muslims never translated the sacred text is rather dubious, as the copious written record preserved in a wide range of vernaculars demonstrates. Needless to say, whether or not such texts should be considered translations forms part of the debate.

In his retort, Wajdī questioned why, if Qur'anic translation were as repugnant an affair as Sulaymān claimed, would the Prophet have sanctioned Salmān's *Fātiḥa*. Furthermore, according to Wajdī, such translation continued throughout the early centuries of Islam. For support, he turned to the Ḥanafī juridical position that those who had yet to master the original Arabic could perform the daily ritual prayers reciting a translation in Persian. This was an argument advanced by the Ḥanafī jurists Abū Yūsuf (d. 182/798) and Muḥammad al-Shaybānī (d. 189/805), who modified the position of their master, Abū Ḥanīfa al-Nuʿmān (d. 150/767), which permitted the unrestricted liturgical use of Persian regardless of one's capacity in Arabic.[37] As a legacy of Ottoman rule, the legal institutions in Cairo upheld Ḥanafī jurisprudence as the normative basis for positive law, and thus arguments based on the history of Ḥanafī praxis carried with them further juridical weight.[38] Wajdī also claimed that the practice of performing ritual prayer in translation could be traced back to the pious forefathers (*salaf*), particularly to the figure of Ḥasan al-Baṣrī (d. 110/728), who was said to have had difficulty with the original Arabic and so recited the Qur'an in Persian during prayer.[39]

Sulaymān responded in *al-Ahrām* with a detailed counterattack. As for Salmān's translation of the *Fātiḥa*, Sulaymān retorted, 'I am immensely sorry that I must say to my friend Professor Muḥammad Farīd Wajdī that this account is not authentic (*ghayr ṣaḥīḥ*); were his Honour to uncover its chain of transmission, this would put us at ease and would help remove the dispute between us.'[40] Likewise, Sulaymān impugned the authenticity of the anecdote ascribed to Ḥasan al-Baṣrī, arguing that the famed *muḥaddith* was known throughout the classical biographical accounts for his eloquent command of Arabic.[41]

This line of argumentation was followed by the judge Muḥammad Muṣṭafā al-Shāṭir, who directly attacked Wajdī's accounts of Salmān and Ḥasan al-Baṣrī in a short pamphlet refuting the lawfulness of Marāghī's project.[42] On the question of Ḥasan al-Baṣrī, Shāṭir concluded that the account was taken from a commentary on the *Musallam al-thubūt*,[43] a work of *uṣūl al-fiqh* by the Ḥanafī Indian Muḥibb Allāh al-Bihārī (d. 1707), where it is Ḥabīb al-ʿAjamī (d. ca. 140/757), a companion of Ḥasan al-Baṣrī, who was said to recite the Qur'an in Persian as he could not properly pronounce the Arabic original.[44]

Turning to Salmān's *Fātiḥa*, Shāṭir set out to dispute the authenticity of the story. The arguments over the report primarily build upon and engage with earlier sources, drawn largely from classical law. Shāṭir argues that there is no historical basis to Wajdī's claim that the Prophet sanctioned Salmān's translation and that the account itself strains all reason:

> I have not found in any of the books of hadith, nor the books of history any basis for [this account]. I have, however, come upon the original report (*al-riwāya al-aṣliyya*) in *al-Mabsūṭ* and there is nothing here to indicate that the Prophet ordered Salmān to do this. Could the Honourable Professor tell us his reference, and if he does not, which will more likely be the case, then he has produced a proof which would go against him . . . O Professor,

> were it established that the Prophet ordered what you have mentioned in your article, then Abū Ḥanīfa would have used it as a proof for his position and the other imams would have been compelled to follow him.[45]

The reference in question is to the Ḥanafī juridical work *al-Mabsūṭ* by the Central Asian jurist Abū Bakr Muḥammad al-Sarakhsī (d. ca. 483/1090). Sarakhsī relates that Abū Ḥanīfa drew authority for his ruling from an account that Salmān had composed the translation of the *Fātiḥa* at the request of Persians who recited it until they grew accustomed to the original Arabic.[46] Shāṭir also turns to the Shāfiʿī encyclopaedia of positive law, the *Sharḥ al-Muhadhdhab* by Abū Zakariyyāʾ al-Nawawī (d. 676/1277), which lists the report as one of the proof texts for the Ḥanafī position.[47] For his part, Nawawī claims that a translation can never equal the Qurʾan, and while he does not directly impugn the authenticity of Salmān's account, he argues that what Salmān produced was merely a commentary (*tafsīr*) of the *Fātiḥa*.[48]

While a prophetic context may well be implied in the account, Shāṭir notes that neither Sarakhsī nor Nawawī clarify whether Salmān's translation was made during the lifetime of the Prophet, nor do they explicitly state that the Prophet condoned Salmān's translation. Likewise, Shāṭir draws the entire historical context into question, as he doubts that there were a significant number of Persian converts at this early period. Even if the account were authentic, Shāṭir argues that the action of a Companion cannot serve as the basis of a juridical proof (*ḥujja*). Furthermore, the isolated reports (*āḥād*) of the story (*qiṣṣa*) are themselves overruled by the established textual authority (*naṣṣ*) of the Qurʾan, which on multiple occasions refers to itself as fundamentally an Arabic revelation.[49]

Coming to Wajdī's defence, the Egyptian religious scholar ʿAbd al-Raḥmān al-Jazīrī (d. 1941) argued that Shāṭir's criticism was entirely unfounded as the accounts of Salmān and Ḥasan al-Baṣrī both form part of the juridical corpus of Ḥanafī law.[50] Best known for the *Kitāb al-Fiqh ʿalāʾl-madhāhib al-arbaʿa*, a work of comparative jurisprudence, Jazīrī published a direct rebuttal to

Shāṭir, and promoted the Azhar translation project as a normative continuation of Qur'anic hermeneutics. Jazīrī claimed that the Azhar position reflected the majority view, while the number of opponents, such as Shāṭir and Sulaymān, could be counted on a single hand.[51] This characterisation may well reflect public sentiment, though it is difficult to assess the accuracy of such a claim, considering that all sides vied for the mantle of consensus.[52]

While Wajdī was by no means the only one to advance Salmān's translation of the *Fātiḥa* as a juridical proof text during the course of the controversy, he vocally upheld this position even in the face of withering criticism.[53] After parliament passed the measure, Wajdī edited an issue of the *Majallat al-Azhar* that focused on the legitimacy of the project; in it he republished a tract by Marāghī written four years earlier on the lawfulness of translation.[54] While Marāghī did not trace the account back to the authority of the Prophet, he did advance the argument that Abū Ḥanīfa drew support for the translation of ritual prayer from the authority of Salmān's Persian *Fātiḥa*.[55]

While Marāghī's plan was criticised by the likes of Sulaymān and Shāṭir, it appears that Wajdī faced more in the way of personal attacks. Yet Wajdī did not let these affronts go unchallenged. His most detailed defence of the matter came with the publication of his own treatise, *al-Adilla al-ʿilmiyya ʿalā jawāz tarjamat maʿānī'l-Qur'ān*, issued as a supplement to the spring volume of *al-Azhar*.[56] Here Wajdī responds point by point to the accusations levelled by Sulaymān and Shāṭir, replying with a similar spiteful tone of public rebuke. One of the centrepieces to the treatise is his affirmation that Salmān indeed produced a Persian translation of the *Fātiḥa*, which the Prophet approved of, and he advances various arguments to support his case.

To the question posed by Sulaymān in *al-Ahrām* concerning the source of the account, Wajdī cites a juridical text by the name of *al-Nihāya wa'l-dirāya*;[57] he adds that the grand mufti, Muḥammad Bakhīt al-Muṭīʿī (d. 1935), drew on the same text when he issued a *fatwā* in 1903, giving licence to Muslims in South Africa to translate the Qur'an.[58] These citations are designed to locate the Prophet's acceptance of the Persian translation of the *Fātiḥa* within the

Ḥanafī juridical tradition and to demonstrate that the account was used as a basis of positive law in modern Egypt. The recourse to Bakhīt served a further purpose, as the grand mufti had published a treatise in 1932 on the juridical question of Qur'anic translation. This treatise was used by both proponents and opponents of Marāghī's translation project.[59] By turning to Bakhīt as an authority on the matter, Wajdī positions the deceased shaykh as an advocate for Qur'anic translation.

In the opening of his treatise, Wajdī argues that the juridical position permitting the translation of the Qur'an and its use in ritual prayer for those who did not know Arabic dates back to the lifetime of the Prophet, 'since Salmān translated the *Fātiḥa* of the Qur'an into Persian and there were Persian converts who would pray using it'. He continues, stating that during the second/eighth century the permissibility of translation became a juridical principle (*aṣlan madhhabiyyan*) in Ḥanafī law, the largest of the juridical schools.[60] He notes that this permissibility was not just theoretical, but put into practice, citing once again the account of Ḥasan al-Baṣrī as authentic and noting that Bakhīt had also turned to the same report in his *fatwā* on the matter.[61] Repeated throughout his treatise is the weight of juridical precedence, as Wajdī advances in his defence the 'numerous Ḥanafī juridical works published in Egypt' which 'all stipulate the permissibility of translating the Qur'an and using it in prayer for those who do not know Arabic'.[62]

Wajdī also turns to Shāṭir's claim that had the Prophet indeed sanctioned the translation, then Abū Ḥanīfa would have used it as a proof for his position and that the other founders of juridical schools would have had to follow him in his ruling. In response, Wajdī argues that there is nothing here which strains reason, for according to Ḥanafī juridical tradition Abū Ḥanīfa indeed used Salmān's translation as the basis for his position. Furthermore, he notes that one of the greatest causes for divergence (*ikhtilāf*) between the juridical schools derives from the founders drawing upon different prophetic sayings and actions to support their own rulings.[63] As to the argument that there were no Persian converts in the region, Wajdī turns to the Persians (*abnā'*) of Yemen who converted during the lifetime of the Prophet and also notes that there could very well have been Persian converts in the Arabian Peninsula, not to mention Mesopotamia, and these converts could have been in contact with Salmān during this period.[64]

To be sure, this tit for tat verges on tautology, with a set of *a priori* assumptions underwriting the entire debate, one claiming that the Prophet would have indeed permitted such a translation and the other arguing the exact opposite. Although Salmān's *Fātiḥa* offers merely one node in a broader constellation of disputes in the larger controversy, it reveals a running tension over the legitimacy of Qur'anic translation and its historical significance. Those debating the issue knew that, if authentic, the account would not only situate the practice of translating the Qur'an in the earliest history of conversion, but it would also position translation in the realm of ritual praxis as a symbolically legitimate replacement of the sacred text for those unable to recite the original. This was not the aim of Marāghī's proposal, which insisted that a translation of the meanings of the Qur'an could never be a substitute for the original text. Yet both Sulaymān and Shāṭir believed that regardless of the real purpose of the project, the result would be the same: a translation which people would use to replace the Qur'an itself.[65]

A Juridical Legacy

While several works of jurisprudence feature as authorities in these debates, arguably the most important is a treatise dedicated to the subject, *al-Nafḥa al-qudsiyya*, composed by the Ḥanafī scholar and leading professor of al-Azhar, Abū'l-Ikhlāṣ al-Shurunbulālī (d. 1658). Although this short tract appears as a source in the writings on the topic prior to Marāghī's parliamentary measure, it was only published in April 1936. The publisher, Farāj al-Sayyid ʿAbd al-ʿĀl, a religious lawyer, states in his preface that the publication was aimed at specifically addressing the recent crisis (*fitna*) and to make more generally known proofs which demonstrate that the translation of the Qur'an is impermissible in any form.[66] The publisher also points out that more than three hundred years have passed since Shurunbulālī collected the positions of the religious authorities on the matter, highlighting, as it were, both the antiquity and authority of the text. Needless to say, Shurunbulālī's treatise is not nearly as programmatic as the preface would suggest, for it gathers a range of early juridical opinions and statements that are at times contradictory and not easily harmonised. To this end, both proponents and opponents of the translation project mined Shurunbulālī's digest to advance their own argumentation.

As mentioned above, Wajdī cites the juridical work *al-Nihāya wa'l-dirāya* as his source for the Prophet's approval of Salmān's translation of the *Fātiḥa*. This source is also referenced within Shurunbulālī's *al-Nafḥa al-qudsiyya* and it is clear from Wajdī's use of the treatise elsewhere that he derived the account from Shurunbulālī. This point is not lost on Shāṭir, who turns his attention to the account as redacted by Shurunbulālī. Shāṭir reworked Shurunbulālī's account in his rebuttal to Marāghī, entitled *al-Qawl al-sadīd fī ḥukm tarjamat al-Qur'ān al-majīd*. He published this in 1936, after Wajdī's *Adilla* and the April (Muḥarram) issue of the *Majallat al-Azhar*, which contained a further defence of the translation project. Here Shāṭir argues:

> [Wajdī] claims in the supplement to the *Majallat al-Azhar* that a translation took place in the time of the Prophet; he relies on what is in *al-Nafḥa al-qudsiyya*, on the authority of *al-Nihāya wa'l-dirāya*. Well, we have never heard of this claim until today. There was no translation of the Qur'an in the time of the Prophet, nor in the time of the Companions. The proof upon which they base their claim is an error in every respect, and thus their conclusion is also an error.[67]

At this point Shāṭir turns to the passage in Shurunbulālī's treatise that describes how the people of Persia wrote to Salmān requesting that he translate the *Fātiḥa* for them. The text explains that Salmān translated the *basmala*, the inchoative benediction to the *Fātiḥa, In the name of God, full of compassion, ever compassionate* (*bismi'llāh al-raḥmān al-raḥīm*), in Persian as *ba-nām-i yazdān bakhshāyand bakhshānīd* ('In the name of God, merciful, forgiving').[68] Shurunbulālī relates that Persian converts would recite Salmān's translation of the *Fātiḥa* in prayer until their tongues became accustomed to the original and that the Prophet had approved of Salmān's translation. Shurunbulālī concludes that the account is related in the *Nihāya* on the authority of Sarakhsī's *Mabsūṭ*. Again, Shāṭir observes that Sarakhsī's report contains neither a translation of the *Fātiḥa* nor an explicit account of the Prophet's approval, and draws into question the authority of the *Nihāya* from which the account is taken. Likewise, Shāṭir notes that the Persian translation does not replicate the *Fātiḥa*, but only the *basmala* and that, furthermore, one could not become accustomed to the original Arabic by reciting a Persian text. From these apparent inconsistencies, Shāṭir concludes that 'it is not possible for a Muslim to draw on the example of this account, for it is invalid in all respects as a basis for arguing that translating the Qur'an took place in various languages during the lifetime of the Prophet'.[69]

Neither Shurunbulālī nor the later authorities who copy from him identify the author of the *Nihāya*, which makes reference to Salmān's translation. However, there is every reason to believe that the juridical collection in question is the *Nihāyat al-kifāya fī dirāyat al-Hidāya* by the Central Asian Ḥanafī jurist Tāj al-Sharīʿa Abū ʿAbd Allāh ʿUmar al-Bukhārī (d. 672/1273–4). This work is, in turn, a commentary on the famed handbook of Ḥanafī law, *al-Hidāya*, by Shaykh al-Islām Burhān al-Dīn Abū'l-Ḥasan al-Marghīnānī (d. 593/1196).[70] While a lithograph edition was printed as a marginal commentary alongside the *Hidāya* in Delhi at the turn of the twentieth century, the *Nihāya* remains unedited and appears to have been entirely unknown in the modern Egyptian disputes, as its author is never directly cited, nor is the full title of the work given. Rather, as mentioned above, all the references to the work are clearly copied from Shurunbulālī's text.

The *Nihāya* of Tāj al-Sharīʿa does indeed report the Persian translation of the *basmala*, and also affirms that Salmān gained the Prophet's approval, ascribing the entire account to Sarakhsī (i.e. *kadhā fī'l-Mabsūṭ*).[71] These details, however, are not found in the two printed editions of Sarakhsī's encyclopaedic juridical compendium.[72] While the manuscript record may indeed prove differently,[73] the point is largely otiose, for, as we shall see, the details of both Salmān's translation and the prophetic approval were in circulation well before Sarakhsī transmitted an abridged version of the account. Sarakhsī's early readers may well have understood the abridged account as alluding to a prophetic sanction given to the translation.

Such objections over the authenticity of Salmān's translation of the *Fātiḥa* were by no means new. Prior to Marāghī's parliamentary proposal, various authorities had challenged the account. There is much to suggest that Wajdī was well aware of these objections. His use of the anecdote as a proof of the legacy of Qur'anic translation speaks to a broader process of contesting the shape and significance of Qur'anic hermeneutics in the course of Islamic history. Before Wajdī took on the post of chief editor of *al-Azhar*, the journal had published in 1932 an article by Shaykh Maḥmūd Abū Daqīqa (d. 1940), a professor in the faculty of Islamic theology (i.e. the Kulliyyat Uṣūl al-Dīn) at the university, taking a rather saturnine view of the lawfulness of Qur'anic translation. As for Salmān's translation of the *Fātiḥa*, Abū Daqīqa argued that the variants separating the material found in the *Nihāya*, the *Mabsūṭ* and in Nawawī's commentary demonstrated how weak the account was and that the very story went against the juridical consensus (*ijmāʿ*), which had agreed that it was unlawful to translate the Qur'an.[74]

In the same year, Muṣṭafā Ṣabrī (d. 1954) the former Shaykh al-Islām in the Ottoman Empire, who was living in exile in Cairo, published a detailed Arabic treatise refuting the modern attempts to translate the Qur'an. A virulent opponent of secular nationalism, Ṣabrī directed much of his ire at the Kemalist support of Turkish translations of the Qur'an and the use of such translations in mosques and for the performance of ritual prayer.[75] However, the treatise was also written in response to both Wajdī and Marāghī, who had published various articles in leading Egyptian newspapers, advocating the translation of the Qur'an.[76] While Ṣabrī acknowledges that the majority of the Muslims throughout the world indeed do not know Arabic, this, he concludes, is no justification for Qur'anic translations; rather, trained religious scholars should explain to these Muslims the meaning of the sacred text.[77] Regarding Salmān's translation, Ṣabrī dismisses the account out of hand, quoting the famed Indian Ḥanafī reformist, Abū'l-Ḥasanāt

'Abd al-Ḥayy al-Laknawī (d. 1886), who wrote an entire study, the *Ākām al-nafā'is*, on the juridical question of the use of the vernacular within the spheres of ritual performance.[78] While material from Shurunbulālī's treatise appears much more frequently, references to Laknawī's *Ākām al-nafā'is* also feature in the Egyptian debates.[79] As for Salmān's *Fātiḥa*, Laknawī notes, 'I have looked into this account, but up until now I have not found it to be reliably transmitted in the books of tradition.'[80]

This is more or less the same position taken by Riḍā on the matter. In 1903, he published a response in his monthly journal *al-Manār* to the *fatwā* issued by Bakhīt. In this *fatwā* Bakhīt cites Shurunbulālī's *al-Nafḥa al-qudsiyya* to argue that one may issue a translation of the Qur'an, but it is only lawful to do so in a manner that maintains the original Arabic side-by-side with the translated text.[81] As noted earlier, Bakhīt also references the report of Salmān's translation of the *Fātiḥa* from *al-Nihāya wa'l-dirāya*, which he clearly derived from Shurunbulālī. In his response, Riḍā questions how Salmān's translation would have offered a means to adapt the Arabic text, as suggested in the account, which states that Persian converts would recite the translation 'until their tongues grew accustomed' (*ḥattā lānat al-alsinatuhum*) to the original. Riḍā concludes that, in any case, this particular tradition is not authentic (*ghayr ṣaḥīḥ*) and thus cannot serve as the basis for law.[82]

It is worth noting that Bakhīt later appears to have reformulated his stance on this particular issue. He still maintained the Ḥanafī position that those who did not know Arabic could use translations for the performance of ritual prayer, citing the Ḥanafī sources redacted by Shurunbulālī in support of this ruling.[83] However, as for the essential Arabic form of the Qur'an, Bakhīt argues that the individual reports (*akhbār āḥād*) concerning the story (*qiṣṣa*) of Salmān al-Fārisī, as mentioned in various books of law, including Sarakhsī's *Mabsūṭ*, do not take precedence over verses of the Qur'an that affirm the Arabic character of the revelation; for, in contrast to this account, the Qur'an has the status of *tawātur*, in other words, it is authenticated by multiple lines of transmission.[84]

For Sulaymān there is no doubt about the matter. In the expanded second edition of his *Ḥadath al-aḥdāth*, he responds directly to

Wajdī's *Adilla* and focuses the brunt of his accusations on the inauthenticity of Salmān's *Fātiḥa*, charging that 'Wajdī lies about the Prophet, about the Companions, about the Successors; with injurious intent he strikes at the revealed law (*sharīʿa*) and without any basis in religious knowledge, he issues rulings to the people.'[85] Sulaymān concludes that the entire account is itself a lie, as it cannot be found in any book of hadith and thus it cannot be relied upon: 'How can al-Azhar permit this mendacious ascription [to the Prophet] and rather than reject it, issue a *fatwā* based upon it?'[86]

Doubt concerning the authenticity of the story continued beyond these heated debates. Such is the case with ʿAbd al-ʿAẓīm al-Zarqānī (d. 1948), a professor of Qur'anic Studies at al-Azhar.[87] In his influential introduction to the study of the Qur'an, the *Manāhil al-ʿirfān*, first published in 1943, Zarqānī contends that there is no historical basis for Salmān's translation. He does this in an extended chapter exploring the lawfulness and linguistic possibility of translating the Qur'an; here he argues that a literal translation that seeks to replace the Qur'an is both impossible linguistically and unlawful juridically, a line of argument most generally agreed upon in the various sides of the debate. However, Zarqānī also advances the position that a translation which does not seek to replace the Qur'an but exegetically explains its meanings is both licit and meritorious, a position that largely conforms to Marāghī's argumentation and al-Azhar's translation project.[88]

With regard to Salmān's translation of the *Fātiḥa*, Zarqānī quotes Shurunbulālī's treatise, and argues that as the transmission of the report is unknown (*lā yurʿafu lahu sanad*), it cannot serve as the basis of law (*fa-lā yajūzu'l-ʿamal bihi*). Like Shāṭir before him, Zarqānī criticises the account, which he asserts is not a translation of the *Fātiḥa*, but only of the *basmala*; furthermore, he argues that the translation of the *basmala* was itself not complete. Zarqānī's transmission of the anecdote is both apocopated and jumbled; here Salmān only offers the community of early converts the following, '*Ba-nām-i yazdān yaḥshayand*', which is a shortened misreading of Shurunbulālī's original account. Nonetheless, Zarqānī contends that the translation lacks a word corresponding to *raḥmān*, which he faults as a deficiency of the Persian language itself.[89]

The historian Abdul Latif Tibawi (d. 1981) echoes many of Zarqānī's points in his English article 'Is the Qur'an Translatable? Early Muslim Opinion', published in 1962. This article has had an enduring influence on the modern western reception of the topic.[90] Though he does not acknowledge it, the 'early Muslim opinion' that Tibawi sets out to unearth is largely a reformulation of what modern Egyptian scholars had collected in their own arguments over the matter. As for Salmān's translation of the *Fātiḥa*, Tibawi asserts: 'A historian will be quick to detect technical reasons, based both on internal as well as external evidence, to reject it altogether. Some jurists will not be far behind the historian in their protests.'[91] Tibawi concludes that there is 'no reliable evidence' that the Prophet had approved of reciting the *Fātiḥa* in Persian during prayer.

Tibawi makes no effort to trace the contexts where Salmān's *Fātiḥa* travelled or the motivations that animated its transmission, though he admits that translations of the Qur'an were indeed produced. While he finds it difficult to establish when these were first attempted, Tibawi claims that the manuscripts of these translations are themselves not particularly old.[92] Such a view can only be obtained by reading solely legal works on the topic, an accusation which Tibawi levels at the authorities themselves.[93] Contrary to his suggestion, the first full translations and commentaries of the Qur'an appear at exactly the same time as the emergence of Early New Persian in the course of the fourth/tenth century, a fact already apparent with the publication of Charles Storey's sweeping treatment of the topic in the first volume of his bio-bibliographical survey of Persian literature, published in 1927.[94] Furthermore, there is much to indicate that this written tradition builds upon even older practices of Qur'anic translation and that the history of Salmān's translation of the *Fātiḥa* is itself tied to this very process of vernacularisation.

Language Politics

While texts like Shurunbulālī's digest feature throughout the controversy, modern religious authorities evince a good deal of resourcefulness in their use of material, often drawing on an array of sources from different genres to marshal their arguments in new and creative ways. Although much of this material is taken from classical sources, the tensions animating the debates were very much part of the unique historical context of the period. As Sulaymān argues, Arabic is the formal language of Islam (*lisān al-Islām al-rasmī*). He continues that Muslims must resist the secularising forces of colonialism, which used the education systems across North Africa, the Levant and India to force French or English upon the local inhabitants.[95]

The writings of the famed Ḥanbalī jurist Ibn Taymiyya (d. 728/1328) are particularly influential in this reformist vision of Arabic as a sacred language that could unite the Muslim community. Perhaps most important is Ibn Taymiyya's polemical treatise *Iqtiḍā' al-ṣirāṭ al-mustaqīm*, which warns Muslims against imitating the practices of infidels, drawing on the prophetic hadith 'whoever resembles a group, belongs to [that group] (*man tashabbaha bi-qawmin fa-huwa minhum*)'.[96] As with other displays of cultural difference, language represents for Ibn Taymiyya one of the many locations of religious identity. Sulaymān cites a famous passage from this treatise in which Ibn Taymiyya argues that speaking languages other than Arabic is juridically detested (*makrūh*), for Arabic is the defining sign or mark (*shiʿār*) of Islam and the Qur'an:

> When the first Muslims settled in the Levant and Egypt, the language of these regions was Greek, and in the region of Iraq and Khurasan it was Persian, and for the people of the Maghrib their language was Berber, and all of the peoples of these regions grew accustomed to Arabic, such that it gained ascendancy amongst both the Muslims and the infidels (*ghalabat ʿalā'l-muslimīn wa'l-kuffār*) of these regions. This used to be the case in Khurasan as well. However, they became careless in the matter of language and they grew accustomed to speaking in Persian, so that Persian predominated amongst them and Arabic became unknown to many of them. There is no doubt that this is detested. Rather, the better course is to become accustomed to Arabic, so that it is taught to the young in schools and used in the home, and so that it manifests as the mark of Islam and its people. Then it would

> become easy for the people of Islam to understand the meanings of the Book and the Sunna and the speech of the pious forefathers (*salaf*), as opposed to those who grew accustomed to another language and then wish to translate [all this].[97]

Here, vernacular exegetical activity is presented as a flawed means of transmitting scripture and religion. Sulaymān builds upon Ibn Taymiyya's views to argue that Arabic has always been the language of true religion and that the translation of the Qur'an, even if it were possible, violates the Arabic essence of Islam. However, it is of note that elsewhere Ibn Taymiyya argues that while it is prohibited to use translations for ritual prayer, translating the Qur'an for the purpose of comprehension, just like commenting upon it, is indeed permitted.[98] Sulaymān, in contrast, refuses to accept the analogy between the two.

While Sulaymān admits that of course non-Arabs did study the Qur'an in their own languages, he is quick to distinguish such interpretive activity from translation. To this end, he turns to the now well-known example of the Basran scholar Mūsā b. Sayyār al-Aswārī (fl. 120/738), who features in a list of prominent eloquent preachers drawn up by the Abbasid intellectual and man of letters, Abū ʿUthmān al-Jāḥiẓ (d. 255/868–9).[99] A descendant of the Sāsānian cavalry (*asbārān asāwira*) that joined forces with the Arabs during the conquest of Iran, Mūsā b. Sayyār is remembered for his prodigious command of both Persian and Arabic.[100] At his renowned assemblies before the mosque of the Asāwira, Mūsā would read a verse from the Qur'an, comment upon it (*yufassiruhā*) in Arabic for the Arabs seated to his right and then turn to the Persians to his left and comment upon it in Persian. Jāḥiẓ concludes that no one could tell in which language he was more eloquent.[101] For Sulaymān, the important point here is not that early Muslims used the vernacular to interpret the Qur'an, but that such acts were done purely for the purposes of explanation (*tafhīm*) and interpretation (*tafsīr*) and not translation (*tarjama*).[102]

Repeated in these debates is an argument over the semantic distinction between translation and interpretation. For instance, Muḥammad Shākir (d. 1939), judge and a vice-rector (*wakīl*) of al-Azhar, also saw the two activities as fundamentally distinct. Shākir famously spoke out against the first Aḥmadī translation, which reached Cairo in 1925, just as he stood in opposition to the Turkish translations of the Qur'an.[103] One of his sources for separating interpretation from translation is the compendium of Shāfiʿī jurisprudence *al-Baḥr al-muḥīṭ*, by the Egyptian religious scholar Abū ʿAbd Allāh Badr al-Dīn al-Zarkashī (d. 794/1392).[104] Zarkashī relates an anecdote from the Shāfiʿī jurist of Transoxiana, Abū Bakr al-Qaffāl al-Marwazī (d. 427/1036), that it was impossible to produce the Qur'an in Persian. To the retort that the same would be true then for any interpretation of the Qur'an, Qaffāl replied that one could determine part of God's intention, but not all of it.[105]

In contrast, the move to issue a translation of the 'meanings' of the Qur'an, as proposed by Marāghī and Wajdī, was designed to keep the activity of translation within the realm of interpretation, an endeavour long considered legitimate in the broader sphere of Qur'anic hermeneutics. Thus, while a literal translation, referred to generally as *tarjama ḥarfiyya* or *lafẓiyya*, is repeatedly ruled out as impossible, an exegetical translation, a *tarjama tafsīriyya* or *maʿnawiyya*, is advanced as entirely licit. Such a hermeneutical division is designed to preserve the sanctity of the divine and inimitable Arabic text, while also opening it up to various vernacular modes of interpretation.[106]

During the run-up to the parliamentary proposal, Shaykh Muḥammad Ḥasanayn Makhlūf al-ʿAdawī (d. 1936), former vice-rector of al-Azhar and head of the religious court in the provincial city of Qena in Upper Egypt, argued in *al-Ahrām* that a *tarjama tafsīriyya* 'without a doubt has been permitted by all the ulama and there is no proof in the Sunna or elsewhere to indicate that it is forbidden'.[107] Makhlūf also concluded that, through the course of history, leading religious scholars have produced commentaries of the Qur'an in Persian and in Hindi, just as they have composed translations of hadith and commented upon them, and in doing so, he said, 'their method has been to understand the original and to express that which they understand in another language and then write that out. No one would say they were translating the Qur'an, rather they have interpreted the Qur'an and then translated their interpretation.' Makhlūf contends, in contrast to those such as Sulaymān and Shākir, that it is a figurative expression (*ḍarb min al-majāz*) to speak of a translation of the Qur'an, for what is meant by translation is really just interpretation.[108] Years earlier, Makhlūf had advanced a similar argument in a treatise he published on the topic, in which he explained that in common usage translation is the interpretation of speech from one language to another.[109] This definition of *tarjama* is entirely in keeping with the classical lexicons.[110]

The grand mufti Bakhīt viewed the matter in similar terms. He maintained that the translation of the Qur'an for the purposes of instruction and comprehension, to warn humanity and to spread Islam is permitted according to all the legal schools without distinction. However, such translations should only be distributed after they have been verified to contain no distortion or falsification of theological meaning (i.e. *taḥrīf*).[111] Bakhīt further argues that just as spreading Islam is a communal obligation (*farḍ kifāya*), so too is translating and explaining the Qur'an, 'for lexically the meaning of translation (*tarjama*) is interpretation (*tafsīr*), and there is no doubt that the interpretation of the Qur'an in Arabic is an expression of it through a translation of its meanings (*'ībāratun 'an tarjamatin li-ma'nāhu*)'.[112] Just as opponents often stated that translation was forbidden by consensus, those in support of the project repeatedly claimed that translation, as an exegetical activity, was not only lawful, but was a religious obligation for the entire community (*farḍ kifāya*).[113] Indeed, the belief that translating the Qur'an was a meritorious duty can be traced throughout the early exegetical and juridical literature on the topic.[114]

Even with this insistence on the probity of Qur'anic translation, advocates generally stressed that such translation can never replace the original Arabic text. The wedding together of meaning and form as the basis of Qur'anic inimitability lies at the heart of the problem. Thus, many modern advocates insisted on the necessity of keeping the Arabic Qur'an alongside the translated text. This line of argumentation is often supported by juridical source texts from Ḥanafī law which state that translations of the Qur'an should always accompany the original text. Such a strategy for managing the vernacular within the sacred space of scripture is entirely congruent with the early emergence of Persian translations of the Qur'an. Rather than reflecting a particularly modern development, the move to subordinate translation to the field of hermeneutics, focusing on the meanings of the Qur'an rather than replacing the inimitable text itself, builds upon established exegetical practices. Yet Shāṭir, who, like Sulaymān and Shākir, also insisted that interpretation and translation were fundamentally distinct, even objected to interlinear translations and vernacular commentaries as contrary to the precepts of Islam.[115]

Such an argument ignores the long tradition of vernacular exegesis in Islamic history and views it instead as unlawful and heretical. It also hinges on a vision of translation as fundamentally replacing the original text. The complete effacement of the source text is not the only manner in which translation as a hermeneutical enterprise operates. The interlinear form of the early Persian translations of the Qur'an very much moves translation into the realm of commentary and interpretation, supplementing, expanding and opening up the Arabic text, but not replacing it. In many senses, the controversy over the authenticity of Salmān's Persian *Fātiḥa* was not only a debate over translation as such. Rather, it was also a dispute over the place and significance of the vernacular in the various fields of religious learning.

Whence Salmān's *Fātiḥa*?

To be sure, Shāṭir was not the first juridical authority to raise objections to the use of vernacular commentaries or interlinear translations. The Ḥanafī jurist of Damascus 'Alā' al-Dīn al-Ḥaṣkafī (d. 1088/1677) contends in his law book *al-Durr al-mukhtār* that while one may write a verse or two in Persian, writing an explanation (*tafsīr*) underneath each verse is to be discouraged (*yukrahu*).[116] This position reflects the concern that people would grow overly dependent upon interlinear translations, which by this period were widely available in Turkish and Persian.[117] Ḥaṣkafī's ruling, in turn, forms the basis for a *fatwā* issued in 1908 by the grand mufti of Egypt, Shaykh Bakrī al-Ṣadafī (d. 1919), in which he discourages the use of such translations.[118] This line of argumentation is designed as a response to an earlier ruling advocated in several early Ḥanafī juridical works from Central Asia. This particular ruling gives licence to interlinear translations, but does not assign their use a degree of approval or disapproval, by which actions are categorised in juridical terms. Thus, for instance, Ḥāfiẓ al-Dīn Abū'l-Barakāt al-Nasafī (d. 710/1310) comments in *al-Kāfī* that while it is forbidden to grow accustomed to reciting the Qur'an in Persian or to write an entire codex (*muṣḥaf*) of the Qur'an in Persian alone, he sees no problem with writing a verse or two of the Qur'an in Persian without the Arabic text and he concludes that 'it is permitted to write underneath each word its explanation (*tafsīr*) and its translation (*tarjama*)'.[119]

More than two centuries earlier, Sarakhsī had made the exact same claim in his commentary on Shaybānī's *al-Jāmiʿ al-ṣaghīr.* Here Sarakhsī similarly forbids the habitualisation of Persian during ritual prayer and the substitution of the entire Qur'an with a Persian translation. However, he also concludes that it is licit to write a Persian explanation and translation underneath each verse of the Qur'an. Sarakhsī substantiates the practice of interlinear translations with a quote from the leading Ḥanafī jurist of Balkh, al-Faqīh Abū Jaʿfar al-Hinduwānī (d. 362/973), who had argued that 'there is no issue with this in our region (*fī diyārinā*), for the masses only grasp its meanings and their inner dimensions in this manner'. Hinduwānī also explains that the Arabs, in their own region, dislike the practice, as they argue, 'the Qur'an was revealed in our language'.[120]

These comments historically align with the emergence of a written corpus of Persian exegetical literature in Khurasan and Transoxiana. A very similar regional justification for the use of Persian is expressed in the opening to the so-called *Tafsīr-i Ṭabarī*, one of the earliest Persian commentaries and translations of the Qur'an. According to its preface, the translation was commissioned in Bukhara by the Sāmānid emir Abū Ṣāliḥ Manṣūr b. Nūḥ (r. 350–65/961–76).[121] One of the rationales given for the project is the argument that while the Qur'an was revealed in the language of the Arabs, 'here in this region (*īnjā ba-dhīn nāḥiyat*), the Persian language [is used] and the kings of this side (*jānib*) are Persian (*'ajam*)'.[122] Hinduwānī, who makes a similar discursive move, appears to have been one of the members of the juridical body assembled by the emir to issue a *fatwā* in support of the state-sponsored translation project.[123] While the historical and cultural motivations are quite different, Marāghī's translation project centuries later was also intimately connected with spheres of state power and religious authority.

From the beginning, vernacular exegetical writing followed patterns laid out in the Arabic field of Qur'anic Studies. Furthermore, the interlinear model, which characterises the earliest surviving translations, highlights in its very form a theological recognition of the supremacy and irreplaceability of the original Arabic. This point is borne out in the juridical opposition to replacing the original Arabic text with a Persian translation. As Abū'l-Ḥasan al-Marghīnānī explained in a work on positive law, *al-Tajnīs*, replacing the Qur'an with a translation is forbidden, 'for it would lead to a devaluation (*tahāwun*) of the importance of the Qur'an'.[124]

While Marghīnānī reaffirms the Ḥanafī argument allowing those who have not yet mastered the Qur'an to use translations in ritual prayer, the position was increasingly discordant with the juridical view that the Qur'an was fundamentally untranslatable and inimitable both in meaning and form. Already in the fourth/tenth century, it is not difficult to trace a discomfort among certain Ḥanafī jurists even with the curtailment of Abū Ḥanīfa's ruling by his two chief disciples, Abū Yūsuf and Muḥammad al-Shaybānī, who permitted the use of Persian in the sphere of ritual performance only for those with no mastery of the original Arabic.[125] The early collections recording Shaybānī's dialogues with his master frame the matter in terms of personal opinion (*ra'y*). In contrast, the accounts of Salmān's translation of the *Fātiḥa* serve to locate the practice historically during the lifetime of the Prophet. As such, the story may well reflect an attempt to grant further legitimacy to this particular juridical position in historical and intellectual contexts where the actions of the early community held greater authority than the individual interpretation of later jurists.

In the surviving material from the early *sīra* literature, the hadith corpus and the exegetical tradition, Salmān often serves as a paradigm for Persian conversion.[126] He also features prominently in the formative currents of Shiʿi esotericism as a Persian inheritor of sacred wisdom who was directly initiated into the family of the Prophet (*ahl al-bayt*).[127] Yet this diverse material makes no direct reference to Salmān's Persian translation. As several of the modern Egyptian authorities surmised, Sarakhsī is one of the first Ḥanafī jurists to mention the account. Yet, there is much to suggest that Salmān's translation had been in circulation as an established proof text in even earlier Ḥanafī circles. Furthermore, the account was not isolated to Ḥanafīs alone. While later Shāfiʿī authorities, such as Fakhr al-Dīn al-Rāzī (d. 606/1209) and al-Nawawī, called the story into question,[128] the Shāfiʿī exegete ʿImād al-Dīn Shāhfūr al-Isfarāʾīnī (d. 471/1079) used the report as a way of justifying the translation of the Qur'an with the direct approval of the Prophet.[129]

Here it would be useful to delineate when and where the story of Salmān's translation first circulated, something that the modern material surveyed here has done only in a very limited way, often with a polemic or apologetic purpose in mind. Admittedly, given the fragmentary state of the archive, such historicisation is rather difficult. If we accept Sarakhsī's statement that Abū Ḥanīfa used Salmān's translation as a basis for his ruling, then the account must have been already a feature of the juridical debates of the time. Yet other than Sarakhsī's claim in the *Mabsūṭ*, we have very little positive evidence to this effect. For the generations of jurists after Abū Ḥanīfa, however, the situation is different. As I have explored in greater depth elsewhere, we have good reason to believe that already in the third/ninth century there circulated amongst certain juridical authorities not only a story of Salmān's translation, but also an actual translation of the *Fātiḥa*.[130]

The Ḥanafī jurist and traditionist of Transoxiana Abū'l-ʿAbbās al-Mustaghfirī (d. 432/1041) preserves a record of the translation in his collection, the *Faḍāʾil al-Qurʾān*. Mustaghfirī quotes Salmān's Persian translation with an *isnād* that stops with a transmitter from the middle of the third/ninth century, a certain Abū Bakr Muḥammad b. Yūsuf, also known as Abū Ḥanīfa the Lesser. His report states, 'It has reached us that the people of Iran requested Salmān to write something of the Qur'an for them in their language'. In response Salmān translated the *Fātiḥa* as follows:

> [1] [*ba*]-*nām-i īzad bakhshāwand bakhshāyishgar* [2] *ushnuhl khīsh* [?] *khudāy-i hama jihān* [3] *bakhshāwand bakhshāyishgar* [4] *khudāy-i rūz-i dādistān* [5] *ka tu-rā parastīm u tu-rā ba-yārī khwāhīm* [6–7] *mā rā rāh-i ān na-dahī ka na-bakhashmī tu bā īshān u na bī-rāhand.*
>
> [1] In the Name of the Lord, the Forgiving, the Merciful [2] gratitude to the Lord of all the world [3] the Forgiving, the Merciful, [4] the Lord of the Day of Judgement, [5] it is You whom we worship and from whom we seek succour; [6–7] do not set us on the path of those with whom You have enmity nor those who have gone astray.[131]

Other than collapsing together the sixth and seventh verses, the translation closely follows the original Arabic. The prayer entirely lacks Arabic vocabulary. This feature would have strengthened the credibility of the document, as it is congruous with what is said to have been its original target audience, namely Persians who, at that point, presumably had not been in linguistic contact with Arabic.

As with Shurunbulālī's account taken from the *Nihāya* by Tāj al-Sharīʿa, the opening expression, *ba-nām-i īzad*, follows the Middle Persian, *pad nām ī yazdān* [PWN ŠM Y yẕḏtn]. This has clear echoes of Zoroastrian liturgical material, as do the terms *bakhshāwand* and *bakhshāyishgar*, both etymologically related to the Middle Persian verb *abaxšāyīdan* ('to forgive').[132] The words are thus evocative of a pre-Islamic religious vocabulary, suggesting in their own right the challenge of using Persian for ritual prayer, as it could very well evoke a set of non-Islamic religious practices and beliefs.

The memory of Salmān's translation circulated in the Ḥanafī juridical milieu of Transoxiana and Khurasan during the course of the fourth/tenth century, while the transmission of the account most likely dates back to preceding generations in Iran and Iraq.[133] However, the historicity of the document, as a reflection of an actual translation made by Salmān al-Fārisī, is rather questionable, particularly as it supports a specific juridical argument. Yet, unlike Sarakhsī's *Mabsūṭ*, no juridical context is explicitly suggested in Mustaghfirī's presentation, which rather pauses on the antiquity of the language. Nonetheless, as many of the transmitters of the account were clearly juridical authorities in their own right, it is not difficult to see the legal implications behind the translation. It is of note that Mustaghfirī's *isnād* does not stretch back to the life of the Prophet or the subsequent generation of Companions and Followers. However, the presentation of the account, with the formula 'it has reached us', would indicate that the story existed in some form prior to its first recorded transmitter.

In addition, the names of the transmitters listed by Mustaghfirī are not particularly well known, save for a reference to Yaḥyā b. Muʿādh al-Rāzī (d. 258/872), who is drawn into the material only after the translation has been presented. The penultimate transmitter, identified as Muḥammad b. Jaʿfar al-Faqīh, was a jurist from the Iranian city of Rayy who asked Yaḥyā about the significance of *ushnuhl khīsh*.[134] While it is not clear what *khīsh* means here, other than perhaps indicating some kind of preposition marker, *ushnuhl* is a perfectly reasonable rendering of *išnōhr* or *šnōhr* [*šnwhl*], a Middle Persian word for propitiation, gratitude, or thanks, which is a religious term used in Zoroastrian literature. Yaḥyā explains that the expression is from *fahlawiyya qadīma* (ancient Pahlavi), and he offers the Persian word *sipās* ('praise' or 'gratitude') as an explanation; this is an interpretation that is entirely in keeping with the original sense of the term.

Why Yaḥyā in particular would have been drawn into the exchange deserves further consideration. He was a popular preacher and renunciant who travelled widely across Iran and Iraq and ultimately settled in Nishapur. Yaḥyā was a contemporary of Ibn Karrām (d. 255/869), the founder of the renunciatory Karrāmī movement. Furthermore, he is said to have praised Ibn Karrām and several modern scholars have suggested that Yaḥyā held Karrāmī sympathies.[135] The Karrāmiyya were particularly instrumental in the process of converting the local population of Khurasan and Central Asia.

The connection between Yaḥyā and Salmān's translation of the *Fātiḥa* points to a broader network of ascetic Persian preachers who were involved in missionary activities along the frontiers and who were associated with vernacular expressions of piety. If we are to accept that the *isnād* accompanying Mustaghfirī's account reflects a historical process of transmission, then it points to the circulation of Qur'anic liturgical material in Persian during the middle of the third/ninth century. Furthermore, by this period, Ḥanafī jurists in the nascent stages of the development of their legal traditions had already circumscribed a space for Persian within the sphere of ritual activity. The same appears to have been the case for the short-lived school of Karrāmī jurisprudence, which, as with many other legal issues, followed the Ḥanafīs on the question of liturgical translation. Like Abū Ḥanīfa, Ibn Karrām is said to have permitted the unrestricted ritual use of translations, regardless of one's capacity in Arabic.[136] Furthermore, both the Ḥanafīs and the Karrāmīs advanced a framework informed by Murjiʾī theology that privileged faith over acts in the process of conversion.[137]

The earliest Ḥanafī treatment of the topic, as preserved by Muḥammad al-Shaybānī and others, makes no reference to Salmān's translation of the *Fātiḥa*. From its presence in Mustaghfirī's hadith collection, we have evidence that a written record of Salmān's *Fātiḥa* had been in circulation for some time. Mustaghfirī's *isnād* stops with the generation of Yaḥyā b. Muʿādh al-Rāzī, and this likely offers a *terminus ante quem* for the use of Salmān's translation as a juridical proof text. The fact that the story appears not to have circulated widely prior to this may indicate its weak historical basis in the eyes of tradition-minded jurists; it may also point to a relatively late date for the emergence of the account. Yet, by the time Sarakhsī composed the *Mabsūṭ*, Salmān's *Fātiḥa* had clearly taken on a measure of authority in Ḥanafī circles as a justification for ritual prayer in translation, rooted in the authority of the Sunna of the early community.

As a document, Salmān's *Fātiḥa* moves the justification for ritual performance in the vernacular beyond merely a hypothetical abstraction of jurisprudence, for it supplies the very textual basis for ritual performance in translation. Indeed, this written record may well substantiate the use of such translations, however limited, in the space of ritual praxis. This is very much the suggestion in the regional history of Bukhara by Abū Bakr al-Narshakhī (d. 348/959), which describes how the first converts of the city in the early second/eighth century performed ritual prayer in translation, as they were unable to master the original Arabic.[138] In this sense, the account of Salmān's Persian translation reduces the complex history of conversion and ritual performance along linguistic frontiers into a discrete and manageable narrative form. Considering the juridical implications, there is good reason to believe that such narrativisation follows after the very ritual practices it seeks to justify.

It is perhaps not entirely inconsequential that we find in the earliest numismatic history of Arab-Sāsānian coins and weights from the first and second centuries of the Islamic era, not only the translation of the testament of faith (*shahāda*) into Middle Persian with 'Prophet of God' (*rasūl Allāh*) rendered *paygāmbar ī yazd* [pgt'mbl Y yz̤d̠t],[139] but also the actual translation of Qur'anic material.[140] As the conversion of non-Arabs necessarily would have been preceded by acts of translation, one may further ponder the extent to which the Ḥanafī and Karrāmī rulings permitting liturgical translation were following rather than establishing a set of normative practices along the frontiers.

The story of Salmān's translation also fits into a discursive process of legitimating vernacular religious learning, which extended beyond Ḥanafī and Karrāmī juridical circles. This is apparent in the introduction to the Persian commentary and interlinear translation of the Qur'an, the *Tāj al-tarājim*, produced by Isfarā'īnī, a Shāfiʿī scholar from Khurasan, in the middle of the fifth/eleventh century. Isfarā'īnī, who was appointed by the powerful Saljuk vizier Niẓām al-Mulk (d. 485/1092) to the Madrasa Niẓāmiyya in Ṭūs, opens his work with a robust defence of translating the Qur'an into any given language where there may be need.[141]

Among the various justifications he offers, the account of Salmān's translation stands out. Isfarā'īnī not only claims that Salmān translated the *Fātiḥa*, but also that, with the Prophet's approval, he produced an entire Persian translation of the Qur'an that preserved the original Arabic with the Persian written underneath. We read that Salmān's translation concluded with a certification in both Arabic and Persian that affirmed 'this is the Qur'an which was revealed to Muhammad'. Unlike the majority of Shāfiʿī scholars, Isfarā'īnī also suggests that converts who have no mastery of the original Arabic may indeed use translations of the Qur'an for purposes of ritual performance.[142]

As often accompanies the process of vernacularisation, the emergence of Persian in spheres once reserved exclusively for Arabic was a source of profound concern. Many of these tensions build upon even older anxieties that followed the waves of early converts in the course of the second/eighth century. For instance, the famed jurist Mālik b. Anas (d. 179/795) detested the use of foreign languages during ritual prayer. Mālik justified this juridical opinion with a report from the second caliph ʿUmar b. al-Khaṭṭāb (r. 13–23/634–44), who is said to have forbidden the wicked whispering prayer (*raṭāna*) used by the Persians.[143] In this formulation, *raṭāna* alludes to the Zoroastrian liturgical practices of chanting,[144] related to the Syriac *reṭnā*, which signifies liturgical chanting, particularly the *reṭnā de-magūšūṭā*, the whispered prayers of the Magi. The *muṣannaf* collections of ʿAbd al-Razzāq al-Ṣanʿānī (d. 211/827) and Ibn Abī Shayba (d. 235/849) transmit similar accounts concerning the whispering (*raṭāna*) of Persians.[145] Ibn Abī Shayba notes that ʿUmar singled out Persian as teaching only wickedness and claimed 'wickedness decreases manliness'.[146] The hadith corpus contains several similar accounts on the deleterious effects of Persian ascribed directly to the Prophet.[147]

Needless to say, Salmān's translation of the *Fātiḥa* could offer an antidote to these sentiments, which Kevin Reinhart associates with 'Arab chauvinism'.[148] We should also recall, nonetheless, that attitudes promoting the superiority of Arabic were by no means limited to Arabs. The early non-Arab clients (*mawālī*), were instrumental in the configuration of Arabic as a cosmopolitan language of learning and salvation, in which language and religious identity were intimately connected in diverse spheres of authority. Many of the staunchest proponents of the soteriological supremacy of the Arabic language were non-Arabs. As a hegemonic language, Arabic could extend beyond ethnicity and even religion. This is a topic treated by those such as Ibn Taymiyya, who supports the universalist reach of Arabic with a saying ascribed to the Prophet, 'whoever speaks Arabic is an Arab'.[149]

In the first half of the twentieth century, the debate over Salmān's translation of the *Fātiḥa* came to reflect larger questions concerning the nature of religious authority and the place of Arabic within the contexts of religious reform. The controversy over Qur'anic translation intersected with the contested role of Arabic as a linguistic force to unite the entire Muslim community. While there are certainly parallels with classical sources on the matter, such mythologies of language were profoundly shaped by the specific histories of modernity and with them the legacy of European colonialism. There are many reasons why the modern debates over the translation of the Qur'an that took place in Egypt did not find direct corollaries in the Persian ecumene or in South Asia, where, like Turkey, vernaculars had long been privileged forms of religious expression.[150] For certain religious officials, the superiority of Arabic as a vehicle for religious authority, and with it the 'transparency' of the Arabic Qur'an, plays an important role in shaping the contours of the controversy.[151] Yet, in Islamic juridical and exegetical material, recourse to Salmān's translation was also an acknowledgment of a universalist current of adaptation, as it has long represented a discursive means of accommodating the vernacular within the spheres of piety and religious learning.

NOTES

1 See Muṣṭafā Ṣabrī, *Mas'alat tarjamat al-Qur'ān* (Cairo: al-Maṭbaʿa al-Salafiyya, 1351/1932–3), p. 4.

2 Muḥammad Farīd Wajdī, 'Ḥadath al-aḥdāth fī'l-islām', *al-Ahrām*, issue 18424 (28 March 1936), pp. 1–2.

3 Travis Zadeh, *The Vernacular Qur'an: Translation and the Rise of Persian Exegesis* (Oxford: Oxford University Press in association with the Institute of Ismaili Studies, 2012), pp. 71, 95, 113–14, 260–63, 369, 374–5 and 478–83.

4 For an illuminating treatment of the topic as it relates to the broader historical context, see M. Brett Wilson, *Translating the Qur'an in an Age of Nationalism: Print Culture and Modern Islam in Turkey* (Oxford: Oxford University Press in association with the Institute of Ismaili Studies, 2014), pp. 184–220. See also in the present volume, Stefan Wild, Chapter 13, pp. 428–31. Further overviews are given in Aḥmad Ibrāhīm Muhannā, *Dirāsat ḥawl tarjamat al-Qur'ān al-karīm* (Cairo: Maṭbūʿāt al-Shaʿb, 1978); Abdelhamid Muhammad Ahmad,

Die Auseinandersetzung zwischen Al-Azhar und der modernistischen Bewegung in Ägypten von Muhammad 'Abduh bis zur Gegenwart (Hamburg: University of Hamburg, 1963), pp. 32–44; Mohammad Ayoub, 'Translating the Meanings of the Qur'an: Traditional Opinions and Modern Debates', *Inquiry/Afkar* 3, no. 5 (1986), pp. 34–9.

5 See M. Brett Wilson, 'The First Translations of the Qur'an in Modern Turkey (1924–38)', *International Journal of Middle East Studies* 41, no. 1 (2009), pp. 419–35, at p. 428. See Muḥammad Rashīd Riḍā, 'Tarjamat al-Qur'ān wa taḥrīf tarjama lahu wa'l-tashkīk fīhi', *al-Manār* 25, no. 10 (1925), pp. 794–7. See also, Richard Hattemer, 'Atatürk and the Reforms in Turkey as Reflected in the Egyptian Press', *Journal of Islamic Studies* 11, no. 1 (2000), pp. 21–42.

6 F. Lyman MacCallum, 'Turkey Discovers the Koran', *Moslem World* 23 (1933), pp. 24–8, at p. 24.

7 Ibid., p. 28.

8 See, for instance, Rashīd Riḍā, 'Bāb al-as'ila wa'l-ajwiba: Tarjamat al-Qur'ān', *al-Manār* 6, no. 6 (1321/1903), pp. 268–70; idem, 'Kitābat al-Qur'ān bi'l-ḥurūf al-inklīziyya', *al-Manār* 6, no. 6 (1321/1903), pp. 274–7; idem, 'Fatāwā'l-Manār: Tarjamat al-Qur'ān', *al-Manār* 11, no. 4 (1326/1908), pp. 268–74. See also, Khwāja Kamāl al-Dīn and Rashīd Riḍā, 'Tarjamat al-Qur'ān wa istiḥālat muṭābiqatihā'l-aṣl', *al-Manār* 17, no. 10 (1914), pp. 793–5. Riḍā reprinted much of this material in an extended article in his lengthy expansion of Muḥammad 'Abduh, *Tafsīr al-Manār*, 2nd edn (Cairo: Maṭba'at al-Manār, 1366/1947), vol. 9, pp. 310–63; this is examined by J. Jomier, *Le commentaire coranique du Manâr* (Paris: G.-P. Maisonneuve, 1954), pp. 338–47.

9 See, for instance, Rashīd Riḍā, 'Tarjamat al-Qur'ān wa taḥrīf tarjama lahu'; idem, 'Mansha' fikrat tarjamat al-Qur'ān wa sababuhā', *al-Manār* 26, no. 7 (1344/1926), pp. 481–96; and idem, 'Tarjamat al-Qur'ān wa kawn al-'arabiyya lughat al-islām', *al-Manār* 32, no. 7 (1351/1932), pp. 535–44.

10 See Muḥammad Shākir, *al-Qawl al-faṣl fī tarjamat al-Qur'ān al-karīm ilā'l-lughāt al-a'jamiyya* (Cairo: Maṭba'at al-Nahḍa, 1925), pp. 23–5. See also, Marmaduke Pickthall, 'Arabs and Non-Arabs and the Question of Translating the Qur'an', *Islamic Culture* 5, no. 3 (1931), pp. 422–33, at p. 424; Muhannā, *Dirāsa*, p. 13; Moch Nur Ichwan, 'Differing Responses to an Ahmadi Translation and Exegesis: The Holy Qur'an in Egypt and Indonesia', *Archipel* 62 (2001), pp. 143–61, at p. 145. For a summary of the debates over translating the Qur'an as they appeared within the Egyptian press during 1925, see Martino Mario Moreno, 'È lecito ai Musulmani tradurre il Corano?' *Oriento Moderno* 5, no. 10 (1925), pp. 532–43.

11 Pickthall, 'Arabs and Non-Arabs', p. 427.

12 Ibid., pp. 423–4. On Marāghī, see 'Abd al-Mun'im al-Khafājī, *al-Azhar fī alf 'ām*, 2nd edn (Beirut: 'Ālam al-Kutub, 1987), vol. 1, pp. 264–79; Khayr al-Dīn al-Ziriklī, *al-A'lām: Qāmūs tarājim li-ashhar al-rijāl wa'l-nisā'* (Beirut: Dār al-'Ilm li'l-Malāyīn, 1979), vol. 7, p. 103; and the monograph, Francine Costet-Tardieu, *Un réformiste à l'université al-Azhar: Œuvre et pensée de Mustafâ al-Marâghî (1881–1945)* (Cairo and Paris: CEDEJ and Karthala, 2005).

13 See Pickthall, 'Arabs and Non-Arabs', p. 425.

14 For a detailed study of the political competition for leadership within al-Azhar, see Rainer Brunner, 'Education, Politics, and the Struggle for Intellectual Leadership: al-Azhar between 1927 and 1945' in Dale Eickleman, ed., *Guardians of Faith in Modern Times: 'Ulamā' in the Middle East* (Leiden: Brill, 2009), pp. 109–40. For a timeline of stages of reform within al-Azhar, see Pierre-Jean Luizard, 'Al-Azhar, Institution sunnite réformée' in Alain Roussillon, ed., *Entre reforme sociale et mouvement national: identité et modernisation en Egypte, 1882–1962* (Cairo: CEDEJ, 1995), pp. 519–48, at pp. 541–7.

15 For the nature of opposition and yet surprising continuity between Ẓawāhirī and Marāghī, see Brunner, 'Education', pp. 121–2. On Ẓawāhirī, see Khafājī, *al-Azhar*, vol. 1, pp. 259–63; and Ziriklī, *al-Aʿlām*, vol. 6, p. 26.

16 Pickthall, 'Arabs and Non-Arabs', pp. 432–3; on the matter of translation, see Costet-Tardieu, *Un réformiste*, pp. 238–46. See Ẓawāhirī's letter to the prime minister, ʿAlī Māhir Pāshā, dated 13 Muḥarram 1355 (5 April 1936), outlining his reasons for not signing the *fatwā* in support of Marāghī's proposal, reprinted in Fakhr al-Dīn al-Aḥmad al-Ẓawāhirī, *al-Siyāsa wa'l-Azhar* (Cairo: Maṭbaʿat al-Iʿtimād, 1945), pp. 349–50.

17 See Pickthall, 'Arabs and Non-Arabs', pp. 432–3.

18 Muḥammad ʿAlī ʿAllūba Pāshā, *Dhikrayāt ijtimāʿiyya wa siyāsiyya*, ed. Aḥmad Najīb Aḥmad Ḥamadī, Jamāl al-Dīn Amīn Muhannā and Nāhid Muṣṭafā Marzūq (Cairo: Markaz Wathā'iq wa Tārīkh Miṣr al-Muʿāṣir, 1988), p. 286; cited in Costet-Tardieu, *Un réformiste*, pp. 242–3.

19 See Jakob Skovgaard-Petersen, *Defining Islam for the Egyptian State: Muftis and Fatwas of the Dār al-Iftā* (Leiden: Brill, 1997), pp. 163–4; Virginia Vacca, 'Lettera del Ministro dell'Istruzione circa il modo di eseguire la traduzione del Corano', *Oriente Moderno* 16, no. 5 (1936), pp. 292–3; Khafājī, *al-Azhar*, vol. 4, pp. 503–7. The *fatwā* is also reproduced in 'Ḥawl Tarjamat al-Qur'ān al-Karīm', *al-Ahrām*, issue 18442 (17 April 1936), p. 2; also in Muḥammad Sulaymān, *Kitāb Ḥadath al-aḥdāth fī'l-islām: al-iqdām ʿalā tarjamat al-Qur'ān*, 2nd edn (Cairo: Maṭbaʿat Jarīdat Miṣr al-Ḥurra, 1355/1936), pp. 46–8; see also Muhannā, *Dirāsa*, pp. 51–3. On ʿAbd al-Majīd Salīm, see Ziriklī, *al-Aʿlām*, vol. 4, p. 149.

20 Muḥammad ʿAlī's speech is reproduced in 'Ḥawl Tarjamat al-Qur'ān al-Karīm', *al-Ahrām*, issue 18441 (16 April 1936), p. 1.

21 'Ḥawl Tarjamat al-Qur'ān al-Karīm' (17 April 1936), pp. 1–2. For more on the political progression of events leading up to and beyond the passage of the bill, see the contemporary Italian digests of the Egyptian press by Virginia Vacca, 'Gili "ʿulama'" di el-Azhar tradurranno il Corano nelle principali lingue straniere?' *Oriente Moderno* 16, no. 4 (1936), pp. 236–7; idem, 'Lettera del Ministro dell'Istruzione'; Carlo Alfonso Nallino, 'Deliberazione della Camera egiziana sul progetto di traduzione del Corano', *Oriente Moderno* 16, no. 10, pp. 560–61; Laura Veccia Vaglieri, 'Nomina della Commissione incaricata della "traduzione dei concetti del Corano"', *Oriente Moderno* 16, no. 12 (1936), p. 710.

22 'Ḥawl Tarjamat al-Qur'ān al-Karīm' (17 April 1936), p. 2; reprinted in Sulaymān, *Ḥadath al-aḥdāth*, pp. 43–4; and in Muhannā, *Dirāsa*, pp. 47–8.

23 Ibid.

24 Ibrāhīm Ḥasan al-Mūjī, 'Al-Bukhari, A Collection of Muhammad's Authentic Traditions, translated into English', *Nūr al-Islām* 5, no. 1 (Muḥarram 1353/April 1934), pp. 1–20. The Arabic title also refers to this as a translation (*tarjama*). Wilfred Cantwell Smith, *Islam in Modern History* (Princeton, NJ: Princeton University Press, 1957), pp. 122–55, examines Wadjī's editorial influence on the journal and the increased use of English. However, contrary to Smith's claim, there is much to suggest that Wajdī intended the English language material not only for Europeans, but also for English-speaking Muslims.

25 Ẓawāhirī, *al-Siyāsa*, pp. 351–4.

26 See Sulaymān, *Ḥadath al-aḥdāth*; this second edition is an expansion of the first version published in May 1936 by al-Maṭba'a al-Salafiyya, see Muhannā, *Dirāsa*, p. 45. Sulaymān published sections of this treatise in various newspapers during the lead-up to the parliamentary vote; see, for instance, 'Ḥadath al-aḥdāth fī'l-islām: al-iqdām ʿalā tarjamat al-Qurʾān', *al-Ahrām*, issue 18420 (24 March 1936), pp. 1 and 3, and *al-Ahrām*, issue 18437 (10 April 1936), pp. 1–3. On Sulaymān, see Ziriklī, *al-Aʿlām*, vol. 6, p. 153. See also the treatise addressed to Marāghī by Muḥammad Muṣṭafā al-Shāṭir, finished on 10 April, *Tadhkira li-ūlī'l-baṣāʾir wa'l-abṣār ilā mā fī tarjamat maʿānī'l-Qurʾān min akhṭār* (Cairo: Maṭbaʿat al-Naṣr, 1355/1936), and a repurposed and expanded version published as *al-Qawl al-sadīd fī ḥukm tarjamat al-Qurʾān al-majīd* (Cairo: Maṭbaʿat Ḥijāzī, Rabīʿ II 1355/June 1936).

27 Sulaymān, *Ḥadath al-aḥdāth*, p. 176; Sulaymān also describes the project as a war on language and nation, ibid., pp. 77–81; cf. Ṣubḥī Maḥmaṣānī, *Falsafat al-tashrīʿ fī'l-islām*, 2nd edn (Beirut: Dār al-Kāshif, 1952), p. 107, tr. Farhat J. Ziadeh as *The Philosophy of Jurisprudence in Islam* (Leiden: Brill, 1961), p. 69, n. 22.

28 See *Oriente Moderno* 16, nos 10, 12 (1936), pp. 560 (Nallino), and 710 (Veccia Vaglieri). On Salīm's role, see Skovgaard-Petersen, *Defining Islam*, pp. 163–4; for Shaltūt, see Wolf-Dieter Lemke, *Maḥmūd Šaltūt (1893–1963) und die Reform der Azhar: Untersuchungen zu Erneuerungsbestrebungen im ägyptisch-islamischen Erziehungssystem* (Frankfurt am Main: Peter Lang, 1980), pp. 113–15.

29 See 'Ḥawl Tarjamat al-Qurʾān al-Karīm' (17 April 1936), p. 2; reprinted in Sulaymān, *Ḥadath al-aḥdāth*, p. 45, and Muhannā, *Dirāsa*, p. 49; see also Vacca, 'Gili "ʿulama'" di el-Azhar', p. 237; idem, 'Lettera del Ministro dell'Istruzione', p. 292; Nallino, 'Deliberazione della Camera egiziana', p. 560; Veccia Vaglieri, 'Nomina della Commissione', p. 710. Wajdī followed a similar exegetical enterprise producing an Arabic paraphrase in his own commentary of the Qur'an, a project which he began in 1906; he titles his Arabic paraphrastic explanations as *tafsīr al-maʿānī*, see Muḥammad Farīd Wajdī, *al-Muṣḥaf al-mufassar* (Cairo: Maṭbaʿat Dāʾirat Maʿārif al-Qarn al-ʿIshrīn, 1925); J.J.G. Jansen, *The Interpretation of the Koran in Modern Egypt* (Leiden: Brill, 1974), pp. 46–7.

30 See Lemke, *Maḥmūd Šaltūt*; Costet-Tardieu, *Un réformiste*, pp. 245–6; cf. Ẓawāhirī, *al-Siyāsa*, p. 354.

31 See Maḥmaṣānī, *Falsafat al-tashrīʿ*, pp. 108–9, tr. p. 70.

32 Even in Salafī circles, the translation of the meanings of the Qur'an became a normative position, upheld, for instance, by the grand mufti of Saudi Arabia, ʿAbd al-ʿAzīz b. ʿAbd Allāh Ibn Bāz (d. 1999), among others in the state agency

for issuing legal rulings, see *Fatāwā'l-lajna al-dā'ima li'l-buḥūth al-ʿilmiyya wa'l-iftā'*, ed. al-Shaykh Aḥmad b. ʿAbd al-Razzāq al-Duwaysh (Riyadh: Dār al-Mu'ayyid, 2003), vol. 4, pp. 132–6; in the Egyptian context, see ʿAbd al-ʿAẓīm al-Zarqānī, *Manāhil al-ʿirfān fī ʿulūm al-Qur'ān*, ed. Fawwāz Aḥmad Zamarlī (Beirut: Dār al-Kitāb al-ʿArabī, 1995), vol. 2, pp. 133–5; cf. the question of reciting a translation in prayer as treated by the grand mufti of Egypt, Faḍīlat al-Shaykh Aḥmad Muḥammad ʿAbd al-ʿĀl Harīdī (d. 1984), 'Tarjamat al-Qur'ān wa tafsīruhu fī'l-ṣalāt mufsidun lahā' (25 April 1961), reprinted in *al-Fatāwā'l-islāmiyya min dār al-iftā' al-miṣriyya* (Cairo: Jumhūriyyat Miṣr al-ʿArabiyya, 1980), vol. 5, pp. 1627–8, no. 712. See also Niloofar Haeri, *Sacred Language, Ordinary People: Dilemmas of Culture and Politics in Egypt* (New York: Palgrave Macmillan, 2003), pp. 12–13.

33 See Maḥmaṣānī, *Falsafat al-tashrīʿ*, p. 107, tr. p. 69.

34 The very title of Muḥammad Sulaymān's article and subsequent treatise, *Ḥadath al-aḥdāth fī'l-islām* is a play on *ḥadath* as both an innovation and a misfortune or a ritual impurity; Wajdī uses the same title for his rejoinder, flipping the meaning around, as it were, suggesting that it was Sulaymān's stance which was deviant; Wajdī, 'Ḥadath al-aḥdāth fī'l-islām'.

35 Sulaymān, 'Ḥadath al-aḥdāth' (24 March 1936), p. 1; see Abū'l-Rayḥān al-Bīrūnī, *Kitāb al-Ṣaydana fī'l-ṭibb*, ed. ʿAbbās Zaryāb (Tehran: Markaz-i Nashr-i Dānishgāhī, 1991), p. 14. For a discussion of this famed passage by Bīrūnī, see Lutz Richter-Bernburg, 'Linguistic Shuʿūbīya and Early Neo-Persian Prose', *Journal of the American Oriental Society* 94 (1974), pp. 55–64, at p. 63.

36 Sulaymān, 'Ḥadath al-aḥdāth' (24 March 1936), p. 3; see Sulaymān, *Ḥadath al-aḥdāth*, p. 21.

37 See Muḥammad b. al-Ḥasan al-Shaybānī, *Kitāb al-Aṣl*, ed. Abū'l-Wafā' al-Afghānī (Beirut: ʿĀlam al-Kutub, 1990), vol. 1, pp. 38–9 and 236; idem, *al-Jāmiʿ al-ṣaghīr* (Karachi: Idārat al-Qur'ān wa'l-ʿUlūm al-Islāmiyya, 1987), pp. 95–6. For further on the early Ḥanafī treatment of the matter, see Zadeh, *Vernacular Qur'an*, pp. 53–72, and passim.

38 See Skovgaard-Petersen, *Defining Islam*, pp. 4, 37 and 50.

39 Wajdī, 'Ḥadath al-aḥdāth' (28 March 1936), p. 1; cf. idem, *al-Adilla al-ʿilmiyya ʿalā jawāz tarjamat maʿānī'l-Qur'an*, 2nd edn (Cairo: Maṭbaʿat al-Raghā'ib, 1355/1936), pp. 61–2.

40 Sulaymān, 'Ḥadath al-aḥdāth' (10 April 1936), p. 3.

41 See also Sulaymān's further retort in his printed treatise, *Ḥadath al-aḥdāth*, pp. 33 and 205–6.

42 Shāṭir, *Tadhkira*, pp. 32–3 and 35–7; idem, *al-Qawl al-sadīd*, pp. 42–4 and 67.

43 Sulaymān, *Ḥadath al-aḥdāth*, p. 205; Shāṭir, *Tadhkira*, pp. 32–3; see Wajdī, *Adilla*, p. 61.

44 The commentary in question is by Baḥr al-ʿUlūm ʿAbd al-ʿAlī al-ʿAyyāsh al-Laknawī (d. 1819), which reads, '*al-Ḥabīb al-ʿAjamī ṣāḥibu Tāj al-Muḥaddithīn Imām al-Mujtahidīn al-Ḥasan al-Baṣrī . . . kāna yaqra'a'l-Qur'ān fī'l-ṣalāti bi'l-fārisiyya . . .*' in *Fawātiḥ al-raḥmūt*, ed. ʿAbd Allāh Maḥmūd Muḥammad ʿUmar (Beirut: Dār al-Kutub al-ʿIlmiyya, 2002), vol. 2, p. 10. The story appears to draw from the account of Ḥabīb and Ḥasan as preserved in Abū'l-Ḥasan al-Hujwīrī (d. ca. 469/1077), *Kashf al-maḥjūb*, ed. Maḥmūd ʿĀbidī (Tehran: Surūsh, 1383 Sh./2004–5), pp. 135–6.

45 Shāṭir, *Tadhkira*, p. 35.
46 Abū Bakr Muḥammad al-Sarakhsī, *Kitāb al-Mabsūṭ*, ed. Abū ʿAbd Allāh Muḥammad al-Shāfiʿī (Beirut: Dār al-Kutub al-ʿIlmiyya, 2001), vol. 1, p. 138.
47 Abū Zakariyyā' al-Nawawī, *Kitāb al-Majmūʿ: Sharḥ al-Muhadhdhab*, ed. Muḥammad Najīb al-Muṭīʿī (Jeddah: Maktabat al-Irshād, 1992), vol. 3, p. 341. Riḍā makes a similar move quoting from Nawawī to discredit the Ḥanafī use of the anecdote in 'Tarjamat al-Qur'ān wa kawn al-ʿarabiyya lughat al-islām', p. 538.
48 Nawawī, *Majmūʿ*, vol. 3, p. 342.
49 Shāṭir, *Tadhkira*, pp. 36–7.
50 ʿAbd al-Raḥmān al-Jazīrī, *Aḥsan al-bayān fī'l-radd ʿalā'l-Shaykh Muḥammad Shāṭir wa ghayrihi min māniʿīn li-jawāz tarjamat tafsīr al-Qur'ān* (Cairo: Maṭbaʿat wa-Majallat al-Irshād, 1936), pp. 54–5.
51 Ibid., p. 5.
52 See Sulaymān's list of authorities opposing Marāghī in 'Ḥadath al-aḥdāth' (10 April 1936), p. 1.
53 See, for instance, ʿAbd al-Raḥmān Ḥasan (president of the Cairo religious court), 'Tarjamat al-Qur'ān ilā'l-lughāt al-ajnabiyya', *al-Ahrām*, issue 18431 (4 April 1936), pp. 1–2.
54 Muḥammad Muṣṭafā al-Marāghī, 'Baḥth fī tarjamat al-Qur'ān al-Karīm wa aḥkāmihā', *Majallat al-Azhar* 7, no. 2 (1355/1936), pp. 77–112; republished two months later as a pamphlet with the same title (Cairo: Maṭbaʿat al-Raghā'ib, 1355/1936).
55 Marāghī, 'Baḥth', p. 91, and in the reissued pamphlet, *Baḥth*, pp. 15–16.
56 Wajdī, *Adilla*, title page; it was first released in May and then again in June with further additions.
57 Ibid., p. 58.
58 Ibid., p. 63; quoted in Rashīd Riḍā, 'Kitābat al-Qur'ān', p. 275.
59 Muḥammad Bakhīt al-Muṭīʿī, *Kitāb Ḥujjat Allāh ʿalā khalīqatihi fī bayān ḥaqīqat al-Qur'ān wa ḥukm kitābatihi wa tarjamatihi* (Cairo: al-Azhar al-ʿIlmiyya, 1350/1932).
60 Ibid., p. 13.
61 Ibid., pp. 57 and 63.
62 Ibid., p. 61.
63 Ibid., pp. 63–4.
64 Ibid., p. 65; on the conversion of the Persian *anbā'* of Yemen, see Mohsen Zakeri, *Sāsānid Soldiers in Early Muslim Society: The Origins of ʿAyyārān and Futuwwa* (Wiesbaden: Harrassowitz, 1995), p. 270, n. 81; on the historical presence of Persians in the Hijaz, see M.J. Kister, 'Al-Ḥīra: Some Notes on its Relations with Arabia', *Arabica* 15, no. 2 (1968), pp. 143–69, at pp. 144–5.
65 Sulaymān, *Ḥadath al-aḥdāth*, pp. 16–18; Shāṭir, *al-Qawl al-sadīd*, pp. 12–13.
66 Abū'l-Ikhlāṣ al-Shurunbulālī, *al-Nafḥa al-qudsiyya* (Cairo: al-Maṭbaʿa al-Raḥmāniyya, 1355/1936), pp. 3–4; on Shurunbulālī, see Muḥammad al-Amīn al-Muḥibbī (d. 1111/1699), *Khulāṣat al-athar fī aʿyān al-qarn al-ḥādī ʿashar* (Cairo: al-Maṭbaʿa al-Wahbiyya, 1284/1868), vol. 2, pp. 38–9.
67 Shāṭir, *al-Qawl al-sadīd*, p. 124. The reference to the supplement of the *Majallat al-Azhar* is to Wajdī's *Adilla*.
68 Ibid., p. 125; Shurunbulālī, *al-Nafḥa al-qudsiyya*, p. 15; the Persian has been slightly garbled in transmission.

69 Shāṭir, *al-Qawl al-sadīd*, p. 126.

70 See Ḥājjī Khalīfa (d. 1067/1657), *Kashf al-ẓunūn ʿan asāmīʾl-kutub waʾl-funūn*, ed. Muḥammad Sharaf al-Dīn Yāltaqāyā and Rifʿat Bīlka al-Kilīsī (Istanbul: Maṭābiʿ Wikālat al-Maʿārif al-Jalīla, 1941), vol. 2, p. 2033. However, on the question of the identity of the author, Tāj al-Sharīʿa, see Ibn Abīʾl-Wafāʾ al-Qurashī (d. 775/1373), *al-Jawāhir al-muḍiyya*, ed. ʿAbd al-Fattāḥ Muḥammad al-Ḥulw (Giza: Hajr liʾl-Ṭibāʿa waʾl-Nashr, 1993), vol. 4, p. 369, no. 2068, n. 1; along with the detailed comments by Abūʾl-Ḥasanāt ʿAbd al-Ḥayy al-Laknawī, *al-Fawāʾid al-bahiyya fī tarājim al-ḥanafiyya*, ed. Aḥmad al-Zuʿbī (Beirut: Dār al-Aqram, 1998), pp. 48, 185–9 and 338 (nos 31, 232 and 442).

71 Printed as a marginal commentary in Burhān al-Dīn Abūʾl-Ḥasan al-Marghīnānī, *al-Hidāya*, ed. Mawlānā Muḥammad ʿAbd al-Aḥad (Delhi: Maṭbaʿ al-Mujtabāʾī, 1332–4/1914–16), vol. 1, p. 86.

72 See Sarakhsī, *Mabsūṭ*, vol. 1, p. 138; idem (Cairo: n.p., 1324–31/1906–13), vol. 1, p. 37.

73 With regard to this passage, the printed editions correspond to Sarakhsī, *Mabsūṭ*, MS Feyzullah Efendi Koleksiyonu 983, Millet Kütüphanesi, Istanbul, fol. 9a; MS 191 Konya Karatay Yusufağa Kütüphanesi, Konya, fol. 22b; cf. Burhān al-Dīn Maḥmūd b. Aḥmad al-Marghīnānī al-Bukhārī (d. 616/1219–20), who, without citing Sarakhsī, appears to be directly copying the passage, *al-Muḥīṭ al-burhānī*, ed. ʿAbd al-Karīm al-Jundī (Beirut: Dār al-Kutub al-ʿIlmiyya, 2004), vol. 1, p. 307; my earlier assessment reflects the reception history of the *Mabsūṭ* and not how it is treated in the published text, see Zadeh, *Vernacular Qur'an*, p. 114.

74 Maḥmūd Abū Daqīqa, 'Kalima fī tarjamat al-Qurʾān al-Karīm', *Nūr al-Islām* 3, no. 1 (1351/1932), pp. 29–35, at pp. 33–4. On Abū Daqīqa, see Ziriklī, *al-Aʿlām*, vol. 7, p. 169; cf. Muhammad Ahmad, *Die Auseinandersetzung Zwischen al-Azhar*, p. 36.

75 See Wilson, 'First Translations', p. 431.

76 Ṣabrī, *Masʾala*, p. 4; Ibrāhīm al-Jabbālī, 'Kalām fī tarjamat al-Qurʾān', *Nūr al-Islām* 3, no. 1 (1351/1932), p. 59.

77 Ibid., p. 14.

78 Abūʾl-Ḥasanāt ʿAbd al-Ḥayy al-Laknawī, 'Ākām al-nafāʾis fī adāʾ al-adhkār bi-lisān al-fāris' in *Majmūʿat rasāʾil al-Laknawī*, ed. Naʿīm Ashrāf Nūr Aḥmad (Karachi: Idārat al-Qurʾān waʾl-ʿUlūm al-Islāmiyya, 1419/1998–9), vol. 4, pp. 333–92. On Abūʾl-Ḥasanāt, see Renate Würsch, 'ʿAbd al-Ḥayy al-Laknawī, Abū l-Ḥasanāt', *EI THREE* (Brill Online).

79 In addition to Ṣabrī, see also, for instance, Sulaymān, *Ḥadath al-aḥdāth*, pp. 83 and 184–7.

80 Laknawī, 'Ākām al-nafāʾis', p. 363; Ṣabrī, *Masʾala*, p. 61.

81 Quoted in Riḍā, 'Kitābat al-Qurʾān', p. 275.

82 Ibid., p. 277. Riḍā goes on to argue that if what is meant here is that Salmān transliterated the account into Persian as a means for converts to pronounce the original Arabic, this would also make little sense, as the Persian and Arabic scripts are themselves nearly the same. Admittedly, Riḍā appears not to be aware that the Arabic script was adapted for the use of Persian much later. See also, Riḍā, 'Tarjamat al-Qurʾān wa kawn al-ʿarabiyya lughat al-islām', p. 538.

83 Bakhīt, *Kitāb Ḥujjat Allāh*, p. 45.

84 Ibid.

85 Sulaymān, *Ḥadath al-aḥdāth*, p. 203.
86 Ibid., p. 204; cf. Wajdī, *Adilla*, p. 75.
87 On Zarqānī, see Ziriklī, *al-Aʿlām*, vol. 6, p. 210.
88 Zarqānī, *Manāhil al-ʿirfān*, vol. 2, pp. 133–5.
89 Ibid., vol. 2, pp. 125–6
90 A.L. Tibawi, 'Is the Qur'an Translatable? Early Muslim Opinion', *Muslim World* 52, no. 1 (1962), pp. 4–16; see for instance, Anna Gade, *The Qur'an: An Introduction* (Oxford: Oneworld, 2010), pp. 101–2.
91 Tibawi, 'Early Muslim Opinion', p. 5.
92 Ibid., p. 15.
93 Ibid., p. 16.
94 Charles A. Storey, 'Qur'anic Literature', in idem, *Persian Literature: A Bio-Bibliographical Survey* (London: Luzac, 1927), vol. 1, part 1, pp. 1–58, vol. 1, part 2, pp. 1189–228. For further overviews in English of the Persian exegetical traditions, see Frank Lewis, 'Persian Literature and the Qur'ān', *EQ*, vol. 4, pp. 55–66; Annabel Keeler, 'Exegesis III. In Persian', *EIr*, vol. 9, pp. 119–23; Mohammad Jafar Yahaghi, 'The Development of Koranic Commentaries in Early New Persian' in Fereydun Vahman and Claus V. Pedersen, eds, *Religious Texts in Iranian Languages* (Copenhagen: Det Kongelige Danske Videnskabernes Selskab, 2007), pp. 247–61. The modern Persian scholarship on the topic is extensive; for general introductions, see, for instance, Ḥasan Sādāt Nāṣirī and Manūchihr Dānishpazhūh, *Hazār sāl-i tafsīr-i Fārsī* (Tehran: Nashr-i Alburz, 1990); Ādhartāsh Adharnūsh, *Tārīkh-i tarjuma az 'Arabī ba Fārsī, az āghāz tā 'aṣr-i ṣafawī*. Volume 1: *Tarjumahā-i Qur'ān* (Tehran: Surūsh, 1375 Sh./1996–7).
95 Sulaymān, *Ḥadath al-aḥdāth*, pp. 77–8.
96 Ibn Taymiyya, *Kitāb Iqtiḍā' al-ṣirāṭ al-mustaqīm li-mukhālafat aṣḥāb al-jaḥīm*, ed. Nāṣir b. 'Abd al-Karīm al-'Aql (Riyadh: Maktabat al-Rushd, 1994), vol. 1, pp. 239–42; for this hadith, see Abū Dāwūd al-Sijistānī (d. 275/889), *Sunan*, Kitāb 33, 'Kitāb al-Libās', Bāb 5, 'Fī lubs al-shuhra', part 2, p. 675, no. 4033, in *Mawsūʿat al-ḥadīth al-sharīf, jamʿ jawāmiʿ al-aḥādīth* (Vaduz: Jamʿiyyat al-Maknaz al-Islāmī, 2000–1); Abū Bakr Aḥmad al-Bayhaqī (d. 458/1066), *al-Jāmiʿ li-shuʿab al-īmān*, ed. 'Abd al-'Alī 'Abd al-Ḥamīd Ḥāmid (Riyadh: Maktabat al-Rushd, 2003), vol. 2, p. 418; cf. 'Abd al-Razzāq al-Ṣanʿānī (d. 211/827), *al-Muṣannaf*, ed. Ḥabīb al-Raḥmān al-Aʿẓamī (Beirut: al-Maktab al-Islāmī, 1970–72), vol. 11, pp. 453–4, no. 20986. More broadly, see M.J. Kister, '"Do Not Assimilate Yourselves . . ." *Lā tashabbahū*', *Jerusalem Studies in Arabic and Islam* 12 (1989), pp. 322–70.
97 Ibn Taymiyya, *Iqtiḍā'*, pp. 468–9; cf. Sulaymān, *Ḥadath al-aḥdāth*, pp. 39–40. See also Kevin Reinhart, 'Fundamentalism and the Transparency of the Arabic Qur'an' in Carl Ernst and Richard Martin, eds, *Rethinking Islamic Studies: From Orientalism to Cosmopolitanism* (Chapel Hill, NC: University of North Carolina Press, 2010), pp. 97–113, pp. 101–2. For a rather clever inversion of this passage for the purposes of advancing Urdu as the mark of Islam and an inheritor of Arabic, see the Deobandi Ḥanafī scholar Ẓafar Aḥmad 'Uthmānī (d. 1974), *Iʿlā' al-sunan* (Karachi: Idārat al-Qur'ān wa'l-'Ulūm al-Islāmiyya, 1401/1980–81), vol. 12, pp. 702–3; discussed in Muhammad Qasim Zaman, *The Ulama in Contemporary Islam: Custodians of Change* (Princeton, NJ: Princeton University Press, 2002), pp. 41–5.

98 Ibn Taymiyya, 'Kitāb fī'l-radd 'alā'l-ṭawā'if al-mulḥida' in *al-Fatāwā'l-kubrā*, ed. Muḥammad 'Abd al-Qādir 'Aṭā' and Muṣṭafā 'Abd al-Qādir 'Aṭā' (Beirut: Dār al-Kutub al-'Ilmiyya, 1987), vol. 6, pp. 323–664, at pp. 572–3.

99 Abū 'Uthmān al-Jāḥiẓ, *al-Bayān wa'l-tabyīn*, ed. 'Abd al-Salām Muḥammad Hārūn (Cairo: Maṭba'at Lajnat al-Ta'līf wa'l-Tarjama wa'l-Nashr, 1948), vol. 1, pp. 368.

100 C. Edmund Bosworth, 'Asāwera', *EIr*; and particularly on Mūsā b. Sayyār, see Zakeri, *Sāsānid Soldiers*, pp. 335–6.

101 For a theoretical reading of the translation process described here, see 'Abd al-Fattāḥ Kīlīṭū, *Lan tatakallama lughatī* (Beirut: Dār al-Ṭalī'a li'l-Ṭibā'a wa'l-Nashr, 2002), pp. 27–46, tr. Waïl S. Hassan as *Thou Shalt not Speak my Language* (Syracuse, NY: Syracuse University Press, 2008), pp. 21–37.

102 Sulaymān, *Ḥadath al-aḥdāth*, p. 196.

103 See Pickthall, 'Arabs and Non-Arabs', pp. 426–8; Muhanna, *Dirāsa*, pp. 14–19; Shākir's treatise, *al-Qawl al-faṣl*, consists of four articles which he published in the Egyptian newspaper *al-Muqaṭṭam* between April and May 1925. The first of these articles, published 15 April (*al-Qawl al-faṣl*, pp. 6–13), was translated by Thomas Arnold as 'On the Translation of the Koran into Foreign Languages', *The Muslim World* 16, no. 2 (1926), pp. 161–5. See also, Moreno, 'È lectio ai Musulamni tradurre il Corano?'.

104 Shākir, *al-Qawl al-faṣl*, pp. 33–4. On Muḥammad Shākir, see Ziriklī, *A'lām*, vol. 6, pp. 156–7.

105 Abū 'Abd Allāh Badr al-Dīn al-Zarkashī, *al-Baḥr al-muḥīṭ fī uṣūl al-fiqh*, ed. 'Abd al-Qādir 'Abd Allāh al-'Ānī *et al.* (Kuwait: Wizārat al-Awqāf wa'l-Shu'ūn al-Islāmiyya, 1992), vol. 1, p. 447, repeated in idem, *al-Burhān fī 'ulūm al-Qur'ān*, ed. Muḥammad Abū'l-Faḍl Ibrāhīm (Cairo: Dār Iḥyā' al-Kutub al-'Arabiyya, 1957), vol. 1, p. 465; the editor of the *Burhān* identifies the Qaffāl referenced here with the famed al-Qaffāl al-Shāshī Abū Bakr Muḥammad Ismā'īl (d. 365/976), also known as al-Qaffāl al-Kabīr; I followed this in *The Vernacular Qur'an*, p. 420, n. 23. However, in *al-Baḥr al-muḥīṭ*, Zarkashī explicitly cites the *fatāwā* of Qaffāl; this most likely refers to the collection of Abū Bakr 'Abd Allāh al-Qaffāl al-Marwazī (d. 427/1036), who records a nearly identical ruling in his *Fatāwā*, ed. Muṣṭafā Maḥmūd al-Azharī (Riyadh: Dār Ibn al-Qayyim, 2011), p. 53; Zarkashī's citation of Qaffāl is copied by Jalāl al-Dīn al-Suyūṭī (d. 911/1505), *al-Itqān fī 'ulūm al-Qur'ān*, ed. Muḥammad Abū'l-Faḍl Ibrāhīm (Cairo: Maktabat al-Mashhad al-Ḥusaynī, 1967), vol. 1, p. 307; this is cited by Shākir, who affirms the legitimacy of commenting on the Qur'an in foreign languages, *al-Qawl al-faṣl*, pp. 25 and 33; see also Ibrāhīm al-Jabbālī, 'Kalām fī tarjamat al-Qur'ān', pp. 58–9; Shāṭir, *Tadhkira*, pp. 60–72; Sulaymān, *Ḥadath al-aḥdāth*, pp. 114–20; Zarqānī, *Manāhil*, vol. 2, p. 135; the account is loosely translated by Tibawi, 'Is the Qur'an Translatable?' p. 15.

106 The ideal of 'literal' translation is, in practice, largely a myth, see David Bellos, *Is That a Fish in Your Ear? Translation and the Meaning of Everything* (New York: Faber and Faber, 2011), pp. 102–16.

107 Muḥammad Ḥasanayn Makhlūf, 'Tarjamat al-Qur'ān al-Karīm', *al-Ahrām*, issue 18424 (28 March 1936), p. 2. On Makhlūf, see Skovgaard-Petersen, *Defining Islam*, pp. 170–71.

108 Makhlūf, 'Tarjamat al-Qur'ān al-Karīm', p. 2.

109 Muḥammad Ḥasanayn Makhlūf, *Risālat ḥukm tarjamat al-Qur'ān al-karīm bi-ghayr al-lugha al-ʿarabiyya* (Cairo: Maṭbaʿat Maṭar, 1343/1925), pp. 3 and 28; cf. Muhannā, *Dirāsa*, pp. 19–24.

110 The Egyptian lexicographer Muḥammad b. Mukarram Ibn Manẓūr (d. 711/1311–12), for instance, explains the verb *tarjama* as 'one's speech has been translated when it is explained in another language' (*qad turjima kalāmuhu idhā fussirahu bi-lisān ākhar*). See Ibn Manẓūr, *Lisān al-ʿArab* (Beirut: Dār Ṣādir, 1955–6), vol. 12, p. 229.

111 Shaltūt quotes Bakhīt's position as articulated in 1925, 'Tarjamat al-Qur'ān', *Majallat al-Azhar* 7, no. 2 (1936), pp. 123–34 and 130.

112 Bakhīt, *Kitāb ḥujjat Allāh*, pp. 55–6; quoted in Shaltūt, 'Tarjamat al-Qur'ān', p. 130.

113 See ʿAbd al-Raḥmān Ḥasan, 'Tarjamat al-Qur'ān' (4 April 1936), p. 2; and the Moroccan statesman, Muḥammad b. al-Ḥasan al-Ḥajawī al-Thaʿālibī, 'Tarjamat al-Qur'ān al-Karīm', *Majallat al-Azhar* 7, no. 3 (1355/1936), pp. 190–98, at p. 190. See also Ayoub, 'Translating the Meanings of the Qur'an', pp. 37–9. Jazīrī offers a critique of Shāṭir's claim to be representing normative consensus, *Aḥsan*, pp. 35 and 42–3.

114 See Shāhfur al-Isfarā'īnī, *Tāj al-tarājim fī tafsīr al-Qur'ān li'l-aʿājim*, ed. Najīb Māyl Harawī and ʿAlī Akbar Ilāhī Khurāsānī (Tehran: Shirkat-i Intishārāt-i ʿIlmī wa Farhangī, 1996), vol. 1, pp. 8–9; see also Abū'l-Qāsim Maḥmūd b. ʿUmar al-Zamakhsharī (d. 538/1144), *al-Kashshāf ʿan ḥaqā'iq ghawāmiḍ al-tanzīl wa ʿuyūn al-aqāwīl fī wujūh al-ta'wīl* (Beirut: Dār al-Kitāb al-ʿArabī, 1947), vol. 2, pp. 538–9 (on Q. 14:4); Ibrāhīm b. Mūsā al-Shāṭibī (d. 790/1388), *Muwāfaqāt fī uṣūl al-sharīʿa*, ed. ʿAbd Allāh Darāz (Cairo: al-Maktaba al-Tijāriyya al-Kubrā, n.d.), vol. 2, p. 68.

115 Shāṭir, *Tadhkira*, pp. 69–70; cf. Jazīrī, *Aḥsan al-bayān*, pp. 23–4.

116 ʿAlā' al-Dīn al-Ḥaṣkafī, *al-Durr al-mukhtār*, ed. ʿAbd al-Munʿim Khalīl Ibrāhīm (Beirut: Dār al-Kutub al-ʿIlmiyya, 2002), p. 67. On Ḥaṣkafī, see Muḥibbī, *Khulāṣa*, vol. 4, pp. 63–4.

117 As quoted in Ibn al-ʿĀbidīn (d. 1252/1836), *Radd al-muḥtār ʿalā'l-durr al-mukhtār*, ed. ʿĀdil Aḥmad ʿAbd al-Mawjūd and ʿAlī Muḥammad Muʿawwaḍ (Beirut: Dār al-Kutub al-ʿIlmiyya, 1994), vol. 2, p. 187. According to Ibn al-ʿĀbidīn, Ḥaṣkafī wrote in the margins to his *Khazā'in* that this position was taken from *al-Mujtabā*, i.e. a commentary by Abū'l-Ḥusayn al-Qudūrī (d. 428/1037), *Mukhtaṣar*, by the Ḥanafī jurist of Khwārazm, Najm al-Dīn Mukhtār al-Zāhidī (d. 658/1259–60); cf. Ḥajjī Khalīfa, *Kashf*, vol. 2, pp. 1592 and 1631. For the broader historical and geographical contexts of post-classical Ḥanafī *furūʿ* literature, see Robert D. McChesney, 'Central Asia's Place in the Middle East: Some Historical Considerations' in David Menashri, ed., *Central Asia Meets the Middle East* (London: Frank Cass, 1998), pp. 25–51, at p. 40.

118 Shaykh Bakrī al-Ṣadafī's *fatwā* is recorded in Harīdī, *al-Fatāwā'l-islāmiyya*, vol. 1, pp. 44–5, no. 3.

119 Abū'l-Barakāt al-Nasafī (d. 710/1310), *al-Kāfī fī sharḥ al-Wāfī*, MS Hk 3502, İl Halk Kütüphanesi, Manisa, fol. 34a (unnumbered); a position repeated in Kamāl al-Dīn ʿAbd al-Wāḥid Ibn Humām (d. 861/1457), *Fatḥ al-qadīr*, ed.

ʿAbd al-Razzāq Ghālib al-Mahdī (Beirut: Dār al-Kutub al-ʿIlmiyya, 1415/1995), vol. 1, p. 291; Shurunbulālī, *al-Nafḥa*, p. 12; cf. Shaltūt, 'Tarjamat al-Qurʾān', p. 129; Shāṭir, *al-Qawl al-sadīd*, pp. 112–13; Makhlūf, *Risāla*, p. 42.

120 As quoted in Bukhārī, *al-Muḥīṭ al-burhānī*, vol. 1, p. 308, cf. Zadeh, *Vernacular Qur'an*, p. 139, n. 92; Ashirbek Muminov, 'Disputes in Bukhara on the Persian Translation of the Qur'an', *Mélanges de l'Université Saint-Joseph* 59 (2006), pp. 301–8. On Hinduwānī, see Ibn Abī'l-Wafāʾ, *al-Jawāhir al-muḍiyya*, vol. 3, pp. 192–4, no. 1345.

121 See Daniel Elton, 'The Sāmānid "Translations" of al-Ṭabarī' in Hugh Kennedy, ed., *al-Ṭabarī: A Medieval Muslim Historian and His Work* (Princeton, NJ: Darwin Press, 2008), pp. 263–98; Shahrokh Mohammad Baygi, 'The First Available Persian Interpretation of the Qur'an Known as the *Tarjumah Tafsīr-i-Ṭabarī*', *Hamdard Islamicus* 19, no. 4 (1996), pp. 31–44.

122 *Tafsīr-i Ṭabarī*, MS Supplément persan 1610, Bibliothèque Nationale de France, Paris, fol. 3a; *Tarjuma-i Tafsīr-i Ṭabarī*, ed. Ḥabīb Yaghmāʾī (Tehran: Intishārāt-i Tūs, 1367 Sh./1988), vol. 1, p. 13.

123 He is listed in MS Supplément persan 1610, fol. 3a as Abū Jaʿfar Muḥammad b. ʿAlī from Bāb al-Hind in Balkh. This appears to be an error of the copyist, as the name given in the biographical authorities is Muḥammad b. ʿAbd Allāh; on Bāb al-Hinduwānī of Balkh, see ʿAbd al-Karīm al-Samʿānī (d. 562/1166), *al-Ansāb*, ed. ʿAbd al-Raḥmān al-Yamānī *et al.* (Hyderabad: Dāʾirat al-Maʿārif al-ʿUthmāniyya, 1962–82), vol. 12, p. 350; see also Elton, 'Sāmānid "Translations"', p. 288, n. 74.

124 Burhān al-Dīn Abū'l-Ḥasan al-Marghīnānī, *Kitāb al-Tajnīs wa'l-mazīd*, ed. Muḥammad Amīn Makkī (Karachi: Idrārat al-Qurʾān wa'l-ʿUlūm al-Islāmiyya, 2004), vol. 1, pp. 477–8, no. 512, cf. vol. 1, p. 478, no. 517. Quoted in Shurunbulālī, *al-Nafḥa*, p. 11; Shākir, *al-Qawl al-faṣl*, p. 26.

125 See, for instance, the position ascribed to Abū Bakr Muḥammad al-Bukhārī (d. 381/991), that only heretics (*zandīq*, dualists?) or the insane (*majnūn*) would pray in Persian, cited in Bukhārī, *Kashf al-asrār*, ed. ʿAbd Allāh Maḥmūd Muḥammad ʿUmar (Beirut: Dār al-Kutub al-ʿIlmiyya, 1997), vol. 1, p. 42; also cited in Ṣabrī, *Mas'ala*, p. 61; Abū Daqīqa, 'Kalima', p. 32; cf. Muhammad Ahmad, *Die Auseinandersetzung Zwischen al-Azhar*, p. 35.

126 Sarah Savant gives an excellent account of the figure of Salmān in this process of historiographical modelling, in '"Persians" in Early Islam', *Annales islamologiques* 42 (2008), pp. 73–91, pp. 80–82, and most recently in ibid., *The New Muslims of Post-Conquest Iran: Tradition, Memory, and Conversion* (Cambridge: Cambridge University Press, 2013), pp. 61–89.

127 See Louis Massignon, *Salmân Pâk et les prémices spirituelles de l'Islam iranien* (Tours: Arrault, 1934); see also Matti Moosa, *Extremist Shiites: The Ghulat Sects* (Syracuse, NY: Syracuse University Press, 1988), pp. 342–51; Mohammad Ali Amir-Moezzi, *The Spirituality of Shiʿi Islam: Beliefs and Practices* (London, I.B. Tauris in association with the Institute of Ismaili Studies, 2011), pp. 97–8, 209–10, 294–5 and 471.

128 Nawawī, *Majmūʿ*, vol. 3, pp. 341; Fakhr al-Dīn al-Rāzī, *Mafātīḥ al-ghayb* (Beirut: Dār al-Fikr, 1981), vol. 1, p. 217; cited in Shāṭir, *Tadhkira*, pp. 46–7.

129 Isfarāʾīnī, *Tāj al-tarājim*, vol. 1, p. 8.

130 The following draws on material examined within the broader context of early Persian exegesis, Zadeh, *Vernacular Qur'an*, pp. 478–83.

131 Abū'l-ʿAbbās Jaʿfar al-Mustaghfirī, *Faḍā'il al-Qur'ān*, ed. Aḥmad b. Fāris al-Sallūm (Beirut: Dār Ibn Ḥazm, 2006), vol. 1, pp. 493, no. 685. Sallūm's transcription leaves much to be desired. My reading is based upon the unicum, MS Esad Efendi 181, Sülaymaniye Library, Istanbul, fol. 96b. The last two lines are admittedly a bit jumbled and may well have been collapsed together in the course of transmission; I have dropped out the '*ka-tu*' which begins line six of the manuscript for the sake of semantic clarity, for it appears here to be pleonastic. The third and tenth lines of the manuscript clearly have *ushtuhl*, which is an error for *ushnuhl* > *shnuhl*, Middle Persian *šnwhl*. The folio is reproduced as figure 9 in Zadeh, *Vernacular Qur'an*.

132 It is common for Zoroastrian manuscripts to begin with the Persian phrase *ba-nām-i khudāy-i bakhshāyanda-i bakhāyishgar*, which functions as a kind of Zoroastrian *basmala*. See also, Philippe Gignoux, 'Pour une origine iranienne du bi'smillah' in Philippe Gignoux *et al.*, eds, *Pad nām i Yazdān: études d'épigraphie, de numismatique et d'histoire de l'Iran ancient* (Paris: Klincksieck, 1979), pp. 159–63.

133 The first two transmitters to Mustaghfirī were from the region: 1) Abū Bakr Muḥammad b. al-Ḥusayn al-Bukhārī, and 2) Abū'l-Ḥasan Naṣr b. Aḥmad al-Sharghī; Shargh (or Jargh), is a village located outside Bukhara, see Samʿānī, *Ansāb*, vol. 7, p. 311. The next transmitter is 3) Abū Bakr Muḥammad b. ʿAbd Allāh b. Yazdād al-Rāzī (fl. 352/963), a baker, who also took up residence in Bukhara; see Samʿānī, *Ansāb*, vol. 8, p. 204 and vol. 9, p. 308. It appears that through him the account circulated in Transoxiana; while in Rayy, he studied with 4) Abū Bakr Muḥammad b. Jaʿfar al-Faqīh al-Ushnānī al-Rāzī; see ʿAbd al-Karīm al-Rāfiʿī (d. 623/1226), *al-Tadwīn fī akhbār Qazwīn*, ed. ʿAzīz Allāh al-ʿUṭāridī (Beirut: Dār al-Kutub al-ʿIlmiyya, 1987), vol. 1, pp. 240–41. The final transmitter, 5) Abū Bakr Muḥammad b. Yūsuf, was a Ḥanafī jurist, as noted by his honorific, Abū'l-Ḥanīfa al-Ṣaghīr (the lesser); this title was used to refer to other scholars who had mastered Ḥanafī law, most notably Hinduwānī; see Ibn Abī'l-Wafā', *al-Jawāhir al-muḍiyya*, vol. 3, pp. 192–4, no. 1345. The appearance of Yaḥyā b. Muʿādh al-Rāzī in the following *isnād*, on the authority of Muḥammad b. Jaʿfar al-Faqīh, dates the transmission of the report; see Mustaghfirī, *Faḍā'il*, vol. 1, p. 494, no. 686.

134 It may well be the case that the jurist Muḥammad b. Jaʿfar had a written version of the account, for he is credited with composing works on both *fiqh* and hadith, see Rāfiʿī, *Tadwīn*, vol. 1, pp. 240–41.

135 For further details, see Zadeh, *Vernacular Qur'an*, pp. 481–2.

136 See ʿAlī b. al-Ḥusayn al-Sughdī (attrib.), *al-Nutaf fī'l-fatāwā*, ed. Ṣalāḥ al-Dīn al-Nāhī (Beirut: Mu'assasat al-Risāla, 1984), vol. 1, pp. 49–50; on the Karrāmī provenance of this juridical collection, see Aron Zysow, 'Two Unrecognized Karrāmī Texts', *Journal of the American Oriental Society* 108, no. 4 (1988), pp. 577–87.

137 See Wilferd Madelung, 'The Early Murji'a in Khurāsān and Transoxania and the Spread of Ḥanafism', *Der Islam* 59 (1982), pp. 32–9. On the Karrāmī association with the Murji'a, see Abū'l-Ḥasan al-Ashʿarī, *Maqālāt al-islāmiyyīn*, ed. Helmut Ritter (Leipzig: Brockhaus in Komm, 1929–33), vol. 1, p. 141. See

also Josef van Ess, *Der Eine und das Andere: Beobachtungen an islamischen häresiographischen Texten* (Berlin: Walter de Gruyter, 2011), vol. 1, p. 664.

138 Abū Bakr Muḥammad b. Jaʿfar al-Narshakhī, *Tārīkh-i Bukhārā*, ed. Muḥammad b. Zufar b. ʿUmar (Tehran: Sanāʾī, 1320 Sh./1940–41), p. 67. See Mohammad Jafar Yahaghi, who views this account, along with Salmān's translation, as shedding light on the early historical tradition of Persian translations, 'An Introduction to Early Persian Qur'anic Translations', *Journal of Qur'anic Studies* 4, no. 2 (2002), pp. 105–9, at p. 105.

139 See Melick Iradj Mochiri, 'A Pahlavi Forerunner of the Umayyad Reform Coinage', *Journal of the Royal Asiatic Society* 2 (1981), pp. 168–72, pp. 170–71; idem, *Arab-Sasanian Civil War Coinage: Manichaeans, Yazidiya and other Khawārij*, tr. Jean Louis Avril and Françoise Graves (Paris: n.p., 1986), p. 57, no. 112; Stuart Sears, 'A Monetary History of Iraq and Iran, ca CE 500 to 750' (Unpublished PhD dissertation, University of Chicago, 1997), vol. 1, pp. 37–8. On the sociopolitical context of the coinage, see Stefan Heidemann, 'The Evolving Representation of the Early Islamic Empire and its Religion on Coin Imagery' in Angelika Neuwirth, Nicolai Sinai and Michael Marx, eds, *The Qur'ān in Context: Historical and Literary Investigations into the Qur'ānic Milieu* (Brill: Leiden, 2010), pp. 149–95, at pp. 168–9.

140 For the bilingual Arab-Sāsānian weight in the Bibliothèque nationale de France (1974.25) with its Middle Persian translation of Q. 5:8, see Raoul Curiel and Philippe Gignoux, who offer a tentative reading of the Middle Persian, 'Un poids arabo-sasanide', *Studia Iranica* 5, no. 2 (1976), pp. 165–9; Ḥasan Riḍāʾī Bāghbīdī attempts to fill in more detail, though with questionable readings, 'Darbāra-i tarjama-i ʿibārātī az Qur'an ba Pahlawī', *Nāma-yi Īrān-ī Bāstān* 1 (1380 Sh./2001), pp. 11–14; Shaul Shaked's explanation is more compelling, 'Mihr the Judge', *Jerusalem Studies in Arabic and Islam* 2 (1980), pp. 1–30, at p. 10, n. 38b.

141 Isfarāʾīnī, *Tāj al-tarājim*, vol. 1, pp. 7–9.

142 Ibid., vol. 1, p. 9; see also Yahaghi, 'Introduction', p. 105.

143 ʿAbd al-Salām b. Saʿīd Saḥnūn (d. 240/855), *al-Mudawwana al-kubrā*, ed. ʿAlī b. al-Sayyid ʿAbd al-Raḥmān al-Hāshim (Abu Dhabi: n.p., 2000), vol. 1, pp. 193–4.

144 On *raṭāna*, related to the Syriac *reṭnā*, as liturgical chanting, see J.C. Greenfield, 'Rṭyn mgwš (The Sorcerer Whispers)' in Benjamin Sidney and Leon D. Stitskin, eds, *Joshua Finkel Festschrift* (New York: Yeshiva University Press, 1974), pp. 63–9; see Ignaz Goldziher, *Muslim Studies*, tr. S.M. Stern (Albany, NY: State University of New York Press, 1967), vol. 1, p. 158, n. 4.

145 ʿAbd al-Razzāq, *al-Muṣannaf*, 'Kitāb al-Manāsik', vol. 5, pp. 496–7, no. 9793; Ibn Abī Shayba, *al-Muṣannaf*, 'Kitāb al-Adab', ed. Ḥamad b. ʿAbd Allāh al-Jumʿa and Muḥammad b. Ibrāhīm al-Luḥaydān (Riyadh: Maktabat al-Rushd, 2004), vol. 8, p. 548, nos 26684–6, cf. vol. 8, p. 549, nos 26687–90; see Goldziher, *Muslim Studies*, vol. 1, p. 157, n. 3; Suliman Bashear, *Arabs and Others in Early Islam* (Princeton, NJ: Darwin Press, 1997), p. 31.

146 Ibn Abī Shayba, *al-Muṣannaf*, vol. 8, p. 548, no. 26684.

147 See al-Ḥākim al-Naysābūrī (d. 405/1014), *al-Mustadrak ʿalāʾl-Ṣaḥīḥayn*, ed. Abū ʿAbd al-Raḥmān al-Wādiʿī (Cairo: Dār al-Ḥaramayn, 1997), vol. 4, p. 184, nos 7080–81.

148 Reinhart, 'Fundamentalism', p. 108.

149 This hadith, which forms part of a larger speech, is notably directed to Ṣuhayb the Greek, Bilāl the Ethiopian and Salmān the Persian, among others. See Ibn Taymiyya, '*fa-man takallama bi'l-'arabiyyati fa-huwa 'arabiyyun*' in *Iqtiḍā'*, vol. 1, p. 410. While Ibn Taymiyya doubts the authenticity of this hadith, he argues that its meaning is authentic. See also Ibn 'Asākir (d. 571/1176), *Ta'rīkh madīnat Dimashq*, ed. Muḥibb al-Dīn al-'Amrawī and 'Alī Shīrī (Beirut: Dār al-Fikr, 1995–2001), vol. 24, pp. 224–5, nos 5227–8; Jalāl al-Dīn al-Suyūṭī, *al-Khaṣā'iṣ al-kubrā*, ed. Muḥammad Khalīl Harrās (Cairo: Dār al-Kutub al-Ḥadītha, n.d.), vol. 3, pp. 10–11; also Roy Mottahedeh, 'The Shu'ûbîyah Controversy and the Social History of Early Islamic Iran', *International Journal of Middle East Studies* 7 (1976), pp. 161–82, at p. 179; Bashear, *Arabs and Others*, p. 56.

150 For an overview of modern Persian commentaries and translations, see my chapter, 'Persian Qur'anic Networks, Modernity and the Writings of "an Iranian Lady", Nusrat Amin Khanum (d. 1983)' in Suha Taji-Farouki, ed., *The Qur'an and Its Readers Worldwide: Contemporary Commentaries and Translations* (Oxford: Oxford University Press in association with the Institute of Ismaili Studies, forthcoming). Within the context of South Asia, see, for instance, Shāh Walī Allāh (d. 1762), *Fatḥ al-Raḥmān fī tarjamat al-Qur'ān* (Meerut: Lithograph, 1867), p. 1. See also the discussion by Abū 'Alā' al-Mawdūdī (d. 1979) of his Urdu translation and commentary in the preface to *Tafhīm al-Qur'ān* (Lahore: Ta'mīr-i Insāniyyat, 1954–65), vol. 1, pp. 1–10; similarly, see 'Uthmānī's robust defence of the early Ḥanafī position on translation during ritual prayer, *I'lā' al-sunan*, vol. 4, pp. 148–57.

151 See Reinhart, 'Fundamentalism', p. 109. More broadly, see Haeri, *Sacred Language*, pp. 25–51, particularly pp. 44–5 and 149.

13

The Qur'an Today: Translating the Translatable*

STEFAN WILD

Introduction

TO TAKE THE Qur'an out of its Arabic context is a problematic and controversial endeavor.[1] In many self-referential statements, the Qur'an insists on the eminent importance of its Arabic character. The major difference between the Qur'an and earlier scripture, such as Jewish and Christian scriptures, was not its content, but the fact that the Qur'an was revealed in Arabic. The relevant self-referential statements of the Qur'an are clear.[2] The Qur'an confirms earlier scripture and it confirms them in Arabic. The Qur'an is primarily an Arabic Qur'an (Q. 12:2, *We have sent it down as an Arabic Koran; haply you will understand*; *innā anzalnāhu Qur'ānan ʿarabiyyan laʿallakum taʿqilūn*).[3] When Muhammad received the message, not all Arabs were Muslims, but all followers of the Prophet spoke Arabic, although some may have also spoken Persian or Ethiopic (Geʿez). The Prophet's recited message was directed initially to speakers of Arabic only. The Muslim community began as a community of speakers of Arabic. Islam was the religion of Arabs, before it became a universal religion.

There are two main theological ideas that have developed in highlighting the Qur'an's unique religious status in comparison with other scriptures. There is, firstly, the affirmation of what is somewhat clumsily called the 'inimitability of the Qur'an' (*iʿjāz*

* I would like to thank Gerrit Bos (Cologne), Stephen Burge (London), Klaus Kreiser (Berlin), Hedda Reindl-Kiel (Bonn) and Travis Zadeh (Haverford, PA) for important information and suggestions.

al-Qur'ān).[4] Secondly, there is the denial of the createdness of the Qur'an, in other words, the assertion that the Qur'an as God's word is uncreated and eternally pre-existent with God – a surprising parallel to the *logos* in the New Testament (John 1:1).[5]

The Qur'an insists that its verses are '*the fairest of stories*' (*aḥsan al-ḥadīth*, Q. 39:23). This can also be rendered in translation as 'the most beautiful word'.[6] But the verse goes on: '*a scripture consistent in its repetition, at which the skins of those who fear their lord crawl; but then their skins and their hearts are softened for the remembrance of God*'. This indicates that the overwhelming power of this recitation is more important than its beauty. The Qur'an itself does not incontrovertibly attest to its primarily aesthetic supremacy. One thing, however, is clear: the Qur'anic voice considers itself supremely matchless. Many verses in the Qur'an refer to this inimitable and perfect character and maintain that neither human beings nor *djinn* could have produced a Qur'anic sura or even a single Qur'anic verse. Muslim scholars called these verses 'the challenging verses' (*āyāt al-taḥaddī*). In post-Qur'anic times, however, the rhetorical beauty of the Qur'anic word became an important part of its inimitability and part of the dogma at the same time. A Qur'anic verse or sura is often seen not so much as the report of a revelation, but as the protocol of a revelation. The awe and attraction that the recitation of the Qur'an evoked in the Muslim community grew throughout the ages. The Qur'an came to be seen as something absolutely and in every respect unique. Many mediaeval Muslim scholars claimed that because of the revelation of the Qur'an the Arabic language as such was a 'sacred language'.[7]

On the other hand, there is only the scarcest scriptural evidence for the second major theological concept relating to the Qur'an, namely the dogma of its uncreatedness. After some theological turmoil, Muslim orthodoxy in its Ashʿarī version accepted the idea of the eternal pre-existence of the Qur'an or at least of some kind of a Qur'anic prototype. The meagre scriptural basis for this dogma is one passage: Q. 85:21–2, *Nay, but it is a glorious Koran, in a guarded tablet* (*bal huwa Qur'ānun majīd fī lawḥin maḥfūẓ*). The notion of the uncreatedness and therefore eternal pre-existence of the Qur'an was developed by early Muslim theology in the third/ninth century.[8]

Scholars combined the two concepts of inimitability and uncreatedness into a kind of firewall in the Muslim collective *imaginaire*. It made the status of Jewish and Christian scripture in the eyes of their believers pale in comparison with the status of the Qur'an in the eyes of a Muslim. There is an element of inter-religious and inter-scriptural outstripping and topping here that, as far as I can see, has not yet received sufficient attention.

In such a context, the competition for scriptural attractiveness played an essential part. For example, the Qur'anic paradise is far more attractive than its counterpart in Christian scripture; conversely the tortures of the Qur'anic hell are much more graphic and cruel than their Christian canonical parallels. It makes sense that the new prophet's message about the Hereafter should be more attractive (paradise) and more terrifying (hellfire) at the same time. Both aspects were part of the struggle for the minds of the new group of followers of the Prophet and of the prospective novices. Following this line, the Qur'an revealed itself as a document to outstrip all other scriptures. The Qur'an was, therefore, from the earliest recitation onward, a highly competitive text. It was also a highly contested text. The emerging young community of 'proto-Muslims' may have had a Jewish, Christian, pagan or other background. They had to incorporate many of these teachings and at the same time distance themselves from competing cultural and religious tendencies and texts – and all this against the general background of Late Antiquity. The Qur'anic text in many verses rejects all attempts to justify a syncretistic mood.[9] Thus, in asserting itself, the Qur'an at the same time defended itself. Its most effective weapon may have been the claim that the recipients of earlier scriptures had tampered with divine revelation (*taḥrīf*).[10] According to this view, only the Qur'an was, and is, the pure and unadulterated word of God.

Given that the Qur'an views its Arabic text as part of a theological statement, contrasting it to other religious scriptures, it is evident that a translation of the Arabic Qur'an into another language is more problematic and complicated than translating the Greek New Testament or the Hebrew (and partly Aramaic) Bible into another language.[11] In this paper I will confine myself to three aspects of the problem of translating the Qur'an: 1.) Qur'anic translation and liturgy – the admissibility of translations of the Qur'an; 2) Kemal Atatürk and the 'Turkish Qur'an'; 3) Lost in Translation: The Politics of Translations.

Qur'anic Translation and Liturgy: The Admissibility of Translations of the Qur'an

For a long time, many Muslim scholars maintained, and many still maintain, that a translation of the Arabic text into another language is strictly impossible – a translated Qur'an cannot claim to be the Qur'an anymore. But a warning is in order: the 'common conflation, of whether it is licit to use translations in prayer and whether it is permissible to produce translations at all, has resulted in a significant misunderstanding in the development of early Qur'anic hermeneutics'.[12] The most lenient law school in this was the Ḥanafī legal tradition. The rule was and still is that the liturgical recitation of the text should be in Arabic. Exegesis was and is impossible without the knowledge of Arabic. The Muslim Law, the immense body of legal knowledge that became the Sharia, could be understood and developed only by those who read and understood the Qur'anic Arabic.

Modern translation experts would agree, first, that all translations are fragmentary, approximate, and interpretive and, second, that literary, poetic, and religious texts are more 'vulnerable' than technical or other everyday texts. The standard Muslim answer to the question of translation was more and more that any attempt to translate could only convey the 'meanings of the Qur'an' (*maʿānī al-Qur'ān*) and any form of these translated 'meanings' necessarily implied comments on, and exegesis of, the Qur'an. The two dogmas of its miraculous inimitability and its uncreatedness further deepened the real and the perceived gulf between the original Arabic Qur'an and any possible translation.

Muslim scholars did not always agree on the exact nature of the inimitability of the holy Text. And in modern Muslim exegesis, interest in the question of the exact nature of Qur'anic inimitability seems to have subsided somewhat. However, in the so-called *tafsīr ʿilmī* ('scientific exegesis'), which finds modern science and technology anticipated in the Qur'an, there are still distinct traces of Qur'anic inimitability.[13] It also seems that the dogma of the uncreatedness of the Qur'an does not receive much theological attention today. However, Qur'anic recitation was, and is, enormously impressive and aesthetically deeply moving for the believer as well as for many a non-believer. Listeners to Qur'anic recitation have been known to faint and even allegedly to die under the shock of the *tremendum* and the *fascinans* of Qur'anic verses and suras.[14]

When a translation of the Qur'an is attempted, much is inevitably lost in translation. In this respect, however, the Qur'an is far from unique – as Muslim Arab scholars found out very early. One of the most famous early representatives of Arabic culture in Abbasid times, Abū ʿUthmān al-Jāḥiẓ (d. 255/868-9), noted about Arabic poetry: 'Arabic poetry is untranslatable and cannot be adapted to another language. When this is attempted its structure is shattered, its metre is destroyed, its beauty disappears and its marvels fall away.'[15] Something similar is true for the Qur'an. The miraculous rhetorical quality that the Qur'anic text has for the believer defies translation. One of the linguistically most sensitive commentators of the Qur'an, Maḥmūd b. ʿUmar al-Zamakhsharī (d. 538/1144), stated in his commentary of Q. 44.43–50: 'the Qur'an is matchless in its rhetoric and in the singularity of its order and styles, and in the subtleties of its meanings and allusions. No other language, Persian or otherwise, can ever hope to attain it.'[16] A translation of the Qur'an that faithfully reflects all its peculiarities, ambiguities, and contextual associations is impossible. In a remarkable way, therefore, the hesitations of Muslim scholars to allow a translation of the Qur'an, on the one hand, and the findings of modern translation theory, on the other, seem to point in the same direction. At the same time however, most contemporary Muslim scholars are aware of the fact that an ever growing majority of Muslims today can neither read nor understand the Arabic Qur'an. For Islam to remain a world religion, the Arabic Qur'an has to be translated and spread in as many languages as possible. This dilemma is at the heart of the problem of how to translate the religiously untranslatable.

Thomas Bauer[17] has argued persuasively that the ambiguities of the Qur'anic text as recited and as written should not be considered a strange anomaly, but should be seen as an essential feature of Islamic revelation. The idea that the Qur'anic text has been revealed in seven different 'ways' or 'forms' (*aḥruf*, sg.: *ḥarf*) goes back to the earliest layers of Muslim exegetical culture – and Bauer insists on the fact that, in these earliest times, the seven *aḥruf* were not identical with the later concept of seven 'canonical' readings (*qirā'āt*) of the Qur'an. Fred Leemhuis is less certain: 'The context of these traditions suggest that with *ḥarf* either a mode of recitation or a manner of pronunciation is meant . . .; however it is clear that in the second/eighth century *ḥarf* was taken to mean the same thing as *qirā'a* in its narrow sense of "variant reading".'[18] The number 'seven' may initially not have to be taken literally, but – like the 'seven heavens' (e.g. Q 17:44) – denote a great but limited number. The ambiguity of the Qur'anic text includes the under-determination of its unpunctuated consonantal written skeleton form (*rasm*). To recite the Qur'an, the reciters had to rely on a primary understanding of the text that in turn was based on often diverging oral traditions of recitation. Furthermore, even after establishing the punctuated Arabic text, there were different ways to vocalise the words, which again led to different 'readings' (*qirā'āt*) of the Qur'an. These 'readings' were collected and documented, and certain prosodic elements in the recitation were later identified and notated – but it took a century or more before the process of canonisation was completed. Sunni Muslim theology developed the idea that the seven or ten or fourteen 'readings' had all been revealed by God and were equally 'valid' (*ṣaḥīḥ*) – and thus refrained from enforcing a single textual version. In pre-modern times, at least, it was never even attempted to notate the markedly different melodies of Qur'an recitation. All these aspects point to the 'tamed ambiguity' (to use Bauer's phrase) of the earliest Qur'anic recitations and to a far-reaching, if prudent and controlled, pluralism. To reproduce the gamut of ambiguities, associations, and variations that inform the Qur'anic source text in a target language is beyond any translator's capacity. It should also be clear that few modern readers or reciters of the Qur'an will share all these ambiguities and associations with the earliest listeners and readers of the Qur'an in the first/seventh century. No text that is read and recited today can ever evoke what was evoked by the same text in its formative period some 1,400 years ago.

If we go back to the earliest period of Islam, the time of the Prophet, the liturgical recitation of any part of the Qur'an was usually performed in Arabic only. That is why, according to traditional Muslim theology, the ritual prayer (*ṣalāt*) that contains as its most important element the first sura, *Sūrat al-Fātiḥa* (the 'opening sura'), must be recited in Arabic and in Arabic only. The Arabic recitation of the Qur'an is at the very heart of the prayer rite.[19] But already in the first centuries of the Muslim expansion, there were dissenting voices. Two of the most famous religious venerable authorities of Islam taught contrary doctrines. Abū Ḥanīfa al-Nuʿmān b. Thābit (d. 150/767) taught that the new Muslims who did not know Arabic could recite the ritual prayer, and that included the *Fātiḥa*, in Persian.[20] Salmān al-Fārisī, a contested and probably semi-legendary figure of earliest Islam, is said to have 'translated the *Fātiḥa* into Persian for the Persians to use during ritual prayer until they became accustomed to the original Arabic'[21] and might have been the first person to translate the Qur'an into a foreign language. In the language of the jurists, reciting the prayer in Persian did not make it 'invalid' (*bāṭil*). Muḥammad b. Idrīs al-Shāfiʿī (d. 204/820), a no less famous authority, opined that for the ritual prayer to be 'valid' (*ṣaḥīḥ*) it had to be said in Arabic. Shāfiʿī's opinion prevailed in the end, but probably more by a twist of history than by better argument. To not fully understand a holy text may enhance rather than diminish its fascination. On the other hand, it is an advantage for any religious community to have a common cultic language. Arabic was in many ways for the Muslim community what Latin was for the Roman Catholic Church until the twentieth century. In view of the fact that the Qur'an so clearly links its Arabic character with the divine origin of the text, it is easy to understand that, for most Muslims even today, recitation of the Qur'an was and is valid only in Arabic.

Insisting that the ritual prayer had to be recited in Arabic did not exclude that passages of the Qur'an or the whole Qur'an might be translated into other languages. That there ever was a formal ban on translating the Qur'an is a myth, but there surely was a marked reluctance, at times coming close to a ban. Zamakhsharī, on the other hand, does not hesitate in his linguistically centred exegesis to posit the necessity of translating the Qur'an into as many languages as possible.[22]

Thus, even if a translation of the (meanings of the) Qur'an was rarely formally prohibited, there was certainly a strong reservation toward translation that survived into modern times. Muḥammad Rashīd Riḍā (d. 1935), one of the most famous 'reformists' of modern Islam, stated in a *fatwā*, *Tarjamat al-Qur'ān wa-mā fīhā min al-mafāsid wa-munāfāt al-Qur'ān*, that both literal and free translations of the Qur'an are illicit.[23] Translating the Qur'an, he states, would create the same problems as those besetting the translations of the Old and the New Testament by Jewish or Christian scholars.[24] Riḍā concluded that reformers of Islam should see to it that all Muslim schools around the world teach Arabic to all students so that for them, at least, a translation would be unnecessary.[25] The Azhar still repeated this somewhat utopian demand in a Fatwa issued as late as in 1953.[26] Riḍā went so far as to say that it was as forbidden to translate the Qur'an as it was forbidden to change a single word in the Qur'an or to replace one word by a different word. According to him, the spread of Islam must be independent of translations of the Qur'an. When the first Muslim British translator Marmaduke Pickthall (1875–1936), a British convert, tried to gain the permission of al-Azhar to translate the Qur'an into English in the 1920s the majority of the Azharis flatly refused.[27]

However, Riḍā's position notwithstanding, Muslim scholars in Egypt who opted for a translation of the (meanings of the) Qur'an in the end succeeded in paving the way to allow such translations. The pioneer was Muḥammad Muṣṭafā al-Marāghī (d. 1945), head of the Ḥanafī *madhhab* in Egypt.[28] After his nomination as Sheikh al-Azhar in 1935, he succeeded in having a law passed by the Egyptian parliament that al-Azhar and the Ministry of Education should collaborate to produce a translation.[29] Today, translations of the Qur'an are completely acceptable even to the most traditional Muslim scholar as long as they insist that they are only translations of its 'meanings'. But more and more Muslim translators call their translations 'translations' and assert implicitly that they are translating only what is translatable. They often choose not to print the Arabic text together with the translation, a feature that is often observed to assure the owner that he or she has, next to the translation, also the Arabic Qur'an in his or her hand. The lack of the Arabic text has one advantage, however: if the Muslim reader uses only a translation of the Qur'an, that allows him or her to take and read the book anywhere without having to worry constantly about the state of ritual purity that he or she is expected to observe when touching the Arabic text. On the other hand, there are still many Salafī voices warning against too readily abandoning the Arabic original in favour of a translation. Muḥammad Muṣṭafā al-Aʿẓamī signals what he believes to be an anti-Muslim strategy, namely: 'to substitute the holy text with vernacular translations, then inflate their status such that they are held on a par with the original Arabic. In this way, Muslim societies, three quarters of which are non-Arab, can be severed from the actual revelation of Allah.'[30] The main-stream opinion, however, seems to be today that Muslim missionary activity (*daʿwa*) outside the Arab-speaking world is next to impossible without referring to translations of the Qur'an.

Kemal Atatürk and the 'Turkish Qur'an'

That the liturgical recitation of the Qur'an should only be done in Arabic was generally beyond doubt – until the dismemberment of the Ottoman Empire after World War One and the rise to power of Mustafa Kemal Atatürk (1881–1938).[31] Already the first inklings of the 'purification' of the Turkish language, in other words, the elimination of Arabic and Persian loanwords, were viewed with grave concern. The aforementioned Riḍā wrote as early as January 1910 in *al-Manar*:

> It became known in Syria, Egypt, and other countries that some Turkish writers call upon their people to take their distance from the Arabs. They even invite them to drop Arabic words used in their language and they call this 'purification' – as if they considered Arabic an impurity that had defiled Turkish. Some people have drawn the logical conclusion that this talk must be

> seen as an attack on the Book of God and the Tradition from the Prophet, and that this call may well be the first step to another call that would logically follow if the first was taken and implemented. That would be the call to apostatise from Islam. For the fundamental basis of Islam is the Noble Book and the Exalted Sunna. Both are in the Arabic language and the Prophet who came was an Arab.[32]

Many Muslims saw the unique status of the Arabic language of the Qur'an endangered as never before when Atatürk, in his push for modernisation, decided in 1928 that the ritual prayer and the call for prayer by the muezzin should henceforth be in Turkish. In the Arabic call to prayer, the formula *allāhu akbar* was replaced by *tanrı uludur.* Already in 1908, after the Turkish Constitution had been proclaimed, a newspaper had 'started to print a (Turkish) translation day by day, but the clergy succeeded in putting a stop to this sacrilege before it had gone very far'.[33] The 'sacrilege' can hardly have been the mere fact of translation. An Ottoman-Turkish translation of the Qur'an had already been printed in Cairo in 1842 and in Istanbul Ottoman translations were printed as early as 1865.[34] Atatürk, however, went further and promoted Turkish translations of the Qur'an to be printed in the newly introduced Latin script. He selected a special commission for this purpose and ordered that this translation should take the place of the Arabic Qur'an. After 1920, three translations appeared, but the public echo was disappointing: 'All the fire and life, the mystery, music and magic of the Koran had been lost. In the hands of the translators the Koran had turned to stone. The Turkish Koran found no place in the mosque, and its functions in the home were largely decorative.'[35] Possibly for that reason, Atatürk did not ban the printing of the Qur'an in Arabic after the reform of the Turkish alphabet.[36]

On 22 January 1932, the Turkish newspaper *Milliyet*, which of course was controlled by the Kemalists, announced that the chief of a Turkish music group of the Presidential Orchestra would 'chant the Turkish Koran at the Yerebatan mosque'.[37] This event caused another general outcry among scholars in Turkey and far beyond in the Muslim world. The state-controlled media, however, celebrated the Turkish version of the Qur'an, even if *Milliyet* recorded: 'For the past day or two certain religious writers have been claiming that the current translations of the Koran are mistaken and faulty and that a worthy translation does not exist.'[38] The Mufti of Istanbul immediately issued an order 'that only those properly qualified by a certificate from his office might publicly read or chant the Turkish Koran'. This seemed to suggest that the Mufti did not mind a Qur'anic sura being recited in Turkish, provided it was done by the right people. But it was probably more a move to keep the new situation under a minimum of control. Ziya Gökalp (d. 1924), one of the founding fathers of Turkish nationalism, had written a poem that prefigured Atatürk's move. It contained the following lines:

> A country where in Turkish the call to prayer is said,
> The meaning of his prayer the villager can understand . . .
> A country in whose schools the Turkish Qur'an is read
> Everyone, young and old, understands the Guide's command . . .
> Oh Turkish son, there is your homeland![39]

For a majority of Muslims worldwide, Atatürk's actions were a sacrilegious attack on the Qur'an and logically followed Atatürk's abolishment of the Caliphate in 1924. His brutal break with the Ottoman Muslim past in the 1920s and 1930s induced a number of Muslims to think that Kemalism with its nationalist modernising secularism was a greater danger to Islam and Muslims than Communism or National Socialism. Muṣṭafā Ṣabrī (1869–1954), erstwhile Seyhülislâm of the Ottoman State in Istanbul, fled to Cairo in 1926, asked for political asylum, and attacked Atatürk's Turkification project from Egypt. In Cairo, he engaged in a memorable and aggressive discussion with the aforementioned Marāghī and with the conservative Muslim intellectual Muḥammad Farīd Wajdī (1875–1940).[40] In a commentary on the Qur'an, the latter had developed a way to re-phrase Qur'anic verses in a simplified Arabic style.[41] Ṣabrī accused Wajdī of extolling Atatürk's replacement of the Arabic letters with European-style letters in Turkish and of trying to persuade Arab Muslims to write the Qur'an in Latin letters resembling those of the new Turkish alphabet. Ṣabrī's critique of the religio-linguistic policy was supported by Riḍā.[42]

For some time in Turkey the state-authorised translation remained by far the most frequently purchased 'commentary'.[43] Its popularity served as a symbol of the success of the Republican efforts to modernise and nationalise religion. The first Turkish translation acceptable to the religious, which, in line with orthodox scholars, called itself an 'interpretation', was the work of the highly respected scholar Elmalılı Muhammed Hamdi Yazır (d. 1942). The translation had the title *Hak dini Kur'an Dili* ('Religion of the Truth, Language of the Qur'an').[44] Later, well known personalities such as Sadi Irmak (d. 1990), the Turkish Prime Minister in 1974–75, also tried their hand at translating the Qur'an.

Since the 1970s at the latest, the state version had to compete with an ever-growing number of alternative translations. Süleyman Ateş (b. 1933), the former head of the huge state-bureaucracy charged with controlling Islam in Turkey, even complained: 'the latest trend is for every religious group to have its own Turkish translation of the Qur'an. This tendency has brought Islam to the verge of division.' Ebu Bekir Sifili, another Qur'anic expert noted: There is a deliberate 'attempt using translation to build a new understanding of religion'. Ahmet Tekir claimed: 'There are almost a hundred translations of the Qur'an on the market . . . nearly one million translations sell each year for up to 70 dollars a copy. There are even those immoral enough to make profit from the Qur'an.'[45] The King Fahd Complex in Saudi Arabia produced a Salafī Turkish version in 1405/1984. The translators of these 'meanings of the Qur'an' were Ali Özek (b. 1932) 'and others'.[46] While widely divergent interpretations of the Qur'an co-exist in present day Turkey, it seems that the violent repercussions of the 'Turkish Qur'an' during the Atatürk era are finally over.

Lost in Translation: The Politics of Qur'an Translations

Translation as a battleground

Generally speaking, translations of the Qur'an did not have the significance for the early spread of Islam that translations of the Bible had for the spread of Christianity.[47] Written translations of the Qur'an into Persian were known as early as the fourth/tenth century.[48] The Ottoman religious bureaucracy, however, allowed Ottoman Turkish translations only in the nineteenth century.[49] But the great impetus to translate the Qur'an in the nineteenth century was linked to three factors: the success of the printing press in the Muslim world, the recognition by the highest Muslim authorities that it was 'unrealistic to expect that the vast majority of Muslims had to learn Arabic in order to understand the Qur'ān',[50] and the growing number of numerous translations of the Qur'an that had been produced by non-Muslims. These were and are suspected of being biased: '[T]he emotional motives behind rendering the Quranic text into languages other than Arabic has always been looked upon with suspicion.'[51]

With the advent of modernity, other reasons beyond a general distrust of Muslim scholars towards translations of the Qur'an emerged that made many Muslims uncomfortable with translations into European languages. The main reason is that, before the 1960s, European translations of the Qur'an were usually done by non-Muslims and for non-Muslims. This approach often bore the imprint of medieval Christian polemics against the Qur'an. One of the first translations of the Qur'an into Latin was produced in 1142/43 at the command of Peter the Venerable, the abbot of Cluny. His version was a theological refutation of Islam. This medieval attitude is not yet completely dead. It was famously re-vivified in the era of colonialism when Christian missionaries studied the Qur'an in order to refute it. Their aim was to Christianise the Muslim world, and their main stumbling block was Islam and its holy Book. A periodical such as *The Moslem World*, founded in 1911 in the United States, called itself 'A Quarterly Review of Current Events, Literature and Thought among Mohammedans, and the Progress of Christian Missionaries in Moslem Lands' and followed precisely this agenda. Samuel M. Zwemer (1867–1952), for thirty-five years editor of *The Moslem World*, wrote almost a hundred books on Islam versus Christianity and on the Qur'an versus the Bible in this spirit. The combination of Christian mission with an overwhelming commercial, political, and military colonial power was deeply resented and has left scars in the, at the time, largely colonised Muslim world that persist until today. The massive missionary effort to convert Muslims to Christianity was by and large singularly unsuccessful. For many Muslim scholars as well as for many average Muslims, the Qur'an and the religion of Islam were for a long time seen as the most effective weapons of resistance against colonialism and foreign domination.

The result of the strong missionary element in many translations of the Qur'an by non-Muslims was, in any case, that the Muslim reader usually saw them as polemically motivated, unfair, and biased. A good example is the translation of the Qur'an by Richard Bell (1876–1951) published in Edinburgh in 1937–39. Its subtitle read: 'Translated with a critical rearrangement of the surahs'. In fact, Bell attempted to restructure the Qur'an in accordance with a fairly arbitrary Bellian chronology that changed the Qur'an into an almost unrecognisable pell-mell text of disjointed verses. Moreover, Bell's comments could be acidly paternalistic. *Sūrat al-Fajr* (Q. 89) begins with a divine oath, and Bell informs the reader that this first verse is an 'absurd oath'.

The best-known contemporary example along such polemical lines was perhaps a notorious remark of the then Pope Benedict XVI at his Regensburg lecture on 'Belief, Reason and the University. Memories and Reflections',[52] delivered on 12 September 2006. He quoted a Byzantine emperor, Manuel II Palaeologos, as saying that 'one will only find bad and inhuman things in the Qur'an such as the prescription to spread the faith with the sword', and he could never completely dispel the impression of Muslim scholars that this quote was not far from what he himself believed. He commented in an excursus on Muslim exegesis:

> The emperor certainly knew that *Sūrat al-Baqara* (Q 2:256) says 'There is no compulsion in religion (*lā ikrāha fī'l-dīn*).' This is probably one of the early suras, which as some experts tell us date from the time in which Muhammad was still powerless and threatened. But the emperor knew, of course, the later rules of holy war as laid down in the Qur'an as well.

Benedict's remarks are factually incorrect. Verse Q. 2:256 was revealed in Medina, and is, therefore, not a verse 'of one of the early suras'. As it stands, it fits into the framework of inter-religious polemics.[53] This type of reflection on the Qur'anic text by a pope continues to draw suspicion from Muslim scholars about the reading of the Qur'an by Christians.

The first British Muslim to translate the 'Meaning of the Glorious Koran' into English, the aforementioned Marmaduke Pickthall,[54] criticised earlier translations because they included 'comments offensive to Muslims' and because 'almost all employed a style of language which Muslims at once recognise as unworthy.'[55] He continues: 'It may be reasonably claimed that no Holy Scripture can be fairly presented by one who disbelieves its inspiration and its message'.[56] Most Muslims would still probably agree, and many Christians and Jews would feel the same way about their own scriptures.

Already before Pickthall's translation appeared, it was clear that many Muslims preferred a translation done by a Muslim to one by a non-Muslim. Often we find today a clear-cut dichotomy: Muslim readers prefer Muslim translations and Muslim translators envisage Muslims as their target readers, while non-Muslim translations cater to non-Muslims. 'Indian Muslims were the first from within the faith to translate the Qur'an to English [. . .] All wrote at a time of British colonialism and intense missionary activity' and all were motivated by a desire to give 'a complete and exhaustive reply to the manifold criticisms of the Koran by various Christian authors'.[57]

The most prominent Muslim agents in translating the Qur'an today are al-Azhar University in Cairo and the King Fahd Complex in Medina. These two organisations compete with each other.[58] Both produce only 'translations of the meanings' of the Qur'anic text. The Azhar orthodoxy has a fairly long tradition of translation. The King Fahd Complex, named after King Fahd b. Abdulaziz (r. 1982–2006), is rigorously Salafī, much better funded, and has been active only since approximately the 1980s.[59] This 'Complex' is now a huge enterprise with about 1,700 employees. It had by 2006 printed more than 136 million copies of publications of, and on, the Qur'an as well as other related Arabic texts, as well as more than 27 million copies of translations. For the year 1427/2005–6 alone, it printed an estimated ten million copies. Every participant in the pilgrimage receives a copy of the Qur'an as a present either in Arabic only or together with a translation. The Complex also publishes translations of 'the meanings of the Qur'an' – of course always together with the original Arabic text. The Complex is under the authority of the Ministry of Islamic Affairs, Pious Foundations, Mission and Guidance and its minister (Nov. 2006) Shaykh Salih ibn ʿAbdul ʿAziz ibn Muhammad Al al-Shaykh, is also the President of the 'High Committee' of the Complex. One of the most audacious projects was for a time a translation of the Qur'an into sign language. As far as I know it has not been finished yet. But there are also other noteworthy developments. The King Fahd Complex sometimes publishes purely oral material. In languages like Oromo (spoken in Ethiopia and Kenya), Malinka (West Africa), and Amharic, the Complex produces translations on cassettes only (as of 2004). English, as the *lingua franca* of modernity, remains, of course, the most coveted target language. 'The Muslim need for translating the Qur'an into English arose mainly out of the desire to combat the missionary effort', says Abdur Rahim Kidwai.[60] But this desire was not without its pitfalls.

The English translation of the Qur'an by Taqi-ud-Din al-Hilali (1893–1987) and Muhammad Muhsin Khan (b. 1927) has been said to be today the 'most widely disseminated Qur'an in most Islamic bookstores and Sunni mosques throughout the English-speaking world'.[61] The King Fahd Complex adopted the Hilali–Khan translation, which had been published in Saudi Arabia in 1996 as *The Noble Qur'ān in the English Language: A Summarized Version of At-Tabari, Al-Qurtubi, and Ibn Kathir with Comments from Sahih al-Bukhari*, but not under the umbrella of the King Fahd Complex.[62] In a later version published by the King Fahd Complex its title was changed to *The Noble Qur'ān: English Translation of the Meanings and Commentary*.[63] The exegetical comments were multiplied, and the sources chosen to justify these comments belong to the most polemical early versions of robustly bellicose Sunni exegesis. A telling example is Q. 1:6–7. The translation by Abdullah Yusuf Ali (1862–1952), which the Complex had initially published in a modified version,[64] had:

> 'Show us the straight way. (7) The way of those on whom Thou has bestowed Thy grace, those whose (portion) is not wrath. And who go not astray.'

The Hilali–Khan 'corrected' version gives:

> 'Guide us to the Straight Way, the way of those on whom You have bestowed Your Grace, not (the way) of those who earned Your Anger (such as the Jews), nor of those who went astray (such as the Christians)'.

Neither Jews nor Christians are mentioned in the Qur'anic text – although it is true that many Muslim exegetes followed this line. Khaleel Mohammed, a leading American Muslim, commented angrily on these and other 'exegetical translations': 'From the beginning, the Hilali-Khan translation reads more like a supremacist Muslim, anti-Semitic, anti-Christian polemic than a rendition of the Islamic scripture.'[65] After 9/11, the Hilali–Khan translation was revised again. In the post-9/11 version, the translation of Q. 1:6–7 was completely changed:

> Guide us to the Straight Way. (7) The Way of those on whom You have bestowed Your Grace, not (the way) of those who earned Your Anger (i.e. those whose intentions are perverted; they know the Truth, yet do not follow it), nor those who went astray (i.e. those who have lost the [true] knowledge, so they wander in error, and are not guided to the Truth).[66]

Christians and Jews had disappeared from the verse. One would like to know the reason that the strongly Salafī redactors backed down from their previous stand. Clearly, translations of the Qur'an are, now more than ever, veritable battlegrounds.

Translations of the Qur'an by Jewish scholars

For political reasons, many Muslims after the advent of Zionism distrusted the few translations done by Jews. Nessim (originally: Naʿim) Joseph Dawood (b. 1927), an Iraqi Jew, published a translation into English for Penguin books in 1956 that sold more than a million copies. In this translation, he followed Richard Bell (see above) in putting the suras into what he believed to be their chronological order. In later editions, however, he restored the traditional order of the suras. Muhammad A.S. Abdel Haleem criticised the translation in the introduction of his own translation of the Qur'an.[67] From the beginning, he says, Dawood's translation was seen as taking 'too many liberties with the text of the Qur'an and to contain many inaccuracies, as was immediately pointed out by reviewers; moreover, many Muslims were deeply offended by the way he translated key terms and by some of the notes to the translation'.[68] This distrust, however, does not extend to Jewish converts to Islam. One of the best known translations of the Qur'an into English was that of Muḥammad Asad. Muḥammad Asad (1900–92) is the Muslim-Arabic name of an Austrian journalist born as Leopold Weiss, grandson of a rabbi from Lemberg. Weiss converted to Islam, was for a time a consultant of Ibn Saud, the King of Saudi Arabia, and in 1952 became the first representative of Pakistan at the United Nations. His translation (*The Message of the Qur'an. Translated and explained by Muhammad Asad* [Gibraltar: Dār al-Andalus, 1980]) was well received inside and outside the Muslim world. This version was in turn translated into Swedish, Turkish and German. The commentary is packed with erudite footnotes that do not always follow the well-trodden path of traditional Muslim exegesis.[69] For the powerful Salafī Saudi faction, the translation and its commentary apparently were too 'liberal', and the Islamic World League, dominated by Saudi Arabia, banned it in 1974.[70]

The advent of Zionism and the creation of the State of Israel (1948) have made translations of the Qur'an into Hebrew and translations of the Qur'an by Jews a special case. To the best of my knowledge, there are four printed Hebrew translations of the Qur'an:

1. Zvi Hayyim (Hermann) Reckendorf (1825–75), *Al-Qor'ān o ha-Miqra. Der Korân aus dem Arabischen ins Hebräische übersetzt und erläutert* (Leipzig: Gerhard, 1857).[71]
2. Joseph Joel Rivlin (1889–1971), *Al-Qor'ān. Tirgem mi-ʿaravit Joseph Joel Rivlin*, 2 vols. (Tel Aviv: Devir, 1936; further editions: 1963, 1972 and 1987);[72]
3. Aharon Ben-Shemesh (b. 1899), *Ha-Qor'ān ha-qadosh, Sefer ha-Sefarim shel ha-Islam. Tirgem miʿaravit Aharon Ben-Shemesh* (Ramat Gan: Massada, 1971, further edition 1978);[73]

4. Uri Rubin, *Ha-Qor'ān. Tirgem mi-'aravit Uri Rubin* (Tel Aviv: Tel Aviv University, 2005).[74]

The Egyptian scholar 'Āmir al-Zanātī al-Jābirī (b. 1969, Associate Professor at the Hebrew Department at Ayn Shams University) read a paper at a congress in Medina in 2006 under the title 'Sūrat Ṭāhā fī'l-tarjama al-'ibriyya li-ma'ānī al-Qur'ān al-karīm'[75] and has nothing but praise for Joel Rivlin's translation. Al-Jābirī emphasises that Rivlin had taken the Hebrew national poet Chaim Nachman Bialik (1873–1934), who became an Israeli national poet after 1948, as his linguistic and stylistic model. Al-Jābirī states that Bialik had at first himself tried to participate in translating the Qur'an into Hebrew, but had later given up this idea. According to al-Jābirī – following the *Enyclopaedia Judaica* (1963) and its entry *Rivlin, Joseph Joel* – Rivlin started with a new translation, trying to downplay Bialik's model. Bialik's linguistic influence on Rivlin's translation of the Qur'an into Hebrew is an interesting parallel to Bialik's literary influence on the early Arabic poetry of Palestinian Maḥmūd Darwīsh (d. 2010).[76] Al-Jābirī recommends the Biblical tone of the Hebrew translation which – he says – is the most appropriate for the Qur'an. He also praises Rivlin's spirit of tolerance, because his translation attacks neither the Qur'an nor Islam and because Rivlin criticises 'Reckendorf's imprecise translation'. According to al-Jābirī, Rivlin has to be considered a great friend of Arabic literature, because he also translated Ibn Hishām's *Biography of the Prophet Muhammad*, the *Arabian Nights* and Ignaz Goldziher's *Lectures on Islam* into Hebrew. Rivlin, who was born in Jerusalem, had taken his doctorate in Frankfurt am Main in 1923. His dissertation dealt with 'Law in the Qur'an: Cult and Rite' ('Gesetz im Koran: Kultus und Ritus'). Sasson Somekh (b. 1933 in Baghdad), one of the best-known Israeli specialists in modern Arabic literature, called Rivlin's translation of the Qur'an 'the most important work of translation from Arabic into Hebrew in the 20th century'.[77] Al-Jābirī finally announces in his article that he intends to correct the mistakes of the existing Hebrew translations of the Qur'an and to pave the way for a complete 'Islamic' translation of the Qur'an into Hebrew. It is likely that this will be a translation sponsored by the King Fahd Complex.

A second contribution in the Medina congress dealt with Uri Rubin's translation: Muḥammad Maḥmūd Abū Ghadīr's paper, 'Tarjamat Uri Rubin li-maʿāni al-Qurʾān al-karīm bi'l-ʿibriyya (ʿarḍ wa-taqwīm)'.[78] The author (b. 1942) is or was Professor of Hebrew at Al-Azhar University and his stance is biased by a mainly political and polemical approach. According to Abū Ghadīr, Uri Rubin had produced his new translation of the Qur'an because Rivlin's translation no longer fitted the *zeitgeist* of modern Israel.[79] Furthermore, Abū Ghadīr states that Uri Rubin's translation cannot be but a failure because the Hebrew language is limited when compared to Arabic and therefore can never reflect the rhetorical splendour of Arabic. To support this, Abū Ghadīr quotes an article written by the Israeli Arabist Joseph Sadan: 'Eight hundred years of translation of the Qur'an. The book that must not be [or: cannot be] translated.'[80] Abū Ghadīr finds fault with the fact that Rubin does not accept that the Qur'an is a revealed book, but considers it a creation of Muhammad. Rubin, he says, is therefore guilty of sowing doubt in the minds of Muslims with regard to the authenticity of the Qur'anic message. He also accuses Rubin of using events such as the Al-Aqsa Intifada in 2000, the attack of 9/11, the US invasion of Afghanistan in 2001 and the US war on Iraq of 2003 to demonise Islam. According to Abū Ghadīr, Uri Rubin's biased translation is also intended to stop a growing movement of Jewish Israelis, mainly Israeli women, from converting to Islam. These conversions, according to Abū Ghadīr, are the result of their reading the Qur'an in Hebrew. Apparently, this refers to a number of Jewish Israeli women who are married to Muslim Palestinians.

Conclusions

Arabic-speaking Muslims are today a minority in the Muslim world, and their percentage is dwindling. This means that the vast majority, approximately three quarters of the Muslim world population, do not know Arabic. If they want to understand the Qur'an, they have to read it in translation. Furthermore, the pressure of growing Muslim missionary activities (*daʿwa*) will make translations of the Qur'an more and more necessary as well as more and more numerous. One of the implications of this is that translations of the Qur'an by Muslims will gradually outnumber those by non-Muslims. The disproportionally strong activity of Salafī- and Saudi-inspired translations will create a greater quantity, and is a result of Saudi financial and economic power.

However, in contrast, liberalising translations by diaspora Muslims, written by those who are in 'Western' societies and beyond the reach of Salafī-networks, will influence the more conventional autochthonous ones. The former will also become more and more divergent.

In conclusion, translations of the Qur'an have become an intra-Islamic battleground and an area of strong intra-religious competition. Theological, liturgical and political differences reach from minor discrepancies to profound cleavages. Verses in the Qur'an, such as the so-called sword-verse (Q. 9:5), can be taken out of context and forced into an often politically motivated one-dimensional scheme. Political expediency frequently triumphs over spirituality.

NOTES

1 Travis Zadeh, *The Vernacular Qur'an: Translation and the Rise of Persian Exegesis* (Oxford: Oxford University Press in association with the Institute of Ismaili Studies, 2012), pp. 194–8: 'A Foreign Qur'an?'.

2 Cf. Stefan Wild, 'An Arabic Recitation: The Meta-Linguistics of Qur'ānic Recitation' in idem, ed., *Self-Referentiality in the Qur'ān* (Wiesbaden: Harrassowitz, 2006), pp. 135–57.

3 Qur'an citations are from Arthur J. Arberry's translation, *The Koran Interpreted* (orig. pub. London: Allen & Unwin 1955).

4 Richard C. Martin, 'Inimitability', *EQ*, vol. 2 pp. 526–35.

5 Richard C. Martin, 'Createdness of the Qur'an', *EQ*, vol. 1, pp. 467–72.

6 William A. Graham and Navid Kermani, 'Recitation and Aesthetic Reception' in Jane Dammen McAuliffe, ed., *The Cambridge Companion to the Qur'ān* (Cambridge: Cambridge University Press, 2006), pp. 115–41, at p. 124.

7 Stefan Wild, 'Arabic *avant la lettre*. Divine, Prophetic, and Heroic Arabic' in Everard Ditters and Harald Motzki, eds, *Approaches to Arabic Linguistics. Presented to Kees Versteegh on the Occasion of his Sixtieth Birthday* (Leiden and Boston: Brill, 2007), pp. 189–208.

8 Josef van Ess, Theologie und Gesellschaft im 2. und 3. Jahrhundert Hidschra. Eine Geschichte des religiösen Denkens im Frühen Islam (Berlin: Walter de Gruyter, 1991–7), vol. 4, pp. 608–12.

9 Claude Gilliot, 'Informants', *EQ*, vol. 2 (2002), pp. 512–18.

10 Hava Lazarus-Yafeh, 'Taḥrīf', *EI*^{2}, vol. 10, pp. 111–12; Shari Lowin, 'Revision and Alteration', *EQ* vol. 4, pp 448–51; Gordon Darnell Newby, 'Forgery', *EQ*,

vol. 2, pp 242–4; and William B. Graham, 'Scripture in the Qur'an', *EQ*, vol. 4, pp. 558–69.

11 Zadeh, *The Vernacular Qur'an*, pp. 1–50.

12 Ibid., p. 10.

13 See J.J.G. Jansen, *The Interpretation of the Koran in Modern Egypt* (Leiden: Brill, 1974), pp. 35ff; and Nidhal Guessoum, 'The Qur'an, Science, and the (Related) Contemporary Muslim Discourse,' *Zygon* 43, no. 2 (2008), pp. 411–31.

14 Beate Wiesmüller, *Die vom Koran Getöteten. Aṯ-Ṯaʿlabīs* Qatlā l-Qurʾān *nach der Istanbuler und den Leidener Handschriften. Edition und Kommentar* (Würzburg: Ergon, 2001).

15 Abū ʿUthmān al-Jāḥiẓ, *Kitāb al-Ḥayawān* (Cairo: al-Maṭbaʿa al-Ḥamīdiyya, 1323–5/1905–7), vol. 1, pp. 74f. Quoted by Adonis, *An Introduction to Arab Poetics*, translated from the Arabic by Catherine Cobham (London: Saqi Books, 1990), pp. 36f.; originally published as *Introduction à la poétique arabe* (Paris: Sindbad, 1985).

16 Maḥmūd b. ʿUmar al-Zamakhsharī, *al-Kashshāf ʿan ḥaqāʾiq ghawāmiḍ al-tanzīl wa-ʿuyūn al-aqāwīl fī wujūh al-taʾwīl*, 2nd edn (Cairo: n.p., 1373/1953), vol. 4, p. 222.

17 Thomas Bauer, *Die Kultur der Ambiguität. Eine andere Geschichte des Islams* (Berlin: Verlag der Weltreligionen, 2011).

18 Fred Leemhuis, 'Readings of the Qur'an', *EQ*, vol. 4, pp. 352–63; see also Yasin Dutton, 'Orality, Literacy, and the "Seven *Aḥruf*" *Ḥadīth*', *Journal of Islamic Studies* 23, no. 1 (2013), pp. 1–49; Christopher Melchert, 'The Relation of the Ten Readings to One Another', *Journal of Qur'anic Studies* 10, no. 2 (2008), pp 73–87.

19 Graham and Kermani, 'Recitation and Aesthetic Reception', p. 120.

20 Zadeh, *The Vernacular Qur'an*, pp. 92–5.

21 Ibid., p. 113; and Abū Zakariyyāʾ al-Nawawī, *Kitāb al-Majmūʿ* (Cairo, Maṭbaʿat al-Taḍāmun, n.d.), p. 380.

22 Zamakhsharī, *Kashshāf*, at Q. 14:3; Hartmut Bobzin, 'Translations of the Qurʾān', *EQ*, vol. 5, pp. 340–58, at p. 341; Bauer, *Ambiguität*, p. 137, n. 12.

23 Muḥammad ʿAbduh and Rashīd Riḍā, *Tafsīr al-Manār* (Cairo: Maṭbaʿat al-Manār, 1344/1926).

24 Cf. Mohammed A.M. Abou Sheishaa: 'A Study of the Fatwa by Rashid Rida on the Translation of the Qur'an', *Journal of the Society for Qur'anic Studies* 1 (2001) and at http://www.islamicwritings.org/quran/language/a-study-of-the-fatwa-by-rashid-rida-on-the-translation-of-the-quran/: 'If the Qur'an is translated by a Turk, a Persian, an Indian, a Chinese, then differences will arise between these translations, such as those that exist between the books of the Christians, namely the Old and the New Testaments.'

25 Muḥammad Rashīd Riḍā, 'Tarjamat al-Qurʾān', *al-Manār* 11 (1907), pp. 268–74 and 25 (1924), pp. 794–6.

26 *Majallat al-Azhar* 24 (1953), p. 852; cf. also Abdelhamid Muhammad Ahmad, *Die Auseinandersetzung zwischen Al-Azhar und der modernistischen Bewegung in Ägypten* (Dissertation, University of Hamburg, 1963), Chapter 4: 'Al-Azhar und die Übersetzung des Korans 32–44'. Muḥammad Shākir had written a book *al-Qawl al-faṣl fī tarjamat al-Qurʾān al-karīm ilāʾl-lughāt al-aʿjamiyya*

(Cairo: Maṭbaʿat al-Nahḍa, 1343/1925) forbidding translations (see pp. 10ff.); first section (pp. 6–19) translated by Thomas Arnold as 'On the Translations of the Koran into Foreign Languages', *The Moslem World* 16, no. 2 (1926), pp. 161–5; cf. also the articles mentioned by August Fischer, 'Der Wert der vorhandenen Koranübersetzungen und Sure 111' in Rudi Paret, ed., *Der Koran* (Darmstadt: Wissenschaftliche Buchgesellschaft, 1975), pp. 3–10, at p. 4, n. 5.

27 Wolf-Dieter Lemke, *Maḥmūd Šaltūt (1893-1963) und die Reform der Azhar: Untersuchungen zu Erneuerungsbestrebungen im ägyptisch-islamischen Erziehungssystem* (Frankfurt am Main: Peter Lang, 1980), p. 97, n. 3.

28 Francine Costet-Tardieu, *Un réformiste à l'université al-Azhar: Œuvre et pensée de Mustafâ al-Marâghî (1881–1945)* (Cairo and Paris: CEDEJ and Karthala, 2005).

29 See Muḥammad Muṣṭafā al-Marāghī's book *Baḥth fī tarjamat al-Qur'ān wa aḥkāmihā* (Cairo: n.p., 1936); Ahmad, *Auseinandersetzung*, p. 38; also Lemke, *Maḥmūd Šaltūt*, pp. 111–15; J. Jomier, *Le Commentaire Coranique du Manâr: Tendances modernes de l'exégèse coranique en Égypte* (Paris: G.-P. Maisonneuve, 1954), particularly the chapter 'Le problème de la traduction du Coran d'après le Commentaire du Manar', pp. 338–47.

30 Muhammad Mustafa Al-Aʿzami, *The History of the Qur'ānic Text, from Revelation to Compilation: A Comparative Study with the Old and New Testaments* (Leicester: UK Islamic Academy, 2003), p. 10.

31 I have not been able to fully incorporate the findings of M. Brett Wilson's exhaustive study *Translating the Qur'an in an Age of Nationalism: Print Culture and Modern Islam in Turkey* (Oxford: Oxford University Press in association with the Institute of Ismaili Studies, 2014).

32 Muḥammad Rashīd Riḍā, *Mukhtārāt siyāsiyya min majallat al-Manār*, edited with an introduction by Wajīh Kawtharānī (Beirut: Dār al-Talīʿa, 1980), p. 150.

33 F. Lyman MacCallum, 'Turkey Discovers the Koran', *The Moslem World* 23 (1933), pp. 24–8; M. Brett Wilson, 'The First Translations of the Qur'an in Modern Turkey (1924–1938)', *The International Journal of Middle East Studies* 41 (2009), pp. 419–35; Hidayet Aydar, 'Kur'an: IX. Tercümesi', *Türkiye Diyanet Vakfı Islâm Ansiklopedisi* (Ankara: Türkiye Diyanet Vakfı, 1988-2013), vol. 26, pp. 404–9.

34 Bobzin, 'Translations of the Qur'an', p. 342.

35 MacCallum, 'Turkey Discovers the Koran', pp. 24f.

36 Arnoud Vrolijk, *Een Turks alphabet op latijnse grondslag: De alfabethervorming in Turkije 1928–1998* (Leiden: Legatum Warnerianum, 1998), p. 81.

37 MacCallum, 'Turkey Discovers the Koran', p. 25.

38 *Milliyet*, 27 January 1932 according to MacCallum, 'Turkey Discovers the Koran', p. 26.

39 Wilson, *Translating the Qur'an*, p. 148.

40 For a more detailed analysis see ibid., pp. 184–220: 'Caliph and Qur'an: English Translations, Egypt and the Search for a Centre'.

41 Jansen, *The Interpretation of the Koran*, pp. 46ff., 78f.

42 Muṣṭafā Ṣabrī, *Mas'alat tarjamat al-Qur'ān* (Cairo: Maṭbaʿa al-Salāfiyya, 1351/1932 3), pp. 146.

43 Cf. Nicholas Birch, 'Turkey: Proliferation of Koran Translations Pushing Turks to "Verge of Division"', http://www.eurasianet.org/node/62703, posted 12 January 2011.

44 Elmalılı Muhammed Hamdi Yazır, *Hak dini Kur'an Dili: Yeni Mealli Türkçe Tefsir* (Istanbul: Matbaa-i Ebüzziya, 1935–39). Cf. Ahmet Karamustafa, 'Elmalılı Muhammed Hamdi Yazır's (1878–1942) Philosophy of Religion', *Archivum Ottomanicum* 19 (2001), pp. 273–9, and Wilson, *Translating the Qur'an*, pp. 226–8, 234–9.

45 All three quotes from Murat Yazıcı, 'Turkey: Proliferation of Koran Translation', http://www.marifah.net, posted 23 January 2011; cf. also Birch, 'Turkey', p. 28.

46 Ali Özek, *Tarjamat ma'ānī al-Qur'ān al-karīm al-ṣādira fī mujamma' al-malik Fahd li-ṭibā'at al-muṣḥaf al-sharīf bi'l-Madīna al-munawwara ḥattā nihāyat 'ām 1425/2004* (Medina: n.p., n.d.), p. 13.

47 Bobzin, 'Translations of the Qur'an', pp. 340f.

48 Zadeh, *The Vernacular Qur'an*, pp. 253–301: 'Early Persian Translations of the Qur'an'.

49 Wilson, *Translating the Qur'an*, pp. 55ff.

50 Fred Leemhuis, 'From Palm Leaves to the Internet' in Jane Dammen McAuliffe, ed., *The Cambridge Companion to the Qur'ān* (Cambridge: Cambridge University Press, 2006), pp. 145–61, at p. 156.

51 Abdur Rahim Kidwai, 'A Survey of English Translations of the Quran', *The Muslim World Book Review* 7, no. 4 (1987), pp. 66–71.

52 This and the following English quotes of Benedict's lecture in German are my translations from: Benedikt XVI. *Glaube und Vernunft. Die Regensburger Vorlesung.* Vollständige Ausgabe. Kommentiert von Gesine Schwan, Adel Theodor Khoury, Karl Kardinal Lehmann (Freiburg: Herder, 2006).

53 Wolfgang Krebs, *Das Papstzitat von Regensburg. Benedikt XVI im 'Kampf der Kulturen'* (Berlin: Rhombos-Verlag, 2007).

54 Marmaduke Pickthall, *The Meaning of the Glorious Koran. An Explanatory Translation*, 1st edn (New York: A.A. Knopf, 1930); cf. Bobzin, 'Translations of the Qur'an', p. 343; Khaleel Mohammed, 'Assessing English Translations of the Qur'an', *Middle East Quarterly* 12 (Spring 2005), pp. 58–71 and at http://www.meforum.org/717/assessing-english-translations-of-the-quran. It is interesting to compare Khaleel Mohammed's essay with the earlier one by Kidwai, 'A Survey of English Translations of the Quran'. Both are written by Muslims living outside the Islamic World. Khaleel Mohammed is a liberal thinker, Abdur Rahim Kidwai a staunch traditionalist. For Kidwai, most translations done by non-Sunni Muslims are nothing but examples of 'the strong sectarian biases of their translators'.

55 Pickthall, tr. *The Meaning of the Glorious Koran*, p. vii; also quoted in the Introduction to M.A.S. Abdel Haleem, tr. *The Qur'an. A New Translation* (Oxford: Oxford University Press, 2004), p. xxviii.

56 Pickthall, tr. *The Meaning of the Glorious Koran*, p. vii.

57 Mohammed, 'Assessing English Translations of the Qur'an', p. 61.

58 This element of competition can be seen in the publishing history of both organisations, see İsmet Binark *et al.*, *The World Bibliography of the Translations of the Meanings of the Holy Quran* (Istanbul: OIC Research Center, 1986). I have discussed the issue of different translations into English adopted by

al-Azhar and the King Fahd Complex in greater detail in Stefan Wild, 'Muslim Translations and Translators of the Qur'an into English' in Johanna Pink (guest-editor), *Journal of Qur'anic Studies* 17, no. 3 (2015, forthcoming).

59 The website of the King Fahd Complex can be found at http://www.qurancomplex.org/ (last accessed 23 April 2014).

60 Kidwai, 'A Survey of English Translations of the Quran', p. 66.

61 Mohammed, 'Assessing English Translations of the Qur'an', p. 64.

62 Taqi ud-Din al-Hilali and Muhammad Muhsin Khan, *The Noble Qur'ān in the English Language: A Summarized Version of At-Tabari, Al-Qurtubi, and Ibn Kathir with Comments from Sahih al-Bukhari* (Riyadh: Darussalam, 1996).

63 Taqi ud-Din al-Hilali and Muhammad Muhsin Khan, *The Noble Qur'ān: English Translation of the Meanings and Commentary* (Medina: King Fahd Complex for the Printing of the Holy Qur'an, 1420/1999–2000).

64 Abdullah Yusuf Ali, *The Holy Qur-ān: English Translation of the Meanings and Commentary. Revised and Edited by the Presidency of Islamic Researchers, Ifta, Call and Guidance* (Medina: King Fahd Holy Qur'an Printing Complex, 1410/1989–90); see Wild, 'Muslim Translations and Translators of the Qur'an into English'.

65 Mohammed, 'Assessing English Translations of the Qur'an', p. 65.

66 al-Hilali and Khan, *The Noble Qur'ān* (Medina: 2006), on Q. 1:6–7.

67 Abdel Haleem, tr., *The Qur'an*, p. xxviii.

68 Ibid.

69 Mohammed, 'Assessing English Translations of the Qur'an', pp. 65–6.

70 Reinhard Schulze, *Islamischer Internationalismus im 20. Jahrhundert. Untersuchungen zur Islamischen Weltliga* (Leiden: Brill, 1990), p. 334, n. 59; see also Mohammed, 'Assessing English Translations of the Qur'an', p. 66, who cites 'creedal issues'. These were most likely the nature of the Qur'anic *jinn* or the question of whether the Prophet's night-journey was a mystical vision or a real journey.

71 'Al-Qur'ān or The Book translated from the Arabic into Hebrew'. Hermann Reckendorf's (1825–75) son (1863–1925), bearing the same name, was the author of the famous *Arabische Syntax* (Heidelberg: C. Winter, 1921).

72 'Al-Qur'an. Translated from the Arabic by Joseph Joel Rivlin'.

73 'The Holy Qur'an. The Book of Books of Islam, Translated from the Arabic by Aharon Ben-Shemesh.'

74 'The Qur'an. Translated from the Arabic by Uri Rubin'. Cf. also Eve Woogen, 'The Best of Stories: Yusuf as Joseph in Hebrew Translations of the Qur'an' (2012). Classics Honors Projects. Paper 15, http://digitalcommons.macalester.edu/classics_honors/15.

75 'Āmir al-Zanātī al-Jābirī, 'Sūrat Ṭāhā fī'l-tarjama al-'ibriyya li-ma'ānī al-Qur'ān al-karīm' ('Surah 20 in the Hebrew Translations of the Meanings of the Noble Qur'an') in *Nadwat al-Qur'ān al-karīm fī'l-dirāsāt al-istishrāqiyya* (Medina: 7–9 November 2006).

76 Maḥmūd Darwīsh, who was fluent in Hebrew, was in his early poetic work influenced by the Hebrew Bible and Bialik's nationalist poetry. Cf. Muhammad Siddiq, 'Significant but Problematic Others: Negotiating "Israelis" in the Works of Mahmoud Darwish', *Comparative Literature Studies* 47, no. 4 (2010), pp. 487–503.

77 Sasson Somekh, *Arabic Literature in Hebrew: Translations and Research in Israel* (Tel Aviv: Bulletin of Israel PEN Centre, August 1971).
78 Muḥammad Maḥmūd Abū Ghadīr, 'Tarjamat Uri Rubin li-maʿāni al-Qur'ān al-karīm bi'l-ʿibriyya (ʿarḍ wa-taqwīm)' in *Nadwat al-Qur'ān al-karīm*.
79 Cf. Hayyim Leshem, *Ha-Qor'ān be-targum ʿivrit ḥadash* (Tel Aviv: n.p., 1993) and Sason Somekh, 'Ha-Qor'ān be-ʿivrit', *Yediʿōt aḥarōnōt*, 12 March 1971.
80 J. Sadan, "Al 800 shanah shel targum ha-Qor'ān. Ha-ṣefer she asūr le-targamo', in *Ha-aretz*, 11 September 2005.

Bibliography

This is a comprehensive bibliography of the sources used for the articles in this volume, but Internet links are not given. An asterisk next to a source denotes that a URL is given in the relevant chapter. Whenever a work is cited only as (MS), references to *GAL* are given in the chapter. Authors have often used different editions of the same primary source; these are listed in the same entry, separated by a semicolon. When different editions have the same title, it has not been repeated in the entry. Variant titles are listed after the semicolon.

Each edition or translation is followed by the initials of the author who has used it, in square brackets, as follows: Chapter 1: Stephen Burge [SB – Intr]; Chapter 2: Kees Versteegh [KV]; Chapter 3: Herbert Berg [HB]; Chapter 4: Christopher Melchert [CM]; Chapter 5: Claude Gilliot [CG]; Chapter 6: Stephen Burge [SB]; Chapter 7: Devin Stewart [DS]; Chapter 8: Toby Mayer [TM]; Chapter 9: Agostino Cilardo [AC]; Chapter 10: Ayesha Chaudhry [ACh]; Chapter 11: M. Brett Wilson [BW]; Chapter 12: Travis Zadeh [TZ]; Chapter 13: Stefan Wild [SW]

Translations of the Qur'an

Abdel Haleem, M.A.S., tr. *The Qur'an: A New Translation*. Oxford: Oxford University Press, 2004. [SB] [SW]

Ali, Abdullah Yusuf, tr. *The Holy Qur'an: Translation and Commentary*. Lahore: 1934–7. [CG]; rev. edn, *The Holy Qur-ān: English Translation of the Meanings and Commentary. Revised and Edited by the Presidency of Islamic Researchers, Ifta, Call and Guidance*. Medina: King Fahd Holy Qur'an Printing Complex, 1410/1989–90. [SW]; *The Holy Qur'ān*, repr. London: Wordsworth, 2000. [SB] [ACh]; *The Meaning of the Holy Qur'ān: Qur'ānic Text (Arabic) with Revised English Translation, Commentary and Index*, 11th edn. Beltsville: Amana Publications, 1427/2006. [SB – Intr]; *The Holy Qur'ān: Text, Translation and Commentary*. Lahore: Shaikh Muhammad Asraf. [AC]

Arberry, Arthur J., tr. *The Koran Interpreted*. London: Allen & Unwin and New York: Macmillan, 1955. [SB] [ACh] [CG] [SW]; New York, NY: Macmillan, 1986. [BW]; Oxford: Oxford University Press, 1998. [SB – Intr] [SB]

Asad, Muhammad, tr. *The Message of the Quran: Translated and Explained*. Gibraltar: Dar al-Andalus, 1980. [BW]

Bakhtiar, Laleh, tr. *The Sublime Quran: Based on the Hanafi, Maliki and Shafii Schools of Law*. Chicago, IL: islamicworld.com, 2007. [SB – Intr]

Ben-Shemesh, Aharon, tr. *Ha-Qor'ān ha-qadosh, Sefer ha-Sefarim shel ha-Islam*. Ramat Gan: Massada, 1971; 1978. [SW]

Blachère, Régis, tr. *Le Coran*. Paris: Maisonneuve-Besson, 1957; orig. pub. 1949–50. [CG]

Fani, Şeyh Muhsin-i (Hüseyin Kâzım Kadri). *Nurü'l-Beyan: Kur'an-i Kerim'in Türkçe Tercümesi*. Istanbul: Matbaa-i Amire, 1924. [BW]

al-Hilali, Taqi-ud-Din, and Muhammad Muhsin Khan, tr. *The Noble Qur'ān in the English Language: A Summarized Version of At-Tabari, Al-Qurtubi, and Ibn Kathir with Comments from Sahih al-Bukhari*. Riyadh: Darussalam, 1996. [SB – Intr] [SW]; *The Noble Qur'ān: English Translation of the Meanings and Commentary*. Medina: King Fahd Complex for the Printing of the Holy Qur'an, 1420/1999–2000. [SW]; *The Noble Qur'ān*. Medina: 2006.* [SB – Intr] [SW]

Jones, Alan, tr. *The Qur'ān: Translated into English*. [Cambridge:] Gibb Memorial Trust, 2007. [CM]

Khalidi, Tarif, tr. *The Qur'ān*. London: Penguin, 2008. [SB]

Khatib, M.M., tr. *The Bounteous Koran*. London: Macmillan, 1986. [CM]

Paret, Rudi, tr. *Der Koran*. Stuttgart: Kohlhammer, 1962. [CG]

Pickthall, Marmaduke, tr. *The Meaning of the Glorious Koran. An Explanatory Translation*, 1st edn. New York and London: A.A. Knopf, 1930. [CG] [BW] [SW]; *The Meaning of the Glorious Quran: Text and Explanatory Translation*. Elmhurst, NY: Tahrike Tarsile Qur'an, 1999. [DS]

Reckendorf, Herman, tr. *Al-Qor'ān o ha-Miqra: Der Korân aus dem Arabischen ins Hebräische übersetzt und erläutert*. Leipzig: Gerhard, 1857. [SW]

Rivlin, Joseph Joel, tr. *Al-Qor'ān*, 1st edn, 2 vols. Tel Aviv: Devir, 1936; further edns publ. 1963, 1972 and 1987. [SW]

Rodwell, J.M., tr. *The Koran*, repr. London: Everyman, 1994. [SB]

Rubin, Uri, tr. *Ha-Qor'ān*. Tel Aviv: Tel Aviv University, 2005. [SW]

Rückert, Friedrich, tr. *Der Koran*, ed. Hartmut Bobzin, 3rd edn. Würzburg: Ergon, 2000; orig. pub. Frankfurt am Main: n.p., 1888. [CG]

Sale, George, tr. *The Korân*, repr. London: Frederick Warne & Co., n.d; orig. publ. London: n.p., 1734. [SB]

Primary Sources

'Abd al-Raḥmān Ḥasan. 'Tarjamat al-Qur'ān ilā'l-lughāt al-ajnabiyya', *al-Ahrām*, issue 18431 (4 April 1936), pp. 1–2. [TZ]

'Abd al-Razzāq b. Hammām al-Ṣan'ānī. *al-Muṣannaf*, ed. Ḥabīb al-Raḥmān al-A'ẓamī. Karachi and Johannesburg: al-Majlis al-'Ilmī, 1390–92/1970–72. [AC] [CM]; 11 vols. Beirut: al-Maktab al-Islāmī, 1983. [HB] [DS] [TZ]

——. *Tafsīr*, ed. Maḥmūd Muḥammad 'Abduh. Beirut: Dār al-Kutub al-'Ilmiyya, 1999. [KV]

'Abduh, Muḥammad, and Rashīd Riḍā. *Tafsīr al-Manār*. Cairo: Maṭba'at al-Manār, 1344/1926. [SW]; 2nd edn, 12 vols. 1366/1947. [TZ]

Abū 'Alī, al-Fārisī. *al-Ḥujja fī'l-qurrā' al-sab'a*, ed. 'Alī al-Najdī Nāṣif *et al.*, 7 vols. Cairo: al-Hay'a al-Miṣriyya, 1403/1983. [CG]; ed. Badr al-Dīn al-Qahwajī, Bashīr Juwayjātī *et al.* Damascus: Dār al-Ma'mūn li'l-Turāth, 1404–19/1984–99. [CG]

Abū Dāwūd al-Sijistānī. *Sunan*, 1 vol in 2 pts, vol. 5 of *Mawsūʿat al-ḥadīth al-sharīf, jamʿ jawāmiʿ al-aḥādīth*, 10 vols. Vaduz: Jamʿiyyat al-Maknaz al-Islāmī, 2000–1. [TZ]

Abū Daqīqa, Maḥmūd. 'Kalima fī tarjamat al-Qurʾān al-Karīm', *Nūr al-Islām* 3, no. 1 (1351/1932), pp. 29–35. [TZ]

Abū'l-Faraj al-Iṣfahānī. *Kitāb al-Aghānī*. Cairo: Dār al-Kutub, 1927–74. [CG]

Abū Ḥanīfa al-Nuʿmān b. Thābit. *Risālat al-Farāʾiḍ*; ed. Agostino Cilardo in 'Un antico documento di diritto ereditario musulmano', *Annali dell'Istituto Orientale di Napoli* 42 (1982), pp. 103–26. [AC]

Abū Ḥātim al-Rāzī, Aḥmad b. Ḥamdān. *Kitāb al-Zīna fī'l-kalimāt al-islāmiyya al-ʿarabiyya*, ed. Ḥusayn b. Fayḍ Allāh al-Hamdānī al-Yaʿburī al-Ḥarrāzī, 2 vols. in 1. Cairo: Maṭbaʿat al-Risāla, 1957–8. [CG]

Abū Ḥayyān al-Andalusī al-Gharnāṭī. *Tafsīr al-baḥr al-muḥīṭ*. Beirut: Dār al-Kutub al-ʿIlmiyya, 1996. [ACh]

——. *Tuḥfat al-arīb bi-mā fī'l-Qurʾān min al-gharīb*, ed. Aḥmad Maṭlūb and Khadīja al-Ḥadīthī. Baghdad: Maṭbaʿat al-ʿĀnī, 1397/1977. [SB]

Abū'l-Layth al-Samarqandī. *Khizānat al-fiqh wa ʿUyūn al-masāʾil*, ed. Ṣalāḥ al-Dīn al-Nāhī, 2 vols. Baghdad: Sharikat al-Ṭabʿ wa'l-Nashr al-Ahliyya, 1385–6/1965–7. [AC]

——. *Tafsīr*, ed. ʿAbd al-Raḥmān al-Zaqqa, 3 vols. Baghdad: Maṭbaʿat al-Irshād, 1985–6. [SB]

Abū Nuʿaym al-Iṣfahānī. *Ḥilyat al-awliyāʾ wa ṭabaqāt al-aṣfiyāʾ*, 10 vols. Cairo: Maktabat al-Khānjī, 1352–7/1932–8. [CM]; 11 vols. Beirut: Dār al-Kutub al-ʿIlmiyya, 1988. [DS]

Abū ʿUbayd al-Bakrī. *Simṭ al-laʾālī fī sharḥ Amāli al-Qālī*, ed. ʿAbd al-ʿAzīz al-Maymanī. Cairo: Lajnat al-Taʾlīf wa'l-Tarjama wa'l-Nashr, 1936. [CG]

Abū ʿUbayd al-Qāsim b. Sallām. *al-Khuṭab wa'l-mawāʿiẓ*, ed. Ramaḍān ʿAbd al-Tawwāb. Cairo: Maktabat al-Thaqāfa al-Dīniyya, 1406/1986. [CM]

——. *al-Gharīb al-muṣannaf*, ed. Ramaḍān ʿAbd al-Tawwāb. Cairo: Maktabat al-Thaqāfa al-Dīniyya, 1989. [CG]; ed. Muḥammad al-Mukhtār al-ʿUbaydī, 2 vols. Tunis: n.p., 1416/1996. [CG]

Abū ʿUbayda. *Majāz al-Qurʾān*, ed. Fuʾād Sazgīn [Fuat Sezgin], 2 vols. Cairo: Muḥammad Sāmī Amīn al-Khānjī, 1954–62. [CG] [KV]; repr. Beirut: Muʾassasat al-Risāla, 1401/1981. [CG]; ed. Aḥmad Farīd al-Mazīdī. Beirut: Dār al-Kutub al-ʿIlmiyya, 2006. [SB – Intr] [SB]

al-Akhfash al-Awsaṭ. *Maʿānī al-Qurʾān*, ed. Fāʾiz Fāris, 2 vols, repr. al-Ṣafāt, Kuwait: n.p., 1981; orig. pub. 1979. [CG]; ed. ʿAbd al-Amīr Muḥammad Amīn al-Ward. Beirut: ʿĀlam al-Kutub, 1405/1985. [CG]

Akseki, Ahmet Hamdi. 'Cevabı Mı? İtirafı Mı?' *Sebilürreşad* 24, no. 600 (1924), pp. 23–6. [BW]

ʿAlī, Muḥammad. [Speech.] Reproduced in 'Ḥawl tarjamat al-Qurʾān al-Karīm', *al-Ahrām*, issue 18441 (16 April 1936), p. 1. [TZ]

ʿAllūba Pāshā, ʿAlī Muḥammad. *Dhikrayāt ijtimāʿiyya wa siyāsiyya*, ed. Aḥmad Najīb Aḥmad Ḥamadī, Jamāl al-Dīn Amīn Muhannā and Nāhid Muṣṭafā Marzūq. Cairo: Markaz Wathāʾiq wa Tārīkh Miṣr al-Muʿāṣir, 1988. [TZ]

Antebi, Mehmet, and İsmail Ferruh. *Tefsir-i Tibyan ve Tefsir-i Mevakib* [published together in one volume]. Dersaadet: Şirket-i Sahafiye-yi Osmaniye, 1902. [BW]

al-Ashʿarī, Abū'l-Ḥasan. *Maqālāt al-islāmiyyīn*, ed. Helmut Ritter, 2 vols. Leipzig: Brockhaus in Komm, 1929–33. [TZ]

al-Aṣmaʿī, ʿAbd al-Malik b. Qurayb. *Dīwān al-Aṣmaʿiyyāt*, ed. Muḥammad Nabīl Ṭarīfī, repr. Beirut: Dār Ṣādir, 1425/2005; orig. pub. 1423/2002. [CG]

Aṭfayyish, Muḥammad b. Yūsuf. *Sharḥ al-Nīl wa shifāʾ al-ʿalīl*, 10 vols. Cairo: n.p., 1343/1925. [AC]

al-Azharī, Muḥammad b. Aḥmad. *Maʿānī al-qirāʾāt*, ed. Muṣṭafā Darwīsh and ʿAwaḍ b. Ḥamad al-Qawzī, 3 vols. Cairo: Maṭābiʿ Dār al-Maʿārif, 1991–3. [CG]

——. *Tahdhīb al-lugha*, ed. ʿAbd al-Ḥalīm al-Najjār, *et al.*, 15 vols. Cairo: al-Muʾassasa al-Miṣriyya al-ʿĀmma li'l-Taʾlīf, 1964–7. [CG]

al-Barqī. *Kitāb al-Maḥāsin*, ed. Jalāl al-Dīn al-Ḥusaynī. Tehran: Dār al-Kutub al-Islāmiyya, 1370; repr. Najaf: al-Maṭbaʿa al-Ḥaydariyya, 1384/1964. [CM]

al-Basīwī, Abū'l-Ḥasan ʿAlī b. Muḥammad. *al-Mukhtaṣar*; tr. Ignazio Guidi as 'Il diritto ereditario musulmano secondo la dottrina degli arabi ibaditi di Zanzibar e dell'Africa Orientale', *Rivista Coloniale* (1906), pp. 173–96 and 335–87. [AC]

al-Bayḍāwī, ʿAbd Allāh b. ʿUmar. *Anwār al-tanzīl wa asrār al-taʾwīl*. Cairo: Muṣṭafā al-Bābī al-Ḥalabī, 1968. [SB]

al-Bayhaqī, Abū Bakr Aḥmad. *al-Jāmiʿ li-shuʿab al-īmān*, ed. ʿAbd al-ʿAlī ʿAbd al-Ḥamīd Ḥāmid, 14 vols. Riyadh: Maktabat al-Rushd, 2003. [TZ]

——. *al-Sunan al-kubrā*, 10 vols. Hyderabad: n.p., 1354–6/1925–7. [AC]

Bint al-Shāṭiʾ, ʿĀʾisha ʿAbd al-Raḥmān. *al-Iʿjāz al-bayānī li'l-Qurʾān wa Masāʾil Ibn al-Azraq*. Cairo: Dār al-Maʿārif, 1971. [DS]

al-Biqāʿī, Ibrāhīm b. ʿUmar b. Ḥasan Burhān al-Dīn. *Naẓm al-durar fī tanāsub al-āyāt wa'l-suwar*. Hyderabad: Maṭbaʿat Majlis Dāʾirat al-Maʿārif al-ʿUthmāniyya, 1972. [ACh]; ed. ʿAbd al-Razzāq Ghālib al-Mahdī, 8 vols. Beirut: Dār al-Kutub al-ʿIlmiyya, 1415/1995. [CG]

al-Bīrūnī, Abū'l-Rayḥān. *Kitāb al-Ṣaydana fī'l-ṭibb*, ed. ʿAbbās Zaryāb. Tehran: Markaz-i Nashr-i Dānishgāhī, 1991. [TZ]

Börekçi, Rifat. 'Beyan-ı Hakikat Müslümanlara', *Sebilürreşad* 24, no. 599 (1924), p. 8. [BW]

al-Bukhārī, ʿAbd al-ʿAzīz b. Aḥmad. *Kashf al-asrār*, ed. ʿAbd Allāh Maḥmūd Muḥammad ʿUmar, 4 vols. Beirut: Dār al-Kutub al-ʿIlmiyya, 1997. [TZ]

al-Bukhārī, Muhammad b. Ismāʿīl. *al-Adab al-mufrad*, ed. Samīr b. Amīn al-Zuhayrī, 2 vols. Riyadh: Maktabat al-Maʿārif, 1419/1998. [CG]

——. *Kitāb al-Taʾrīkh al-kabīr*, 8 vols. Hyderabad: Maṭbaʿat Jamʿiyya Dāʾirat al-Maʿārif al-ʿUthmāniyya, 1360–64. [CM]; repr. 1377/1958. [CM]; repr. with added index vol. Beirut: Dār al-Kutub al-ʿIlmiyya, n.d. [CM]

——. *Ṣaḥīḥ al-Bukhārī*, ed. Ludolf Krehl. Leiden: Brill, 1862–1908. [CG]; ed. Muḥammad Muḥammad ʿAbd al-Laṭīf, 24 vols. Cairo: n.p., 1351–6/1932–8. [AC]; ed. Qāsim al-Shammāʿī al-Rifāʿī. Beirut: Dār al-Qalam, 1987. [HB]; tr. Octave Houdas and William Marçais as el-Bokhâri, *Les Traditions islamiques*, 4 vols. Paris: Adrien Maisonneuve, 1977; orig. publ. 1903–14. [CG] al-Bukhārī, Tāj al-Sharī'a Abū 'Abd Allāh 'Umar. *Nihāyat al-kifāya fī dirāyat al-Hidāya*, as a marginal commentary in al-Marghīnānī, *al-Hidāya*, ed. Mawlānā Muḥammad 'Abd al-Aḥad, 2 vols. Delhi: Maṭba' al-Mujtabā'ī, 1332–4/1914–16. [TZ]

al-Ḍaḥḥāk b. Muzāḥim. *Tafsīr al-Ḍaḥḥāk: Jam' wa dirāsa wa taḥqīq*, ed. Muḥammad Shukrī al-Zāwiyyatī. Cairo: Dār al-Salāma, 1419/1999. [KV]

al-Dāraquṭnī, 'Alī b. 'Umar. *al-Sunan*, ed. 'Abd Allāh Hāshim Yamānī al-Madanī, 4 vols. Medina: n.p., 1386/1966. [AC]

al-Dārimī, Abū Muḥammad 'Abd Allāh b. 'Abd al-Raḥmān. *al-Sunan* (also known as *al-Musnad al-jāmi'*). Damascus: Maṭba'at al-I'tidāl, 1349. [CM]; ed. 'Abd Allāh Hāshim Yamānī al-Madanī, 2 vols. Cairo: n.p., 1386/1966. [AC]

Dhahabī, Muḥammad b. Aḥmad Shams al-Dīn. *Siyar a'lām al-nubalā'*, ed. Shu'ayb al-Arna'ūṭ *et al.*, 25 vols. Beirut: Mu'assasat al-Risāla, 1401–9/1981–8. [CG]

——. *Ta'rīkh al-islām wa ṭabaqāt al-mashāhīr wa'l-a'lām*, ed. Bashshār 'Awwād Ma'rūf, 17 vols. Beirut: Dār al-Gharb al-Islāmī, 1424/2003. [CG]

Fani, Şeyh Muhsin-i (Hüseyin Kâzım Kadri). 'Diyanet İşleri Riyasetinin "Beyan-ı Hakikat"' Unvanlı Makalesine Cevap' in *Nurü'l-Beyan*, Appendix, pp. 2–7. [BW]

——. 'Hazret Şeyh'ın Sebil'e İlk ve Son Cevabı', *Sebilürreşad* 24, no. 599 (1924), p. 8. [BW]

——. *İstikbale Doğru*. Istanbul: Ahmed İhsan ve Şürekası Matbaacılık Osmanlı Şirketi, 1913–14. [BW]

——. *Nurü'l-Beyan*. *See* Translations of the Qur'an, Fani, Şeyh Muhsin-i.

——. *see also* Kadri, Hüseyin Kâzım.

al-Farrā', Abū Zakariyyā' Yaḥyā b. Ziyād al-Kūfī. *Ma'ānī al-Qur'ān*, ed. Aḥmad Yūsuf Najātī and Muḥammad 'Alī al-Najjār. Cairo: Maṭba'at Dār al-Kutub al-Miṣriyya, 1955. [HB] [CG]; repr. Beirut: 'Ālam al-Kutub, 1980. [CG]; repr., 1983. [BW]

al-Fīrūzabādī, Muḥammad b. Ya'qūb. *al-Qāmūs al-muḥīṭ*. India: n.p., n.d. [SB – Intr] [SB]

——. (attrib.). *Tanwīr al-miqbās min tafsīr Ibn 'Abbās*, with, in the margin, Suyūṭī, *Kitāb Lubāb al-nuqūl fī asbāb al-nuzūl*, and Ibn Ḥazm, *Kitāb Fī ma'rifat al-nāsikh wa'l-mansūkh*. Cairo: Muṣṭafā al-Bābī al-Ḥalabī, 1370/1951. [CG]

Furāt b. Furāt al-Kūfī. *Tafsīr Furāt al-Kūfī*, ed. Muḥammad al-Kāẓim, 2 vols. Beirut: Mu'assasat al-Nu'mān, 1412/1992. [AC]; repr. Tehran: Mu'assasat al-Ṭab' wa'l-Nashr, Wizārat al-Thaqāfa wa'l-Irshād al-Islāmī, 1416/1995. [SB]

al-Ghazālī, Abū Ḥāmid Muḥammad b. Muḥammad. *Iḥyā' 'ulūm al-dīn*; tr. Nabih Amin Faris as *The Mysteries of Fasting – Iḥyā' 'ulūm al-dīn: Kitāb Asrār al-ṣawm*. Lahore: SH. Muhammad Ashraf, 1992. [BW]

al-Ḥajawī al-Tha'ālibī, Muḥammad b. al-Ḥasan. 'Tarjamat al-Qur'ān al-Karīm', *Majallat al-Azhar* 7, no. 3 (1355/1936), pp. 190–98. [TZ]

Ḥājjī Khalīfa. *Kashf al-ẓunūn 'an asāmī'l-kutub wa'l-funūn*, ed. Muḥammad Sharaf al-Dīn Yāltaqāyā and Rif'at Bīlka al-Kilīsī, 2 vols. Istanbul: Maṭābi' Wikālat al-Ma'ārif al-Jalīla, 1941. [TZ]; ed. and tr. Gustav Flügel as *Lexicon Bibliographicum et Encyclopaedicum*, 7 vols. Leipzig: Oriental Translation Fund of Great Britain and Ireland, 1835–58. [CG]

al-Ḥākim al-Naysābūrī. *al-Mustadrak ʿalā'l-Ṣaḥīḥayn*, ed. Abū ʿAbd al-Raḥmān al-Wādiʿī, 5 vols. Cairo: Dār al-Ḥaramayn, 1997. [TZ]

al-Harawī, Abū ʿUbayd. *Kitāb al-Gharībayn*, ed. Maḥmūd Muḥammad al-Tinaḥī. Cairo: Lajnat Iḥyāʾ al-Turāth al-Islāmī, 1970. [CG]

Harīdī, Faḍīlat al-Shaykh Aḥmad Muḥammad ʿAbd al-ʿĀl. 'Tarjamat al-Qurʾān wa tafsīruhu fī'l-ṣalāt mufsidun lahā' (25 April 1961), reprinted in *al-Fatāwā'l-islāmiyya min dār al-iftāʾ al-miṣriyya*. 2nd edn, 20 vols. Cairo: Jumhūriyyat Miṣr al-ʿArabiyya, 1997. [TZ]

Hārūn b. Mūsā al-Qāriʾ al-Aʿwar. *al-Wujūh wa'l-naẓāʾir fī'l-Qurʾān al-karīm*, ed. Ḥātim Ṣāliḥ al-Ḍāmin. Baghdad: Wizārat al-Thaqāfa, 1988. [DS]

al-Ḥaṣkafī, ʿAlāʾ al-Dīn. *al-Durr al-mukhtār*, ed. ʿAbd al-Munʿim Khalīl Ibrāhīm. Beirut: Dār al-Kutub al-ʿIlmiyya, 2002. [TZ]

al-Ḥillī, Jaʿfar b. al-Ḥasan. *Sharāʾiʿ al-islām fī masāʾil al-ḥalāl wa'l-ḥarām*, ed. ʿAbd al-Ḥusayn Muḥammad ʿAlī, 4 vols. Najaf: Maṭbaʿat al-Ādāb, 1389/1969. [AC]; tr. A. Querry as *Droit Musulman: Recueil de lois concernant les musulmans schyites*, 2 vols. Paris: Imprimerie Nationale, 1871–2. [AC]

Hūd b. Muḥakkam al-Hawwārī. *Tafsīr Kitāb Allāh al-ʿazīz*. Beirut: Dār al-Gharb al-Islāmī, 1990. [ACh]

al-Hujwīrī, Abū'l-Ḥasan. *Kashf al-maḥjūb*, ed. Maḥmūd ʿĀbidī. Tehran: Surūsh, 1383 Sh./2004–5. [TZ]

el-Hüseyni, Seyyid Süleyman. *Zübdet'ül-Beyan*. Istanbul: Amidi Matbaası, 1924. [BW]

Ibn ʿAbbās, ʿAbd Allāh (attrib.). *Masāʾil al-Imām al-Ṭastī ʿan asʾilat Nāfiʿ b. al-Azraq wa ajwibat ʿAbd Allāh Ibn ʿAbbās*, ed. ʿAbd al-Raḥmān ʿUmayra, 2 vols in 1. Cairo: Dār al-Iʿtiṣām, n.d. [CG]

——. *Masāʾil Nāfiʿ b. al-Azraq ʿan ʿAbd Allāh Ibn ʿAbbās* (MS Ẓāhiriyya; recension of Abū Bakr ʿAbd Allāh b. Jaʿfar al-Khuttalī), ed. Muḥammad A. al-Dālī. Limassol: Jaffān wa'l-Jābī, 1992. [CG]

Ibn al-ʿĀbidīn. *Radd al-muḥtār ʿalā'l-durr al-mukhtār*, ed. ʿĀdil Aḥmad ʿAbd al-Mawjūd and ʿAlī Muḥammad Muʿawwaḍ, 12 vols. Beirut: Dār al-Kutub al-ʿIlmiyya, 1994. [TZ]

Ibn Abī'l-Dunyā. *al-Zuhd*, ed. Yāsīn Muḥammad al-Sawwās. Damascus: Dār Ibn Kathīr, 1420/1999. [CM]

Ibn Abī Ḥātim al-Rāzī. *Tafsīr al-Qurʾān al-ʿaẓīm*, ed. Asʿad Muḥammad al-Ṭayyib, 10 vols. Mecca and Riyadh: al-Maktaba al-ʿArabiyya al-Saʿūdiyya, 1417/1997. [CG]; Mecca: Maktabat Nizār Muṣṭafā al-Bāz, 1419/1999. [CM]

Ibn Abī Shayba. *Kitāb al-Muṣannaf fī'l-aḥādīth wa'l-āthār*, ed. Muḥammad ʿAbd al-Salām Shāhīn, 9 vols. Beirut: Dār al-Kutub al-ʿIlmiyya, 1995. [DS]; ed. Ḥamad b. ʿAbd Allāh al-Jumʿa and Muḥammad b. Ibrāhīm al-Luḥaydān, 16 vols. Riyadh: Maktabat al-Rushd, 1425/2004. [CM] [TZ]

Ibn Abī'l-Wafāʾ al-Qurashī. *al-Jawāhir al-muḍiyya fī ṭabaqāt al-ḥanafiyya*, ed. ʿAbd al-Fattāḥ Muḥammad al-Ḥulw, 5 vols. Cairo and Riyadh: n.p. 1978–88. [CG]; 2nd edn; Giza: Hajr li'l-Ṭibāʿa wa'l-Nashr, 1993. [CG] [TZ]

Ibn Abī Zamanīn. *Tafsīr al-Qurʾān al-ʿazīz li-Ibn Abī Zamanīn*. Cairo: al-Fārūq al-Ḥadītha li'l-Ṭibāʿa wa'l-Nashr, 2002. [ACh]

Ibn Abī Zayd al-Qayrawānī, ʿAbd Allāh. *al-Risāla*; ed. Léon Bercher as *La Risâla ou Epître sur les éléments du dogme et de la loi de l'Islâm selon le rite mâlikite*, 5th edn. Algiers: J. Carbonel, 1960. [AC]

Ibn ʿĀdil, Sirāj al-Dīn Abū Ḥafṣ ʿUmar b. ʿAlī al-Dimashqī al-Ḥanbalī. *al-Lubāb fī ʿulūm al-Kitāb*, ed. ʿĀdil Aḥmad ʿAbd al-Mawjūd and ʿAlī Muḥammad Muʿawwaḍ, 20 vols. Beirut: Dār al-Kutub al-ʿIlmiyya, 1419/1998. [CG]

(Ibn) al-Anbārī. *Kitāb al-Aḍdād*, ed. Muḥammad Abū'l-Faḍl Ibrāhīm. Kuwait: Dā'irat al-Maṭbūʿāt wa'l-Nashr, 1960. [KV]

——. *al-Zāhir fī maʿānī kalimāt al-nās*, ed. Ḥātim Ṣāliḥ al-Ḍāmin, 2 vols. Baghdad: Dār al-Rashīd, 1979. [CG]

Ibn ʿAsākir, Thiqat al-Dīn ʿAlī b. al-Ḥasan. *Ta'rīkh madīnat Dimashq*, ed. Muḥibb al-Dīn al-ʿAmrawī and ʿAlī Shīrī, 80 vols. Beirut: Dār al-Fikr, 1995–2001. [CG] [TZ]

Ibn ʿĀṣim, Muḥammad b. Muḥammad. *Tuḥfat al-ḥukkām*; ed. and tr. Octave Victor Houdas and F. Martel as *Traité de Droit Musulman: La Tohfat d'Ebn Acem. Texte arabe avec traduction française, commentaire juridique et notes philologiques*. Algiers: Gavault Saint-Lager, 1882. [AC]

Ibn al-Athīr, Majd al-Dīn. *al-Nihāya fī gharīb al-ḥadīth*, ed. Ṭāhir Aḥmad al-Zāwī and Maḥmūd Muḥammad al-Ṭināḥī, 5 vols. Cairo: ʿĪsā al-Bābī al-Ḥalabī, 1383–4/1963–4. [CG]; repr. Beirut: Dār Iḥyā' al-Turāth al-ʿArabī, n.d. [CG]

Ibn ʿAṭiyya al-Andalusī. *al-Muḥarrar al-wajīz fī tafsīr al-Kitāb al-ʿazīz*, ed. ʿAbd al-Salām ʿAbd al-Shāfī Muḥammad, 5 vols. Beirut: Dār al-Kutub al-ʿIlmiyya, 1413/1993. [CG]; Beirut: Manshūrāt Muḥammad ʿAlī Bayḍūn, 2001. [ACh]

Ibn Bābawayh al-Qummī (al-Shaykh al-Ṣadūq), Abū Jaʿfar Muḥammad b. ʿAlī. *Kitāb Man lā yaḥḍuruhu'l-faqīh*, 4 vols. Najaf: Dār al-Kutub al-Islāmiyya, 1377–8/1957–9. [AC]

Ibn Bāz, ʿAbd al-ʿAzīz b. ʿAbd Allāh (lead author). 'Tarjamat maʿānī'l-Qur'ān' in *Fatāwā'l-lajna al-dā'ima li'l-buḥūth al-ʿilmiyya wa'l-iftā'*, ed. al-Shaykh Aḥmad b. ʿAbd al-Razzāq al-Duwaysh, 23 vols. Riyadh: Dār al-Mu'ayyid, 2003, vol. 4, pp. 132–6. [TZ]

Ibn Durayd. *Kitāb Jamaharat al-lugha*, repr. Baghdad: al-Muthanna Library, n.d. [SB – Intr] [SB]

Ibn Fāris. *al-Ṣāḥibī fī fiqh al-lugha*, ed. Moustafa Chouémi. Beirut: A. Badran, 1964. [CG] [KV]

Ibn Ḥajar al-ʿAsqalānī, Aḥmad. *Fatḥ al-bārī fī Ṣaḥīḥ al-Bukhārī*, ed. ʿAbd al-ʿAzīz b. Bāz *et al.*, numeration of the traditions by Muḥammad Fu'ād ʿAbd al-Bāqī, under the direction of Muḥibb al-Dīn al-Khaṭīb, 13 vols + Muqaddima. Cairo: al-Maṭbaʿa al-Salafiyya, 1379–90/1960–70. [CG]; repr. Beirut: al-Maʿrifa, n.d. [ca. 1980]. [CG]

——. *Lisān al-mīzān*, ed. Amīr Ḥasan al-Nuʿmānī *et al.*, 7 vols. Hyderabad, Dā'irat al-Maʿārif al-Niẓāmiyya, 1330–31/1912–13; repr. Beirut: Mu'assasat al-Aʿlamī, 1986. [CG]

——. *Tahdhīb al-tahdhīb*, ed. Muṣṭafā ʿAbd al-Qādir ʿAṭā. Beirut: Dār al-Kutub al-ʿIlmiyya, 1994. [HB]

Ibn Ḥanbal, Aḥmad. *Kitāb al-Zuhd*, ed. ʿAbd al-Raḥmān b. Qāsim. Mecca: Maṭbaʿat Umm al-Qurā, 1357/1938. [CM]; Beirut: Dār al-Kutub al-ʿIlmiyya, 1403/1983. [CM]

——. *al-Musnad*, ed. Muḥammad al-Zuhrī al-Ghamrāwī, 6 vols. Cairo: al-Maṭbaʿa al-Maymaniyya, 1313/1895. [CG] [CM]; ed. Aḥmad Muḥammad Shākir, Ḥamza A. al-Zayn *et al.*, 20 vols. Cairo: Dār al-Ḥadīth, 1416/1995. [CG]; ed. Shuʿayb al-Arnaʾūṭ *et al.* Beirut: Muʾassasat al-Risāla, 1413–21/1993–2001. [CM].

Ibn Hāniʾ al-Naysābūrī. *Masāʾil al-imām Aḥmad b. Ḥanbal*, ed. Zuhayr al-Shāwīsh. Beirut: al-Maktab al-Islāmī, 1400. [CM]

Ibn Ḥazm, ʿAlī b. Aḥmad. *Kitāb Fī maʿrifat al-nāsikh waʾl-mansūkh*. Cairo: Muṣṭafā al-Bābī al-Ḥalabī, 1370/1951. [CG]

——. *Kitāb al-Muḥallā*, ed. Aḥmad Muḥammad Shākir, 11 vols. Beirut: al-Maktab al-Tijārī, 1389/1969. [AC]

——. *Marātib al-ijmāʿ fīʾl-ʿibādāt waʾl-muʿāmalāt waʾl-muʿtaqadāt*. Beirut: Dār al-Kutub al-ʿIlmiyya, 1978. [AC]

Ibn Hishām, ʿAbd al-Malik. *al-Sīra al-nabawiyya*, ed. Muṣṭafā al-Saqqā, Ibrāhīm al-Abyādī and ʿAbd al-Ḥāfiẓ Shalabī. Beirut: Dār al-Maʿrifa, n.d. [HB]

Ibn Humām, Kamāl al-Dīn ʿAbd al-Wāḥid. *Fatḥ al-qadīr*, ed. ʿAbd al-Razzāq Ghālib al-Mahdī, 10 vols. Beirut: Dār al-Kutub al-ʿIlmiyya, 1415/1995. [TZ]

Ibn Isḥāq, Muḥammad. *Kitāb al-Siyar waʾl-maghāzī*, ed. Suhayl Zakkār. Beirut: Dār al-Fikr, 1978. [HB]

Ibn al-Jawzī, Abūʾl-Faraj. *Zād al-masīr fī ʿilm al-tafsīr*. Damascus: al-Maktab al-Islāmī liʾl-Ṭibāʿa waʾl-Nashr, 1964. [ACh]

Ibn Jinnī, Abūʾl-Fatḥ ʿUthmān. *[Kitāb] al-Khaṣāʾiṣ fī ʿilm uṣūl al-ʿarabiyya*. Cairo: 1371/1952; Cairo: 1374/1955. [TM]

——. *al-Muḥtasib fī tabyīn wujūh shawādhdh al-qirāʾāt*, ed. ʿAlī al-Najdī Nāṣif *et al.*, 2 vols. Cairo: al-Majlis al-Aʿlā, 1386–1415/1966–94. [CG]

Ibn Jurayj. *Tafsīr Ibn Jurayj*, ed. ʿAlī Ḥasan ʿAbd al-Ghanī. Cairo: Maktabat al-Turāth al-Islāmī, 1992. [KV]

Ibn Juzayy al-Gharnāṭī. *Kitāb al-Tashīl li-ʿulūm al-tanzīl*. Beirut: Dār al-Kitāb al-ʿArabī, 1973. [ACh]

Ibn Kathīr, Ismāʿīl b. ʿUmar. *Tafsīr al-Qurʾān al-ʿaẓīm*, ed. ʿAbd al-ʿAzīz Ghunaym, Muḥammad A. ʿĀshūr and Muḥammad Ibrāhīm al-Bannā, 8 vols. Cairo: Dār al-Shaʿb, 1390/1971. [CG]; *Tafsīr al-ʿaẓīm li-Ibn Kathīr*. Damascus: Dār Ibn Kathir, 1994. [ACh]; *Tafsīr al-Qurʾān al-karīm*. Cairo: Dār al-Fikr, n.d. [SB]

Ibn Khallikān. *Wafayāt al-aʿyān wa anbāʾ abnāʾ al-zamān*, ed. Iḥsān ʿAbbās, 8 vols. Beirut: Dār Ṣādir, 1968–77. [CG]

Ibn Khayr al-Ishbīlī. *Fahrasa mā rawāhu ʿan shuyūkhihi* . . . [*Index librorum de diversis scientiarum* . . .], ed. Francisco Codera and Julián Ribera y Tarragó. Caesaraugustae [Saragossa]: n.p., 1894–5. [CG]

Ibn Maktūm, Tāj al-Dīn Abū Muḥammad ʿAbd Allāh. *Talkhīṣ akhbār al-naḥwiyyīn*, MS 3069, Dār al-Kutub, Cairo. [CG]

Ibn Manẓūr, Muḥammad b. Mukarram. *Lisān al-ʿArab*, 20 vols. Cairo: Būlāq, 1300–8/1883–91. [BW]; 15 vols, Beirut: Dār Ṣādir, 1955–6. [TZ]; 6 vols and 3 vol. indexes. Cairo: Dār al-Maʿārif, 1400–1/1979–80. [CG]; ed. Amīn Muḥammad ʿAbd al-Wahhāb and Muḥammad al-Ṣādiq al-ʿUbaydī, 18 vols. Beirut: Dār Iḥyāʾ al-Turāth al-ʿArabī, 1999. [SB – Intr] [SB]

Ibn al-Mubārak. *Kitāb al-Jihād*, ed. Nazīh Ḥammād. Beirut: Dār al-Nūr, 1391/1971. [CM]; repr. Beirut: al-Maktaba al-ʿAṣriyya, 1409/1988. [CM]

——. *al-Zuhd wa'l-raqā'iq*, ed. Ḥabīb al-Raḥmān al-Aʿẓamī. Malegaon: Majlis Iḥyā' al-Maʿārif, 1386. [CM]; repr. Beirut: Dār al-Kutub al-ʿIlmiyya, 1419/1998. [CM]

Ibn al-Murtaḍā, Aḥmad b. Yaḥyā. *Kitāb al-Baḥr al-zakhkhār al-jāmiʿ li-madhāhib ʿulamā' al-amṣār*, ed. ʿAbd Allāh Muḥammad al-Ṣiddīq and ʿAbd al-Ḥafīẓ Saʿd ʿAṭiyya, 5 vols. Cairo: Maktabat al-Muthannā, 1366–8/1947–9. [AC]

Ibn Qudāma, Muḥammad b. Aḥmad. *al-Kāfī fī fiqh al-imām Aḥmad b. Ḥanbal*, 3 vols. Damascus: n.p., 1964. [AC]

——. *al-Mughnī*, 12 vols. Cairo: n.p., 1341–8/1922–30. [AC]

——. *al-Muqniʿ fī fiqh imām al-sunna Aḥmad b. Ḥanbal*, 2nd edn, 3 vols. Cairo: al-Maṭbaʿa al-Salafiyya wa-Maktabatuhā, 1382/1962–3. [AC]

——. *al-ʿUmda fī fiqh imām al-sunna Aḥmad b. Ḥanbal al-Shaybānī*. Cairo: n.p., 1385/1965–6. [AC]

Ibn Qutayba, ʿAbd Allāh b. Muslim. *Kitāb ʿUyūn al-akhbār*, ed. A. Zakī al-ʿAdwī. Cairo: Dār al-Kutub, 1925–30. [CG]

——. *Tafsīr gharīb al-Qur'ān*, ed. al-Sayyid Aḥmad Ṣaqr. Beirut: Dār al-Kutub al-ʿIlmiyya, 1398/1978. [CG]

Ibn Saʿd, Muḥammad. *Kitāb al-Ṭabaqāt al-kubrā*, Foreward by Iḥsān ʿAbbās on the basis of the edition by Eduard Sachau *et al.* Beirut: Dār Ṣādir, 1960–68. [HB]

Ibn al-Sikkīt. *Iṣlāḥ al-manṭiq*, ed. Aḥmad Muḥammad Shākir and ʿAbd al-Salām Muḥammad Hārūn. Cairo: Dār al-Maʿārif, 1970; orig. pub. 1949. [CG]; also repr. 1987. [CG]

Ibn Taymiyya. 'Kitāb fī'l-radd ʿalā'l-ṭawā'if al-mulḥida' in *al-Fatāwā al-kubrā*, ed. Muḥammad ʿAbd al-Qādir ʿAṭā' and Muṣṭafā ʿAbd al-Qādir ʿAṭā', 6 vols. Beirut: Dār al-Kutub al-ʿIlmiyya, 1987, vol. 6, pp. 323–664. [TZ]

——. *Kitāb Iqtiḍā' al-ṣirāṭ al-mustaqīm li-mukhālafat aṣḥāb al-jaḥīm*, ed. Nāṣir b. ʿAbd al-Karīm al-ʿAql, 2 vols. Riyadh: Maktabat al-Rushd, 1994. [TZ]

——. *Muqaddima fī uṣūl al-tafsīr*, ed. ʿAdnān Zarzūr. Kuwait: Dār al-Qur'ān al-Karīm, 1971. [SB]

Ibn Wahb, ʿAbd Allāh. *al-Jāmiʿ: Tafsīr al-Qurʿān (Die Koranexegese)*, ed. Miklos Muranyi. Wiesbaden: Otto Harrassowitz, 1993. [HB]

al-Isfarā'īnī, Shāhfur. *Tāj al-tarājim fī tafsīr al-Qur'ān li'l-aʿājim*, ed. Najīb Māyl Harawī and ʿAlī Akbar Ilāhī Khurāsānī (partial edn), 2 vols. Tehran: Shirkat-i Intishārāt-i ʿIlmī wa Farhangī, 1996. [TZ]

al-Jabbālī, Ibrāhīm. 'Kalām fī tarjamat al-Qur'ān', *Nūr al-Islām* 3, no. 1 (1351/1932), p. 59. [TZ]

al-Jāḥiẓ, Abū ʿUthmān. *al-Bayān wa'l-tabyīn*, ed. ʿAbd al-Salām Muḥammad Hārūn, 4 vols. Cairo: Maṭbaʿat Lajnat al-Ta'līf wa'l-Tarjama wa'l-Nashr, 1948. [TZ]

——. *Kitāb al-Ḥayawān*, 7 vols in 2. Cairo: al-Maṭbaʿa al-Ḥamīdiyya, 1323–5/1905–7. [SW]

al-Jazīrī, ʿAbd al-Raḥmān. *Aḥsan al-bayān fī'l-radd ʿalā'l-Shaykh Muḥammad Shāṭir wa ghayrihi min māniʿīn li-jawāz tarjamat tafsīr al-Qur'ān*. Cairo: Maṭbaʿat wa Majallat al-Irshād, 1936. [TZ]

al-Jīlī, ʿAbd al-Karīm b. Ibrāhīm. *al-Insān al-kāmil fī maʿrifati'l-awākhir wa'l-awā'il*. Cairo: n.p., 1402/1981. [TM] al-Jishumī, al-Ḥākim. *Tahdhīb fī tafsīr al-Qur'ān*; introduction tr. Suleiman A. Mourad in 'Towards a Reconstruction of the Muʿtazilī Tradition of Qur'anic Exegesis: Reading the Introduction to the *Tahdhīb* of al-Ḥākim al-Jishumī (d. 494/1101) and Its Application' in Karen Bauer, ed., *Aims, Methods and Contexts of Qur'anic Exegesis (2nd/8th–9th/15th c.)*. Oxford: Oxford University Press in association with the Institute of Ismaili Studies, 2013, pp. 101–37. [SB - Intr]

al-Jurjānī, Abū'l-ʿAbbās Aḥmad b. Muḥammad. *Kitāb al-Kifāya fī maʿrifat al-farā'iḍ wa qismat al-mawārīth* (MS). [AC]

Kadri, Hüseyin Kâzım (Şeyh Muhsin-i Fani, pseud.). *Meşrutiyet'ten Cumuriyet'e Hatıralarım*, ed. İsmail Kara. Istanbul: İletişim Yayınları, 1991. [BW]

——. *Türk lûgati; Türk dillerinin iştikakı ve edebi lûgatleri: Uygur, Çağatay, Kazan, Azeri ve Garp Türkçeleriyle, Koybal, Yakut, Altay, Çuvaş, ve Kırgız lehçelerinin lûgatlerini ve Garp Türkçesinde kullanılan Arap ve Acem kelimelerini şevahidi ve emsaliyle havidir.* Istanbul: Devlet Matbaası, 1927. [BW]

——. *See also* Fani, Şeyh Muhsin-i.

al-Kalbī, Muḥammad. *Tafsīr*, MS 4224 Chester Beatty Library, Dublin. [KV]

Kamāl al-Dīn, Khwāja, and Rashīd Riḍā. 'Tarjamat al-Qur'ān wa istiḥālat muṭābiqatihā'l-aṣl', *al-Manār* 17, no. 10 (1914), pp. 793–5. [TZ]

al-Khalīl b. Aḥmad. *Kitāb al-ʿAyn*. Beirut: Dār al-Iḥyā' al-Turāth al-ʿArabī, 2001. [SB - Intr] [SB]

Khalīl b. Isḥāq al-Jundī. *Mukhtaṣar*; ed. and tr. Ignazio Guidi and David Santillana as *Il "Mukhtaṣar" o Sommario del diritto malechita*, 2 vols. Milan: Hoepli, 1919. [AC]

al-Khaṭīb al-Baghdādi. *Ta'rīkh Baghdād*, ed. Muḥammad Saʿīd al-ʿUrfī, 14 vols. Cairo: Maṭbaʿat al-Saʿāda and Maktabat Amīn al-Khānjī, 1931–49; repr. Beirut: Dār al-Kitāb al-ʿArabī, 1970–80. [CG]

al-Khāzin al-Baghdādī. *Tafsīr al-Khāzin: al-Musammā Lubāb al-ta'wīl fī maʿānī al-tanzīl*. Baghdad: Maktabat al-Muthannā, 1975. [ACh]

al-Khiraqī, Abū'l-Qāsim. *Mukhtaṣar al-Khiraqī ʿalā madhhab al-imām Aḥmad b. Ḥanbal*, in Ibn Qudāma, *al-Mughnī*. Cairo: n.p., 1341–8/1922–30. [AC]

Kīlīṭū, ʿAbd al-Fattāḥ. *Lan tatakallama lughatī*. Beirut: Dār al-Ṭalīʿa li'l-Ṭibāʿa wa'l-Nashr, 2002. [TZ]; tr. Waïl S. Hassan as *Thou Shalt not Speak my Language*. Syracuse, NY: Syracuse University Press, 2008. [TZ]

al-Kulaynī, Muḥammad b. Yaʿqūb. *al-Kāfī*; ed. ʿAlī Akbar al-Ghaffārī as *al-Uṣūl min al-Kāfī. Al-Furūʿ min al-Kāfī. Al-Rawḍa min al-Kāfī*, 8 vols. Tehran: Dār al-Kutub al-Islāmiyya, 1388–9/1967–8. [AC]; repr. as *Ṣaḥīḥ al-Kāfī*. Beirut: n.p., 1401/1980. [TM]

al-Laknawī, Abū'l-Ḥasanāt ʿAbd al-Ḥayy. 'Ākām al-nafā'is fī adā' al-adhkār bi-lisān al-fāris' in *Majmūʿat rasā'il al-Laknawī*, ed. Naʿīm Ashrāf Nūr Aḥmad, 6 vols. Karachi: Idārat al-Qur'ān wa'l-ʿUlūm al-Islāmiyya, 1419/1998–9, vol. 4, pp. 333–92. [TZ]

——. *al-Fawā'id al-Bahiyya fī tarājim al-ḥanafiyya*, ed. Aḥmad al-Zuʿbī. Beirut: Dār al-Aqram, 1998. [TZ]

al-Laknawī, Baḥr al-ʿUlūm ʿAbd al-ʿAlī al-ʿAyyāsh. *Fawātiḥ al-raḥmūt*, ed. ʿAbd Allāh Maḥmūd Muḥammad ʿUmar, 2 vols. Beirut: Dār al-Kutub al-ʿIlmiyya, 2002. [TZ] al-Maḥallī, Jalāl al-Dīn, and Jalāl al-Dīn al-Suyūṭī. *Tafsīr al-Jalālayn*. Damascus: Maṭbaʿat al-Mallāḥ, 1389/1969. [SB]; *al-Qurʾān al-karīm: biʾl-rasm al-ʿUthmānī wa bi-hāmishahu tafsīr al-Jalālayn; Mudhayyalan bi-Kitāb Lubāb al-nuqūl fī asbāb al-nuzūl*. Beirut: Dār al-Qalam, 1982. [ACh]; tr. Feras Hamza as *Tafsīr al-Jalālayn: An Annotated English Translation of the Commentary of the Two Jalāls*. Louisville, KY: Fons Vitae Ammoni: Royal Aal al-Bayt Institute for Islamic Thought, 2008. [SB] [BW]

al-Majlisī. *Biḥār al-anwār*, 110 vols. Tehran: al-Maktaba al-Islāmiyya, 1956–72. [DS]

Makhlūf, Muḥammad Ḥasanayn. *Risālat ḥukm tarjamat al-Qurʾān al-karīm wa qirāʾatihi wa kitābatihi bi-ghayr al-lugha al-ʿarabiyya*. Cairo: Maṭbaʿat Maṭar, 1343/1925. [TZ]

——. 'Tarjamat al-Qurʾān al-Karīm', *al-Ahrām*, issue 18424 (28 March 1936), p. 2. [TZ]

Mālik b. Anas. *Kitāb al-Muwaṭṭaʾ*, with the *Sharḥ Muwaṭṭaʾ* by Muḥammad b. ʿAbd al-Bāqī b. Yūsuf al-Zurqānī, 4 vols. Cairo: n.p., 1373/1954. [AC]; ed. Ḥasan ʿAbd Allāh Sharaf. Cairo: Dār al-Rayyān liʾl-Turāth, 1988. [BW]

al-Marāghī, Muḥammad Muṣṭafā. 'Baḥth fī tarjamat al-Qurʾān al-Karīm wa aḥkāmihā', *Majallat al-Azhar* 7, no. 2 (1355/1936), pp. 77–112. [TZ]; republished as a pamplet, *Baḥth fī tarjamat al-Qurʾān wa aḥkāmihā*. Cairo: Maṭbaʿat al-Raghāʾib, 1355/1936. [SW] [TZ]

al-Marghīnānī, Burhān al-Dīn Abūʾl-Ḥasan. *al-Hidāya*, ed. Mawlānā Muḥammad ʿAbd al-Aḥad, 2 vols. Lithograph, Delhi: Maṭbaʿ al-Mujtabāʾī, 1332–4/1914–16. [TZ]

——. *Kitāb al-Tajnīs waʾl-mazīd*, ed. Muḥammad Amīn Makkī, 2 vols. Karachi: Idrārat al-Qurʾān waʾl-ʿUlūm al-Islāmiyya, 2004. [TZ]

al-Marghīnānī, Burhān al-Dīn Maḥmūd b. Aḥmad al-Bukhārī. *al-Muḥīṭ al-burhānī*, ed. ʿAbd al-Karīm al-Jundī, 9 vols. Beirut: Dār al-Kutub al-ʿIlmiyya, 2004. [TZ]

al-Marwazī, Abū Bakr ʿAbd Allāh al-Qaffāl. *Fatāwā*, ed. Muṣṭafā Maḥmūd al-Azharī. Riyadh: Dār Ibn al-Qayyim, 2011. [TZ]

al-Māturīdī, Abū Manṣūr. *Kitāb al-Tawḥīd*, ed. Bekir Topaloğlu and M. Aruçi. Ankara: Türkiye Diyanet Vakfi (Isam), 2003. [CG]

——. *Taʾwīlāt ahl al-sunna*, ed. Fāṭima Yūsuf al-Khaymī. Beirut: Muʾassasat al-Risāla Nāshirūn, 1425/2004. [SB - Intr]

——. *Taʾwīlāt al-Qurʾān*, 13 vols, ed. Ahmet Vanlioğlu *et al.* Istanbul: Mizan Yayinevi, Imam Ebû Hanīfe ve Imam Mâtürīdī Arastirma Vakfi, 2005–8. [CG]

al-Māwardī, Abūʾl Ḥasan. *al-Nukat waʾl-ʿuyūn*, ed. al-Sayyid b. ʿAbd al-Maqṣūd b. ʿAbd al-Raḥīm. Beirut: Dār al-Kutub al-ʿIlmiyya and Muʾassasat al-Kutub al-Thaqāfiyya, n.d. [CM]; 1992. [ACh]; *Tafsīr al-Māwardī*, published with *Muṣḥaf al-taḥajjud*. Cairo: Dār al-Ṣafwā liʾl-Ṭibāʿa waʾl-Nashr, 1413/1993. [SB]

al-Mawdūdī, Abū ʿAlāʾ. *Tafhīm al-Qurʾān*, 6 vols. Lahore: Taʿmīr-i Insāniyyat, 1954–65. [TZ]

Mubarrad, Muḥammad b. Yazīd. *al-Kāmil*, ed. Muḥammad A. al-Dālī. Beirut: Muʾassasat al-Risāla, 1406/1986. [CG]; ed. William Wright as *The Kamil of El-Mubarrad*. Leipzig: F.A. Brockhaus, 1864–92. [CG] al-Muḥibbī, Muḥammad al-Amīn. *Khulāṣat al-athar fī aʿyān al-qarn al-ḥādī ʿashar*, 4 vols. Cairo: al-Maṭbaʿa al-Wahbiyya, 1284/1868. [TZ]

Mujāhid, Abū'l-Ḥajjāj b. Jabr al-Makkī al-Makhzūmī. *Tafsīr Mujāhid*, ed. Muḥammad ʿAbd al-Salām Abū Nīl. Cairo: Dār al-Fikr, 1989. [BW]; ed. ʿAbd al-Raḥmān al-Ṭāhir al-Sūratī. Beirut: al-Manshūrāt al-ʿIlmiyya, n.d. [HB]; Islamabad, n.d. [KV]

Muqātil b. Sulaymān al-Balkhī, Abū'l-Ḥasan. *Tafsīr al-khams miʾat āya min al-Qurʾān al-karīm*, ed. Isaiah Goldfeld. Shfaram: Al-Mashriq Press, 1980. [KV]

——. *Tafsīr Muqātil b. Sulaymān*, ed. ʿAbd Allāh Maḥmūd Shiḥāta, 5 vols. Cairo: al-Hayʾa al-Miṣriyya al-ʿĀmma li'l-Kitāb, 1979–89. [HB] [SB] [CG] [KV]; repr. Beirut: Mūʾassasat al-Tārīkh al-ʿArabī, 2002. [BW]

al-Muṣʿabī, ʿAbd al-ʿAzīz b. Ibrāhīm. *Kitāb al-Nīl wa shifāʾ al-ʿalīl*, 2 vols. Cairo: n.p., 1305/1887–8. [AC]

al-Mustaghfirī, Abū'l-ʿAbbās Jaʿfar. *Faḍāʾil al-Qurʾān*. MS Esad Efendi 181, Süleymaniye Library, Istanbul. [TZ]; ed. Aḥmad b. Fāris al-Sallūm, 2 vols. Beirut: Dār Ibn Ḥazm, 2006. [TZ]

al-Muṭīʿī, Muḥammad Bakhīt. *Kitāb Ḥujjat Allāh ʿalā khalīqatihi fī bayān ḥaqīqat al-Qurʾān wa ḥukm kitābatihi wa tarjamatihi*. Cairo: al-Azhar al-ʿIlmiyya, 1350/1932. [TZ]

al-Muzanī, Abū Ibrahīm Ismāʿīl b. Yaḥyā b. Ismāʿīl. *Mukhtaṣar*, on the margins of vols. I–V of Muḥammad b. Idrīs al-Shāfiʿī, *Kitāb al-Umm*. Cairo: Būlāq, 1321–5/1903–8. [AC]

al-Narshakhī, Abū Bakr Muḥammad b. Jaʿfar. *Tārīkh-i Bukhārā*, ed. Muḥammad b. Zufar b. ʿUmar. Tehran: Sanāʾī, 1320 Sh./1940–41. [TZ]

al-Nasafī, Abū'l-Barakāt. *al-Kāfī fī sharḥ al-Wāfī*. MS Hk 3502, İl Halk Kütüphanesi, Manisa. [TZ]

——. *Tafsīr al-Nasafī: al-Musammā bi-Madārik al-tanzīl wa ḥaqāʾiq al-taʾwīl*. Beirut: Dār al-Qalam, 1989. [ACh]

al-Nawawī, Muḥyī'l-Dīn Abū Zakariyyāʾ Yaḥyā. *Kitāb al-Majmūʿ*. Cairo: Maṭbaʿat al-Taḍāmun, n.d. [SW]; ed. Muḥammad Najīb al-Muṭīʿī, 23 vols. Jeddah: Maktabat al-Irshād, 1992. [TZ]

——. *Minhāj al-Ṭālibīn*; ed. and tr. L.W.C. van den Berg as *Le Guide des Zélés Croyants: Manuel de Jurisprudence musulmane selon le rite de Châfiʿî*, 3 vols. Batavia: Imprimerie de Gouvernement, 1882–4. [AC]

Nazif, Süleyman. 'Ramazan Musahabesi II', *Resimli Gazete*, 19 April 1924 (19 Nisan 1340). [BW]

al-Nuʿmān, al-Qāḍī Abū Ḥanīfa. *Daʿāʾim al-islām wa dhikr al-ḥalāl wa'l-ḥarām wa'l-qaḍāyā wa'l-aḥkām ʿan bayt rasūl Allāh*, ed. ʿĀṣif b. ʿAlī Aṣghar Fayḍī [Asif A.A. Fyzee], 2 vols. Cairo: Dār al-Maʿārif 1379–83/1960–63. [AC]; 3rd edn. Cairo: Dār al-Maʿārif, 1969. [CM]; repr. Beirut: al-Manāra, n.d. [CM]

——. *Kitāb al-Iqtiṣār*, ed. Muḥammad Waḥīd Mīrzā. Damascus: Institut Français de Damas, 1376/1957. [AC]

——. *Minhāj al-farāʾiḍ*; ed. and tr. Agostino Cilardo as *The Early History of Ismaili Jurisprudence: Law under the Fatimids. A Critical Edition of the Arabic Text and English Translation of al-Qāḍī al-Nuʿmān's* Minhāj al-farā'iḍ. London: I.B. Tauris in association with the Institute of Ismaili Studies, 2012. [AC]

——. *Mukhtaṣar al-āthār fī-mā ruwiya 'an al-a'imma al-aṭhār* (MS). [AC]

Qālī, Abū 'Alī Ismā'īl al-Qāsim. *Kitāb Dhayl al-Amālī*, 2 vols. Cairo: Dār al-Kutub al-Miṣriyya, 1344/1926. [CG]

al-Qifṭī, al-Wazīr 'Alī b. Yūsuf. *Inbāh al-ruwāt 'alā anbāh al-nuḥāt*, ed. Muḥammad Abū'l-Faḍl Ibrāhīm, 4 vols. Cairo: Dār al-Fikr al-'Arabī, 1950–73. [CG]

al-Qudūrī, Abū'l-Ḥusayn Aḥmad b. Muḥammad. *Mukhtaṣar*. Cairo: n.p., 1367/1948. [AC]

al-Qummī, 'Alī b. Ibrāhīm. *Tafsīr al-Qummī*, ed. Ṭayyib al-Mūsawī al-Jazā'irī, 2 vols. Najaf: Maṭba'at al-Najaf, 1387/1967. [SB – Intr] [SB] [CM]

al-Qurashī, Abū Zayd Muḥammad b. Abī'l-Khaṭṭāb. *Jamharat ash'ār al-'Arab*, ed. 'Alī Muḥammad al-Bijāwī. Cairo: Dār Nahḍat Miṣr, 1981; orig. pub. 1967. [CG]

al-Qurṭubī, Muḥammad b. Aḥmad. *al-Jāmi' li-aḥkām al-Qur'ān*, ed. Aḥmad al-Bardūnī *et al.*, 2nd edn, 20 vols. Cairo: al-Hay'a al-Miṣriyya al-'Āmma li'l-Kitāb, 1952–67. [CG]; Cairo: Dār al-Kutub al-'Arabī, 1387/1967. [SB]; ed. 'Abd al-Razzāq al-Mahdī. Beirut: Dār al-Kitāb al-'Arabī, 1418/1997. [ACh] [CM]; ed. 'Abd Allāh b. 'Abd al-Ḥasan al-Turkī and Muḥammad Riḍwān 'Arqusī. Beirut: Mu'assasat al-Risāla, 2006. [BW]

al-Rāfi'ī, 'Abd al-Karīm. *al-Tadwīn fī akhbār Qazwīn*, ed. 'Azīz Allāh al-'Uṭāridī, 4 vols. Beirut: Dār al-Kutub al-'Ilmiyya, 1987. [TZ]

al-Rāghib al-Iṣfahānī, Abū'l-Qāsim al-Ḥusayn b. Muḥammad. *al-Mufradāt fī gharīb al-Qur'ān*, ed. Muḥammad Sayyid Kīlānī. Beirut: Dār al-Ma'rifa, 1961. [DS]

al-Rāzī, Fakhr al-Dīn. *Kitāb al-Arba'īn fī uṣūl al-dīn*. Hyderabad: Maṭba'at Majlis Dā'irat al-Ma'ārif al-'Uthmāniyya, 1353/1934–5. [SB – Intr]

——. *Mafātīḥ al-ghayb* [*Tafsīr*], ed. Muḥammad Muḥyī'l-Dīn 'Abd al-Ḥamīd, 'Alī Ibrahīm al-Ṣāwī *et al.*, 32 vols. Cairo: al-Maṭba'at al-Bahiyya al-Miṣriyya, 1933–62. [CG]; *al-Tafsīr al-kabīr*. Tehran: Dār al-Kutub al-'Ilmiyya, n.d. [SB – Intr] [SB] [TM]; Beirut: Dār al-Fikr, 1981. [TZ]; *al-Tafsīr al-kabīr*. Beirut: Dār Iḥyā' al-Turāth al-'Arabī, 1997. [ACh]

Riḍā, Muḥammad Rashīd. 'Bāb al-as'ila wa'l-ajwiba: Tarjamat al-Qur'ān', *al-Manār* 6, no. 6 (1321/1903), pp. 268–70. [TZ]

——. 'Fatāwā'l-Manār: Tarjamat al-Qur'ān', *al-Manār* 11, no. 4 (1326/1908), pp. 268–74. [SW] [TZ]

——. 'Kitābat al-Qur'ān bi'l-ḥurūf al-inklīziyya', *al-Manār* 6, no. 6 (1321/1903), pp. 274–7. [TZ]

——. 'Mansha' fikrat tarjamat al-Qur'ān wa sababuhā', *al-Manār* 26, no. 7 (1344/1926), pp. 481–96. [TZ]

——. *Mukhtārāt siyāsiyya min majallat al-Manār*, edited with an introduction by Wajīh Kawtharānī. Beirut: Dār al-Ṭalī'a, 1980. [SW]

——. 'Tarjamat al-Qur'ān', *al-Manār* 25 (1924), pp. 794–6. [SW]

——. 'Tarjamat al-Qur'ān wa kawn al-'arabiyya lughat al-islām', *al-Manār* 32, no. 7 (1351/1932), pp. 535–44. [TZ]

——. 'Tarjamat al-Qur'ān wa taḥrīf tarjama lahu wa'l-tashkīk fīhi', *al-Manār* 25, no. 10 (1343/1925), pp. 794–7. [TZ]

Rūmī, Mawlānā Jalāl al-Dīn Muḥammad. *Kitāb Fīhi mā fīhi*, ed. Badī' al-Zamān Farūzānfar. Tehran: Mu'assassa-yi Intishār-i Amīr Kabīr, 1362 Sh./1983. [TM]; tr. A.J. Arberry as *Discourses of Rūmī*. London: John Murray, 1961. [TM]

Ṣabrī, Muṣṭafā. *Mas'alat tarjamat al-Qur'ān*. Cairo: al-Maṭba'a al-Salāfiyya, 1351/1932–3. [SW] [TZ]

al-Ṣafadī, Khalīl b. Aybak. *al-Wāfī bi'l-wafayāt* [*Das biographische Lexicon des Ṣalāḥaddin Ḫalīl Ibn Aibak aṣ-Ṣafadī*], ed. Helmut Ritter *et al.*, 30 vols. Istanbul, then Beirut: Deutsche Morgenländische Gesellschaft, Wiesbaden, then Stuttgart, 1931–2004. [CG]

Saḥnūn, 'Abd al-Salām b. Sa'īd. *al-Mudawwana al-kubrā*, 16 vols. Cairo: n.p., 1323–4/1905. [AC]; ed. 'Alī b. al-Sayyid 'Abd al-Raḥmān al-Hāshim, 12 vols. Abu Dhabi: n.p., 2000. [TZ]

Sait, Cemil [Dikel]. *Kur'an-i Kerim Tercümesi*. Istanbul: Şems Matbaası, 1924. [BW]

Salīm, 'Abd al-Majīd (signitory). 'Fatwa' in 'Ḥawl Tarjamat al-Qur'ān al-Karīm', *al-Ahrām*, issue 18442 (17 April 1936), p. 2. [TZ]; and in Muḥammad Sulaymān, *Kitāb Ḥadath al-aḥdāth fī'l-islām: al-iqdām 'alā tarjamat al-Qur'ān*. Cairo: Maṭba'at Jarīdat Miṣr al-Ḥurra, 1355/1936, pp. 46–8. [TZ]

al-Sam'ānī, 'Abd al-Karīm. *al-Ansāb*, ed. 'Abd al-Raḥmān al-Yamānī *et al.* 13 vols. Hyderabad: Dā'irat al-Ma'ārif al-'Uthmāniyya, 1962–82. [TZ]

al-Sarakhsī, Muḥammad b. Aḥmad. *Mabsūṭ*. MS Feyzullah Efendi Koleksiyonu 983, Millet Kütüphanesi, Istanbul. [TZ]; MS 191 Konya Karatay Yusufağa Kütüphanesi, Konya. [TZ]; *Kitāb al-Mabsūṭ*, 30 vols. Cairo: Maṭba'at al-Sa'ādah, 1324–31/1906–13. [AC] [TZ]; ed. Abū 'Abd Allāh Muḥammad al-Shāfi'ī, 30 vols in 15. Beirut: Dār al-Kutub al-'Ilmiyya, 2001. [TZ]

al-Ṣarīfīnī, Abū'l Ḥasan 'Abd al-Ghāfir. *al-Muntakhab min al-siyāq li-ta'rīkh Naysābūr*. Beirut: Dār al-Kutub al-'Ilmiyya, 1989. [CG]

al-Shāfi'ī, Muḥammad b. Idrīs. *Kitāb al-Umm*, 7 vols. Cairo: Būlāq, 1321–5/1903–8. [AC]

Shāh Walī Allāh. *Fatḥ al-Raḥmān fī tarjamat al-Qur'ān*. Lithograph, Meerut: 1867. [TZ]

al-Shahrastānī, Muḥammad b. 'Abd al-Karīm. *Kitāb Nihāyat al-iqdām fī 'ilm al-kalām*, ed. and partially tr. by Alfred Guillaume, *The Summa Philosophiae of al-Shahrastānī*. Oxford: Oxford University Press, 1934. [TM]

——. *Mafātīḥ al-asrār wa maṣābīḥ al-abrār*, MS 8086/B78, Library of the Islamic Consultative Assembly in Tehran. [TM]; *Tafsīr al-Shahrastānī al-musammā Mafātīḥ al-asrār wa maṣābīḥ al-abrār*, ed. Muḥammad 'Alī Ādharshab, 2 vols. Tehran: Mīrās-i Maktūb, 2008. [TM]; tr. Toby Mayer as *Keys to the Arcana: Shahrastānī's Esoteric Commentary on the Qur'an. A Translation of the Commentary on* Sūrat al-Fātiḥa *from Muḥammad b. 'Abd al-Karīm al-Shahrastānī's* Mafātīḥ al-asrār wa maṣābīḥ al-abrār.

Oxford: Oxford University Press in association with the Institute of Ismaili Studies, 2009. [SB – Intr] [TM]

——. *Majlis-i Maktūb-i Shahrastānī-i munʿaqid dar Khwārazm*; translated into French by Diane Steigerwald (with Jalālī Nāʾinī's edition of the Persian text) as *Majlis: Discours sur l'ordre et la création*. Saint-Nicolas: Les Presses de l'Université Laval, 1998. [TM]

Shākir, Muḥammad. *al-Qawl al-faṣl fī tarjamat al-Qurʾān al-karīm ilāʾl-lughāt al-aʿjamiyya*. Cairo: Maṭbaʿat al-Nahḍa, 1343/1925. [SW] [TZ]; first section (pp. 6–19) translated by Thomas Arnold as 'On the Translation of the Koran into Foreign Languages', *The Muslim World* 16, no. 2 (1926), pp. 161–5. [SW] [TZ]

Shaltūt, Maḥmūd. 'Tarjamat al-Qurʾān', *Majallat al-Azhar* 7, no. 2 (1936), pp. 123–34. [TZ]

al-Shāṭibī, Ibrāhīm b. Mūsā. *Muwāfaqāt fī uṣūl al-sharīʿa*, ed. ʿAbd Allāh Darāz, 4 vols. Cairo: al-Maktaba al-Tijāriyya al-Kubrā, n.d. [TZ]

al-Shāṭir, Muḥammad Muṣṭafā. *al-Qawl al-sadīd fī ḥukm tarjamat al-Qurʾān al-majīd*. Cairo: Maṭbaʿat Ḥijāzī, Rabīʿ II 1355/June 1936. [TZ]

——. *Tadhkira li-ūlīʾl-baṣāʾir waʾl-abṣār ilā mā fī tarjamat maʿānīʾl-Qurʾān min akhṭār*. Cairo: Maṭbaʿat al-Naṣr, 1355/1936. [TZ]

al-Shaṭṭī, Muḥammad al-Ṣādiq. *Risāla fī Masāʾil al-imām Dāwūd al-Ẓāhirī*. Damascus: n.p., 1330/1912. [AC]

al-Shawkānī, Muḥammad b. ʿAlī. *Fatḥ al-qadīr al-jāmiʿ bayna fannayʾl-riwāya waʾl-dirāya fī ʿilm al-tafsīr*, 4 vols. Cairo: Muṣṭafā al-Bābī al-Ḥalabī, 1349/1930. [CG]; repr. Beirut: Dār al-Fikr, 1973. [CG]

al-Shaybānī, Muḥammad b. al-Ḥasan. *al-Ḥujja fī ikhtilāf ahl al-Kūfa wa ahl al-Madīna* (MS); partly edited by Mahdī Ḥasan al-Kīlānī al-Qādirī as *Kitāb al-Ḥujja ʿalā ahl al-Madīna*. Hyderabad: n.p., 1385/1965. [AC]

——. *al-Jāmiʿ al-ṣaghīr*. Karachi: Idārat al-Qurʾān waʾl-ʿUlūm al-Islāmiyya, 1987. [TZ]

——. *Kitāb al-Aṣl*, ed. Abūʾl-Wafāʾ al-Afghānī, 4 vols. Hyderabad: Maṭbaʿat Majlis Dāʾirat al-Maʿārif al-ʿUthmāniyya, 1966–73. [TZ]

al-Shirbīnī, Muḥammad b. Aḥmad. *Tafsīr al-Khaṭīb al-Shirbīnī: al-musammā al-sirāj al-munīr fīʾl-iʿāna ʿalā maʿrifat baʿḍ maʿānī kalām Rabbinā al-ḥakīm al-khabīr*. Beirut: Dār al-Kutub al-ʿIlmiyya, 2004. [ACh]

al-Shurunbulālī, Abūʾl-Ikhlāṣ. *al-Nafḥa al-qudsiyya fī aḥkām qirāʾat al-Qurʾān wa kitābatihi biʾl-fārisiyya*. Cairo: al-Maṭbaʿa al-Raḥmāniyya, 1355/1936. [TZ]

al-Subkī, Tāj al-Dīn ʿAbd al-Wahhāb b. ʿAlī. *Ṭabaqāt al-shāfiʿiyya al-kubrā*, ed. Maḥmūd Muḥammad al-Ṭināḥī and ʿAbd al-Fattāḥ al-Ḥulw, 10 vols. Cairo: ʿIsā al-Bābī al-Ḥalabī, 1964–76. [CG]

al-Suddī, Ismāʿīl b. ʿAbd al-Raḥmān (al-Suddī al-Kabīr). *Tafsīr al-Suddī al-Kabīr*, ed. Muḥammad ʿAṭā Yūsuf. al-Manṣūra: Dār al-Wafāʾ, 1993. [KV]

Sufyān al-Thawrī b. Saʿīd Abū ʿAbd Allāh. *Kitāb al-Farāʾiḍ*; ed. Hans-Peter Raddatz as 'Frühislamisches Erbrecht nach dem *Kitāb al-Farāʾiḍ* des Sufyān al-Thawrī', *Die Welt des Islams* 13 (1971), pp. 26–78. [AC]

——. *Tafsīr al-Qur'ān al-karīm* (*Tafsīr Sufyān al-Thawrī*), ed. Imtiyāz ʿAlī ʿArshī. Rāmpūr: n.p., 1385/1965. [AC]; repr. Beirut: Dār al-Kutub al-ʿIlmiyya, 1403/1983. [HB] [AC] [KV]

al-Sughdī, ʿAlī b. al-Ḥusayn (attrib.). *al-Nutaf fī'l-fatāwā*, ed. Ṣalāḥ al-Dīn al-Nāhī, 2 vols. Beirut: Mu'assasat al-Risāla, 1984. [TZ]

Sulaymān, Muḥammad. 'Ḥadath al-aḥdāth fī'l-islām: al-iqdām ʿalā tarjamat al-Qur'ān', *al-Ahrām*, issue 18420 (24 March 1936) and *al-Ahrām*, issue 18437 (10 April 1936). [TZ]

——. *Kitāb Ḥadath al-aḥdāth fī'l-islām: al-iqdām ʿalā tarjamat al-Qur'ān*. Cairo: Maṭbaʿat Jarīdat Miṣr al-Ḥurra, 1355/1936, pp. 46–8. [TZ]

Suyūṭī, Jalāl al-Dīn. *Asrār tartīb al-Qur'ān*, ed. Muḥammad Abū'l-Faḍl Ibrāhīm. Cairo: Dār al-Iʿtiṣād, 1376/1976. [SB]

——. *Bughyat al-wuʿāt fī ṭabaqāt al-lughawiyyīn wa'l-nuḥāt*, ed. Muḥammad Abū'l-Faḍl Ibrāhīm, 2 vols. Cairo: Maṭbaʿat ʿĪsā al-Ḥalabī, 1964–5. [CG] [KV]

——. *al-Durr al-manthūr fī'l-tafsīr bi'l-ma'thūr*. Cairo: Dār al-Maʿarifa, 1978. [SB]; ed. ʿAbd Allāh ʿAbd al-Muḥsin al-Turkī, 18 vols. Cairo: Dār Hajr, 1424/2003. [CG]

——. *al-Khaṣā'iṣ al-kubrā*, ed. Muḥammad Khalīl Harrās, 3 vols. Cairo: Dār al-Kutub al-Ḥadītha, n.d. [TZ]

——. *[Kitāb] al-Itqān fī ʿulūm al-Qur'ān*, ed. Muḥammad Abū'l-Faḍl Ibrāhīm, 4 vols in 2. Cairo: Maktabat al-Mashhad al-Ḥusaynī, 1967. [TZ]; Beirut: Dār al-Kutub al-ʿIlmiyya, 1407/1987. [TM]; Beirut: Dār al-Fikr, 1423/2003. [SB]; tr. Ḥamid Algar, Michael Schub and Ayman Abdel Ḥaleem as *The Perfect Guide to the Sciences of the Qur'ān: al-Itqān fī ʿulūm al-Qur'ān*. Reading: Garnet, 2011. [SB] [TM]

——. *Lubāb al-nuqūl fī asbāb al-nuzūl*. Tunis: Dār al-Tūnisiya, 1981. [SB]

——. *al-Muhadhdhab fī-mā waqaʿa fī'l-Qur'ān min al-muʿarrab*. Beirut: Dār al-Kutub al-ʿIlmiyya, 1988. [SB]

——. *al-Mutawakkilī*; ed. and tr. William Y. Bell as *The Mutawakkilī of as-Suyūṭī*. Cairo: Nile Mission Press, 1924. [SB – Intr] [SB]

——. *al-Muzhīr fī ʿulūm al-lugha wa anwā'ihā*. Cairo: ʿĪsā al-Bābī al-Halabī, 1954–7. [SB]

——. and Jalāl al-Dīn al-Maḥallī. *Tafsir al-Jalālayn*. *See* al-Maḥallī.

al-Ṭabarī, Abū Jaʿfar Muḥammad b. Jarīr. *Jāmiʿ al-bayān ʿan ta'wīl āy al-Qur'ān* [*Tafsīr*]. Cairo: Būlāq, 1905–12. [SB]; ed. Muṣṭafā al-Saqqā *et al.*, 30 vols. Cairo: Muṣṭafā al-Bābī al-Ḥalabī, 1373–7/1954–7. [CG] [DS]; 3rd edn, 1968. [KV]; ed. Maḥmūd Muḥammad Shākir and Aḥmad Muḥammad Shākir, 16 vols (incomplete: to Q. 14:27). Cairo: Dār al-Maʿārif, 1374–89/1954–69. [AC] [CG]; repr. Cairo: Maktabat Ibn Taymiyya, n.d. [BW]; rev. ʿAlī ʿĀshūr, 30 vols in 15. Beirut: Dār Iḥyā' al-Turāth al-ʿArabī, 1421/2001. [CM]; *Tafsīr al-Ṭabarī al-musammā Jāmiʿ al-bayān fī ta'wīl al-Qur'ān*. Beirut: Dār al-Kutub al-ʿIlmiyya, 1992. [HB]; repr. 1999. [ACh].

——. *Ṣarīḥ al-sunna*, in Dominique Sourdel, 'Une profession de foi de l'historien al-Ṭabarī', *Revue des études islamiques* 36 (1968), pp. 177–99. [CM]

——. *Tafsīr-i Ṭabarī*, MS Supplément persan 1610, Bibliothèque Nationale de France, Paris. [TZ]

——. *Ta'rīkh al-rusul wa'l-mulūk*; ed. Muḥammad Abū'l-Faḍl Ibrāhīm as *Ta'rīkh al-Ṭabarī*. Cairo: Dār al-Ma'ārif, 1960–69. [CM]; ed. M.J. de Goeje, *et al.* as *Annales quos scripsit Abu Djafar Mohammed ibn Djarir at-Tabari*, 3 series in 16 vols. Leiden: Brill, 1879–1901. [CM]

——. *Tarjuma-i Tafsīr-i Ṭabarī*, ed. Ḥabīb Yaghmā'ī, 3rd edn, 7 vols. Tehran: Intishārāt-i Tūs, 1367 Sh./1988. [TZ]

al-Ṭabrisī (or al-Ṭabarsī), Amīn al-Dīn al-Faḍl b. al-Ḥasan. *Majma' al-bayān fī tafsīr al-Qur'ān*. Sidon: Maṭba'at al-'Irfān, 1333–56. [CM]; 30 vols. in 6. Beirut: Dār Maktabat al-Ḥayāt, n.d.; repr. of Beirut: n.p., 1380/1961. [CG]

al-Ṭaḥāwī, Aḥmad b. Muḥammad. *Bayān i'tiqād ahl al-sunna wa'l-jamā'a*, appended to Aḥmad Ibn Ḥanbal (attrib.), *Kitāb al-Wara'*, ed. Zaynab Ibrāhīm al-Qārūṭ. Beirut: Dār al-Kutub al-'Ilmiyya, 1403/1983, pp. 198–205. [CM]

——. *Mukhtaṣar*, ed. Abū'l-Wafā' al-Afghānī. Cairo: n.p., 1370/1950. [AC]

al-Tha'ālibī, 'Abd al-Raḥmān. *Tafsīr al-Tha'ālibī: al-musammā bi'l-Jawāhir al-ḥisān fī tafsīr al-Qur'ān*. Beirut: Dār Iḥyā' al-Turāth, 1997. [ACh]

al-Tha'labī, Abū Iṣḥāq Aḥmad b. Muḥammad. *al-Kashf wa'l-bayān 'an tafsīr al-Qur'ān*, ed. Abū Muḥammad b. 'Āshūr, revised by Naẓīr al-Sā'idī, 10 vols. Beirut: Dār Iḥyā' al-Turāth al-'Arabī, 2002. [CG] [DS]; tr. and ed. Isaiah Goldfeld as *Qur'ānic Commentary in the Eastern Islamic Tradition of the First Four Centuries of the Hijra: An Annotated Edition of the Preface to al-Tha'labī's 'Kitāb al-Kashf wa'l-Bayān an Tafsīr al-Qur'ān'*. Acre: Srugy, 1984. [CG]

al-Ṭūsī, Abū Ja'far Muḥammad b. al-Ḥasan (Shaykh al-Ṭā'ifa). *al-Fihrist*, ed. Muḥammad Ṣādiq Āl Baḥr al-'Ulūm. Najaf: al-Maṭba'a al-Ḥaydariyya, 1937. [CM]; repr. 1960. [CM]

——. *al-Istibṣār fī-mā'khtulifa min al-akhbār*, ed. Ḥasan al-Mawsawī al-Khurāsānī, 2nd edn, 4 vols. Najaf: Dār al-Kutub al-Islāmiyya, 1376/1957. [AC]

——. *Kitāb al-Khilāf*, 3 vols. Najaf: Sharikat Dār al-Ma'ārif al-Islāmiyya, 1956. [AC]

——. *Tahdhīb al-Aḥkām*, 10 vols. Najaf: Dār al-Kutub al-Islāmiyya, 1377–82/1957–62. [AC]

——. *al-Tibyān fī tafsīr al-Qur'ān*, ed. Āghā Buzurg al-Ṭihrānī *et al.*, 10 vols. Najaf: al-Maṭba'a al-'Ilmiyya, 1376–83/1957–63. [AC]; *Tafsīr*, 10 vols. Beirut: Dār Iḥyā' al-Turāth al-'Arabī, n.d. [CG]; reprint of Najaf: al-Maṭba'a al-'Ilmiyya, 1367–83/1957–63. [CG]

al-Tustarī, Sahl b. 'Abd Allāh. *Tafsīr*; tr. Annabel Keeler and Ali Keeler as *Tafsīr al-Tustarī*. Louisville, KY: Fons Vitae / Royal Aal al-Bayt Institute for Islamic Thought, 2011. [SB – Intr] [SB]

Ubeydullah, Mehmet. 'Cuma Mev'izeleri', *Vatan*, 16 May 1924 (16 Mayıs 1340). [BW]

al-'Ukbarī, Abū'l-Baqā'. *Imlā' mā manna bihi al-Raḥmān min wujūh al-i'rāb wa'l-qirā'āt fī jamī' al-Qur'ān*, ed. Ibrāhīm 'Aṭwa 'Awaḍ. Cairo: Dār al-Ḥadīth, 1992. [CG]; orig. pub. 2 vols. in 1. Cairo: Muṣṭafā al-Bābī al-Ḥalabī, 1380/1961. [CG]; also without the name of the editor. Beirut: Dār al-Kutub al-'Ilmiyya, 1399/1979. [CG]; ed. 'Alī Muḥammad al-Bijāwī as *al-Tibyān fī i'rāb al-Qur'ān*, 2 vols. Cairo: 'Īsā al-Bābī al-Ḥalabī, 1396/1976. [CG]

——. *Iʿrāb al-qirāʾāt al-shawādhdh*, ed. Muḥammad al-Sayyid A. ʿAzzūz, 2 vols. Beirut: ʿĀlam al-Kutub, 1417/1996. [CG]

ʿUthmānī, Ẓafar Aḥmad. *Iʿlāʾ al-sunan*, 22 vols. Karachi: Idārat al-Qurʾān wa'l-ʿUlūm al-Islāmiyya, 1401/1980–81. [TZ]

al-Wāḥidī, Abū'l-Ḥasan ʿAlī b. Aḥmad al-Naysābūrī. *al-Tafsīr al-basīṭ*, ed. Muḥammad Ṣāliḥ b. ʿAbd Allāh al-Fawzān *et al.*, 25 vols. Riyadh: Jāmiʿat al-Imām Muḥammad b. Suʿūd, 1430/2010. [CG]

——. *al-Wajīz fī tafsīr al-Kitāb al-ʿazīz*. Damascus: Dār al-Qalam, 1995. [ACh]

Wajdī, Muḥammad Farīd. *al-Adilla al-ʿilmiyya ʿalā jawāz tarjamat maʿānī'l-Qurʾān ilā'l-lughāt al-ajnabiyya*, 2nd edn. Cairo: Maṭbaʿat al-Raghāʾib, 1355/1936. [TZ]

——. 'Ḥadath al-aḥdāth fī'l-islām', *al-Ahrām*, issue 18424 (28 March 1936). [TZ]

——. *al-Muṣḥaf al-mufassar*. Cairo: Maṭbaʿat Dāʾirat Maʿārif al-Qarn al-ʿIshrīn, 1925. [TZ]

Wakīʿ. *al-Zuhd*, ed. ʿAbd al-Raḥmān ʿAbd al-Jabbār al-Faryawāʾī. Medina: Maktabat al-Dār, 1404/1984. [CM]; repr. Riyadh: Dār al-Ṣumayʿī, 1415/1994. [CM]

Yāqūt b. ʿAbd Allāh al-Ḥamawī al-Rūmī. *Muʿjam al-buldān*; ed. Ferdinand Wüstenfeld as *Jacut's Geographisches Wörterbuch*, 6 vols. Leipzig: F.A. Brockhaus, 1866–73; repr. 1924. [CG]

——. *Muʿjam al-udabāʾ aw Irshād al-arīb ilā maʿrifat al-adīb*, ed. Iḥsān ʿAbbās. Beirut: Dār al-Gharb al-Islāmī, 1993. [CG]

Yazır, Elmalılı Muhammed Hamdi. *Hak Dini Kur'an Dili: Yeni Mealli Türkçe Tefsir*, 9 vols. Istanbul: Matbaa-i Ebüzziya, 1935. [BW] [SW]

al-Zabīdī, Muḥammad b. Muḥammad Murtaḍā. *Tāj al-ʿarūs min jawāhir al-qāmūs*, ed. ʿAbd al-Sattār Aḥmad Farāj *et al.*, 40 vols. Kuwait: Maṭabaʿat Ḥukūmāt al-Kuwayt and al-Majlis al-Waṭanī li'l-Thaqāfa wa'l-Funūn wa'l-Ādāb, 1385–1422/1965–2001. [SB – Intr] [SB] [CG] [BW]

al-Zajjāj, Abū Isḥāq Ibrāhīm b. al-Sarī. *Maʿānī al-Qurʾān wa iʿrābuhu*, Beirut: al-Maktaba al-ʿAṣriyya, 1973. [ACh]; ed. ʿAbd al-Jalīl ʿAbduh Shalabī, 5 vols. Beirut: ʿĀlam al-Kutub, 1408/1988. [CG]

al-Zajjājī, ʿAbd al-Raḥmān b. Isḥaq. *Ishtiqāq asmāʾ Allāh*, ed. ʿAbd al-Ḥusayn al-Mubārak, repr. Beirut: Muʾassasat al-Risāla, 1406/1986. [CG]

al-Zamakhsharī, Abū'l-Qāsim Maḥmūd b. ʿUmar. *Asās al-balāgha*. Beirut: Dār Ṣādir, 1979. [CG]

——. *al-Kashshāf ʿan ḥaqāʾiq al-tanzīl*, 4 vols. Cairo: Dār ʿĀlam al-Maʿrifa, n.d. [DS]; *al-Kashshāf ʿan ḥaqāʾiq ghawāmiḍ al-tanzīl wa ʿuyūn al-aqāwīl fī wujūh al-taʾwīl*, 4 vols. Beirut: Dār al-Kitāb al-ʿArabī, 1947. [TZ]; 2nd edn. Cairo: n.p., 1373/1953. [SW]; Beirut: Dār al-Maʿrifa, 1987. [SB]; Beirut: Dār al-Kutub al-ʿIlmiyya, 2003. [ACh]

——. *Nukat al-aʿrāb fī gharīb al-iʿrāb fī'l-Qurʾān al-karīm*, ed. Muḥammad Abū'l-Fatūḥ Sharīf. Cairo: Dār al-Maʿārif, 1986. [SB]

al-Zarkashī, Abū ʿAbd Allāh Badr al-Dīn. *al-Baḥr al-muḥīṭ fī uṣūl al-fiqh*, ed. ʿAbd al-Qādir ʿAbd Allāh al-ʿĀnī, *et al.*, 6 vols. Kuwait: Wizārat al-Awqāf wa'l-Shuʾūn al-Islāmiyya, 1992. [TZ]

——. *al-Burhān fī ʿulūm al-Qurʾān*, ed. Muḥammad Abū'l-Faḍl Ibrāhīm, 4 vols. Cairo: Dār Iḥyāʾ al-Kutub al-ʿArabiyya, 1957. [TZ] al-Zarqānī, ʿAbd al-ʿAẓīm. *Manāhil al-ʿirfān fī ʿulūm al-Qurʾān*, ed. Fawwāz Aḥmad Zamarlī. Beirut: Dār al-Kitāb al-ʿArabī, 1995. [TZ]

Ẓawāhirī, Muḥammad al-Aḥmadī. 'Letter to the Prime Minister', dated 13 Muḥarram 1355/5 April 1936 in Fakhr al-Dīn al-Aḥmad al-Ẓawāhirī, *al-Siyāsa wa'l-Azhar*. Cairo: Maṭbaʿat al-Iʿtimād, 1945, pp. 349–50. [TZ]

Zayd b. ʿAlī. *Tafsīr gharīb al-Qurʾān*, ed. Ḥasan Muḥammad Taqī al-Ḥakīm. Beirut: al-Dār al-ʿĀlamiyya, 1992. [KV]; ed. Muḥammad Jawād al-Ḥusaynī al-Jalālī. Tehran: Markaz al-Nashr al-Tibāʿ li-Maktabat al-Iʿlām al-Islāmī, 1376 Sh./1418/1997. [SB]

al-Zubaydī, Muḥammad b. al-Ḥasan. *Ṭabaqāt al-naḥwiyyīn wa'l-lughawiyyīn*, ed. Muḥammad Abū'l-Faḍl Ibrāhīm. Cairo: M. Sāmī Amīn al-Khanjī, 1373/1954. [CG]

Secondary Sources

ʿAbd al-Bāqī, Muḥammad Fuʾād. *al-Muʿjam al-mufahras li-alfāẓ al-Qurʾān al-karīm*, repr. Riyadh: Dār al-Ḥadīth, 1417/1996. [SB]

ʿAbd al-Tawwāb, Ramaḍān. *Das Kitāb al-Gharīb al-muṣannaf von Abū ʿUbaid und seine Bedeutung für die nationalarabische Lexikographie*. Munich: Heppenheim, 1962. [CG]

Abdel Haleem, M. 'Grammatical Shift for Rhetorical Purposes: *Iltifāt* and Related Features in the Qur'ān', *Bulletin of the School of Oriental and African Studies* 55, no. 3 (1992), pp. 407–32. [DS]

Abou Sheishaa, Mohammed A.M. 'A Study of the Fatwa by Rashid Rida on the Translation of the Qur'an', *Journal of the Society for Quranic Studies* 1 (2001).* [SW]

Abrahamov, Binyamin. 'The Creation and Duration of Paradise and Hell', *Der Islam* 79 (2002), pp. 87–102. [KV]

——. 'Faḫr al-Dīn al-Rāzī on the Knowability of God's Essence and Attributes', *Arabica* 49, no. 2 (2002), pp. 204–30. [SB – Intr]

Abū Ghadīr, Muḥammad Maḥmūd. 'Tarjamat Uri Rubin li-maʿāni al-Qurʾān al-karīm bi'l-ʿibriyya (ʿarḍ wa-taqwīm)' in *Nadwat al-Qurʾān al-karīm fī'l-dirāsāt al-istishrāqiyya*. Medina: 7–9 November 2006. [SW]

Adharnūsh, Ādhartāsh. *Tārīkh-i tarjuma az ʿArabī ba Fārsī, az āghāz tā ʿaṣr -i ṣafawī*. Volume 1: *Tarjumahā-i Qurʾān*. Tehran: Surūsh, 1375 Sh./ 1996–7. [TZ]

Adonis. *An Introduction to Arab Poetics*, tr. Catherine Cobham. London: Saqi, 1990; orig. pub. as *Introduction à la poétique arabe*. Paris: Sindbad, 1985. [SW]

Ahmad, Abdelhamid Muhammad. *Die Auseinandersetzung zwischen Al-Azhar und der modernistischen Bewegung in Ägypten*. Dissertation, University of Hamburg, 1963. [SW] [TZ]

Ahmad (Jullandri), Rashid. 'Qurʾānic Exegesis and Classical Tafsīr', *Islamic Quarterly* 12 (1968), pp. 71–119. [HB]

Ahmed, Shahab. 'Ibn Taymiyya and the Satanic Verses', *Studia Islamica* 87 (1998), pp. 67–124. [SB]

Ahmed, Shukri B. *Aristotelian Logic and the Arabic Language in Alfārābī*. Albany, NY: State University of New York Press, 1991. [SB]
Aichele, George. *Sign, Text, Scripture: Semiotics and the Bible*. Sheffield: Sheffield Academic Press, 1997. [SB – Intr]
——, and Gary A. Phillips. 'Exegesis, Eisegesis, Intergesis', *Semeia* 69/70 (1995), pp. 7–18. [SB – Intr]
Albayrak, Ismail. 'The Qur'anic Narratives of the Golden Calf Episode', *Journal of Qur'anic Studies* 3 (2001), pp. 47–69. [SB]
Ali, Kecia. 'Money, Sex, and Power: The Contractual Nature of Marriage in Islamic Jurisprudence'. Unpublished PhD Dissertation, Duke University, 2002. [ACh]
——. *Sexual Ethics in Islam: Feminist Reflections on Qur'an, Hadith and Jurisprudence*. Oxford: Oneworld, 2006. [ACh]
——. *Marriage and Slavery in Early Islam*. London: Harvard University Press, 2010. [ACh]
ʿAlī Akbār Qurashī. *Qāmūs-i Qur'ān*. Tehran: Dār al-Kutub al-Islāmiyya, 1973–6. [SB – Intr]
Alí-de-Unzaga, Omar. 'The Conversation between Moses and God (*munāǧāt Musā*) in the *Epistles* of the Pure Brethren' in Daniel De Smet, Godefroid de Callataÿ and Jan van Reeth, eds, *Al-Kitāb: La sacralité du texte dans le monde de l'Islam, Actes du Symposium international tenu à Leuven et Louvain-la-Neuve du 29 mai au 1 juin 2002*. Brussels: Société Belge d'Etudes Orientales, 2004, pp. 371–87. [CM]
——. 'Citational Exegesis of the Qur'an: Towards a Theoretical Framework for the Construction of Meaning in Classical Islamic Thought. The Case of the *Epistles of the Pure Brethren* (*Rasā'il Ikhwān al-Ṣafā'*)' in Abdou Filali-Ansary and Aziz Esmail, eds, *The Construction of Belief: Reflections on the Thought of Mohammed Arkoun*. London: Saqi Books in association with the Institute for the Study of Muslim Civilisations, 2012, pp. 168–93. [SB – Intr]
Allen, Graham. *Intertextuality: The New Critical Idiom*, 2nd edn. London: Routledge, 2011. [SB – Intr]
Ambros, Arne A., with Stephan Procházka. *A Concise Dictionary of Koranic Arabic*. Wiesbaden: Reichert Verlag, 2004. [SB – Intr]
Amir-Moezzi, Mohammad Ali. *The Spirituality of Shiʿi Islam: Beliefs and Practices*. London, I.B. Tauris in association with the Institute of Ismaili Studies, 2011. [TZ]
Arazi, Albert, and Salmā Maṣāliḥa. *al-ʿIqd al-thamīn fī diwāwīn al-shuʿarā' al-sitta al-jāhilliyyīn*. Jerusalem: al-Jāmiʿa al-ʿIbriyya fī Ūrushalayim, 1999. [SB]
Awn, Peter J. *Satan's Tragedy and Redemption: Iblīs in Sufi Psychology*. Leiden: Brill, 1983. [SB – Intr]
Ayoub, Mohammad. 'Translating the Meanings of the Qur'an: Traditional Opinions and Modern Debates', *Inquiry/Afkar* 3, no. 5 (1986), pp. 34–9. [TZ]
Al-Aʿzami, Muhammad Mustafa. *The History of the Qur'ānic Text, from Revelation to Compilation: A Comparative Study with the Old and New Testaments*. Leicester: UK Islamic Academy, 2003. [SW]

Baalbaki, Ramzi. 'Early Arab Lexicographers and the Use of Semitic Languages', *Berytus* 31 (1983), pp. 117–27. [CG] [KV]

Badawi, Elsaid M., and Muhammad Abdel Haleem. *Arabic-English Lexicon of Qur'anic Usage*. Leiden: Brill, 2008. [SB – Intr] [CG]

al-Badr, Badr b. Nāṣir b. Badr. *Aqwāl Abī 'Ubayda fī Tafsīr al-Ṭabarī wa mawqifuhu minhā*. Riyadh: Jāmiʿat al-Imām Muḥammad b. Su'ūd, 1428/2007. [CG]

Bāghbīdī, Ḥasan Riḍā'ī. 'Darbāra-i tarjama-i ʿibārātī az Qur'an ba Pahlawī', *Nāma-yi Īrān-ī Bāstān* 1 (1380 Sh./2001), pp. 11–14. [TZ]

Bar-Asher, Meir M. *Scripture and Exegesis in Early Imāmī Shiism*. Leiden: Brill, 1991. [SB – Intr]; Leiden: Brill, and Jerusalem: The Magnes Press, 1999. [SB]

al-Bāriqī, 'Abd al-Raḥmān b. Ḥasan b. 'Abduh. *al-Naḥw fī'l-Tafsīr al-wasīṭ li'l-Wāḥidī*. Mecca: University of Umm al-Qurā, 1426–7/2005–6. [CG]

Barthes, Roland. 'The Death of the Author' in idem, *Image, Music, Text*, tr. Stephen Heath, repr. London: Flamingo, 1984, pp. 142–8; orig. pub. as 'La mort de l'auteur', *Manteia* 5 (1968), pp. 12–17. [SB – Intr]

——. 'From Word to Text' in *Image, Music, Text*, pp. 155–64; orig. pub. as 'De l'œuvre au texte', *Revue d'esthétique* 3 (1971), pp. 225–32. [SB – Intr]

Bashear, Suliman. *Arabs and Others in Early Islam*. Princeton, NJ: Darwin Press, 1997. [TZ]

Bauer, Karen. '"Traditional" Exegesis of Q 4:34', *Comparative Islamic Studies* 2 (2006), pp. 129–42. [ACh]

——. 'Room for Interpretation: Qur'ānic Exegesis and Gender'. PhD Dissertation, Princeton University, 2008; published as *Gender Hierarchy in the Qur'an: Medieval Interpretations, Modern Responses*. Cambridge: Cambridge University Press, 2015. [ACh]

——. '*The Male Is Not Like The Female* (Q 3:36): The Question of Gender Egalitarianism in the Qur'ān', *Religion Compass* 3, no. 4 (2009), pp. 637–54. [ACh]

——. '"I Have Seen the People's Antipathy to this Knowledge": The Muslim Exegete and his Audience, 5th/11th–7th/13th Centuries' in Asad Q. Ahmed, Behnam Sadeghi and Michael Bonner, eds, *The Islamic Scholarly Tradition: Studies in History, Law, and Thought in Honor of Professor Michael Allan Cook*. Leiden: Brill, 2011, pp. 293–314. [SB – Intr]

——. 'Introduction' in Karen Bauer, ed., *Aims, Methods and Contexts of Qur'anic Exegesis (2nd/8th–9th/15th c.)*. Oxford: Oxford University Press in association with the Institute of Ismaili Studies, 2013, pp. 1–16. [SB – Intr] [SB]

——. 'Justifying the Genre: A Study of Introductions to Classical Works of *Tafsīr*' in Bauer, ed., *Aims, Methods and Contexts of Qur'anic Exegesis*, pp. 39–65. [SB – Intr]

Bauer, Thomas. *Die Kultur der Ambiguität: Eine andere Geschichte des Islams*. Berlin: Verlag der Weltreligionen, 2011. [SW]

Baygi, Shahrokh Mohammad. 'The First Available Persian Interpretation of the Qur'an Known as the *Tarjumah Tafsīr-i-Ṭabarī*', *Hamdard Islamicus* 19, no. 4 (1996), pp. 31–44. [TZ]

Bell, Richard. *A Commentary on the Qur'ān*, ed. Clifford Edmund Bosworth and Mervin Edwin John Richardson. Manchester: University of Manchester Press, 1991. [CG]

Bellos, David. *Is That a Fish in Your Ear? Translation and the Meaning of Everything*. New York: Faber and Faber, 2011. [TZ]
Benedikt XVI. *Glaube und Vernunft. Die Regensburger Vorlesung*. Vollständige Ausgabe. Kommentiert von Gesine Schwan, Adel Theodor Khoury, Karl Kardinal Lehmann. Freiburg: Herder, 2006. [SW]
Berg, Herbert. 'Ṭabarī's Exegesis of the Qur'ānic Term *al-kitāb*', *Journal of the American Academy of Religion* 63, no. 4 (1995), pp. 761–74. [SB - Intr] [HB]
——. *The Development of Exegesis in Early Islam: The Authenticity of Muslim Literature from the Formative Period*. Richmond, Surrey, and London and New York: Curzon, 2000. [HB] [SB] [KV]
——. 'Competing Paradigms in the Study of Islamic Origins: Qur'ān 15:89–91 and the Value of *Isnāds*' in idem, ed., *Method and Theory in the Study of Islamic Origins*. Leiden: Brill, 2003, pp. 259–90. [HB]
——. 'Ibn ʿAbbās in ʿAbbāsid-Era *Tafsīr*' in James E. Montgomery, ed., *Abbasid Studies: Occasional Papers of the School of Abbasid Studies, Cambridge, 6–10 July 2002*. Leuven: Peeters Publishers, 2004, pp. 129–46. [HB]
——. "Abbasid Historians' Portrayals of al-ʿAbbās b. ʿAbd al-Muttalib' in John Nawas, ed., *Abbasid Studies II: Occasional Papers of the School of Abbasid Studies, Leuven, 28 June - 1 July 2004*. Leuven: Peeters Publishers, 2010, pp. 13–38. [HB]
Bergenholz, Henning, and Rufus S. Gouws. 'A Functional Approach to the Choice between Descriptive, Prescriptive and Proscriptive Lexicography', *Lexikos* 20 (2010), pp. 26–51. [SB - Intr]
Binark, İsmet *et al*. *The World Bibliography of the Translations of the Meanings of the Holy Quran*. Istanbul: OIC Research Center, 1986. [SW]
Birch, Nicholas. 'Turkey: Proliferation of Koran Translations Pushing Turks to "Verge of Division"'.* [SW]
Birkeland, Harris. *Old Muslim Opposition against Interpretation of the Koran*. Oslo: Jacob Dybwad, 1955. [HB]
Blachère, Régis. 'Origine de la théorie des *aḍdād*' in Jacques Berque and Jean-Paul Charnay, eds, *L'ambivalence dans la culture arabe*. Paris: Editions Anthropos, 1967, pp. 397–403. [KV]
Blau, Joshua. 'The Role of the Bedouins as Arbiters in Linguistic Questions and the *Mas'ala az-Zunburiyya*', *Journal of Semitic Studies* 8, no. 1 (1963), pp. 42–51. [SB]
Bohas, George, and Jean-Patrick Guillaume. *Étude des theories des grammairiens arabes. I. Morphologie et phonologie*. Damascus: Institut Française de Damas, 1984. [SB]
Boullata, Issa J. 'Poetry Citation as Interpretive Illustration in Qur'ān Exegesis: *Masā'il Nāfiʿ ibn al-Azraq*', reprinted in Mustafa Shah, ed., *Tafsīr – Interpreting the Qur'ān: Critical Concepts in Islamic Studies*. London: Routledge, 2013, pp. 65–77. [SB]
Bravmann, Meir Max. *The Spiritual Background of Early Islam: Studies in Ancient Arab Concepts*. Leiden: Brill, 1972. [CG]
Brigaglia, Andrea. 'Two Published Hausa Translations of the Qur'ān and Their Doctrinal Background', *Journal of Religion in Africa* 35, no. 4 (2005), pp. 424–49. [SB - Intr]

Brockelmann, Carl. *Geschichte der arabischen Litteratur* (*GAL*). Leiden: Brill, 1943–9. [AC] [CG]

Brown, Francis, S.R. Driver, and Charles A. Briggs. *Hebrew and English Lexicon of the Old Testament*. Oxford: Clarendon Press, 1968. [TM]

Brown, Jonathan. *The Canonization of al-Bukhārī and Muslim: The Formation and Function of the Sunnī Ḥadīth Canon*. Leiden: Brill, 2007. [HB] [SB]

Brunner, Rainer. 'Education, Politics, and the Struggle for Intellectual Leadership: al-Azhar between 1927 and 1945' in Dale Eickleman, ed., *Guardians of Faith in Modern Times: 'Ulamā' in the Middle East*. Leiden: Brill, 2009, pp. 109–40. [TZ]

Bultmann, Rudolf. 'Is Exegesis without Presuppositions Possible?' in idem, *Existence and Faith: Shorter Writings of Rudolf Bultmann*, tr. M. Ogden. London: Hodder and Stoughton Ltd., 1961, pp. 342–51; orig. pub. as 'Ist voraussetzungslose Exegese möglich', *Theologische Zeitschrift* 13 (1957), pp. 409–17. [SB – Intr]

Burge, S.R. 'The Angels in *Sūrat al-Malā'ika*: Exegeses of Q. 35.1', *Journal of Qur'anic Studies* 10 (2008), pp. 50–70. [HB] [SB]

——. *Angels in Islam: Jalāl al-Dīn al-Suyūṭī's* al-Ḥabā'ik fī akhbār al-malā'ik. London: Routledge, 2012. [DS]

——. 'Jalāl al-Dīn al-Suyūṭī, the *Mu'awwidhatān* and the Modes of Exegesis' in Bauer, ed., *Aims, Methods and Contexts of Qur'anic Exegesis*, pp. 277–307. [SB – Intr] [SB]

——. 'Scattered Pearls: al-Suyūṭī's Hermeneutics and Use of Sources in *al-Durr al-manthūr fi'l-tafsīr bi'l-ma'thūr*', *Journal of the Royal Asiatic Society* 24, no. 2 (2014), pp. 251–96. [SB]

——. 'The Search for Meaning: *Tafsīr*, Hermeneutics, and Theories of Reading', *Arabica* 62, no. 1 (2015), pp. 53–73. [SB – Intr]

Burton, John. '"Those are High Flying Cranes"', *Journal of Semitic Studies* 15 (1970), pp. 246–65. [SB]

——. *The Collection of the Qur'ān*. Cambridge: Cambridge University Press, 1977. [TM]

——. *Abū 'Ubaid al-Qāsim b. Sallām's* K. al-Nāsikh wa-l-mansūkh *(MS Istanbul, Topkapı, Ahmet III A 143), edited with a commentary*. Bury St. Edmunds: St. Edmundsbury Press, 1987. [KV]

——. 'Linguistic Errors in the Qur'an', *Journal of Semitic Studies* 33, no. 2 (1988), pp. 181–96. [DS]

——. 'The Qur'an and the Practice of *wuḍū*'', *Bulletin of the School of Oriental and African Studies* 51 (1988), pp. 21–58. [KV]

——. *The Sources of Islamic Law: Islamic Theories of Abrogation*. Edinburgh: Edinburgh University Press, 1990. [KV]

Calder, Norman. 'Tafsīr from Ṭabarī to Ibn Kathīr: Problems in the Description of a Genre, Illustrated with Reference to the Story of Abraham' in G.R. Hawting and Abdul-Kader A. Shareef, eds, *Approaches to the Qur'ān*. London: Routledge, 1993, pp. 101–40. [SB – Intr] [CM] [KV]

Caner, Daniel. *Wandering, Begging Monks: Spiritual Authority and the Promotion of Monasticism in Late Antiquity*. Berkeley, CA: University of California Press, 2002. [CM]

Carter, Michael G. 'Language Control as People Control', *al-Abḥath* 31 (1983), pp. 65–84. [SB]
Ceylan, Yasin. *Theology and Tafsīr in the Major Works of Fakhr al-Dīn al-Rāzī*. Kuala Lumpur: International Institute of Islamic Thought and Civilization, 1996. [SB – Intr] [SB]
Chaudhry, Ayesha S. 'The Problems of Conscience and Hermeneutics: Some Contemporary Muslim Approaches', *Comparative Islamic Studies* 2 (2006), pp. 157–70. [ACh]
——. *Domestic Violence and the Islamic Tradition: Ethics, Law and the Muslim Discourse of Gender*. Oxford: Oxford University Press, 2013. [ACh]
Cilardo, Agostino. 'The Position of the Grandfather with Regard to the Germane or Consanguine Brothers in the Islamic Law of Inheritance. A Reconsideration' in idem, *Studies on the Islamic Law of Inheritance, Annali dell'Istituto Universitario Orientale di Napoli* 50, Supplement 63 (1990), pp. 1–32. [AC]
——. *Teorie sulle origini del diritto islamico*. Rome: Istituto per l'Oriente, 1990. [AC]
——. 'The Position of the Slave in the Islamic Law of Inheritance. A Reconsideration (Conference of the School of Abbasid Studies, University of St Andrews, Scotland, July 31–August 5, 1989)' in *Studies of the Islamic Law of Inheritance*, pp. 43–57. [AC]
——. *Diritto ereditario islamico delle scuole giuridiche ismailita e imamita. Casistica*. Rome and Naples: Istituto per l'Oriente – Istituto Universitario Orientale, 1993. [AC]
——. 'The Transmission of the Patronate in Islamic Law' in F. de Jong, ed., *Miscellanea Arabica et Islamica. Dissertationes in Academia Ultrajectina prolatae anno MCMXC, Proceedings of the XVth Congress of the U.E.A.I. (Utrecht, September 13–19, 1990)*. Louvain: Uitgeverij Peeters en Departement Oriëntalistiek, 1993, pp. 31–52. [AC]
——. *Diritto ereditario islamico delle scuole giuridiche sunnite (ḥanafita, mālikita, šāfiʿita e ḥanbalita) e delle scuole giuridiche zaydita, ẓāhirita e ibāḍita. Casistica*. Rome and Naples: Istituto per l'Oriente – Istituto Universitario Orientale, 1994. [AC]
——. '"The Superimposition Theory" in the Islamic Law of Inheritance' in Alexander Fodor, ed., *Proceedings of the 14th Congress of the Union Européenne des Arabisants et Islamisants: Budapest, 29th August–3rd September, 1988*. Budapest: Eötvös Loránd University Chair for Arabic Studies: Csoma de Koőrös Society, Section of Islamic Studies, 1995, pp. 33–41. [AC]
——. 'Preliminary Notes on the Qur'ānic Term *Kalāla*' in U. Vermeulen and J.M.F. van Reeth, eds, *Law, Christianity and Modernism in Islamic Society. Proceedings of the Eighteenth Congress of the Union Européenne des Arabisants et Islamisants, held at the Katholieke Universiteit Leuven (September 3–September 9, 1996)*. Leuven: Uitgeverij Peeters, 1998, pp. 3–12. [AC]
——. 'Some Peculiarities of the Law of Inheritance: The Formation of Imami and Ismaili Law', *Journal of Arabic and Islamic Studies* 3 (2000), pp. 127–37. [AC]

——. *The Qur'ānic Term* Kalāla: *Studies in the Arabic Language and Poetry,* Ḥadīṯ, Tafsīr, *and* Fiqh. *Notes on the Origin of the Islamic Law.* Edinburgh: Edinburgh University Press, 2005. [AC]

Cook, David. 'The Prophet Muḥammad, Labīd al-Yahūdī and the Commentaries to *Sūra* 113', *Journal of Semitic Studies* 45 (2000), pp. 323–45. [SB]

Corriente, Federico. 'Some Notes on the Qur'ānic *lisānun mubīn* and its Loanwords' in Juan Pedro Monferrer-Sala and Urbán Ángel, eds, *Sacred Text: Explorations in Lexicography.* Frankfurt am Main: P. Lang, 2009, pp. 31–46. [KV]

Costet-Tardieu, Francine. *Un réformiste à l'université al-Azhar: Œuvre et pensée de Mustafâ al-Marâghî (1881–1945).* Cairo and Paris: CEDEJ and Karthala, 2005. [SW] [TZ]

Curiel, Raoul, and Philippe Gignoux. 'Un poids arabo-sasanide', *Studia Iranica* 5, no. 2 (1976), pp. 165–9. [TZ]

Czapkiewicz, Andrzej. *The Views of the Medieval Arab Philologists on Language and Its Origins in Light of 'As-Suyūṭī's* ''al-Muzhīr'. Krakow: Naktadem Uniweisytetu Jagiellońskiego, 1988. [SB]

Daftary, Farhad. *Ismaili Literature: A Bibliography of Sources and Studies.* London: I.B. Tauris in association with the Institute of Ismaili Studies, 2004. [CG]

Dagorn, René. *La geste d'Ismaël d'après l'onomastique et la tradition arabes.* Geneva: Librairie Droz, 1981. [KV]

Darwīsh, 'Abd Allāh. 'Mu'jam Tahdhīb al-lugha li-Abī Manṣūr al-Azharī', *Revue de l'Academie Arabe de Damas* (*RADD*) 18 (1968), pp. 71–8. [CG]

al-Dāwūdī, Muḥammad b. 'Alī. *Ṭabaqāt al-mufassirīn*, ed. 'Alī Muḥammad 'Umar, 2 vols. Cairo: Maktabat Wahba, 1392/1972. [CG]; repr. 2008. [CG]

Denny, Frederick. 'Some Religio-Communal Terms and Concepts in the Qur'ān', *Numen* 24 (1977), pp. 26–59. [KV]

Dihkhudā, 'Alī Akbar *et al. Lughatnāma.* Tehran: Dānishgāh-i Tihrān, 1946–. [DS]

Donner, Fred M. *Narratives of Islamic Origins: The Beginnings of Islamic Historical Writing.* Princeton, NJ: Darwin Press, 1998. [CM]

——. *Muhammad and the Believers: At the Origins of Islam.* Cambridge, MA: Belknap Press of Harvard University Press, 2010. [CM]

Dutton, Yasin. 'Orality, Literacy and the "Seven *Aḥruf*" *Ḥadīth*', *Journal of Islamic Studies* 23, no. 1 (2013), pp. 1–49. [SW]

Eco, Umberto. *The Role of the Reader: Explorations in the Semiotics of Text.* Bloomington, IN: University of Indiana Press, 1979. [SB – Intr]

Elder, E.E. 'Al-Ṭaḥāwī's "Bayān al-sunna wa'l-jamā'a"' in *The Macdonald Presentation Volume.* Princeton, NJ: Princeton University Press, 1933, pp. 131–44. [CM]

Elmarsafy, Ziad. 'Translations of the Qur'ān into Western Languages', *Religion Compass* 3, no. 3 (2009), pp. 430–39. [SB – Intr]

Elton, Daniel. 'The Sāmānid "Translations" of al-Ṭabarī' in Hugh Kennedy, ed., *al-Ṭabarī: A Medieval Muslim Historian and His Work.* Princeton, NJ: Darwin Press, 2008, pp. 263–98. [TZ]

van Ess, Josef. *Theologie und Gesellschaft im 2. und 3. Jahrhundert Hidschra. Eine Geschichte des religiösen Denkens im Frühen Islam*, 6 vols. Berlin: Walter de Gruyter, 1991–7. [CM] [SW]

——. *Der Eine und das Andere: Beobachtungen an islamischen häresiographischen Texten*. Berlin: Walter de Gruyter, 2011. [TZ]

Fatani, Afnan H. 'The Lexical Transfer of Arabic Non-core Lexicon: Sura 113 of the Qur'an – *al-Falaq* (The Splitting)', *Journal of Qur'anic Studies* 4 (2002), pp. 61–81. [SB]

Fischer, August. 'Der Wert der vorhandenen Koranübersetzungen und Sure 111' in Rudi Paret, ed., *Der Koran*. Darmstadt: Wissenschaftliche Buchgesellschaft, 1975, pp. 3–10. [SW]

Fischer, Wolfdietrich. *Farb- und Formbezeichnungen in der Sprache der altarabischen Dichtung: Untersuchungen zur Wortbedeutung und zur Wortbildung*. Wiesbaden: Otto Harrassowitz, 1965. [SB – Intr] [KV]

Frank, Richard. 'Meanings Are Spoken of in Many Ways: The Earlier Arab Grammarians', *Le Muséon* 94 nos 3–4 (1981), pp. 259–319. [SB – Intr]

Fück, Johann. *Arabiyya: Untersuchungen zur arabischen Sprach- und Stilgeschichte*. Berlin: Akademie Vorlage, 1958. [SB]

Fudge, Bruce. *Qur'ānic Hermeneutics: Al-Ṭabrisī and the Craft of Commentary*. Abingdon and New York: Routledge, 2011. [CG]

Gadamer, Hans-Georg. *Truth and Method*, tr. Joel Weinsheimer and Donald G. Marshall, 2nd rev. edn. London: Continuum, 2004; orig. pub. as *Wahrheit und Methode: Grundzüge einer philosophischen Hermeneutik*. Tübingen: Mohr, 1960. [SB – Intr]

Gade, Anna. *The Qur'an: An Introduction*. Oxford: Oneworld, 2010. [TZ]

Galli, Ahmad Mohmed Ahmad. 'Some Aspects of al-Māturīdī's Commentary on the Qur'ān', *Islamic Studies* 21, no. 1 (1982), pp. 3–22. [SB – Intr]

Gignoux, Philippe. 'Pour une origine iranienne du bi'smillah' in Philippe Gignoux *et al.*, eds, *Pad nām i Yazdān: études d'épigraphie, de numismatique et d'histoire de l'Iran ancient*. Paris: Klincksieck, 1979, pp. 159–63. [TZ]

Gilliot, Claude. 'Portrait "mythique" d'Ibn 'Abbās', *Arabica* 32 (1985), pp. 127–84. [HB] [SB – Intr] [KV]

——. *Exégèse, langue et théologie en islam: L'exégèse coranique de Tabari*. Paris, Vrin, 1990. [CG]

——. 'Muqātil, grand exégète, traditionniste et théologien maudit', *Journal Asiatique* 279 (1991), pp. 39–92. [CG]

——. 'Textes arabes anciens édités en Égypte au cours des années 1987 à 1990', *Mélanges de l'Institut dominicain d'études orientales du Caire* (*MIDEO*) 20 (1991), pp. 301–504. [CG]

——. 'Textes arabes anciens publiés en Égypte au cours des années 1992 à 1994', *Mélanges de l'Institut dominicain d'études orientales du Caire* (*MIDEO*) 22 (1992), pp. 271–412. [CG]

——. 'Textes arabes anciens édités en Égypte au cours des années 1996 à 1999', *Mélanges de l'Institut dominicain d'études orientales du Caire* (*MIDEO*) 24 (2000), pp. 115–346. [CG]

——. 'Textes arabes anciens édités en Égypte au cours des années 1999 à 2002', *Mélanges de l'Institut dominicain d'études orientales du Caire* (*MIDEO*) 25–26 (2004), pp. 193–475. [CG]

——. 'Kontinuität und Wandel in der "klassischen" islamischen Koranauslegung', *Der Islam* 85 (2010), pp. 1–155. [CG]

——. 'The "Collections" of the Meccan Arabic Lectionary' in Nicolet Boekhoff-van der Voort, Kees Versteegh, and Joas Wagemakers, eds, *The Transmission and Dynamics of the Textual Sources of Islam: Essays in Honour of Harald Motzki*. Leiden: Brill, 2011, pp. 105–33. [KV]

——. 'Mujāhid's Exegesis: Origins, Paths of Transmission and Development of a Meccan Exegetical Tradition in its Human, Spiritual and Theological Environment' in Andreas Görke and Johanna Pink, eds, *Tafsīr and Islamic Intellectual History: Exploring the Boundaries of a Genre*. Oxford: Oxford University Press in association with the Institute of Ismaili Studies, 2014, pp. 63–111. [CG]

Gimaret, Daniel. *Les noms divins en Islam*. Paris: Le Cerf, 1988. [CG]

Gleave, Robert. *Scripturalist Islam: The History and Doctrines of the Akhbārī Shīʿī School*. Leiden: Brill, 2007. [SB - Intr]

——. *Islam and Literalism: Literal Meaning and Interpretation in Islamic Legal Theory*. Edinburgh: Edinburgh University Press, 2012. [SB - Intr]

Goldfeld, Isaiah. 'The *Tafsīr* of Abdallah b. 'Abbās', *Der Islam* 58 (1981), pp. 125–35. [KV]

Goldziher, Ignaz. *Muhammedanische Studien*, 2 vols. Halle, Max Niemeyer, 1888; repr., Hildesheim: G. Olms, 1971. [KV]; tr. S.M. Stern as *Muslim Studies*, 2 vols. Albany, NY: State University of New York Press, 1967. [TZ]

——. *Die Richtungen der islamischen Koranauslegung*. Leiden: Brill, 1970. [KV]

Graham, William A., and Navid Kermani. 'Recitation and Aesthetic Reception' in Jane Dammen McAuliffe, ed., *The Cambridge Companion to the Qur'ān*. Cambridge: Cambridge University Press, 2006, pp. 115–41. [SW]

Greenfield, J.C. 'Rṭyn mgwš (The Sorcerer Whispers)' in Benjamin Sidney and Leon D. Stitskin, eds, *Joshua Finkel Festschrift*. New York: Yeshiva University Press, 1974, pp. 63–9. [TZ]

Greimas, A.J. *Maupassant: La sémiotique du texte*. Paris: Editions du Seuil, 1976. [SB - Intr]

——. *Sémantique structurale. Recherche de méthod*. Paris: Larousse, 1966; tr. D. McDowell, R. Schleifer and A. Velie as *Structural Semantics: An Attempt at a Method*. London: Nebraska University Press, 1983. [SB - Intr]

Guessoum, Nidhal. 'The Qur'an, Science, and the (Related) Contemporary Muslim Discourse', *Zygon* 43, no. 2 (2008), pp. 411–31. [SW]

Gully, Adrian. *Grammar and Semantics in Medieval Arabic: A Study of Ibn-Hishām's* 'Mughni l-Labīb'. Richmond, Surrey: Curzon Press, 1995. [SB]

Haeri, Niloofar. *Sacred Language, Ordinary People: Dilemmas of Culture and Politics in Egypt*. New York: Palgrave Macmillan, 2003. [TZ]

Halevi, Leor. 'The Paradox of Islamization: Tombstone Inscriptions, Qur'ānic Recitations, and the Problem of Religious Change', *History of Religions* 44 (2004–5), pp. 120–52. [CM]

Hämeen-Antilla, Jaako. 'Al-Aṣmāʿī, Early Lexicography and *Kutub al-Farq*', *Zeitschrift für Geschichte der arabisch-islamischen Wissenschaften* 16 (2004–5), pp. 141–8. [SB]

Hamza, Feras, tr. *Tafsīr al-Jalālayn*. *See* Primary Sources, al-Maḥallī and al-Suyūṭī. *Tafsīr al-Jalālayn*.

—— and Sajjad Rizvi with Farhana Mayer, eds. *An Anthology of Qur'anic Commentaries. Volume 1: On the Nature of the Divine*. Oxford: Oxford

University Press in association with the Institute of Ismaili Studies, 2008. [SB – Intr] [SB]

Harrison, Victoria S. 'Hermeneutics, Religious Language and the Qur'an', *Islam and Christian-Muslim Relations* 21, no. 3 (2010), pp. 207–20. [SB – Intr]

al-Ḥasnāwī, Muḥammad. *al-Fāṣila fī'l-Qur'ān*. Beirut: al-Maktab al-Islāmī, 1986. [DS]

Hattemer, Richard. 'Atatürk and the Reforms in Turkey as Reflected in the Egyptian Press', *Journal of Islamic Studies* 11, no. 1 (2000), pp. 21–42. [TZ]

Haywood, John A. 'The Entry in Medieval Arabic Monolingual Dictionaries: Some Aspects of Arrangement and Context' in Reinhard R.K. Hartmann, ed., *The History of Lexicography: Papers from the Dictionary Research Centre Seminar at Exeter, March 1986*. Amsterdam: J. Benjamins, 1986, pp. 107–13. [SB – Intr] [SB]

Heath, Peter. 'Creative Hermeneutics: A Comparative Analysis of Three Islamic Approaches', *Arabica* 36, no. 2 (1989), pp. 173–210. [SB – Intr]

Heidegger, Martin. *Being and Time*, tr. John Macquarrie and Edward Robinson, repr. Oxford: Blackwell, 1978; orig. pub. as *Sein und Zeit*. Tübingen: Max Niemeyer, 1927. [SB – Intr]

Heidemann, Stefan. 'The Evolving Representation of the Early Islamic Empire and its Religion on Coin Imagery' in Angelika Neuwirth, Nicolai Sinai and Michael Marx, eds, *The Qur'ān in Context: Historical and Literary Investigations into the Qur'ānic Milieu*. Brill: Leiden, 2010, pp. 149–95. [TZ]

Heinrichs, Wolfhart. 'On the Genesis of the *Ḥaqīqa-Majāz* Dichotomy', *Studia Islamica* 59 (1984), pp. 111–40. [CG] [KV]

——. 'Contacts between Scriptural Hermeneutics and Literary Theory in Islam: The Case of *Majāz*', *Zeitschrift für Geschichte der arabisch-islamischen Wissenschaften* 7 (1991–2), pp. 253–84. [SB] [CG]

El-Hibri, Tayeb. 'The Redemption of Umayyad Memory by the 'Abbāsids', *Journal of Near Eastern Studies* 61, no. 4 (2002), pp. 241–65. [KV]

Himmelfarb, Martha. *Tours of Hell: An Apocalyptic Form in Jewish and Christian Literature*. Philadelphia, PA: University of Pennsylvania Press, 1983. [SB]

Hodgson, Marshall G.S. *The Venture of Islam*, 3 vols. Chicago, IL: University of Chicago Press, 1974. [CM]

Ichwan, Moch Nur. 'Differing Responses to an Ahmadi Translation and Exegesis: The Holy Qur'an in Egypt and Indonesia', *Archipel* 62 (2001), pp. 143–61. [TZ]

Innis, Robert E. 'Pragmatics of Reading', *Transactions of the Charles S. Peirce Society* 34, no. 4 (1998), pp. 869–84. [SB – Intr]

Iser, Wolfgang. *The Act of Reading: A Theory of Aesthetic Response*. London: Routledge & Kegan Paul, 1978. [SB – Intr]

Izutsu, Toshihiko. *The Concept of Belief in Islamic Theology: A Semantic Analysis of* Īmān *and* Islām. Tokyo: Keio Institute of Cultural and Linguistic Studies, 1965. [CG]

al-Jābirī, 'Āmir al-Zanātī. 'Sūrat Ṭāhā fī'l-tarjama al-'ibriyya li-ma'ānī al-Qur'ān al-karīm' in *Nadwat al-Qur'ān al-karīm fī'l-dirāsāt al-istishrāqiyya*. Medina: 7–9 November 2006. [SW]

Jansen, J.J.G. *The Interpretation of the Koran in Modern Egypt*. Leiden: Brill, 1974. [SW] [TZ]

Jawharjī, Muḥammad ʿAdnān. 'Raʾy fī taḥdīd ʿaṣr al-Rāghib al-Iṣfahānī', *Majallat Majmaʿ al-Lugha al-ʿArabiyya fī Dimashq* 61, no. 1 (1986), pp. 191–200. [DS]

Jeffery, Arthur. *The Foreign Vocabulary of the Qurʾān*. Baroda: Oriental Institute, 1938. [CM] [DS]; repr. Lahore: al-Biruni, 1977. [CM]

Jomier, J. *Le commentaire coranique du Manâr: tendances modernes de l'exégèse coranique en Égypte*. Paris: G.-P. Maisonneuve, 1954. [SW] [TZ]

Juynboll, G.H.A. 'Some Thoughts on Early Muslim Historiography', *Bibliotheca Orientalis* 49 (1992), pp. 685–91. [HB]

Kaḥḥāla, ʿUmar Riḍā. *Muʿjam al-muʾallifīn*, 15 vols. in 8. Damascus: al-Maktaba al-ʿArabiyya, 1957–61. [CG]; repr. Beirut: al-Muthannā and Dār Iḥyāʾ al-Turāth al-ʿArabī, n.d. [CG]

Karamustafa, Ahmet. 'Elmalılı Muhammed Hamdi Yazır's (1878–1942) Philosophy of Religion', *Archivum Ottomanicum* 19 (2001), pp. 273–9. [SW]

Keeler, Annabel. *Sufi Hermeneutics: The Qur'an Commentary of Rashīd al-Dīn al-Maybūdī*. Oxford: Oxford University Press in association with the Institute of Ismaili Studies, 2006. [SB – Intr]

Key, Alexander. 'Al-Raghīb al-Iṣfahānī' in Terri de Young, ed., *Essays in Arabic Literary Biography. Volume 1*. Wiesbaden: Harrassowitz, 2011, pp. 298–306. [SB – Intr]

——. 'A Linguistic Frame of Mind: al-Rāghib al-Iṣfahānī and What it Meant to be Ambiguous'. Unpublished PhD Dissertation, Harvard University, 2012. [DS]

al-Khafājī, ʿAbd al-Munʿim. *al-Azhar fī alf ʿām*, 2nd edn. Beirut: ʿĀlam al-Kutub, 1987. [TZ]

Khan, Mohammad-Nauman. *Die exegetischen Teile des* Kitāb al-ʿAyn*: Zur ältesten philologischen Koranexegese*. Berlin: K. Schwarz, 1994. [CG] [KV]

Khaṭīb, ʿAbd al-Laṭīf Muḥammad. *Muʿjam al-qirāʾāt*. Damascus: Dār Saʿd al-Dīn li'l-Ṭibāʿa wa'l-Nashr wa'l-Tawzīʿ, 2002. [CG]

Khoury, Raif Georges. *Wahb b. Munabbih*. Volume 1: *Der Heidelberger Papyrus PSR Heid Arab 23*, Codices arabici antiqui. Wiesbaden: Otto Harrassowitz, 1972. [CM]

——. 'Quelques réflexions sur les citations de la Bible dans les premières générations islamiques', *Bulletin d'études orientales* 29 (1977), pp. 269–78. [CM]

Kidwai, Abdur Rahim. 'A Survey of English Translations of the Quran', *The Muslim World Book Review* 7, no. 4 (1987), pp. 66–71. [SB – Intr] [SW]

Kister, M.J. 'Al-Ḥīra: Some Notes on its Relations with Arabia', *Arabica* 15, no. 2 (1968), pp. 143–69. [TZ]

——. '"Do Not Assimilate Yourselves ..." *Lā tashabbahū*', *Jerusalem Studies in Arabic and Islam* 12 (1989), pp. 322–70. [TZ]

Köbert, R. 'Das Gottesepitheon *aṣ-Ṣamad* in Sure 112, 2', *Orientalia* 30 (1961), pp. 204–5. [SB]

Koç, Mehmet Akif. 'A Comparison of the References to Muqātil b. Sulaymān (150/767) in the Exegesis of al-Thaʿlabī (427/1036) with Muqātil's Own Exegesis', *Journal of Semitic Studies* 53 (2008), pp. 69–101. [CG]

Kofler, Hans. 'Das *Kitāb aḍdād* von Abū 'Alī Muḥammad Quṭrub ibn al-Mustanīr, herausgegeben und mit erklärenden Anmerkungen versehen', *Islamica* 5 (1931–32), pp. 241–84, 385–461, 493–544. [KV]

Kopf, Lothar. 'Religious Influences on Medieval Arabic Philology', *Studia Islamica* 5 (1956), pp. 33–59. [CG] [KV]; repr. in Moshe H. Goshen-Gottstein, ed., *Studies in Arabic and Hebrew Lexicography*. Jerusalem: The Hebrew University, 1976, pp. 19–45. [CG]

Kraemer, Jörg. 'Studien zur altarabischen Lexicographie nach istanbuler und berliner Handschriften', *Oriens* 6 (1953), pp. 201–38. [CG]

Krebs, Wolfgang. *Das Papstzitat von Regensburg. Benedikt XVI im 'Kampf der Kulturen'*. Berlin: Rhombos-Verlag, 2007. [SW]

Kulinich, Alena. 'Representing "a Blameworthy *Tafsīr*": Mu'tazilite Exegetical Tradition in *al-Jāmi' fī tafsīr al-Qur'ān* of 'Alī ibn 'Īsā al-Rummānī (d. 384/994)', Unpublished PhD Dissertation, School of Oriental and African Studies, University of London, 2011. [SB – Intr] [SB]

Lagarde, Michel. *Index du Grande Commentaire de Faḫr al-Dīn al-Rāzī*. Leiden: Brill, 1996. [SB]

Lane, Andrew J. *A Traditional Mu'tazilite Qur'ān Commentary: The* Kashshāf *of Jār Allāh al-Zamakhsharī (d. 538/1144)*. Leiden: Brill, 2006. [SB]

Lane, Edward William. *An Arabic-English Lexicon*. London: Williams and Norgate, 1863–93. [CM] [DS] [BW]; 2 vols. Cambridge: Islamic Texts Society, 1984. [SB] [CG]

Langhade, Jacques. 'Grammaire, logique, études linguistiques chez al-Farabi', *Historiographica Linguistica* 8 (1981), pp. 365–77. [SB]

Lawḥī, Sayyid 'Alī Mīr. *Rāghib-i Iṣfahānī: zindigī va āthār-i ū*. Isfahan, Sāzimān-i Farhangī-yi Tafrīḥī-yi Shahrdārī-yi Iṣfahān, 2008. [DS]

Lecker, Michael. *The 'Constitution of Medina': Muḥammad's First Legal Document*. Princeton, NJ: Darwin Press, 2004. [CG]

Leemhuis, Fred. 'From Palm Leaves to the Internet' in McAuliffe, ed., *The Cambridge Companion to the Qur'ān*, pp. 145–62. [SW]

Lemke, Wolf-Dieter. *Maḥmūd Šaltūt (1893–1963) und die Reform der Azhar: Untersuchungen zu Erneuerungsbestrebungen im ägyptisch-islamischen Erziehungssystem*. Frankfurt am Main: Peter Lang, 1980. [SW] [TZ]

Leshem, Hayyim. *Ha-Qor'ān be-targum 'ivrīt ḥadash*. Tel Aviv: n.p., 1993. [SW]

Lowry, Joseph E. *Early Islamic Legal Theory: The Risāla of Muḥammad ibn Idrīs al-Shāfi'ī*. Leiden: Brill, 2007. [CM]

——. 'Early Islamic Exegesis as Legal Theory: How Qur'ānic Wisdom (*Ḥikma*) Became the Sunna of the Prophet' in Natalie B. Dohrmann and David Stern, eds, *Jewish Biblical Interpretation and Cultural Exchange: Comparative Exegesis in Context*. Philadelphia, PA: University of Pennsylvania Press, 2008, pp. 139–60, 286–95. [CM]

Lubin, Timothy. 'The Virtuosic Exegesis of the Brahmavadin and the Rabbi', *Numen* 49 (2002), pp. 427–59. [TM]

Lucas, Scott C. *Constructive Critics, Ḥadīth Literature and the Articulation of Sunnī Islam*. Leiden: Brill, 2004. [KV]

Luizard, Pierre-Jean. 'Al-Azhar, Institution sunnite réformée' in Alain Roussillon, ed., *Entre reforme sociale et mouvement national: identité et modernisation en Egypte, 1882–1962*. Cairo: CEDEJ, 1995, pp. 519–48. [TZ]

MacCallum, F. Lyman. 'Turkey Discovers the Koran', *The Moslem World* 23 (1933), pp. 24–8. [SW] [TZ]

Madelung, Wilferd. 'Aspects of Ismāʿīlī Theology: The Prophetic Chain and the God beyond Being' in S.H. Nasr, ed., *Ismāʿīlī Contributions to Islamic Culture*. Tehran: Imperial Academy of Philosophy, 1398/1977, pp. 51–65. [TM]

——. 'The Early Murjiʾa in Khurāsān and Transoxania and the Spread of Ḥanafism', *Der Islam* 59 (1982), pp. 32–9. [TZ]

Mahdī, Jūda Muḥammad Muḥammad. *al-Wāḥidī wa manhajuhu fīʾl-tafsīr*. Cairo: Wizārat al-Awqāf, 1978. [CG]

al-Mālikī, Muḥammad. *Juhūd al-Ṭabarī fī dirāsāt al-shawāhid al-shaʿriyya fī 'Jāmiʿ al-bayān ʿan taʾwīl al-Qurʾān': Dirāsa lughawiyya adabiyya fī tafsīr al-Qurʾān al-karīm*. Ribat: Maṭbaʿat al-Maʿārif al-Jadīda, 1994. [SB]

Marín, Manuela. 'Disciplining Wives: A Historical Reading of Qurʾān 4:34', *Studia Islamica* 97 (2003), pp. 5–40. [ACh]

Massignon, Louis. *Essay on the Origins of the Technical Language of Islamic Mysticism*, tr. Benjamin Clark. Notre Dame, IN: University of Notre Dame Press, 1997; orig. publ. as *Essai sur les origins du lexique technique de la mystique musulmane*. Paris: Paul Geuthner, 1922. [CM]

——. *Salmân Pâk et les prémices spirituelles de l'Islam iranien*. Tours: Arrault, 1934. [TZ]

Mayer, Toby, tr. *Keys to the Arcana: Shahrastānī's Esoteric Commentary on the Qur'an*. *See* Primary Sources, al-Shahrastānī, *Mafātīḥ al-asrār wa maṣābīḥ al-abrār*.

——. 'Shahrastānī's Ḥanīf Revelation: A Shiʿi Philosophico-Hermeneutical System' in Farhad Daftary and Gurdofarid Miskinzoda, eds, *The Study of Shiʿi Islam: History, Theology and Law*. London: I.B. Tauris in association with the Institute of Ismaili Studies, 2014, pp. 563–83. [TM]

McAuliffe, Jane Dammen. 'Quranic Hermeneutics: The Views of al-Ṭabarī and Ibn Kathīr' in Andrew Rippin, ed., *Approaches to the History of the Interpretation of the Qurʾān*. Oxford: Clarendon Press, 1988, pp. 46–62. [SB - Intr]

——. 'Exegetical Sciences' in Andrew Rippin, ed., *The Blackwell Companion to the Qurʾān*. London: Blackwell, 2006. [SB]

McChesney, Robert D. 'Central Asia's Place in the Middle East: Some Historical Considerations' in David Menashri, ed., *Central Asia Meets the Middle East*. London: Frank Cass, 1998, pp. 25–51. [TZ]

McLean, B.H. *Biblical Interpretation and Philosophical Meaning*. Cambridge: Cambridge University Press, 2012. [SB - Intr]

Melchert, Christopher. 'Early Renunciants as *Ḥadīth* Transmitters', *The Muslim World* 92 (2002), pp. 407–18. [CM]

——. 'The Piety of the Hadith Folk', *International Journal of Middle East Studies* 34 (2002), pp. 425–39. [CM]

——. 'Baṣran Origins of Classical Sufism', *Der Islam* 82 (2005), pp. 221–40. [CM]

——. 'The Relation of the Ten Readings to One Another', *Journal of Qur'anic Studies* 10, no. 2 (2008), pp. 73–87. [SW]

——. '"God Created Adam in His Image"', *Journal of Qur'anic Studies* 13 (2011), pp. 113–24. [CM]
——. 'Quotations of Extra-Qur'anic Scripture in Early Renunciant Literature' in Agostino Cilardo, ed., *Islam and Globalisation: Historical and Contemporary Perspectives. Proceedings of the 25th Congress of L'Union Européenne des Arabisants et Islamisants*. Leuven, Peeters, 2013, pp. 97–107. [CM]
Meyer, Jonas. *Die Hölle im Islam*. Basel: Universitäts-Buchdrucherei, 1901. [DS]
Mochiri, Melick Iradj. 'A Pahlavi Forerunner of the Umayyad Reform Coinage', *Journal of the Royal Asiatic Society* 2 (1981), pp. 168–72. [TZ]
——. *Arab-Sasanian Civil War Coinage: Manichaeans, Yazidiya and other Khawārij*, tr. Jean Louis Avril and Françoise Graves. Paris: n.p., 1986. [TZ]
Mohamed, Yasien. 'The Ethical Philosophy of al-Rāghib al-Iṣfahānī', *Journal of Islamic Studies* 6, no. 1 (1995), pp. 51–75. [DS]
——. 'Knowledge and Purification of the Soul: An Annotated Translation of Iṣfahānī's *Kitāb al-Dharīʿa ilā Makārim al-Sharīʿa* (58–76; 89–92)', *Journal of Islamic Studies* 9, no. 1 (1998), pp. 1–34. [DS]
Mohammed, Khaleel. 'Assessing English Translations of the Qur'an', *Middle East Quarterly* 12 (Spring 2005), pp. 58–71.* [SW]
Moosa, Matti. *Extremist Shiites: The Ghulat Sects*. Syracuse, NY: Syracuse University Press, 1988. [TZ]
Moreno, Martino Mario. 'È lecito ai Musulmani tradurre il Corano?' *Oriento Moderno* 5, no. 10 (1925), pp. 532–43. [TZ]
Mottahedeh, Roy. 'The Shuʿûbîyah Controversy and the Social History of Early Islamic Iran', *International Journal of Middle East Studies* 7 (1976), pp. 161–82. [TZ]
Motzki, Harald. 'The Collection of the Qurʾān: A Reconsideration of Western Views in Light of Recent Methodological Developments', *Der Islam* 78 (2001), pp. 1–34. [TM]
——. 'The Question of the Authenticity of Muslim Traditions Reconsidered: A Review Article' in Herbert Berg, ed., *Method and Theory in the Study of Islamic Origins*. Leiden: Brill, 2003, pp. 211–58. [KV]
——. 'The Origins of Muslim Exegesis. A Debate' in Harald Motzki with Nicolet Boekhoff-van der Voort and Sean W. Anthony, *Analysing Muslim Traditions: Studies in Legal, Exegetical and Maghāzī Ḥadīth*. Leiden: Brill, 2010, pp. 231–303. [HB] [SB] [KV]
Muhannā, Aḥmad Ibrāhīm. *Dirāsat ḥawl tarjamat al-Qurʾān al-karīm*. Cairo: Maṭbūʿāt al-Shaʿb, 1978. [TZ]
al-Mūjī, Ibrāhīm Ḥasan. 'Al-Bukhari, A Collection of Muhammad's Authentic Traditions, Translated into English', *Nūr al-Islām* 5, no. 1 (Muḥarram 1353/April 1934), pp. 1–20. [TZ]
Müller, Friedrun R. *Untersuchungen zur Reimprosa im Koran*. Bonn: Selbstverlag des Orientalischen Seminars der Universität, 1969. [DS]
Muminov, Ashirbek. 'Disputes in Bukhara on the Persian Translation of the Qur'an', *Mélanges de l'Université Saint-Joseph* 59 (2006), pp. 301–8. [TZ]
Muranyi, Miklos. 'Neue Materialien zur *Tafsīr*-Forschung in der Moscheebibliotek von Qairawan' in Stefan Wild, ed., *The Qurʾān as Text*. Leiden: Brill, 1996, pp. 225–55. [KV]

Nagel, Tilman. '*Die Qiṣāṣ-al-anbiya'*: Ein Beitrag zur arabischen Literaturgeschichte'. Bonn, Rheinische Friedrich-Wilhelms-Universität, 1967. [HB] [CM]

Nallino, Carlo Alfonso. 'Deliberazione della Camera egiziana sul progetto di traduzione del Corano', *Oriente Moderno* 16, no. 10, pp. 560–61. [TZ]

Nāṣirī, Ḥasan Sādāt, and Manūchihr Dānishpazhūh. *Hazār sāl-i tafsīr-i Fārsī*. Tehran: Nashr-i Alburz, 1990. [TZ]

Naṣṣār, Ḥusayn. *al-Muʿjam al-ʿarabī: nasha'tuhu wa taṭawwuruhu*. Cairo: Dār Miṣr li'l-Ṭibāʿa, 1965. [CG]; repr. 1968. [CG]; repr. n.d. [SB]

Nasser, Shady Hekmat. *The Transmission of the Variant Readings of the Qur'ān: The Problem of* Tawātur *and the Emergence of* Shawādhdh. Leiden: Brill, 2013. [KV]

Neuwirth, Angelika. *Studien zur Komposition der mekkanische Suren*. Berlin: Walter de Gruyter, 1981. [DS]

——. 'Die *Masā'il Nāfiʿ b. al-Azraq*. Éléments des "Portrait mythique d'Ibn 'Abbās" oder ein Stück realer Literatur? Rückschlüsse aus einer bisher unbeachteten Handschrift', *Zeitschrift für Arabische Linguistik* 25 (1993), pp. 233–50. [CG]

Newman, Andrew. *The Formative Period of Twelver Shīʿism: Ḥadīth as Discourse Between Qum and Baghdad*. Richmond, Surrey: Curzon, 2000. [SB – Intr]

Nguyen, Martin. *Sufi Master and Scholar: Abū'l-Qāsim al-Qushayrī and the* Laṭā'if al-ishārāt. Oxford: Oxford University Press in association with the Institute of Ismaili Studies, 2012. [SB – Intr]

Nöldeke, Theodor. *Geschichte des Qorans*, ed. Friedrich Schwally, Gotthelf Bergsträsser and Otto Pretzl, 2nd edn, 3 vols. Leipzig: Dieterich, 1909–38; repr. Hildesheim: G. Olms, 1961. [HB] [DS]

——. 'Zur Sprache des Korāns' in idem, *Neue Beiträge zur semitischen Sprachwissenschaft*. Strasbourg: K.J. Trübner, 1910, pp. 1–30; translated into French by G.-H. Bousquet as *Remarques critiques sur le style et la syntaxe du Coran*. Paris: Maisonneuve, 1953; translated into English by Ibn Warraq as 'On the Language of the Koran' in Ibn Warraq, ed., *Which Koran? Variants, Manuscripts, Linguistics*. Amherst, NY: Prometheus Books, 2011, pp. 85–129. [CG]

Ory, Solange. 'Aspects religieux des texts épigraphiques du début de l'Islam' in Alfred-Louis de Prémare, ed., *Les premières écritures islamiques*. Aix-en-Provence: Édisud, 1990, pp. 30–39. [CM]

O'Shaughnessy, Thomas. 'The Seven Names for Hell in the Qur'ān', *Bulletin of the School of Oriental and African Studies* 24 (1961), pp. 444–69. [SB] [DS]

Özek, Ali. *Tarjamat maʿānī al-Qur'ān al-karīm al-ṣādira fī mujammaʿ al-mālik Fahd li-ṭibāʿat al-musḥaf al-sharīf bi'l-Madīna al-munawwara ḥatta niḥāyat ʿām 1425/2004*. Medina: n.p., n.d. [SW]

Paret, Rudi. 'Der Ausdruck *ṣamad* in Sure 112, 2', *Der Islam* 56 (1979), pp. 294–5. [SB]

——. *Der Koran: Kommentar und Konkordanz*, repr. Stuttgart: Kohlhammer, 1980. [CG]

Peña Martín, Salvador. *Corán, palabra y verdad: Ibn al-Sid y el humanismo en al-Ándalus*. Madrid: Consejo Superior de Investigaciones Científicas, 2007. [CG]

Pennacchio, Catherine. *Les emprunts à l'hébreu et au judéo-araméen dans le Coran*. Paris: Maisonneuve, 2014. [KV]

Penrice, John. *A Dictionary and Glossary of the Qur'an*, repr. Lahore: al-Biruni, 1976. [SB - Intr]

Peters, J.R.T.M. 'La théologie musulmane et l'étude du langage', *Histoire Épistémologie Langage* 2 (1980), pp. 9–19. [SB]

Pickthall, Marmaduke. 'Arabs and Non-Arabs and the Question of Translating the Qur'an', *Islamic Culture* 5, no. 3 (1931), pp. 422–33. [TZ]

Poonawala, Ismail K. *Bibliography of Ismāʿīlī Literature*. Malibu: Undena Publications, 1977. [TM]

——. 'Ismāʿīlī *ta'wīl* of the Qurʾān' in Rippin, ed., *Approaches to the History of the Interpretation of the Qurʾān*, pp. 199–222. [SB - Intr]

Powers, David Stephan. 'The Islamic Law of Inheritance Reconsidered: A New Reading of Q. 4:12b', *Studia Islamica* 55 (1982), pp. 61–94. [AC]

——. *Studies in Qurʾān and Ḥadīth: The Formation of the Islamic Law of Inheritance*. Berkeley, CA: University of California Press, 1986. [AC]

——. *Muḥammad is Not the Father of Any of Your Men: The Making of the Last Prophet*. Philadelphia, PA: University of Pennsylvania Press, 2009. [AC]

Pregill, Michael. 'Isrāʾīliyyāt, Myth, and Pseudepigraphy: Wahb b. Munabbih and the Early Islamic Version of the Fall of Adam and Eve', *Jerusalem Studies in Arabic and Islam* 34 (2008), pp. 215–84. [CM]

de Prémare, Alfred-Louis. 'Wahb b. Munabbih, une figure singulière du premier Islam', *Annales. Histoire, Sciences Sociales* 60 (2005), pp. 531–49. [CM]

Pulcini, Theodore. *Exegesis as a Polemical Discourse: Ibn Ḥazm on Jewish and Christian Scriptures*. Atlanta, GA: Scholars Press, 1998. [TM]

Rahman, Y. 'Hermeneutics of al-Baydawi in his Anwar al-Tanzil wa Asrar al-Ta'wil', *Islamic Culture* 71 (1997), pp. 1–14. [SB]

Reinhart, Kevin. 'Fundamentalism and the Transparency of the Arabic Qur'an' in Carl Ernst and Richard Martin, eds, *Rethinking Islamic Studies: From Orientalism to Cosmopolitanism*. Chapel Hill, NC: University of North Carolina Press, 2010, pp. 97–113. [TZ]

Richter-Bernburg, Lutz. 'Linguistic Shuʿūbīya and Early Neo-Persian Prose', *Journal of the American Oriental Society* 94 (1974), pp. 55–64. [TZ]

Rippin, Andrew. 'Ibn ʿAbbās's *Lughāt fī'l-Qurʾān*', *Bulletin of the School of Oriental and African Studies* 44, no. 1 (1981), pp. 15–25. [SB]

——. 'Ibn ʿAbbās's *Gharīb al-Qurʾān*', *Bulletin of the School of Oriental and African Studies* 46, no. 2 (1983), pp. 323–33. [KV]

——. 'Al-Zuhrī, *Naskh al-Qurʾān* and the Problem of Early *Tafsīr* Texts', *Bulletin of the School of Oriental and African Studies* 47, no. 1 (1984), pp. 22–43. [SB] [KV]

——. 'Lexicographical Texts and the Qurʾān' in idem, ed., *Approaches to the History of the Interpretation of the Qurʾān*, pp. 158–74. [SB - Intr] [SB]

——. 'Syriac in the Qurʾān: Classical Muslim Theories' in Gabriel Said Reynolds, ed., *The Qurʾān in Its Historical Context*. London: Routledge, 2008, pp. 249–61. [DS]

Robinson, Neal. *Discovering the Qur'an: A Contemporary Approach to a Veiled Text*. London: SCM Press, 1996. [SB]; 2nd edn. London: SCM Press, 2003. [CM]

——. 'Sectarian and Ideological Bias in Muslim Translations of the Qur'an', *Islam and Christian-Muslim Relations* 8, no. 3 (1997), pp. 261–78. [SB - Intr]

Robson, James. 'Is the Moslem Hell Eternal?' *Muslim World* 28 (1938), pp. 386–96. [DS]

Rosenblatt, Louise M. *The Reader, the Text, the Poem: The Transactional Theory of the Literary Work*. Carbondale, IL: Southern Illinois University Press, 1978. [SB - Intr]

Rothstein, Gustav. *Die Dynastie der Laḫmiden in al-Ḥīra*. Berlin: Verlag von Reuther & Reichard, 1899. [CG]

Rubin, Uri. '*al-Ṣamad* and the High God - an Interpretation of Sura CXII', *Der Islam* 61 (1984), pp. 197–217. [SB]

Rustomji, Nerina. *The Garden and the Fire: Heaven and Hell in Islamic Culture*. New York: Columbia University Press, 2009. [DS]

Sadan, J. 'Some Literary Problems Concerning Judaism and Jewry in Medieval Arabic Sources' in M. Sharon, ed., *Studies in Islamic History and Civilization in Honour of Professor David Ayalon*. Jerusalem and Leiden: 1986, pp. 353–98. [CM]

——. 'Al 800 shanah shel targum ha-Qorʾān. Ha-ṣefer she asūr le-targamo', *Ha-aretz*, 11 September 2005. [SW]

Saleh, Walid A. *The Formation of the Classical Tafsīr Tradition: The Qurʾān Commentary of al-Thaʿlabī (d. 427/1035)*. Leiden: Brill, 2004. [SB - Intr]

——. 'Hermeneutics: al-Thaʿlabī' in Andrew Rippin, ed., *The Blackwell Companion to the Qurʾān*. Oxford: Blackwell, 2006, pp. 323–37. [SB - Intr]

——. 'The Last of the Nishapuri School of Tafsīr: Al-Wāḥidī (d. 468/1076) and His Significance in the History of Qur'anic Exegesis', *Journal of the American Oriental Society* 126 (2006), pp. 223–43. [CG]

——. 'Ibn Taymiyya and the Rise of Radical Hermeneutics: An Analysis of *An Introduction to the Foundation of Qurʾānic Exegesis*' in Yossef Rapoport and Shahab Ahmed, eds, *Ibn Taymiyya and his Times*. Lahore: Oxford University Press, 2010, pp. 123–62. [SB]

——. 'Preliminary Remarks on the Historiography of *tafsīr* in Arabic', *Journal of Qur'anic Studies* 12 (2010), pp. 6–40. [CM]

——. 'The Introduction of Wāḥidī's *al-Basīṭ*: An Edition, Translation and Commentary' in Bauer, ed., *Aims, Methods and Contexts of Qur'anic Exegesis*, pp. 67–100. [CG]

Sanni, Amidu. 'The Arabic Science of Lexicography: State of the Art', *Islamic Studies* 31, no. 2 (1992), pp. 141–68. [CG]

Savant, Sarah. '"Persians" in Early Islam', *Annales islamologiques* 42 (2008), pp. 73–91. [TZ]

——. *The New Muslims of Post-Conquest Iran: Tradition, Memory, and Conversion*. Cambridge: Cambridge University Press, 2013. [TZ]

Schacht, Joseph. *The Origins of Muhammadan Jurisprudence*, 3rd rev edn. Oxford, Clarendon Press, 1959. [HB]

Schleiermacher, Friedrich D.E. *Hermeneutics and Criticism and Other Writings*, tr. and ed. Andrew Bowie. Cambridge: Cambridge University Press, 1998; orig. pub. as *Hermeneutik und Kritik mit besonderer Beziehung aus das Neue Testament*. Berlin: Reimer, 1838. [SB – Intr]

Schleifer, Ronald. *A.J. Greimas and the Nature of Meaning: Linguistics, Semiotics and Discourse Theory*. London: Croom Helm, 1987. [SB – Intr]

Schöck, Cornelia. *Koranexegese, Grammatik und Logik: Zum Verhältnis von arabischer und aristotelischer Urteils-, Konsequenz- und Schlusslehre*. Leiden: Brill, 2006. [KV]

Schoeler, Gregor. 'Die Frage der schriftlichen oder mündlichen Überlieferung der Wissenschaften im frühen Islam', *Der Islam* 62 (1985), pp. 201–30. [HB]

——. *Charakter und Authentie der muslimischen Überlieferung über das Leben Mohammeds*. Berlin and New York: de Gruyter, 1996. [KV]

Schöller, Marco. '*Sīra* and *Tafsīr*: Muḥammad al-Kalbī on the Jews of Medina' in Harald Motzki, ed., *The Biography of Muḥammad: The Issue of the Sources*. Leiden: Brill, 2000. [KV]

Schulze, Reinhard. *Islamischer Internationalismus im 20. Jahrhundert. Untersuchungen zur Islamischen Weltliga*. Leiden: Brill, 1990. [SW]

Sears, Stuart. 'A Monetary History of Iraq and Iran, ca CE 500 to 750'. Unpublished PhD Dissertation, University of Chicago, 1997. [TZ]

Serjeant, Robert Bertram. 'The "Constitution of Medina"', *Islamic Quarterly* 8 (1964), pp. 3–16. [CG]

——. 'The Sunnah Jāmiʿah, Pacts with the Yathrib Jews, and the Taḥrīm of Yathrib: Analysis and Translation of the Documents Comprised in the so called "Constitution of Medina"', *Bulletin of the School of Oriental and African Studies* 41 (1978), pp. 1–42. [CG]

Sezgin, Fuat. *Geschichte des arabischen Schrifttums* (*GAS*), 9 vols. Leiden, Brill, 1967–84. [HB] [AC] [CG]

Shah, Mustafa. 'The Philological Endeavours of the Early Arabic Linguists: Theological Implications of the *tawqīf-iṣṭilāḥ* Antithesis and the *majāz* Controversy – Part I', *Journal of Qur'anic Studies* 1, no. 1 (1999), pp. 27–46. [SB – Intr] [TM]; Part II, *Journal of Qur'anic Studies* 2, no. 1 (2000), pp. 43–66. [TM]

——. 'The Quest for the Origins of the *Qurrā'* in the Classical Islamic Tradition', *Journal of Qur'anic Studies* 7, no. 2 (2005), pp. 1–35. [KV]

——. 'Classical Islamic Discourse on the Origins of Language: Cultural Memory and the Defense of Orthodoxy', *Numen* 58 (2011), pp. 314–43. [SB] [TM]

Shaikh, Saʿdiyya. 'Exegetical Violence: *Nushūz* in Qur'ānic Gender Ideology', *Journal for Islamic Studies* 17 (1997), pp. 49–73. [ACh]

Shaked, Shaul. 'Mihr the Judge', *Jerusalem Studies in Arabic and Islam* 2 (1980), pp. 1–30. [TZ]

al-Shaybī, Kāmil Muṣṭafā. *al-Ṣila bayna'l-taṣawwuf wa'l-tashayyuʿ*. Baghdad: Maṭbaʿat al-Zahrā', 1382–3/1963–4. [CM]

——. *al-Fikr al-shīʿī wa'l-nazaʿāt al-ṣūfiyya*. Baghdad: Maktabat al-Nahḍa, 1386/1966. [CM]

Shaykhū, Luwīs [Louis Cheiko], *Shuʿarā' al-naṣrāniyya*, repr., 2 vols. Beirut: Dār al-Mashriq, 1986; orig. pub. 1901. [CG]

Siddiq, Muhammad. 'Significant but Problematic Others: Negotiating "Israelis" in the Works of Mahmoud Darwish', *Comparative Literature Studies* 47, no. 4 (2010), pp. 487–503. [SW]

Sinai, Nicolai. 'The Qur'anic Commentary of Muqātil b. Sulaymān and the Evaluation of Early *Tafsīr* Literature' in Görke and Pink, eds, *Tafsīr and Islamic Intellectual History*, pp. 113–43. [KV]

al-Sistani, Ayatullah Ali. 'Dialogue on Sawm (fasting)'.* [BW]

Skovgaard-Petersen, Jakob. *Defining Islam for the Egyptian State: Muftis and Fatwas of the Dār al-Iftā*. Leiden: Brill, 1997. [TZ]

Smith, Jane I., and Yvonne Y. Haddad. *The Islamic Understanding of Death and Resurrection*. Albany, NY: State University of New York Press, 1981. [DS]

Smith, Wilfred Cantwell. *Islam in Modern History*. Princeton, NJ: Princeton University Press 1957. [TZ]

Somekh, Sasson. *Arabic Literature in Hebrew: Translations and Research in Israel*. Tel Aviv: Israel PEN Centre, 1971. [SW]

——. 'Ha-Qor'ān be-ʿivrīt', *Yediʿōt aḥarōnōt* (12 March 1971). [SW]

Speight, R. Marston. 'The Function of *ḥadith* as Commentary on the Qurʾān, as Seen in the Six Authoritative Collections' in Rippin, ed., *Approaches to the History of the Interpretation of the Qurʾān*, pp. 63–81. [HB] [SB]

Sprenger, Aloys. 'Notes on Alfred von Kremer's Edition of Wakidy's Campaigns', *Journal of the Asiatic Society of Bengal* 25 (1856), pp. 53–74, 199–220. [HB]

Stewart, Devin J. '*Sajʿ* in the Qurʾān: Prosody and Structure', *Journal of Arabic Literature* 21 (1990), pp. 101–39. [DS]

——. 'Poetic License in the Qurʾān: Ibn al-Ṣāʾigh al-Ḥanafī's *Iḥkām al-rāy fī aḥkām al-āy*', *Journal of Qurʾanic Studies* 11, no. 1 (2009), pp. 1–54. [SB – Intr] [DS] [BW]

——. 'The Mysterious Letters and Other Formal Features of the Qurʾān in Light of Greek and Babylonian Oracular Texts' in Gabriel Said Reynolds, ed., *New Perspectives on the Qurʾān: The Qurʾān in Its Historical Context 2*. London: Routledge, 2011, pp. 321–46. [DS]

——. 'Divine Epithets and the *Dibacchius*: *Clausulae* and Qurʾānic Rhythm', *Journal of Qurʾanic Studies* 15, no. 2 (2013), pp. 22–64. [DS]

Storey, Charles A. 'Qur'anic Literature', in idem, *Persian Literature: A Bio-Bibliographical Survey* (London: Luzac, 1927), vol. 1, part 1, pp. 1–58; vol. 1, part 2, pp. 1189–228. [TZ]

Strothmann, Rudolf. 'Das Problem der literarischen Persönlichkeit Zaid ibn ʿAlī', *Der Islam* 10 (1923), pp. 1–52. [SB]

Ṣubḥī Maḥmaṣānī. *Falsafat al-tashrīʿ fī'l-islām*, 2nd edn. Beirut: Dār al-Kāshif, 1952. [TZ]; tr. Farhat J. Ziadeh as *The Philosophy of Jurisprudence in Islam*. Leiden: Brill, 1961. [TZ]

Sviri, Sara. '*Wa-rahbāniyyatan ibtadaʿūhā*', *Jerusalem Studies in Arabic and Islam* 13 (1990), pp. 195–208. [CM]

Talmon Rafael. *Arabic Grammar in its Formative Age:* Kitāb al-ʿAyn *and its Attribution to Ḫalīl b. Aḥmad*. Leiden: Brill 1997. [SB] [CG]

Tayob, Abdulkader. 'An Analytical Survey of al-Ṭabarī's Exegesis of the Cultural Symbolic Construct of *Fitna*' in Hawting and Shareef, eds, *Approaches to the Study of the Qurʾān*, pp. 157–72. [SB – Intr]

Thomas, David. *Anti-Christian Polemic in Early Islam: Abī ʿĪsā al-Warrāq's 'Against the Trinity'*. Cambridge: Cambridge University Press, 1992. [SB]

Thomassen, Einar. 'Islamic Hell', *Numen* 56 (2009), pp. 401–16. [DS]

Tibawi, A.L. 'Is the Qur'an Translatable? Early Muslim Opinion', *Muslim World* 52, no. 1 (1962), pp. 4–16. [TZ]

Todorov, Tzvetan. *Symbolism and Interpretation*, tr. Catherine Porter. Cornell: Cornell University Press, 1986; orig. pub. as *Symbolisme et interprétation*. Paris: Editions du Seuil, 1978. [SB – Intr]

Toorawa, Shawkat M. 'Hapaxes in the Qur'ān: Identifying and Cataloguing Lone Words (and Loanwords)' in Gabriel Said Reynolds, ed., *New Perspectives on the Qur'ān: The Qur'ān in its Historical Context 2*. London: Routledge, 2011, pp. 193–246. [KV]

Tottoli, Roberto. 'Origin and Use of the Term *Isrā'īliyyāt* in Muslim Literature', *Arabica* 46 (1999), pp. 193–210. [KV]

——. 'Tours of Hell and Punishment of Sinners in *Miʿrāj* Narratives: Use and Meaning of Eschatology in Muḥammad's Ascension' in Christiane J. Gruber and Frederick S. Colby, *The Prophet's Ascension: Cross-Cultural Encounters with the Islamic* Miʿrāj *Tales*. Bloomington, IN: University of Indiana Press, 2010, pp. 11–26. [SB]

Touati, Houari. *Islam et voyage au Moyen Âge: histoire et anthropologie d'une pratique lettrée*. Paris: Seuil, 2000; tr. Lydia G. Cochrane as *Islam and Travel in the Middle Ages*. Chicago, IL: University of Chicago Press, 2010. [CM]

Vacca, Virginia. 'Gili "ʿulama'" di el-Azhar tradurranno il Corano nelle principali lingue straniere?' *Oriente Moderno* 16, no. 4 (1936), pp. 236–7. [TZ]

——. 'Lettera del Ministro dell'Istruzione circa il modo di eseguire la traduzione del Corano', *Oriente Moderno* 16, no. 5 (1936), pp. 292–3. [TZ]

Veccia Vaglieri, Laura. 'Nomina della Commissione incaricata della "traduzione dei concetti del Corano"', *Oriente Moderno* 16, no. 12 (1936), p. 710. [TZ]

Vermes, Geza. 'Biblical Proof-Texts in Qumran Literature', *Journal of Semitic Studies* 34 (1989), pp. 493–508. [SB – Intr]

Versteegh, Cornelis [Kees] H.M. 'Logique et grammaire au dixième siècle', *Histoire Épistémologie Langage* 2 (1980), pp. 39–52. [SB]

——. 'Grammar and Exegesis: The Origins of Kufan Grammar and the *Tafsīr Muqātil*', *Zeitschrift der Deutschen Morgenländischen Gesellschaft* 67 (1990), pp. 206–42. [KV]

——. *Arabic Grammar and Qur'ānic Exegesis in Early Islam*. Leiden: Brill, 1993. [CM] [KV]

——. 'Linguistic Attitudes and the Origin of Speech in the Arab World' in Alaa Elgibali, ed., *Understanding Arabic: Essays in Contemporary Arabic Linguistics in Honor of El-Said Badawi*. Cairo: The American University in Cairo Press, 1996, pp. 15–31. [TM]

——. 'Zayd ibn ʿAlī's Commentary on the *Qur'ān*' in Yasir Suleiman, ed., *Arabic Grammar and Linguistics*. London: Curzon Press, 1999, pp. 9–29. [KV]; repr. RoutledgeCurzon, 2003. [SB]

——. 'The Name of the Ant and the Call to Holy War: al-Ḍaḥḥāk ibn Muzāḥim's Commentary on the Qur'ān' in Boekhoff-van der Voort,

Versteegh and Wagemakers, eds, *The Transmission and Dynamics of the Textual Sources of Islam*, pp. 279–99. [KV]
Vishanoff, David R. *The Formation of Islamic Hermeneutics: How Sunni Legal Theorists Imagined a Revealed Law*. New Haven, CT: American Oriental Society, 2011. [SB - Intr]
——. 'An Imagined Book Gets a New Text: Psalms of the Muslim David', *Islam and Christian–Muslim Relations* 23 (2011), pp. 85–99. [CM]
Vrolijk, Arnoud. *Een Turks alphabet op latijnse grondslag: De alfabethervorming in Turkije 1928–1998*. Leiden: Legatum Warnerianum, 1998. [SW]
Vuckovic, Brooke Olson. *Heavenly Journeys, Earthly Concerns: The Legacy of the* Miʿrāj *in the Formation of Islam*. London: Routledge, 2005. [SB]
Wadud, Amina. *Qur'an and Woman: Rereading the Sacred Text from a Woman's* Perspective. Oxford: Oxford University Press, 1999. [ACh]
Wagtendonk, K. *Fasting in the Koran*. Leiden: Brill, 1968. [CM] [BW]
Walker, Paul E. *Early Philosophical Shiʿism: The Ismaili Neoplatonism of Abu Ya'qub al-Sijistani*. Cambridge: Cambridge University Press, 1993. [TM]
Wansbrough, John. '*Majāz al-Qur'ān*: Periphrastic Exegesis', *Bulletin of the School of Oriental and African Studies* 33 (1970), pp. 247–66. [SB] [CG] [KV]
——. 'Review: Friedrun Müller, *Unterzuchungen zur Reimprosa im Koran*', *Bulletin of the School of Oriental and African Studies* 33 (1970), pp. 389–91. [DS]
——. *Quranic Studies: Sources and Methods of Scriptural Interpretation*. Oxford: Oxford University Press, 1977. [HB] [DS] [KV]; new edn. Amherst, NY: Prometheus Books, 2004. [SB]
——. *The Sectarian Milieu: Content and Composition of Islamic Salvation History*. Oxford, Oxford University Press, 1978. [HB]
Watt, W. Montgomery. *Muhammad at Mecca*. Oxford, Oxford University Press, 1953. [HB]
——. 'Belief in a "High God" in Pre-Islamic Mecca', *Journal of Semitic Studies* 16 (1971), pp. 35–40. [SB]
——. 'The Qur'ān and a Belief in a "High God"', *Der Islam* 56 (1979), pp. 205–11. [SB]
——. *Islamic Philosophy and Theology*, 2nd edn. Edinburgh: Edinburgh University Press, 1985. [SB - Intr]
——. *Islamic Creeds*. Edinburgh: Edinburgh University Press, 1994. [CM]
Weiss, Bernard George. 'Language in Orthodox Muslim Thought. A Study of "*Waḍʿ al-lughah*" and its Development'. Unpublished PhD Dissertation, Princeton University, 1966. [CG]
——. 'Medieval Discussions of the Origin of Language', *Zeitschrift der Deutschen Morgenländischen Gesellschaft* 124 (1974), pp. 33–41. [SB] [TM]
Wensinck, A.J., ed. *Concordance et indices de la tradition musulmane*. Leiden: Brill, 1936–88. [SB] [AC] [CG]
Whittingham, Martin. 'The Value of *taḥrīf maʿnawī* (Corrupt Interpretation) as a Category for Analysing Muslim Views of the Bible: Evidence from

al-Radd al-jamīl and Ibn Khaldūn', *Islam and Christian–Muslim Relations* 22 (2011), pp. 209–22. [TM]

Wiesmüller, Beate. *Die vom Koran Getöteten: Aṯ-Ṯaʿlabīs* Qatlā l-Qurʾān *nach der Istanbuler und den Leidener Handschriften. Edition und Kommentar.* Würzburg: Ergon, 2001. [SW]

Wild, Stefan. *Das Kitab al-ʿAin und die arabische Lexikographie.* Wiesbaden: Otto Harrassowitz, 1965. [SB]

——. 'Arabische Lexicographie' in Helmut Gätje, ed., *Grundriss der arabischen Philologie: II – Literaturwissenschaft.* Wiesbaden: Ludwig Reichert, 1987, pp. 136–47. [CG]

——. 'An Arabic Recitation: The Meta-Linguistics of Qurʾānic Recitation' in idem, ed., *Self-Referentiality in the Qurʾān.* Wiesbaden: Harrassowitz, 2006, pp. 135–57. [SW]

——. 'Arabic *avant la lettre.* Divine, Prophetic, and Heroic Arabic' in Everard Ditters and Harald Motzki, eds, *Approaches to Arabic Linguistics. Presented to Kees Versteegh on the Occasion of his Sixtieth Birthday.* Leiden and Boston: Brill, 2007, pp. 189–208. [SW]

——. 'Muslim Translations and Translators of the Qur'an into English' in Johanna Pink (guest-editor), *Journal of Qur'anic Studies* 17, no. 3 (2015, forthcoming). [SW]

Williams, Jay G. 'Exegesis-Eisegesis: Is there a Difference?' *Theology Today* 30 (1973), pp. 218–27. [SB – Intr]

Wilson, Barrie A. 'Bultmann's Hermeneutics: A Critical Examination', *International Journal for Philosophy of Religion* 8 (1977), pp. 169–89. [SB – Intr]

Wilson, M. Brett. 'The First Translations of the Qur'an in Modern Turkey (1924–1938)', *International Journal of Middle East Studies* 41 (2009), pp. 419–35. [SB – Intr] [BW] [SW] [TZ]

——. *Translating the Qur'an in an Age of Nationalism: Print Culture and Modern Islam in Turkey.* Oxford: Oxford University Press in association with the Institute of Ismaili Studies, 2014. [BW] [SW] [TZ]

Woogen, Eve. 'The Best of Stories: Yusuf as Joseph in Hebrew Translations of the Qur'an' (2012). Classics Honors Projects. Paper 15.* [SW]

Wright, W. *A Grammar of the Arabic Language*, 3rd edn, 2 vols, repr. Cambridge: Cambridge University Press, 1981. [DS]

Yahaghi, Mohammad Jafar. 'An Introduction to Early Persian Qur'anic Translations', *Journal of Qur'anic Studies* 4, no. 2 (2002), pp. 105–9. [TZ]

——. 'The Development of Koranic Commentaries in Early New Persian' in Fereydun Vahman and Claus V. Pedersen, eds, *Religious Texts in Iranian Languages.* Copenhagen: Det Kongelige Danske Videnskabernes Selskab, 2007, pp. 247–61. [TZ]

Yazıcı, Murat. 'Turkey: Proliferation of Koran Translation'.* [SW]

Zadeh, Travis. *The Vernacular Qur'an: Translation and the Rise of Persian Exegesis.* Oxford: Oxford University Press in association with the Institute of Ismaili Studies, 2012. [SB – Intr] [KV] [SW] [TZ]

——. 'Persian Qur'anic Networks, Modernity and the Writings of "an Iranian Lady", Nusrat Amin Khanum (d. 1983)' in Suha Taji-Farouki, ed., *The Qur'an and Its Readers Worldwide: Contemporary Commentaries and*

Translations. Oxford: Oxford University Press in association with the Institute of Ismaili Studies, forthcoming. [TZ]
Zaehner, R.C. 'Abū Yazīd of Bisṭām: A Turning Point in Islamic Mysticism', *Indo-Iranian Journal* 1 (1957), pp. 286–301. [CM]
Zakeri, Mohsen. *Sāsānid Soldiers in Early Muslim Society: The Origins of ʿAyyārān and Futuwwa*. Wiesbaden: Harrassowitz, 1995. [TZ]
Zaman, Muhammad Qasim. *The Ulama in Contemporary Islam: Custodians of Change*. Princeton, NJ: Princeton University Press, 2002. [TZ]
Zammit, Martin R. *A Comparative Lexical Study of Qurʾānic Arabic*. Leiden: Brill, 2002. [CG]
al-Ziriklī, Khayr al-Dīn. *al-Aʿlām: Qāmūs tarājim li-ashhar al-rijāl waʾl-nisāʾ*. Beirut: Dār al-ʿIlm liʾl-Malāyīn, 1979. [TZ]
Zysow, Aron. 'Two Unrecognized Karrāmī Texts', *Journal of the American Oriental Society* 108, no. 4 (1988), pp. 577–87. [TZ]

Index of Qur'anic Citations

Index of Qur'anic Citations

Index of Qur'anic Citations

Index of Qur'anic Words and Phrases

General Index